THE

GREAT LAKES STATES

OF AMERICA

BY NEAL R. PEIRCE

THE MEGASTATES OF AMERICA

THE PACIFIC STATES OF AMERICA

THE MOUNTAIN STATES OF AMERICA

THE GREAT PLAINS STATES OF AMERICA

THE DEEP SOUTH STATES OF AMERICA

THE BORDER SOUTH STATES

THE NEW ENGLAND STATES

THE MID-ATLANTIC STATES OF AMERICA
(WITH MICHAEL BARONE)

THE GREAT LAKES STATES OF AMERICA
(WITH JOHN KEEFE)

THE PEOPLE'S PRESIDENT

THE
GREAT LAKES
STATES

OF AMERICA

People, Politics, and Power

in the Five Great Lakes States

NEAL R. PEIRCE
AND JOHN KEEFE

W·W·NORTON & COMPANY

NEW YORK   LONDON

FIRST EDITION

W. W. Norton & Company, Inc. 500 Fifth Avenue, New York N.Y. 10110
W. W. Norton & Company Ltd. 25 New Street Square, London EC4A 3NT

Library of Congress Cataloging in Publication Data
Peirce, Neal R
    The Great Lakes States of America.
    Bibliography: p.
    Includes index.
    1. Great Lakes region.   I.   Keefe, John, 1942–
joint author.   II.   Title.
F551.P44   1980   977   80–13702

ISBN 0–393–05619–8

1 2 3 4 5 6 7 8 9 0

CONTENTS

FOREWORD

THIS IS A BOOK ABOUT the Great Lakes states, the last of a series covering the story of each major geographic region and all of the 50 states of America in our time. The objective is simply to let Americans (and foreigners too) know something of the profound diversity of peoples and life styles and geographic habitat and political behavior that make this the most fascinating nation on earth.

The previous books in this series began in 1972 with *The Megastates of America*, treating America's 10 most heavily populated states. (Three chapters from that book—Illinois, Ohio, and Michigan—are included in this volume, substantially updated, revised, and expanded.) The series of eight regional volumes began, also in 1972, with publication of *The Mountain States of America* and *The Pacific States of America*, followed by *The Great Plains States of America* (1973), *The Deep South States of America* (1974), *The Border South States* (1975), and *The New England States* (1976), and, with Michael Barone joining Neal Peirce as coauthor, *The Mid-Atlantic States of America* (1977).

In this book, John Keefe, author, writer, and consultant from Madison, Wis., joins Peirce as coauthor. In addition, acknowledgment is made to Jerry Hagstrom, Carol Steinbach, and George Hatch for substantial editorial assistance. Others to whom the authors are particularly indebted are Evan Thomas, senior editor, and Calvin Towle, copy editor, of W. W. Norton & Company. Credit goes to Russell Lenz, former chief cartographer of the *Christian Science Monitor*, for the state and city maps.

The authors express their thanks to all the persons in the various Great Lakes States who gave so generously of their time and knowledge to help them in preparing this book.

THE
GREAT LAKES STATES
OF AMERICA

THE
GREAT LAKES STATES

TROUBLED HEARTLAND

THE GREAT LAKES STATES—mention them and instantly the romantic epithets of the poets leap to mind: the heart of the Midwest, the heart of the heartland, the builders of the nation, the breadbasket of the world! Whatever else may be said of this region, once robust but challenged now in its economic supremacy, people of the Great Lakes States do not think of themselves in diminutive terms.

More mundanely, the Great Lakes States conjure up visions of interminable miles of sometimes undulating, sometimes just plain flat plains, of manicured cornfields, and of barn-studded pasture land; of grimy and glutted industrial complexes and congested metropolises with their social perplexities, and of sprawling suburban communities neatly laid out amid meandering treeless sidestreets. Culturally, it brings to mind small town boredom and big city bustle, and the contrasting life styles that attach themselves to both. For countless thousands, the Great Lakes States present a way of life somewhat remove from mainstream America, reminiscent of what the U.S.A. used to be and still is in many parts of the five-state region.

As Theodore H. White wrote in his *Making of the President 1968:*

> Somewhere out beyond the Alleghenies, the old culture of America still persists, people who think Boy Scouts are good, who believe that divorce is bad, who teach Bible classes on Sunday, enjoy church suppers, wash their children's mouths with soap to purge dirty words, who regard homosexuals as wicked,

whose throats choke up when the American flag is marched by on the Fourth of July.

Politically, the heartland area has become synonymous with conservatism, isolationism, McCarthyism, steadfast independence, and an often-voiced resentment that wonders "why the hell the government is meddling around with this anyway." In some quarters, in lesser degrees, these political sentiments do find sustenance in the Great Lakes States, but they are the minority's opinion, stereotypes which no longer apply to vast numbers yet have still to be erased from the nation's consciousness. More than ever, the challenges of an urban economic society are invading the heartland, alternately coaxing and pushing the political decision-makers out of the mold formed by their fathers and grandfathers.

With a heritage that goes back even before the Northwest Ordinance of 1787 opened the wilderness to westward expansion, the Great Lakes States today are developing the wrinkles of economic maturity. As the last two decades of the 20th century advance, the region is feeling the full force of the age of decrepitation. In 1970, its 40,313,000 inhabitants accounted for 19.8 percent of the country's population; by the end of the decade, the signs of a slipping vitality were all too prevalent. Its population grew less than one million during the 1970s, and its share of the national total slipped under 19 percent (18.9 percent in 1977) with no consistent signs of relenting in its downward direction. Population loss may involve advantages, of course. More critically, the region's continued prosperity and last century of persistent economic development were threatened by the multitudinous challenges of the more aggressive Sun Belt States, by energy shortages and transportation system degeneration, and by the vexing problems of a dilapidated industrial plant that not infrequently predated World War II.

Illinois, Indiana, Michigan, Ohio, and Wisconsin all had Republican governors as the 1980s dawned, a fact that could bode well for the states if their leaders could forget their independent ways long enough to foster a regional mentality and the political clout to accompany it. Together, these states contributed 96 electoral votes toward the election of a President in 1980, almost a fifth of the total, a fact not likely to be overlooked by candidates of either party. In Congress, their voices had been muted in the past by partisan divisions and parochial fragmentation which, perhaps, accurately reflected the sentiments of the people but not necessarily their long-term interests. The competition between and among the five Great Lakes States has created a mind-set that approached stubbornness and shortsightedness at times, each state seeing itself pitted in mortal economic combat with its neighbors, refusing to recognize the advantages that might come from a cooperative and united front in economic planning and national political maneuvering. Newspaper columnist Michael J. McManus observed in 1979 that Midwestern governors still were bent on voting their states' ideology more than their self-interest. They "don't seem to know why they need to cooperate," he observed. It was a harsh judgment, but not undeserved.

Regions Within a Region

Even if modern-day competition has pulled apart the common bonds of the Great Lakes States, there was a time when it stood as a single territory, extending nearly 800 miles from southeastern Ohio to the westernmost point on Lake Superior and an equal amount from north to south. With the exception of 100 miles on Ohio's eastern border and 50 miles on Wisconsin's northwestern boundary, the Great Lakes States are entirely separated by water from their surrounding states. These natural boundaries comprise three of the greatest waterway systems in the country and give the five states a role as major exporters of both agricultural and industrial products, notwithstanding their land-locked location. Winding its way along the southern borders of Ohio, Indiana, and Illinois is the 981-mile Ohio River. In pioneer days, the Ohio was the interstate system of its era, bringing settlers by raft to homestead in the new lands of the Northwest Territory; today it is a commercial artery of the first rank, its traffic slowed only by the annual spring floods and the occasional winter freezes. Along the western edges of Illinois and Wisconsin is almost half of the mighty Mississippi River, the grand-daddy of North American rivers at 2,348 miles from its headwaters in Minnesota to the deltas of Louisiana. From east to west along the northern tier are the Great Lakes themselves, some, like Lake Superior, still an aesthetic spectacle rivaled nowhere in North America, equal in size to all of Michigan and Indiana combined, and the endpoint of the St. Lawrence Seaway and its window to the sea—and to the world at large.

For all their natural boundaries, for all their common interests, for all their similar heritage, the Great Lakes States remain a region of virtually endless diversity. In reality, geographically, economically, and culturally, this area of America is more like four subregions than five states. First there is the southern hill country, with the fertile farm belt to the north of it. Inserted in the farm belt as it nears the Great Lakes are the immense urban and industrial centers; finally comes the Northwoods, where the winters are long, the people scarce, and the scenery superb. The southern hill country falls roughly south of the Old National Road, later U.S. Highway 40 and, in contemporary times, Interstate 70. The Old National Road, the first great highway building venture of the federal government, was constructed in the early 1880s, moving out from Cumberland, Md., and bisecting such cities as Columbus in Ohio, Indianapolis in Indiana and Vandalia in Illinois (with a later extension, built by Illinois, to reach St. Louis). Here, in the southern hill country, can be found people every bit as poor and poverty-ridden as the destitute in Appalachia or the Ozarks, where many of the people have their roots. Indeed, the countryscape closely resembles the foothills of the Appalachias and the Ozarks, contoured with endless ridges and hollows that have a rustic attractiveness of their own, except where the scars of the coal mines have been left without restoration. The first settlers were hardy Southerners, Virginians and Kentuckians for the most part, a bloodstream since diluted but with vestiges that still persist, especially when it comes to race relations.

Just to the north is the farm belt, extending like a giant wedge across central and northern Ohio, Indiana, and Illinois to the Mississippi River. The farm belt's northern perimeter is more ill-defined, interrupted by the urban industrial masses along the lakes, but it does extend northward to include the orchards of Michigan and the dairy farms of Wisconsin. When other Americans think of the Midwest, this is the flat land they picture. Here is where 42 percent of the nation's corn is grown, 26 percent of the hogs are raised, and 11 percent of both cattle and wheat are produced.

In 1800, the government sold the land of the farm belt at two dollars an acre to induce settlers to homestead. At today's prices, it can cost more than $1 million just to buy an average size farm in Illinois, where the rich soil is made even more fertile by modern productive technology. The family farm since pioneer days has been the primary stabilizer of the farm belt economy, but the pressures of technology, escalating costs, and an aging rural population are taking their toll, leaving the land more and more to the bigger, more efficient operators, be they individuals or corporations.

Scattered throughout the farm belt are the medium-sized cities, some within the northern Megalopolis, some without, often seemingly like concrete extensions of the cornfields. Rockford, Moline, Champaign, Terre Haute, Muncie, Ft. Wayne, Green Bay, Lansing, Pontiac, Battle Creek, Warren, Lima, Zanesville, Columbus: they differ greatly in size but all retain common qualities. John Gunther rather unkindly described the middle cities of the Midwest as

> the ugliest, least attractive phenomena in the United States. They represent more bluntly than anything else in the country the worst American characteristics—covetousness, ignorance, tolerance of slums, absence of aesthetic values, get-rich-quickism, bluster, lack of vision, lack of civic spirit, excessive standardization, and immature and undisciplined social behaviour.

After 35 years, many of the traits Gunther saw still flourish. But the general image has ameliorated as the insularity of the region has been broken down by the population's mobility (especially young executives brought in to run the old and new industry), by mass communications (primarily network television, although the local media usually reflect the traditional establishment), by new social legislation (often resisted but implemented to degrees), and the force of economic change (the language the power establishments and local elites understand best). A paternalistic air swirls around most community projects, whether drives for the United Fund, symphony orchestra, art galleries, or donated parks. But that paternalism, compared to the "me generation" values of many other parts of America, seemed far less reprehensible in 1980 than in 1940 or 1950—indeed there were many Americans, among them quite sophisticated folk, who wished the old-fashioned, tight-knit American community values symbolized by the older Midwestern cities, places with a legitimate and deep sense of communal interdependence, had not been so totally eclipsed in many parts of the nation. The farm belt cities harbor severe problems, of course. In dealing with minorities, many of them are but microcosms of Chicago, Detroit, Milwaukee, and Cleveland, tolerating ghettos and substandard housing and marginal schools and inadequate job opportunities that contrast so starkly with the part of town the city fathers live in.

Hugging the shores of Lake Erie and Lake Michigan is the third major subregion, the great metropolitan masses and industrial centers. It is more than just Chicago, Detroit, Cleveland, and Milwaukee: here too are Youngstown, Akron, and Toledo, Flint and Grand Rapids, Gary, Hammond, and East Chicago, Racine and Kenosha, not to mention all the sinewy environs of Chicagoland. Notwithstanding their reputation as the breadbasket of the world, the Great Lakes States are primarily urban (ranging from 65 percent in Indiana to 83 percent in Illinois). Half of the region's people, more than 20.7 million of them, live in the metropolitan areas in this 200-mile-wide band. These cities, once the haven for thousands of European immigrants— the Irish, the Poles, the Slavs, and the Germans, seeking steady work in the auto plants, steel mills, and meat-packing factories—have all but ceased to grow, their central cities actually declining precipitously. The 1970s saw an ominous fall-off in the manufacturing jobs and a foreboding increase in the proportion of poor living in the central cities and dependent upon the largesse of the government for their subsistence. It is here, in the cities, that the future of the Great Lakes States will unfold, determining their course toward renewed vitality or a continued plummeting toward what, at the worst, could be economic calamity.

In northern Michigan and Wisconsin lie the Northwoods, distinct from all three other subregions, an area sorely depressed economically since World War II but showing significant signs of regeneration during the 1970s. Like the southern hill country, the Northwoods' population seems to be in inverse proportion to the number of pines and hardwoods that cover its surface (even as new people move in, portions of the land are cleared, prompting environmentalists to question if the new-found growth will be worth the price paid). Poverty exists here too, but not in the concentrated form of the cities or even of the southern hill country. In addition to Michigan's Upper Peninsula, still largely a forsaken area, the Northwoods includes the northern third of Michigan's lower peninsula plus most of the upper half of Wisconsin. Once rich in resources, first from the pelts of fur-bearing animals, then timber, later from copper and iron ore, parts of the Northwoods resemble ghost towns. For reasons still not entirely clear, people in the 1970s began moving into the Northwoods area, shattering previous economic dictates that people follow jobs. In detecting the return of population growth, demographers for the Upper Great Lakes Regional Commission said the new residents were migrating north with or without jobs, sometimes retreating in fear and frustration from the urban scene, usually seeking some kind of quality of life lacking in their previous home. Significant for the economic well-being of the North-woods, commercial and industrial development, albeit on limited scales, was following the new residents on their new migration route.

Diverse Political Cultures

Politically, many Americans view the Great Lakes and the Midwest in general as a distinctly conservative monolith, much as Midwesterners envision the East as a solid strip of concrete from Washington to Boston. It is true the political atmosphere is tainted still by some of the same ancient Midwestern suspicions that drove the 19th century progressives and Grange organizations to rail against Eastern financiers, monopolistic railroads, or—worse yet—foreign corrupters of all stripes. Up until the late 1970s, it would be more accurate to break the region into two fundamentally different political cultures, although each state has its own peculiar strains of political development. The southern tier of states bordering on the Ohio River—Illinois, Indiana, and Ohio—had experienced strong two-party competition for more than a century. These states saw politics in terms of jobs and spoils, not issues; they saw government as something to protect the people from, as they strove to keep taxes and the services they might provide to an absolute minimum. Federal mandates, in terms of environmental standards, civil rights legislation, worker safety (especially in the coal mines in the southern parts of the three states), social welfare, and highway building programs, have all led the government to intrude more and more in the lives of individuals, in the eyes of Illinoisans, Indianians, and Ohioans, at least, slowly but surely altering the traditional role government has played in these states.

To the north, in Michigan and Wisconsin, one-party politics—Republican politics—had been the primary political mileu, at least up until the Great Depression. Since then, strong Democratic parties have emerged, oriented to issues, not the rewards political office has to bestow. These two states have taxed heavily, but the taxpayers' return on their dollar has been manifest in the superior levels of schools, parks, social services, and the quality of life and the environment in general.

History explains much of the difference between the two tiers of Great Lakes States. Illinois, Indiana, and Ohio, as we noted earlier, welcomed large contingents of Southerners before the Civil War and harbored spirited Copperhead sentiments during that conflict; the result was a pronounced Democratic legacy in numerous rural counties near the Ohio River, a sentiment which the dominant Republicans in the states associated with rebellion and treason. To this day, the great- and great-great grandchildren of those steadfast Democrats often support the party of their ancestors, although contemporary television, universal education, and easy mobility have eroded some of the once lopsided majorities. When the New Deal arrived, big-city European ethnics and later the newly arrived blacks from the South joined the traditional Democrats to swing the balance of power, at least occasionally. Opposed to them were the more Republican descendants of New England and Middle Atlantic Yankees, deeply imbued with the work ethic and proud of the fact they had climbed to positions of wealth or stature, or both, through their own sweat and blood. After World War II, Republicans remained fairly unified, but the Democrats in the three states were afflicted by recurring divisions between their old-line rural (and usually conservative) followers and the disadvantaged blacks and ethnics in the big cities. Eventually, even the blue collar, unionized ethnics in the urban areas took on the conservative trappings of Middle Class America and broke their political alliance with blacks, while remaining within that broadest of all tents, the Democratic party. In Illinois, with the overwhelming dominance of Chicago Democrats, their machine reigned supreme until the mid-1970s, when the winds of political change began to leave marks of wear on the organization. In Indiana and Ohio, the Democrats remained geographically splintered throughout many medium-sized cities, uncertain of what they really stood for, still more inclined to play politics for the sake of the job, the contract, the patronage, rather than the issue or the cause. In all three states, one still found no small amount of bipartisan collusion for corrupt ends, a practice with wide acceptance but carried to its fullest flower in Illinois and only slightly less so in Indiana.

The heritage of the two northern Great Lakes States is almost diametrically different. No large number of Southerners made their way here, except for the late-arriving blacks who trekked to the cities directly before and after World War II. Michigan and Wisconsin fought wholeheartedly on the side of the Union during the Civil War, afterwards leaving no Democratic party worth the name. In these states, the new Scandinavian immigrants and the free-thinking but fundamentalist Germans found their way to compromise where necessary and work with the Republican Yankees who had preceded them. When agrarian protest rose late in the 19th century, and still later when the Progressive movement gained momentum, the dissent was concentrated within the Republican party. Immediately after World War II, there was reason to think the northern tier might return to their traditional Republican moorings. In Wisconsin, Progressive Senator Robert LaFollette Jr. (son of the turn-of-the-century Progressive champion) was defeated in the 1946 Republican primary, impelling his more liberal followers into the then-moribund Democratic party. Across the lake in Michigan, a decision was made by organized labor to join the Democrats, providing the crucial enthusiasm and organizational talents to revive the party there. As has been pointed out by John H. Fenton, perhaps the most perceptive political scientist in studying the long-term political geography of the Midwest, there already was an institutional base for an issue-oriented Democratic party in both states—the LaFollette Progressive movement in Wisconsin and the politically attuned United Auto Workers under the impetuous Walter Reuther in Michigan. It was relatively simple for these liberal elements to move in and assume control of the weak shell that then passed for the Democratic party in both states. With strong civil service traditions which encouraged political participation for public policy reasons, not jobs, it was not long before the newcomers were in control, pushing aggressively for their socially oriented government programs.

In more recent years a new dimension has appeared, the product of the national ticket-splitting phenomenon that became so dominant during the 1960s and more so in the 1970s. The result has been a kind of schizophrenic political organization in both parties. On the one hand, there has been a perceptible shift toward the middle of the political spectrum, especially by statewide candidates dependent on the massive independent vote for election, with a concurrent (although frequently reluctant) acceptance of more government in people's lives. On the other hand, beneath the electoral politics at the organizational level, the traditional ties and allegiances to the rewards of political office remain an implicit but less spoken cornerstone, particularly in the southern tier of Great Lakes States. Republicans still field conservative candidates, but the ones who win more frequently are more moderate and progressive persons such as Senators Charles Percy of Illinois and Richard Lugar of Indiana, and Governors William Milliken of Michigan, James Thompson of Illinois, and Lee S. Dreyfus of Wisconsin. Similarly, liberal Democrats can still win, but the successful ones—Indiana Sen. Birch Bayh and former Wisconsin Gov. Patrick Lucey are examples—pay more than simple lip service to notions once considered the purview of conservatives only.

One can detect the changing political coloration of the Great Lakes States by looking at their political leaders. Once, in the southern tier, they tended toward the nonideological like Chicago Mayor Richard Daley and Ohio Gov. and Sen. Frank Lausche (a Democrat who might as well have been Republican), and such conservative Senators as Illinois' Everett McKinley Dirksen (a pragmatist, though, to the bone), Ohio's Robert A. Taft (the intellectual voice of American conservatism), and Indiana's William Jenner and Homer Capehart (both far to the right). In contrast, the northern states elected liberals or moderates in both parties—Michigan's G. Mennen Williams, Philip A. Hart, and Donald Riegle (a former Republican) on the Democratic side; George Romney as well as Milliken on the GOP side; in Wisconsin, there were Gaylord Nelson, John Reynolds, and William Proxmire (although Proxmire exhibited a streak of financial conservatism to match his liberal positions). While there are exceptions, the contemporary trend more and more is toward a dual constituency—independent voters who choose increasingly on personality and issues rather than on partisanship, paralleled by the traditional organizational politicians within each party, who proved alternatively reluctant to part with their allegiance to the spoils, as in Illinois, Indiana, and Ohio, or with their causes as in Michigan and Wisconsin.

Lest one begins to think that the Great Lakes States represent nothing more than politics and massive urban problems, we need to pause momentarily to look at the way of life in the small towns and rural areas that cuts across all of the region outside the cities. The people here make up just a quarter of the population but inhabit the bulk of the land. They are the people of such small villages as Longview, Broadlands, Kendall, and Williams Corners, hardly more than a "bump in the road," as the local gentry would say. But they, along with the farmers, would be missed if they were to fade from the American scene, taking with them the comfortable and reassuring values they and the country grew up with. John Steinbeck, in his *Travels with Charley*, did not miss this part of Midwestern reality by far when he wrote:

> Almost on crossing the Ohio line, it seemed to me that people were more open and more outgoing. The waitress in a roadside stand said good morning before I had a chance to, discussed breakfast as though she liked the idea. . . . Strangers talked freely to one another without caution.
> I had forgotten how rich and beautiful is the countryside—the deep topsoil, the wealth of great trees, the lake country of Michigan handsome as a well-made woman, and dressed and jeweled. It seemed to me that the earth was generous and outgoing here in the heartland and perhaps the people took a cue from it.

There is a certain nostalgia in this part of the Great Lakes, a certain attachment to a more basic way of life. But even here that way of life is eroding to a degree: small industry, finding lower-wage and harder-working employees in the rural area, have built some of their new plants here, providing an invigorating alternative to the youngsters who no longer are all that intent on moving to the city but who have no yearning to follow in the footsteps of their farmer or merchant parents. Even for some farmers, the planting, cultivating, and harvesting are worked in and around a second job in a nearby town, as they find inflation no longer allows them to make ends meet by tilling the soil alone. Nor are these communities so immune from modern reality that they have been spared the travails of ills more acutely pronounced in the urban areas—the drugs, the unemployment, the crime, the divorces and disintegration of family life. Even if life in these out-of-the-way spots may not be quite as idyllic as Steinbeck's Charley would believe as he passed through, neither is it as onerous as that often imposed by the urban centers.

Shadows Over the Economy

Historically, the Great Lakes States could stake a valid claim to having a dynamic dual economic base—agriculture as well as heavy industry. To be sure, the farmland still exists, producing better than ever. And the region still has its heavy industry, its steel and automobiles, its rubber and earth-moving equipment, its machines and tools, located along the Great Lakes, the inevitable result of a central continental location close to major markets and midway between the iron ore of the Mesabi Range and the coal of the Appalachians. But the 1970s saw the exacerbation of the exodus of industry that began almost undetected two decades before. The economic hemorrhaging of the automobile industry, highlighted by the necessity of federal intervention to save the great Chrysler Motor Corporation, was the most visible and perhaps serious example, since so much Midwestern industry depended in one form or another on auto production. But there had already been serious signs that the region's dynamic growth and expansion of a century had been slowed—in some instances shrinking, in somes case actually stopped.

The case of Zenith Radio Corporation is but one of many that could be cited, but it well illustrates the dilemma confronting the industrial and political decision-makers of the Great Lakes States, to say nothing of the employees and their families. In 1977 the Chicago-based maker of radios and televisions announced it was shifting the production of all its color television set components to Taiwan and Mexico, eliminating 5,600 jobs, most of them in the heartland. Zenith was the last of the television manufacturers to capitulate to the competition and pricing squeeze and move its component production out of the country. By making the television set parts in Mexico, for example, Zenith could replace $6-an-hour American workers with $1-an-hour Mexican employees, thus permitting the firm to price its sets more competitively and perhaps recoup some of the market and profits it had lost in recent years. The destination of companies leaving varies. Frequently, the company doesn't leave the country, but just trades the chill of the Snow Belt for the warmth (and wintertime energy savings) of the low-wage, non-unionized Sun Belt states; at other times, the company simply leaves the central city for a new plant (with enticing tax breaks and modern equipment) in an adjacent suburb. The impact on the community abandoned, however, in terms of taxes, jobs, and income lost is no less agonizing, whatever the reasons precipitating a move. What it adds up to is the slow sapping of the Great Lakes States' economic life blood.

In an unusual and rather hesitant response to their growing dilemma, the governors set up a Committee for Great Lakes Economic Action late in the 1970s. After an initial survey, the committee recognized the region was facing "its first severe test" as a result of the decision of so many manufacturers to leave the central cities. "The leadership of the region faces the question of how best to aid the older manufacturing centers in their transition from heavy reliance on manufacturing to a more diversified and balanced economic basis," its 1977 report said. It went on to describe the causes of the stagnation:

Beginning in 1950, and accelerating in the 1960s and 1970s, a number of changes began to take place in the national economy as it moved from an economy dominated by manufacturing into a postindustrial era. For industry, many of the traditional advantages associated with a location in the industrial Midwest began to change. Population concentration started to shift to the West and South for reasons of climate and amenities. Many household-serving industries looked to new markets in these new growth areas outside of the region. . . . Many kinds of industries were becoming increasingly footloose, that is, they could choose to carry out their manufacturing operations with equal advantage in many parts of the United States. While it had been unthinkable in the 19th century to make iron and steel far from coal and iron ore, computers, digital watches, and airplanes could be manufactured in almost any state in the Union. Industry, then, began to follow the people.

The impact of these new facts of economic life was enough to send chills through the local chambers of commerce. We previously mentioned the near no-growth of the population during the 1970s and the region's shrinking share of the total national citizenry. While the U.S.A. was gaining 6.4 percent in population, none of the five Great Lakes States achieved the national average, and only Wisconsin (with 5.3 percent) came remotely close to matching it. In the critical nonagricultural employment sector, the region's 10.4 percent growth significantly trailed the national average of 16.2 percent and dramatically fell behind the almost 26 percent surge in both the South and the West. In Illinois, Ohio, and Indiana, manufacturing employment actually dropped 173,400 between 1970 and 1977, a slippage which Michigan's and Wisconsin's combined 66,300 increase could not offset. Where the industry was heading was clear from the hefty increases exceeding 11 percent in both the southern and western states. While investment in new capital equipment almost doubled in the West and increased 130 percent in the South, Ohio could hardly point with pride at its 25 percent increase, and Illinois and Indiana were not that much ahead with their growth of 50 percent each. (Again, Michigan and Wisconsin both nearly doubled their capital investments, exceeding the national average of 82.5 percent.) Unemployment figures also reflected the traumas of an aging economy, and the Great Lakes States suffered more and suffered longer than their regional counterparts in the South and West during the recurring recessionary valleys and inflationary peaks of the 1970s.

It must be noted that the economic distress of the Great Lakes States was not unique to them. The Northeastern States likewise have passed into the postindustrial era. Sensing their common plight, members of the U.S. House of Representatives from the two regions in 1976 formed the Northeast-Midwest Congressional Coalition, set up to analyze their mutual problems and lobby for remedies. It didn't take long for its research to verify that federal policies were encouraging growth in the South and West, at the expense of the Great Lakes and the Northeast. Analysis of federal funding formulas and spending policies, especially those of the Defense Department, confirmed what had been suspected. As one of the coalition's reports in 1979 stated:

Federal tax and spending policies have inadvertently hastened the drain of economic activity from the Northeast and Midwest. . . . Some federal policies still respond to the regional economic problems of earlier decades, favoring what are now the healthiest, fastest growing section of the nation.

Tax policies continue to encourage business expansion in areas outside the

Northeast and Midwest by favoring new construction rather than maintenance and rehabilitation of old structures. And because federal tax policies are progressive and based on nominal, rather than real, disposable income, they are higher in the Northern regions of the country than in the South and West. After putting more money into the federal treasury, the Northeast and Midwest receive appreciably less in federal spending than do the South or West.

How much less do they receive? In 1976, the *National Journal* analyzed the balance of payments problem between states and the federal government and found the five Great Lakes States paid $62 billion to the treasury the year before, only to get back $43.6 billion, a deficit of nearly $20 billion. The roll call for the Great Lakes States was ominous—Illinois, a $5.3 billion deficit; Michigan, $5 billion; Ohio, $4.6 billion; Indiana, $2 billion, and Wisconsin, $1.7 billion. While the spending disparity was spread through many agencies, the gap in the Defense Department's regional allocations offered a glaring discrepancy: in the Midwest, defense payrolls and contracts amounted to $210 per person; in the Far West, the figure was almost triple the amount, $620 per capita. There was a time when some in the Midwest were proud the nefarious Defense Department had few tentacles in their states, an attitude now being scrutinized. And where was that $20 billion imbalance of payments going? It was easy to trace: the South had a payment surplus of $11.5 billion, the *National Journal* survey showed, and the West $10.6 billion. In times of prosperity, the Great Lakes States could afford to be the rich uncle to what traditionally have been the poorer states; the region had the wealth and the government's income redistribution policies purposefully shifted the surplus to states with less to spend and more of a need. But as the South and West themselves prospered, such policies became targets for the new have-nots of the nation to question. The Northeast-Midwest Congressional Coalition, later in the decade, conducted a similar survey and reached nearly identical conclusions as did the *National Journal*. The only difference in its 1979 analysis was that the gap was growing: the Great Lakes States were losing more, and the southern and western states were the recipients of an even larger surplus, $33.4 billion compared to the $22.1 billion the *National Journal* found.

Metropolitan Movements

In the major urban centers—Chicago, Detroit, Cleveland, and Milwaukee, and to a lesser extent in Indianapolis, Gary, Dayton, and Columbus—the region's economic distress is intensified by racial tensions and other social ills. The 1960s saw a burst of federal activities to combat urban decay, especially after the racial riots in Detroit, Chicago, Newark, and Watts. But, in retrospect, the federal dollars and initiatives did little to alleviate the mixture of terror and suspicion that convinced many individuals and corporate citizens they would be better off in the suburbs. The consequences of urban abandonment can readily be seen by contrasting the central city of Detroit, where blacks now are a majority, and the scores of sparkling steel-and-glass commercial and industrial developments that spring up like mushrooms as soon as one crosses Eight Mile Road and enters suburban Oakland County just north of the city. It is the difference between the water-parched desert and the luscious green oasis; only the oasis surrounds the increasingly financially strapped deserts in the inner cities. Here, in the great metropolitan areas, one finds the unemployed and the unemployable, the school systems more intent on passing students than educating them, the crime rates undeterred by better trained and higher paid police officers, the neighborhoods decaying for want of incentives to rehabilitate them, and, above all, the racial animosity that makes cooperation and progress difficult in the best of times.

The federal solicitude waned as the 1970s advanced, and the state governments—with the exception of Gov. Milliken's foresight in Michigan and former Gov. Lucey's efforts in Wisconsin—did little to pick up the slack. The still pervasive rural and small-town attitudes of state legislatures usually prevailed when the problems of the cities were broached. The lawmakers from beyond the central cities could not appreciate, or would not support, the kinds of financial commitments that are necessary to salvage the inner cities. The home-rule tradition, with each community protecting its rights to decide its own destiny, runs deep in the Great Lakes States, deep enough that it can justify ignoring the real problems eating away at the urban insides. As the final two decades of the 20th century approached, the major urban areas of the Great Lakes were seemingly held together only by a patchwork system of federal, state, and local programs that, as often as not, conflicted and thwarted meaningful and coherent progress.

Yet it was also true that a degree of indigenous revival was occurring in a number of cities. "Gentrification" by middle class people who would previously have opted for the suburbs began to appear; many of the young affluent were developing a taste for the architecture, entertainment, neighborhoods, and varied life style of cities, no matter how severe their problems. Simultaneously, as their parents had rejected city living, they began to dismiss suburban living as dull and monotonous and a potentially foolish option in an era of impending severe gasoline shortages. By 1980 all of this still represented a minority movement in the Great Lakes States, much smaller in proportion than the comparable inner-city revival on the East and West Coasts (perhaps because the Midwestern cities were more exclusively manufacturing-based, less places of high culture and communications than their counterparts on the coasts). But the trend was still significant. In Chicago, for instance, major pressure was being felt to convert apartments to condominiums. Among the less elite, strong indigenous pressure to revive ethnic urban neighborhoods was being felt across the region. Benefiting from such trends, there were early signs that such cities as Columbus, Cincinnati, Madison, Milwaukee, and possibly even Detroit might be on the verge of a legitimate comeback.

Economically, the energy crisis threatened to play havoc with the Great Lakes States' economy. Detroit, Motor City U.S.A., felt the brunt of the initial Arab oil embargo and cutbacks, as did the many other cities in Michigan, Indiana, Ohio, and Wisconsin which rely on the auto industry's assembly plants and the manufacturers of the parts that go into the cars and trucks. The auto industry began some conversion to smaller cars, despite its long-standing insistence that Americans preferred powerful engines over fuel economy. By the end of the decade record numbers of the smaller vehicles were rolling off the assembly lines—but not in sufficient proportion, it turned out, when gasoline shortages in 1979 turned out to be even more serious than those of 1974. The mighty Chrysler Corporation, a massive Midwestern employer, found itself with a surfeit of large vehicles and an inability to make smaller cars at a profit; thus it was turning to the federal government to save it from bankruptcy. And the prospect of decades of reduced petroleum availability cast a very long shadow over the economy of that region, among all America, most solidly based on the internal combustion engine.

Of Rails and the Waters

The erosion of the nation's rail system did little to put the Great Lakes into a more competitive economic system. For years, the railroads consciously postponed maintenance on their marginally profitable lines; then they sought and usually got authority to abandon them. When Penn Central and six other bankrupt lines were allowed to merge and form Conrail early in the 1970s, and in the process abandon lines with little traffic, the days of convenient transportation were numbered for many Great Lakes businesses. Then, in the mid-1970s, two major Midwestern lines (the Penn Central had substantial Midwestern trackage, too) filed for bankruptcy; first the Chicago, Rock Island and Pacific, later the Milwaukee Road. The Rock Island survived its cash crisis, but midway through 1979 the Milwaukee Road was living off subsidies and reluctantly granted government loans. Even if it continued to operate, the Milwaukee Road's intention was to drop its unprofitable branches: in 1979, it had begun proceedings to halt operations on 37 percent of its 10,074 miles of track. Hundreds of Great Lakes firms along these lines were forced to seek an alternative—and usually more costly—means of bringing in their raw materials and shipping out their finished products. Michigan, practically alone among the Great Lakes States, showed the foresight to step in and help subsidize continued operations of some of its rail lines threatened with abandonment. In 1976, Michigan assumed funding of 850 miles of nonpassenger track, spending more than $3 million annually for operating expenses and several million more for capital improvements. The experiment could prove an expensive failure in Michigan. But at least Michigan could say it tried, something its sister states could not claim with equal veracity. Wisconsin and Michigan also sought alternatives to the demise of Lake Michigan's rail ferries, carriers of railroad cars laden with manufactured goods and raw materials. The rail ferries saved many companies many miles and considerable time by shipping across the lake instead of around it, but the two states had only limited success.

The sporadic efforts to save Midwestern rail service served not just the function of sustaining the region's economic vitality. Rail transport is far more energy efficient, mile for mile of freight carried, then petroleum consuming motor transport. Every step to preserve the rails reduced potential petroleum demand; each gallon of oil saved made the nation less dependent on OPEC oil and helped to undergird, rather than undermine, the United States' national security.

The Great Lakes are a grand expanse of 94,710 square miles containing 20 percent of all the fresh water in the world. As the largest reservoir of fresh water on earth, the five Great Lakes—Superior, Michigan, Huron, Erie, and Ontario—are said to hold 67 trillion gallons of water, enough to cover the continental United States to a depth of 10 feet. They have aptly been called the freshwater Mediterranean of the western hemisphere (although Lake Erie, because of pollution, has on occasion been referred to as America's Dead Sea). With their 2,342 miles of connecting waterways, the lakes form the largest inland water transportation system on earth, a resource which might well be the key to overcoming the economic stagnation of the region. The completion of the St. Lawrence Seaway in 1959, linking Superior, Wisconsin, and Duluth, Minnesota, with the Atlantic Ocean, created a new seacoast in the midst of the heartland. The prospects of the inland shipping potential raised hopes far beyond what has ever been realized, as we shall see in a moment. What the Atlantic and Pacific oceans are to life, commerce, and culture on the east and west coasts, the Great Lakes are to the heartland Megalopolis: no great world culture has ever prospered without water transportation, a fact critical to the economic futures of Detroit, Chicago, Toledo, Milwaukee, and Cleveland and all the other cities and farms which see the ports as their doorways to world markets. The one great difference between the coastal ports and those of the Great Lakes is the oceans themselves. By virtue of their salinity and sheer magnitude, the oceans still seem relatively inviolate to the pollution of man, notwithstanding the coastal degradation and occasional oil spills. The same cannot be said of the Great Lakes. In the 1960s, the Great Lakes, especially Lake Erie, were on the verge of an ecological death, choked and smothered by the thousands of tons of insidious wastes poured into them daily. But the tidal wave of environmental concern, fostered by the likes of Wisconsin's Sen. Gaylord Nelson, forced federal clean-up mandates and the expenditures of billions of dollars in treatment facilities by industry as well as state, local, and federal governments. By 1980, no self-respecting ecologist would yet pronounce the Great Lakes cured of all their ingested ailments. But there had been enough success stories to show that concerted antipollution campaigns can make a crucial difference. The message was manifestly clear: while much has been done, much more remained to be done if the lake shore beaches were to see children frolic in their waters again, if the fish were to spawn and thrive again, if the water was to cease to be a health hazard and an aesthetic cesspool.

John Gunther's curt summation of the impact of the Great Lakes, in his *Inside U.S.A.*, is hardly less valid today:

Aside from much else, they feed half the nation with (a) grain and (b) steel. From the western tip of Lake Superior . . . flows an inordinate, colossal tonnage of iron ore and wheat destined for the furnaces and breadbasket of the East. In return, coal flows up. The life of the great freighters carrying this cargo has an authentic romance hard to match in contemporary affairs.

The romance, and tragedy, of these Great Lakes is as real today as ever. In the mid-1970s, a 729-foot taconite ore carrier, the *Edmund Fitzgerald*, sank in Lake Superior during one of the treacherous storms for which that lake is deservedly notorious. Romanticized in 1976 by a hauntingly popular ballad by Gordon Lightfoot, the *Edmund Fitzgerald* went down without a trace. None of its 29 crew members was ever found, a fate not at all uncommon on tumultuous Lake Superior.

Heavy cargoes and agricultural products still dominate the Great Lakes trade—limestone (another vital ingredient in making steel), petroleum, newsprint, and wood pulp, in addition to those mentioned by Gunther. The trade agreements with Russia during the 1970s allowing shipments of grain added a new port of call to the outgoing Great Lakes freighters. Since the completion of the St. Lawrence Seaway, automobiles and other machinery no longer have to travel overland before leaving for overseas.

The St. Lawrence Seaway, for all the glittering hopes held out for it after completion in 1959 as a joint project with Canada, has not lived up to expectations. Long dreamt of by Midwesterners as a fourth American seacoast, a way to transform cities like Cleveland and Chicago into New Yorks and Rotterdams of world trade, the seaway was bitterly opposed by eastern interests and the railroads. It would be ironic if the collapse of the railroads became the catalyst to achieving its potential. Approved during President Eisenhower's first administration, the seaway can handle ships of up to 29,000 tons and 730 feet. Foreign vessels venturing as far as Duluth rise almost 600 feet above the Atlantic through an intricate series of locks not only in the St. Lawrence but connecting the lakes as well. But as part of the legislative battle to win approval, the seaway was required—through tolls—not only to support its running expenses but also to repay its construction costs and bond interest—a provision peculiarly omitted for similar projects such as the Houston Ship Canal. As a result, the cost of each iron ore freighter passing up and down the passage has not been as competitive as hoped for and overall traffic has been less than once anticipated. As the *Wall Street Journal* forbodingly reported about a decade after its opening, the seaway is "a flop. . . . Shippers shun it. Shipbuilders curse it. Ship operators ignore it. It is deeply in debt, in disrepair, and almost obsolete." Some caustic observers were predicting early in the 1970s that Great Lakes shipping would not survive the decade. While the prognostication turned out to be premature, the seaway did continue to encounter obstacles.

As the 1980s advanced, however, two developments held out a promise of better things to come. One was the energy crisis, the very circumstance that had done so much to undermine the Midwest's manufacturing capability. The port of Toronto's general manager, Ernest B. Griffith, told a 1979 conference of Great Lakes shippers that the rising energy costs and diminishing fuel supplies could be a double-edged sword and force manufacturers and grain exporters to rely more extensively on the Great Lakes and the Seaway. But he had some words of caution: long-term Great Lakes shipping activity would grow only if a compromise could be reached with environmentalists, ports continued to be upgraded, the shipping season was extended to 11 months (instead of eight), and ports would increase their own promotional efforts. By the end of the 1970s, the ports had in place or were planning for upgraded facilities that would handle the container ships that almost sounded the death knell for Great Lakes shippers a decade earlier.

The second promising development came from Washington. Great Lakes States' Congressmen mounted an offensive of their own to pressure federal agencies to use their ports more often for transportation of goods from the Midwest. As one example, Chicago area Congressmen complained that President Carter was promoting Great Lakes development, only to have the agencies ignore the directives and bypass their ports. If the region's representatives could succeed in shifting shipping to the Great Lakes, the potential could be dramatic indeed: 37 percent of the nation's gross national product originates within 300 miles of Chicago. Illinois ranks first in the nation in agricultural exports and second in manufactured goods, and the other Great Lakes States rank correspondingly high. Yet the Port of Chicago handles only 3 percent of the nation's exports, the other Great Lakes ports even less. The fledgling congressional efforts to force a reexamination of federal policies in this area were motivated by parochial interests, to be sure, but it was the first step toward the kind of regional cooperation that could offer a far greater return, both for the Midwest and for the nation as a whole.

Sadly, none of the Great Lakes has been spared from people's propensity to leave wastes wherever they have been. In 1967, the Chicago *Tribune* initiated a series entitled "Save Our Lakes," a detailed look at the contamination of the Great Lakes and their tributaries. The accounts read like a requiem for the waterways of a region:

A stream of poison pours into Lake Michigan from the Indiana harbor— a contender as champion of polluted waterways. . . . These waters stand as an open indictment of Indiana Calumet area industry. The waters cry for help.
"These are the sewers for industry here. That's the way they use waterways," said (one federal official). . . . 37,000 gallons of oil are discharged by Calumet

area industries into the Indiana harbor every day. That is equivalent to three tank cars. Add to that 32,000 pounds of iron wastes and 280 pounds of cyanide coming from the United States Steel plant in Gary alone each day. There are two other steel plants almost as large feeding their wastes into the harbor. . . . Each of the three draws about 1 billion gallons of water from Lake Michigan every day and returns it loaded with wastes via the river and the harbor canal.

Around the Great Lakes went the *Tribune* reporters: the Fox River leading into Green Bay ("the largest stream in the Lake Michigan basin" and "filthiest waterway in Wisconsin"); the Milwaukee River ("a slime-coated cauldron of filth"); Cleveland's Cuyahoga River ("one of the few rivers in the world that is a fire hazard. . . . Some say that anyone who falls into the Cuyahoga does not drown—he decays"); the Detroit River (one of the sources "turning Lake Erie into a swamp"). The river and the lake changed, the dosage of pollutants changed, names of the polluters changed as the *Tribune* went from city to city, but the story remained essentially the same. The Great Lakes were in bad shape.

In the mid-1970s, the *Tribune*'s Environment Editor, Casey Bukro, went back for a second look at the lakes and reported slow and often reluctant progress, but progress nonetheless. Of the Indiana Harbor, he said:

Its waters once looked and flowed like a melted chocolate bar heavy with the refuse of one of the nation's thickest concentrations of steel mills and oil refineries. It became a national proving ground, pitting the clout of industrial giants against the zeal of newcomers carrying the banner of environmental protection. The conflict has left the canal cleaner if still polluted. (You'd sink in if you tried to walk on it now, said [one federal official]). It's much better in appearance and chemically, but the canal has a long way to go.

At Cleveland, developers were constructing $48 million worth of shops, offices, and restaurants on the banks of the Cuyahoga, a testimonial to their conviction that the river was no longer the fire hazard it once was. Fox River watchers worried about a new threat to game fish—sea lampreys which prey on game fish but cannot live in polluted waters. Fishermen dropped their lines into the Detroit River in the downtown area, and Milwaukee approved a $501 million project to separate its storm water and sewer lines, a major cause of pollution there. As Bukro noted, seeing results from the Great Lakes clean-up is "like watching a glacier move." But there was movement.

Industry was not the only foot-dragger in the clean-up campaign. In some respects, it produced better results than the government. By the end of the 1970s, industry ranked behind both municipal treatment facilities and run-offs from storm sewers, agricultural fertilizers and wastes, and other nonpoint sources as contaminators of the lakes. The federal government, initiator of the pollution control standards and purveyor of millions of dollars of grants, was sending out mixed messages. In 1972 it signed an agreement with Canada to clean up the Great Lakes cooperatively. Conceived with good intentions, the agreement has been plagued by suspicions. After the first four years, Canada could report it had completed target sewage treatment projects serving 97 percent of its population. The United States lagged, completing projects serving only 60 percent of the people in the targeted area. In 1979 Canadian concerns again were raised when President Carter requested a budget for the Great Lakes project equal to only half of the amount of a year before.

The case of the Reserve Mining Company on Lake Superior stands out as a classic instance of the environmental-economic confrontation that seems to result in a stand-off. Lake Superior, the largest, the deepest, and the most exhilarating of the Great Lakes, is threatened by the 67,000 tons of power-fine fiber wastes dumped daily into it by Reserve Mining since 1955. Two federal courts ruled that the tailings, containing possible cancer-inducing fibers, threatened the health of 200,00 persons drinking Lake Superior's waters. Reserve Mining, which employed 2,800 persons and indirectly provided jobs for another 2,700 in an otherwise economically destitute area, argued it could not afford the solution proposed by ecologists, a $677 million processing plant 40 miles inland. It opted instead for a $252 million disposal site five miles from the lake. All the while the protracted court struggle went on, the taconite tailings continued to be dumped into Lake Superior, health hazard or not. The Reserve Mining situation served to remind all of the consequences of cleaning up as well as not cleaning up the pollution. The good news was that Reserve Mining's on-land disposal site was ready to go into use in the early 1980s.

Lake Erie was once called America's Dead Sea, and it still remains in a comatose state. "So far the struggle to save Lake Erie is a stand-off," reported the *Wall Street Journal* midway through the 1970s. Erie's waters, it continued, had stopped getting worse, but it would be years before much more improvement could be seen, and added:

> Any real improvement in Lake Erie's health would carry a steep price tag. Just providing adequate facilities to treat municipal sewage going into the lake would cost another $17 billion, using current technology, the U.S. Environmental Protection Agency estimates. Industry will have to spend roughly $2 billion more to meet federal water pollution standards, a Cleveland consulting firm reports. And scientists seem to discover new sources of pollution as fast as plans are developed to deal with older ones. . . . The Lake Erie experience shows that cleaning up the nation's inland waters will be far more expensive and difficult than expected only a few years ago.

One sign of improvement in Lake Erie was the area of the lake devoid of oxygen during summer months. Without oxygen, most life forms cannot grow; in short, the lake dies. In earlier years, some 4,000 squares miles of Lake Erie bottom, close to 90 percent, were considered dead for want of oxygen. By the mid-1970s, the size of the oxygen-starved area had ceased to grow, although it still had not shrunk appreciably.

To the casual observer, many parts of Lake Erie, even at its worst period a decade ago, reflected vitality—the great ships passing through the seaway and the amenities of life—Euclid Beach, Sandusky Bay, amusement parks, marinas for small pleasure craft, elegant summer homes tree-shielded from curious roadways, breakwaters spiny with the antennae of fishing poles. But, to a large extent, that was a dilution of reality, an ignoring of the fact that the lake had aged some 15,000 years in just half a century.

One could go on endlessly citing the successes and failures of the Great Lakes clean-up. Perhaps we should close with one more happier note, the improvement of the Detroit River. As *Newsweek* recounted in 1978:

> The Detroit River, flowing between Lake St. Clair and Lake Erie, was dismissed as terminally polluted a decade ago. Grease balls 10 inches across floated on its oily surface, and ducks died after landing in the water. But after a vigorous chemical attack on the effluents, the river is recovering fast. By 1979, about $700 million will have been invested in new sewage plants. Even in downtown Detroit fishermen routinely catch small-mouth bass, coho salmon and sturgeon—although they are advised not to eat their haul because of a lingering threat of mercury poisoning.

A far more encouraging precedent for the Great Lakes states was the success in cleaning the great Ohio River, which was so contaminated at the end of World War II that fish could not live in its waters or people swim in it. An interstate authority of the eight Ohio basin states was set up in 1948 with power to enforce antipollution orders and haul offenders into court. At that time, virtually 100 percent of the sewage discharged into the Ohio was untreated; after 15 years and $1 billion, the figure was reduced to 1 percent and the river was clean enough so that any city, at reasonable cost, could make the water pure enough to drink. An interesting aspect of the eight-state authority was that it operated entirely independently of the federal government.

Just as the Great Lakes are the lifeline of the heartland's north, so is the Ohio River for the region's southern reaches. The industrial growth of the Ohio represents one of the encouraging advances of the American economy after World War II. Construction by Indiana during the 1970s of two new port facilities on the Ohio River added impetus to its cargo-carrying capacity, which now equals 70 million tons a year. Of the Ohio and its ways, however, we will have more to say as it passes Cincinnati.

In a very real sense, the effort to clean up the great waterways of the Midwest was symbolic of the region's perplexing challenges in the last decades of the 20th century. Here was a region that grew to greatness through its pioneer spirit, the vigor of entrepreneurs, the power of local decision-making. The best of those qualities would have to be retained for a worthwhile future. But in water clean-up, as in so many other areas, the new and greater problem this region faced in its struggle for economic viability was how to foster cooperation between a thousand and one powers, economic and governmental. It would be unreasonable to expect that the Great Lakes region could retain its overwhelming share of the nation's industry and agricultural wealth for all time to come: as the nation expanded westward and southward, the relative share was sure to drop. Yet conversely, the resources of the states surrounding the Great Lakes—resources of coal and ore and grain, of industry and commerce, human resources—were still immense, being both regional and national. It was in the way the people of the region chose to use those resources that the future would be told: of a region still buoyant and strong and resourceful, or one consigned by lack of vision and leadership to needless and disheartening decline.

The choice was not only a critical one for the people of these five states. This region was not named the nation's heartland by whim: that indeed it has been, and will remain. All Americans would find their lot enhanced or diminished to a major degree according to the health of the national heartland.

ILLINOIS

AND THE MIGHTY LAKESIDE CITY:

WHERE CLOUT COUNTS

I. CHICAGOLAND

CHICAGO—CHICAGO—how can one adequately describe it? The heart of the heartland, or as a visiting Sarah Bernhardt said some 80 years ago, "the pulse of America," this lusty, masculine, beauty and terror-filled metropolis remains the archetype of all our cities. It throbs with life and energy, it worships Mammon without qualm, it attracts and repels, it is perennially young yet perennially decaying. It is the one place on the continent where the exercise of power—raw, unfettered, physical, economic, and political power—has been brought to its apex. Chicago is the glory and damnation of America all rolled up into one. Not to know Chicago is not to know America.

Thus our story of Illinois must begin with this mighty lake city, for in its shadow every other aspect of Lincoln's prairie state slides toward afterthought. A native son, John Gunther, sets the stage:

Being a Chicagoan born and bred I can recall much. . . . The icy wind screaming down snow-clogged boulevards; the sunny haunch of Lincoln Park near the yacht moorings in torrid summers; the angry whistles of angry traffic cops and the automobilelike horns of the Illinois Central suburban trains; the steady lift of bridges, bridges, bridges; holes, bumps and yawning pits in the streets; the marvelous smooth lift of the Palmolive Building and how the automobiles seem to butt each other forward like long streams of beetles; the tremendous heavy trains of the North Shore slipping like iron snakes through the quivering wooden suburban stations; the acrid smell from the stockyards when the wind blew that way, and the red flush of the steel mills in black skies—all this is easy to remember.

The feel of Chicago remains true to the Guntherian image; some of the specifics are transformed. The stockyards, victims of decentralization of the packing house business, lie quiet like a deserted battlefield, no longer filled with thousands of animals awaiting their moment of terror and dissection. The Palmolive Building stands, but now overwhelmed in a great crush of higher buildings and its name, indignity of indignites, actually changed to Playboy Building, symbol of the first (now passé) sex breakthrough of the postwar era. The North Shore Line is gone, and one's eyes are easily diverted to the screaming jets landing and taking off in an incessant stream from O'Hare. Chicago's raw interchange of man and machine remains; so does the jewel of the city, her beautiful and unspoiled shoreline off which white sails sparkle on a summer day.

People Count and Economic Clout

Chicagoland—to borrow the descriptive if somewhat nauseous term popularized by the Chicago *Tribune*—is the home and workshop for well over half the 11 million people of Illinois. The reader can take his pick of three levels of population analysis: the city of Chicago alone, Cook County (which embraces Chicago and a multiplicity of close-in suburbs), or the six-county Chicago metropolitan area. The population of Chicago alone, since 1890 second only to New York's, was 3,366,957 according to the 1970 Census and had been static for 30 years, declining in fact by 7 percent between 1950 and 1970. The dropoff became even more precipitous in the first half of the 1970s, falling by more than a quarter of a million people to 3,062,881, a full 9 percent loss in five years. Cook County had grown more than 35 percent in the 30 years before 1970, but even it lost 150,000 in the first half of the 1970s. In 1977, Cook County's population was estimated at 5,309,763. The suburban "collar counties" have continued to grow, however, allowing Chicagoland to recapture in 1976 its position as the second largest metropolitan area in the U.S.A., a distinction it had temporarily ceded to Los Angeles during the California boom of the 1960s.

What raw population counts fail to reflect adequately is the remarkable economic resilience of the "Chicagoland" economy, which grew more rapidly than the country at large for most of the postwar years and had a substantially lower unemployment rate. Except for its several hundred thousand or so people living under established "poverty line" definitions, the Chicago area is a great place to make money, and a lot of people are making a lot of it.

What gives Chicago its economic dynamism? The basic fact is an amazingly well diversified economy, with finance, manufacturing, and transportation its great mainstays—and virtually no defense industries. By one estimate, the Chicago area contributed 4.6 percent of the gross national product though it has only 3.2 percent of the U. S. population. The city is both a great headquarters town (with home offices of 40 of the 500 largest industrials listed by *Fortune*) and a great branch office town. The long list of man-made items of which Chicago makes the most includes such disparate items as household appliances, radios, candy, athletic goods, television sets, plastics, railroad equipment, diesel engines, telephone equipment, and soap. More steel and machinery are fabricated in the Chicago area than anywhere else in the world, and food processing remains a multi-billion-dollar business. Chicago is also the nation's biggest wholesaling center, its traditional mail order headquarters (Sears and Montgomery Ward), and through its Board of Trade and Mercantile Exchange, the world's busiest commodity market and trader in livestock futures. Amazingly successful businesses include the switched-on world of consumer electronics (Zenith, Admiral, Motorola, etc.), printing and publishing (R. R. Donnelly & Sons Co. is the world's largest commercial printing company), and conventions. Chicago is one of the five largest financial centers of the U.S.A.; of course it has the Federal Reserve Bank for its region.

The recital of these superlatives has not even touched on transportation. Chicago has long been the world's greatest railhead. O'Hare Airport is the busiest commercial field in the world and in 1978 handled 49 million people in 760,000 scheduled plane movements, an average of almost three flights every other minute, day-in and day-out. O'Hare has been expanded several times, in anticipation of even more travelers, but its growth has fallen short of the 80 million-plus passengers once forecast for 1980. Plans to ease the pressure for landings by revitalizing Midway Airport and by building an airport on water—eight miles out in Lake Michigan—failed to materialize. The airport-on-the-lake, hotly contested by environmentalists, provides ample testimony, however, to the colossal heights to which the builders of Chicago aspire. Chicago also boasts of having a "Fourth Seacoast" because of its capacity for global freight shipments through the St. Lawrence Seaway; the city is the busiest Great Lakes port and eighth largest in the nation, even though the business on the Seaway has not lived up to early expectations.

Chicago has been at the center of the new atomic age; it was on a snowy day in 1942 that Dr. Enrico Fermi and his colleagues, working under the plank board seats of the abandoned football stadium at the University of Chicago, succeeded in accomplishing the first sustained controlled production of atomic energy in human history. The Atomic Energy Commission's impor-

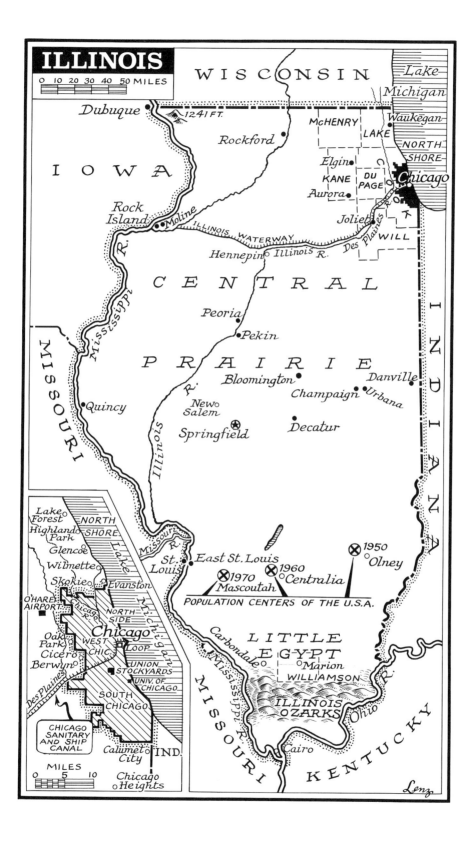

ILLINOIS

0 10 20 30 40 50 MILES

WISCONSIN

Lake
Michigan

Dubuque • ▲1241 FT.

Rockford •

McHENRY

LAKE

Waukegan

NORTH
SHORE

I O W A

Elgin •

KANE

DU
PAGE

Chicago

Aurora •

Rock
Island

Moline

ILLINOIS WATERWAY

Joliet

Des Plaines R.

WILL

Hennepin Illinois R.

C E N T R A L

I N D I A N A

Peoria •

Pekin •

P R A I R I E

Danville •

Bloomington •

Champaign

Urbana

Quincy •

New
Salem

Decatur •

Springfield

POPULATION CENTERS OF THE U.S.A.

Lake
Forest
Highland
Park
Glencoe
Wilmette
Skokie
Evanston

NORTH
SHORE

⊗ 1950
Olney ○

St.
Louis

East St. Louis

⊗ 1970
Mascoutah

⊗ 1960
Centralia

O'HARE
AIRPORT

NORTH
SIDE

Oak
Park
Cicero
Berwyn

WEST
CHIC.
LOOP

Chicago

UNION
STOCKYARDS

UNIV. OF
CHICAGO

Carbondale

L I T T L E
E G Y P T

Marion

WILLIAMSON

SOUTH
CHICAGO

ILLINOIS
OZARKS

Ohio R.

CHICAGO
SANITARY
AND SHIP
CANAL

Calumet
City

IND.

Cairo

K E N T U C K Y

MILES
0   5   10

Chicago
Heights

M I S S O U R I

Lenz

tant Argonne National Laboratory for research and development is at suburban Lemont. In 1969, ground was broken at Weston, a little town 30 miles southwest of Chicago, for an AEC atom-smasher, named, appropriately enough, Fermilab. The "scientific prize of the century" as the New York *Times* called the world's largest proton accelerator, has been both a boom and a bane for the tiny hamlet of Weston. To win the prize, Weston residents rose above principle to pass a fair-housing ordinance when congressional hearings brought charges that it discriminated against blacks; later the facility grew so large that the town voted itself out of existence, and the village buildings remain as lab facilities, providing a bizarre rural flavor to the highly technical mission of the project. The lab's $50 million annual budget apparently enriches the local economy to make the prize worth the price.

As a final nuclear note, Chicago's Commonwealth Edison Company built one of the earliest nuclear energy plants at Dresden near Morris in 1960 and has since built two more units there, plus two others at Zion north of Chicago and two more in the Quad City area around Rock Island-Moline. With another pair of plants under construction, Commonwealth Edison was to have the nation's most powerful concentration of nuclear-powered electrical generating facilities in the nation, with the 6,200 megawatts projected by the early 1980s to produce 55 percent of its electricity. While environmentalists protested their construction and pointed to safety hazards, utility officials claimed economic efficiency, with rates running around one-fifth, for instance, of what New Yorkers paid.

Chicago is not without its economic worries, however. From the mid-1960s to mid-1970s, the central city lost 211,000 jobs, and the trend was continuing at the decade's end. Major industries such as the stockyards and steel mills became outmoded, and the sad fact, economists noted, was that Chicago was not moving fast enough to create industries based upon modern technologies such as electronics. Nor was Chicago emphasizing its potential in education and research, finance and communications—sectors that appeared to be growing in other central cities.

"Chicago is getting old," said Dick Simpson, a University of Illinois professor who founded several innovative political institutions in the city. "Despite the Potemkin façade of the Lakefront and the Loop, despite some new office buildings, major changes must occur if Chicago is to survive economically."

The Architectural Lodestone of Chicago

Power, we have said, is the essence of Chicago; many who know it well refer to it as "clout"—a peculiarly brutal, raw kind of power. It must be examined in its many faces: economic, political, criminal, religious, racial, even architectural. Since the architecture is what first meets the eye, we will start there.

Chicago, city of the Big Shoulders, regards itself with good reason as the world capital of modern architecture. Indeed, the gigantic structures of steel and glass and concrete which thrust at the sky along the lakefront and around the Loop * are a symphony of might and mass—and excellence—that few world cities can compete with. Henry Fairlie commented in the Washington *Post* in 1978 that any other city can be duplicated, but not Chicago:

The almost unbelievable gift of Chicago to our sense of our urban civilization is the power of its commercial architecture. Not its public buildings, not its monuments, but its commercial buildings. The "Miracle Mile" of North Michigan Avenue puts every other commercial city today to shame. One tries to think of the equivalent—Wilshire Boulevard in Los Angeles—but that is like a drawn-out shopping mall. In Chicago, the commercial architecture bursts on you, seizes you, carries you with it on its brassy, unangelic wings. One actually reels back, to look up and up, along and along, through and through, to catch every glimpse. And this was built by business? This is the doing of commerce?

There have been two great eras of Chicago architecture. The first began a century ago, when Chicago rebounded from its disastrous Great Fire of 1871 to give birth to the first skyscrapers of the world. Many still stand, making the Loop a kind of outdoor architectural museum. Here architect William Jenney shifted from the 5,000-year old tradition of buildings with weight-bearing walls to designing the first steel skeleton building of history. Here the masters of the Chicago School built classic high buildings that rejected Victorian gingerbreadism in favor of a simplicity in which "form follows function."

In the early years of this century, little of distinction was built. A second golden era of Chicago architecture was inaugurated in the mid-1950s and continues unabated to this day; its dominant figure until his death in 1969 was Ludwig Mies van der Rohe, a stonemason's son from Germany who never took an architectural degree but by his later years was widely regarded as the dean of world architecture. The new Chicago classicism which Mies fathered is true to the spirit of the first golden age: simple, direct expression using modern techniques in which newer kinds of steel span vast distances. Mies designed modern classics of structural clarity, stripped of adornment; one of the finest examples is his four "glass house" apartment towers on Lake Shore Drive, their black-coated metal and shimmering glass mirroring the clouds and the lakefront. Mies' building at the Federal Center, according to Chicago journalist/architectural critic W. M. Newman, "fills its great envelope of space with mysterious rightness, daring to hurl its regimental rhythms along an entire block. This is the best new federal building in any city."

Another prime example of the Miesian "skin and bones" principle is the 1966 Chicago Civic Center, in which the steel skeleton is close to being one and the same with the outside of the building. Chief designer of the Civic Center was Jacques Brownson, a pupil of Mies who became a master himself. He directed that the building be finished in an alloy that weathers to a deep bronze; to grace the noble plaza before the center, the city commissioned

* The Loop, Chicago's mercantile and financial center, gains its name from the elevated tracks which encircle it.

Pablo Picasso to design a great five-story-high steel sculpture which has been executed in a steel alloy that oxidizes to a russet color akin to that of the center. (The abstract Picasso design triggered great controversy among those who saw in it everything from Picasso's dog to a baboon to a great dragon fly; Picasso settled the dispute by saying it was a woman's head. To the authors—as to many—it is a threatening, brooding, fascinating structure of a thousand faces, not at all unconsonant with the Chicago political machine that rules from across the street in City Hall.)

There are dozens of other modern Chicago buildings by Mies or his school, structures which have literally transformed the city in a few short years. Some prime examples are the Time-Life Building with tinted mirrored glass that reflects a bright orange to the outside world; the twin tube-like towers of Marina City on the Chicago River front; and the First National Bank Building, soaring 850 feet over the Loop, sheathed in glistening white granite and shaped like a long, thin stick of butter that has begun to melt at the bottom.

As one drives along Lake Shore Drive and glances inland, the landmarks of the latest surge of development meets the eye—the great skyscraper race. Three of the world's tallest buildings now grace the Chicago skyline. To the north, along the "magnificent mile" on North Michigan Avenue, stands the first of the towering triumvirate, the tapered design of the John Hancock Building, a 1,127-foot structure of such mass and height that it dwarfs all near it. Newman, writing for the *Daily News* before it folded, called the Hancock Building "some large horned animal, gazing serenely along the rim of the world." He also described the building as a symbol of the dangers of "giantism,"—the "hard, impersonal power of overwhelming technology, the dwarfing of man, the dehumanizing of the city." Good Chicagoan that he is, Newman quickly added: "It took boldness and guts to put it up that way, it is very impressive, very Chicagoan." By those standards, the white marble Standard Oil of Indiana headquarters, two blocks to the south of the Chicago River, must be a bit more bold, a little more impressive: "Big Stan," as the natives refer to it, stands nine feet taller than "Big John," making it the fourth highest building in the world. The accolade as the "most Chicagoan" building of them all, however, is left for Sears Tower, near the southwest corner of the Loop, at 1,454 feet the tallest of the tall. With 110 stories, the Sears Tower surpasses the twin towers of New York's World Trade Center by 100 feet and the Empire State Building by 200 feet. As the *National Geographic* noted in 1978, "if this skyline lacks quite the dramatic compression, the almost Gothic verticality of Manhattan's, it compensates with a broad-shouldered massiveness, a stupendous horizontality that takes second place to none." It is unquestionably Chicagoan.*

Perhaps the most negative note of the present-day building boom is that

---

* The Sears Tower is also unquestionably Chicagoan from another vantage, the politics surrounding its City Council approval. Part of the deal involved the city selling Sears, Roebuck one block of Quincy Street, which bisected the proposed project. Selling public thoroughfares is not unheard of in Chicago, but Gordon Metcalf, Sears' board chairman, negotiated a rather favorable agreement.

many of the historic structures of the late 1800s are falling before the wrecker's ball; among these have been three-quarters of the 92 buildings of Louis
Sullivan, whose superb designs, combining ornamentation with functional
austerity, influenced great architects like Frank Lloyd Wright. The last Sullivan office building in the Loop, the 13-story Old Stock Exchange, built in
1894, was demolished in 1971. A city landmarks commission was created in
1968, but in its first six years the commission was able to award designations
to only three downtown commercial buildings. No building in Chicago is
sacred: the ponderous yet compelling Chicago Public Library, on the corner
of Randolph and Michigan, was saved from the late Mayor Richard Daley's
dictum to demolish only by the rare intrusion of his wife. "The number of
classic American buildings torn down here in recent years is enough to make
an architectural historian cry," noted Ira Bach, author of *Chicago on Foot*.
"Many have been replaced by parking garages and undistinguished office
buildings." His lament is shared by a few, but not the City Fathers, who see
development as new jobs, new taxes, and new contracts to keep the political
machine running. As one developer contemplating the removal of five homes
in the Astor Street landmark district explained: "We are not anxious to destroy Chicago. But if anybody is going to have a chance to make money on
it, it might as well be us."

The Machine and the Leaders

"Organization, not machine. Get that. Organization, not machine,"
Mayor Richard J. Daley insisted when the subject came to the Cook County
Democratic organization. But this "antique and high-powered juggernaut," as
one observer has described it, is a political machine if the term has any meaning. And until Daley's death, no one considered it anything less than the best
functioning machine in America.

Chicago, said one-time alderman Leon M. Despres a few years ago, "is
governed by a firmly run, businesslike organization of about 35,000 persons
who live off politics. . . . Indeed, it is really a business. It controls the mayoralty, 38 of the 50 members of the city council, the school board, the park
board, the library board, the housing authority, the transit authority, two-
thirds of the county board, nearly all the county offices, many suburban governments, the judiciary." Until 1969, the governor and attorney general of
Illinois were also organization men and the machine had a decisive voice in
the designation of federal judges and other local federal officials through its
close ties with the Kennedy and Johnson administrations. In the late 1970s
it still controlled the comptroller and treasurer, a chunk of the state legislature, and almost all of the Chicago Congressmen.

The sale price of $130 a square foot (total $2.8 million) was about $40 more than the going price
for streets and alleys; but the city agreed to foot the bill for relocating water and sewer lines, which
had the effect of saving Sears, and costing the city taxpayers, about $1.1 million.

Under this authoritarian, hierarchical organization, some 500 patronage jobs are allotted to each ward. Virtually every precinct committeeman has a city job; the public, in effect, subsidizes the system by salaries paid to patronage workers. Many ward committeemen own insurance agencies and do a land-office business with retailers and real estate owners who see an obvious way to get access to City Hall. But the ward and precinct committeemen, in turn, are under tremendous pressures to contribute and work on election day, or they can expect to be thrown out on the street. The machine knows what they are doing, and it brooks no election day inefficiency—or dissent. Adlai Stevenson III has called it "a feudal system that rewards mediocrity or worse, with jobs for the blind party faithful, special favors for business, and ineffectual civil service." But its power is so great that he, like his father before him and that otherwise fearless United States Senator, Paul H. Douglas, made his peace with it.

According to their own particular "clout," Chicago's varied ethnic groups are allowed to queue up for the rewards of power. Irish get the top jobs like mayor, president of the county board, county assessor, and state's attorney, plus the major local patronage slots beneath them; the Poles get jobs like city clerk or a couple of seats in Congress; Jews get some judgeships but are generally dealt the lesser cards. Other ethnic groups, assuming they are part of the coalition, pick up the scraps from the table; among these are Italians, including some who have influence from participation in organized crime. Blacks, the most faithful election-time supporters, have traditionally been shortchanged worst of all.

For the ambitious Cook County Democrat, a seat in the U.S. Senate or House or the General Assembly in Springfield, as juicy a political plum as each might appear, is but a stepping stone to higher (more lucrative) things at the local level. Once in power, Cook County Democrats do not behave in traditional textbook terms. According to Milton Rakove, who spent 10 years as part of the organization preparing for his book, *Don't Make No Waves . . . Don't Back No Losers: An Insider's Analysis of the Daley Machine:*

> The Democratic organization in Chicago is nonideological. It is dedicated primarily to gaining and retaining offices and reaping the rewards of office. Its movers and shapers are relatively unconcerned with philosophical terms like liberalism, conservatism, or any other "ism" except pragmatism and materialism. . . . This attitude toward politics and public office is the key to an understanding of the dynamics of the Democratic political organization of Cook County. . . . Their primary concern is their own self-interest. This is not to say that they have no concern for the public good, but rather that that concern is secondary to their own interests.

Chicago emerged from World War II under the tight control of a city-wide Democratic machine controlled by Mayor Edward J. Kelly, a master of private profiteering in public office, and Patrick Nash, sewer contractor and Democratic boss since the 1930s. In the Kelly-Nash era, everything could be bought or sold, organized crime prospered, and the center city was dying rapidly. But the machine's gross inefficiencies in public services, together with severe school administration problems, weakened Kelly so much that the Democratic machine ousted him in 1947 in favor of a reform-flavored candidate, Martin Kennelly. A clean and handsome millionaire warehouseman who had previously fought the local machine as director of the Chicago Crime Commission, Kennelly was sponsored by one of the cleverest politicians of modern Chicago, Col. Jacob M. Arvey. (Arvey, a diminutive, bald attorney who mixed idealism with a background in corrupt ward politics, was visible for many years after he had ceased to be a power in the machine. In 1976, at age 81, he appeared at Daley's funeral, a forlorn figure, a titular leader with no clout. Less than a year later, he too died.)

In office, Kennelly turned out to be too naive (and vain) for tough Chicago, and the hoodlums and political machine carried on as before. In 1955 he was defeated in a primary fight by none other than Richard J. Daley, prototype of the good Irish ward politician. Many viewed Daley as little more than a hack politician, the machine's last gasp. Daley's reply: "I would not unleash the forces of evil. It's a lie. I will follow the training my good Irish mother gave me—and Dad. If I am elected, I will embrace mercy, love, charity, and walk humbly with my God." *

In his prime, Daley represented far more than an average ward politician, even if his heavy-set looks and jowls, and a sometimes awesome temper, set the image of a strong-armed boss from the smoke-filled rooms. He had a thorough grasp of the details of Chicago government; he was a master of finance and introduced cost accounting in city administration; he was a keen judge of the level of performance and influence of thousands of Chicagoans in and out of government. When new power bases arose in the city, Daley found ways to incorporate them—or if their holders declined his muscular embrace, to freeze them out. His working alliance with Chicago's big business and labor unions, as we shall see later, was extremely close, and it was under his administration that Chicago began its great postwar central building boom. Daley was extremely hard working and strong willed, a man whose personal honesty was never seriously questioned. He succeeded in curbing the bolder thieves in his organization, even though ward and precinct bosses were allowed to carry on "clean graft" of a type that would not embarrass the regime.

Yet, despite all, this master of political weight-balancing remained a product of the simple Irish neighborhood of Bridgeport (40,000), where he

---

* This was one of Daley's more grammatical statements; in his early years as mayor he was still doing violence to the English language in everyday speech, referring, for instance, to Chicago's "Nort' Side and Sout' Side." Later most rough corners had been rubbed off His Honor's speech, though the press recorded such Daley gems as these:
"I resent the insinuendos."—*Chicago Daily News,* May 15, 1965.
"Together we must rise to ever higher and higher platitudes."—*Newsweek,* March 13, 1967.
"It is amazing what they will be able to do once they get the atom harassed."—*Life,* February 8, 1960.
". . . . for the enlightenment and edification and hallucination of the alderman from the 50th ward"—*Life,* February 8, 1960.
"They have vilified me, they have crucified me, yes they have even criticized me."—*Harper's,* August 1968.
An entire volume of Daleyana, *Quotations from Mayor Daley,* compiled by Peter Yessne, was published in 1966 by G. P. Putnam's Sons.

was born the son of a sheet-metal worker; he lived in a modest bungalow on a street of inexpensive but creditably well painted and tended homes. Like many Chicago neighborhoods, Bridgeport retains clear-cut community and ethnic identity. Some 40 percent are immigrants or the children of immigrants; the typical resident has a ninth-grade education and lives in a very modestly priced house; blacks are not permitted to buy homes here and indeed are said to be afraid to walk its streets at night. A good family man, Daley returned here almost every evening for dinner at home with wife and children. Every day he attended Mass, though, as writer David Halberstam pointed out, his religion was pre-Ecumenical, pre-John XXIII, where there was individual sin but little social sin. He could tolerate small and petty graft, excuse an occasional roaring drunk or failing of business virtue, but could not excuse adultery nor understand or tolerate a man who fathers a family and then deserts it.

Next to mother Church, Bridgeport's first loyalty is to the Democratic party, a lesson Daley learned well as a boy from the age of 12 when he started doing small political chores. Four successive mayors of Chicago came from the 11th Ward, of which Bridgeport is the heart. "All this political clout," Chicago *Sun-Times* columnist Mike Royko commented, "means nearly every family has got somebody on a government payroll. In the East, some families register a newborn son at Harvard or Yale. In Bridgeport, they sign him on with the city water department." While most wards got about 500 patronage jobs, Bridgeport, as the most equal among the wards, generally was estimated to have about 2,000 public positions allocated to its ward committeeman, before Mayor Jane Byrne cut back jobs to the area.

For the patronage favors Daley did offer black neighborhoods, he expected gratitude, and he was all the more shocked when bitterness and rioting were the answer. For a native of Bridgeport, it was indeed difficult to understand the desperate plight of blacks in ghettos like the raw, tough West Side. When Daley entered such areas, his coming and going were rapid in his Cadillac limousine; he never thought of walking the streets of an explosive black neighborhood as John Lindsay of New York had done. His information on the black communities came instead from a police intelligence network and black politicians often beholden to him. David Halberstam reported in *Harper's* that when a militant civil rights activist nun working on the West Side went to Daley and pleaded with him to come out and witness the deplorable condition of the children and their schools, he replied, "Look, Sister, you and I come from the same background. We know how tough it was. But we picked ourselves up by our bootstraps."

One key to Daley's success was his dual roles: mayor of Chicago and chairman of the Cook County Democratic Central Committee. Holding those two jobs was a bit like being Premier of the U.S.S.R. and First Secretary of the Communist Party at the same time. The vast power of the two offices permitted Daley, with his well developed political skills, to become an authoritarian ruler of his city, a Buddha-like figure whose slightest word was law. As each election approached, for instance, Daley appointed a Democratic slatemaking committee, usually with himself as chairman. The sessions were secret, and potential candidates were asked to come; they never, if really serious, invited themselves. One by one, hat in hand, the office-seekers were allowed to appear and make a brief review (rarely for more than three minutes or so) outlining their qualifications, their potential financial and group support. Then they were expected to show their unqualified fealty to the party by offering to run for *any office* that the party might stipulate. The slatemaking sessions were a mysterious affair; the public had no idea of what went on behind the closed doors. They were also scheduled so close to the primary filing deadline that it was hard for any independent candidacy to get organized afterward.

Indeed, were it not for the machine, even the slated candidates would have had difficulty getting the required number of names on nomination papers that close to the filing deadline. One candidate unexpectedly slated for the county board of commissioners had sought a countywide office. He had no idea how he'd get 8,000 signatures for his slated post, until he walked into county party headquarters and asked for help. He was steered to a nearby table, where his stack of petitions with 8,000 names was waiting for him. "This is an organization we are running here," he was curtly reminded.

The election-day pluralities which the mighty Democratic machine could produce were sometimes nothing less than phenomenal; in 1948, 558,111 for Harry Truman for President; in 1960, 456,312 for John F. Kennedy for President; in 1967, 516,208 for Richard Daley for mayor; in 1968, 421,199 for Hubert Humphrey for President; in 1970, 521,353 for Aldai Stevenson III for U.S. Senator. It was on the basis of such one-sided votes that Daley wielded the power he did in national Democratic politics.

In the early 1970s, however, Daley's ironclad grasp on Chicago began to slip after a series of election losses and the indictments and convictions of close associates. The first major blow came in 1971 when federal judge and former Gov. Otto Kerner, a Chicago aristocrat, son-in-law of former Mayor Anton Cermak and a Daley protegé, was indicted and later sent to prison for his involvement in a racetrack stock deal that earned him $150,000. Behind Kerner's indictment was an ambitious and aggressive young Republican U.S. Attorney, James Thompson, appointed by President Nixon. Thompson made public corruption cases his special domain and Daley's charmed circle his special target. In four years, Thompson obtained indictments of more than 350 Illinois officials and their cronies and won convictions in 97 percent of the cases. Among the more prominent were Kerner and some of Daley's closest confidants and friends including: Thomas Keane, chairman of the City Council's finance committee and Daley's right-hand man, found guilty of 17 counts of mail fraud and one count of conspiracy to buy 1,900 tax delinquent properties and resell them to public agencies at a profit; Earl Bush, Daley's press secretary since his first day in office in 1955, on 12 counts of mail fraud and one count of extortion in connection with his secret ownership of a company with an exclusive contract with O'Hare Airport; Alderman Paul T. Wigoda, for receiving a $50,000 payment to rezone a golf club in his ward; County Clerk Edward J. Barrett, for accepting a $187,000 bribe to guarantee purchase of 900 voting machines; Matthew Danaher, clerk of the patronage-rich circuit court, former alderman of Daley's own 11th Ward and a man with a future in the organization, for income tax evasion and conspiracy on a real estate deal that netted him and his brother-in-law $400,000.

Thompson also obtained the convictions of 18 vice detectives and a traffic chief for shaking down tavern and nightclub owners, a prosecution that pressured Daley into sacking Police Commissioner James B. Conlisk and replacing him with James Rochford. Rochford unnerved the department by demanding 70 top officers take lie detector tests. Thompson convicted more than 50 of Chicago's finest for bribetaking. Daley himself was taken to task publicly when word got out that he had ordered $2 million in city insurance business placed with an Evanston firm that employed his son John. Reformers and Democratic politicians who felt the mayor was crowding in on their own business territory joined in a chorus of criticism. Daley's response: "If a man can't put his arms around his son's, then what's the world coming to? And if they don't like it, they can kiss my ass."

While the corruption charges were mounting, Daley's longtime nemesis on the City Council, reform alderman William Singer, teamed with the Rev. Jesse Jackson to unseat the 59 legally elected Chicago machine delegates to the 1972 Democratic National Convention. In a see-saw battle that ran through federal and state courts onto the convention floor, Singer and Jackson succeeded in proving that the machine delegates failed to reflect the reform guidelines of the Democratic Party's McGovern Commission. The reformers were seated, and Daley, symbol of the bloody 1968 Democratic convention in Chicago, was publicly humiliated before a national television audience.

The 1972 Illinois state races brought even harder knocks to Daley's machine. The Democratic gubernatorial nomination was settled in an open primary as Lt. Gov. Paul Simon, endorsed by the Daley organization, lost to Daniel Walker, who had been the author of the controversial "Walker Report" that condemned police activities at the 1968 Democratic National Convention. Walker announced that he would disdain Daley's slatemaking procedure altogether. Walker's insurgent candidacy gave Illinois Democrats their first contested gubernatorial primary since 1960 and only the fourth (the others were in 1936 and 1952) in 40 years. Walker brought modern campaign tactics to Illinois. In 1971 he made a walking tour of more than 100 days and 1,000 miles throughout Illinois and then turned to computerized election returns of recent years to concentrate on precincts that had voted heavily Democratic in general elections but failed to turn out big primary votes.

In 1972, Daley also lost control of the state attorney's office, considered indispensable to keeping the machine away from government investigators. The machine dumped incumbent state's attorney Ed Hanrahan after he was indicted for conspiracy to suppress evidence in the 1970 slaying of two Black Panther members during a raid he ordered. Hanrahan won the primary and received machine backing once again, but angry black leaders refused to work for him, and Republican Bernard Carey won in the general election.

In 1976, Daley achieved one last, sweet partial victory. Walker was planning on a second term but had never made his peace with the machine. As Secretary of State Michael Howlett described the relationship, "the basis of the problem is that we have elected a governor who hates Daley and thinks this is the way to get elected president of the United States." Howlett became the machine's gubernatorial candidate, and Daley was able to use Walker's alienation from his own supporters and the organization's power to beat Walker in the primary by 229,000 votes, or 63 percent of the total. But it was a short-lived victory. In the November elections, Republican James Thompson, the man who had successfully prosecuted so many of Daley's allies, won the governor's seat, and the 425,000-vote plurality Chicago gave Jimmy Carter was not enough to keep Gerald Ford from winning Illinois. Perhaps worst of all for the organization, Carey was reelected to the state's attorney office, the first time in Daley machine history a Republican won re-election to that sensitive post.

Six weeks after the election, on Dec. 23, 1976, Daley visited his doctor on North Michigan Avenue for treatment of a recurring chest pain that was slowing his pace. The doctor was preparing to hospitalize him when Daley fell out of his chair and slumped to the floor. The last of the powerful American machine mayors, an anachronism yet a dominating figure of his time, was dead at 74.

Mike Royko, the persistent critic of Daley and author of the biography *Boss*, called the mayor both the best and the worst of Chicago.

In some ways, he was Chicago at its best—strong, hard-driving, working feverishly, pushing, building, driven by ambitions so big they seemed Texas-boastful. In other ways, he was this city at its worst—arrogant, crude, conniving, ruthless, suspicious, intolerant.

He wasn't graceful, suave, witty or smooth. But then, this is not Paris or San Francisco. He was raucous, sentimental, hot-tempered, practical, simple, devious, big and powerful. This is, after all, Chicago.

Chicago A.D.

On February 27, 1979, 26 months after Daley's death, Chicago voters went to the polls in unprecedented numbers and handed the machine its most resounding defeat in 50 years. The nominee for mayor: Jane Byrne, a long-time Daley protegée who had broken with Daley's successors. Five weeks later, on April 3, Byrne's easy general election victory made her Chicago's first woman mayor and first nonmachine mayor since 1931. To the Chicagoans and national political pundits who had long speculated on what Chicago would be like After Daley, Byrne's election at first appeared to trigger a revolution in local politics. But then Byrne moved quickly to dispel notions of the machine's end. Her quarrel, she said, was not with machine politics, but with the corruption of that kind of politics under interim Mayor Michael J. Bilandic and the "cabal of evil men" surrounding him. She soon established working relationships with those power groups over which she had triumphed in her primary victory.

What indeed had happened in Chicago; what would the future be like in the new era, After Daley? Starting with the first transition meeting after Daley's death, it was clear that Chicago A.D. would be different. Daley had left no heir apparent. The lusty politicians who survived him were left squabbling, for the first time in decades without a Superman to lead them. The slatemakers faced several sobering problems. Chicago's reputation as "the city that works" and its double-A bond ratings were so strongly tied up in Daley's iron-fisted rule that bondholders were calling local bankers to inquire about selling their stake at whatever the market would bear. The blacks and Poles whom Daley had discriminated against saw his death as a new and golden opportunity to make real headway in Chicago politics. Wilson Frost, president pro tem of the city council and leader of the black caucus, insisted his position automatically made him acting mayor. Frost tried to move into the mayor's office but found it locked; he then marched into the council chambers to announce his claim to the press, only to be interrupted in the finest tradition by workmen who created a din ostensibly to prepare for a Daley memorial service. Black businessmen notified the media, however, and Clayton Kirkpatrick, editor of the Chicago *Tribune*, told the slatemakers that if Frost were treated unfairly, his newspaper might have to editorialize against the transition process.

The end result was a halfway redivision of power. Frost was appointed chairman of the city council finance committee, a position with genuine prestige and clout. Daley's key roles, chairman of the Cook County Democratic Central Committee and mayor, were divided. George W. Dunne, president of the Cook County Board of Commissioners and Daley's trusted lieutenant, was named party chairman. Dunne was a poor speaker and campaigner and lacked Daley's toughness, but seasoned observers depicted him as "1,000 percent honest" and admired his careful bookkeeper's approach to the affairs of government. Dunne was officially given control of patronage.

The real power, including final say on patronage, was turned over to the acting mayor, Michael J. Bilandic, a 53-year-old successful corporate lawyer from Daley's own 11th ward. Bilandic, a relatively inexperienced politician who had been appointed finance chairman after Thomas Keane's conviction, proved to be hopelessly dull for a city accustomed to the dynamism of a boss. Single until he took office, "Mayor Bland" married a socialite and found money in his budget for jogging paths. As Mike Royko lamented, "Daley must have done this on purpose to seem big in death."

On substantive matters, Bilandic's administration turned out to be a continuation of Daley's policies with a few departures. When the firemen's union tried to overturn Daley's longstanding rule that labor agreements would be formalized with a handshake rather than a written agreement, Bilandic quietly made plans to fire all striking firemen and persuaded the leaders of the 10,000 civilian trade workers employed by the city to support the firings. The Daleyesque maneuver forced the firemen to retreat meekly. Bilandic did reverse Daley's pattern of confrontation with the federal government over charges of racial discrimination and promotion policies in the police department by curtailing plans to appeal a court decision withholding federal revenue sharing money. By settling the police discrimination case, Bilandic not only eliminated a blemish on the city, but also obtained the money to repay $55 million in bank loans that Daley had arranged (at an extremely favorable rate of 4.5 percent) when the revenue sharing money was withheld. Bilandic also acquiesced to federal intrusion into the city's vaunted patronage system by repaying the Labor Department $1 million in federal aid which had been illegally spent to hire applicants with "political referral letters." Bilandic courted Chicago's middle class much more actively than Daley ever did by starting a $100 million tax free revenue bond program to finance middle class home mortgages at a rate two points below the market. The mortgage bond program caught fire nationally and became Bilandic's questionable political legacy to the country.

It was the snowstorm of 1979 that sealed Bilandic's political fate. Twelve inches fell on January 1, 1979, and eventually seven feet of snow inundated the city. Garbage from more than 800,000 homes and apartments went uncollected for weeks. The Chicago transit system, famous for working in all kinds of weather, ignominiously ground to a standstill at times, stranding thousands of commuters. Hundreds of city buses were stalled and temporarily lost in mountainous snowdrifts. In the midst of the winter snow-in, transit officials tried to improve service to white areas by cutting all rush hour elevated train service to the most populous black areas of the south and west sides, depriving blacks of their way to work and often the wages for those days. In the midst of these lapses in service, the Chicago *Tribune* revealed that Kenneth Sain, the former deputy mayor under both Daley and Bilandic, had received two nonbid contracts totaling $90,000 to plan snow and ice removal from Chicago's streets.

This wintertime despair set the stage for the political rise of Jane Byrne, a former Daley official who declared war on the machine. Byrne had started in politics in John F. Kennedy's 1960 presidential campaign, when she was a 25-year-old widow of a Marine pilot with a year-old daughter to raise. Byrne spurned offers from the Kennedy Administration to go to Washington to work, staying in Chicago, pursuing a master's degree so she could teach, and fascinating Daley, who could not figure out a woman who worked for Kennedy but did not accept a job with the administration or deal with his organization. Daley taught her all about the organization, placed her in apprenticeship positions in her precinct and ward, named her to a city anti-poverty post. In 1968 he said he wanted to make Byrne "the first woman commissioner in any major city in the United States." She became commissioner of consumer sales, weights and measures and later cochairman of the Cook County Democratic Central Committee and Illinois Democratic national committeewoman.

Byrne's anger with Bilandic's "new machine" and the "cabal of evil men" which she said ran the city started when she accused Bilandic of greasing fare increases for taxicab companies. Bilandic, in response, fired her as commissioner. Until primary day, her candidacy stirred more ridicule than enthusiasm. She had a snowball's chance in hell to win, detractors said—but then hell froze over. On primary day, black voters turned out in massive numbers, giving Byrne 67 percent of their votes and playing the key role in the election. The blacks had long been angry over police brutality and machine opposition to Ward Three's choice of a successor to the late Rep. Ralph Metcalfe. And the snowstorm and the machine's treatment of Wilson Frost gave them new reason to seek a political change. White ethnic voters were also angry that for years City Hall had paid too much attention to downtown while neighborhoods were slowly crumbling. Citywide 51 percent of the votes went antimachine.

Byrne did not try to recentralize power. Resentful of Bilandic's old boy control over City Hall, she turned over complete control of patronage to Democratic party chairman Dunne. But even before the April general election, Byrne hastened to build a new coalition with the elements of the machine. "I never ran against the organization," she said. "I love the Democratic party."

Not long after Byrne's accession to power, the old question of whether the machine would survive Daley's death gave way to much graver questions of Chicago's survival. In her first year in office, Byrne earned the nickname "Calamity Jane" as Chicago was faced by a series of crises that most other older American cities had experienced years before: the debt-ridden school board missed paychecks and ordered job cutbacks, the teachers went on strike, and the firemen followed. The city's credit rating was lowered by two New York rating services. Standard and Poor's dropped it twice in five months from AA to A+ and then A—, and Moody's from AA to A. The ratings services noted that Chicago was still losing productive workers and thus its ability to repay bond principal and interest. Said Byrne: "The so-called city that works hasn't really worked in some time. We had a half-dozen years of Band-Aid government—of ignoring problems and dipping into (bond interest) escrow accounts to pay bills. It was going to blow up eventually, and it finally did. I intend to face the problems and call things as I see them. If that upsets some people, so be it."

Upset some people, Byrne did. She fired her budget director after an alleged $29 million error raised property taxes by 6.7 percent instead of the intended 4.4 percent; later she decided to keep the money anyway because the city needed it. After categorically assuring high Carter administration sources that she would endorse the President for re-election in 1980, Byrne suddenly came out for the nomination of Sen. Edward M. Kennedy instead, an apparent effort to head off a political flanking attack from Richard Daley, the ambitious son of the late mayor. That Byrne was incapable of wielding the clout of her former mentor clearly was reflected in the widespread pre-primary dissidence among party leaders—openly flaunted in public, a cardinal sin in the machine of old—as well as the primary outcome. Carter outpolled Kennedy almost 2–1 in Chicago wards (the President did slightly better statewide), and limited the Massachusetts Senator's share of convention delegates to only 14 of the 49 selected from Chicago congressional districts.

Chicago seemed unable to make up its mind about the blonde who challenged the most macho political system in the country. "Chicago is kind of nutty. People say, 'Oooh, she's in political trouble.' Well, that is what happens when you open up a political system," said Mike Royko. But Royko also called Byrne's appointees "as amazing a collection of political connivers, wheeler-dealers, misfits, incompetents, and deadbeats as I've ever seen." Polls showed that the public recognized that some of the troubles were not entirely of Byrne's making. A January 1980 poll showed that over half the citizens contacted blamed either Daley or Bilandic for the city's financial ills. Even a former Daley stalwart, Alderman Edward (Fast Eddie) Vrdolyak, proclaimed to the city council that, "The city that works was for 20 years the city that juggled its books."

Given Chicago's weak mayor-strong council form of government, it appeared that any revolutionary political reform in Chicago still seemed out of character and legally difficult. The traumatic events of the late 1970s only served to exacerbate the problems and frustrate the idealism of those who would pursue reform. The character of the community, as Professor Milton Rakove has written, supports the machine. "Chicago is a politically conservative, culturally diffuse, governmentally weak community which is resistant to change, fragmented in its constituencies and tolerant of its longtime politics," Rakove wrote. "The political machine has survived and prospered in Chicago because it is representative of the community's cultural differences, adaptive to changes in the city's social and political environment and efficient in its political practices." But others disagreed: Richard Simpson, the former alderman, called Byrne a "transitional figure from government-by-machine to something else. I think she'd like to reshape the machine to suit herself, but it's probably gone too far for that. The most likely outcome, is that for better or worse, Chicago will have the personal, news-media-oriented politics other big cities have."

A small cloud on the machine's traditional style was the election in 1979 of younger, more liberal, and more pragmatic aldermen than their predecessors. The long-term prospects for Chicago's machine, however, depended on how well its leaders could cope with a host of problems that came mostly from outside the machine itself: population decline, difficult relations with other areas of Illinois that were growing in population and voter strength, race rela-tions, a declining number of jobs and industries in the city, the declining tax base, court cases that challenged the patronage system, public employee unionization, and finally increasing demands for better city services.

But whatever its future problems may be, the truth is that the Chicago Democratic machine has endured, robust and healthy, years after the atrophy or death of big-city machines like those in New York and Philadelphia, Kan-sas City and Jersey City. The same reasons given for the decline of the others —increasingly sophisticated electorates and the substitution of government aid, often federal, for breadbaskets—should apply equally in Chicago. Why have they not? Strong leadership and able management of the Chicago ma-chine were certainly major reasons under Daley. Yet even with the death of the heavy-handed father figure, the city remained supportive of the machine concept. For an explanation, we must look further to the powerful allies the Chicago machine has made and kept—big and little business, organized labor, and organized crime—and to that most time-honored of all methods of maintaining power, plain old vote stealing.

Machine Allies: State Street, Captive Unions

For 20 years before his 1975 retirement from the City Council, Alderman Leon Despres argued consistently, even eloquently, for reform—to little avail. But Despres' proximity to the seat of power did sharpen his perspective. Many agreed with his 1968 assessment of the Democratic machine's ties to big business,* which remained little changed as Chicago entered the 1980s:

Chicago's most pampered neighborhood is the central business area, com-prising downtown and the near North Side along Lake Michigan. When visitors speak of Chicago's "dynamic, modern progress," they usually refer to the central business area. There you see bold new buildings, daytime vigor, and excellent city maintenance. New projects are always in the works. Speedy public transit con-verges on the area. Hundreds of millions of dollars in expressway pour people into the area by day and back to the suburbs at night. Get off the subway anywhere in the central business area and you won't find a broken city sidewalk. Get off the subway anywhere else, and you will. Between the central business area and the outskirts lie large, almost uninterrupted gray areas of urban dry rot. There is where most Chicagoans live.

The pampered central business area evidences the basis of Chicago politics, the unwritten compact between Chicago's Democratic political machine and the business and financial interests. Under this tacit agreement the business and finan-cial interests receive luxurious support for the central business area, subsidies of valuable public works, indulgent business-oriented drafting and enforcement of ordinances regulating business, and, for the rest of Chicago, a firm hand on the city's tiller and on the till. In exchange, the business and financial interests pro-vide the machine what it needs in money and Republican backing, and deliver nearly full support of all parts of the public opinion media.

* From "The Chicago the Delegates Won't See," *The Progressive*, August 1968.

Bilandic turned to many corporate executives, especially A. Robert Abboud, chairman of the First National Bank, John Perkins, president of Continental Illinois National Bank, and Thomas Ayers, chief executive officer for Commonwealth Edison, as informal advisors. In the primary after Daley's death, they supported Bilandic, and the general manager of the Merchandise Mart warned businessmen that "the alternative to Mayor Bilandic is chaos." But despite Byrne's pledges to spend more money in the neighborhoods, business achieved a rapprochement with Byrne within one week of election. The political-business partnership, Perkins said, "will continue to play a significant role in maintaining Chicago's stature as the city that works." But to Despres, the situation proved that the politicians and businessmen were "quarreling over who is coming out on top, not over the purpose of the machine itself."

In the words of Emmett Dedmon, vice-editorial director of the Chicago *Sun-Times,* "Chicago, far from being run by its ethnic groups, has been run by its puritanical, white Anglo-Saxon Protestant minority from years ago. There is a business establishment which functions pretty much as an extra government within the city—and that's what has given it its continuity." This business community, Dedmon told us, "has been free to develop its own interests as long as it does not interfere in the political sphere" in a way hostile to the controlling party of the moment. "The system endures in Chicago," Dedmon said, "because of the traditional alliance between politics, business, and labor."

Just how effective that alliance is can be illustrated by the excellent police protection of the Loop, the extremely efficient snow removal usually provided for downtown, and low tax assessments imposed by the machine-controlled county tax assessor. In 1971 investigative reporters discovered that P.J. (Parky) Cullerton had granted millions of dollars in tax breaks to real estate developers who were big Democratic contributors and members of the committee for Cullerton's reelection as assessor. Later a story broke about underassessment of five of the largest Chicago banks. One of the banks was Continental Illinois Bank, which had saved $1.8 million by the preferential treatment. The chairman of the board of Continental Illinois at the time was Donald M. Graham, cochairman of the 1971 businessmen's Nonpartisan Committee to Reelect Mayor Daley.

The mutual aid flows in hundreds of big and small ways. Even though the Loop is the center of the syndicate, downtown continuously ranks as one of the safest sections of the city, thanks to effective foot patrols as well as squad car patrols. When merchants complained about the growing losses from shoplifting, a special court was created to handle the cases, increasing the conviction rate and decreasing the problem. In 1968 there was scarcely a murmur of protest from these Chicago heavies to Daley's strong-arm tactics in controlling demonstrations at the Democratic National Convention—even when the daughter of one business leader was arrested and roughed up by police. Daley strongly supported the creation of a special tax district to finance construction of a subway in the Loop and get rid of its ugly, rumbling overhead rapid transit; when that did not pan out, Daley successfully founded a Regional Transit Authority, including the suburban counties, to provide subsidies for the capital-starved Chicago Transit Authority (CTA) and eliminate a potentially major tax burden for landowners in the central business area.

In the late 1970s, however, the political-business alliance appeared to have trouble coping with the economic and social flux that challenged State Street as the premier downtown shopping center in America. As late as 1974, the *Christian Science Monitor* had referred to State Street as one of the two "remaining viable downtown areas in the nation." The annual gross of State Street merchants rose from almost $400 million in 1970 to $600 million at the end of the decade. But competition arrived in the form of the Magnificent Mile, a 14-block complex of high-fashion stores, luxury hotels, elegant restaurants, stylish theaters, and expensive condominiums (some over $250,000) along North Michigan Avenue. Even Marshall Field's opened a "branch store" in Water Tower Place, the 74-story showpiece of the new district. State Street merchants were also worried about the Loop's new reputation as a work area for whites during the day and entertainment for blacks and Latinos by night. Not only had the clientele changed but, according to urbanologist Pierre de Vise, estimates of those who shop, work, and play on the Loop's streets at night had fallen from 70,000 in the 1950s to under 25,000 by the early 1970s.

Striving valiantly to maintain its position, State Street merchants, with the cooperation of City Hall of course, planned a tree-lined mall the length of the Loop, passing in front of each of four major downtown department stores. Scheduled for completion in late 1979, the mall was to include plazas and sidewalk cafés to attract middle class shoppers. Just south of the Loop lies another possible salvation for State Street: the Dearborn Park project, an attempt to build all at once a complete middle class neighborhood of 3,000 high-rise, middle-rise apartments and townhouses on 51 acres of what used to be mighty railyards. Begun during the Daley years at the behest of downtown businessmen and strongly encouraged by Bilandic, the project was plagued by expensive cost overruns and numerous delays and opening rents starting at a very un-middle class $448 for a one-bedroom apartment. There was the possibility, however, that the mere presence of such housing could do wonders for the stability of the Loop area. Across the nation, big retail developers were saying that middle-to-upper income housing in center city areas is a prerequisite to full-scale revival. The reason: the on-the-streets presence of higher income people automatically cuts crime and creates an atmosphere of greater safety for shoppers.

Organized labor has a similarly close relationship with the machine; in fact, the ties are sometimes so close that one could well say that in Chicago the Democratic party is not in the hip pocket of labor, but rather that labor is in the hip pocket of the Democratic party. Edward Brabec, head of the plumbers union and probably labor's most consistent member of the power coalition, explained the relationship. "In other cities, organized labor doesn't have the influence and input with the mayor that we have. We treasure that.

Here, we're part of the process, part of the organization."

No major Chicago union ever opposed Daley, nor had there been a major public strike of significant duration in the city—until the tense firemen's walkout early in 1980. In some unions, Daley could dictate who would be elected to leadership positions. In 1971 labor staged a gigantic dinner in Daley's honor, attended by 10,158 in cavernous McCormick Place. Sitting on the dais flanked by a praetorian guard of the labor elite and beneath a Mao-sized portrait of himself, Daley could gaze out on 1,100 tables—275 occupied by Teamsters, 190 by building trades, 50 by Steelworkers, etc. In return for this subservience, labor got special breaks and privileges. Joseph Germano, a district Steelworkers director and powerful man in the national union, once was given a voice in party slatemaking. The building trades, Teamsters, and janitors' unions are especially close to the mayor's office; gross featherbedding has been reported in city jobs, and a Chicago garbage truck driver and hauler are among the best paid in the country.*

The close relationship, however, does not mean that Daley regarded the unions as equals. During the 1965 session of the legislature, some Democrats sponsored a bill to extend collective bargaining rights to public employees. But the word came through Governor Kerner that Daley was opposed and the bill would be killed. Why, asked some of the Democrats; isn't labor our friend? The reply (roughly) was as follows: "We're not going to give them anything. We don't want them across the table as equals. We want them to come to us, so we can get something from them."

After Daley's death, machine relations with the unions became a little more complex. In 1978 the Illinois AFL-CIO broke with tradition and supported Republican Sen. Charles Percy for reelection. Bilandic intervened directly or indirectly in five major labor disputes during his first six months in office and, as noted, used strong-arm tactics to keep the firemen in line. But Bilandic also rewarded labor by sponsoring the appointment of Brabec as a director of the Federal Reserve Bank of Chicago, the first union leader ever appointed to any Federal Reserve board. In her campaign, Byrne broke with machine tradition to support collective bargaining, but her ability to maintain that position in the face of a real confrontation remained questionable, especially in the wake of the acrimonious firemen's strike.

Vote Theft and Ties to the Mafia

Unadulterated vote stealing is another underpinning of the Democratic machine; in the 1950s and 1960s, by reliable estimates, between 50,000 and 60,000 unlawful votes were regularly registered in Chicago for the straight

---

* A critical study of Chicago's refuse collection practices, compiled by independent aldermen in 1978, showed Chicago used three loaders on each truck, while many other cities used only two. Chicago's drivers were paid $9.30 an hour, the study said, while those in Philadelphia got $6.48 on the average and, in Baltimore, $5.73 at the top rate. Chicago's garbage loaders likewise were better off, making $7.63 an hour, compared to Philadelphia's $5.81 and Baltimore's $5.23 an hour, the study said.

Democratic ticket. Nowhere in America was vote theft practiced on so grandiose a scale. The importance of this was graphically demonstrated in the 1960 presidential election, when John Kennedy squeaked through in Illinois by a plurality of 8,858 votes in a close national contest. Just two more votes in each of Cook County's 5,199 precincts would have given Nixon Illinois' 27 electoral votes, and after checking only 699 paper-ballot precincts, Republicans charged that Nixon was entitled to at least 4,539 more votes than the Democratic-controlled election board credited him with in those precincts alone. Contempt charges were brought against 677 election officials and precinct workers, but a special judge disposed of all the cases without requiring the persons cited to respond and explain what had happened in their precincts on election day. Charging a "whitewash," the Chicago *Tribune* editorialized: "The net result of this judicial mummery is that election officials have received further assurance that stealing votes is no crime in Chicago."

Illegal registrations, coercion of voters by Democratic precinct captains, and intimidation of Republican poll watchers (who in many wards sell out to the Democrats and collaborate in vote theft) are all part of the Chicago pattern. Since 1960, reformer Republican prosecutors and the lack of cooperation by disaffected blacks have cut back some in the degree of vote stealing. On election day 1976, on the orders of the Republican-held state's attorney and U.S. attorney's offices, an army of close to 800 state and federal legal officials, marshals, and FBI agents fanned out to the precincts to monitor the polls and investigate complaints. Chicago's highly respected Better Government Association (BGA), which pioneered in investigating the machine's vote thefts, had its own teams watching selected wards with a history of ghost voting. The 1976 pollwatching effort showed real progress, BGA's chief investigator Bill Recktenwald told us: "In the old days when we watched out there, we had people thrown out and threatened with guns."

Vote fraud isn't dead in Chicago, however. The 1979 Byrne-Bilandic mayoral primary, Republican state's attorney Bernard Carey told us, produced 2,000 complaints of irregularities, including one charge that a troop of Gi Scouts was illegally handing out campaign literature outside a polling place. The girls told investigators that they had been promised merit badges for their electioneering effort.

The difficulty with reforming Chicago's voting methods is that the history of abuse starts at such an outrageous level. In 1968 the BGA dispatched Recktenwald to register in skid-row hotels under fictitious names—at the McCoy Hotel (owned by Charles Swibel, chairman of the Chicago Housing Authority) under the name of James Joyce, at Workingmen's Palace as Jay Gatsby, at the Legion Hotel as Henry Locke. Sure enough, when the registration sheets for the November election were inspected later, the fictitious names were miraculously registered to vote. On precinct registration day, BGA investigators saw highly paid city employees paying derelicts $2 each to register. One $12,000-a-year sewer inspector, they discovered, registered from the Starr Hotel at 610 West Madison (the same flophouse murderer Richard

Speck once lived at), even though the official was also registered at another address in the city and somehow was able to afford a $70,000 Chicago home and a $100,000 Wisconsin summer home. Among other BGA findings:

Chicago police officers double as precinct captains.

Thousands of persons were registered to vote from empty lots and burned-out buildings, or from expressway cloverleafs, city parks, and many parking lots.

Numerous persons who had died years before were carried on the voter rolls.

As a result of the BGA's investigations, seven election officials resigned before the election, and in 1969 two Democratic precinct captains were convicted of vote fraud. In the reformist 1970s, the same kind of skulduggery was reported. Reporters said they saw machine-controlled election judges repeatedly enter the voting machines and draw the curtains before the polls opened. In one precinct, reporters with binoculars watched voters receiving yellow slips at the polling place, which were then taken around the corner and exchanged for money. In 1972 the Chicago *Tribune* infiltrated the Board of Elections and uncovered more than 1,000 registration frauds and other irregularities that helped lead to numerous indictments and the Pulitzer Prize. The fears of greater voter fraud in Chicago remained so strong that in 1977 John Hanly, then chairman of the Chicago Board of Elections, pleaded with a congressional committee not to pass national legislation allowing registration on election day. "Believe me, anything going wrong in smaller jurisdictions will be compounded a hundredfold in Chicago," Hanly candidly testified.

The Better Government Association is the only one of its kind in the country—a privately sponsored, unofficial watchdog agency to ferret out malfeasance in government. (A $600,000-a-year budget is contributed by business and professional leaders.) BGA's staff of aggressive investigators, headed by J. Terrence Brunner, a former Justice Department attorney specializing in organized crime, has no subpoena power or shred of legal authority. Nevertheless, it has worked effectively to reveal scores of scandals in city, suburban, and state government and save Illinois taxpayers millions of dollars. BGA's standard operating method is to select one of Chicago's fiercely competitive newspapers or television stations to work with it on an investigation, or to cooperate with reporters from one of the papers when they turn up first leads on a potential scandal.

One BGA investigation revealed that some of Chicago's worst slum buildings were owned by officials of the city buildings department, and that lackadaisical or compromised code enforcement was causing thousands of Chicagoans to live in indescribable filth in dangerously unsafe tenements.

A BGA investigation into crime syndicate political alliances in the Veterans Park District, which administers local parks in five western suburbs, led to the indictment of six men on charges ranging from grand theft to forgery, conspiracy, and official misconduct; five were subsequently convicted. The Oak Forest police chief was fired after BGA men photographed him lounging at the racetrack with Mafia hoods. In 1969 the BGA was able to document lucrative graft and corruption at the Illinois State Fair. Its allegations of rampant waste, inefficiency, and loafing by employees of Chicago's vast Park District and the Cook County Forest Preserve roused the ire of Mayor Daley, who accused the BGA of being an arm of the Republican party. But other BGA probes have embarrassed Republicans just as much.

During the late '70s the BGA and the Chicago *Sun-Times* secretly took over a tavern operating near downtown, the Mirage, to find out through close surveillance if the tales of extortion and petty graft among Chicago's inspectors were true. They were. The BGA and the *Sun-Times* documented a parade of city inspectors ignoring health and safety codes for payoffs ranging from $10 to $100; private contractors routinely acting as go-betweens for city inspectors hesitant to take bribes directly from strangers; accountants and tax preparers offering counsel on ways to keep two sets of books; vending machine distributors skimming cash off the top of their weekly collections from pinball and other amusement machines; and shakedowns by state liquor inspectors. Subsequently, 11 city inspectors were suspended from their jobs for their negligence and worse at the Mirage. But the action was less than the reforms the BGA proposed.

In substantial measures, then-BGA director George Bliss told us in 1970, Chicago has put behind it the days when the syndicate mobsters terrorized and virtually ruled the city, the era of wide-open red light districts, Prohibition bootleg profiteering, Al Capone, and raw murders in the streets. But the mob—variously referred to as the Syndicate, Cosa Nostra, Mafia, and other titles—still has a Chicago branch that Ovid Demaris in his 1969 book *Captive City* described as "the most politically insulated and police-pampered 'family' this side of Sicily." Unlike the many-headed Mafia structure of the New York-New Jersey area, the Chicago syndicate is a single system. The first postwar leader was Tony Accardo, onetime bodyguard to Al Capone; when he got embroiled in an income tax evasion case in 1956, Accardo turned the reins over to Sam Giancana, the prime suspect in countless murder investigations and a man who was once described by one police official as "a snarling, sarcastic, ill-mannered, ill-tempered, sadistic psychopath." In the late 1960s, Giancana in turn had a scrape with the law and stepped down in favor of William (Willie Potatoes) Daddano, alleged assassin, torturer, gambling and pinball machine czar and convicted burglar. In 1976 Giancana was murdered, and Accardo once again was back on top of the syndicate, only to find himself the prime suspect in a Justice Department inquiry into the gangland-style killing of five presumed burglars who were believed to have broken into Accardo's home in 1978. When federal agents searched Accardo's River Forest home after the incident, they found —and seized—$275,000 in neat stacks of $5,000 bills. Accardo brazenly appealed for return of the money.

While Dan Walker was president of the Chicago Crime Commission, he published reports listing the names of more than 100 firms and 200 individuals with crime syndicate connections. The notoriety forced many companies out of business. One firm, with an American Stock Exchange listing, was forced to reorganize. Demaris charged that tens of thousands of Chicagoans were involved in organized crime, a vast army of "burglars, hijackers, fences, counterfeiters, moonshiners, panderers, prostitutes, B-girls, cab-drivers, bartenders, extortionists, narcotics peddlers, juicemen, collectors, torturers, assassins, (corrupt) cops, venal judges and politicians, union and business fronts, plus an array of gamblers including bookies, steerers and policy runners."

A measure of the Chicago syndicate's efficiency is that while there have been more than a thousand mob slayings in the city since Capone arrived there in 1919, only a handful have been solved. By contrast, the police are able to solve 62 percent of all run-of-the-mill killings—those committed by average men and women in the passion of a moment.

And there is a seemingly endless web of interconnection between the Chicago mob and Chicago politicians, amply documented over the years by the BGA, the Chicago Crime Commission, the Chicago newspapers, and writers like Demaris. The prime example is the First Ward, a downtown area including the Loop, the banks, City Hall, museums and luxury hotels, slum homes of derelicts, newly arrived immigrants, and the dispossessed. Up to the mid-1960s, this was a strongly Italian area; in 1962 it was estimated to hold 30,000 Italians, 15,000 blacks, 14,000 Mexicans and Puerto Ricans, 10,000 Poles and Bohemians, and smaller assortments of Chinese, Jews, Irish, and Greeks. (Since then urban renewal has shifted the population focus and poor blacks now dominate.) For years, the First was the heart of Chicago gangsterism and corrupt politics; here flourished such figures as "Bathhouse" John Coughlin and Hinky Dink Kenna, the diminutive 5-foot, 100-pound ward committeeman for 50 years (1895–1944) who ran a flourishing red-light district and fostered countless hoods, including the infamous Al Capone himself. As Demaris tells the story,

> Kenna and Coughlin collected votes and tribute for every racket and vice operation in their baliwick. . . . They had their own policemen, prosecutors, judges, state legislators and always at least one United States Congressman for speechifying on patriotic occasions. . . . Some precinct captains were gamblers, bootleggers and male madams. Whatever their origin, precinct captains had a slice of the rackets, especially bookmaking. . . .

> Back in his Blackstone Hotel suite, the Dink was guarded by city policemen and Syndicate gunmen. . . . Finally, in 1946, at the age of 86, he died. He left $1,100,000 in cash to relatives who proved to be just as greedy as he was—they ignored his request for a $30,000 mausoleum for his wife and himself; instead, their graves were marked by $85 headstones.

An illustrious First Ward leader for several decades was Roland ("Libby") Libonati, who defended accused murderers in some 200 trials and looked the picture of a mob member himself. Asked about his friendship with Al Capone in 1947, Libonati told a reporter: "Mr. Capone showed me

great respect as a person of Italian extraction who represented one of the
pioneer families of Chicago, and naturally I . . . ah . . . returned . . . I returned . . . I treated him in accordance with . . . I treated him with respect
as I would do any American. . . . You know, politically that man was not a
politician. If people treat me nice, I treat them nice." On other occasions
Libonati delighted listeners with such pronouncements as "Nobody can
speak asunder of the government's reputation. . . . Not by any creeping of
the imagination. . . . I am trying not to make any honest mistakes. . . . The
moss is on the pumpkin. . . ."

Libonati served in the legislature for 22 years, where he was an able member of the "West Side bloc," a bipartisan group that strove to kill all anti-
crime legislation. In 1957 the mob chose Libonati to go to the U.S. Congress,
where two interesting things happened to him: he was immediately placed on
the House Judiciary Committee (to the horror of some of his more scrupu-
lous colleagues), and he found it wise to take on as a congressional aide a
young attorney named Anthony P. Tisci—the son-in-law of none other than
the man who had decided Libonati would be Congressman, syndicate boss
Sam Giancana.

In 1963 Libonati suddenly announced a desire to retire; as widely assumed at the time and proven by a secret federal report printed by Demaris,
this was at Giancana's orders.* Giancana picked Frank Annunzio, an above-
average First Ward product who had indeed been Governor Adlai Stevenson's
labor director, to succeed Libonati, and the party and voters in customary
fashion ratified his choice with 85.9 percent of the vote. Although Annunzio
took a congressional interest in consumer fraud and veterans affairs that made
him more than a mere Mafia figurehead, no one doubted that he would retire if the syndicate told him to. He was redistricted out of a seat in the 1970s
but moved to the Northwest Side and won election there.

The most charitable view one can take of City Hall's attitude toward
the mob-infested First Ward and the downtown congressional district is that
it deliberately ignored the brazen control of criminal elements. In the mid-
1960s, the FBI was able to establish clear connections between four leading
First Ward politicians and the syndicate's shakedowns, payoffs to police, and
vice and gambling networks in the area. The U.S. Attorney, Edward Hanrahan, was given specific information about two payoffs totaling $30,000 from
Giancana to First Ward politicians. Yet Hanrahan, loyal son of the city
Democratic machine, refused to press for indictments. (U.S. Attorneys are
presidential appointees who serve four-year terms.) When press agitation
mounted for Hanrahan's resignation, Mayor Daley leaped to his defense, saying, "Hanrahan's reputation for integrity, intelligence, and courage is un-

* Why did Giancana force Libonati to retire? According to one report, Libonati backed a
weakening amendment to the 1963 civil rights bill at a crucial point in committee deliberations. Robert
F. Kennedy, then attorney general, called Daley to protest and by some accounts said if Libonati returned to Congress, Kennedy would see to it that he went to jail. Daley apparently got the word to
Giancana and Libonati was axed. Libonati told our reporter friend Andrew Glass that he "was caught
in the switches" and "given a Mickey Finn."

equaled." (This was before Hanrahan's troubles with the Black Panthers led the machine to dump him.)

Yet when questioned at press conferences about the corrupt leadership of the First Ward, Daley became general, evasive, the master of platitude. His most specific answer to reporters' questions about the skulduggery: "The leadership of the First Ward is selected by the people of the ward. . . . I am proud of the leadership I have exerted in this entire community." Daley's reasons for professed ignorance of pervasive and frequently documented corruption was not hard to divine: the First Ward turned in four- and five-to-one margins for Democratic candidates on election day. The machine could count on pluralities of 100,000 and more—not only a major asset in state and county contests, but, as 1960 showed, perhaps even vital in electing a President of the United States.

Population losses and reforms have shriveled the First Ward's election margin to half, but the syndicate still has special access to power. When the slatemakers met after Daley's death to pick a successor, the gathering included Alderman Fred (Peanuts) Roti, who *Chicago* magazine said serves within the council as the "eyes and ears" of the First Ward and crime interests in nine other wards. As *Chicago* noted, "Roti was the only person present throughout the week of meetings who did not hold a major leadership post or a staff position in the inner circle. His role here, too, was to watch and listen."

The Police, the Syndicate, and the Democratic Convention

Corruption is as endemic to the Chicago police force as patronage to its political system. For decades, there have been policemen on the take—accepting penny-ante payoffs for minor infractions * or, at the highest levels of the department, senior commanders accepting bribes to let the mob carry on its work of numbers games, prostitution, and extortion, unmolested by honest cops. Up to 1960, according to Sandy Smith, *Time-Life's* former investigative reporter in Chicago, "Commanders in police headquarters were on the Mob's payroll. The graft system, or the Fix, worked almost openly in most station houses where the payoff distributor—the bagman—was easily identifiable. Gangsters who operated rackets in a district sometimes held enough political power to dictate the choice of a district captain."

In 1960 came perhaps the worst scandal ever to rock the Chicago Police Department, as eight policemen were arrested and sent to jail for burglary. Daley fired the police superintendent of the moment and appointed in his stead the highly respected Orlando Wilson, dean of the school of criminology at the University of California. Wilson cleaned up the most blatant corrup-

---

* Mort Sahl once said Chicago's Outer Drive was "the last outpost of collective bargaining."

tion, built new police stations, installed a $2 million highly computerized communications system considered one of the finest in the world. But the system of ingrained corruption was more than even a man of Wilson's stature could deal with adequately. A secret FBI report, prepared in 1963 under orders from Attorney General Robert Kennedy, named 43 Chicago policemen allegedy working in collusion with the underworld. One of those specifically named was Lt. Paul Quinn, one of Wilson's chief aides (and later a top deputy to Wilson's successor, Superintendent James B. Conlisk, Jr.). Quinn had liaison duties with City Hall and was known as "the mayor's man" at police headquarters. The FBI alleged that Quinn had received $200 monthly from the mob "in compensation for this activity as a tipoff man for North Side hoodlums." Another man named in the federal report, Captain James Riordan, commander of the Central Police District, was alleged to be protecting strip-tease honky-tonks and to have "sanctioned" the distribution of payoffs.

Mayor Daley said he had not read the FBI report but nonetheless attacked it as a "vicious document." Wilson also brushed aside the FBI's allegations. But when he retired in 1967, Wilson acknowledged that the Cosa Nostra was so entrenched in Chicago that he had barely scratched its surface. And he said he had not been able to eradicate corruption on the police force.

Much of business as usual returned to police headquarters with the accession of Conlisk, a man close to Daley and member of an old Chicago police family (his father had been one of the nine "old men" who resigned from the force when the 1960 scandal broke). Indeed, Conlisk had been in office less than a year when he sacked the courageous chief of the department's anti-mobster Intelligence Unit, Captain William Duffy. Duffy had just led a raid, in conjunction with federal authorities, on a North Side headquarters for "bolita," the Cuban numbers game. The raid turned up "ice lists"—the mob's list of protection payoffs it had made to police, including members of the Vice Control Division, which is supposed to be responsible for suppressing gambling in the city. The monthly graft payroll to the Chicago police paid by this single operation had been $8,020, or nearly $100,000 a year. In the wake of the raid, one of the mob's gambling bosses reportedly boasted: "We got a promise that Duffy will go." And shortly, on Conlisk's orders, Duffy did go—to a 4 P.M. to midnight job as watch commander in the quiet, Jewish district of Albany Park.

As Sandy Smith of *Time-Life* summed up the situation, "There is a climate around Chicago police in which organized crime thrives like jungle shrubbery. There are good cops in Chicago—but not enough of them." The same situation prevailed to the end of the '70s: while police corruption had taken on a lower profile, there was widespread assumption in the city of continuing syndicate influence.

In calmer times, a compromised Chicago police force might have presented no clear and present dangers. Before the 1960s, the Chicago police had been even more corrupt and the people of Chicago seemed to accept it. But the late 1960s were also the time of black revolt, and a huge majority of the force was made up of men from white ethnic communities that had the least natural empathy for militant blacks. During the explosive protest marches led by Martin Luther King, Jr., in 1967, the police handled themselves well. In the spring of 1968, when the tumultuous West Side ghetto erupted into a major riot in the wake of King's assassination—leading to arson that destroyed blocks of buildings, widespread looting, sniper battles, and the calling up of 12,000 National Guard and federal troops—Daley assigned the elite police units to guard the Loop and let the ghetto streets go undermanned; nevertheless, the police on the West Side acted with general restraint, despite some questionable deaths. But then Mayor Richard Daley let the genie of police violence out of the bottle. Provoked, confused, angered by the rioting in his beloved city, Daley said he had told Conlisk "very emphatically and very definitely that an order be issued immediately and under his signature to shoot to kill any arsonist or anyone with a Molotov cocktail in his hand in Chicago because they're potential murderers, and to issue a police order to shoot to maim or cripple anyone looting any stores in the city." It mattered little that the next day Daley said that the police would use only "minimum force" in carrying out orders, and blandly asserted, "There wasn't any shoot-to-kill order. That was a fabrication." As D. J. R. Bruckner, the Los Angeles *Times'* Midwestern correspondent, pointed out, "The mayor's repentence will always be suspect. . . . The revelation of his inner anger has set loose evil spirits which may never be laid to rest again."

Only four months later, the Democratic National Convention of 1968 opened in Chicago, and with it came thousands of youthful demonstrators bent on protest against the Vietnam war and discrediting the old-line political system that was about to nominate the Johnson administration's candidate, Hubert Humphrey, for the Presidency. Raw intelligence from FBI files raised the specter of widespread street violence, of disruption of convention proceedings, of LSD in the water system or uprisings in the black ghettos. The reports frightened Daley and his colleagues and put them in a frame of mind to use whatever force might be necessary to maintain order.

Into the city streamed a motley band of hippies, yippies, SDS'ers in search of a confrontation—but also thousands of McCarthy-style liberals who abhorred any kind of violence, and thousands of innocent bystanders swept up in it. No repetition is needed here of the agonizing story of repeated and escalated street clashes between protestors and police, of tear-gassing and the senseless nighttime curfew at Lincoln Park and the bludgeoning of the curfew-breakers by police in the dark, of the cruel violence perpetrated before television cameras, of obscene provocation on the one side and brutal police attacks on the other. "It left a scar on the city of Chicago," *Newsweek* commented, "that may become as indelible a part of its violent history as the Haymarket Riot and the St. Valentine's Day Massacre." *

---

* *Newsweek* might have added that Chicago's violent history also included the Pullman strike of 1893, in which federal troops were called in to quiet rioters; the race riot of 1919, which took the lives of 38; the Republic Steel strike of 1937, in which 10 died.

At the request of the National Commission on the Causes and Prevention of Violence, a 212-member staff under Chicago attorney Daniel Walker interviewed thousands of witnesses to prepare a report on just what had happened at the convention. Some highlights from its report:

The Chicago police were the targets of mounting provocation by both word and act. It took the form of obscene epithets, and of rocks, sticks, bathroom tiles and even human feces hurled at police by demonstrators. That was the nature of the provocation. The nature of the response was unrestrained and indiscriminate police violence on many occasions, particularly at night. That violence was made all the more shocking by the fact that it was often inflicted upon persons who had broken no law, disobeyed no order, made no threat. . . .
On the part of the police there was enough wild club-swinging, enough cries of hatred, enough gratuitous beating to make the conclusion inescapable that individual policemen, and lots of them, committed violent acts far in excess of the requisite force for crowd dispersal or arrest. To read dispassionately the hundreds of statements describing at first hand the events of Sunday and Monday nights is to become convinced of the presence of what can only be called a police riot.

One incident within the 343-page Walker report bears special relevance to the story of Chicago's police over the years. A deputy commissioner of police, distraught by the attacks of individual policemen on demonstrators, started to pull his men away, crying, "Stop, damn it, stop. For Christ's sake, stop it." But these police were not to be controlled, even by their officers. In a police force honeycombed with payoffs and favors from the syndicate, involving officers and their men alike, and in a city where a mayor talks of shooting to kill, it was not surprisng to hear that police discipline evaporated in a moment of stress.

Whatever the problems of the Chicago police, it was sure that they remained totally, indiscriminately loyal to the political machine. In 1977, 15 current and former state legislators revealed that the Chicago police had spied on them and compiled dossiers. The legislators' common crime: all had at one point or another dared to raise objections to Daley and his policies.

The Church: Catholic and Ecumenical

For many decades, the Roman Catholic Archdiocese of Chicago and the Cook County Democratic organization have been closely allied—if for no other reason than the fact that they share the same heavily Irish, Polish, and Italian constituencies. George Cardinal Mundelein, who gained world renown for his public denunciation of Hitler in the early 1930s, was a personal friend of President Roosevelt; in Chicago he cooperated extensively with the mayor and party boss of the era, Ed Kelly. John Cardinal Cody, leader of the flock of 2.5 million (the largest Roman Cathlic archdiocese in North America) since 1966, is an authoritarian figure similar to Mayor Daley, and in fact the two men had a close working relationship.

The machine-church ties extend to a parish precinct connection too. Irish priests in Chicago are as prominent as Irish politicians, and many priests have family members whose jobs depend on the machine. Despite the presumed American separation of church and state, the churches are recipients of services. One priest told us of a parish where the school got its playground resurfaced and vapor lights installed by the city. "That's where the buy-off occurs," the priest explained. "The clergy are basically sympathetic to the machine."

But just as reform movements and black militancy threaten the Democratic machine, so the winds of change symbolized by the Vatican Council and Pope John started a decline in the authoritarian regime of the church. Under Cody's two direct predecessors, Samuel Cardinal Stritch and Albert Cardinal Meyer, many new and creative ideas were introduced: a Catholic Interracial Council, work with the Catholic workers movement, cooperation with Chicago's pioneer community organizations such as The Woodlawn Organization, and an Interreligious Council on Urban Affairs which led to deep involvement of Catholics, Protestants, and Jews together on inner-city problems.

Cardinal Cody, outspoken for the record on equal rights in race matters,* attempted to cork the bottle of change and ecumenicism among both the clergy and laity. One of his first moves was to remove from his key diocesan urban affairs post a foremost spokesman for racial amity and inner-city social work, Monsignor John Egan. Egan had also been the first outspoken critic within the church of Daley and the Democratic machine. Cody cut off contributions to the Metropolitan Area Housing Alliance and blocked a $50,000 grant from outside sources to a Chicago area coalition of churches to help rejuvenate the parishes on the grounds that the priests had acted without his approval. The atmosphere within the church had shifted from one of openness and innovation under Cardinal Meyer to a stifling of initiative and creativity under Cody.

Dozens of Chicago area priests have found the situation intolerable and have left the priesthood in recent years. Another form of response, begun in 1965, was the Association of Chicago Priests, a forerunner of various priests organizations across the country. About 900 of the 2400 priests in the archdiocese joined originally; in 1979 the number of priests in the association had dipped to 572. The group pressed for a strong church social action program (including work in the ghettos), lifting the requirement of celibacy, permitting men to be worker priests, and consideration of team ministries which would eliminate the pastor as an authority figure and include priests, laity, and sisters working together as a "pastoral team." To some degree, Cody succeeded in "squashing" the activist clerics, a priest told us. But in early 1979, the Association showed signs of life when it made public its year-

---

* Theory and practice in church race policies may not always go together. The Rev. Rollins Lambert, who in 1949 became the first black priest in the Chicago Archdiocese, has described Cody and "the whole white church" as "unconsciously racist." In 1978, one could still count the number of black priests in Chicago on your fingers, a cleric said.

long diplomatic effort to make the Vatican aware of Cody's "arbitrary exercise of authority" and the priests' conviction that Chicago needed a new archbishop. Shortly thereafter, the Rev. Andrew Greeley, a Chicago priest and author, asserted in his book *The Making of the Popes, 1978* that three Popes had tried to remove Cody and failed. "That's a dirty lie," Cody replied.

In fairness, it should be noted that Cody did reallocate funds to provide subsidies for about three dozen Catholic schools serving the poor, inner-city areas. The subsidies were continued despite a furious battle during mid-decade which raged within the Priests' Senate, pitting the pastors of the black and poor city neighborhoods against those serving the more affluent suburban communities. The split in the Senate was reflective of the intensely felt schism on liberal and racial attitudes among Catholics at large in Chicagoland, wherein lay part of Cody's difficulties. The middle-aged, wage-earning ethnic, and especially the older generation of retired Catholics, do not accept change readily. They were reared on a conservative dogma, with respect taught for the authoritarian priest figure and the value of neighborhood and homes among one's own people. Vatican II, the racial pressures, and the liberal attitude of younger priests and some laity threatened those values. Even if Cody had been disposed toward socially progressive change, he would have found it difficult to get the sheep to follow the shepherd when they fear the wolves in the shadows. That task remained for a new generation of shepherds.

Social Work in the Melting Pot; Back of the Yards and Saul Alinsky

One of America's most complex and colorful melting pots, Chicago has been making a major effort to ease conditions for its polyglot immigrants ever since Jane Addams started Hull House to help newly arrived Greeks, Lithuanians, Italians, Jews, Irish, Germans, and Poles more than 90 years ago. Chicago's very first settlers, the American Indians, numbered only 400 in the city in 1940 but have risen to several tens of thousands in population, necessitating their own Indian Center with a salaried director. Today valiant community organizers are just beginning to provide help to the newest of Chicago immigrants, the Latinos, many of whom are illegal aliens. Totally unorganized politically, the Latinos face language problems and exploitative labor practices equal to those of immigrants a century ago.

Chicago deserves to be remembered as the city that gave birth to the modern community organization techniques of confrontation, sit-downs, boycotts, and militancy that have become a vogue in recent years. The man probably most responsible for this was Chicagoan Saul Alinsky, a sharp-witted nonconformist who died at 63 in 1972. Alinsky, who enjoyed the sobriquet "The Professional Radical" given him by *Harper's Magazine*, traveled all over the U.S.A. helping numerous community organizations get their start: The

Woodlawn Organization in South Chicago, the FIGHT organization to mobilize blacks to deal with Eastman Kodak in Rochester, and inspiring César Chávez to start the organization of California grape pickers.

The test tube for Alinsky's method was the sprawling steeple-and-smoke-stack neighborhood of stockyard workers living in the late 1930s in the area in back (to the west) of the famous Chicago Stockyards, close to Daley's Bridgeport. The area was afflicted with severe problems of poverty, juvenile delinquency, health, housing, unemployment, but perhaps most serious of all, deep-seated hostilities among its 24 various nationality groups. Joseph B. Meegan, who worked with Alinsky in founding the Back of the Yards Council and is still its director, recalls that "the Poles didn't speak to the Lithuanians or the Slovaks to the Bohemians or the Slovenians to the Ukrainians, and the Irish called them all foreigners." Stockyards workers were earning 39 cents an hour but were so hostile to each other that the Packinghouse Workers were experiencing great difficulties in organizing them. One of the first things the Back of the Yards Council did was to arrange a unity meeting of some 16,000 packinghouse workers; under threat of a strike, an immediate increase of 17 cents an hour was obtained; later on, strikes were actually called and, in some, clergy joined the picket line.

The principal groups which threw in their lot with the Back of the Yards Council were the workers, the churches (virtually all Roman Catholic, but split up into Polish, Lithuanian, Mexican, Irish parishes, etc.), and the small merchants of the area. The plan succeeded spectacularly in drawing the community together, and major accomplishments were ticked off year by year: first labor organization to get living wages for the packinghouse workers and to make sure men from the neighborhood got the available stockyards jobs, then a broad school lunch program, an infant care clinic, water fluoridation, employment counseling for workers (especially necessary as the stockyards later declined and gave way to light industry*), and sustained efforts to control street gangs and help out youngsters as soon as they are arrested for a first juvenile offense. The Council has sustained a painstaking record-keeping program to track the ownership and condition of every house and piece of land in the area, in order to encourage maximum property maintenance. We have seen few other American communities in which so many low-cost homes have been so well tended; one may question the tastefulness of stucco applique or aluminum siding, but the tenant's love of hearth and home is there for all the world to see. No less than 80 percent of the homes are owner occupied.

Since Alinsky's death, his work has been carried on by the Industrial Areas Foundation, which teaches tactics of community organizing. In 1975 Alinsky's

---

* The century-old Union Stockyards, which inspired Carl Sandburg to call Chicago "Hog Butcher for the world" and Upton Sinclair to write *The Jungle,* culminated a long decline by dropping handling of the last farm animals in February 1971. The decline began in the 1950s when the big packers like Swift, Wilson, and Armour shifted their slaughtering to more efficient, one-story plants at locations near the farms and feed lots where cattle and hogs are born and fattened. Rapid truck transport of the already slaughtered animals made the decentralization feasible. Now the stockyards are rapidly turning into an industrial park, and the hardy ethnics whose fathers and grandfathers once sweated to earn 15¢ an hour in the steaming slaughter rooms are employed in small factories or on Chicago's many construction projects.

followers reached a new level of success with the passage of the federal legislation to end bankers' vicious practice of refusing to grant mortgages in the
nation's inner-city neighborhoods. The force behind the new law was Gale
Cincotta, the first woman to lead an Alinsky style group and a typically Chicagoan figure: the daughter of a Greek father and a Latvian mother, high
school educated, the widow of a service station manager, and mother of six
sons. Cincotta started out applying pressure tactics to real estate agents, businessmen, and politicians in her Westside neighborhood of Austin in the late
1960s, a time when real estate sales people were encouraging panic selling as
the first blacks moved in. Soon she moved on to other issues, employing tactics that Alinsky would love. When a local savings and loan association would
not provide enough money for mortgages in the neighborhood, Cincotta and
her neighborhood group organized a "bank-in," tying up the facility for an
entire day with children cashing in their piggy banks and adults buying $5
money orders. When one slumlord failed to respond to demands to repair his
property, neighborhood activists leafleted the suburban Little League baseball
game where he was coaching, asking parents if they wanted their children
under the influence of a man who tolerated such rotten living conditions for
his tenants. One alderman found a rat nailed to his door when he failed to
show up for a community rat control meeting; within a week, city rat abatement crews had made the rounds in the neighborhood, not once, but twice.
"You can't win by being nice," Cincotta said.

After becoming head of the Metropolitan Area Housing Alliance, this
amply proportioned "mama of community organizing," as Cincotta was
known, formed National People's Action, a coalition of 300 neighborhood
groups around the country, and took on Washington. Within a year, Cincotta
and other national neighborhood leaders had muscled through Congress the
Community Reinvestment Act of 1975, which required the nation's banks and
other lenders to disclose by zip code where they make home loans, a major
step toward curbing "redlining" of neighborhoods. In 1977 Cincotta and company took on the insurance industry's unwillingness to issue fire and homeowners policies in deteriorating neighborhoods. Scared to death of the same
federal regulation the neighborhood movement had wrought on the bankers,
the insurance companies quickly fell in line; for example, Allstate Insurance
Company, a subsidiary of the Chicago based Sears Roebuck and Company,
pledged to funnel $1 million in housing rehabilitation and improved finance
services in inner cities, with substantial portions targeted for six Chicago
neighborhoods. Aetna Life & Casualty went a step further by announcing in
late 1979 a commitment to invest $15 million in housing projects in six of
the scrappiest neighborhoods in Cincotta's organization, plus a $225,000 grant
for training by the neighborhood groups of housing specialists.

The sad note to this saga of Alinsky success in the 1970s was that while
his tactics continued to help poor people in other places, community organizing was not doing well in its home base of Chicago. As Cincotta spent more
time on national politics, her local organizations became less effective and less

powerful as a political force. Alinsky-trained organizers established effective community organizations for Latinos in Los Angeles and San Antonio but did relatively little among the same group in Chicago. Ironically some of Chicago's strongest neighborhood groups sprang up in the bastions of white ethnic power, such as Marquette Park on the Southwest side. Their cause, however, was to maintain the status quo, to curb the power of Chicago's growing black and Latino populations, a far cry from Alinsky's advocacy of social and economic change to benefit the underprivileged.

The Balkanized Black Nation in Chicago and a Footnote on the Unorganized Latin Minority

For half a century, and most spectacularly in the decades immediately after World War II began, the cars of the Illinois Central Railroad transported vast numbers of blacks up the Mississippi River Valley, from Louisiana and Mississippi, Arkansas and Tennessee, into the city of Chicago. According to the 1970 Census figures, there were at least 1,102,620 blacks in Chicago. In reality, because of the problem of Census undercounts in minority areas, the figure was probably much higher.

During the 1970s the great black northward movement slowed to a trickle, but the relative importance of blacks as a cultural and voting force in Chicago continued to grow as whites fled to the suburbs. The black percentage of the Chicago population went up from only 8 percent in 1940 to 14 percent in 1950, 23 percent in 1960, and 33 percent in 1970. A 1978 University of Chicago study, which estimated the number of blacks at 1.2 million, said that blacks made up 40 percent of the city's population. (Whites made up 49 percent, and Latinos made up the bulk of the other 11 percent.)

The black civilization of Chicago is so multifaceted—from the great national black media *The Defender*, its daily paper of great pride and vigor, and its popular black magazines *Ebony* and *Jet*, to the longtime headquarters of the Black Muslims, to its enormous, usually unexercised political potential—that we can only sample some aspects of the political, economic, and social life of black Chicago in this chapter.

With the possible exception of Cleveland, no city is as rigidly segregated in its housing patterns as Chicago. In the 1950s and 1960s, whites would flee like locusts whenever a black family moved onto the block. In 1968, 5.2 blocks a week in Chicago shifted from white to black; reform legislation (persistently pursued by several community organizations) curtailed some of the abuses in the '70s, but the latent panic that could sweep a neighborhood still existed. Whites sometimes organized to stem the black expansion; certain streets on the Southwest Side stretched like great Chinese Walls of Segregation, and certain parks remained sanctified holy lands for the ethnics, areas blacks could transgress only out of ignorance or militance.

There are two great black population concentrations in Chicago. The first, and by far the largest, is the South Side. Many of its neighborhoods—Woodlawn, Kenwood, Grand Boulevard, and the like—have been black for decades now; many others, clear down to the city border, are more recently black or turning black. Only a handful, most notably Hyde Park, North Kenwood, and the South Commons area,* have witnessed successful and durable integration. Especially in its southern sections, the South Side has some prosperous, middle-class black neighborhoods; the more desperate slums are in its more northern sections. One South Side area, Woodlawn, is home of the first and probably most effective community organization in any American ghetto (a story to which we will return in a few pages). In all, the South Side has about as settled a feeling as any large black section of a U.S. city.

In the violent 1960s, the raw, volatile ghetto of the city was in Lawndale and other West Side sections—Jewish communities until the '50s or the '60s which then experienced a lightning transformation into all-black islands. As Chicago's overall black immigration slowed in the '70s, the West Side lost some of the social instability associated with an immigrant center. Still when West Side blacks began to make some money, the most frequent pattern was for them to escape to better-to-do sections of the South Side.

The sociologist Pierre de Vise reported in his 1967 book, *Chicago's Widening Color Gap*, that compared to the white Chicagoan or white suburbanite the average black of the city was less likely to find a job, even less likely to hold a managerial position, traveling farther to the job, living in housing smaller and more dilapidated but just as costly as a white person's and earning only two-thirds as much. Between 1970 and 1975, de Vise later told us, conditions deteriorated. The medium income of white families in the Chicago metropolitan area rose from $14,760 to $15,720 while the median income for blacks actually fell from $9,380 to $8,300.

Yet at the same time, thousands of blacks were able to move into middle class status. The contrast is "simply striking," said former HUD regional director Francis Fisher, when one remembers that in 1952, the Yellow Cabs in Chicago had not a single black driver, only one State Street store had black sales people, and only one or two Loop restaurants served blacks. "The bright, educated person in Chicago today knows he or she can get a good job—in contrast to the discouragement and desperation of a few years back."

This is not a solution, Fisher acknowledged, for the 16-to-18-year-old school dropouts with police records or for families mired in the worst slums. The outlook for black Chicagoans living in poverty is poor indeed. By any indicator, the quality of public education is shameful for a city that supposedly works. "The public schools are just jungles," a Catholic priest told us. The parochial schools are not just havens for ethnic whites seeking to avoid interracial contact, but also for poor black families, many not even Catholic, who make incredible sacrifices to pay the tuition to get their children into

---

* South Commons, a completely new area with 4,000 residents, has succeeded as an integrated community because the entrepreneur who built it had the guts to build in a quarter-million-dollar school, which he then succeeded in leasing to the city. With a quality, integrated school, many young white families have been kept who might otherwise have fled to the suburbs.

parochial school, the priest said. But for the poorest of the blacks, dependence on the public schools means that they are not receiving the education to prepare them for advanced jobs. There has been a protracted battle to improve the education of black children by integrating the schools, but the machine stymied the effort for so long that it has become a moot question unless the suburbs are involved. Enrollment figures for 1978–79 showed that white children made up only a fifth of the pupil population, blacks three-fifths, and Hispanics the rest.*

Many Chicago blacks would like to move, but the question is where? Squeezed by low incomes and hemmed in by ethnic neighborhood barriers, their options are limited. There is ample evidence to show that the segregated housing patterns in Chicago, which in turn are the major cause of school segregation, are fostered by government itself. In 1968 a federal district court ruled that the Chicago Housing Authority, a creature of the city government which uses federal funds to put up public housing, was guilty of racial discrimination in choosing building sites and assigning tenants. Of 54 public housing projects in Chicago, containing some 30,000 units, all but four had been constructed in black neighborhoods and had black tenant rates of 99 percent. By contrast, there were four projects in white sections of the city; these had a black occupancy rate of only 1 to 7 percent (set by quota), and the most lily-white of all was located just nine blocks from Mayor Daley's Bridgeport home.

The real villain in this scenario is probably not the housing authority, but the city council. Aldermen from white districts invariably veto any proposed public housing in their areas, and thus it is not built. Federal Judge Richard B. Austin took note in the 1968 decision of a "desperately intensifying division of whites and Negroes in Chicago." His court orders to put more projects in white areas did have some limited effect, but not without a typical display of objections from Daley and the aldermen who sought to frustrate the decisions. In 1972, HUD pulled back $20 million of urban renewal funds and spent it elsewhere, because of continued foot-dragging. Another $26 million was impounded. Judge Austin minced no words when he likened Daley to Alabama's Governor George Wallace:

There have been occasions in the past in other parts of the country where chief executives have stood in schoolhouse and statehouse doorways with their faces livid and their wattles flapping and have defied the federal government to enforce its laws and decrees. It is an anomaly that the chief executive of this city should challenge and defy the federal law. Apparently, law and order only applies to state and municipal ordinances.

Perhaps the most deplorable housing project of Chicago is a string of 28 high-rise buildings along the railroad tracks near South State Street, known as

* In the late 1960s, integration would have been possible. In 1968 the gap between black and white pupils was less than 10 percent, with blacks making up slightly more than 50 percent and white almost 45 percent. A 1976 analysis by the Chicago *Reporter*, a respected monthly publication dealing with racial issues, surveyed Chicago schools and found half the 669 public schools were at least 95 percent black, 68 others were at least 95 percent white.

the Robert Taylor Homes. Of the 28,000 people once in the project, 20,000 were under 21. The residents, according to a Chicago newspaper reporter, were "all poor, grappling with violence and vandalism, fear and suspicion, teen-age terror and adult chaos, rage, resentment, official regimenting. They're second-class citizens living in a second-class world, and they know it, and hate it." One wonders how this misuse of federal money came to be, and hears the story that Col. McCormick's wife, riding on the 20th Century Limited from the East, would wake up early in the morning as the train entered Chicago and see the terrible slums. So she asked the Colonel if something couldn't be done about the eyesore, and that led to Chicago *Tribune* support and construction of a project which may be even worse than what preceded it.

Opening up the suburbs, a seemingly workable solution to blacks' problems, has had mixed results. In a 1976 landmark decision, *Hills* vs. *Gautreux*, the U.S. Supreme Court ruled that federal judges could order HUD to administer federal housing programs throughout the six-county Chicago metropolitan area, to help remedy the effects of past racial bias in Chicago's public housing. Some editorial writers suggested that the ruling was as important as the *Brown* vs. *Board of Education* school desegregation ruling. Surveys initially showed that 40,000 poor families were eligible for the subsidized move to the greener pastures in the suburbs. But by 1978 only 375 families had found suburban apartments under the plan, and some of them said on national television that they missed their old neighborhoods. Chicago black leaders also charged that the almost total concentration on suburban public housing siphoned off federal dollars that could have been better spent rehabilitating inner-city homes and apartments.

The subjugation of Chicago's black population was made all the more poignant by the demonstration of blacks' voter power when they coalesced around Jane Byrne and won the primary election for her. Yet no Chicago political observer suggested that the show of strength had transformed the black community into any kind of monolithic bloc that could follow through in future political battles. "Black voters reacted individually and spontaneously," Leon Davis, the black chairman of the board of governors of Illinois State Colleges and Universities, noted following the strong black vote for Byrne. "Black voters do not threaten the Democratic organization," he said. "There is no ongoing political education of the black constituency, no forum to review issues and hold black officeholders accountable."

The machine has a long history of neutralizing effective political opposition in the ghettos and indeed making the black vote a mainstay of its power. For almost 30 years, the principal agent of machine power in the black wards was Georgia-born Congressman William L. Dawson, who had failed in politics as a Republican but then succeeded brilliantly after Mayor Kelly picked him as his black plantation chief. Elected in 1942 as the second black Congressman of the century, Dawson rose to become the first black congressional committee chairman in U.S. history (the Government Operations Committee), but he never introduced major legislation and showed scant interest in the civil rights drive of the 1960s. At 84 years of age, he died in 1970.

Dawson's base of power was his position as Second Ward Democratic committeeman; from it he built, in the words of former Chicago *Defender* editor Chuck Stone, "a black political machine that was as efficient and vicious as the city-wide Democratic machine." Ill-educated blacks were often led to believe that if they defied him, they might lose welfare benefits or be turned out of public housing. For the South Side black in search of a job or a favor or a bailbondsman, Dawson's organization was the place to go. As a lawyer before his election to Congress, Dawson had specialized in defense of black gamblers; as boss, he permitted the numbers racket, organized prostitution, and illegal bookmaking to flourish in exchange for support of his organization.

As long as Dawson remained in good health, his fiefdom of his own Second Ward plus four other South Side wards could be depended upon for 50,000 to 70,000 Democratic votes, making the wards, in Rakove's words, the "bulwark of Democratic strength in city elections." But within two years of Dawson's death, the black machine disintegrated. Dawson's successor in Congress, Ralph H. Metcalfe, a machine alderman for 16 years and an Olympic sprinter in the 1936 games, broke with Daley after the 1969 Black Panther raids and later sided with reform Alderman William Singer to embarrass Daley at the 1972 Democratic Convention.

In the 1976 primary, Daley slated Erwin France, director of the model cities program, 30 years Metcalfe's junior and well educated and obviously well financed by the machine, but Metcalfe won with 72 percent of the vote. Yet when Metcalfe died just before the 1978 election, the machine-slated candidate, Bennett M. Stewart, a nondescript alderman who some critics said took orders so well he had a plantation mentality, won easily. Part of the reason for Stewart's success, according to reform Alderman Clifford Kelley, was a poor voter turnout. The sad fact is that Chicago blacks do not appear to turn out unless angered by a specific event such as the shutdown of their transportation system in the case of the Byrne election or the sense of outrageous racial insult when they reelected Metcalfe.

Michael Preston, a black researcher at the University of Illinois, found that only 40 percent of eligible black voters turned out for the 1977 elections while 57 percent of white ethnics turned out. Preston also concluded that black voter participation declined from 1971 to 1977 not only in the inner-city traditional machine wards but in the middle class black wards. There are many analyses of why blacks have made so little real headway in Chicago politics. Alderman Kelley blamed some black leaders who encouraged blacks not to vote as an act of defiance against the machine. Preston claimed blacks stopped going to the polling booth because "they voted, voted, voted, and voted, and very little changed." Still the election of Frost as finance committee chairman did add some stature to the black community, and as the black percentage of the city population increases the possibility of a black, charismatic mayoral candidate cannot be ignored.

Despite the inability of reformers to make broad advances through elective politics, Chicago has still produced national models for self-assertion in the United States through The Woodlawn Organization and the Rev. Jesse Jackson.

Located just south of the University of Chicago on the city's South Side, Woodlawn by the 1950s had become a neighborhood of absentee landlords, decaying buildings, boarded up shops, and, in the words of one local clergyman, "spray-paint graffiti on buildings and fences to remind everyone of the explosive mixture of hope and suppressed rage to be found in every young person who roams the streets." Here in 1959, in a unique ecumenical effort, one Roman Catholic and three Protestant pastors combined forces to start a strong umbrella-type community organization. After prolonged controversy, they decided to invite the colorful Saul Alinsky, of Back of the Yards fame, to advise and consult with the newly forming group, The Woodlawn Organization (TWO).

In succeeding years, with more than 100 community organizations participating, TWO mounted an Alinsky-style program of issue confrontation and action on an amazingly broad scale. Early undertakings included an attack on unscrupulous businessmen for sales tactics that antagonized local residents, the first rent strike in the U.S.A. to force absentee white landlords to make necessary repairs to buildings, and a crucial battle with the gigantic University of Chicago to make it compromise on its monstrous urban renewal plans, which in their first forms would have consumed a major portion of the Woodlawn area. Through a sit-in in Mayor Daley's office, TWO finally got an agreement that no urban renewal demolition would begin until construction could actually begin on a large (502-unit) low-cost housing project on Cottage Grove Avenue to house potential displacees; it was the first agreement of that kind any community organization in the country had evoked from government. In another unique move, the residents were called in to say what the new housing should be like before it was even designed. Their almost unanimous judgment: build no high rises; we want a dense, low-rise community with no buildings over five stories. What they wanted to avoid was the kind of high-rise vertical ghetto horror symbolized by the Robert Taylor Homes. So the promotional folders for the Cottage Grove literally and truthfully claim: "Designed by the residents of Woodlawn."

TWO took the lead in closing up the infamous "Sin Corner" in Woodlawn, a fountainhead of dope traffic and prostitution, by means of a localized prohibition ordinance. And TWO was able to get an experimental decentralized school board established in which community residents, in conjunction with the University of Chicago and the Board of Education, actually ran a local high school and several feeder grade and junior high schools. Local people received the major say in hiring of the administrator, teacher assignment, and curriculum.

Alinsky used to glow with pleasure when he thought of some of the unconventional tactics TWO has occasionally improvised. Examples: "TWO got Mayor Daley to deal with them after they threatened to tie up all the rest rooms at O'Hare—keeping all the booths occupied. O'Hare is one of Daley's sacred cows. Another time TWO people piled rats on the steps of City Hall. Daley got that message too."

One of the most controversial projects TWO ever became involved with was a national poverty programs grant of $975,000 to set up a special kind of youth project in its area, an admittedly "high-risk venture" that would utilize the existing structures of street gangs such as the Blackstone Rangers and the Devil's Disciples. Gangs are nothing new to Chicago; back in the 1920s the Moran, O'Banion, and Capone gangs ruled the streets and murdered at will; there are still violence-prone gangs in many lower class white areas. In the postwar era it was almost inevitable that a new and virulent form of gangism would emerge among the desperate youths of the black ghettos. Individual members of gangs like the Rangers (later called the Black P. Stone Nation) have been charged with all manner of crimes—including robbery, murder, rapings, knifings, extortion, and traffic in narcotics *—especially in connection with their ongoing feud against the Disciples, who refused to join with them. (Many lesser South Side gangs, ranging from the Maniacs to the Pharaohs, once found it advisable to join the Rangers, so that total membership apparently ran between 3,500 and 8,000 boys and men.) But at the same time, the Ranger Nation was credited with keeping the South Side "cool" when West Side ghettos erupted in the wake of King's assassination, and Rangers reportedly used their persuasion to keep alcoholics, prostitutes, and drug peddlers out of their neighborhood.

Predictably, the TWO program with the gangs involved the organization in semi-scandals and the intense conflict between the police and gang members. Some of the worst alleged abuses were aired in June 1968 hearings before Senator McClellan's Senate Investigations Subcommittee. The program became a liability for the national Office of Economic Opportunity and was discontinued. Years later, Leon Finney, president of TWO, defended the work with the gangs. "We really had no alternative," Finney told us. "They were at war, and I am confident if we had not worked with them we would have had a major riot in the community. There would have been no hope."

As TWO matured, it continued to encounter scandal from time to time, and it was unable to counter a population loss so great that the neighborhood's public utility usage dropped by half. But as John Hall Fish concluded in his 1973 book *Black Power/White Control*, TWO refused to give up, and every Chicago neighborhood had benefited from its leaders' demands. By the late 1970s, TWO had lost much of its colorful character and people-to-people strength, but it could easily be argued that TWO's later projects were the natural outcome of an organization that had won some battles and respect. When supermarket chains closed their Woodlawn outlets due to high crime and red ink, TWO went into partnership with Hillman Foods, used its com-

---

* The worst violence was perpetrated by "gang-bangers"—boys in their early teens who liked to fight with firearms; older Rangers disdained the youngsters but could not control them. By their mid-twenties, a friend of the Rangers told us, "they're either in jail, dead, or they've changed their sinful ways."

munity reputation to minimize pilferage and vandalism, and turned a profit. TWO also undertook a massive housing rehabilitation project that forced the organization to learn how to deal with City Hall, how to get necessary permits, zoning changes, and inspection approvals and how to achieve complicated financial arrangements with downtown moneylenders. TWO's property management company adopted some very tough standards for the occupants of its housing units: an investigation before renting, home visits to make sure the property is maintained, and for those tenants who tear up their apartments, eviction with court order by the organization's own 50-man armed security force. The goal, Finney said, was to create a community integrated in race, economic mixture, and age—and a socially viable community as well.

Chicago's gift to national black leadership has been Jesse Louis Jackson, Baptist preacher, son of South Carolinian poverty, organizer of economic boycotts, fiery battler for black rights, politician and prophet. In the spring of 1968, Jackson was talking with Martin Luther King, Jr., on the balcony of the Lorraine Motel in Memphis when the sniper's bullets cracked across the void. Jackson cradled the dying man in his arms; less than a day later, standing in a sweater stained with King's blood in the City Hall chambers in Chicago, he responded to a platitudinous testimonial by Mayor Daley with a shout to the Chicago political establishment assembled. "His blood is on the hands of you who would not have welcomed him here yesterday!"

"That gesture demonstrated both the militant indignation and the dramatic flair that mark Jackson's charismatic style," writer Arthur Kretchmer noted in *Playboy*.

Jackson was a director of King's Southern Christian Leadership Conference until he split with the SCLC to form his new "PUSH" ("People United to Save Humanity") in 1972. But by that time, the Operation Breadbasket which he had nurtured within the black nation in Chicago had established itself as one of the most impressive demonstrations in America of black economic power and self-determination. Through use or threat of boycott, great corporations doing business in the ghettos were led to sign some far-reaching agreements with Operation Breadbasket—to hire stipulated numbers of blacks, to stock their shelves with products produced by black-owned companies, to use black construction firms to build their ghetto stores, to bank with black-owned banks, even to use black-owned janitorial and exterminating services for their ghetto installations. Late in 1969, Operation Breadbasket sponsored a three-day Black Expo in Chicago, described by *Ebony* as "undoubtedly the largest, most successful black trade fair ever held;" the attendance was a scarcely believable 900,000. By 1971, the Black Expo had grown to 500 commercial booths (90 percent sponsored black concerns) and even Richard Daley was impressed enough to pay a personal visit. After that, attendance tapered off, and the show was closed down after 1976, a victim of changing times and Jackson's interest in other issues.

In the mid-1970s, Jackson began a new national campaign to rid black Americans of the welfare mentality and the assumption that racism is the sole reason for their low status in society. Jackson's new theme emerged from his own realization on a White House picket line that his followers, especially the young, were too often too drunk or too high on drugs to do anything beyond protesting. "Blacks must buckle down and apply to academic studies the same formula which they have used so successfully in athletics: sacrifice, discipline, and perseverance," Jackson told both parents and youths in speaking appearances around the country. In 1979 Jackson also branched off into foreign affairs. He toured South Africa to the cheers of the thousands of blacks there and the discomfort of whites when he said "apartheid is worse than Hitler." Jackson was also the first black leader to come to the defense of U.S. Ambassador to the United Nations Andrew Young Jr. when Young resigned after holding a meeting .with the Palestine Liberation Organization that was not authorized by the U.S. government. Jackson subsequently undertook a highly controversial trip to the Middle East, meeting with Palestinian leaders and traveling in Israel as well. He urged both sides in the conflict to emulate the civil rights movement's tactics of nonviolence and said the United States should recognize the Palestinian cause. In the future, Jackson said, black Americans would want a much greater voice in U.S. foreign policy making.

But while Jackson obviously earned a national following and national press, the mercurial nature of his approach never impressed Chicago politicians. In the Chicago wards, where points are made for long and arduous work in the precinct vineyards, Jackson was considered something of a charlatan, quick to capture headlines on practically any issue, but rarely following through to achieve substantive change. Jackson had some solid local political successes in the late 1960s when he led a "hunger march" of some 3,000 on the state capitol in Springfield and got then-Governor Richard Ogilvie and then-House Speaker Ralph T. Smith to withdraw their proposal for cutting some $25 million in welfare aid. But a quick-change pattern emerged. In 1971 Jackson seriously considered running for mayor but reversed course. Some segments of the Chicago black press even ignored his penchant for supporting voter registration one week, black colleges the next, and economic development after that. The disdain with which he was regarded locally was vividly reflected when black aldermen gathered after Daley's death to chart a course of action. Jackson showed up for the meeting but was pointedly asked to leave—and did. One black leader contended that "Jackson is a hero because the whites made him—he's a creation of the white press. He'll create a problem, make an issue of it, and that's the end of it." Jackson has never hidden his belief in alliances with whites and desire for national publicity. He admitted his failure to follow through is legitimate criticism, but argued, "My responsibility is to raise issues. . . . Must I be expected to toss the rock and tend to the concentric circles too?"

The predominantly black South Shore district was also aided beginning in the late 1970s by another unique institution, the South Shore National Bank, the nation's first bank founded to preserve a neighborhood. The South

Shore went from 99 percent white in the 1950s to 85 percent black in 1979, and as the blacks moved in, the businesses moved out. The South Shore bank began to cut its services, made investments in other neighborhoods, and planned to close. After obtaining $4 million in financing from foundations and other philanthropic groups, Ronald Gryzwinski and three partners took over the bank with the avowed intent of "greenlining" a neighborhood that other banks were "redlining." The bank plowed money back into the community, helping rehabilitate houses, apartments, and commercial buildings, supporting neighborhood crime prevention efforts, child care, senior citizen centers, providing up-to-date banking services—and making a profit. University of Chicago studies showed that the bank played a significant role in improving the South Shore community and residents' confidence. Welfare rates declined, and the median selling price of homes went from $19,000 to $25,000 in the first two years of operation and continued to rise thereafter. Bankers and developers around the nation were attracted to the enterprise, proving once again Chicago's role as an innovator in community organization.

Since the early 1950s, another wave of immigrants has been arriving in Chicago quite literally changing the language of the streets and threatening the blacks' claim to most underprivileged and disenfranchised. First Puerto Ricans, then Mexicans, and most recently Central and South Americans have been moving northward, working themselves up from farm work to urban status and urban jobs. The story of the Latino community—as the various Hispanic groups are collectively referred to in Chicago—is one of constant movement from neighborhood to neighborhood. The Puerto Ricans first moved into the deteriorating and forsaken streets such as Clark and LaSalle on the western edge of Chicago's near North Side. They were then displaced by urban renewal, but knowing little of American politics and often not holding citizenship, they did not fight back. The bright spot in Latino development in Chicago came in 1970 when the Lakeview Latin American Coalition joined with Una Puerta Abierta, an unemployment agency associated with Jane Addams' House, to convince the city colleges of Chicago to create the Universidad Popular, the only community-controlled educational institution in Chicago's college system. In the late 1970s, the Latinos in Chicago remained sadly disorganized, although national Latin leaders said Chicago could one day play a special role in creating a national Hispanic movement because the city's Latin population included people from so many countries.

Suburban Cook County and the Collar Counties: The Emerging Political Keystone

Chicago has a bewildering variety of suburbs, in both Cook County and the five so-called "collar counties" which make up metropolitan Chicago. Together the Cook County and collar suburbs were home of about 4.25 million people by 1980, nearly a third more than the city and approaching 40 percent of the total state population. Traditionally most (though definitely not all) of the suburbs were Republican. In recent elections, however, these suburbs, like those surrounding other cities across the nation, have become ticket splitters, choosing carefully among partisan candidates and issues. In rough terms, the suburbs may be divided into four groups.

Oldest and most settled in their ways are the North Shore "establishment" suburbs—cities and villages like Evanston (population 72,019), Wilmette (31,374), Glencoe (9,836), Highland Park (31,983), and Lake Forest (15,222), many of them places of stately trees lining streets of gracious older homes. In the more outlying areas there are also quantities of high-grade postwar residential developments; starting in the '60s, apartment buildings for young singles began to sprout up. Census figures show these areas ranking at the very top of national surveys of income and educational levels. They are overwhelmingly white and Protestant, though in recent years some have received immigration of Jews, and in Evanston there is a substantial black community. The voting pattern of the North Shore has been traditionally Republican, but there are many more independents now, and Democratic Senator Adlai Stevenson and Republicans Senator Charles H. Percy and Governor James Thompson have received equally lopsided majorities. The North Shore's independent politics were epitomized by the issue-oriented and expensive campaigns of Rep. Abner J. Mikva, the South Side Chicago liberal who found a final electoral home in the suburbs after he was reapportioned out of his city seat by the 1970 Census. Mikva was defeated in 1972, won by 124 votes in 1976, and quadrupled his margin to 650 votes in 1978 before resigning to become a judge on the U.S. Court of Appeals, a job with more security.

At the opposite geographic and ethnic pole are the industrialized middle and lower income suburbs to the south of Chicago. Some of the larger towns are Oak Lawn (62,198), Calumet City (39,548), and Chicago Heights (38,806). They are peopled with white laboring folk who have "made it" through diligent saving and are mainly concerned with escaping the problems of the inner city. The population is mostly ethnic: Polish, Italian, Slavic, although Chicago Heights, East Chicago Heights, and Robbins all have significant black populations, and nearby Blue Island has a smaller black ghetto. The area has many cheap postwar tract housing developments that are literally coming apart at the seams with normal use. In general, the resistance to integration remains the fiercest in the areas with the lower education and income levels.

To the west, southwest, and northwest of Cook County, subdivisions each year consume thousands of acres of prairie in the fast-growing suburban counties of Will, McHenry, and DuPage. DuPage is the most densely populated of the three: it is almost completely residential, except for the part of sprawling O'Hare Airport straddling its eastern boundary and connected only by a pipeline-like strip of land to Chicago. With the exception of a few major towns like Joliet (72,102), a decaying industrial center and home of the decrepit state prison, the rest of the area epitomizes urban sprawl with all of its rewards (for developers), its problems (for public officials coping with gargantuan growth), its amenities (for young professional people who either commute to Chicago or indirectly make their living off the big city), and its frustrations (for the farmers on the fringes trying to pay urban taxes out of agricultural incomes). Despite the urbanization in these counties (400,000 acres of farmland disappeared from 1954–74 in the six-county area), the incongruous sight of major manufacturing plants and corporate complexes rising out of what used to be cornfields, however, is becoming more and more commonplace. While the political complexion is usually Republican, Democratic candidates no longer can be written off as knights errant.

Finally, there are the three close-in westside suburbs of Cicero (60,483), and Berwyn (47,799), both aging bastions of the middle and lower class ethnic—Bohemian, Polish, and other Slavic—and Oak Park (56,691), architecturally as well as financially affluent and somewhat more progressive in its attitudes toward integration and community development. The business streets of Cicero and Berwyn are dreary, but the homeowners keep immaculate lawns and faithfully shovel the snow from their sidewalks. Cicero has a notorious heritage as hangout of Al Capone and the crime syndicate and still harbors some vice and gambling despite periodic raids. (Another Chicago suburb, River Forest, is known for being the home turf for top leaders of the syndicate.)

Many of the suburbs, especially the older ones close in to the city, are facing the same racial integration pressures which confronted Chicago's neighborhoods in the last 30 years. Their responses are varied, from exclusionary zoning and building codes to planned integration. While we cannot examine here the hundreds of suburbs that ring the city, we can single out one, Oak Park, that is trying to demonstrate that the segregationist patterns established in Chicago need not be repeated in the suburbs. Oak Park might be an example of what Chicago could have done and what other suburbs still could do.

Oak Park is, in fact, in many ways a showplace suburb, with more than 300 buildings of historical or architectural significance. It is best known for the two dozen homes and buildings designed by Frank Lloyd Wright when he lived there early in his career. In 1970 Oak Park was peaceful, affluent, and almost 100 percent white, but its location, immediately across Chicago's western border, Austin Boulevard, made it an easy target for the blockbusting and quick sales tactics practiced by unscrupulous real estate agents in the city. Rather than knuckling under, the village fathers anticipated the changes in racial and economic makeup and developed a plan emphasizing the community architectural heritage and promoting integration. A fair housing ordinance was adopted, and the Oak Park Community Relations Commission was given subpoena power and the authority to review and initiate complaints. To give the commission a positive image, it was also charged with promoting the village and counseling prospective homebuyers and apartment dwellers.

When Oak Park businesses began moving out of a major commercial strip close to Austin Boulevard, the village built its new $4.5 million village hall on the site as a symbol of its faith. The police department was increased from 68 to 115 people, the number of patrol cars doubled, and officers were given special sensitivity training to avoid touching off racial flare-ups. Code enforcement was strict to head off the development of any slums. The result was a slow but stable integration; blacks have risen from 1 percent in 1970 to 7 percent in 1979. Blacks are scattered throughout much of the village, although the largest concentration is in the southeast neighborhoods closest to the all-black ghettos across Austin Boulevard in Chicago. Housing values have not dropped, but in fact increased between $2,000 and $5,000 per year. An International City Management Association team studied Oak Park in 1978 and issued generally favorable remarks, although it noted that Oak Park preferred to attract middle-income blacks who would complement the white middle-income majority already there and was not addressing the needs of Chicago's poor blacks.

For many years, Chicago's suburbanites were superbly served, at least in comparison to any other American metropolis, in one area: public transportation for commuters. With some justification, Chicagoland leaders boasted of having the "finest commuter railroad service in the world." Hard times—financially and climatically—have pressed in on the transportation system, tarnishing its image, even before the calamitous effect of the blizzard of '79. That was on top of the periodic accidents, including the 1972 collision between two Illinois Central commuter trains that killed 44 persons and injured 350. The dollar crunch hit early in the 1970s, with both the Chicago Transit Authority (CTA) and the commuter lines facing a multitude of problems—bankruptcies, labor strikes, fare increases, cutbacks in service, tracks in disrepair, and equipment held together by hope. Then the "Blizzard of '79" swooped through Chicago, causing cancellation of many runs, forcing delays for weeks after the storm and generally exposing the frailty of the operations. The breadth of service is excellent, however. In normal weather, no fewer than eight rail commuter lines operate. The Chicago and Northwestern (CNW) and the Milwaukee Road radiate out to the north and west, the Burlington and Rock Island (probably the best equipped lines) serve the west and southwest, the Illinois Central-Gulf (ICG) moves south along the lake and southwest to Joliet and the South Shore ringing the lake on its way to South Bend, Ind.

Since so many suburbanites left the city to avoid its depressing array of burdens, it was hardly surprising that deep-seated animosity arose when Mayor Daley and the state legislature began talking about ways to subsidize the CTA and the commuter rail lines. When it became apparent the solution would involve a Regional Transit Authority (RTA), with a separate taxing power, the animosity became outright hostility. The establishment of the RTA was approved in 1973 but had to be ratified by a referendum in the six-county area. It won, by only 13,000 votes, with the machine dutifully turning out the margin to offset the overwhelming opposition in the suburbs. From the start, the RTA has been plagued by the continuing suburban-city split. It took seven months to break the stalemate over electing the first chairman, with the post finally going to Milton Pikarski, former Chicago public works commissioner, CTA chairman, and long-time aide to Daley. Before he resigned in 1978, Pikarski was besieged with constant calls from suburban officials to resign, and suburban legislators continued to sponsor bills to undermine the RTA's authority or eliminate it entirely (a dozen such debilitating proposals were introduced in the 1977 legislative session). House Speaker W. Robert Blair, a Park Forest Republican, was voted out of office because of his support of the RTA. The RTA did pump millions of new dollars into the system (the CTA sought a $193 million subsidy in 1979 alone). First the funds were only to subsidize operations, then the RTA expanded aid to help buy new equipment and repair existing stock, probably preventing a total collapse of the metropolitan transit sytem. But frequent criticism was heard about the way the RTA was running its railroads (and CTA). In assessing the RTA in 1978, the *Sun-Times'* Dennis Byrne said the RTA had allowed the city to "merrily go on its own way" pursuing an expensive downtown subway and the O'Hare rapid transit extensions, projects estimated to cost $800 million. "So, who is making the decisions about what transit projects are most important if the RTA isn't," Byrne asked. "Seemingly, it's a combination of a shadowy bureaucratic arrangement and the roll of the political dice." Apparently, changing the administrative structure and infusing outside funds does little to alter the way decisions are made in Chicagoland.

It was typical of both the Chicago press and the United States in general in the 1970s, however, that the problems affecting a regional transit authority were all too often allowed to overshadow the fact that (1) the entire postwar government subsidy system in the Uinted States, and in localities, had been skewed heavily to highways over transit; (2) that without mass transit, highways would become even more incredibly congested—and those in and around Chicago offer some of America's champion traffic jams; (3) that in any successful city of the world, effective mass transit, if not built in from the start, is eventually seen as a major necessity; and (4) that in the impending petroleum shortages (if not disastrous cutoffs) of the 1980s and beyond, a sound mass transit system, including rapid rail, would be one of the United States' most important lifelines. On those tests, the Chicago area system, for all its failings, was leagues ahead of the competition in most American metropolises.

Chicago Miscellany: The Media, the Universities, the Environment

Illinois has traditionally been regarded as two distinct entities—Chicago and "downstate." By Chicago, people also meant Cook County; by downstate, every other place in Illinois from the Wisconsin border to where the Ohio River meets the Mississippi at Cairo. But former Gov. Richard D. Ogilvie told one of the authors a decade ago that the dominant region of

Illinois today is "the Chicago viewing area"—the territory within the 65-mile viewing radius of the Chicago television stations with 70 percent of Illinois' population.* Television makes Chicago news and personalities pre-eminent in Illinois, Ogilvie said. By general agreement, the most influential person in television during the 1970s was Len O'Connor, who commented editorially from WMAQ-TV, the NBC outlet; with a whiff of understate-ment, Ogilvie said of O'Connor: "I'd rather have him as friend than as enemy."

This introduction is clearly intended to make the reader ask what ever happened to the Chicago *Tribune*, described by John Gunther as "more than a mere newspaper, more than even the 'World's Greatest Newspaper,' as it fondly calls itself, a domain, a kind of principality." The *Tribune* is still there, and doing very nicely, thank you, with circulation of some 757,000 weekdays and 1,156,000 Sundays; its conservative, Republican way of looking at the world doubtless continues to influence millions of Midwesterners. But the winds of change have enveloped the Tribune Tower, and the mighty clout is gone. Fewer and fewer people read the *Tribune*, even as the popula-tion rises. Television gives *Tribune* readers a new view of reality. Colonel Robert R. McCormick, the grand, domineering, ferocious ruler of the *Tribune* empire for 45 years, went to his grave in 1955. The days of rampaging anti-New Deal, anti-British, anti-Russian editorials are definitely past. The paper remains staunchly Republican, though along with the other Chicago dailies, it backed Daley's reelection bids; some saw a connection in the fact that the tax assessment of the Tribune Tower building was suspiciously low. A Sunday section, *Perspective*, occasionally features the world of blacks, the young, and women as the old *Tribune* would never have done. In 1971 a new "op-ed" page was inaugurated, including cartoonists and columnists of moderate to liberal opinions. It took on its own black columnist, Vernon Jarrett, and hired black reporters. The changes can be attributed to a post-McCormick generation of editors now coming to power; they are no flaming liberals, but less erratic, far more responsible than their predecessors. The *Tribune* main-tains a high quality reporting staff and won five Pulitzer prizes in the 1970s, three of them for local reporting.

Chicago remains a competitive newspaper town, but the death of two of its dailies in the last decade has left an unfillable void in the spirit of rivalry that once prevailed. For years, the *Tribune*'s conservative slant was offset by two Marshall Field entries in the Chicago news field, the morning *Sun-Times* and the evening *Daily News*, offering moderate to liberal viewpoints and lively, issue-oriented news coverage. But on March 4, 1978, the *Daily News*, with all the bravado of a captain going down with his ship, said "So Long, Chicago," in swaggering type across the top of its front page, ending 103 years of glory and tribulation. When Field Enterprises bought the *Daily News* in 1959, it had a circulation of 600,000; when it closed down, circula-

* Ogilvie got the idea from our friend Norton Kay, former political correspondent for *Chicago Today* and press secretary for former Gov. Daniel Walker.

tion had fallen by almost half, and the operating deficit the last year was $11 million. The *Sun-Times* absorbed about 90 of the editorial staff from its step-sister, including the *Daily News* columnist of 19 years, Mike Royko, an authentic Chicago institution himself. Five years earlier, the *Tribune*'s afternoon counterpart, *Chicago Today*, also had folded. Frequently chastised for its lack of taste, *Chicago Today* nonetheless had given the competition a run for its money with its spunkiness and aggressiveness. With *Chicago Today* gone, the *Tribune* initiated round-the-clock editions and modified its staid image a bit when it took on some more sprightly offerings. With only the two giants left in the field, Chicagoans often are treated to journalistic one-upmanship, shades of the good old days. But even with a market split two ways instead of four, the *Tribune* and *Sun-Times* face a struggle for survival in an increasingly television-conscious age. In influence, however, the Chicago newspapers far outshine any others in the state.*

Chicago is also a center of the black press in America. John H. Johnson publishes *Ebony*, modeled after *Life*, which has a circulation of 1.3 million, as well as the newsweekly *Jet* (circulation 342,518). A daily tabloid, the *Chicago Defender*, is the flagship of a chain of 10 papers whch are owned by publisher John H. Sengstacke. The *Defender*'s circulation is only 22,079, small potatoes compared to the 500,000 claimed by another Chicago-based publication, *Muhammad Speaks*, the propaganda organ of the Black Muslims. But *Muhammad Speaks* is sold on a pushy, shakedown basis, so that its influence is easily overrated. (It should be noted, however, that the overt hostility of Black Muslims toward whites moderated perceptibly during the 1970s, with an unspoken truce declared by Elijah Muhammad. Imam Wallace Deem Muhammad, his son and successor of the Chicago-based sect, told us that times and conditions had simply shifted since the earlier days of his father's career, requiring a new orientation. The Muslims had found their work in prisons, he noted, much more accepted by white administrators than in earlier years. And the church in general, renowned for its immense resources, made a clear shift toward black independence instead of freedom from "white devils.")

In broadcasting, Chicago has never produced serious competition to Manhattan or even Los Angeles, although ABC News did make Chicago one of its three major anchor cities in a national television format developed in the late 1970s. And the city remained (by his insistence) the point of origin for the daily news-and-opinion broadcasts of Paul Harvey, self-styled "voice of the silent majority" who provides listeners on hundreds of ABC affiliate stations with a kind of political fundamentalism loyal to all the old American values and suspicious of all the new.

Chicago harbors 30 colleges and universities and with its five medical

* The papers outside Chicago taken most seriously by the politicians include the Rockford *Morning Star* and *Register Republic*, the Peoria *Journal Star*, the Bloomington *Pantagraph*, the Springfield *State Journal*, and the two interlopers from across the Mississippi—The St. Louis *Globe-Democrat* and *Post-Dispatch*, both heavily read downstate. The *Post-Dispatch* is especially influential.

schools trains a goodly share of America's physicians. One of the nation's outstanding inner-city university branches is the magnificently designed Chicago Circle campus of the University of Illinois which opened its doors in 1965 (after 20 years at a temporary site on the Navy Pier). Other outstanding institutions include Northwestern University at Evanston and the Catholic institutions of Loyola and DePaul.

But the University of Chicago, founded in 1890 through the largesse of John D. Rockefeller, remains the greatest of all. Since its founding, the institution has had more than 30 Nobel Prize winners on its faculty. The University established the first sociology department in the United States in 1893, and its commitment to urban problems and studies has remained strong over the years. Pioneer work on planned parenthood was done at Chicago, and the faculty has in recent years included Milton Friedman, the renowned economist.

Despite its prominence in social science, Chicago is not as prominent as it once was. Nevertheless, the University continues its reputation as a premier educational institution. A 1979 survey for the Chronicle of Higher Education added another chapter to its long list of credentials when it ranked 12 of Chicago's academic departments as one of the five best in the nation. Not only was it recognized for its social science excellence (in economics, history, political science, sociology) but for a range of other disciplines as well (business, chemistry, English, education, law, mathematics, philosophy, and physics).

One of the most fascinating case studies of a large inner-city university's relationships with its community is provided by the University of Chicago. In contrast to the turmoils Columbia experienced at Morningside Heights, it is largely a success story. The fate of the University in its Hyde Park-Kenwood neighborhood hung in the balance, however, for some years following World War II. Low-income blacks began to inundate the neighborhood, slum landlords chopped up apartments into units to house five times as many residents as originally planned for, and real estate owners engaged in unscrupulous "blockbusting." The undergraduate enrollment declined from 3,200 to 1,300 and recruiting faculty became increasingly difficult. The University trustees seriously considered moving the campus lock, stock, and barrel to a suburban location or even to another city.

In the early '50s, however, the University decided to stay put and to throw its full power and prestige behind a fight against neighborhood blight. It formed a private citizens' organization, the Southeast Chicago Corporation (SECC), to lead the battle by court action against housing code offenders and by pressing for widescale urban renewal in the area. Julian Levi, a professor of urban affairs with good City Hall connections and a talent for wheeling and dealing, became SECC's head and showed no compunctions about forcing out low-income blacks. But eventually he and SECC came to accept stable, middle-income blacks, and after 1956 a neighborhood population balance of 38 percent black was achieved. As comedian Mike Nichols explained it: "This is Hyde Park, whites and blacks, shoulder to shoulder against the lower classes."

Today the renewal of Hyde Park-Kenwood must be judged a major success. Hundreds of new townhouses and high-rise apartment buildings have gone up and many old ones have been renovated; there are restaurants of wide gastronomic variety, coffee houses, and theatres. The crime rate is one of the city's lowest, due in part to the large sum the University spends each year on a security force to augment Chicago police in the area. Adding to all this, the spacious Midway strip is a little architectural showplace all on its own, with buildings by Wright, Mies van der Rohe, Saarinen, and Edward Durrell Stone.

Despite its traditionally radical student body, the University of Chicago demonstrated unusual skill in dealing with the student protests of the '60s, even while great institutions like California, Harvard, and Cornell—and even the rurally set Champaign-Urbana campus of the University of Illinois— were in the throes of violent demonstrations. This has not been because of an absence of agitators; the Students for a Democratic Society, in fact, led a 16-day-and-night takeover of the administration building in 1969. The university administration met the crisis by avoiding what Dean Wayne Booth called the twin traps of "calling in the cops, which is disastrous, and amnesty, which only brings more and more sit-ins."

One resident of the University community who made a unique contribution to the neighborhood was Mrs. Laura Fermi, widow of the late great physicist. She related that in 1959 she noticed that during the winter months, everything in her Hyde Park apartment was covered with grime from the coal-burning furnaces of the area. Aroused by the nuisance, Mrs. Fermi and a group of other women, mostly faculty wives, set up a committee to fight the local smog wave. She delighted in telling the story of how her little band of smog battlers "undertook the education of the University of Chicago," which is the greatest real-estate holder in Hyde Park, persuading it to agree to a schedule for conversion to non-coal heating.

Bit by bit, government agencies, aided and often prompted by private conservationist groups, have made some progress in reducing the amount of Chicago's air and water pollution. Even the Chicago Sanitary District, a big "wholesaler" of sewage disposal for Chicago and 115 other municipalities in Cook County, finally took an interest.* U.S. Steel, one of the most egregious polluters of Lake Michigan and the Chicago area's air, in 1971 bowed to pressure from the Sanitary District and a state attorney general's suit and agreed to a plan to try to end the daily dump of 36,000 pounds of chemicals and suspended solids into the lake from its enormous South Works plant,

---

* The Sanitary District is a favorite target of downstaters who say it sends Chicago's effluent their way in the waters of the Chicago River. The District reversed the flow of the Chicago River in 1910 to prevent the epidemics of cholera and typhoid Chicago had suffered when open sewage dumped into the river entered the lake and thus returned in the city's water supply. In later years, the agency acquired a sordid history of great and petty graft.

built in the 1880s. Environmental groups also persuaded the U.S. Environmental Protection Agency to heed a little known 1899 law and withhold permission for seven heavy-industry companies, including U.S. Steel, to discharge waste into the southern end of Lake Michigan. While the area is hardly pollution-free even yet, the results of the efforts were beginning to show by the end of the 1970s. Fishermen reported they regularly could see the bottom of the lake through 20 feet of water, and the salmon and trout which were restocked in the southern part of Like Michigan were thriving, much to the anglers' delight. Some impressive progress was made by the state government too. A muscular Environmental Protection Agency (EPA), embracing the pollution control functions previously performed by several agencies, was created by the legislature in 1970, along with a rule-making Pollution Control Board and research-oriented Institute for Environmental Quality. The new Illinois system was considered unique because it avoided the device of a single environmental superagency and deliberately separated the jobs of environmental research, prosecution, and adjudication of cases. The idea was to introduce an element of tension into the process, so that more violations were in fact tracked down and stopped. One way this was accomplished was by giving not only the EPA, but also the attorney general and any interested citizen, the right to bring action against an environmental offender.

II. STATEWIDE AND DOWNSTATE

Politics of Party, Patronage, and Corruption

Illinois presents the classic picture of the big Democratic city against the Republican countryside. But the modern equation must figure in the Chicago suburban vote, now substantially larger than Chicago's, growing pockets of Democratic strength in cities like Peoria in the rich farmbelt of central Illinois, and "Little Egypt," the depressed southernmost counties where Democratic strength remains at least competitive through vestiges of Civil War antagonisms fused with modern economic issues.

From the Civil War to the advent of the New Deal, Illinois had a political pattern practically the reverse of what has been familiar in recent years. Northern Illinois, which had sympathized with the Union, was staunchly Republican; Southern Illinois, with strong Southern ties, was comparatively more Democratic. The Republicans held the balance of power and won all but two presidential and gubernatorial elections between 1860 and 1928.

But starting around the turn of the century, Bryan's silver policies began to eat away at Democratic loyalties in downstate. And by the middle of the New Deal, virtually all the rural counties and small towns outside of Little Egypt, revolted against Franklin Roosevelt's free-spending policies. Today, rural Illinois is big Farm Bureau territory.* The heart of Democratic strength is in the big industrial cities with high numbers of low-income ethnic group voters and blacks in uneasy alliance—Chicago, Moline and Rock Island, East St. Louis. The big-city coalition was large enough to give the Democrats vic-

* As in other states, the Farm Bureau's political clout is but a shadow of what it was in former days.

tory in all but two presidential elections between 1932 and 1964. But it has seen its share of the statewide vote shrink from 45 to 26 percent since Harry Truman's 1948 election, making it only half as important as it once was and prompting pundits to suggest Illinois may become a consistently Republican state. This transition becomes more pronounced with each passing election, with political analysts ascribing the balance of power in Illinois variously to the suburbs, to the "other 96 counties," as downstate is now referred to, or to the independent-minded ticket splitters.

The importance of the increasing electoral power of the suburbs should not be underestimated, Peter Colby and Paul Green, professors at Governors State University in Park Forest South, wrote in a 1978 analysis of voting trends in *Illinois Issues*, the state's fine foundation-sponsored political magazine. "Despite the success of a few overwhelmingly popular Democrats in the suburbs, in recent years," Colby and Green said, "the underlying base of party support for the Republicans is greater than ever, great enough to offset the Chicago base of party support for the Democrats. The downstate vote is more closely contested and is likely to hold the balance of power in close statewide elections."

"Under primary, under convention, under despotism or under a pure democracy, Illinois would be corrupt and crooked. . . . It is in the blood of the people," William Allen White opined over 50 years ago. The judgment was harsh and categorical, but there is ample evidence to show it is as true today as when it was made. Within this century, Adlai Stevenson III pointed out during a 1969 interview, there has been no true reform movement in Illinois state government. A primary reason, he said, is the division of Democratic big-city politics and Republican downstate politics. Each produces its own disciplined, well structured party apparatus. Ten years later, Illinois had elected two self-styled reformer governors, Daniel Walker and James Thompson, but the corruption endured. A high proportion of Illinois state officers and state legislators are in politics for profit or patronage and show minimal interest in issues of public service. In California, the governor has 120 patronage positions to fill, in Oregon 12, in Iowa 35, in Wisconsin 26. But in Illinois until the 1970s the governor and other cabinet officials had 15,000 patronage positions in their control, and there were at least twice that many patronage jobs in Cook County, and thousands more in county courthouses where Republican-sponsored venality is just as egregious as the venality of the big-city Democrats. Whether this system would truly survive into the 1980s was thrown into doubt by a 1979 decision of a federal judge in Chicago that the patronage system was unconstitutional. Predictably, Mayor Byrne and Cook County Board President George Dunne promised to appeal the ruling.

In recent years, a number of Illinois politicians have spent time in jail, including former Gov. Otto Kerner, some legislators, and one former house speaker charged with taking $30,000 in bribes to pass a bill increasing load limits for cement trucks. Republican State Auditor Orville E. Hodge in 1956 was sentenced to 20 years in prison for embezzling at least $1,612,639 in state funds to pay for his own lush living. But relatively few Illinois politicians actually go to jail for corrupt practices, largely because prosecutors' offices and the courts are often compromised.

The classic example of all time has to be that of Paul Powell, the self-styled "country boy" from impoverished southern Illinois who died in 1970 leaving an estate of about $3.1 million—even though his lifetime earnings, all in 36 years of public service, had come to less than $300,000. When Powell died in 1970, his body lay on the same catafalque that once bore Lincoln. A thousand officeholders and politicians crowded the crepe-draped rotunda of the State Capitol to honor the most powerful of all downstate Democrats. Governor Ogilvie and Mayor Daley were on hand to eulogize Powell. Only two and a half months later was the public suddenly told that $750,000 in cold cash had been found crammed into an old shoe box, a bowling-ball bag, and other containers in the closet of Powell's modest hotel room in Springfield. Then all the sordid details of Powell's way of operating came spilling out, with a flurry of talk (fruitless, it later turned out) about stiff new financial disclosure requirements for public officials.

Of course the politicians had known all along what Powell was up to. The late Adlai Stevenson once said of Powell that he could have been one of the great political figures of American history "if only he didn't believe that the shortest distance between two points is a curve." Powell had close ties to Chicago's infamous syndicate-controlled West Side Bloc; in fact the Bloc made Powell speaker of the Illinois house in 1963 by instructing two Republican legislators it controlled, Republicans who held jobs on the Chicago Sanitary District, to vote for Powell instead of the Republican candidate. The house was so closely divided that the defection caused Powell's election as speaker. Later, as secretary of state, Powell had big contracts to award and was revealed to be receiving several thousands of dollars a year from a racetrack for consulting services.

Following Powell's death, even more details came out, especially in regard to the hundreds of thousands of dollars of racetrack stock Powell had acquired at a minimal price years ago and financed through a loan repaid out of dividends. His estate also included a substantial chunk of stock in Illinois-based small banks and insurance companies, whose interests Powell had assiduously defended in the legislature. Powell's effects turned up hundreds of thousands of dollars in negotiable securities made out to the Paul Powell Dinner Committee, although under Illinois law campaign contributions are not to be converted into personal wealth. Details of two girl friends to whom he left hundreds of thousands of dollars, an extra Springfield apartment known as "Powell's love nest," and his tight-fistedness to maids and doormen who had served him for many years, also came to light.

How did Powell's constituents react to his shenanigans? "He was always a hero to the downstate voter," John Gardner, editor of the *Southern Illinoisan* at Carbondale, was quoted as saying. "He was the guy who out-slicked the city slickers." The reaction is a little like Harlem's long-time toleration of Adam Clayton Powell as long as he was beating the white man at his own game. But now it is all over for Paul Powell, and while the Internal Revenue Service, state agencies, and legatees went into years of litigation, Powell lies under a gravestone with the words chiseled as he had directed in his will: "Here lies a life-long Democrat."

The important point about Powell was that he was no bizarre aberration, but simply a master practitioner of a familiar game. In 1964 state senator Paul Simon (now a member of Congress) wrote an article for *Harper's* in which he estimated that about a third of Illinois legislators took payoffs— some in the form of payments for legal services, public relations work, or as campaign contributions, and a smaller number in the shape of outright bribes. In 1971 federal investigators discovered that former Gov. Otto Kerner, other leading Chicago Democrats, and some Republicans had realized large profits from racetrack stock transactions in the 1960s—transactions hidden at the time from the public. The transactions were made when Kerner controlled, through his appointive power, the membership of the Illinois Racing Board.

In 1965 former Republican Governor William G. Stratton (1953–61) came to trial on a federal income tax fraud indictment. Stratton did not dispute the government's charge that he had received $93,959 which he failed to report as income; his defense was that the money was in nontaxable gifts from prominent Republican politicians and others. Stratton was acquitted on the criminal charges, but the court testimony is fascinating reading. Stratton argued that expenses for vacations, formal clothes, and trips to the beauty parlor for his wife, or for the use of a luxurious lodge and houseboat, were all necessary political entertaining. Senate Republican Leader Everett M. Dirksen flew to Illinois to testify for Stratton, maintaining that the governor was justified in accepting "contributions that came to him from time to time." Dirksen said he had "clocked" his own expenses over six months and found that they "ran at the rate of a hundred dollars a day," so that he too was pleased to receive "contributions from those who recognize the difficulty that public service interposes for you."

When this many scandals come to light, one can imagine what goes on in secret and is never revealed. Of course there have been and are men of great personal integrity in Illinois state government. But when we asked veteran state political reporters to name the high state officials of the postwar period they were convinced were absolutely honest, the list was embarrassingly short. It included former Governor Adlai Stevenson II, and his son Adlai III (former state treasurer and later a United States Senator); Joseph Lohman, Democratic state treasurer in the late 1950s (who was crushed by the organization when he tried to run for governor and left the state brokenhearted); Latham Castle, Republican attorney general who prosecuted Hodges; Elbert Smith, Republican state auditor in the 1950s; and the bipartisan team—Republican Governor Richard B. Ogilvie, Lieutenant Governor Paul Simon, a crusader for higher ethics in government, and George Lindberg, the state's first elected comptroller, and father of the ethics act.

Men like U. S. Senator Charles H. Percy, and his predecessor, Paul H. Douglas, would have qualified for the integrity list, but neither ever held a position in state government. This may be no accident. Percy, a successful businessman who had made his fortune as head of Bell & Howell in Chicago, was obviously an alien force to the "system" and had less than full support from the downstate courthouse Republicans when he ran for governor in 1964. Douglas, a professor at the University of Chicago and pillar of integrity, would have liked to run for governor in 1948 but was slated for the U. S. Senate instead by Jake Arvey, then undisputed Cook County Democratic boss. Arvey did slate Stevenson for governor that year; he may have felt Stevenson would be more pliable than Douglas and in any event probably thought both men would lose in the anticipated Republican sweep of '48 that never materialized.

A story about Jake Arvey, related by John H. Fenton in *Midwest Politics*, may illustrate a reason why essentially corrupt party machines sometimes slate top men for statewide office. The story is borrowed from Boss Plunkett of Tammany Hall but is just as applicable for Illinois. It appears that a candidate for lesser office complained to Arvey that his name was never used on radio and television or on campaign posters, while Stevenson monopolized the publicity. "Look," said Arvey, "have you ever watched a boat dock along the lakefront?" "Yes," was the reply. "And did you notice the garbage and the trash that was drawn into the dock by the boat?" "Uh huh," said the candidate. "Well," Arvey concluded, "Stevenson is the boat and you are the garbage."

The inevitable result of a politics of patronage and payoff is a low level of service for the people. The state's per capita income was $7,768 in 1977, eighth highest in the United States. But Illinois spent less than the national per capita average for higher education, for local government aid, for public welfare, and for health and hospitals. The adoption of an income tax in 1969 made available more revenue than ever before, but over most of its history Illinois has been a rich state that chose not to do more for its people.

Illinois Governors: From Stevenson to Thompson

Two postwar Illinois governors have served with unusual distinction. The first was Adlai Stevenson II, elected in 1948 by a record-breaking plurality of 572,067 votes. Though he served just a single four-year term, Stevenson was able to double state aid to school districts, place the state police under a merit system, and effect a big increase in gasoline tax and truck license fees to expedite highway construction. But Stevenson's more important contribution was to bring a fresh breeze of integrity and a higher quality of official service into the musty corridors of the state capitol at Springfield; for many, he restored a belief in the viability and purpose of government. Even in defeat, he made a similar contribution to the nation through his eloquence and leadership in two unsuccessful campaigns for the presidency. Stevenson's distinguished public service, running through the years he served as U.S. Ambassador to the United Nations before his death in 1965, has won him a secure place in history and requires no further recital here.

Business as usual returned to Springfield under Stevenson's two successors, Republican William Stratton (1953–61) and Democrat Otto Kerner (1961–68). Stratton was a capable technician and does deserve credit for pushing through the first reapportionment of the legislature in half a century. Kerner's major contribution was outside of Illinois government—in his chairmanship of the Civil Disorders Commission to study racial divisions in America following the great urban riots of 1967. In Springfield, Kerner was strictly Daley's man. His office issued an "idiot sheet" to Democratic legislators telling them how they should vote; on issues of importance, the line was invariably set by Daley, not Kerner himself.

Richard B. Ogilvie, another one-term governor, was a totally different commodity from any of his recent predecessors. In demeanor, Ogilvie lacked the Stevensonian charisma or many politicians' physical glamour. A stocky, stolid man, he speaks with a hoarse voice and reminds many people of a small-town banker. As a tank commander in World War II, he was struck by shell fragments that ripped into the left side of his face; plastic surgery left him with a grim, set expression that proved a special liability on television. But few recent American governors demonstrated natural executive skill equal to Ogilvie's. His approach to problems was pragmatic, businesslike, and low-keyed. And he was a gutsy man, willing to undergo stiff criticism if he thought he was right. His great promise was cut short not by any scandal (so characteristic in Illinois) but the contrary: he dared to place the commonweal above political expediency. He supported—strenuously—the state's first income tax. "I knew damn well then it was probably signing my political death warrant as governor," Ogilvie recollected to us in a 1975 interview. "But everything I had in mind doing was contingent on our having additional revenues—school needs, social service requirements. All those things required a hefty transfusion of additional money." Asked if he would have done anything different, he said not. "I never viewed myself as being anointed to be anything," he replied. "I wasn't governor of Illinois by any right; I was entrusted with a responsibility. The question was, 'Did I want to be a mediocre eight-year governor or a really good four-year governor?' "

Ogilvie got his start in the tough world of Cook County politics, upsetting Mayor Daley's man to become county sheriff in 1962. In that post, he cracked down hard on the crime syndicate and won fame through a successful prosecution of mobster Tony Accardo. In 1966 he again upset the Democrats to be elected Cook County board president. Normally a Cook County politician would face stiff opposition from downstate Republicans in a gubernatorial primary, but Ogilvie's glowing reputation as an antagonist of the Daley machine helped him win the 1968 GOP gubernatorial nomination with ease and go on to win the general election with a 127,794-vote plurality.

But Illinois was hardly prepared for the flurry of creative activity that Ogilvie would unleash when he hit Springfield. Within a few months he had chalked up more concrete major accomplishments than any other governor of modern Illinois history. By executive order, he created a powerful management tool by establishing a bureau of the budget (modeled after the federal bureau), thus taking from the dawdling and often compromised legislature the right one of its committees had long enjoyed to pass on departmental budget requests before they even reached the governor's office. To staff the budget bureau, Ogilvie then installed a group of young "whiz kids," some direct out of federal service and all beholden to him rather than the old-line political structure of the state. State support for local schools was increased 75 percent, with special weighting provisions to give additional help to some urban school districts—though not enough to tackle the gut problems in ghetto schools. A full department of law enforcement, with an IBI modeled on the FBI, was created to wage war on organized crime in the state, though in practice it tended to concentrate more on chasing students for drugs and peace demonstrations than pursuing the syndicate.

Finally, with Illinois government on the point of bankruptcy because of rising expenditures, Ogilvie forced through a reluctant legislature the first income tax in the state's history. "For 50 years," the Chicago *Sun-Times* commented when Ogilvie unveiled his tax program, "Illinois has talked about a state income tax, and for 50 years the politicians and the citizens have dodged the issue." But despite the howls of protest from timid legislators, Ogilvie got the tax approved in a single session. Ogilvie asked for a flat 4 percent rate, but the legislature modified it to 2½ percent for individuals, 4 percent for corporations. The personal tax was essentially progressive because a liberal $1,000 personal exemption was allowed each taxpayer and each of his dependents, meaning that poor families would pay little if any tax. But the tax was on total gross income after those exemptions, and thus not subject to the myriad deductions which plague many tax structures (including the federal).

An important element of the Illinois income tax was that one-twelfth of the revenues were earmarked for direct, no-strings-attached sharing by city and county governments on a simple per capita basis. The provision not only had appeal as a precursor of the national revenue-sharing plan, but sweetened the tax package for reluctant state legislators. It even helped Ogilvie get some Cook County votes he needed to pass the program. By 1977, the shared income tax revenues amounted to $13.48 a person, almost twice as much as in 1970.

Ogilvie proved unable to survive the severe backlash from the income tax. The conservative Bourbon Republicans of downstate Illinois were so furious with him that they tried to dump him in the primary. But he was finally beaten by a scant 77,494 of 4.7 million votes cast in the 1972 general election. The winner was Democrat Daniel Walker, a superb campaigner who hiked 1,197 miles from the tip of southern Illinois to the Wisconsin border and back to Chicago preaching an evangelistic, antimachine, populist message designed to play on the resentment of workers who felt betrayed by Ogilvie's support of the income tax.*

A somewhat self-righteous Naval Academy graduate, Walker not only refused to play the typical Illinois politician's back-scratching game but was aloof from normal and necessary dealings with legislators, seeming to prefer town meetings and news conferences in assorted Illinois cities to the real business of governing. "The only way to shake things up is to go over the heads of the politicians and appeal to the people," he once said. None of this was appreciated in normal political circles. One old hand in Illinois politics told us that few in the Statehouse trusted Walker after his first few months in office. "He was the biggest public liar I've ever seen in politics and that includes Paul Powell," the source said. State Treasurer Alan Dixon (later secretary of state) said Walker didn't govern at all. "He spends all his time looking for fights, and his chief object is simply to dominate the news." Another political observer called Walker a "cross between Elmer Gantry and Huey Long."

It is impossible to record a single real accomplishment of Walker's term. He did pare the public payrolls, which had become overloaded with the beneficiaries of a bloated patronage system, but while reducing the number of employees from 117,941 to 110,443, he allowed state salaries to explode, increasing the payroll by one third. Mostly Walker vetoed everything, including school aid and tax relief. He used his powers so extensively that he broke the Illinois tradition of printing veto messages, forcing the Legislative Council to compile the veto message itself to maintain a centralized record. Finally, the legislature ignored his recommendations, passing budgets hundreds of millions of dollars above his requests.

One of Walker's most strident causes was campaign disclosure, and on taking office, he signed an executive order requiring his appointees to disclose their income and assets and then fought for the state's first campaign disclosure law. But neither act has substantially altered the wheeling and dealing that prevails, several statehouse reporters told us. "Clean Dan" hurt his own image when he refused to respond to questions the *Sun-Times* raised about possible illegalities in his campaign and when he was forced to cancel a $1.1 million construction contract his administration approved when it was discovered the firm had syndicate ties and had contributed to his campaign. Walker issued another executive order requiring firms to disclose campaign contributions if they did business with the state, but the court threw out the order.

In the end, Walker was defeated by his own party and the Daley machine. Walker took pride in challenging Daley, vetoing school aid when Chicago schools needed more aid, vowing that a cross-town expressway

---

* Walker banned pictures of himself in state offices but had his Abercrombie and Fitch hiking boots bronzed and displayed in the Capitol.

would never be built while he was governor (it wasn't) and finally openly fielding his own slate of independent candidates for office in 1974 and setting up an alternative campaign committee aimed at undermining the machine's control of the pursestrings. "I learned there is simply no making peace with the machine," Walker insisted. "Unless you do things on their terms, there's no compromise. And I refuse to do things on their terms." Other Illinois politicians questioned Walker's personal campaign against Daley. Said one Congressman with machine backing: "Not in 30 years of public life do I remember a governor treating a mayor with such disregard. It borders on contempt." In the March 16, 1976 primary, Daley got his revenge. The machine-backed Democratic candidate, Secretary of State Michael Howlett, defeated Walker 811,721 to 696,380.

Howlett lost in the general election, however, to Republican James R. Thompson, the U.S. Attorney whose crime-busting achievements were detailed earlier in this chapter. Thompson amassed the largest plurality of any governor in Illinois history, almost 1.4 million votes. In office, he turned out to be a compromiser rather than a crusader; for a period of time it appeared his mind was more on presidential aspirations than on governing Illinois. Thompson adopted a strategy of avoiding conflict, keeping a low profile, offering modest legislative programs, and not raising taxes. His approach to state government earned him the somewhat paradoxical distinction of being named to the Chicago *Tribune*'s list of Illinois' 20 most powerful people (by virtue of his office) and to its satirical list of Illinois' least powerful. "No one has seen anyone less interested in state government since the Queen of Romania passed through in the 1920s," the *Tribune* commented.

But Thompson may have been right when he mused more than once that "maybe the mood of the people of Illinois after four years of Walker, fighting and confrontation, was to have two years of nothing bad happening to them." It fell to Thompson to undo the damage that took place during the Walker regime. He improved the relations between the governor's office and the legislature and built up the state reserves that had dwindled under Walker to the point that the state had trouble paying its day-to-day bills. Thompson did not prove to be a social innovator, but he did respond to overcrowding and rioting in the state prison by building two new 750-bed prisons, the first in Illinois in decades.

State Government Miscellany: Legislature, Constitution, Education

We have heard such words as "very average," "thoroughly mediocre," and "very corrupt" applied to the Illinois legislature over the years. To a degree, the negative image has been accurate enough. One could fill volumes with the wheelings, dealings, and conflicts between Cook County machine Democrats, reformers in both parties, conservative downstate Republicans, the downstate Democratic contingent, and the sometimes crime syndicate elements in both parties.

It is also fair to say, however, that Illinois began to elect a somewhat different breed of legislators in the late 1960s and the 1970s. "Each crop of freshman legislators," said Charlie Wheeler, Springfield correspondent for the Chicago *Sun-Times*, "has a greater percentage willing to do their homework, willing to find out about issues, not so steeped in one philosophy that they can't compromise." Sessions became annual and the number of full-time legislators increased from seven in 1963 to 75 in 1973. Corroborating the brightening picture of those years, the Citizens Conference on State Legislatures in 1971 said the Illinois legislature had registered "a rapid rate of improvement" since reapportionment; the group even accorded Illinois a high ranking of third in the U.S. on its tests of year-round staffing, uniform rules, public committee rollcall votes, and the like.

There were two problem areas in the move to excellence. One was described by former Rep. George Burditt, who quit the legislature when he found he could not manage his 30-person Chicago law firm and fulfill his elected duties simultaneously. The legislature, he noted, was losing not only lawyers from the big city firms but farmers as well. A "citizen" legislature with many members holding outside interests, he believed, would be more efficient, less expensive, and less eager to pass bills.

The second problem was the ancient Achilles heel of the legislature—ethics. The state was unable, even during the reformist 1970s, to pass more than a weak lobby disclosure bill. The legislative reaction to testimony for a stiffer ethics bill, offered by the executive director of Illinois Common Cause, Lee Norrgard, was illustrative. The big question the legislators had for Norrgard was not on the merits of the bill he backed, but what was his salary. Norrgard replied: $15,800. The reaction of State Sen. John Knuppel: "Any man who doesn't earn more than this guy and has a college degree must not have any balls. I vote no."

Reapportionment had long been opposed by a bipartisan cabal of downstate Republicans and Democrats who both stood to lose if it were approved. The first house reapportionment since 1901 came in the early 1950s, but the senate was not reconstituted on a full population basis until federal court orders forced such a move in the 1960s. Reapportionment has had the greatest effect on the senate, where the old rural GOP oligarchy that long held sway has been dispersed, and the Democrats in 1970 were actually able to win control for the first time in 30 years. But the senate Republicans have changed too, with a shift away from downstate and toward Chicago suburban leadership. Cook County now has many more legislative seats than it used to, but it is not a unified force because of the split between Chicago machine Democrats and suburban Republicans.

Reapportionment has cut down the once mighty clout of the Farm Bureau lobby. Lobbies of most influence include the Illinois Manufacturers Association (which helps finance many Republican campaigns), the Illinois

Chamber of Commerce, coal operators, insurance companies like State Farm and Allstate, the Illinois Education Association, and the Illinois Medical Society (Chicago is AMA headquarters), AFL-CIO unions (especially the Steelworkers), retail merchants, and the racetracks—the latter a key source of patronage with many legislators owning racetrack stock. Many special interests now exert influence in Springfield by getting their own employees or operatives elected to legislative seats. And the chambers are packed with lawyers, real estate, and insurance people who often find the special interests throwing business their way, making them more and more beholden. Thus the technique of direct bribery became passé, almost an anachronism. The lobbyists have responded with fervor to the increasingly sophisticated legislative staff. One organization, we were told, has two lobbyists: one whose job is to wine and dine the lawmakers, another who specializes in the legislative staff.

The Chicago *Tribune* wields great influence in the legislature, although not as blatantly as when its former Springfield correspondent, George Tagge, served as a kind of father confessor to the Republican party. Pushing an idea of Colonel McCormick, Tagge lobbied successfully for legislation that would divert racetrack tax revenues to finance McCormick Place on the lakefront. The building's informal nickname: Tagge's Temple. Actually the first version, an architectural monstrosity, burned down, forcing the Democrats to hold their 1968 convention at the old International Amphitheatre beside the odoriferous Chicago stockyards. The new version of McCormick Place has a low, black silhouette. It is an invasion of the lakefront but not as offensive as its predecessor.

In 1970, Illinois voters approved a fresh constitution. It did purge anachronistic sections of the 1870-vintage constitution which Illinois had been living under, including provisions on cartways, drains and ditches, lotteries, and "World's Columbian Exposition." It changed the legislature from semiannual to annual sessions, included an innovative clause giving any citizen the right to sue polluters to secure his "right to a healthy environment," shifted primary responsibility for financing public schools to the state, gave local governments some more flexibility in reforming their own structures, and included a long Bill of Rights article with an explicit open-housing and fair employment provision. The governor was given both an amendatory and a reduction veto. The amendatory authority allows the governor to send vetoed bills back to the legislature with suggested changes, which then become law if approved by both houses. The reduction veto permits the governor to lower the spending levels of appropriation bills. They are elements in the veto power rarely granted to governors in state constitutions.

But the new constitution actually made the revenue system more restrictive rather than more flexible, failed to reduce the vastly oversized state house of representatives (177 members), and did not effect the far-reaching structural reforms needed in state and local government. Fearful that the whole constitution might go down to defeat if encumbered with controversial provisions, the authors submitted four separate vote proposals to (1) abolish election of judges and have them appointed by the governor from nominees submitted by judicial nominating conventions; (2) abolish the death penalty; (3) lower the voting age to 18; and (4) abolish the confusing cumulative voting system for legislative candidates in three-man districts (a device which breeds lack of competition and cozy relationships between the parties).

Thanks in part to belated but clear support from Mayor Daley, the constitution itself was approved by a 1,122,452 to 838,168 vote. But all the controversial separate proposals went down to defeat. The most interesting test of "old" versus "new" politics was the vote on appointment of judges. Governor Oglivie, three of the four Chicago dailies, civic organizations, many law school professors and other "good government" forces were for the provision with its so-called "merit selection plan" similar to existing provisions in Missouri and California. But Daley wanted to keep the elective system because judgeships and the jobs which go with them are big plums in the Democrats' patronage system. Downstate Republican organizations felt the same way about *their* own patronage. Only the suburbs were strongly in favor. So a blizzard of negative Chicago city and downstate votes stopped "merit selection" in its tracks.

The whole effort for constitutional change might never have begun had it not been for the 20-year campaign in behalf of reform launched by Chicago attorney Samuel Witwer. He was chosen president of the convention and helped to smooth over the fiery clashes that erupted among the delegates. If the speed of reform in Illinois seems glacial, it may be because the prevailing climate discourages all but a few civic-minded leaders with Witwer's determination.

By most modern day progressive standards, Illinois state government has few innovations or accomplishments to be proud of. The exception is in higher education. Although the state's per capita expediture for higher education is almost 10 percent under the national average, the University of Illinois system of 10 universities and 39 community colleges stands out as one of the country's finest in many disciplines. A 1977 *Chronicle of Higher Education* national survey of college faculty ranked Illinois highest in engineering, education, and music and gave commendations in biology, business, chemistry, languages, mathematics, physics, and psychology. The library at the University of Illinois-Urbana is one of the five largest in the country. Illinois residents make good use of the system. In the 1978–79 academic year, over 689,000 full-time and part-time students were enrolled, twice the number of a decade earlier. Sadly, however, the state has taken a provincial attitude toward student recruitment, and the schools lack the national and international student bodies that characterize the universities of Michigan, Wisconsin, Minnesota, and California.

Illinois in Washington

The outstanding legislators Illinois has sent to Washington in the post-war years have reflected the state's many images: the intellectual community represented by Senator Paul Douglas, rural and small-city Illinois symbolized by Senator Everett Dirksen, suburban and new industrial Illinois in Senator Charles Percy.

The outstanding members of the House delegation are even more of a microcosm: Daniel Rostenkowski, a keen big-city spokesman who was Mayor Daley's man; Abner J. Mikva, brilliant but sole representative of the Democratic reform contingent of the Chicago area delegation until he resigned to accept a federal judgeship; House minority whip Robert Michel, reflecting his conservative Peoria constituency with annual amendments to cut the federal social service budget; Melvin Price, the East St. Louis lawmaker who emerged from 34 years of near obscurity to become chairman of the powerful Armed Services Committee; Paul Simon, the bright, promising, and affable downstater who retained his reform inclinations after years of frustration as a legislator, lieutenant governor, and Daley's gubernatorial candidate in 1972; Robert McClory, the aging but ranking minority member of the House Judiciary Committee, who finally cast a fragmented vote for impeachment of Nixon even though his district voted for Goldwater in 1964; Philip Crane, the good-looking and dogmatic Mount Prospect Congressman and president of the American Conservative Union who ran for President in 1980; and Paul Findley of the Springfield and west congressional district, a Republican who started as a super conservative but became interested in issues like North Atlantic union and expanding agricultural trade with the communists (pleasing incidentally the exporting farmers in his constituency).

In 1969 the delegation lost one of its most promising members when the youthful North Shore Congressman, Donald Rumsfeld, resigned to become director of the federal Office of Economic Opportunity and later Counselor to President Nixon with Cabinet rank and director of operations for the Cost of Living Council. Under President Ford, Rumsfeld ran the White House staff transition, served two years as Secretary of Defense, and had a tour as U.S. Ambassador to NATO. When Ford was defeated, Rumsfeld left politics for private business, becoming head of the troubled Chicago drug firm, G.D. Searle. A progressive by inclination, Rumsfeld subordinated his own ideological preference in service to President Nixon, but his political acumen and high reputation as a government manager continued to feed speculation that he might one day reemerge as a potent Illinois political figure in his own right.

An even greater national impact was to be made a dozen years later, however, when John B. Anderson, a veteran House member from the booming Rockford area northwest of Chicago, leaped into the presidential race—

first as a Republican, then as an independent. A self-described "one-time conservative who has been steadily jogging leftward," Anderson had been chairman of the House Republican Conference before his decision to run for President. Anderson's independent presidential candidacy was a marked departure from independent or third-party bids of the 20th century since he was a candidate in the nation's ideological mainstream rather than a representative of the far right or left.

Now senior Senator from Illinois is Charles H. Percy, a man who has been in the national eye since, at 29 years of age, he became president of the Bell & Howell camera firm. Then the youngest chief executive of any major U.S. corporation, Percy showed a business genius that carried Bell & Howell from $5 million to $160 million in annual sales during the 15 years he was in command. In the process, Percy earned all the money he would ever need: in 1967 he estimated his personal worth at "conservatively" $6 million.

After an abortive start in elective politics in 1964, when he ran for governor but lost in the Goldwater debacle, Percy shook some of the brashness which had characterized his first campaign (and been especially offensive to downstate Republican old-liners) and in 1966 won election to the Senate over incumbent Paul Douglas. The strongest margins for Percy came in the suburbs; it is this "new Illinois" which his image matches: the successful buinessman, pragmatic, centrist in his political views. (Indeed, it was that image that saved Percy from near defeat at the hands of a conservative Democratic opponent in 1978.) In the Senate, Percy steered a moderate liberal Republican course, rose to be ranking Republican on the Government Operations Committee, and frequently made constructive suggestions (i.e., a home ownership plan for the poor or, during the Vietnam war, an "All-Asian" peace conference to settle that conflict). As a chief Illinois patronage dispenser during the Nixon-Ford years, he backed Thompson as U.S. Attorney and could take credit for the naming of several outstanding individuals to the U.S. bench.

Tragedy crossed Percy's path in 1966 when his 21-year-old daughter Valerie was murdered in the family's lakeshore Kenilworth home. Ten years later the $50,000 reward was still out for the killer, and Percy told of the life of dread he and his family had continued to live with the murderer at large. The joyous counterpart is the happy life his other daughter, Sharon, is leading as the wife of John D. Rockefeller IV, governor of West Virginia. Percy once was frequently spoken of as a presidential candidate, but there are those who think his daughter Sharon may be the family member who ends up living in the White House.

Adlai Stevenson III, elected to Illinois' other Senate seat in 1970, lacked the grace and wit that made his father an illustrious national and international figure. But he seemed to have about everything else going for him. His performance, first as a state legislator in the famous "blue ribbon" legislature of 1965–66, when he was named that body's outstanding member, and later as state treasurer, a job in which he opened account ledgers to the public and increased investment returns to the state by millions of dollars, helped Stevenson build on the inherent advantages of a famous name. By the end of the 1970 Senate campaign, it was also clear that he was an astute politician. His opponent, interim Senator Ralph Smith, was a glib statehouse politician who tried to "radicalize" Stevenson's image through a series of innuendo-packed commercials that depicted Stevenson as an enemy of the police cut from the same cloth as yippie agitator Jerry Rubin. "When I see Adlai, I see red," Smith said in one speech. The commercials backfired with ordinary voters, and Stevenson skillfully deflected the attack by putting an American flag in his lapel, saying he "detested" violence whether "by Black Panthers, white students, or state troopers," and then making Thomas Foran, prosecutor of the "Chicago Seven," a co-chairman of his campaign. (Dan Walker was his regular campaign chairman, however.) As noted earlier, Stevenson won in a veritable landslide, even carrying downstate Illinois.

In the Senate, Stevenson rarely took the lead on major issues, preferring to labor in the background on the more mundane structural and procedural reforms in government. His ratings by the Americans for Democratic Action and labor groups revealed a consistently liberal record which led to a short campaign for the presidential or vice presidential nomination in 1976. But Stevenson did not like the oxen-like pace of reform in the Senate or the superficial treatment of issues in the "media" politics of the 1970s and announced that he would not seek reelection in 1980. He proposed formation of a third party, but confounded his followers by refusing to lead it himself.

Paul Douglas, elected to the U.S. Senate in 1948, fell victim to old age and the swirling new tides of suburban politics which propelled his onetime student, Charles Percy, into the seat in 1966. But Douglas merits a word of note before the tides of history obscure the contributions of a brave, proud man who, like many Quakers, never doubted the righteousness of what he stood for. Though a pacifist, Douglas was convinced of the justifiability of World War II; he entered the Marines at age 52 as a private and was twice wounded in combat. (Douglas was later a vigorous cold war warrior and remained a "hawk" on Vietnam to the end.) In the Senate, he demonstrated both great intellectual skill and sharp partisan wit; he was at once an author of liberal measures like the landmark 1949 Housing Act and a prime opponent of "pork barrel" federal public works spending. (In 1962, Douglas credited himself with saving the taxpayers nearly $2 billion through economy amendments.) Douglas served as chairman of the Joint Economic Committee, pioneered in consumer protection legislation (especially "truth in lending") and was a long-time battler of the congressional seniority system, which he claimed was a device to let Southern conservatives control committees in league with conservative Republicans. Such views precluded his ever becoming a member of the Senate "club."

Everett McKinley Dirksen, by contrast, was a personification of the Senate inner circle and perhaps the most powerful single Senator during the decade of the '60s. Apparently a conservative by natural inclination, he first won national attention when he pointed at Thomas E. Dewey from the rostrum of the 1952 Republican National Convention and intoned angrily: "We followed you before and you took us down the road to defeat." (Dewey was for Eisenhower for the nomination, Dirksen for Taft.) In his 33 years in Congress, Dirksen was variously regarded as an isolationist and an internationalist, a New Dealer and a conservative, a friend and foe of civil rights. Though opposed to Ike's nomination in 1952, he became his valued lieutenant when elected minority leader in 1959. "I am a man of principle, and one of my first principles is flexibility," he once said. It was Dirksen's personal change of position which shifted enough conservative Republican Senators to make possible passage of numerous Kennedy-Johnson measures, including the Nuclear Test Ban Treaty and the Civil Rights Act of 1964 ("an idea whose time has come," said Dirksen). Yet he was a defender of Senator Joseph McCarthy, nominated Barry Goldwater for President in 1964, and was the leading figure in a failing effort to turn back the clock on the Supreme Court's reapportionment and school prayer decisions.

In his excellent biography, *Dirksen: Portrait of a Public Man*, Neil Mac-Neil, *Time*'s chief congressional correspondent since 1958, said Dirksen was "committed to the idea of compromise as a good in itself" and was a man who "played the game of politics for the zest of the game itself, for its fascination, for its exhilaration." Toward the end of his career, *Newsweek* and other publications suggested an underlying theme of venality in Dirksen's activities, pointing to his extraordinary interest in legislation affecting certain industries (drugs, chemicals, gas pipelines, steel, and lending institutions), his placement of "Dirksen men" in federal regulatory agencies, and his bitter opposition to any requirement that members of Congress disclose their income or holdings. It seemed the suspicions were being borne out when the attorneys handling his estate were more than a year remiss in filing a full inventory, and when the inventory was finally made public it included $53,-379.43 in unspent campaign funds in a Washington lock box at the time of his death. But Dirksen's total estate, even counting a valuation of $150,000 placed on 11 crates of personal papers, was only $302,235, certainly slim pickings in comparison to what Dirksen's *opportunities* for under-the-table money had been. MacNeil was probably correct when he said that Dirksen "sought power and influence, not money."

Robert Novak, reviewing MacNeil's book, provided a fitting epitaph:

Everett Dirksen's place in history is as ambiguous as was his own ideology. His flexibility time and again prevented deadlock of the legislative process and produced legislation where, otherwise, there might have been none. But that same flexibility kept him from charting even a broad course for himself, his party, and his nation, and this may exclude him from the first order of American statesmen.

Downstate Illinois: Prairie, City, Farm, and Factory

For the past quarter century, the population center of the United States has been creeping westward across southern Illinois. In 1950 it was in the little town of Olney, not far from the Indiana border; in 1960 not far from a small city prophetically named Centralia; in 1970 in farmer Lawrence Friederich's fallow soybean field 5.3 miles east of Mascoutah—and 23 miles to the east of East St. Louis. But, as others have noted in the past, this is not the only sense in which Illinois is the "state in the middle" or "the most American." In the downstate Illinois of plowed fields in spring and rows of drying corn in the autumn, there still flourishes a conservative yet concerned way of life, a pride in self, soil and workmanship, and entrenched independence that has diminished in urban America. The naturalist-writer and Illinois native Donald Culross Peattie a few years ago proclaimed that "Illinois is the best state precisely because it is so American. More, it is heartland. As Castile is of Spain, as the plain of Beauce is the granary of France, or Tuscany of Italy, so Illinois is core America. . . ."

Outside of the Chicago metropolis, Illinois remains essentially rural; in the 381 miles of her length, the top north of Boston, the bottom south of Louisville, there are only a handful of significant cities. The largest of these is Rockford (1975 population 140,667—only a twentieth of the Chicago figure), a healthy manufacturing center set in the forests and low hills of the Rock River valley of north central Illinois. The flavor is strongly Scandinavian and conservative; the city once struggled with its political conscience before finally accepting urban renewal funds to help rebuild its center city. But with a growing black and Latino population, more factories, and more union members (many belonging to the UAW local at Chrysler's nearby Belvidere plant), the tone has moderated considerably. Rockford developed one of the most successful "scattered site" public housing projects in America and elected—and more surprisingly reelected—a Democratic mayor, Robert McGaw.

Peoria (pop. 125,724), set in the midst of Central Illinois' endless cornfields, used to be so renowned for municipal corruption, whiskey bootlegging, and unsolved murders that John Gunther called it "one of the toughest towns on earth." The past two decades have brought an infusion of reform politicians and a constant fight to renovate the decaying central city. Indicative of the new spirit, Caterpillar Tractor, largest Peoria employer with a local payroll of some 33,000, moved its national headquarters into the city proper. But many merchants abandoned downtown in 1973 when a suburban mall opened. In 1979, Hiram Walker and Sons staggered Peoria with the announcement that it would close its whiskey distillery and lay off 850 employees by 1981. When it opened in 1934, the plant was the world's largest distillery, and in 1978 it was still Peoria's 11th largest employer and paid $1.3 million in local taxes. Peoria's dynamic young Republican mayor Richard Carver (in his late 30s) has fought the economic problems by accumulating once-distrusted federal and state dollars, taking in more than $10 million in his first term and convincing the University of Illinois to locate its regional medical school in an urban renewal area. Carver in 1979 became head of the U.S. Conference of Mayors and attempted to create a bigger voice for the medium and small town mayors in the group; Carver was frequently mentioned as a possible statewide Republican candidate.

The major business of Springfield (pop. 87,520) is politics and state government, despite a scattering of industries. As a state capital with considerable tradition, Springfield has a social strata of sorts; there are still many names that were prominent in Lincoln's day. True to the Lincolnian heritage, this territory remains staunchly Republican. Springfield, like most other Illinois cities, is agonizing over the decay of its downtown, but it has capitalized on the Lincoln name and undertaken the renovation of the old Capitol, constructed a mall area around Lincoln's home, and developed a new convention center and hotels.

Diversified industry and dull politics typify most of Illinois' other downstate cities in the 40,000 to 90,000 population bracket—Decatur (89,690), self-proclaimed "soybean capital of the world"; Moline (47,299), home of John Deere and "farm implement capital of America"; Rock Island (47,299), site of the government's largest military arsenal; Champaign (59,519), which shares with neighboring Urbana the site of the main campus of the University of Illinois; Aurora (78,544); Alton (34,488); Danville (41,478); Elgin (61,690); the old river town of Quincy (42,326) on the Mississippi; and Bloomington-Normal (twin cities with 77,361), an insurance-rich community which also is the ancestral home of the Stevenson family.

For all of Illinois' industrial might, farming remains its biggest single industry. Rich black glacial soil that goes as deep as 75 feet—called gumbo by early settlers, who had difficulty plowing it—covers all of Illinois except the southern counties, and no less than 80 percent of the state is in farmland. Fully 90 percent of this land is rated "prime" by the state Soil Conservation Service, and Illinois has approximately 9 percent of all such high quality soil within the United States. Modern agricultural techniques, machinery, fertilizer, and hybrid seeds have all contributed to phenomenal production increases which industry only dreams about, allowing Illinois farmers to export $3 billion of their products annually.

Outside of Chicago, principal industrial growth is coming along the Illinois Waterway, a combination of the Cal-Sag Canal and the Des Plaines and Illinois rivers stretching 300 miles from Chicago to Joliet, Peoria, and then into the Mississippi River north of St. Louis.* A major industrial corridor is developing along the Waterway, which can deliver coal, iron ore, chemicals, petroleum products, and construction materials by cheap barge

* The Waterway provides the direct link between the Great Lakes and the Gulf of Mexico.

transportation. Most of central and northern Illinois is prime corn belt territory, and the state vies with Iowa for number one position among the states in corn harvestings and trails only Iowa in hog production. Illinois is also strong in beef production and second only to Iowa as a meat packer; throughout the state new, automated packing plants have filled the gap created by the demise of the Chicago stockyards. In the north, there are also Wisconsin-like dairylands. Illinois ranks number one among the states in soybeans, the great (and versatile) crop of U.S. agriculture in the postwar period. Overall, Illinois farmers register $6.1 billion in receipts each year, ranking behind only California, Iowa, and Texas. But the tremendous production overshadows an alarming shrinkage of farm acreage. James Krohe, Jr., outlined the scope of the problem in *Illinois Issues:*

> Farmland in the state is being paved, flooded, stripmined and sodded over at an average annual rate of 100,000 acres. That's 281 acres, or nearly one average-sized Illinois farm, every day, seven days a week. In 17 years, Illinois' farmland inventory has shrunk from 30.7 to 29 million acres, a loss equivalent to eight average-sized counties. If current rates of loss continue unabated, another eight counties' worth of farmland will be gone by the turn of the century. One recent study shows that 18,000 acres a year are lost to forest, 19,000 to mining (including strip mining of coal), 64,000 to parks and reservoirs, 80,000 to large-lot rural residences, 84,000 to subdivisions, 83,000 for new industrial and commercial development, and 52,000 for miscellaneous uses such as highway. The 1,300-mile Illinois interstate highway system alone has eaten up 48,000 acres of land since its first mile was laid in 1957. And it is an incontrovertible biological fact that, although it's possible to ship corn on an interstate, it's not possible to grow it on one.

What neither Illinois nor the other Great Lakes States (nor many in the nation, for that matter) offer is a coherent land use plan to conserve open spaces and farmland in particular. The resulting sprawl development causes immense extra energy use, especially in petroleum, and chips away at the best land for agricultural production which the nation needs desperately to pay for its foreign oil imports and provide a stable base for the United States in the world economy into the 21st century.

Egypt and Its Cairo; East St. Louis

Far from booming "Chicagoland" and ranging southward from the rich glacier-tilled prairie of central Illinois lies a 31-county region of hilltop and bottom country wedged between the Ohio, Wabash, and Mississippi Rivers that looks like, thinks like, and acts like the American Southland. Perhaps because of its similarity to the deltalands of the Nile, the region has long been known as Egypt (or Little Egypt) and comes complete with towns named Cairo, Karnak, Thebes, and Dongola. It is not only a land of levees and overflowing rivers, but of the Illinois Ozarks with their valleys and hills where the first settlers hacked farmsteads out of the magnificent hardwood forests of walnut, oak, beech, sycamore, and poplar.

Egypt lies south of prosperity and indeed has been in a spiraling economic decline for several decades. About 15 percent of the families in southern Illinois live on $3,000 or less a year (mid-1970s dollars), the average education still stops halfway through high school, and high unemployment is perpetual. Since the 1890s, coal has been a major industry of the region, and the state still has enough coal to supply the world for almost a century. But even though Illinois ranks fourth in the nation in coal production (behind West Virginia, Pennsylvania, and Kentucky), the coal is cursed by its high sulfur content, which runs it afoul of modern federal pollution standards. Few companies are willing to install the expensive pollution control equipment necessary to make Illinois coal clean enough to use. Two-thirds of Illinois' 57 coal mines are also of the land-despoiling strip variety. The national concern over energy in the late 1970s brought new hope for Illinois coal, but any real effects on the regional economy lay down the road. Illinois' Egypt, blessed with many idyllic settings, holds a potential for recreation and tourism, and the creation of several major lakes has attracted more fishermen. But young people leave the region in droves despite the efforts of such institutions as the Southern Illinois University at Carbondale to expand technical education in varied fields.

Those who know the region have written of Southern Illinois as an "intemperate land" of "great and bitter passions." It was in Williamson County that one of the most gruesome episodes in American labor history took place in 1922, as 500 striking miners massacred 19 strikebreakers (a story graphically recounted in Paul Angle's *Bloody Williamson*).

And in the 1960s new kinds of terror and trouble began to stalk across Southern Illinois, centered in the town of Cairo and the city of East St. Louis.

Cairo (pronounced Kerro), perhaps the only walled city in the U.S.A., is a squat, drab river town set behind 60-foot levees at the very point of confluence of the Ohio's gray waters and Mississippi's yellow tide.

In its heyday, Cairo was a great port of call for river crews, a trading and cotton production center, crossroads for seven railroads, and county seat where close to 20,000 people lived. It was also a wide open town, very wet during Prohibition, a place where riverboat crews could always find women and gambling. The economy began a long decline a generation ago, and the town now has just 5,437 people. Up until early 1970s, it was wracked by the bitterest conflicts between blacks and whites of almost any town in America. In 1969 alone, fires were reported to have destroyed over $1 million of business property in Cairo. A 1973 report by the U.S. Commission on Civil Rights said the community had suffered a "breakdown in law and order" during the turbulence, and criticized the exclusionary practices in the police department, jobs, schools, housing, and medical care.

East St. Louis, a town of 53,902 people some 170 miles northwest of Cairo on the Mississippi opposite St. Louis, has a raucous and violent history that dates back to 1885 when the first mayor was assassinated by a disgruntled city employee. Up to World War I the town was largely white, but then the industries (railroads and big meat packers) imported Southern blacks as strikebreakers; the result in 1917 was the worst race riot of the first half of the 20th century, in which 39 blacks and nine whites were killed, more than 300 buildings and 44 railroad cars burned in three days of mob rule.

A big clean-up of organized vice and crime came under Mayor Alvin Fields in the 1950s, but most of the postwar years spelled a compounding of misery for East St. Louis. Three major employers—Swift, Armour, and Alcoa —pulled out of the city. Poorly educated northbound blacks from the South flooded in in ever increasing numbers, and by 1978 the city was 80 percent black, 28 percent unemployed, and 60 percent on welfare.

As the poverty level rose and the tax base dwindled, the East St. Louis government for 25 years was obliged to resort to what is euphemistically called "judgment financing"—a ploy by which the city lets its cash balance go down to zero, creditors go to court and get a judgment against the city, and the city may then (under Illinois law) issue bonds to cover the indebtedness.

The hard-working East St. Louis blacks thrown onto relief when the packing houses closed were not of the rioting type, but their sons and daughters turned militant by the mid-1960s. Most of the protesting youngsters refrained from violent protest, but there were disturbances in 1967 and 1968. Then a small element of black hoodlums, capitalizing on the black revolution, began a wave of terror that drove law-abiding blacks and whites alike behind locked doors at home each night. Murders and strong-armed robberies increased sharply, and between early 1968 and mid-1969 there was a wave of unexplained snipings that wounded dozens and killed several.

Up to the late 1960s East St. Louis was ruled by an antique, patronage-based Democratic machine with a cadre of ill-educated white precinct committeemen who curried favor by paying occasional grocery or light bills for families in trouble, providing dinners for wakes, getting people out of jail after fights or drinking bouts, and paying up to $3 a vote on election day. But gradually blacks took over committeeman and leadership posts, the local antipoverty campaign, and the model cities program; everyone knew that the future of East St. Louis was as a black-run town. The question was what kind of black leadership—militant, reformist, or old-line political—would emerge. One answer came in 1971 when Fields retired voluntarily, and a "clean" reform slate of moderate blacks (with one white ally) took control of the mayoralty and a majority of the city council. The new mayor was James E. Williams, Sr., 49, a political novice who ran on a pledge not to be a puppet for a political machine. He scored an upset victory over another black, city commissioner Virgil E. Calvert, who had been the favorite.

But Williams' election was no true harbinger of lasting reform or of an end of a corrupt tradition. Among the notable differences were the fact that blacks and not whites controlled the patronage and corruption and that votes now cost $5 instead of $3. Williams was succeeded as mayor by former school Supt. William Mason, whose administration was embarrassed in 1977 with the indictment and conviction on gambling charges of three former aides, the police chief, a police lieutenant, and a special assistant to the mayor himself.

For the third time in the decade, voters of East St. Louis elected themselves a new mayor in 1979, ousting incumbent Mason by almost a 2–1 margin. In his place, they chose a youthful (27 years old) undertaker, Carl E. Officer, who insists his vocation is not symbolic of the future of the city. A former administrative assistant to Secretary of State Alan Dixon, Officer pledged to bring in a cadre of professionals to replace the deadwood patronage workers in City Hall. "I'm not saying you'll see a turnaround immediately, but I promise you you'll see the beginning of that turnaround," he said in a pre-election speech.

Steven Sargent of the Illinois Municipal League reminded us that many people unfairly characterize southwestern Illinois by East St. Louis. While it indeed is the most notorious, he pointed out that the area also includes a combination of comfortable middle-class communities and several thriving industrial towns (Belleville, Alton, Edwardsville, Granite City, Collinsville, and Wood River, to cite a few).

Nevertheless, it is the continued presence of an East St. Louis, with its overwhelming burden of social and governmental distress, that both confuses and confounds the visitor. Why, in a state of such affluence and industrial and agricultural and financial might, must such conditions persist? The conclusion is inescapable: Illinois state government, constitutionally and morally responsible for the cities and counties within its borders, chooses to ignore the festering social sore. Illinois is not alone in that negligence: every other Great Lakes State, and indeed most in the Union, harbor similar pockets of poverty and desperation. By special intergovernmental subsidies, industrial tax incentives for target areas, and the like, European and Canadian national and provincial governments most frequently find ways to cope with such situations. That success record makes the failure of the American states even more apparent and discouraging and dictates a healthy measure of skepticism about the claimed successful progress of American governments in this century.

WISCONSIN

TRADITION, MAVERICKS, AND GOOD GOVERNMENT

LIKE A BRIGHT METEOR sailing through a midnight sky, Wisconsin in the first years of this century showed the nation what an individual state, if it has the will, can do to enhance the life and security of its people. The trailblazer was Robert Marion LaFollette; the tradition he created was called Progressivism.

But there is far more to Wisconsin than LaFollette or Progressivism. The state bred not only LaFollette and his political descendants (by bloodline or ideology or both), but also Sen. Joseph McCarthy, the man whose Hitler-like red-baiting eventually made its way into dictionaries as *sui generis*. The fact is that Wisconsin is an amalgam of strong political traditions and self-perpetuating political myths, of high government expectations and high taxes to prove it, of economic diversity in the extreme (cows to heavy machinery), and a distinctive quality of life found in few of its sister states.

It is true that Wisconsin's strain of Progressive politics, born when the people revolted against hard times in 1900 and ousted the corporate magnates and corrupt political bosses they blamed for their misfortunes, runs exceedingly deep, reflected not only in a high level of government activity but also in extraordinarily clean politics. Wisconsin's rich ethnic heritage (Germans and Scandinavians dominate) played a major part in making the state receptive to such diverse politics, ranging from McCarthy to Progressivism, from Milwaukee's dominant Socialism for half of this century, to a sedated version of agrarian Populism late in the 19th century, to say nothing of the modern-day mavericks like U.S. Sen. William Proxmire and the anti-establishment Republican governor who took office in 1979, Lee Sherman Dreyfus.

The Wisconsin reputation for honesty in public life is well deserved. While other states expect (and thus often get) bribery and corruption from their public officials, the people of Wisconsin will make a major issue of incidents considered penny-ante elsewhere.

A small example. In 1978 three legislators were charged with abusing their publicly-issued and publicly paid for telephone credit cards by making personal calls with them and allowing friends and relatives to do likewise. Altogether, the phone tolls cost about $1,700. When two judges dismissed the charges, newspaper editorials chastised the actions. "The taxpayer could be forgiven if he believes he has been had, both by the Legislature and the judiciary," lamented the LaCrosse *Tribune,* which along with the Racine *Journal-Times* had dug up the original allegations. Yet the saga did not end with the dismissal. In the 1978 elections, two of the three legislators (both committee chairmen) were defeated for reelection. Increased scrutiny of phone records saw a 40 percent drop in the long-distance calls made by the legislature, and the state senate decided not to issue phone credit cards at all for the 1979 session. "Using state telephones for personal calls or allowing others to use their telephone may not equal the shenanigans that periodically crop up in Washington or Illinois," the Madison *Capital Times* editorialized in the wake of the "scandal," "but it is a matter of grave concern to Wisconsinites who have come to expect high integrity from their legal representatives. To underscore this judgment, it is noteworthy that only one state lawmaker and not a single major state officer was indicted for any kind of corruption in the 1970s. Before that, the last time legislators were accused of violating the public trust was in the late 1960s, when one lawmaker was accused of accepting a $100 bribe and another a $50 bribe. Both charges ultimately were dropped, but not before one went to the state supreme court.

Wisconsin pays a price for the quality of government it demands. In 1965, for instance, the state ranked fourth in the nation, and second only to Minnesota among states of significant population, in combined state and local tax revenue as a percentage of personal income. But by 1977, thanks largely to the austerity administrations of Gov. Patrick J. Lucey, this ranking had slipped to ninth, behind a number of major states including New York, Massachusetts, California, and again Minnesota. Seen another way, the Wisconsin personal tax burden was 120 percent of the national average in 1965 but was down to 112 percent by 1977.

Paul Hassett, president of the state's major industrial trade association, told us in an interview that he now counsels his corporate president members to stop complaining about Wisconsin's high taxes. "I've given up complaining about taxes, because I believe the people want them. It's part of the sense of a progressive society," he said. For those high taxes, though, Wisconsinites get service to match: only Alaska, New York, and New Jersey spent more per pupil for elementary education (in 1976–77); the university at Madison, an integral part of the progressive tradition, stands out as a prestigious institution with deserved national acclaim; one-seventh of the state's 56,154 square miles are devoted to public parks and forests, assuring that Wisconsin's wealth of lakes and waterways, scenic retreats, and wildlife resources will remain truly accessible to the public; the state Medicaid program is one of the most generous in the country, spending $623 million in 1975–79 for the 325,000 poor and needy residents, including many services private insurance plans don't provide; no tollway will be found in Wisconsin, and the major state and federally financed highways are complemented by an excellent network of state-aided county and town roads (where the tourist preferring a leisurely pace will see the best of Wisconsin's scenery).

All of this government service does not mean there is no resistance to "progress" in the state. In 1976 a farmer named Ed Klessig and his family moved part of their dairy herd to the lawn of the state capitol, where they set up tents and holding pens for a month to protest the construction of an interstate road from Sheboygan to Green Bay, which would slice off a few acres of their dairy farms. In the finest tradition of Robert LaFollette himself, Klessig railed against the "county boards, the chamber of commerce, the state highway commission, the steel and cement people, (and) the labor unions," who he said were "all determined to lay their hands on so-called free federal trust fund money and build the biggest damn thing they could." (We later spent a day talking with Klessig at his lovely dairy farm; we found a man that not only could rail against the establishment but had a deep love of his own land and a determination, through the network of friends he had built in his anti-freeway struggle, to prevent the state highway department from building redundant, land-consuming parallel roads in rural areas across the entire state.) Corporate interests as well as the individual farmer also rebel today against the stringent regulations imposed by Wisconsin state agencies, as the paper mills forced to clean up their wastes before dumping them into rivers and utilities planning giant atomic energy plants (until halted by a state-dictated moratorium) can well attest.

Known as the "dairy state," Wisconsin offers much more economically than just cows and farmland. True, the 1.8 million milk cows make up the largest herd of any state, and the state does lead the nation in production of milk and cheese (as well as hay and alfalfa). The dairy interests once exhibited such formidable political power that it was not until 1967 that the oleomargarine interests could persuade the legislature to eliminate an extraordinary tax on the artificial spread and allow it to be sold in colored form.

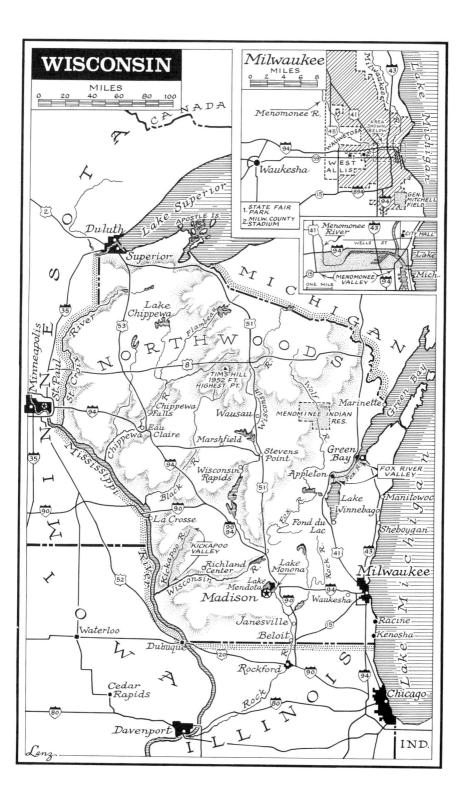

WISCONSIN

MILES
0   20   40   60   80   100

Milwaukee
MILES
0 2 4 6 8

Menomonee R.
WAUWETOSA
Waukesha
WEST ALLIS
AREA SHOWN BELOW
GEN. MITCHELL FIELD
1. STATE FAIR PARK
2. MILW. COUNTY STADIUM

Menomonee River
CITY HALL
WELLS ST.
MENOMONEE VALLEY
ONE MILE
Lake Mich.

C A N A D A

M I N N E S O T A

Lake Superior

Duluth
Superior
APOSTLE IS.

M I C H I G A N

Minneapolis
St. Paul
St. Croix River

Lake Chippewa
Flambeau R.

N O R T H W O O D S

TIMS HILL 1952 FT. HIGHEST PT.

Chippewa Falls
Eau Claire
Chippewa R.
Marshfield

Wausau

Wisconsin R.
Wolf R.
MENOMINEE INDIAN RES.

Marinette

Green Bay

Stevens Point

Mississippi River

Black R.

Wisconsin Rapids

Appleton
Fox R.

FOX RIVER VALLEY

Manitowoc

Lake Winnebago

La Crosse

Kickapoo R.
KICKAPOO VALLEY

Richland Center

Fond du Lac

Sheboygan

Wisconsin R.

Lake Monona

Rock R.

Lake Mendota
Madison

Milwaukee

Waukesha

W   A

Janesville
Beloit

Racine
Kenosha

Waterloo

Dubuque

Rock R.

Rockford

Cedar Rapids

I L L I N O I S

Chicago

Davenport

IND.

Lenz

Lake Michigan

Green Bay

But political reality was merely catching up with economic. In addition to its bucolic farms, Wisconsin is also one of the top dozen industrial states in the Union; such industries as beer, paper, heavy machinery, automobiles, and food processing add up to 40 percent of the state's income. Four of the country's largest breweries have Wisconsin headquarters (Miller, Schlitz, and Pabst in Milwaukee and Heileman in LaCrosse).*

The world's largest concentration of paper mills produces major income while crowding and polluting the Fox River between Appleton and Green Bay. The largest private employer in the state is American Motors, which has all its domestic car production plants in Kenosha and Milwaukee. Most of the state's 4.7 million people live and work in a triangle in the southeastern part of the state, roughly from Milwaukee-Kenosha-Racine, up to Green Bay and over to Madison, 70 miles west of Milwaukee. But studies in the late 1970s detected a reversal of the migration to the cities and the long decades of population decreases in the Northwoods counties, long stagnant economically and dependent upon forests and lakes to attract the tourists, fishermen, hunters, and seasonal residents with second homes. The recreation industry is the third leg of Wisconsin's economy, continuing to attract about $1.4 billion a year even after the gasoline shortages of the 1970s.

Viewing Wisconsin politics, the reader should be forewarned: Wisconsin is not as liberal as many have assumed, its progressive tradition often being confused with stereotype liberalism. Wisconsin progressivism is a mutation of old-fashioned individualism with the traditional values it espouses and a kind of humanistic recognition of the needs of the poor and downtrodden, all stirred together with a fervent insistence that public officials be responsive to the people. Sometimes it comes out liberalism, but as often as not it produces conservatism. And, in fact, some of LaFollette's basic progressive tenets (short terms of office, limited patronage appointments, part-time commissions running state agencies) have been overturned in recent years as the state adapted to modern demands. David Carley, one of Wisconsin's more liberal politicians and an extraordinarily successful businessman, for one, has consistently argued the state is not nearly as liberal as its reputation suggests. Wisconsinites opposed the Vietnam War earlier and more vociferously than most, living up to its liberal reputation. But its isolationism goes back generations: antidraft riots occurred in the Civil War, LaFollette steadfastly resisted entrance into World War I and broke with President Wilson on the issue, and his son Philip flirted openly with Nazi notions and voiced reluctance to go to war against Germany in World War II. Then, antiwar sentiments were not known as liberal causes but as reactionary attitudes.

---

* Milwaukee owes its position as the beer capital of the world to the families of fine German brewers who came to the city as immigrants before the Civil War, as well as the Great Chicago Fire of 1871. The fire wiped out most Chicago breweries, with the result Milwaukee beer sales soared 44 percent in 1872, allowing the "relatively small city of Milwaukee (to overtake) such great brewing centers as New York, Philadelphia, and St. Louis as the greatest beer exporting center in the nation," as the Chamber of Commerce effused that year. After introducing the first bottled beer in 1875, there was no stopping the industry, except for the pause during Prohibition years.

Complicating Wisconsin politics has been the long line of mavericks sent to Washington and to the state capitol in Madison. In addition to all the LaFollettes and many of the Progressives, one must add the Senators of the 1940s to 1970s—including McCarthy, Alexander Wiley, Gaylord Nelson, and William Proxmire. All have been known to stand alone. Proxmire, as a freshman Senator, had the audacity to stand on the Senate floor and chastise Majority Leader Lyndon B. Johnson; his government economizing issues in later years made him a Senator-set-apart. Nelson was one of the first to oppose the Vietnam War, one of three Senators refusing to vote for the Gulf of Tonkin resolution. And on the home front, Wisconsin in 1978 elected a populist-style Republican governor, Lee Sherman Dreyfus, a former university professor and administrator who joined the Republican Party less than a year before he began campaigning. Dreyfus [correctly] sensed another of the anti-government moods that periodically invade the Wisconsin politico-scape, and he rode an anti-establishment campaign into office, first defeating the party-endorsed GOP candidate, then the incumbent Democratic governor.

Viewed from a national perspective, "maverick" easily describes those leaders and movements arising in Wisconsin that seem to be ahead of or out of step with the mainstream flow of American politics. But simply to dismiss them as mavericks ignores their roots in Wisconsin's traditions—the abhorrence of political bossism and insistence on open government, the irrelevance of partisan labels and the appeal of a candidate with a sense of concern, the expectation of good government by honest officials, the insistence upon the protection and preservation of the state's natural resources, the contributions of the great university at Madison. Any simplistic view also obscures Wisconsin's rich ethnic and religious roots, the concurrent commitment to individual rights and collective compassion, the appeal of Milwaukee-style socialism as well as LaFollette Progressivism and stalwart Republicanism, and the ever-present tension among the stand-patters, the movers, and the independents in between. A glance at some of these traditions and the way they continue to flourish and affect politics today will better set the context of Wisconsin's style of government and politics.

Plundering and Protecting Resources:
From Glaciers to Nuclear Power

When Jean Nicolet, reputedly the first white man to step on Wisconsin soil, arrived in 1634 in quest of the fabled Northwest Passage to India, he found an outdoor paradise, virgin white pines so big two men could not reach around them and join hands, pristine streams teeming with luxuriant beavers, whose pelts were so much in demand in Quebec and Paris, lakes so clear and full of fish that no man, woman, or child need go hungry. Most of the northern and eastern regions of Wisconsin were sculpted by the glaciers that first descended across the state at least a million years ago but finally retreated about 17,000 years ago. By a quirk of nature, the glaciers did not touch much of the southwestern part of the state, creating the geologically unique "Driftless Area," so called because it lacks the glacial deposits or drift found elsewhere in the upper Midwest. The topography here reveals rock formations far older than in the rest of the state, much of it sandstone and limestone outcroppings that have created some breathtaking formations, buttes, ridges, and mesas, especially for the canoeists willing to paddle the Kickapoo River in the west or the Wisconsin River in the area of Wisconsin Dells. It was the preservationists' instinct, for instance, that objected during the 1970s to the building of a dam across the Kickapoo to control nearly annual flooding of communities downriver, on the grounds that much of the area's unique geologic formations and vegetation would be lost to future generations. Here too in Mineral Point and New Diggins can be found the remains of the lead mines, Wisconsin's first statehood industry, as well as the more pastoral hills and ridges around New Glarus and Monroe that attracted a colony of Swiss settlers in the 19th century, because it reminded them so much of their native homes. The Swiss—and their delectable Swiss cheese—still dominate the area.

The "Driftless Area" is a scenic contrast to the rest of the state, which includes the flat, sandy plains of the central area, fertile enough for the potato and other vegetable farmers and interspersed with the cranberry bogs that rank Wisconsin either first or second in the nation, depending on the year.

The Northwoods offer a refreshing respite from both the "Driftless Area" and the urban centers in the southeastern sectors. The glaciers, as they sliced off the outcroppings and mountaintops and carved out the depressions which filled with water as the final thaw occurred, left nearly 8,800 lakes and ponds in Wisconsin. They range from the shallow, 214-square mile Lake Winnebago between Appleton and Fond du Lac inland from Lake Michigan to those of only a few acres. Despite the 785-mile shoreline along Lakes Michigan and Superior, two-thirds of the state drains into the Mississippi River basin through an extensive network of rivers. These rivers, the Wisconsin, the Chippewa, the Flambeau, the St. Croix, and the Black, formed the link in the late 1800s between the northern forests (mostly pine but some hardwoods as well) and the markets for a growing nation moving westward. As in Michigan, Minnesota, and wherever else great stands of harvestable timber stood, the lumber barons of the late 19th century laid utter waste to inconceivably wide swaths of Wisconsin, cutting it over, leaving debris that became kindling for forest fires. These plunderers never gave any thought to reforestation. It has been said fires consumed more timber than ever was harvested, a frightening thought when it is considered that 1.25 billion board feet were cut in Wisconsin in 1873 alone and production did not peak until the early 1890s. It was at Peshtigo, in northeastern Wisconsin, that the nation's most deadly holocaust occurred in 1871. Fire literally exploded through the dry timber around Peshtigo, where the cut-over debris often was piled higher than a lumberman's head, killing 1,182 persons. The disaster was upstaged, however, by the more famous Chicago Fire, which occurred the day before and received by far the greater publicity although only 250 perished there.

Huge fortunes were made from timber, but at the cost of forsaking any preservation. A Menomonie company was said to be the largest lumber corporation in the world in 1870, but it was soon overshadowed by the aggressive (and destructive) tactics of Frederick Weyerhaeuser, a name that endures even today in the lumber industry. The lumber baron who most completely combined wealth with political power in Wisconsin, however, was Philetus Sawyer, the U.S. Senator from 1881 to 1893 and probably the prime symbol of corrupt Republican bossism in the eyes of an aspiring young politician of the day named Robert Marion LaFollette.

It was out of this record of exploitation that Wisconsin's concern for its natural resources developed. A latent concern always existed: the state's 1848 constitution declared all navigable waterways part of the public domain, clearly establishing a regulatory authority, albeit one little used for decades afterwards. A state forestry commission and later a fish commission were both established in the 19th century, and as early as 1885 three fish wardens were appointed to watch over all of the Great Lakes fisheries. The tradition also was built and perpetuated by the likes of John Muir, who grew up and fell in love with "that glorious Wisconsin Wilderness," as he called it, and later became the father of the national park system and founder of the Sierra Club; the naturalist-scientists of the University of Wisconsin, ranging from Increase A. Lapham, father of the Wisconsin conservation movement (his 1867 "Report of the Disastrous Effects of the Destruction of Forest Trees Now Going on So Rapidly in the State of Wisconsin" was far ahead of its times), to Charles Van Hise, the geologist-president of the University of Wisconsin, to the renowned Aldo Leopold, professor of game management (the first such professorial seat in the country); and the countless other resources-conscious citizens who formed the natural history, fishing, game, horticulture, and bird-watching clubs (Wisconsin had one of the first Audubon Society chapters), and kept raising their voices to preserve more of Wisconsin's natural resources.

Jeffrey Smoller, a former aide to Gov. Patrick Lucey subsequently with the State Dept. of Natural Resources (DNR), observed in a discussion with us that all of Wisconsin's major growth industries up to modern times had their origins in the state's resources. First, he said, there were trapping and fur trading, followed by the free use of waterways by loggers, brewers, and farmers, coupled with the raping of the timberlands. The mining industry contributed more than its share of degradation of the landscape, first by the lead miners in southwestern Wisconsin and then, more flagrantly, by the producers of iron ore in the northwestern regions after the Gogebic range discoveries in 1885. "With all of this, Wisconsin gave up a lot," he said. "Before the Depression, there were parts of Wisconsin that were worse than Appalachia."

With the reorganization of the State Conservation Commission in 1927, the preservationists were able to do battle with the plunderers more evenly. It was not until the 1960s, however, that demonstrable progress was shown. Then-Gov. Gaylord Nelson won approval of landmark legislation to acquire and develop prime scenic land, for which his Outdoor Recreation Act Program (ORAP) set aside $50 million in 1961. Twice since then, under governors of both parties, the program has been expanded. The creation under Nelson of the Resource Development Dept., later merged with the old Conservation Commission to form the Dept. of Natural Resources, gave the state the enforcement impetus to go after the polluters of the lakes and streams—the paper mills, the cheese factories, the farmers, and the city sewage treatment plants, hitherto sacred cows not to be coerced or interfered with. Fortified with grants from the Federal Environmental Protection Agency, the DNR went after the worst of the polluters and demonstrated that preservationists now had the upper hand. And none too late: in the 1960s, the Chicago *Tribune* and others ranked the lower Fox River between Appleton and Green Bay with the infamous Cuyahoga River in Cleveland as the dirtiest tributaries of the Great Lakes. More than three dozen paper mills lined the 37 miles of the lower Fox, making it the greatest papermaking concentration in the world. But they were only a part of the industrial, municipal, and agricultural pollution that wiped out fish and plant life in portions of the river, making massive fish kills periodic occurrences in other parts. Not without considerable protest, the paper mills in the 1970s met and in some cases exceeded the stringent water quality standards laid down by the state and EPA, spending about $375 million statewide during a single decade, according to the Wisconsin Paper Council. In the mid-1950s, the DNR said 450,000 pounds of biochemical oxygen demand (the waste substances that dissolve in water but still eat oxygen needed by fish and plants to survive) were being poured into the lower Fox each day. In July 1978, the level had declined to 39,699 pounds daily, an 85 percent reduction. People still wouldn't drink water straight from the lower Fox, but fish are being discovered in portions of the stream where not long ago it wouldn't have been worth even dropping a line into the water.

With this kind of tradition of protecting natural resources, it was hardly surprising to find staunch opposition to a Navy plan that surfaced in 1968, Project Sanguine, to build an underground antenna grid in northern Wisconsin to communicate with submarines. Arguments that the low-voltage antenna could harm wildlife proved stronger than the presumed economic benefits such a project might have for the area. Likewise, ecologists' concerns spearheaded the move to curtail use of nuclear power in Wisconsin, finally forcing the major state utilities in 1977 to drop plans for building twin giant nuclear reactors alongside Lake Koshkonong southeast of Madison and pressuring the State Public Service Commission (PSC) a year later to impose a moratorium on all nuclear plant-building. (Republican Gov. Lee Dreyfus named a woman physicist, openly pro-nuclear development, as one of his first appointees to the PSC, but opposition forced her to withdraw before she was confirmed. The final chapter on nuclear power undoubtedly has not been written in Wisconsin.)

A Great State University: The Wisconsin Idea

"The boundaries of the campus are the boundaries of the state," declares a long-heeded dictum at the University of Wisconsin at Madison. That meant the concept of public service, for which it became famous, was intended to apply to all 56,154 square miles of Wisconsin, stretching 320 miles from the Illinois border to the Apostle Islands in Lake Superior, and the 295 miles from the tip of the peninsular Door County in the east to the rambunctious St. Croix River on the west. The exact origins of the sense of obligation of the university community to serve the public, which became embodied as the Wisconsin Idea, long since have been obscured by time. It first reached practical application, however, during the tenure of John Bascom, president of the university (1874–87), a man imbued with the demands of the social gospels of Christianity. It was during his administration that the College of Agriculture established its agricultural short courses and institutes to bring the fruits of agricultural research and knowledge to the farmers themselves.

The contributions of many other early UW professors were prevalent in the scientific cataloguing of the state's topography and natural resources, as noted earlier. University extension centers were first created in 1890 to sponsor discussions about the ideas of the new social scientists just coming into vogue. It was not until the Panic of 1893 focused attention on the problems of the economy that a young professor at the university gained national attention and, in the process, firmly implemented the Wisconsin Idea as noblesse oblige. Richard Ely extended Bascom's ideas into the realm of political economics; his message of social and human progress clashed sharply with the high-handed notions of laissez-faire industrialists and their political henchmen, especially as it encouraged the organization of workers. A conservative member of the board of regents accused Ely of radicalism in 1894, and his case became a national cause for academic freedom. In vindicating Ely and academic freedom, the board of regents adopted a resolution that has become a cornerstone of the Wisconsin Idea: "Whatever may be the limitations which trammel inquiry elsewhere, we believe the great State University of Wisconsin should ever encourage that continual and fearless sifting and winnowing by which alone the truth can be found." These words were later placed on a brass plaque that still hangs on a wall outside Bascom Hall, reminding all that the quest for truth is not to be limited by political demagogues, though some have tried in the ensuing years.

Thus, by the time LaFollette and the Progressives assumed political power in 1901, the tradition of the university as a public service institution was firmly entrenched. What LaFollette and his progressive successor, Francis

McGovern, did was to draw on the energies and ideas of the new social scientists and convert them into practical legislation. The list of contributors here is extensive. A few of the more notable include John R. Commons, an economic colleague of Ely's who helped draft the civil service act of 1905 and the nation's first state workmen's compensation law in 1911; Charles McCarthy, a student of the UW historian Frederick Jackson Turner, who went on to create the nation's first Legislative Reference Library (supposedly a bill-drafting office but in reality a front for McCarthy's one-man brain trust of progressive ideas); President Van Hise, already mentioned for his geologic research, but also a champion of the university's public service mandate after his former classmate LaFollette had him named head of the university. Frederic C. Howe, author of *Wisconsin, An Experiment in Democracy* in 1912, wrote that "the university is largely responsible for the progressive legislation that has made Wisconsin so widely known as a pioneer."

The progressive spirit has by no means made the university immune from attack and criticism. During and after World War I, certain antiwar speakers were banned from the campus. Again, in the 1960s, Wisconsin's campus became the scene of frequent national attention when many of its students protested the Vietnam conflict. Most of the protests were at most clamorous, with minimal property damage, but one was not. In August of 1970, an explosion ripped through Sterling Hall, which housed, among other facilities, Army Mathematics Research Center, recipient of federal research grants which funded some defense-related projects. Long a target of antiwar protesters, the math research center was demolished by the home-made bomb, one graduate student was killed, and years of painstaking academic research were mutilated and destroyed. By 1979, only one of the four persons accused of the bombing had not yet been caught, tried, and convicted. The bombing shattered more than the lives and facilities of those associated with the Army Math Research Center; its violence repulsed many antiwar sympathizers, and so stigmatized the movement that it never regained popular support on the university campus.

One contemporary historian has suggested the idea of public service at the university has been exaggerated by public relations experts seeking to connect the hallowed memories of the Progressives with modern-day affairs. Noting that Prof. Commons himself once disclaimed frequent and widespread faculty involvement, UW History Prof. Robert Nesbit commented: "He [Commons] might have added that at any given time, nine-tenths of the faculty occupied itself with other scholarly concerns and had no interest in the boundaries of the university, or its impact upon practical politics." That has become even more accurate as the "publish or perish" edict has consumed more time and attention of scholars, and the major rewards for faculty members go not to the practitioners of the earlier credo of public service but to those with the capability of attracting major research grants. John Wyngaard, the dean of the Madison Capitol press corps, noted in the 1970s that the public service mission seemed to be dying out, with few academicians found in key state policymaking or advisory positions. This brought a rebuttal from Prof. Charles Cicchetti, at the time chairman of the Public Service Commission, which issued the nuclear power plant moratorium. As the 1970s ended, however, Cicchetti was one of the few genuine university voices to be heard in progressive governmental circles. The debate remained unresolved —whether the Wisconsin Idea is more myth than reality.

Using contemporary national standards, however, Wisconsin undoubtedly is an outstanding university. By virtue of its reputation, it retains many scholars who could earn far more elsewhere. Its researchers attract numerous federal grants, totaling $56.7 million in 1977–78 (third in the nation), plus another $34.8 million from other sources. Considerable research support also is generated by the Wisconsin Alumni Research Foundation (WARF), a remarkable institution which initially grew largely through the generosity of Harry Steenbock, a biochemist who in 1923 discovered a successful process for fortifying food with vitamin D. Steenbock sold the patent rights to WARF for $10, which reaped $8 million in royalties to underwrite much of WARF's early scientific research. Since 1925, WARF has given the UW about $80 million. In 1971 the university at Madison was merged with the state university system (formerly the nine state teacher colleges), causing critics to predict a significant dilution of the quality of education on the Madison campus, a prediction which has yet to come to pass. The merger, a Republican proposal brought to fruition by a Democratic governor, Patrick Lucey, created a system with 143,440 students. The university tried to attract a larger percentage of black students early in the 1970s, but the effort met with only moderate success; in 1979 it still had only 473 black students on the Madison campus. As UW-Madison entered the 1980s, its reputation for educational excellence remained intact, still an academic rival of such prestigious national universities as Harvard, Michigan, Princeton, Yale, and California at Berkeley.

Progressivism and LaFollette

While concern for resources and a passion for academic freedom are part of the foundation of the Wisconsin idea, it remained for the surge of reform after the Panic of 1893 to translate it into legislation and politics. And it remained for Robert M. LaFollette to crystalize the antiestablishment reformers into a political organization, although he preferred to call his organization "the public." As the story of LaFollette and Progressivism has been told and retold, it has taken on the simplistic shades of black and white, good versus evil. LaFollette, the champion crusader, advocating the rights of "the people," assailed the political bosses and corporate plunderers, demanded an open political system, and in large part through sheer force of his intensive personality and extensive organization, muscled the reforms sought by the growing ranks of disenchanted voters through the legislature. Much of this was true.

Railroad regulation, civil service reform, the direct primary, and taxation reform were the major landmarks of his administration as governor from 1901 to 1906, when he resigned to go to the U.S. Senate. His other notable accomplishment before going to the Senate was the takeover of the Republican party, toppling the boss-ridden stalwarts and replacing them with Progressive Republicans of his own ilk.

LaFollette's proclamation that he represented "the people," however, obscured much of the factionalism within Progressive ranks. His hand-picked candidate lost the state's first gubernatorial primary to another anti-LaFollette Progressive. He had a falling out with the next Progressive governer, Francis McGovern, and tried subverting parts of his initiatives. The storybook version clouds the fact that the landmark Progressive legislation passed into law under McGovern at least equaled and even surpassed that of "Fightin' Bob." While LaFollette reformed the political structure, it was McGovern who extended the Progressive philosophy into the economic and industrial realm, creating the nation's first workmen's compensation law, and an industrial commission to administer it, the first state income tax law (progressively graduated to tax the richer more heavily than those in the lower and middle class), a state life insurance fund, factory safety legislation, restrictions on working hours for women and children, a comprehensive waterpower conservation law, and a revitalized forest commission. The needs of rural voters were not forgotten by the Milwaukeean McGovern, as he supported and enacted laws encouraging cooperatives, farm improvement loans, and extension of agricultural education. "It is manifestly unfair to label the accomplishments under McGovern's leadership as simply the fruition of reforms advanced by LaFollette," wrote historian Robert Nesbit in 1973. "They went well beyond LaFollette's basic concern with the machinery of democracy, the curbing of monopolies, equitable taxation, and regulation of irresponsible financial power."

The myth of Progressivism overlooks the fact that Wisconsin largely has lived on its early-in-the-century reputation for more than half a century. The state has maintained the honesty, openness, and responsiveness of the political system, to be sure. But with the exception of its pioneering unemployment compensation law in 1932 (three years before any other state), Nelson's outdoor recreation land acquisition program in 1961, and a farmland preservation law in 1977, Wisconsin has passed no legislation that could be considered a major innovation serving as a model for other states.

The Progressive movement in Wisconsin actually was divided into two segments, the first from Old Bob's election as governor in 1900 to the end of McGovern's term in 1915. While LaFollette himself continued on in the Senate until his death in 1925, making his mark as one of the nation's leading voices for regulating corporations and splitting up monopolies, the surge of reform in Wisconsin had dissipated. Throughout the early period, the Progressive movement in Wisconsin was fought from within the Republican Party, giving Wisconsin factionalized one-party rule similar to that of Democrats in Southern states. Succeeding him after his death was his oldest son, Robert, Jr. In the mid-1930s, Young Bob joined with his brother Philip to form a separate Progressive Party that actually became the majority party for a few years, while the Democrats dwindled to a skeletal force. Philip was first elected governor in 1930 as a Republican but was defeated in the Democratic landslide in 1932. The Progressive Party gradually withered after his defeat in 1938, when seeking a fourth term. His brother Bob's persistent preoccupation with his senatorial duties in Washington only compounded the decline. The Progressive Party formally disbanded in 1946 when Young Bob decided to return to the party of his father and run as a Republican, even though many Democrats courted his candidacy at the head of their ticket. His choice proved unfortunate, for he was beaten in the primary by a relatively unknown county judge from Appleton named Joseph R. McCarthy. By the 1970s, the LaFollette legacy was carried on through Bronson LaFollette, the son of Bob Jr. He was attorney general and is likely to remain so only until one of the current Democratic Senators retires and he can assume his father's and grandfather's seat, an aspiration he has denied.

Much has been said and written about the legacy of Joe McCarthy, whose name has found its way into dictionaries as meaning "the use of indiscriminate, often unfounded, accusations, sensationalism, inquisitorial investigative methods, ostensibly in the suppression of communism." From the time McCarthy was elected in 1946, to the time he ran for reelection six years later, his record was noteworthy only for its lack of accomplishment. Many have attributed his crusade against communism as simply an effort to generate a campaign reelection issue. Perhaps it was. But once McCarthy had stood on the stage in Wheeling, W. Va., during that memorable Lincoln Day dinner speech on Feb. 9, 1952, and declared he had "here in my hand a list of 205 that were known to the Secretary of State as being members of the Communist Party and who, nevertheless, are still working and shaping policy in the State Department," the issue was to snowball beyond even his wildest expectations. The question has been raised innumerable times: "How could a Progressive state like Wisconsin elect a man like McCarthy?" The answer lies partly in the confusion surrounding the storybook version of LaFollette and the Progressives, and in the character of the people in the state. Communism raised the specter of political control, an anathema to Wisconsin voters since LaFollette threw out the Republican bosses. Wisconsinites also have a staunch isolationist tradition, encouraged for years by the LaFollette family itself. McCarthy usually managed to contrast atheistic communism with God-fearing Christians protecting democracy, another theme likely to tap a responsive chord among the many Catholics and Lutherans making up a state majority. Progressivism was able to focus political energies on the need to cooperate for the common good; McCarthy appealed instead to the latent —but still present—selfish character of the populace: fear fed by isolationist instincts, the dogmatism of some of the state's religious and ethnic roots, and a manipulation of fundamental values of individualism, property, and patriotism. The composite stimulated an emotional reaction, with grave consequences.*

In the midst of all the McCarthy-induced hysteria, in Wisconsin and elsewhere, there remained some with the independent courage that is part of the LaFollette tradition. One such person was Leroy Gore, editor of a weekly newspaper in Sauk City, a small community 20 miles north of Madison along the Wisconsin River. Gore described himself as a "thoroughly respectable, thoroughly conservative, thoroughly smug Republican country editor" before that March 1954 afternoon when he decided to write an editorial declaring that "Joe Must Go." The call was reported in front pages of newspapers all around the country, which placed Gore at the forefront of those who wanted to oppose McCarthy, but who up to Gore's stand, were unwilling to risk an attack by the pugnacious McCarthy or the verbal and economic abuse of his legions of supporters. The "Joe Must Go" recall effort failed, falling about 65,000 signatures short of the 400,000 necessary. But progressive Wisconsinites like to believe that the effort gave heart to many who had been petrified by McCarthy's tactics. That Gore's recall effort came five months before the conclusion of the Army-McCarthy hearings and eight months before the U.S. Senate censured McCarthy 67–22 earned for the country editor a special niche in the annals of political courage in Wisconsin.

Because Wisconsin is far removed from the bossism LaFollette sought to displace, distinctions need to be made about Wisconsin politics today. At the national level, its elected officials generally do reflect the liberal tendencies ascribed to Progressivism. But at the state and local level, it is far more complicated, with Wisconsinites usually liberal on political process issues, often progressive on social issues, and frequently out-and-out conservative on economic issues.

The Liberal Side of Progressive Politics

Few states, if any, so jealously guard the public's right to know about and participate in policymaking as Wisconsin does. Starting from the time LaFollette overthrew the boss-dominated conventions and established the direct open primary, the state has made extraordinary progress in narrowing the gap between the theory and reality of open government. Its open meeting law, zealously protected by a vigilant press, provides public access in fact as well as principle, even if the public chooses not to attend, as it often does. Few officials would risk the wrath of their constituents by trying secretly to ram through major policy without public hearings. For years, the legislature had an unwritten rule that every bill would get a hearing, a practice that

---

* Indicative of the fear that existed among Wisconsinites at the time was a survey taken on the Fourth of July, 1951, in a Madison park by a reporter for the *Capital Times.* The reporter carried copies of the Declaration of Independence and the Bill of Rights and asked 112 people if they would sign his "petitions." Only one agreed to sign. If such was the reaction in a liberal community like Madison, it left little doubt about the fearful gut reactions of the rest of the state.

slipped as a nearly full-time legislature generated more bills than could be handled. Lobbying and lobbyists, another target of LaFollette, remain suspect and subject to rigid reporting laws, including prohibition against offering food, drink, or "anything of value" to public officials. Even state agency employees are required to make quarterly reports if they have more than 13 "unsolicited" contacts with lawmakers for the purpose of influencing legislation. Wisconsin has one of the nation's tougher campaign expenditure reporting laws, stipulating the public listing—before elections—of expenditures and donors. (For some offices, all persons giving as little as $10 must be listed.) After an outcry of legislating in secret caucuses in the mid-1970s, even some party caucuses in the legislature are now open to the press and public.

LaFollette's campaign against the bosses and rigged party conventions had the effect of leaving the official political parties in Wisconsin largely impotent. Statutory parties are only a shell, existing to meet legal requirements, while the major party functions (recruitment, fund-raising, and organization) are left to candidate organizations. "In Wisconsin, when a person is elected (governor), he develops his own party," said one former Republican executive. Democrats refuse to indulge in pre-primary endorsements (and frequently suffer the consequences through bitter primary contests), while Republicans endorse only for statewide candidates. At the local level, municipal and judicial elections are nonpartisan and held in the spring, removing a source of grassroots partisanship. All this does not mean Wisconsin is politically pure, for loopholes in the laws do exist; but they are more difficult to squeeze through, there is vigilant monitoring of the filing reports by the media, and politicians grow up on the notion of good, responsive government, making the intent more of a reality than in most other states.

For the first half of the 20th century, political battles and elections were limited primarily to the Stalwart Republicans and the Progressives. Democrats were often no more than bystanders in elections: only two Democrats held U.S. Senate seats in this century until Proxmire won a special election in 1957 to fill Joseph McCarthy's vacancy, and only one sat in the governor's office (and that thanks to Franklin Roosevelt's long coattails in 1932) until Gaylord Nelson won his first term in 1958.* From the end of World War I through World War II, Democrats were a dispirited third party in Wisconsin at best. In the 1920s, the Milwaukee Socialists elected more legislators than did the Democrats (the state senate had no Democrats at all from 1923 to 1931), while the Progressive Party of Young Bob LaFollette and brother Phil garnered most of the liberal support throughout the 1930s.

When World War II ended and the Progressive Party disbanded, the more liberal remnants of the LaFollette tradition faced a dilemma—to return to the Republican party as Young Bob did, or to try to resurrect the moribund Democratic Party. A handful of young liberals meeting in a Green Bay hotel in 1949, including John Reynolds (later governor and a federal

---

* One long-time legislator recalled Democrats were so disorganized and feeble in the Depression years that one of their candidates elected to the legislature in 1932 thought he had been elected to Congress and did not find out the truth until after boarding a train for Washington.

judge in Milwaukee), James E. Doyle (for years the federal judge in Madison), and Patrick J. Lucey (subsequently governor and Ambassador to Mexico), decided on the latter course and the modern Democratic Party in Wisconsin was born. With new life and new leadership, the Democrats slowly created a two-party state. The first signs of the incremental advances were in the size of its legislative minority. The big breakthrough came in 1957 with Proxmire's Senate victory and was as surprising to Republicans as to Democrats. Proxmire, a persistent carpetbagger who had moved to Wisconsin because of its fertile opportunities for a politician of Democratic persuasions, had run three times earlier in the 1950s for governor, including two losses to Walter Kohler, Jr. When the Republicans nominated Kohler for McCarthy's seat, most Wisconsinites envisioned an encore of the previous contests. Aided by a low turnout in the special election, Proxmire stunned Kohler and won 56 percent of the vote. Democrats had finally come of age in Wisconsin. The following year came the twin triumphs of Nelson defeating the incumbent Republican governor, Vernon Thomson (later to sit in Congress for 14 years) and the Democrats winning a majority in the lower house of the legislature for only the second time since 1893 (the other was in 1932). Since then, the parties have competed fairly evenly, although the Democrats finally won a Senate majority in 1975 to give them complete control of the statehouse. Republican fortunes had reached low ebb, a level raised only slightly when the GOP won the governor's office in 1978.

For decades, the quadrennial Wisconsin presidential primary has drawn major candidates; indeed, before the spate of early primaries created by other states in the 1970s, Wisconsin's primary was second in time only to New Hampshire and universally regarded as a testing ground of major importance. Even with several other states' primaries now intervening, the Wisconsin test is still regarded as important, partly because of its history. Memories run back to 1960 when John F. Kennedy was catapulted toward the Democratic nomination by defeating Wisconsin's neighboring "third Senator," Hubert H. Humphrey. In 1968 the Wisconsin test confirmed Lyndon Johnson's decision to pull out of that year's contest in view of advance polls showing Eugene McCarthy would beat him in Wisconsin. (The final primary result, a few days after Johnson's formal withdrawal, was McCarthy 56.2 percent, Johnson 34.6 percent.) The Wisconsin primary was extremely influential in 1972, when it provided a critical plurality for George McGovern (who won almost a third of the vote in a crowded field and all but eliminated Alabama Gov. George C. Wallace, Sen. Edmund S. Muskie of Maine, and a host of also-rans).

It has been the Kennedy, McCarthy, and McGovern campaigns, coupled with the vocal antiwar sentiments, that have reinforced in recent years the notion of Wisconsin as a liberal state. But it is a liberalism that cannot be taken for granted, and often does not extend too far beyond those who cast their ballots in the Democratic primary. For while Kennedy, McCarthy, and McGovern won in the spring primaries, it was Richard M. Nixon who won a majority of Wisconsin's presidential votes in the November election in all three of those years. That independent streak in the Wisconsin voters, perhaps tapping the same wellsprings as did Joe McCarthy a dozen years earlier, was revealed again in the 1964 primary, when Governor Wallace picked up an embarrassingly high 33.8 percent of the vote against the favorite son stand-in for President Johnson, then-Gov, John Reynolds. That campaign showed a substantial number of Wisconsinites, especially among the labor classes in Milwaukee, Racine, and Kenosha counties, plus the conservatives in the Fox River Valley and suburban Milwaukee, could be reached with populist-like appeals of race-tinged tirades against governmental bureaucracy. Again, in 1976, the liberal philosophy of U.S. Rep. Morris Udall of Arizona was expected to assure Wisconsin's convention delegates would be his. Two networks actually called Udall the winner on primary night, but the war issue was gone, Wisconsin voters had moved to the center, and the late-arriving rural and small-town ballots gave Jimmy Carter a one percentage point victory. In the fall, Carter and Gerald R. Ford split the two million votes almost evenly. Carter finally won by a 34,000-vote margin.

Many have questioned the validity of Wisconsin's presidential primary as a reflection of Democratic sentiment in the state, because under Wisconsin law voters may cast their ballot for candidates of either party on election day (the so-called "open primary"). Cross-over voting is notorious, however, with Republicans doing most of the switching since most of the contested presidential primaries have been on the Democratic side. The open primary, however, was the vehicle that Fightin' Bob LaFollette championed to destroy the party boss control of nominating conventions and to guarantee the people the right to chose their candidates for office. Wisconsin children have been reared on the idea the open primary is as much a right as the vote itself. When the Democratic National Committee, at the suggestion of Senator McGovern's reform commission in the early 1970s, called for eliminating open primaries, it discovered Wisconsin Democrats and Republicans standing arm-in-arm in opposition. A closed primary would promote party control and remove the nominating process from the control of the people, leaders of both Wisconsin parties objected. After the state senate came under Democratic control in 1975, the party could no longer argue that Republicans were blocking the reform. Gov. Patrick Lucey, considered as strong a political boss Wisconsin has had since Old Bob himself, half-heartedly tried to persuade Democratic legislators to buy a watered down primary—a proposal for a dual election, one a popular "beauty contest" for anyone and a second to elect convention delegates open only to those who declare their party allegiance. But that failed too. By 1980 Wisconsin still held out, even in the face of the unexercised threat from the Democratic National Committee that the state's delegates would not be seated at future conventions without a change.

Since 1967, it is worth noting, Wisconsin law has provided for inclusion on the ballot of all presidential contenders whose "candidacy is generally advocated or recognized in the national news media throughout the United

States." The preference primary winner gets to pick his own convention delegates from Wisconsin. Previously, voters had only been able to vote for delegate slates of those individual candidates who had decided Wisconsin would be an advantageous state to enter. The net result: Wisconsin is an exceedingly difficult state for nationally recognized candidates to avoid.

Republican primaries, on the whole, have drawn less attention than the Democratic, but some have been decisive. In 1944 the Wisconsin contest proved to be the "killer primary" when Wendell Willkie, the Republicans' 1940 standard bearer, lost ignominiously to Thomas E. Dewey and then dropped out of the presidential race. In 1940 the primary shattered Arthur Vandenberg's presidential hopes, in 1948 Douglas MacArthur's.

As the record shows, Wisconsin has over the years had more than its share of maverick candidates and maverick public officials.* For explanations one looks back to the Progressives statewide and the Socialists in Milwaukee, all of whom undoubtedly contributed to Wisconsinites' willingness to look beyond the partisan label at the individual and sometimes risk a vote on the maverick. U.S. Rep. Alvin O'Konski, a free-wheeling Congressman seemingly impervious to the normal ethics of the state, represented a sprawling northern Wisconsin district from 1942 until redistricting threw him into a race against another incumbent in 1972 and he lost. We have already noted the appeal of Wallace and Joseph McCarthy, Proxmire and Lee Sherman Dreyfus, all of whom fit the same mold. In addition, the Wisconsin legislature has been filled with renegades of one stripe or the other, ready to spurn positions and party dominance at the start of any rollcall vote.

The example of Wisconsin's Seventh Congressional District offers ready evidence that Wisconsin's voters are far more attracted to the candidates and their ideas than their party. The Seventh District used to include the north-central part of the state, straddling the Wisconsin River from Stevens Point northward. For 16 years, it was the domain of Melvin R. Laird, a chief strategist in the House leadership and confidant of Gerald Ford as minority leader, chairman of the Platform Committee of the Goldwater Convention in 1964, and a respected power on the House Appropriations Committee before he resigned to become Nixon's Secretary of Defense. Laird was no ideologue, but the consummate political pragmatist. He took care of his constituents, and they responded by giving him consistent margins of 2–1. When he resigned, Republicans assumed it was a safe seat. In the special election in 1969, however, the aggressive and intense young Wausau liberal Democrat David Obey, who had been in the Assembly leadership ranks for two of his four

---

* Harvey Breuscher, the long-time Associated Press correspondent at Madison now in an administrative position at the University of Wisconsin, related to us his own unique and interesting theory about mavericks in the state. "I always thought, 'how in hell did Wisconsin get to be the home of the circus?'" he mused. "But, to get corny for a minute, I think there's a loneliness to living in Wisconsin. We are not that many people, there are a lot of trees, and it gets cold, and you entertain yourself. And if you think on it, you can see how a populace like this could get enamored with circuses. And I think, once you get a place that likes circuses, you know what? They get to like the clowns in politics too. . . . If you like circuses, I think you like mavericks. I see some parallel here. We in Wisconsin are ready to take a chance with someone who jiggles your juices, and gets you stirring, even if he's from another party."

terms, won narrowly. In subsequent elections, he built the margin to a size comparable to what Laird had done a few years before. Obey created for himself a comfortable seat, but it was clear that if he were to leave, the right Republican with a good organization could win back the district.

In recent years, the rise of influence of women in Wisconsin politics also has added another layer of evidence to the liberal notion, if one looks at the surface. The state has a well organized Women's Political Caucus, generally small in numbers but with a voice that increasingly is listened to in statehouse politics. The caucus maintains a nonpartisan stance officially, because it includes Republicans as well as Democrats. Yet, most of the time, it can be expected to take a liberal position. "The women's movement has moved more into the halls of government in Wisconsin, instead of in the streets," according to Rita Wlodarczyk, a former state coordinator of the Caucus. "In other states, the movement is still in the streets." She noted the state already has de-sexed its laws (the state level equivalent of the Equal Rights Amendment nationally, which Wisconsin was among the first to ratify); it has reformed its divorce code, allowing for no-fault divorce, made it illegal for lending institutions to discriminate against women in giving credit and loans, and reformed its marital property laws. Gov. Lucey appointed Shirley Abrahamson as the first woman justice on the Supreme Court, and she won election in her own right in 1979. Another woman, Vel Phillips, a black from Milwaukee, also was elected in 1978 as secretary of state. By 1980 the number of women in Wisconsin politics had not only risen significantly (10 percent of the state house of representatives, for instance), but many more women were running for office—and not infrequently against each other.

Wisconsin's Liberals in Washington

Wisconsin's reputation as a liberal state has been more than enhanced by its congressional delegation. Cases in point: Senators William Proxmire and Gaylord Nelson. Both scored high in the ratings by the Americans for Democratic Action (Nelson as high as 100 percent some sessions; Proxmire somewhat less consistently), and five of the seven House Democrats generally ranked above 80 percent in the late '70s. Nelson became easily one of the most popular Senators and has staked out the environment as his area of expertise, an issue sure to win him votes back home. When the banking industry wanted to influence legislation, it had to go to Wisconsin men in both houses: Proxmire as chairman of the Senate Banking, Housing, and Urban Affairs Committee, Henry Reuss of Milwaukee as chairman of the counterpart committee in the House. Reuss, a member of an aristocratic Milwaukee German family, is a uniquely skilled legislator in such areas as international finance, the environment (it was he who unearthed the long-forgotten 1899 Refuse Act which flatly prohibits dumping of pollutants in interstate waterways), and urban affairs. As Banking, Finance and Urban Affairs Committee chairman, he established a special Subcommittee on the City which has looked with care, and in depth, at urban problems and solutions both in the United States and abroad.

Not all Wisconsin's congressional leaders have been liberal, however. Clement Zablocki, the southside Milwaukeean who was an avowed hawk on the Vietnam War and votes with the ADA only half the time, climbed into the leadership ranks the traditional way—through seniority. After 32 years, he was chairman of the House International Relations Committee. Up and coming young liberals in Wisconsin include both Racine's Les Aspin, an economics Ph.D. who built his reputation as a fly in the Pentagon's ointment, and Wausau's David Obey, part of the hardworking reform-minded contingent in Congress which early caught the leadership's eye. Obey was named to head a special committee that wrote and got passed a tough ethics code for his colleagues in the late 1970s (tougher than many wanted to see). He also won a prize appointment in his freshman term to the House Appropriations Committee. In 1979, he also was elected chairman of the Democratic Study Group.

Proxmire came to enjoy a particularly schizophrenic image. A self-proclaimed fiscal conservative, he was applauded by liberals when he attacked the defense budget but attracted their enmity when he questioned subsidies to the cities or revenue sharing. Proxmire was sure never to be part of the Senate's Inner Circle, although he shed the robes of the rampant maverick in which he clothed himself during his early Senate days. A faithful jogger and an inveterate campaigner in his home state, he was said to have shaken the hand of three million persons in his three decades of public life. The most popular vote-getter in the state's history, he occasionally carried every county, averaging about 70 percent of the vote, and in one campaign of the 1970s he spent only $2,000 (with no advertising) on his reelection.

Nelson became influential in liberal circles in another way. A rare Senator who harbored no presidential aspirations, Nelson shunned notoriety and assiduously avoided the self-righteousness flaunted by some liberals. On certain issues, however, he was willing to stand alone, as he did when he became one of the first Senators to publicly decry continued involvement in Vietnam, voting against funds for the war as early as 1965. In Wisconsin, that made him a prophet. He also made his mark on environmental and consumer issues, founding the Earth Day movement in 1970 and spearheading reforms in car safety standards, generic drug laws, and hospital cost containment efforts. As a high-ranking Democrat on the Finance committee, he consistently supported liberal tax reform but still was considered a good friend of the conservative chairman, Louisiana's Russell Long. He has passed up chances for greater prestige and power, turning down George McGovern's overture in 1972 to be his running mate on the presidential ticket. Some critics accuse Nelson of laziness, but a former staff aide, William Bechtel, refuted the suggestion. "He generates issues, but he's selective in the issues he takes on. He doesn't want to run the country. He doesn't want to tell people what to do, and he doesn't want to wield power. What he wants is to develop an issue and deal with it," Bechtel told us.

Before leaving the Washington scene, we must note the death of William Steiger, the moderate Republican from Oshkosh who died after his reelection to a seventh term in 1978. The energetic and personable Steiger, a veteran in the House at the age of 40, offered one of the few hopes for progressive leadership in the otherwise depleted ranks of Wisconsin and House Republicanism.

The Two-Party System Arrives

Wisconsin rested on the progressive laurels of the LaFollette and McGovern years for almost four decades until, in 1958, the Democrats broke the Republican stranglehold on state government and elected Nelson governor. Gaylord Nelson's four years as governor did set in motion a renewed dynamic, not LaFollette Progressivism in its truest sense, as its adherents would maintain, but a modern-day progressive response to the demands of the moment. Responsiveness was the key: in the 1960s, with the postwar babies reaching college age, it was a time of rapid expansion, burgeoning taxes, equal opportunities, high expectations, and higher frustrations as riots broke out on campuses and in the cities. Wisconsin was no exception. In the 1970s, however, a mood of retrenchment settled in, and the liberal Gov. Patrick Lucey astutely sensed it long before most of his political brethren; he guided a quasi-conservative administration—austere, he called it—that stressed consolidation and redistribution of state dollars, not more dollars for everyone.

In the old tradition of protecting public resources, Nelson assured he would be known as the "environment" governor when he proposed and won passage of his program to buy and develop recreation lands. Without the $50 million in bonding which was approved, he argued, countless acres of unique scenic, recreation, and archeologically significant areas would be gobbled up and developed, their beauty and wonderment forever lost. Financed by a penny-a-pack tax on cigarettes, the program enabled the state to buy almost 225,000 acres in practically every corner of the state. Under Republican Governor Knowles (1965–71) the program was expanded, with another $200 million in bonding provided. The second extension was added in 1978 under Acting Gov. Martin Schreiber, a Democrat. Squabbles periodically developed whether it was better to emphasize land acquisition (while it was still available) or land development of existing properties (so citizens could enjoy it). But there was always widespread support for the concept, a lasting testimonial to Nelson's foresight and to the fact the tradition of resource protection had not died.

Republicans, so long accustomed to ruling with only token opposition, did not adjust immediately to Democrats in places of power. They continued to control the Senate and the Assembly most of the 1960s, creating a degree of partisanship novel for Wisconsin. Gov. John Reynolds, considered by many as the only "real" liberal governor Wisconsin has had in modern times, bore the brunt of the partisanship. It forced him out of office after only two years (1963–65). Reynolds had campaigned against a sales tax expansion, and Republicans vowed to force the expanded tax (new in Wisconsin at that time) on him. Even more detrimental was the partisan decision, bordering on the irresponsible, that saw the Republican senate refuse action for up to two years on most of Reynolds' key state agency appointments. When Reynolds left, the bitter taste of undue partisanship remained.

Wisconsin traditionally has had a strong legislature, dominating state government. Partly because of their own initiatives, partly because of the changing times, the administrations of Nelson and Reynolds also precipitated a struggle between the executive and legislative branches that continues today. Out of the rivalry, however, has come a better-staffed, better-paid, and better-educated legislature, confronting a better-organized and better-staffed executive branch. Nelson consolidated a number of housekeeping functions into a strong Department of Administration that included staff for centralized budget-making. Within a few years, the legislature had created a Fiscal Bureau to provide independent staff in reviewing the budget. From a start with only four analysts, it grew by the 1970s to 26, giving the legislators information that often was considered more accurate than that coming out of the governor's office. The "one-man, one-vote" decision on reapportionment had even more impact on the legislature, forcing it out of its rural-dominated mold. The state supreme court ended up redrawing district lines after legislative Republicans and Governor Reynolds could not agree in 1964. The part-time legislator, whose experience had come from living life, was nearing the end of his time. The "colorful characters" of the legislature were dying or retiring. Earl Leverich, who had served in the senate almost 30 years, had led fellow dairy farmers on their famous march on the Capitol during the 1930s protesting the sale of oleomargarine. Gordon Roseleip, a self-proclaimed protector of the American flag and butter, once bombastically predicted he could tell the difference between butter and oleo blindfolded. Put to the test surrounded by reporters and interested observers, he promptly called butter the artificial spread. Characters came from Milwaukee, too, where legislative seats were not always perceived as political plums. Norman Sussman left a string of malapropisms that always made the state senate worth watching. (Once, defending a pet proposal from attack, Sussman waved off the criticism with a comment, "We'll jump off that bridge when we get there.") Then there was Leland (Packy) McParland, who once leaped from his seat and interrupted a colleague's speech when it was suggested that whiskey ought to be among restricted drugs. "Whiskey!" McParland uttered with no little animation. "That's food!"

Not all the veteran legislators were characters. There also were those whose political sagacity and down-to-earth sensitivity earned them respect from both sides of the aisle. Robert Huber, a brewery worker from West Allis, rose to be speaker of the Assembly when Democrats controlled it in 1959 and again in 1965. He was an unflappable gentleman who could play tough politics but always fair politics. On the other side of the aisle was the venerable Walter Hollander, who got his schooling on a county board and served as senate cochairman of the Joint Finance Committee for 12 years. Rarely did he need a staff aide to tell him about any issue, and often he could be counted upon to ignore partisanship and support Democrats on key issues, if his conscience thought it best. He was a living argument against a mandatory retirement age: 80 years old and still as shrewd as ever when defeated by a youthful Republican a third his age in a 1976 primary, Hollander was the last of the influential old breed.

The legislature as it entered the 1980s reflected the changing times. Annual sessions were constitutionally required in 1971, forcing many of the part-time lawmakers to quit. By 1979, 55 representatives and 13 senators considered their lawmaking duties full-time. Some lawyers were saying they no longer could afford the time demanded in Madison, and in 1975, for the first time, there were no farmers in the Senate (the Assembly had only 14). The younger, better-educated (in a formal sense) lawmaker was very much in evidence: in 1965 the average senator was 55 and his counterpart in the Assembly was 48. By 1979, that had dropped to 43 in the senate and 42 in the lower house. One former legislative official told us that while the new legislators were better educated in a formal sense, they "have little practical experience, and are without sufficient judgment" in many cases to make good policy decisions. On top of that, the legislature increasingly is viewed as a stepping-stone, he said. "The person who's elected and stays 10–25 years is a thing of the past. More and more, we're seeing the up-and-out syndrome," as they seek higher elective or appointive office. When Nelson was elected governor in 1959, only 43 percent of the legislators had college degrees, while 31 percent had never gone beyond high school. By 1979, two-thirds of the members had college degrees (half with advanced degrees and five with doctorates), and those with only high school educations had been cut in half. Despite public howls every time legislative salaries were increased, the pay has expanded eightfold in two decades, going from $2,400 in 1957 to $19,767 in 1979 (not to mention the many fringe benefits). The increased staffing (tripled in two decades) offered incentives to those who saw their responsibility as more than merely accepting the suggestions of the governor, state agencies, or the lobbyists. By 1980, the legislature resembled the staffing patterns of Congress, with aides for not just the budget-reviewing committee but also for the party caucuses, individual members, and standing committees. Gone were the days when a Wisconsin legislator would work off a desk in the Assembly or Senate chambers, answering his (or her) own mail and sharing a typist with 10 colleagues.

Wisconsin legislators have gone far beyond the traditional role of policymaking, questioning much of the daily administration of state agencies and performing a watchdog function found in few states. One veteran lobbyist noted he no longer could simply tell a legislator what recommendation was best; he had to show why it was best before he could expect to win the vote. At times, legislative involvement seems to impede state agency implementation of programs. In the administrative rule-making process, not only does an agency have to hold public hearings, but the proposed regulations must be reviewed by at least three separate standing committees. It's little wonder some Wisconsin citizens consider their government cumbersome and bureaucratic.

Warren Knowles, silver-haired, courtly, and with a temperament so placid it seemed to contrast with the idea of executive leadership, was thought to be part of the old-line conservative legislators when he restored the governor's office to the Republicans in 1965 after six years of Democratic rule. For 20 years, he had been either lieutenant governor or a state senator. His six years as chief executive turned out to be more moderate than expected, but they still reflected his conviction that the governor proposed and the legislature disposed. "He allowed things to happen," one Democrat said. Given the growth demands of the 1960s, when the biennial state budget was ballooning 71 percent to $4.8 billion in Knowles' administration alone, he could have done much worse. While passive on executive leadership, he was aggressive on promoting economic development. At a time when college educations were considered by many as a panacea, he reorganized the state vocational-technical educational system (initially established by Governor McGovern in that tide of 1911 legislation) and expanded the opportunity for people without college aspirations to obtain an extended education. With the expanded facilities and added state aid, vocational-technical education reached almost 400,000 persons annually by 1979, twice the number of 1967.

Few people are aware of it, but Knowles' most lasting legacy probably was his adamant refusals to cave in to those vehement voices demanding that he close down the University of Wisconsin in Madison during the raucous riots in the late 1960s when antiwar protesters marched and disrupted classes, sometimes commandeering whole buildings. With many of his own Republican colleagues clamoring for a hard-line response, including punitive action, Knowles agreed with UW officials that the school should remain open and the demonstrators be assured due process. Knowles also maintained a secret pipeline to many of the students through his brother Robert, then a state senator. Robert Knowles would spend many of his evenings during those years in the student dormitories and living quarters, talking one-on-one with students about gripes and beliefs, without ever seeking a shred of publicity for his efforts to improve communication between campus and Capitol.* Senior faculty and administrators at UW-Madison still talk about Governor Knowles' resolute courage in the face of the anti-university forces, according

---

* An intelligent and highly principled man, Robert Knowles might have made just as good a choice as his brother to be governor. He served for a period as president of the state senate (off the record always fully candid about some of his more Neanderthal colleagues) and took a major interest in federal-state relations, serving as a member of the Advisory Commission on Intergovernmental Relations.

to Harvey Breuscher, a former newsman now with the UW. Breuscher noted that Knowles always spoke of the UW "with reverence; he really believes it is a valued resource." Such is the depth of the Wisconsin Idea, even in contemporary political feuds.

Warren Knowles also encouraged moves that would have profound influences on the shape and direction of state government, although it would be left to Patrick Lucey to extend and fully implement them. The first involved the creation of a cabinet system of state government, replacing the system of multitudinous part-time policymaking commissions and boards with a set of full-time department heads appointed by the governor. (One of the major cornerstones of Robert LaFollette Sr.'s political philosophy was thus being dismantled and disregarded, having thoroughly outlived its time, one could argue.) Recommendations by a Knowles-appointed task force provided the major initial impetus toward cabinet government, although his shifts left several critical department heads still appointed by commissions and failed to provide more than a cosmetic realignment of department organization. Lucey, in his drive to centralize power and control of state agencies which he found unresponsive to public and political demands, would almost complete the task. Knowles also initiated a major shift in state-local government relations. Wisconsin long had a "home-rule" tradition in local government relations, with the state interfering little with the way localities made decisions or spent their money. Another Knowles study committee laid much of the groundwork that helped Lucey to push through major changes in state-local relations, with the state both issuing mandates in several realms reserved for local discretions and reallocating state aids to localities to make sure the directives were carried out.

In 1967 the state constitution was amended to permit four-year instead of two-year terms for the governor and other statewide officers. Lucey, the first governor elected under the new provision, demonstrated the difference a guaranteed four years in office could make. Before resigning in 1977 to become Ambassador to Mexico, he produced a plethora of new initiatives, the likes of which had been unseen since 1911. University merger, redistribution of state aids to cities and schools, increased property tax relief coupled with elimination of an onerous property tax on corporate machinery and equipment, tighter regulation of power plant siting and power line routes, and a host of open meeting, campaign reform, and financial disclosure legislation all bore his imprint. An implementer and political manipulator without peer in recent Wisconsin history, Lucey deserved more credit than any other single person for building the Democratic party. The accomplishment was all the more remarkable because, given Wisconsin's antiboss traditions and suspicions of centralized authority, Lucey often was forced to mask his political wheeling and dealing.

The 1970s brought a new mood to Wisconsin, and with it a simultaneous expansion of the progressive tradition and a departure from it. "Rather than follow the LaFollette tradition, we have followed the New Democratic tradition, a new progressive tradition mixed with a huge dose of reality," observed Dale Cattanach, our long time friend who directed the Legislative Fiscal Bureau for 14 years. "The Democrats, and Patrick Lucey was the first person in Wisconsin to see that clearly, have adjusted the ideology, mixing the past tradition with what the public is willing to accept today." After the campus and city riots, the biennial tax increases, and the gigantic expansion of state services in the 1960s, the public was willing to accept less. Lucey, the liberal, brought in three straight budgets without tax increases, "conservative budgets in the name of good government, not fiscal conservatism," Cattanach noted. Within those budgets were packed the policy changes, however, that resulted in a plethora of new legislation the likes of which had been unseen since McGovern's initiatives in 1911–15. Much of it followed the progressive tradition of spreading the wealth—redistribution of state aids to cities (which might well prevent Milwaukee from becoming another Cleveland or New York, as one observer said), shifting of school aids away from income-rich communities to property-poor districts, a state-imposed lid on local property tax rates (a mortal blow to "home-rule" advocates)—all were Lucey legacies. Other aspects deviated from the Progressive tradition, such as the overt tax breaks for business—the elimination of property taxes on corporate machinery and equipment, removing the sales tax on pollution abatement equipment (worth $15 million to the paper mills alone), and the exemption from the sales tax of fuel used in manufacturing products. The breaks were worth $150 million a year to businesses. "LaFollette must be thumping up and down in his grave," Cattanach said. But it also did much to reverse the image of Wisconsin's antibusiness climate, and kept economic productivity high even during the recession in the mid-1970s. Wisconsin's economic health surpassed that of all its neighboring Midwestern states during those tough times, prompting the *Wall Street Journal* to tag the state with the accolade, the "star of the snow belt." At the same time, Lucey's program responded to the consumers and the plight of the "little people." He endorsed and fought the utilities to win stringent controls on the location of new power plants and power lines; he sought to place more consumers and women on policymaking boards and commissions; and he pushed for campaign reform, financial disclosure laws, and strong ethics codes that would reassure the people that his administration was open and responsive.

For all the burst of new programs and policies, Lucey borrowed profusely from the ideas of others (the merger of the university system was a Republican proposal, for instance). But he knew how to make the system move and succumb to his will because he was a politician of the first rank. Lucey would be remembered first as a politician, only secondarily as an administrator. Given his background, it could hardly have been otherwise. He served one term as a legislator in 1949, ran for Congress and lost, and then moved to Madison. While building a successful real estate business, he became state Democratic Party chairman and built an even more successful state organization. He was an early and critical supporter of John Kennedy in the

1960 Wisconsin presidential primary, a move that made him one of the most trusted of the non-Washington Kennedy advisers. Some Wisconsinites thought Lucey abused power, politicizing the office of governor like none before him. He thought nothing of conducting fund-raising efforts out of his East Wing Capitol office, calling up businessmen and quizzing them on why they hadn't contributed to his campaign, a blatant act which would have created sharp editorial rebuke had it been known at the time.

Lucey's use of power would tax the imagination of the naive, and ran the gamut of devices, depending on the issue and the person he was trying to influence. He would persuade constantly and intimidate when necessary, dangling patronage appointments and highway contracts before wavering legislators and ocassionally going to great lengths to get what he wanted. Usually he knew what he could get.* Occasionally, however, Lucey would pursue a futile proposal just for the principle involved.

Years after Lucey's departure for Mexico City, debate continued whether he had overstepped the bounds of political propriety in his unceasing battle to make the bureaucracy responsive to him. He refined cabinet government as a tool to be used for the governor's advantage and made a controversial bid for control of the state civil service system, a doddering and archaic process (rather than the fortress against political manipulation LaFollette had intended) by the 1970s. The Progressive tradition, carried to its logical extreme, led to so many protections in government that executive governing became exceedingly difficult. Sometimes adroitly, sometimes in a crude way, Lucey set out to make the state government responsive to the governor's will. His legacy was unquestionably a more *governable* state—for any chief executive with the skill to govern.

In 1978 Lee Dreyfus charged onto the political scene in Wisconsin clothed in the garments of the maverick reformer, complete with anomalies. A public employee all his life, as professor and chancellor of the University of Wisconsin-Stevens Point, he railed against bureaucracy. He was the outsider among Republicans, never joining the party until 10 months before his campaign; but he put together a low-budget campaign that included an old school bus painted up to look like a locomotive and traveled the state with a local high school band drumming up support. Wisconsinites—Republicans, Democrats, and independents—loved it and believed he could take more risks and be beholden to fewer interests than either acting Gov. Martin Schreiber or Republican Rep. Robert Kasten, Jr., the Milwaukee-area Congressman who had the blessing and dollars from the regular GOP.

For years, Dreyfus had worn a scarlet red vest whenever in public. That, coupled with his glib repartee along the campaign trail, gave him the easy-to-recall symbols he needed to overcome the endorsed GOP candidate and the incumbent governor. The regular GOP had had a chance to hear Dreyfus, who had addressed the state Republican convention in 1977. "I told them they had

* One former aide swore Lucey could look at a computer printout of the effect of a proposed tax redistribution and within minutes tell you what the final legislative rollcall votes would be. He rarely was off more than a few votes, the aide said.

made a terrible mistake trying to make the Wisconsin Republican Party a conservative party and ignoring the LaFollette tradition of progressivism," Dreyfus recalled later. "I told them they had to make room for students and young people and farmers and blacks and get the party out of the country club if they ever wanted to win."

Dreyfus put together the coalition needed to put him in office; but like many reformers, he quickly discovered the difference between campaigning and running a state government with an $11.9 billion biennial budget. He showed he could compromise, as he needed to do to realize his campaign pledge to cut taxes. The Democratic-controlled legislature and Dreyfus, within two months of his taking office, agreed on a compromise tax rebate of $942 million. His budget and the rest of his legislative program reflected his lack of experience, as he found himself vacillating in some areas and making ill-informed, hasty decisions in others. One insider noted, only half facetiously, that Lucey used to ruthlessly grill his aides and analysts about policy questions before making decisions, Schreiber often didn't ask any questions, and Dreyfus would make decisions and ask questions later.

Industry and Labor's Unholy Alliance

Wisconsin had a business development image problem when it entered the 1970s: its taxes were high, its politics seemed too liberal, and businesses were packing up and leaving, or expanding elsewhere. A decade later, the problem had been eliminated or at least mitigated. Wisconsin still suffered from the same stagnating malaise afflicting the Midwestern and Northeastern industrial states. But compared with its neighboring states, which lost more jobs, had greater unemployment and gained fewer people, Wisconsin survived the economic tribulations of the 1970s quite well. The decade saw Wisconsin's population increase 4.3 percent, no great surge compared to some of the Sun Belt states, but eminently better than the four other Great Lakes States, which were growing at half or less of that rate. While the rest of the Midwestern states were losing 7.3 percent of their manufacturing jobs from 1970–77, Wisconsin was gaining a percentage point, the only one except Iowa to show any improvement. In sharp contrast to Michigan's domination by the auto industry, Wisconsin staked a claim on its manufacturing diversity (which produced 40 percent of its income). A quick rundown of the 15 largest publicly held companies told a lot about the state. The five biggest were a paper company (Kimberly-Clark), a machinery manufacturer (Allis-Chalmers), a meat packer (Oscar Mayer), a brewer (Schlitz), and an oil company (Clark Oil, a regional firm). The biggest brewer, Miller's, was no longer Wisconsin-owned, having been bought out in 1973 by Philip Morris, the cigarette maker which descended upon the beer industry with millions of advertising dollars and revolutionized the marketing techniques of what was a staid and structured industry.

Going on down the list, one found extraordinary numbers of machinery manufacturers ranging from the small lawnmower engines made by Briggs and Stratton to the mammoth mining and construction equipment of both Bucyrus-Erie and Harnischfeger to the electrical equipment of Johnson Controls. Interspersed were another brewer (Pabst), the world's largest maker of writing pens (Parker Pen at Janesville), and a producer of floor covering (Congoleum). Wisconsin also had major car and truck assembly lines (American Motors at Kenosha and General Motors at Janesville), producing nearly 575,000 vehicles in 1977.

Industrial plants are geographically concentrated, mostly in the Milwaukee area and the Fox Valley (11 of the top 15 are in Milwaukee or its suburbs), one reason why Wisconsin could rank so high in manufacturing but still be perceived as an agricultural and recreation state. The image Wisconsin held at the start of the 1970s was vividly recounted in a *Wall Street Journal* article in 1977. Calling Wisconsin the "star of the snow belt," it said:

> In the battle among states for people and jobs, Wisconsin has all the attributes of a loser.
>
> First, there is the weather. Milwaukee, the state's largest city, is colder than any other major U.S. city except Minneapolis-St. Paul. Farther north, Superior has almost 80 inches of snow each year and a January daily temperature average of just nine degrees—among the coldest readings in the U.S. outside Alaska.
>
> Then there are the high taxes that go with the state's left-of-liberal political tradition. Wisconsin residents pay $138 in state and local taxes for each $1,000 they earn; that compares with the national average of $123 and is seventh highest among the 50 states.
>
> Wisconsin labor is expensive; the state's average manufacturing wage is more than $6 an hour, compared with the national average of about $5.50. And Wisconsin workers are more heavily unionized than those in all but 10 other states.

What was surprising, the *Wall Street Journal* commented, was how well Wisconsin was doing economically, compared with its neighbors. The explanation—in addition to the diversity—was said to lie in Lucey's package of tax incentives for industry (passed, incidentally, over the objections of municipalities standing to lose property tax revenues), a growing sophistication in the relations between labor and management, and quite simply, the fact that Wisconsin was a good place to live. Shortly after the Lucey tax cuts in 1973, which totaled $155 million, a UW survey showed one-third of the state's businesses had expanded in the state, and another 15 percent had canceled plans to move out. Wisconsin business leaders were finally beginning to feel wanted, but it took a liberal Democratic governor to pull it off. (Undoubtedly, a Republican proposing the same breaks would have been pummeled politically by Democrats.)

While Wisconsin workers are heavily unionized, that should not be mistaken to mean they are strongly liberal (except perhaps for the leadership of the United Auto Workers, a union unto itself in Wisconsin). Unions in the state and particularly in the Milwaukee area, former Milwaukee Socialist Mayor Frank Zeidler told us, have been consumed by the "Gompers philosophy." What's that? we asked. "No particular philosophy except *more*," he replied. But he quickly added, "They are reflecting the rank and file." While they have been generally successful at the bargaining table, most Wisconsin unions are not as hungry politically as they were half a century ago. But many Wisconsin employers feel they get what they pay for. "The quality of workmanship is excellent," said one industrialist, even if the cost of labor is high. Another manufacturing leader said he knows of two companies which expanded out of state, only to move their skilled labor operations back to Milwaukee, just to have access to the workers who ply their trade with the pride of a guild craftsman.

Over the years, labor-management clashes have occurred, some of them protracted and bitter. The classic case in Wisconsin was the eight-year strike at the Kohler Company, maker of bathtubs and toilets. When the unions walked out in 1954, one of the company's ruling elite, Walter Kohler, Jr., was governor. When the strike finally ended in 1962, Kohler was but an elder statesman in the state Republican party. Notwithstanding all the Progressive rhetoric about greedy corporations, labor unions in Wisconsin have found their interests often coincide with those of industry. The state AFL-CIO helped business lobbyists and Governor Lucey convince Democratic legislators in 1973 that the governor's tax breaks for industry meant more jobs for union members. It might come as a surprise to Progressive initiators of the unemployment compensation and workmen's compensation laws (both Wisconsin innovations) that a tacit agreement exists between unions and business on all bills changing these laws or their benefits. The legislature won't even consider any changes in the two programs unless both sides have previously agreed on them. And more than a few eyebrows were raised when the state AFL-CIO and the State Association of Commerce and Manufacturers joined hands to form an "Energy Coalition" to promote energy growth—including both nuclear and coal-fired generating plants—to offset the crescendoing voices of environmentalists.* For the unions, energy growth and nuclear power plants could be translated into construction and jobs. While the coalition generally was considered pronuclear, its program extended beyond that issue to promote conservation and alternate energy sources, as well as fostering a state regulatory climate to encourage reasonable growth of energy supplies. Called the "unholy alliance" in many quarters, the coalition nonetheless demonstrated the kind of ties that transcend the usual labor-management conflicts and provide a further restraint on Wisconsin as a liberal state in the purest sense. The unions are economically liberal, in their demand for "more," but socially and politically cautious and sometimes even conservative.

The public employee unions in Wisconsin offer a partial exception to the rule. Municipal employee unions won the right to bargain collectively on wages and fringe benefits in the 1960s. But it wasn't until 1973 that state

* The AFL-CIO and the Association of Commerce and Manufacturers were the dominant members of the coalition, but it also included such interesting partners as the Wisconsin Federation of Cooperatives, Wisconsin State Grange, Wisconsin Farm Bureau, the Wisconsin Association of School Boards, and several pro-energy individuals in industry and at the University of Wisconsin.

employees won comparable rights. Reflecting the aggressive stance of Jerry Wurf's American Federation of State, County, and Municipal Employees (AFSCME), the state workers lost no time organizing units and pushing for new economic and working condition gains. Despite prohibitions against strikes, the unionized employees (although not all of them) left their jobs in 1977 for nearly two weeks. They won some key concessions from that strike, but after that their momentum faltered, and even state employee representatives in Wisconsin were encountering resistance to further organization. The National Labor Relations Board reported that for the region covering most of Wisconsin, unions won more than 55 percent of the representation elections in 1965–75. In the last half of the 1970s, the companies were winning the majority of elections, as more employees decided to stay nonunion, the NLRB said.

As the 1980s advanced, Wisconsin faced a new threat to its economic independence—loss of critical rail lines. In January 1979, the state's Rail Service Advisory Committee told the governor that "a long developing cycle of rail line decline, poor financial conditions in the rail industry and government policy have combined to confront Wisconsin with a rail abandonment crisis." In 1977 the Milwaukee Road, one of the two largest lines serving the southern half of the state and with a quarter of all track in Wisconsin, declared bankruptcy, leaving many businesses relying on the line in a state of limbo. The Milwaukee Road had 542 of its 1,318 miles of track proposed for or considered likely to be abandoned by 1982. Altogether, 918 miles of all the railroads' 5,291 miles in Wisconsin were considered primary targets for abandonment. Railroads were one of the principal ogres on LaFollette's list of political monsters, leading to his railway regulatory reforms in 1905. But at the 1970s rate of abandonment, there soon will be little left to regulate, and countless manufacturers and industrialists would have to convert to other (usually more costly) transportation for their products. If the rail lines collapsed, and no public body intervened to subsidize them, the economic growth of the 1970s could be sorely altered for these companies in the 1980s.

America's Dairyland, Where the Cow Is Queen

Wisconsin is known, perhaps even more than for its beer, for its milk and cheese. The license plates of its cars let the world know it is "America's Dairyland," an appellation justly deserved. Its 1.8 million dairy cows (largest herd in the country) produce enough milk to provide every man, woman, and child in the U.S.A. more than nine gallons a year. Largely because of its dairy output, Wisconsin ranked ninth in the nation in agricultural production in the 1970s, with 60 percent of its $3.5 billion farm income derived from the Holsteins, Jerseys, Guernseys, Brown Swiss, and other dairy cows.

Wisconsin was not always a dairy state. For that, it can thank the collapse of the wheat markets after the Civil War (wheat was king at that time), an influx of New Yorkers and Swiss, Dutch, German, and Scandinavian immigrants late in the 1800s who brought with them their skills as cheese-makers, and the energy and ideas of William D. Hoard. Hoard was an extraordinary apostle for the embryonic dairying industry: he moved to Wisconsin from New York, worked on odd jobs, settled into farming, turned to newspapering and lobbying for dairy improvements and assistance from the UW, and ultimately spent a term as governor (1889–91) and headed the UW's board of regents. In 1885 he started the magazine *Hoard's Dairyman*, which at its zenith was the last word on all things tried and untested in dairying. Hoard popularized the slogan, "Speak to a cow as you would to a lady!" A century later, his campaign was still successful: in Wisconsin, the cow remained queen.

During the frontier days, raw milk was almost worthless except for local consumption. To sell it in large quantities and transport it to the eastern and foreign markets, dairymen turned to making cheese. Even here, they encountered obstacles in the exorbitant rates charged by the railroads, initially pricing them out of the eastern markets. But after Hoard helped found the Wisconsin Dairymen's Association in 1872 and then persuaded the railroads to cut the rates in half, the cheese industry was ready to grow. By the end of World War I, Wisconsin was making two-thirds of the nation's cheese, a veritable delicatessen of Swiss and limburger, muenster and cheddar, plus Wisconsin's own original creation, colby, a milder, moister variety of cheddar. Altogether, Wisconsin produces 200 kinds of cheese, including about a quarter as much Italian-style varieties as all of Italy itself makes. By the 1970s the state produced almost 40 percent of the nation's 3.4 million pounds of cheese.

For awhile in the 1960s, it seemed a share of Wisconsin farmers were becoming more militant in demanding greater support prices. In 1964 the National Farmers Organization (NFO) conducted a 42-day livestock withholding action, which led to the deaths of two farmers at a demonstration at Bonduel. The situation did not reflect the majority of farm views, however, which traditionally have been divergent. The conservative Farm Bureau for years was the dominant voice, with the aggressive NFO and the more liberal Farmers Union maintaining significant memberships. Ironically, the NFO, according to a 1965 study, didn't attract just the small dairyman: most of their members' farmers were larger and their sales greater than the Wisconsin average. Another significant influence in Wisconsin agriculture has been the cooperatives, although these did not flourish until this century. In recent years Wisconsin has had more than 500 cooperatives (only Minnesota and North Dakota have more), with three-quarters of the state's dairymen buying supplies through co-ops and half marketing through them. Co-ops also responded to another rural need by generating and distributing their own electricity. Dairyland Power Company, for instance, built Wisconsin's first nuclear power plant, at Genoa along the Mississippi River in 1969.

Not surprisingly, much of Wisconsin's grain production is not for the commercial markets, but for the towering silos that rise like sentinels from the rolling hills and dells and for the haymow in the barns. A leader in corn production and first nationally in hay harvesting, Wisconsin uses the crops to feed her cows during the long winter months when the pasture land is layered with crusted snow. For every farm in Wisconsin, there are about 6.3 jobs created in agricultural-related industries. Names such as J.I. Case of Racine, an early developer of the thresher, and Allis-Chalmers of Milwaukee, the maker of tractors (among other industrial equipment) stand out in the machinery industry, while Oscar Mayer of Madison and Packerland Packing Company of Green Bay dominate the food processing field. Wisconsin also gave the malted milk to the world, a concoction of dried milk mixed with malted wheat and barley developed by William Horlick of Racine before 1900.

Significant changes have occurred in the dairying and agricultural business in Wisconsin since the Depression, diminishing its clout in legislative halls and raising the question of survival of the small family farm. The elimination of the ban on selling colored oleomargarine in 1967 was like the last blow to the farm-dominated legislature. When the name of the State Agriculture Department was changed in the mid-1970s to the Agriculture, Trade, and Consumer Protection Department, it was clear the private fiefdom of the farmer had been invaded by those with a broader interest.

Not only is the number of farms declining, from 200,000 in the Depression to 95,000 in 1979, but the age of the farmers is increasing, a sign that the youngsters are heading off for college or "better jobs" in the city. Always largely dependent on the moods of Mother Nature, farming has more and more become a business, with college degrees and access to computers demanded of the farmer if he is to be successful. The start-up costs are enough to make the young novice think twice. UW Extension estimated in the '70s that it took close to $300,000 to buy all the land, equipment, and cows to begin dairying. By national standards, farms in Wisconsin were small (averaging 184 acres), but they were getting bigger, driving the family farm against the wall of economic survival and attracting more and more corporate investors. Rural legislators and Congressmen have sought (with moderate success) to place restrictions on corporate farming and thereby protect the livelihoods of the family farmer. A dairy plant security law, assuring payments to dairymen if their milk plants default, was passed by the state legislature in 1968, offering some protection in times of a volatile economy. In the 1970s, a new face showed up on the Wisconsin farm scene, the international investor, primarily from the oil-rich Middle East and from Japan. With their fat pocketbooks, the foreigners were able to pay high prices for Wisconsin acreage, prompting a new concern for the family farmer. Legislation did limit the amount of land which corporations or aliens could own, but the small, independent family farmer still had to struggle to compete in the increasingly technical realm of agriculture.

Every growing season, central Wisconsin becomes home for thousands of migrant workers. Mechanization has replaced the need for some of them, but migrant men, women, and children still spend long back-breaking hours in the fields cultivating and harvesting the peas, potatoes, beets, snap beans, and other vegetables for the canneries. The flat, sandy-based soils of central Wisconsin are well suited for the vegetable canning industry. So fertile is this land that Wisconsin produces 25 percent of the country's peas, 30 percent of its beets, 25 percent of its kraut cabbage, 24 percent of its sweet corn, and 19 percent of its snap beans. The conditions under which migrants once lived and worked bordered on the abominable, with one-room shacks housing whole families, without modern sanitation facilities, with nonexistent health services, and wages reminiscent of the pre-1900 sweat shops. But state pressure in the 1960s and 1970s forced the employers to upgrade facilities and provide the migrants with a modicum of dignity. Not unlike the capitalists at the turn of the century, many migrant employers resisted and resented this intrusion on their private property (and profits). So much of the squalor was eliminated, though, that a number of the families left the migrant stream and settled in Wisconsin, creating Spanish-speaking populations in many small communities.

Interspersed with the sandy soil in the central plains region of Wisconsin are clusters of peat bogs, which have become the center of the state's flourishing cranberry industry. The state traditionally vies with Massachusetts as the foremost producer of cranberries, annually growing a full third of the country's supplies. While cranberries will never replace the cow as the state's top farm income source, they—along with peppermint, tobacco, maple syrup, ginseng root, and frozen bull semen—add to the diversity of Wisconsin's agricultural base.

The Germans and Other Ethnic Vestiges

It has been eight decades since the rush of European immigrants into Wisconsin passed its peak. Today, the vestiges of the culture and values they brought with them endure, mostly nostalgically, sometimes in reality. The popularity of the beer and bratwursts of the Germans in Milwaukee, Sheboygan, and other Lake Michigan communities is one of the continuing realities. So too are the periodic feasts of Norwegian lutefisk and *musical sangerfests* in Stoughton and Madison, the Cornish pasties in Mineral Point, and the Swiss cheese in New Glarus. More nostalgic are the images of the Swedish meatballs and coffee *klatschen* in St. Croix Valley; the Danish *kringle* in Racine; the square-logged homes (with the sauna out back) of the Finns around Superior; the sausage, *sokols* (physical development centers), and three-day wedding ceremonies of the Poles in Steven Point and Milwaukee; the wooden Dutch shoes and the factories along the Lower Fox River that made them (the last cobbler quit in the 1940s). Pockets of French Canadians, Belgians, Russians, Czechs, and Italians scattered around the state only added to the cultural traditions that became rooted in many areas.

So heavy was the immigration that the first settlers, the Yankees from New York and New England, almost became a cultural minority themselves. At the turn of the century, foreign tongues were almost as prevalent as English, with fully four out of every 10 persons born outside the U.S.A. Milwaukee Socialists in 1910 found it necessary to distribute political circulars printed in 12 languages. Now the foreign born are the rarity, and the total of first and second generation Americans in Wisconsin barely reaches 15 percent. The largest of the foreign stock remains the Germans (5.3 percent of the population), while Poles and Norwegians account for less than 3 percent between them. But a 1970 survey found 40 percent of state residents were of German descent.

Assimilation has taken its toll, as the sons and daughters and grandchildren have become the victims (or beneficiaries, depending on the view) of a public education, television, the tug to move to the suburbs, and all the other modernizing influences. Even the so-called Polish South Side of Milwaukee is no longer Polish, but a potpourri of nationalities, and many of those that still live there ignore the old traditions. At St. Stanislaus, the gigantic Catholic citadel in the heart of what once was Milwaukee's Polish community, for instance, one is struck by the paucity of churchgoers on a Sunday morning.

The Old World immigrants brought their religion—or lack of it—with them, providing cause for tensions and animated political debates that eased only in recent years. Splitting the Germans were the Catholics from southern Germany, the Lutherans from the north, and the anticlerical, free-thinking refugees from the Revolution of 1848, to say nothing of the variant religious beliefs of the socialists. That breakdown for the state as a whole is perpetuated today, although the Catholics have declined from the 40 percent they once were reputed to have had. At late as 1960, when John Kennedy won Wisconsin's presidential primary, the Catholics (then numbering 31 percent) were a critical component in his victory. Kennedy's appeal was especially telling in the Fox River Valley, which includes three of the nation's most heavily Catholic counties (Brown, Outagamie, and Kewaunee), all long-time bastions of Republicanism. Of the Protestants, Lutherans by far and away are the dominant religion.

The people of Wisconsin, perhaps because of their ethnic heritage and the sense of belonging it nourished, love celebrations. Throughout the state, certain community festivals have become famous, either as a retelling of part of their ethnic past or simply as an out-and-out tourist attraction. Some have criticized the exploitation of the past, and have rightfully suggested the ethnic festival of today is an artificial re-creation of the past, at best. Yet, whether or not the criticism is valid, some have endured. Stoughton celebrates Syttende Mai, the Norwegian day of independence, for three days; the Swiss in New Glarus stage an entrancing outdoor pageant in September depicting the Swiss struggle for independence as part of their Wilhelm Tell festival; and the Dutch of Cedar Grove turn out in July for a Holland Festival that includes real street scrubbing with brooms and brushes and a wooden shoe dance. The biggest extravaganza of all, though, is Milwaukee's Summerfest, a 10-day celebration of the country's cultural heritage that includes the "World's Greatest Music Festival." For those communities without an ethnic past, the fun-loving Wisconsinites often create a reason for a celebration. Folks at Rhinelander pay homage to "Hodag Days," in honor of a mythical monster of the woods, and the people of Poynette, the watermelon capital of the world (they say), once a year attract thousands for their watermelon seed-spitting contest.

Milwaukee: Beer and Government with a German Flavor

Milwaukee surely is the smallest big city in the U.S.A.—and proud of it. With 620,000 people, it was shrinking in the '70s, sure to drop from its 12th place ranking among major cities when the 1980 census was completed. But the fact didn't seem to perturb too many other than a few officials. Milwaukee is a city where many of the German ethnic traditions have fallen by the wayside, but where the individualistic German values of civic responsibility, public order, frugality, and pride in property ownership continue to thrive. "Milwaukee is a nice place to live, but you wouldn't want to visit there," was the way the Boston *Globe* put it in 1978 in a portrait of the city that made beer famous. "It is everything a Bostonian would expect, and less. But things get done. In fact, people expect their city to work. They have not yet developed the cynicism of the urban East. . . . Milwaukee is still—almost naively, it seems to an Easterner—American."

The city, one may add, has none of the taste of Boston or New Orleans, less of the cosmopolitanism of New York or San Francisco. Excitement borders on the humdrum. When the city dump caught fire and burned for several months in 1968, it became one of the best shows in town. "Why?" asked author and newspaper columnist Robert Wells. "Well, because it was there. And because watching a good dump fire doesn't cost a cent." People in Milwaukee go to antique shows not to buy, but with their pencil and paper to jot down the prices so they can get the market price at their next garage sale. The city does have its culture: it brings in the Chicago Symphony occasionally, and it has built a startling modern white stone Performing Arts Center as well as the Milwaukee Exposition and Convention Center and Arena (MECCA), in downtown Milwaukee, both only a few blocks from the magnificently refurbished turn-of-the-century Pabst Theatre. Over on Lake Michigan, there is also the modernistic Milwaukee Art Center, housing both contemporary and primitive art from Europe and earlier American periods.

For the vast majority of Milwaukeeans, however, culture is to be found in the beer bars and bowling alleys or, when in season, at County Stadium (home of baseball's Milwaukee Brewers) or the Arena (home of basketball's Bucks). It's no accident the city has almost 1,650 taverns and the metropolitan area claims to have 2,600 bowling alleys. It is a blue collar, unionized town, where the first-shift workers in the heavy machinery plants frequently brace themselves for their day with a couple of shots of brandy and beer chasers—before reporting to work at 6 A.M.* The worst of the freeway congestion is over by 5:30 P.M. in the summer, because so many Milwaukeeans hurry home to fuss and putter in their yards, meticulously manicuring their lawns and keeping the grass from growing between the cracks in the sidewalk. More than half of Milwaukeeans own their own home, another of the lingering Old World values that made owning a lot and a small house the symbol of success in America. Few of the people speak German or Polish as their first language, and the once numerous foreign language newspapers are gone. Yet the feeling of *Gemutlichkeit* has yet to be lost, especially at the Friday night fish fries such as can be found at Serb Hall on the southwest side. The feeling even pervades many of the more elegant restaurants or busier stores, where the customer is likely to be told to "have a good day."

Much of this sense of community was fostered by the Socialist Party in Milwaukee, which controlled the mayor's office for more than 40 years of the 20th century. Milwaukee's socialism was not the left-of-liberal brand usually associated with such ideologies. Instead, it was a frugal, almost penny-pinching brand of municipal management, stressing practical, basic, and efficient services. So focused was it on the basic government services that it was often referred to as a "sewer socialism," in contrast to the more ideological, anti-capitalistic rhetoric practiced elsewhere. Daniel Hoan, the Socialist city attorney of Milwaukee before he began his 24-year tenure as mayor in 1916, has been classed as a "shrewd politician in his own right who was one-tenth socialist and nine-tenths businessman." Hoan and his Socialist colleagues dealt with LaFollette and the Progressives in statewide power at the start of his career, but Milwaukee Socialism could never be considered an urban extension of the Progressives. Emil Seidel, the first Socialist elected mayor, in 1910, rode into office on the crest of a citizen revolt (including businessmen, professional, and working people) fed up with the corruption of the Republicans and Democrats of the day. They promised good government, and they produced. "Milwaukee did not express for Socialism," one writer of the period noted. "It merely gave a vote of confidence to the Socialists." That was typical of Milwaukeeans, then and now. They care less about the label than about the product. Paul Hassett, a Republican and now president of the Wisconsin Association of Commerce and Manufacturers, recalled in an interview with us his youth growing up in Milwaukee under a Socialist administration: "Fifty-three years ago, I played basketball Monday, Wednesday, and Friday nights at a social center in a school, open to me without cost and to everyone in the city who wanted to. . . . I learned to swim at 16th and North Avenue in an indoor natatorium. I was nobody in Milwaukee, nobody. In fact, my parents were unemployed. But I learned to swim indoors in Milwaukee

---

* This fact helps explain in part why Wisconsin, with only 2 percent of the population, annually consumes more brandy than any other state. Wisconsinites down 20 percent of all brandy drunk in the United States.

over 50 years ago. What I'm trying to point out is that Milwaukee made these things available, the parks, the zoo, the museum, and therefore the legislators who grew up in Milwaukee and people who grew up in Milwaukee became used to a high service . . . and while a few people complain about high taxes, I think generally speaking most people accept the cost of the high service they want."

When Hoan was defeated in 1940, according to his biographer Edward Kerstein, he

left many monuments of his unprecedented public service in the form of a great harbor, pleasant social centers and parks, honest police department, efficient fire department, an outstanding water department owned by the city, a dependable street illuminating system, better housing, properly regulated public utilities, a great public health department and a clean government.

That may inflate the accomplishments of the Socialists somewhat; it certainly completely ignored the fact that they did pitifully little to prepare the city for the racial and social problems that were to confront Milwaukee in the 1960s and 1970s. But the 1940 defeat did not end the Socialist era in Milwaukee. Eight years later, the city elected Frank Zeidler (brother of the Republican who had beaten Hoan), who would continue Hoan's brand of Socialism, stressing basic government services, for another 12 years. It is a startling realization that Milwaukee's last Socialist left office the same year John F. Kennedy was elected President.

Frank Zeidler, by the late 1970s, was the elder statesman of American Socialists. In his mid-sixties, he was national chairperson of the Socialist Party of U.S.A., working out of a run-down third-floor office within sight of City Hall. He was considered an urban expert, frequently lecturing, helping set up neighborhood organizations, and serving as critic-in-residence of the man who succeeded him in the mayor's office, Henry Maier. Surrounded by posters of Karl Marx and an Austrian social democrat, others supporting the American Indian Movement and opposing forced sterilization, Zeidler recounted for us the decline of the Socialists in Milwaukee. It began as early as World War I, he told us, when those with British ancestry pulled out of the movement. But the crushing blows came from 1930 to 1945, he said, when the party encountered opposition from Catholics and later the Catholic leadership of the labor unions. "Socialism was anathema to the Catholic population of Milwaukee, which constitutes the bulk of voters," he related. "Milwaukee really reflects the conservative German Catholic philosophy. Maybe now it might be said the leaders represent more of the Polish Catholic philosophy. It represents a conservative type of philosophy, which has only one liberal aspect: the mass of people would vote Democratic nevertheless on labor issues." When the labor leadership became Catholic in the 1930s and the national labor leaders ordered its members out of the Norman Thomas-led Socialist movement, Milwaukee Socialism lost its tie-in with the unions. The deaths of young men in World War II, who might have formed a base on which to rebuild, plus internal dissension with Trotskyites, sealed the fate of Milwaukee Socialism, Zeidler said. When he became mayor, he admitted, he was "just a caretaker" unable to rebuild the past. Yet he undoubtedly extended for another generation the expectations of good municipal government which Socialists had given Milwaukee.

A new wave of immigrants was entering Milwaukee during Zeidler's time in office—the poor blacks from the South, seeking a job and a reprieve from the poverty of the sharecropper's life. In 1940 about 9,000 blacks lived in Milwaukee. The black population increased so noticeably in the 1950s that Zeidler felt compelled to run in 1956 just to refute the whisper campaign that he had ordered billboards erected in Alabama and Mississippi inviting blacks to the city of *Gemutlichkeit*. Milwaukee had almost 60,000 blacks when he left office in 1960, a total that would double in the following two decades. According to official 1970s estimates, 18 percent of Milwaukee was black, but Zeidler insisted the 1980 census would reveal a much larger number, perhaps as much as 25 percent. With few exceptions, the Milwaukee brothers who voted for the Socialists didn't want to rub shoulders with the black immigrants. To this day, finding a black living on the South Side of Milwaukee is like meeting an Arab in Tel Aviv. Blacks do work on the South Side, but when the shift ends they go back to the straining Inner City, as the ghetto is called. As the black population grew, the ghetto boundaries moved further north and west, but never south of the Menomonee Valley.

The Valley is the heart of Milwaukee's industrial might, a congested, often polluted expanse of heavy manufacturers, factories, warehouses, and scrap yards surrounding the converging Menomonee, Milwaukee, and Kinnickinnic rivers. This half-mile-wide valley covering 4.5 square miles from the lake inward is where 30,000 people work. But it is also a dividing line, an inverted Wall of China. Especially after the riots of 1967, there was a frequently repeated story about one of the bridges across the Valley. "What's the longest bridge in the world?" the story began. "The 16th St. Viaduct: it connects Poland and Africa," went the response. The Valley also has been described as Milwaukee's Mason-Dixon line, an epithet which took on additional meaning in 1967 when Fr. James Groppi, a Catholic cleric who has since left the priesthood, led civil rights marchers across the bridge into the South Side to demand an open housing ordinance. For more than 200 days they marched, bringing their protest about unequal housing opportunities in various white enclaves throughout the city and even some suburbs. Finally, but not before violence occurred (whites attacked some blacks in the South Side Kosciuszko Park), the city council passed an open housing law. Hailed as a civil rights triumph at the time, experience has proven it more a symbol than a cure. That same summer, exactly one week after the far more violent riots in Detroit, a roving gang of 300 black youths began breaking windows and tossing rocks at cars passing through their segregrated neighborhood. A shootout ensued with police, with two persons killed and six injured. With visions of the televised holocaust in Detroit still vivid, Mayor Henry Maier moved with Prussian-like efficiency to head off any repeat of Detroit or Watts. The

National Guard was called out and a strictly enforced curfew slapped on the city.

Critics questioned whether the curfew was necessary, and some wags observed Milwaukee was so law-abiding and respectable that "it couldn't even put on a real riot," or so reported Robert Wells in his book, *This Is Milwaukee*. Necessary or not, it was effective, and Maier's political stock soared, assuring his reelection the following year. Racial tensions remained taut for months after that, but the would-be riot did prompt improved communications between the black and white communities, even if the South Side stayed a sacrosanct citadel of exclusionist ethics. On both the city and state levels, officials reached out behind the scenes to respond to the legitimate complaints about jobs, housing, and schooling raised by the black communities. Republican Governor Knowles, for instance, made repeated unannounced trips to talk informally with black leaders and Inner City residents, including the youthful "Commandoes," the rebellious activists spearheading the open housing marches. Without fanfare, Maier's administration also began making more room for black job opportunities.

Two years later, it was not difficult to suggest that Milwaukee blacks had progressed little. The Inner City residents were poorer, more likely to be jobless, and in worse health than other Milwaukeeans. Ben Johnson, the black president of the city council, provided a voice for his constituents, but he chose not to wield power, and blacks generally found themselves without political muscle in either city hall, the county courthouse, or the state Legislature. Housing remained dilapidated in many parts of the Inner City; integration was still limited, and then only on the North Side. One exception was in the Washington Park neighborhood on the near west side, not too far west of the Marquette University campus. There, a group of foresightful residents, black and white, formed a neighborhood group to promote integration and thwart the blockbusting tactics some realtors encouraged to turn white neighborhoods into black ones almost overnight. Washington Park has many fine, old homes ideal for families, and the neighborhood association has tried to attract blacks who would keep it that way. Regrettably, the neighborhood was an exception in Milwaukee.

By the late 1970s the Inner City crime rate was not ideal, but it was far less of a problem than in any other major urban centers. The job opportunities had expanded some. "There is a feeling that things are good here, the belief that they can work and the hope they can get better," said Johnson. Part of that hope could be attributed to the honest efforts of Milwaukee's business leadership before, during, and after the confrontation era to open up jobs through such devices as National Alliance of Business programs. "We Milwaukeeans," a combined group of Milwaukee's business-civic elite and a cross-section of black professionals, held monthly dialogue sessions for several years and organized committees to work on education, housing, health, and welfare problems. Both Schlitz and Miller breweries signed agreements early in the 1970s with the Rev. Jesse Jackson's Operation PUSH to funnel millions of dollars over a period of years into the pockets of minority employees and minority enterprises in Milwaukee and elsewhere in the country. Less than optimistic opinions are still easy to find. John Givens, a black associate director of the city's Community Development Department, has seen some jobs for blacks dry up, as alleged quotas have been set, shoving already high unemployment rates among blacks even higher. "There's more hopelessness, because the problems are more difficult to get at," Givens contended. "The prejudice is more sophisticated. White people look at the numbers and think everything's OK."

In 1976, Federal Judge John Reynolds (the former governor) sent a shudder through order-loving Milwaukee when he found the city's school unconstitutionally segregated. Acting on a case filed two years before Father Groppi's marches, Reynolds ordered the school board to come up with an integration plan, which, given Milwaukee's rigidly segregated housing patterns, could mean only one thing: busing. The previous year, busing orders in Boston and Louisville spawned racial ugliness and violence. And Milwaukee's ethnics were not any different from those in Boston, some were saying. The school board gave every indication of fulfilling that prophecy, appealing to higher courts and loudly protesting, even after Reynolds in 1978 further ruled that the board had intentionally maintained segregated schools "at least since 1950." But, in a way peculiar to Milwaukee, with its tradition of civic responsibility and proclivity for stability, the court and the school board simultaneously persisted in working out a compromise that lessened the past practices even as they argued about their existence. Finally, in March 1979, a settlement was reached, short of full integration but one likely to be accepted by both the blacks and the blue-collar families of Milwaukee. It required at least 75 percent of the students to be in desegregated schools, which could include anywhere from 20–60 percent blacks. While it would require all white students to have at least some black schoolmates, it allowed about a third of the blacks to stay in about 20 all-black or nearly black schools. According to the school board president, "75 percent was the most the system and the city could effectively deal with." Integration purists argued about the equity, but the pragmatists (and Milwaukee is full of them) responded by noting the city had a desegregation plan replete with busing, already partly implemented, with none of the racial turmoil that characterized such efforts in other major cities. In their own way, Milwaukeeans took a certain unvoiced pride in that. But German frugality suffered a bit when Judge Reynolds ordered the school board to pay $892,778 in fees to the court-appointed attorney and to the lawyer for the black children who had filed the suit 14 years before.

Reynolds' decision also allowed another exception—for the small (about 6–7 percent) but concentrated Latino population in Milwaukee. Four elementary schools offered a bilingual educational program, to meet the special needs of the Mexican, Puerto Rican, and other Spanish-speaking schoolchildren; in these, the ratio of minorities was to be smaller, to avoid forced dispersion of the Spanish-speaking pupils. The exact number of Latinos could only be guessed at, but generally was placed around 40,000–45,000, all but a handful compacted into two neighborhoods. One is in the deteriorating neighborhood of Walker's Point, on the Near South Side, the other just north of the freeway and west of downtown. Although Latinos have lived in Milwaukee for 50 years, it has only been in the last decade that they have started to overcome their small numbers and great apathy about the political process. Many of the Spanish-speaking immigrants have jobs paying between $6 and $8 an hour, which is the kind of news relayed to family back in California and Texas and entices more relatives to join the trek to Milwaukee. "Maybe later on we can get a better house in a better neighborhood and keep progressing up, up, up," said one Mexican worker. The same sentiments were expressed in earlier decades by the Germans, Polish, and other immigrants.

Mayor Henry Maier was described by the Milwaukee *Journal's* Michael Bauman as a "little like a father figure but more like a rich uncle." Not everyone likes him, but no one wants to offend the man who has run Milwaukee for 20 years plus. His decisiveness in 1967 in slapping a curfew on the city instantly immortalized him in the minds of Milwaukee's voters, forever tinging their future images of him with the Teutonic notion that he was a leader who would take care of them. At the same time, Maier's raging temper tantrums are legendary, striking out with ferocity at the Milwaukee Journal Company, the state government, the suburbs, the federal agencies, intimidating many who would otherwise question him or his policies. He is little short of a genius, one appointee noted, in creating the "them and us syndrome," in which courageous Mayor Maier paternalistically takes on "them" (i.e., the haughty suburbs or the arrogant Journal Company) in defense of "us," all Milwaukeeans, against this outside evil standing in the way of the city's progress (and the mayor's proposal). This tactic allows Maier to "identify with the blue collar and working class people," said the businessman appointee. "It's the key to his success." But there is much more to this man, who hides a steel trap mind and a presidential-sized ego behind a pipe-smoking, casual demeanor that has wide appeal. Not even his divorce and remarriage in the mid-1970s made any noticeable impact on his large Catholic constituency.

Twenty years after first winning the mayoralty against later-to-be-Congressman Henry Reuss and the business community elite, Maier remained an enigma to many, a source of contradictions to others. Considered a liberal Democrat nationally and one of the most outstanding practicing urbanologists in the country, he alienated his liberal backers through his tough stand in the civil disturbances of the 1960s and his continuing refusal to take a more active and vocal stance in dealing with the city's social problems.

Maier, with all his contradictions, remains one of the strongest mayors in the country, without any of the patronage or political organizations found in the city of Big Shoulders 90 miles to the south. Ostensibly, Milwaukee has a weak mayor and a strong city council system; in reality, it is the reverse. Maier has been sagacious or fortunate, or both, in selecting generally top-notch people as his appointees and placing them in charge of city departments, from which he exercises control of the council, the city, and all its dominions. For the most part, the city runs well, "certainly well enough not to be on the public mind," as one businessman put it. That effectively eliminates the issues that might spawn a viable political opponent. Talk to any city officials for any length of time, and invariably reference is made at least once to the city's Triple A bond rating, a symbol of more than just a financially solvent city (always contrasted to New York or Cleveland). More importantly, that Triple A bond rating symbolizes all the good city services, all the good German traditions, and all the high public expectations that Milwaukeeans consider as their way of life.

One department head ascribed Maier's success to his vote pluralities. But it goes beyond that, to his ability to manage policy and government through his department appointees and to the force of his own personality, a combination of intimidation and cogent persuasion. "In Maier's view," comments Milwaukee *Sentinel* political reporter Kenneth Lamke, "a chief source of power is prestige or status. It inclines people to follow the mayor's suggestions even when he has no formal power over them. Maier guards his prestige as a banker guards his deposits."

Among the nation's mayors, Maier stands apart, for his longevity as well as his ideas on urban revitalization. With the longest tenure of any large-city mayor in the country, Maier commands an audience wherever he goes, in Washington, on college campuses, in other cities. At one time or the other, Maier has been president of the U.S. Conference of Mayors, the National League of Cities, and the National Conference of Democratic Mayors, forums which he uses well to expound upon the needs of financially strapped cities pinned between declining populations, deteriorating housing and commercial bases, and rising service demands. He has been called one of America's 60 most influential men (by *U.S. News and World Report*), has been a spokesman for the cities in responding to presidential urban policy pronouncements, and early-on advocated a radical reallocation of national resources to aid central cities.

Downtown Milwaukee development languished for several decades before the 1970s. Most of the development—and it wasn't much to brag about—was privately initiated and privately financed. Why? First, there was the business community's traditional reluctance to cozy up to a City Hall dominated so long by Socialist mayors. Then there was the fact key business elites had opposed Maier's initial election. Finally, there was Maier's need to forge a consolidated base of power within the city departments before turning to tangible projects downtown. It took him 10 years, for instance, to turn a one-man operation known as the Division of Industrial Development within his office into a major consolidated city agency, the Department of City Development, headed by his appointee with the power to produce results. As 1980 approached, some sign of results finally was emerging, beyond the already completed public facilities—such as the Performing Arts Center and the convention center (MECCA). Next to the convention center, a Hyatt Regency hotel was rising, the first new downtown hotel in decades. The Department of City Development was coordinating creation of a $50 million downtown retail center, providing a climate-controlled pedestrian walkway through the heart of the major department stores and specialty shops. The project, a joint city effort with the quasi-private Milwaukee Redevelopment Corporation, was set for completion in 1982. Another project still on the drawing board involved a proposed new federal office building, which some developers have talked about constructing with private offices, shops, and condominiums atop the federal facilities. With outside help (including federal development grants and state-approved tax incremental financing legislation), Milwaukee's City Hall and the community private sector finally seemed to be producing something other than friction.

Maier's celebrated feud with the Milwaukee Journal Company—hardly paralleled anywhere in the U.S.A. for its bitterness—finally subsided during the 1970s, revived only periodically by the mayor when the *Journal* took stands in opposition to him or perhaps during an election campaign when he needed an ox to gore.* For Milwaukee, the results of the feud were tragic, even if not readily apparent: with both distinguished newspapers and a brilliant mayor, the city's attention for years was diverted from its very real problems of race, unemployment, and housing. The influence of the *Journal* in Milwaukee remains prodigious, at least in the minds of those seeking to mold public opinion. In the first weeks after the school desegregation decision, when fears of racial violence were rampant, integregationists courted the *Journal* and counted heavily on its progressive editorial voice. The *Journal*, acutely aware of its position in the community, responded like the dignified, public-spirited citizen it is.

Journal publisher Irwin Maier (no relation to the mayor) acknowledges that Milwaukee has suffered from the mass and almost total migration of its business leaders to the suburbs, reducing the pool available for civic duty. But he insists that groups such as the Greater Milwaukee Committee (GMC), a blue-ribbon citizens' committee started by himself and other business leaders in 1939, has fostered a metropolitan-wide attitude that is neither narrow nor suburban-oriented. GMC also has included leaders in labor, education, and medicine and been the prime mover in such undertakings as the Eero Saarinen-designed War Memorial building on the lakefront, a fresh bold facility housing the Milwaukee Art Center. GMC also obtained new land west

* Maier alleged that the Milwaukee Journal Company, which has owned the *Journal* for almost a century (begun in 1882) and the *Sentinel* since 1962, enjoys a monopoly position in violation of anti-trust laws and should divest itself of the morning *Sentinel*. Ironically, 80 percent of the *Journal*, which also owns WTMJ radio and WTMJ-TV, the local NBC affiliate, is owned by its employees, not a single owner or family. The founder of the Milwaukee *Journal*, Lucius Nieman, incidentally, also bequeathed the funds to Harvard University that support the prestigious Nieman Fellowships for journalists.

of the city in which the Zoological Gardens could expand, so that Milwaukee now has one of the world's best zoos. The group was the force behind the $10 million raised by citizens for construction of the Performing Arts Center. In 1973, GMC spawned the Milwaukee Redevelopment Corporation (MRC), a limited profit corporation formed with $3 million seed money from 40 civic-minded stockholders interested in promoting growth downtown. It was the MRC, under the prodding of Francis Ferguson, president of Northwestern Mutual Insurance Company, which was the primary mover in the private sector behind the downtown retail center.

A genealogist would have a field day untangling the lines of intermarriage which connect Milwaukee's old German beer baron and industrial families—Uihlein, Pabst, Miller, Pritzlaff, Falk, Harnischfeger, Kopmeier, Nordberg, Friend, Gallun, Trecker, Bunder, and the like. They still represent a tight coterie of social control and possess great wealth, even though many of their corporations have gone public or been eaten up by the conglomerates. Milwaukee, caught geographically between the two great trade and transportation centers of Chicago and Minneapolis, never has developed into a regional capital with strength to maintain a high degree of local ownership. Its largest bank, First Wisconsin, ranks no higher than 52nd in the nation. There are exceptions, of course, such as Northwestern Mutual, eighth largest life insurance firm in the nation, and MGIC, the largest mortgage insurer in the country. The geographic factor of Lake Michigan on the east also has drawbacks. A shining exception to the trend of selling out is provided by the Uihlein family, which still owns Schlitz breweries and substantial interest in banks and real estate. The Uihleins disproved Milwaukee's reputation of stinginess in philanthropy by giving generously to the Performing Arts Center and spending—through Schlitz—some $300,000 a year for the Fourth of July parade featuring the circus wagons from the Circus World Museum of Baraboo.

Beer, while still consumed in vast quantities, no longer is the giant it once was in Milwaukee's economy. In fact, decentralization and automation have reduced the payrolls of all the big breweries to the point where they account for only 2 percent of the beer city's total employment. Products like mechanical and electrical machinery and parts for automobiles now provide the mainstay of the economy. The completion of the St. Lawrence Seaway was long and eagerly anticipated by Milwaukee port officials. But the opening of the linkage to the Atlantic never produced the port traffic hoped for; now, cargo shipments from the port are barely more than a third of the 9 million tons handled annually 50 years ago. Up to the late 1970s, concern about holding land for potential port facilities placed a damper on potential lakefront recreational development. But opinions were changing rapidly, suggesting that Milwaukee—a city that already boasts miles of handsome parklike setting along the lake—might be able to convert even more, at the very heart of the city, to enhancement of the city's quality of life.

Of Suburbs, Madison, and Other Cities

The suburbs of Milwaukee have survived easily and generally prospered in recent times, notwithstanding the verbal onslaughts of Mayor Maier and the financial adjustments forced by what for them was a painful redistribution of state educational aids, based more on need than place of residence, instituted during Patrick Lucey's governorship.

The most affluent of the Milwaukee area elite migrated many decades ago to such rich Republican enclaves as Shorewood, River Hills, Fox Point, and Whitefish Bay along the North Shore. To the west of Milwaukee is suburban Waukesha County, Wisconsin's fastest growing area for the last two decades, with nearly a 25 percent spurt since 1970 (on top of a 46 percent increase during the 1960s). Initially, Waukesha county attracted staunch conservatives, including substantial John Birch Society activity. While the Birchers have slipped into obscurity and significant pockets of right-wing Republicanism remain, Democrats have made some tangible inroads. They at least field creditable candidates now, invariably win around 40 percent of the vote, and occasionally (as Patrick Lucey did in 1974) capture a majority.

One of the Milwaukee area cities sharply hurt by the state tax revisions of 1973 was West Allis (pop. 66,791), a heavily industrialized Milwaukee County suburb that is Wisconsin's sixth largest city and home of the state fair. Just to the west of Milwaukee is another upper middle class suburb, Wauwatosa (pop. 54,416), an older community which has experienced a small-scale outmigration of its own in the 1970s. To the south lie heavily Polish Catholic, conservative, and blue collar communities such as St. Francis (10,269), Cudahy (named after the meat packing family; 21,144), and South Milwaukee (22,673), as well as some of the more recently developed suburbs, Oak Creek (16,070) and Greenfield (30,250).

There are now 1.8 million people living in southeastern Wisconsin, heavily concentrated in Milwaukee and its suburban ring, but including also Racine (177,337), another industrial city with a significant proportion of blacks; Kenosha (125,808), home of a sizable Italian community, the main plant of American Motors, and the largest UAW local in the state; and Waukesha (50,572), once a tired county seat which has suddenly found itself in the midst of the urban sprawl movement.

The continued growth of much of the Milwaukee area was severely threatened during the mid-1970s after the State Department of Natural Resources (DNR) issued a moratorium on hooking up new customers to the area's sewer system, throwing developers and other growth advocates into a panic. Treatment facilities for the Milwaukee Metropolitan Sewerage District were already overloaded, causing frequent spillages of raw sewage into Lake Michigan, especially when heavy rains overflowed the connecting storm sewer system. The cost of modernizing Milwaukee's sewage treatment facilities to full DNR standards would nearly bankrupt the sewerage district, but the action served to prod it in the direction of compliance. The DNR relaxed the moratorium later, but only after eliciting promises of developing plans that ultimately would meet the water quality standards most of the other major cities in the state were already maintaining.

Few American state capitals can even start to compete with the multi-splendored attributes of Madison, Wisconsin. The town offers lake-studded beauty, the university's intellectual stimulation and vitality of oft-clashing ideas, white collar economic vigor, and a fair dash of cosmopolitan attitudes. With all this, one also finds a certain small-town intimacy. The 280-foot-high Vermont granite State Capitol (with an 18-foot gilded statue of Miss Forward at its crest) is unique for its four identically shaped wings spreading out from a magnificent central dome. The Capitol, set in the midst of a land-scaped, four-square-block park, is set on the high ground of a narrow isthmus between Lakes Mendota and Monona. (City ordinances prohibit any building in the area of the State Capitol to be taller than the base of the dome, assuring that modern developments do not block out the towering beauty of the structure.) Employment by the state government, the University of Wisconsin (located exactly one mile to the west of the Capitol on the shores of Lake Mendota), and a scattering of research firms made Madison one of the fastest growing Midwestern cities during the postwar years, mushrooming the county's population from 130,000 in 1940 to 250,000 in 1970. While the area continued to grow during the 1970s, the city's populace stabilized around 168,000.

Madison is set in Dane County, the cradle of Wisconsin Progressivism by virtue of LaFollette's birth on a farm in the nearby town of Primrose. The county remains the most liberal in Wisconsin; it gave a solid 59 percent of its vote in 1972 to McGovern and Shriver over Nixon and Agnew and in 1976 reluctantly supported Jimmy Carter after all their favorite liberals had been overwhelmed. The university has been the well-spring for liberal and even radical thought for generations. But part of the credit for this pulsating brand of liberal activism also must go to the Madison *Capital Times*, founded in 1917 by William T. Evjue, whom John Gunther precisely described as "one of the last of the great line of salty, individualistic liberal editors that once distinguished the Middle West." Evjue imbued his paper with almost a messianic attitude, proclaiming its editorial positions as the public will and all those who doubted it as public enemies. True to the LaFollette Progressive line, Evjue proselytized that all politicians were corrupt, all lobbyists were suspect, all attempts to build or control power were evil. The paper's unorthodox, shrill stance as "protector of the people" profoundly influenced the political climate during its first half-century of existence. More recently, however, it is viewed with more tolerance than appreciation, considered by many a journalistic anachronism which has failed to keep abreast of the times. Some insiders have predicted that if the *Capital Times'* circulation ever dipped below 40,000, its days were limited. In 1978, in the midst of a strike against it and its morning counterpart, *The Wisconsin State Journal* (circulation 73,000 daily; 120,000 Sunday), the *Cap Times* slipped under 40,000. The strike against the two papers and the company that prints them badly undercut the *Cap Times'* liberal reputation. Within a few weeks of the strike in October 1977, the *Cap Times* hired replacements, raising cries of hypocrisy against the paper. Early in 1979, the two papers finally settled with their reporters on strike—though most still out didn't get their jobs back.

One other media source has helped perpetuate Wisconsin's and Madison's liberal image, the *Progressive Magazine,* founded in 1909 by Old Fighting Bob LaFollette himself. It has had its ups and downs over the years, and had about 40,000 circulation in 1979. That was just before it became a *cause célèbre* when a federal court issued an injunction against the magazine's publication of an article about hydrogen weapons, including how bombs are put together. The U.S. Justice Department sought the injunction on the grounds the article contained "restricted data" that would damage national security. The case marked the first time in the history of the country that the courts had infringed on freedom of the press to stop publication of an article.

Madison elected a "radical-boy-mayor" in 1973, Paul Soglin, a former student antiwar activist and city council member. Conservative doom-saysers portrayed the 28-year-old Soglin as a radical intent on destroying Madison for the "decent people" and ready to push the remains into the lakes. Soglin proved to be neither so radical as some expected (he lost support of some of his student supporters) nor as boyish as his years would have suggested. When he left office in 1979, he had revitalized the city bus system, pushed through a major State Street mall and Capitol Concourse project, and ended a 25-year stalemate over where to build a downtown civic auditorium. Befitting Madison's intellectual ferment, the auditorium issue was emotionally tied up in a struggle between foes and proponents of Frank Lloyd Wright, the renowned and politically liberal architect who lived much of his later life at Taliesen, his home and school near Spring Green, a community a half hour's drive west of Madison. Wright at one time designed an auditorium to overlook Madison's downtown Lake Monona, but his enemies blocked the plan—and in the process thwarted every other alternative from the early 1950s until Soglin took office. Soglin abandoned Wright's auditorium on the lake, negotiated to buy and renovate a theater on State Street, and accomplished what his less liberal predecessors had failed to do. The cost of renovations far overshot estimates, and the project encountered many delays, but they were nothing compared to the 25-year wrangle over what to do. The auditorium opened in early 1980.

Economically, Madison is virtually depression-proof; the bulk of jobs come from the state government and the university, neither of which pare back much in hard times. In the private sector, the city has more home-based insurance companies per capita than any other city save Hartford, Conn. It could be argued that Madison, like Austin, Texas, Berkeley, Calif., Boulder, Colo., and some other cities experimenting with "radical" governments could easily afford to do so because they didn't face the harsh economic realities of more economically exposed (and less publicly supported) towns.

Outside of Milwaukee and Madison, the heaviest populations and strongest economic growth are found in the Lake Michigan cities, the Fox River Valley, and the Wisconsin River Valley. We mentioned Racine and Kenosha earlier, both heavily unionized manufacturing centers. To them must be added Sheboygan (pop. 48,371), famous for its tangy bratwursts, and Manitowoc (32,957), a significant shipbuilding center. All the Lake Michigan cities are ethnic polyglots and overwhelmingly Democratic. The Fox River Valley in northeastern Wisconsin—including Green Bay (pop. 89,289), Appleton (56,158), and Oshkosh (50,259)—is equally ethnic but of a different mixture, more German, more Catholic, and decidedly more conservative.

Green Bay, home of a dozen paper mills that still emit layers of sulfur fumes over downwind residents, grew with the late-arriving immigrants, the Dutch, the Poles, and Bohemians, in addition to the Germans. What practically all Americans know Green Bay for is its professional football team, the Packers (winners of the first two Super Bowls and assorted other honors). Virtually the only blacks in town play for the Packers, giving them an acceptance they might not find in other small towns, and making Green Bay perhaps the only city in America where the earnings of blacks average more than that of whites. As a Great Lakes port city, it's not unusual to hear a multitude of foreign languages on Green Bay's streets whenever sailors disembark from their ships. Green Bay now has a graduate-level campus of the University of Wisconsin, with a curriculum uniquely designed around its special mission of ecological studies. St. Norbert's College, the Catholic institution where Fr. Robert Cornell teaches after serving two terms in Congress, is in nearby DePere.

Appleton, at the other end of the lower Fox, likewise is a paper mill town. Actually, Appleton is just part of the Fox Cities, a collection of cities, villages, and towns that add almost 90,000 more to the population strung out up and down river. Appleton, though, is the economic as well as the cultural heartbeat of the Fox Cities. It boasts a small but first-class liberal arts university, Lawrence, which was headed by Nathan Pusey before he went to Harvard and later by Curtis W. Tarr before he succeeded Gen. Lewis B. Hershey as director of the Selective Service System in the waning days of the Vietnam War. Appleton also holds some distinction for being one of the few cities across the country that have been able to keep a viable downtown shopping area. Its main shopping area still straddles seven blocks of College Avenue, a clean, landscaped, and prosperous area that until now has held its own against the fringe shopping areas. But as 1979 drew to a close, one major department store, despite vehement protests from the mayor, was threatening to foresake downtown Appleton for a mall planned on the outskirts of town. If other stores follow, the city's retailing could be severely eroded.

Both the Appleton *Post-Crescent* and Green Bay *Press-Gazette* are second only to the Milwaukee and Madison papers in circulation, and for years their coverage of the State Capitol through their veteran correspondent, John Wyngaard, rivaled the big-city competitors. They are generally conservative, as one might expect, but cast off the far-right image associated with one-time favorite son, Joseph McCarthy. Oshkosh (pop. 50,259), a few miles south of the shore of Lake Winnebago, is a strait-laced town, still old-fashioned in many ways. Its dull old-line newspaper, the *Daily Northwestern*, was challenged in the late 1960s by a bright, well-financed upstart, *The Paper*, owned by the Miles Kimball family of the mail order business. But *The Paper* discovered that not even high-quality offset printing, superb use of pictures, a fresh approach by a talented staff—and a reported $5 million in five years—was enough to seriously dent the doughty *Northwestern*. At the end of five years, it threw in the towel. But the brief competition forced the *Northwestern* to alter its stodgy vertical style make-up, even if Oshkosh natives, like so many other small-town Wisconsinites, insisted on the status quo.

The Wisconsin River Valley in the central part of the state encompasses three counties with significant growth rates (10–17 percent) during the 1970s, even though their major cities have remained static. Wausau (pop. 33,164) is the largest, followed by Stevens Point (23,631), home of Sentry Insurance and the UW campus formerly headed by Lee Dreyfus, Wisconsin Rapids (18,361) and Marshfield (17,290). As along the Fox, paper mills line the Wisconsin River in this area, providing both the major industrial lifeblood as well as a significant amount of despoliation of the waters. Clean-up orders by the DNR have curtailed the pollution and helped restore the waterway to better ecological health. Beyond the river as it winds southward are the farms, mostly dairying operations in the north around Wausau and sizable truck farms (especially potatoes) in the south around Stevens Point.

Over in the western part of the state are the Mississippi River towns of LaCrosse (48,332), probably the most rigidly conservative large city in the state, and Eau Claire (47,364), almost as Democratic as LaCrosse is Republican. Both have major UW campuses and a sprinkling of industry (including the nation's seventh largest brewer, Heileman's in LaCrosse).

The Northwoods

North of a line from Green Bay to Hudson on the St. Croix River lie the Northwoods of Wisconsin, geographically, politically, and economically distinct from the rest of the state. Here is where the first French explorers and trappers trekked through the majestic virgin forests and canoed the beaver-laden streams and rivers. The early pristine wilderness has long since been mindlessly plundered; yet huge expanses have been replanted. Most of the state's 450,000 acres of forests are in northern Wisconsin, as are two expansive national preserves, the Chequemegon and Nicolet National Forests. The woods, coupled with the thousand of lakes and streams, draw vacationers and outdoorsmen alike to the region's pacific beauty and contribute a significant part to the state's $2.5-billion-a-year tourist and recreational industry. Until the last decade, when state regulations closed them up, town dumps provided one of the major Northwoods attractions: bears scavenging for food in the dumps.

In contrast to the beauty of the region, the politics of the Northwoods often resembles the Western frontier of 100 years ago—abrupt, aggressive, parochial, and sometimes even vindictive. Local politics can assume a venal character more akin to Chicago or Gary than Milwaukee or Madison. The northern counties are notorious for sending mavericks to Washington or Madison, usually elected as Republicans but bolting party ranks whenever personal whim or advantage or local pressures (which are frequent) demand it. One northern state legislator in the late 1970s, after serving three terms, renounced his Republican Party and joined the Democrats; he won reelection easily. The senate Republican minority leader, Clifford Krueger of Merrill, was a former Progressive, and many counties in the Northwoods harbor the traditional Progressive sentiments that make party less important than the personality or issue of the moment.

The largest city of the Northwoods is Superior (pop. 29,424), perched on the westernmost point of Lake Superior, just across the St. Louis River from Duluth, Minn. Superior's port facilities, combined with those of Duluth, are the second largest on the Great Lakes, behind only Chicago. More than 32 million tons of grain (Superior has the biggest grain elevator in the world), iron ore (mostly from the Minnesota iron range), and other products are shipped from its docks every year, more than Detroit, Toledo, Indiana harbor, or Cleveland, and far more than the 3.5 million tons passing through the port of Milwaukee. The iron ore excavated from Wisconsin soil has all but been depleted (except for a low grade ore called taconite), but the 1970s saw a new breed of miner scouring the Northwoods. This time, the object of their quest was copper and zinc. The Exxon Corporation announced in 1976 it had discovered in Forest County a copper lode that it estimated could be among the 10 largest in North America. Kennecott was developing another copper mine further west, near Ladysmith. Many other mining companies were close behind, but the actual development of the new-found mineral wealth could be far off. The state, sensing the potential revenue lodestone, quickly revised its mining tax laws and increased the levies the mining companies would have to pay the state and local governments, as well as made sure stringent controls were in place, true to Wisconsin's progressive traditions. Exxon and Kennecott fought the changes furiously but to no avail. Afterwards, the corporations said the added tax and regulations might not allow them to develop and mine the copper, although state officials noted the declining world copper market also had a bearing in their decision to postpone actual development. The issue also generated another typical schism between the Northwoods communities and the state government in Madison. The northern natives have long felt Madison ignored them and their economic needs, and the imposition of the mining controls and the subsequent cooling of the copper fever only exacerbated the attitudes.

The post-World-War-II economic decline of the Northwoods region has contributed to the political isolation from Madison. The economic erosion may be changing, according to William Bechtel, federal cochairman of the Upper Great Lakes Regional Commission, which includes northern counties in Wisconsin, Michigan, and Minnesota. "The 1970s have clearly established a pattern of 'turnaround' throughout this once depressed region," Bechtel said. "Measured in terms of various demographic, economic, and social indicators, this region is experiencing a dramatic economic and social recovery." Where population declines were the rule since the end of World War II, the 1970s saw only one county—Ashland (off 2.8 percent)—continuing that trend. Eleven other counties could boast of increases of 10–12 percent, while one (Vilas) grew more than 20 percent. A study by the Population Studies Center of the University of Michigan showed outmigration patterns had been reversed, and that growth was faster than in both the three-state area and the country as a whole. Unemployment, however, still remained a problem. Brightening the economic picture were the new jobs created in the Northwoods counties—more than 80,000 since 1970—and the increase in manufacturing payrolls—63 percent compared to 49 percent nationally. One amazing thing about the shift to the Northwoods country, according to Bechtel, was the apparent noneconomic motives. "It's an antimetropolitan move," he told us in an interview. "People traditionally have followed the economy, but this isn't so any more. They're moving [to the northern counties] whether or not they have a job." For the ecologically minded citizens, the new migration raises a host of gnawing concerns about the nature of growth, where it occurs, how it is planned—or not planned—and the impact it will have on the fish and wildlife, the pristine forests and waterways that made the Northwoods attractive in the first instance.

Northern Wisconsin remains the home for more than 10,000 Native Americans, most of them Chippewas, Menominees, Oneidas, and Winnebagos living on 11 reservations. An almost equal number of Indians live in urban Wisconsin settings, many in Milwaukee. The largest reservation is that of the Menominees, located within an hour's drive northwest of Green Bay. In 1954 the Menominees became the subject of a 20-year federal experiment that would fail abjectly. Congress terminated the Menominees' status as a tribal reservation, as part of a project to see if Native Americans could survive without the dependency on the federal government that had come to be associated with reservation status. Throughout the 1960s, Menominee County struggled. Its primary resources were its 221,549 acres of tribal-owned land that produced the trees for its tribal-owned sawmill, and patchwork assistance from the state government. But three days before Christmas in 1973, the experiment was officially acknowledged as unsuccessful and Menominee County reverted to reservation status, wards of the federal government. The Menominees (2,300 of them live on the economically destitute reservation) have long been a free-spirited and very democratic nation. A woman, Ada Deer, was head of the ruling tribal council during much of the agonizing early 1970s, a time of severe (but not unusual) factionalism among the Menominees. One manifestation of the conflict occurred early in 1975, when 40 members of the Menominee Warrior Society, a faction opposing Ms. Deer's clique, seized an abandoned 64-room religious abbey just outside the reservation and demanded it be given to the tribe. For 34 days, they stayed barricaded in the aging mansion, while the mobilized National Guard stood watch outside. Tensions between the Indians and the white community in nearby Shawano, often racial-tinged in the best of times, were strained to the breaking point. Eventually, the Warriors surrendered and the religious order owning the abbey turned the title over to the tribe.

The Last Word

When every major aspect of Wisconsin's life has passed in review, one remains still impressed—almost overwhelmed—by the state's insistence that government and politics can and should mirror that elusive reality, the "public good." But can this be "for real"? Can Wisconsin government be *that* clean? Do the state's people feel theirs is truly the "good life," something superior to almost all other states of this Union?

We have traveled throughout those other states, from Maine to Hawaii, from Florida to Alaska. And along the way, we have discovered not a few communities and even states with ideas similar to the "Wisconsin Idea." But few others—Minnesota, Vermont, Washington, and Oregon spring to mind as possible competitors—so often *realize* their high expectations.

But what do the people of Wisconsin say? For that, we turn to a public opinion survey, vintage late 1978, conducted by Peter Hart Associates for the Madison-based Wisconsin Center for Public Policy (a nonprofit research center that focuses on practical politics and government policymaking). The Center's survey was part of a series it has conducted to maintain an accurate assessment of the political pulse and attitudes of Wisconsin's citizenry. The poll showed that a surprisingly high percentage of Wisconsin citizens—59 percent—felt that the state was heading in essentially the right direction. Only 26 percent felt it was on the wrong track. Compared to other states, Wisconsin's livability also drew remarkably positive answers. Thirty-three percent considered it one of the best, another 35 percent ranked it above average, 27 percent just average, only 2 percent below average.

Hope for the future was also buoyant, with 32 percent of the statewide sample anticipating Wisconsin would be a better place to live in for five years into the future and only 12 percent expecting the state to deteriorate. Predictably, the people considered taxes Wisconsin's biggest problem (35 percent). But in keeping with Wisconsin tradition, the issue of second greatest concern was the environment (12 percent).

Yet as if to prove once again their maverick streak and the fact that they are not quite the liberals outsiders so often assume, exactly one half of the persons polled said they would vote for a California-like Proposition 13 to reduce taxes radically. Only 19 percent said they would oppose such a proposal.

Confident about their own civilization, expecting a great deal from it, believing in their way of life, doubtful about paying the bill, willing to upset established orders—these are the Wisconsinites. In this state, where the public will loom so large in the tradition of how things are done, it seems appropriate to let the public have the last word.

MICHIGAN

AUTO EMPIRES AND UNIONS

THE STATE OF MICHIGAN is the keystone of the Great Lakes. The waters of Lakes Michigan, Superior, Huron, and Erie wash up against her shores along a coastline 3,121 miles in length (greater than any other state save Alaska). And the Straits of Mackinac, separating Lake Huron from Lake Michigan, in fact divide Michigan into two separate geographic entities, also a distinction among the states.* So separate is the Upper Peninsula that many of the natives periodically feel isolated and without responsive representation in Lansing. At these times, a secession movement gathers short-lived momentum in the Upper Peninsula, spreading publicity about the ignored needs; but few south of the Straits of Mackinac take the idea of a 51st state seriously.

But it is not the division of Upper Peninsula and Lower Peninsula, so apparent from the map, which really divides Michigan. (In fact, the two since

* The sheer physical size of Michigan warrants notice; the distance from Ironwood on the Upper Peninsula to Detroit, for instance, is 595 miles—more than the distance from Detroit to New York City. Another oddity: Ironwood is west of St. Louis; Port Huron is east of Greenville, S. C.

1957 have been joined by the graceful five-mile span of the Mackinac Bridge.) Michigan is like Caesar's Gaul—really three parts:

Across the whole of the Upper Peninsula and the northern half of the Lower Peninsula is a vast expanse of wooded hills, lakes, and resorts, a territory shorn of its virgin forests by the lumber barons of yesteryear. This is a land of depleted mines, of poor soil, and few inhabitants. Even with a quarter of the land mass of the state, the Upper Peninsula's 315,000 people account for less than 4 percent of the state's population. But the 1970s saw a population explosion of sorts in the northern half of the Lower Peninsula—with 17 of 27 counties increasing more than 20 percent.

Spread throughout the southern half of the Lower Peninsula are rich fruit and dairy farms and quiet towns and villages whose frame houses and steepled churches evoke the spirit of the New England and New York pioneers who first settled there. Here, too, there are few people.

Finally, there is industrial Michigan—bustling, materialistic, seat of one of the greatest industrial and labor empires ever developed by man but now threatened by overseas competition and the changing world energy picture. It thrives in bruised but still brawny Detroit and smaller carbon copies like Flint, Lansing, Grand Rapids, Saginaw, and Muskegon, all in southern Michigan. Three quarters of Michigan's 9,104,000 people live here. So do the wealth, the power, and the principal troubles of the state today. Industrial Michigan and its great hallmarks—the automotive behemoths, the sinewy and socially conscious United Auto Workers, and "programmatic," issue-oriented politics— are the essential Michigan story. First we will examine those phenomena, then state government, then the plight of the Michigan cities and suburbs.

The Auto World

The history of the auto industry is littered with the wrecks of the 2,000-odd makes once introduced but eventually doomed to extinction in one of the world's most fiercely competitive industries. Such illustrious makes as Duryea, Mercer, LaSalle, Pierce Arrow, and Stanley Steamer succumbed long before World War II, and later years have seen the demise of such once great stalwarts as Packard and Hudson. The only firms of any consequence surviving are General Motors, Ford, Chrysler, and American Motors. As the 1970s ended, grave questions were seriously raised whether Chrysler and possibly even Ford could avoid the fate of the illustrious Pierce Arrow and Stanley Steamer without an infusion of federal dollars. The auto industry found itself entering the 1980s confronted, to a certain extent even confounded, by forces seemingly beyond its control. The Arab oil cartel controlled the price of oil (increasing it more than 50 percent in 1979 alone), and thus threatened the steady supplies of gasoline. The Japanese, with lower wages and higher productivity, were far ahead of Detroit in producing the smaller fuel-efficient cars that had severely eroded the U.S. industry's reliance on more

profitable big cars. On another front the success of the United Auto Workers (UAW) in representing the monetary interests of their members also drove costs upward. With the cost of labor standing at 34 percent of revenues in 1980 (compared with less than 30 percent in 1965), management presented a posture of hopelessness. Without a doubt, the turbulent events of the 1970s left the industry reeling: even after the traditionally conservative corporate managers concluded they were dealing with something more than a passing fad, they were technically restrained by the three-to-four-year time frame needed to redesign, retool (at a cost of billions during times of high interest rates), and replace their large cars with the smaller ones in demand. On top of it all, the rippling impact of all these problems no longer could be considered just a nemesis affecting Detroit. All four of the car-makers have their headquarters in Detroit or its suburbs, although American Motors, a feeble fourth in the industry with only 3 percent of GM's 1977 output, in fact has no actual Michigan production. Assembly plants have spread increasingly across the continent in the postwar period; now 33 percent of automobiles and trucks produced roll off Michigan production lines, with Missouri, California, Ohio, and Georgia among the other leading states with assembly locations.

It would be easy to raise the specter of an industry's death in surveying what the 1980s may hold for the automakers. But as the *National Journal's* Robert J. Samuelson astutely noted in the spring of 1980:

America's love affair with the automobile has been declared dead so many times that anyone writing about the car's future is almost honor bound to stick with the same metaphor. Well, the love affair may be dead, but the marriage isn't. Divorce is out of the question, and recent events widely deplored by Americans—higher gasoline prices and occasional gasoline lines—have probably improved the union's prospects considerably. . . . But the ultimate significance of the marriage between Americans and their cars is not defined by Detroit's health so much as a simple statistic: about 85 percent of all travel in the United States is by auto.

General Motors is one of the most gigantic industrial corporations the world has ever seen. For years, it ranked as the largest corporation, but the energy problems of the 1970s curtailed sales and profits, so it followed Exxon for a few years on the list of largest industrial corporations, only to surge ahead again in 1977 with record-high sales. On its global payrolls were 850,000 men and women* at 121 plants in 21 states and more than 60 cities in the United States. In 1977, its sales were almost $55 billion, its tax bill $4.7 billion, and its profits $3.3 billion—more than any industrial corporation. Its vulnerability, however, to the nation's economic vicissitudes was reflected by the fact it dramatically cut its dividend to stockholders after an unnerving first quarter in 1980, during which domestic car sales slumped. Traditionally, GM has had a resiliency and adaptability that has allowed it to bounce back significantly after each of the economic downturns of the 1970s. The firm's gross still is twice as large as the budget of any of the states and its profit is, in fact, larger

---

* Only eight cities in the United States have more population than GM has employees: New York, Chicago, Los Angeles, Philadelphia, Houston, Detroit, Baltimore and Dallas.

than the total budget of three-fifths of the states. Aside from producing about half of the passenger autos of the United States (Chevrolet, Buick, Oldsmobile, Cadillac, Pontiac), GM has gigantic divisions producing trucks, buses, refrigeration equipment, diesel motors, marine engines, aircraft engines, earthmoving equipment, inertial navigation systems, and space components. The corporation is the tenth largest military contractor, but so large are its total operations that military and space work account for only 3 percent of its total sales.

From a corporation with such immense national and international power, one can fairly demand innovative leadership not only in technological breakthroughs and advanced planning in its own field of vehicle manufacture, but in social and political fields as well—areas in which General Motors has been shockingly negligent over most of its history. Not only has it failed to lead, but it has often been a poor follower. Smugness and complacency were long the hallmarks of its executive leadership; critics were to be dismissed as unworthy of consideration, because GM knew what was right. The nation got a brief glimpse of this in the Senate Armed Forces Committee hearings on the nomination of GM president Charles E. Wilson to the post of Secretary of Defense in the Eisenhower cabinet, when Wilson uttered his famous line: "What is good for the country is good for General Motors, and what's good for General Motors is good for the country." The problem was that GM, neither then nor for many years afterward, had a single person among its 600,000 to 700,000 employees specifically assigned to looking far ahead and seeing what GM and the entire auto industry could and should be doing to meet conditions in a changing world—the safety, size, and ultimate disposal problems of automobiles, their impact on cities and the natural landscape, the potentiality of exerting a creative and positive impact on the development of governmental policies all the way from Detroit to the international scene. GM waited until 1978, for instance, to initiate any significant civic action, a neighborhood rehabilitation project on the back doorstep of its corporate headquarters in Detroit.

The problems of auto safety, for example, were known long before Ralph Nader came on the scene. And, in fact, some inventive people in GM would develop new safety features and the styling staff might sell them to the engineers, but when they got to the car divisions, the general managers would veto the ideas, saying that "this safety stuff won't sell." Apparently the basic policy issues were never brought to their proper forum—the GM board of directors. Yet since GM so dominated the industry, it was incumbent on it to lead; the other companies, competitively, were simply in no position to take risky initiatives.

GM's insistence, again with the rest of the industry tagging along, that the American public demanded large cars powered by high-horsepower, low-mileage engines, provides another example of GM-style leadership. The big car trend was throttled only by the convergence of three external forces—pressure by the federal government, higher gasoline prices prompted by the

Arab oil embargo, and the encroachment of smaller foreign imports on the American market. After the rapidly rising sales of Japanese and European cars in the 1970s disproved the industry's claims that Americans insisted upon big cars, GM, as well as Ford and Chrysler, belatedly decided to forego their more profitable big cars and settle for smaller margins on compacts. By then, though, even some auto insiders were admitting the industry had made some incredible miscalculations and bad decisions. Joseph Kraft, writing in early 1980 in *The New Yorker,* quoted one auto executive about the decision-making process in the board rooms of Detroit. According to the executive, the decision to downsize was a classic example of the way things change in the industry. The decision to downsize, he said,

> . . . may look obvious to outsiders, but it wasn't obvious to the auto indus-try—especially not to GM. To begin with, the auto companies aren't innovators. . . . The premium hasn't been on technological change. After about 1920, the premium was on mass production—on doing the same thing over and over again, always at a little less cost if possible. The penny-pinchers rose in the auto indus-try—especially at GM. Even when there were changes, they tended not to be changes in the basic product. They were changes in style and appearance, changes in fashion.

Reflective of its massive financial prowess, GM moved with its dollars out front when it finally did decide to downsize. Between 1974 and 1980, Kraft noted, the firm invested $20 billion in the changeover, a sum, inciden-tally, which Chrysler could not raise without the federal bailout it sought in 1979.

Indicative of GM's *modus operandi* is that it dispenses virtually no char-itable contributions on a national scale, but rather contributes in the local communities where its plants are located—and local good will can be ob-tained. Instructions to plant managers have run along these lines: Don't ini-tiate any movement to start something like a new hospital or YMCA building in your community. But if someone else initiates such an idea and comes to you for help, well, then give a nominal amount of assistance.

When General Motors did break with this noninitiative policy in 1978, its corporate leaders unveiled a $20 million proposal to rehabilitate homes, apartments, and businesses in a neighborhood just north of its Detroit head-quarters. The project, GM Board Chairman Thomas A. Murphy noted, was "far and away the most ambitious program of its kind that GM has initiated anywhere." Some skeptics in Detroit commented at the time that GM's share of the $20 million was only $1.2 million, that it came 11 years after Detroit's riots, and that it was the "most ambitious" only because the company had never recognized its social and civic responsibilities before. Others, especially in City Hall, saw the plan as a hopeful sign that General Motors now con-sidered Detroit a good place for making an investment, and perhaps it would serve as a catalyst for other neighborhood development by other private businesses.

In partisan politics, GM traditionally placed pressure on its employees on the senior bonus roll (those eligible for bonuses in addition to salaries) to contribute to the Republican party of Michigan. They received cards on which to record their contributions (in some years with the name of the Michigan GOP actually printed thereon) and were expected to send them not to the party but the business manager of their departments at GM. David L. Lewis, a former GM public relations officer and now professor of business history at the University of Michigan, explained that "the checks were then presented to the party and GM—not the donors—got the thanks." According to Stuart Hertzberg, treasurer of the Michigan Democratic party, "GM had no bipartisan contribution program until 1968, when we talked them into it. We didn't get a dime out of GM until then." After that, Hertzberg told the *National Journal*, GM employees had given about $2,000 a year to the Michigan Democrats and, based on state filings, between $100,000 and $200,000 a year to the Michigan GOP.

Yet, as unimaginative as GM may be in many aspects, the fact is that in areas of the most pressing social concern directly related to it—auto safety, pollution control, and minority hiring—it has begun to move forward. And being the biggest, it has become the inevitable top target of reformers—an effort institutionalized in 1970 under the Nader-inspired Campaign to Make General Motors Responsible. This "Campaign GM" began by focusing on GM's accountability in the fields of safety, pollution, and minority employment. The odd coalition of forces working within "Campaign GM"—ranging from students to churches, foundations, and universities—seemed at first blush to be repulsed. But it was not long after that GM announced a new "public policy committee" and elected Philadelphia's Reverend Leon Sullivan to the GM board, the first black man ever to sit on that august body. Seven years later, in discussing GM's management and production "turn-around," *Fortune* magazine concluded the public policy committee was more than public relations puffery. The opinions voiced in the committee were heard. New blood from outside the company—a radical break with past policy— also was infused at key junctures within the management structure, a fore- sighted move which some credit as being critical to GM's successful adjust- ments during the 1970s.

Yet old habits don't die immediately. When the government began to pressure the auto industry to achieve better gasoline mileage after the 1973 energy crisis, GM was among the first to suggest it could do so only if pollu- tion control standards were relaxed. The deadlines for some of the standards were delayed several times, but the industry also "discovered" better mileage could be accomplished by building less heavy—i.e., smaller—cars. Ironically, the early 1980s brought with them an air of optimism from Detroit that the 27.5 mile-per-gallon standard by 1985 indeed was not only possible but very likely to be met.

By the late 1970s, the average wage of GM workers was close to $15 an hour (including fringe benefits). But for financial remuneration the great prizes went to its top executives. Board Chairman Murphy drew $996,000 in salary, bonuses, and other fees in the record sales year of 1977.* The other gainers were 1,237,000 stockholders, living in every U.S. state and Canadian province plus more than 80 foreign countries. The bulk of the stock, however, has traditionally been held by a narrow group of U. S. banks plus insurance companies, foundations, universities, and retirement funds.

Old Henry Ford, the brilliant titan of the automobile industry, inventor of the assembly line, and introducer of the then revolutionary five-dollars-a-day wage in 1914, has been dead since 1947. But the Ford Motor Company, third largest U.S. industrial corporation with annual sales of $37.8 billion, retained to 1980 intensely personal, family-flavored leadership through chairman of the board Henry Ford II. This grandson of the founder, a callow youth of 28 when he took command in 1945, was, as *Time* commented in 1970, "perhaps the most psychologically secure chief executive in the U.S.," possessed of immense wealth, bearing the family name with its aura of power, the man to whom all major questions, suggestions, ideas, and issues in the Ford empire had to be brought for final decision. As Ford approached retirement, he also took an extremely active interest in the revitalization of Detroit. Recognized by the Detroit *News* in 1978 as one of the seven most influential men in metropolitan Detroit, Ford was the power broker and financial force behind the $350 million Renaissance Center complex that became the symbol of downtown development resurgence.

When Ford took over in the 1940s, it was only by forcing his aged grandfather to give up control of a financially troubled company that was losing $10 million a month; through sound fiscal management and the building of good relations with the United Auto Workers, Ford guided the company to its phenomenal postwar success. Through the same years, quiet but significant influence was also exerted by his mother, Mrs. Edsel Ford, who lived the life of a *grande dame* in Grosse Pointe Farms until her death in 1976.

That Ford is really still a family-held corporation was underscored once again in mid-1978 when Henry Ford reshuffled the executive leadership to assure a member of the family at the helm after his retirement. "When it gets down to a confrontation, it's still the family against the world," observed one company insider in the wake of the shifts. A month before, in a move with reverberations throughout the auto industry, Henry Ford had ousted his oft-flamboyant president, Lee A. Iacocca, a possible obstacle to continued family leadership. There were other factors in the firing of Iacocca—whom Henry Ford let go after 32 years with the curt explanation, "I just don't like you." Iacocca, according to *Monthly Detroit* magazine, had devised a plan to put Ford near the top of the small-car market in 1979. But Ford reportedly

* Even at that range, Murphy was not the highest paid auto executive. That prestigious reward went to Henry Ford II, who was paid $682,000 in salary and bonuses. But when his other fees were added in, he received $1,011,000. The compensation for the other auto maker chief executives reflect their companies' ranking in the industry. Chrysler's John J. Riccardo received a total compensation package of $443,000 that year, while Gerald C. Meyers, then chief executive at American Motors, was paid only $160,000, *Forbes* magazine reported. The deposed president of Ford, Lee A. Iacocca, jumped companies and became president of Chrysler late in 1978. According to the *Wall Street Journal*, "To land Mr. Iacocca, Chrysler had to agree to pay him several million dollars in cash and give him options on huge amounts of Chrysler stock."

denied the corporate funds necessary to finance the development and production of small Fords in America—what Iacocca later called "the greatest strategic error in 50 years at the Ford Motor Company." The result, financially, was near to disastrous for Ford—an estimated $1 billion 1979 loss in its North American division because the company simply didn't have small autos in sufficient quantity to compete with foreign manufacturers when the energy shortage hit again following the shutdown of oil exports from Iran. Ford was also having severe safety and quality problems with its product: it led the industry in mandatory recalls in 1978, was charged with (but finally acquitted of) reckless homicide in regard to its Pinto model, and agreed with the federal government in 1980 to warn consumers that 6 million Fords have had engine defects.

Iacocca's dismissal was followed by elevation of Ford's younger brother, William Clay Ford, into a "top policymaking position" in the firm, which "provides for the continuity of Ford family representation in the senior level of management," the chairman of the board stated. While William Clay Ford had been more closely identified with his ownership of the Detroit Lions and their move out of the city to the Silverdome in Pontiac, 25 miles to the north, there was no mistaking Henry Ford was moving to bolster the family heritage on the board. Even after he named Philip Caldwell in October 1979 as the new chairman of the board—the first non-Ford in that position in the company's history—it was generally assumed the hand of Henry Ford would not soon be lifted from the helm. Some close observers of company politics noted that Henry's son, Edsel B. Ford II, approaching 30 at the time, was serving his proper apprenticeship in the lower levels of management, and could well restore the name of Ford as head of the company in the not-too-distant future. An even greater appreciation of the extent of family control can be gained by examining the stock structure. Through the wills of old Henry and his son Edsel, a major chunk of Ford stock went to the Ford Foundation (avoiding the punitive 91 percent inheritance tax). But the Ford Foundation stock was nonvoting, so that effective control remained with the family through its own stock holdings in the firm. Even today, despite the millions of shares owned by outside investors, the Ford family still has effective control through its 40 percent weighted share of the voting stock.

Since World War II, nothing so unsettled the auto magnates of Motor City as the twin challenges from across the oceans—the energy crisis of 1973–74, instigated by the Arab oil embargo, and the Japanese and German encroachment on the American carmakers' share of the market. At the worst, no oil meant no gasoline, and no gasoline meant millions of cars on the road and on the drawing boards would become the dinosaurs of the 20th century. The worst didn't occur immediately, although gloom and doom spread throughout the industry during the mid-1970s. What did occur was bad enough, forcing upon the American consciousness the awesome implications of oil dependency. New car sales plummeted from the record 9,676,000 in 1973 to 7,454,000 in 1974, a staggering 23 percent drop-off. In 1975, domestic car sales decreased another 400,000. Profits shriveled even more: GM's $2.4 billion net income in 1973 sank to less than $1 billion in 1974, and Chrysler's balance sheet showed a net loss of $52 million that year. Inventories backed up, and so did the unemployment lines as massive layoffs followed, soaring to over 100,000 in the Big Three plants alone and thousands more as suppliers were forced to cut back employment too. The state of Michigan, to meet the crunch created in the unemployment offices, estimated it would have to hire 1,000 new workers to handle the claims. The recession and effect of the dramatic increase in foreign, small car imports in 1979–80 produced similar effects, both in profits (Chrysler and Ford both posted deficits while GM's profits plunged precipitously) and in employment (layoffs from the industry climbed past 250,000 early in 1980).

If the Arabs with their oil embargo didn't completely convince the Detroit automakers that Americans would give up their large, high-powered, gadget-laden, sleek cars, the Japanese, the Germans, the Swedes, and the other manufacturers of foreign imports cooled whatever may have been left of the ardor for the golden era of big cars. Traditionally, the foreign import share of the American auto market amounted to 15 percent. After the gasoline crunch, the import share of the market began creeping upward until by 1980 it was approaching 25 percent. In an industry where a single percentage point difference in sales translates into millions of dollars, the encroachment of the small imports sent a terrifying message to Detroit.

The industry would retool, would think small, would think high-mileage. It would be a slow process, since it ordinarily takes three or four years for a newly designed car to get from the drawing board to the highway. It was reflected in mileage figures: in 1973, passenger cars averaged 13.1 miles per gallon; three years later, that had edged upward to only 13.7 miles per gallon. But by 1977, the new breed of intermediates, compacts, and subcompacts were regularly rolling off the assembly lines. Adding impetus to the change-over was the Energy Policy and Conservation Act of 1975. That law set the standards for Detroit to aim for: 18 miles per gallon in 1978, 20 by 1980, and 27.5 miles per gallon by 1985. The acceptance of the switch to small cars also was evident in the long-range planning of the industry. Chevrolet General Manager Robert Lund said in 1978 that 7 out of every 10 Chevrolets sold in 1985 might well be compacts and subcompacts, compared with the 40 percent small car mix it was selling at the time. Even more to the point was the flat-out recognition by GM President Elliott M. Estes that his company, at least, could meet the 27.5-miles-per-gallon standard: "We're working on three or four scenarios for getting to 27.5 miles per gallon by 1985," Estes told *Fortune* magazine in 1978. "It's a problem now of economics—how can we do it for the least cost?" The attitude—in complete contrast to the industry's foot-dragging response to pollution control standards and earlier laments about mileage demands—was as remarkable as the hope it held out.

By the end of the decade, the future of the automobile industry seemed shakier than it had perhaps at any time past. Gasoline prices across the nation had soared beyond the dollar-per-gallon watermark, even as the Arab ministers predicted new increases in oil prices. In the years immediately following the Arab oil embargo of 1974, the American public turned to the highways in greater abundance than before. The Motor Vehicle Manufacturers Association reported that Americans traveled 74 billion more miles in 1978 than in 1976. And the miles traveled in 1976 by passenger cars alone already was 57 billion more than 1973. Not until the gasoline shortages and skyrocketing petroleum prices of 1979–80 did the demand curve slacken. Finally, a national consensus seemed to be brewing which recognized the permanence of rising gas prices and the need to foster more mass transit and other alternative transportation forms.

By 1979, however, Chrysler's future was clearly in serious trouble. The firm suffered a staggering $1.097 billion loss for 1979, and was expected to suffer another of $1.05 billion in 1980. Congress finally approved a loan guarantee plan to bail out the firm, involving $3.5 billion from a combination of private and government-underwritten loans. Yet there were many who wondered if Chrysler ever could recover fully—and some who were entertaining the same doubts about Ford.

The energy crisis-prompted dramas of the late '70s and the '80s joined a continuing saga of the Motor City's triumphs and failures. Those stories—of flashy fins, of Chrysler's ups and downs, of scrappy little American Motors and George Romney's now-prophetic assault on the "gas-guzzling dinosaurs" of the Big Three, and a myriad of other tales—could well fill chapters.

Yet it is perhaps best to forget the colorful specifics and say the obvious: that the endless stream of automobiles pouring out of Detroit and its satellite factories for the past two-thirds of a century has had an impact on Americans' everyday life second to no other modern invention save electricity. The dividends in mobility and convenience are simply stupendous, and the industry has given birth to others which themselves are giants of the modern American economy: petroleum, tires, road and superhighway construction. Without the automobile, we might well have remained an essentially rural nation.

Even preceding the '70s energy crisis, the U.S.A., as if in a great rush of horrified awakening, began to see the bane mixed with the blessing in what Detroit had wrought. Cars created problems as well as opportunities, and the public through the government demanded accountability. The problems:

SAFETY. Between 1950 and 1979, more than 1,300,000 Americans met their deaths in automobile accidents, a carnage far exceeding the battlefield casualties of all the wars the nation has ever fought (636,000 through Vietnam). Yet as recently as 1965, the official Detroit attitude had been that the culprit in all this was the driver behind the wheel, and that automobiles were as safe as they could be expected to be. "Safety doesn't sell," Ford executives used to say. But then, virtually singlehandedly, a young attorney named Ralph Nader changed the nation's mind on that subject. Nader's book, *Unsafe at Any Speed*, showed Detroit putting style, horsepower, comfort, and sales ahead of safety.

General Motors then committed a monumentally foolish act of the kind usually reserved for great heads of state. It put private investigators on Nader's trail (a deed to which it confessed), and at the same time Nader was approached by questionable women, harassed with late-night telephone calls, and questioned on his sex life, potential anti-Semitism, and professional competence by various private agencies. Called before a Senate committee, General Motors president James Roche was obliged to apologize to Nader before national television "to the extent that General Motors bears responsibility" for the harassment. (Later, Nader's invasion-of-privacy suit against GM was settled out of court for $425,000.)

The GM episode gave instant national exposure to Nader and his views. The first automobile and highway safety acts of American history sailed through Congress in a few months with scarcely a murmur of opposition.

Soon the federal government was requiring scores of safety modifications in new cars, ranging from seat belts and padded dashboards and windshield visors to collapsible steering columns.* Tire standards were also put into effect, causing some declines in the highway death rate. But not until the 55-miles-per-hour national speed limit imposed after the oil embargo of 1973–74 did the fatality rate fall precipitously. Slowly the auto makers accepted, grudgingly perhaps, but accepted nonetheless the fact that safety considerations had to be part of their decision-making. By the end of the 1970s, they were talking as if they had invented auto safety about the time Henry Ford the elder offered his Model T to the public, an ironic footnote to their obdurate attitude a decade earlier.

Whether cars actually were safer could be debated. Certainly, however, the industry no longer was able to ignore its responsibility for its product once off the assembly line. A vivid testimonial to the delayed-but-no-less-significant consequences of Nader's efforts were the periodic recalls of defective vehicles —the scourge of the auto industry in the 1970s. From 1966, when federal legislation took effect, to 1972, more than 36,000,000 domestic and foreign vehicles were recalled for repairs. The numbers mounted, with more than 12,000,000 recalled during each of 1976 and 1977. Of the 195 separate recall campaigns during 1977, only 16 were ordered by the National Highway Traffic Safety Administration (NHTSA). The rest were termed "voluntary." But the club which the NHTSA quietly wiggled behind its back undoubtedly prompted the industry to act first to avoid public hassles that might bespoil its self-conceived image.

POLLUTION. Late in the 1960s, Americans for the first time became concerned about the growing pollution of their air. And it was discovered that at least 60 percent of the pollutants in the atmosphere came from the internal combustion engine. By one estimate, automobiles spewed forth 8 percent of all particulates in the air (bits of solid matter, including lead), 42

---

* By 1971, one impartial Michigan source suggested, the industry effected or programmed about 85 percent of the safety features that can probably be expected. If the U. S. is really serious about reducing highway injuries and fatalities, it will have to crack down next on perennially careless drivers and people driving under the influence of alcohol.

percent of the nitrogen oxides (which give the air a brownish tinge and act as fertilizers, thus inducing harmful growth of algae in lakes and rivers when they settle from the atmosphere), 63 percent of the hydrocarbons (unburned fuel that helps cause smog), and 92 percent of the carbon monoxide (a lethal gas). In some cities' smog belts, auto emissions accounted for as much as 92 percent of the air pollution; each year American automobiles dumped 90 million tons of pollutants into the air (and potentially the lungs). GM vehicle-generated pollution alone was said to account for 35 percent of the total air-pollution load of the United States.

At one time, auto spokesmen blithely dismissed air pollution as the responsibility of car owners; for many of the postwar years, the industry regularly spent $1 million a year on pollution-control research, one tenth of one percent of what it spent each year to change over its models. A growing national cry of protest—and government pressure—made the industry change its mind. By 1970, the big four had in the test stage a total of 26 different cars powered by everything from steam, gas turbine, and electricity to the type of fuel cells used for moon spacecraft. President Nixon set a goal for production of a "virtually pollution-free" car in five years, but even he must have been surprised when Sen. Edmund Muskie's amendments were adopted to the 1970 Clean Air Act, requiring by statute a 90 percent reduction in exhaust pollutants by 1975 (with a possible one-year extension).

The cry emanating from the Motor City was "impossible," and it became more audible after the energy crunch hit. But lo, with only a year's extension, the industry almost accomplished the impossible. With no small amount of pride, the Environmental Protection Agency (EPA) called attention to the fact that emissions for 1976 model cars were 85 percent less than from those produced in 1968. Compliance did not come without use of the regulatory club. In 1973, Ford agreed to a $7 million fine by the government on charges of tampering with cars undergoing federal pollution control tests. The action, coupled with the drastic reductions in emissions after the industry insisted it couldn't be done, hurt the automakers' credibility. The astute auto executives learned a lesson, accepted the fact they would have to live with Washington-made decisions, and quietly softened the shrillness of their antiregulatory pronouncements. The last few steps toward complete compliance have been slower, with Congress and the EPA shoving back deadlines several times and indicating continued flexibility.

To another form of pollution—the thousands of auto graveyards which scar the American landscape from Maine to Los Angeles—no clear answer was in sight, despite the obvious possibilities (with the right technology) of reducing the hulks to basic materials for recycling through the industrial machine.

And finally, there is the noise pollution, the nemesis of all those living near the thousands of miles of freeways and boulevards. For those people, large-scale mass transit would be one solution, but not as long as America's love affair with the auto persists.

PROLIFERATION. With the vehicle population approaching 150 million and on its way to 200 million by the year 2000, there were increasingly difficult questions of where to put them all—especially in large cities, where the vehicle population growth is greater than the human population growth. Parking costs have skyrocketed into the billions; it costs, for instance, $4.75 to park an automobile in some downtown Detroit lots for half an afternoon, not to mention the astronomical rates in New York City and other major metropolises. The interstate highway system, built with government largesse to accommodate the automobile, will finally cover some 42,500 miles at a cost of $104.3 billion, devouring (with right of way) a territory equal to one and a half times the size of Rhode Island.

Yet Detroit, despite its inventive genius, took a head-in-the-sand attitude toward mass transit or intercity transportation up until the mid-1970s. Then it only paid token attention to the possibilities. Bus production did increase 39 percent in the decade 1968–78, while auto production was up 36 percent. But if Detroit no longer had its head in the sand, it had yet to show it was willing to devote sizable resources to mass transit needs.

RACE AND POVERTY. The automobile industry was one of the first in the United States to open wide-scale job opportunities for blacks, and high UAW-won wages have indeed created a stable class of homeowning blacks in the $18,000–$20,000 bracket with a real stake in society. Some plants, like Ford's River Rouge complex, have 50 percent black employment. But Detroit has more than its share of destitute blacks, and in the wake of the 1967 riots the auto industry began a determined effort to find jobs for the once-thought-unemployable black. Of the Big Three, Chrysler developed sensitivity in the hiring of blacks much earlier and more comprehensively than General Motors, and somewhat ahead of Ford. By 1971, some 35 percent of Chrysler's 150,000 employees and 10 percent of its foremen and high-ranking workers belonged to minority groups, the best record in the industry. The smallest of the Big Three also was the first to name a black man as plant manager, promoting Lowell Perry in 1973 to head its 1,800-employee Detroit Universal Division. Chrysler could also take credit for the biggest single government contract for training the hard core, and it was the only auto company to adopt a ghetto school, donating a completely stocked auto-repair shop. All of this is of special importance in Detroit, where Chrysler production so far outweighs that of its competitors that it is considered the home-town auto. Chrysler had another reason for being responsive to the black population. As Detroit's largest employer, with more than 80,000 men and women from the area on the payroll in 1977, it simply had more black employees.

But it was Ford that got the most headlines and showed the most imaginative approach in the immediate post-riot era. Henry Ford threw his full personal prestige behind minority hiring and became the first national chief of the National Alliance of Business to hire hard-core unemployables. In Detroit, Ford's company not only relaxed its old hiring criteria—a written examination and insistence that a new employee have no police record—but went into the ghetto to recruit new men, setting up special hiring locations to attract hard corers and instructing interviewers to screen "in" instead of screen "out." The program was spectacularly successful; the day Ford opened its ghetto employment offices, more than 2,000 men showed up to apply. In two years Ford hired 5,800 of the 7,800 men it interviewed at its inner-city locations, as well as thousands more who appeared at the plant gates. While absenteeism was higher, the actual retention rate among the hard core was just a little higher than that of other employees. The auto companies still have a long way to go in hiring a fair share of blacks in skilled trades or in management positions, but they are making a serious effort to go beyond mere tokenism.

The dearth of black dealerships has been a second sore spot. In 1969, for instance, blacks held only .008 percent of the 30,000 auto dealerships in the country, even though American blacks spent $3.8 billion for new and used cars in that year alone. For many years, Ed Davis, a Chrysler-Plymouth dealer in Detroit, was the only black new-car dealer in the U.S.A. Up to 1967, there was not a single GM dealership owned by a black in the United States. But then everyone "got religion" and a spate of new black dealerships opened under auspicies of all the big auto makers. Unfortunately, all the perils of doing business in the ghetto awaited—pilferage and theft, high insurance premiums, credit turndowns on about half the potential sales, lack of qualified black personnel as middle managers, and on top of it all, the recession that began in 1969. Several failed, including the lonely pioneer, Ed Davis. As late as 1978, many urban areas still didn't have a black dealership. When Indianapolis, for example, got its first black dealer in August 1978, the situation was so novel the mayor held a ceremony in city hall to announce it.

A POSTSCRIPT. By the end of the 1970s, a compelling question about the automobile industry was quite simply: How sincerely, how much had it changed from its old ways? Some observers were discouraged. "I don't see that they are any different," William Serrin, author of *The Company and the Union* and former Detroit newsman, told us in an interview. "They've done some things—like pollution controls—only because they were mandated." Social responsibility? Mixed, at best, Serrin argued. "What they give, they take away," he said, citing Ford's support of the Renaissance Center in Detroit while at the same time building a huge new shopping center in Dearborn named after his Ford Fairlane model.

Compelling arguments are found on the other side of the issue. David Lewis, former GM public relations official and now a business professor at the University of Michigan, believes the industry "really has come a long way in the last ten years, further in ten years, I suppose, in terms of the concept of social responsibility, than they've come in the previous seventy. Before they did only what they had to do and did it begrudgingly. Now, you see things like the Renaissance Center and GM's revitalization of the New Center area, which they really weren't required to do, but felt they should."

Prof. Eugene E. Jennings, a management professor at Michigan State and a close watcher of GM's hierarchy for 20 years, has likewise noted an outward attitude which is the antithesis of past policy. "In the late 1960s and the early 1970s, GM was one of the most insular and inner-directed companies around," he told *Fortune* magazine in 1978. "Now, more than any other company in the auto business, and more than most companies anywhere, it has moved up to a higher level of organizational effectiveness. It has learned how to be outer-directed and strategic—to use its head, rather than trying to use its clout."

In the political arena, however, other opinions were being heard. Republican presidential candidate Ronald Reagan, addressing the Detroit Economic Club in May 1980, warned: "The U.S. auto industry is being regulated to death. The auto industry remains the best in the world. It simply needs the freedom to compete, unhindered by whimsical bureaucratic changes in energy, environmental, and safety regulations."

The UAW: Powerful Engine of Change

Michigan has the most powerful labor movement of any state of the American Union. There are 1,255,000 union members—one of every 17 unionists in the U.S.A. Michigan factory workers have been so successful that their average weekly pay is 40 percent greater than the national average.

The Depression did a good job of turning auto workers to the left. In 1928, the booming industry turned out close to five million cars and there were 435,000 workers earning an average pay of $33 a week. Then came the massive layoffs. "These are really good times," Henry Ford said in March 1931, "but only a few know it." Five months later he shut down his plants, throwing 75,000 men out of work. The other manufacturers closed down as well, banks busted, and schoolmarms were paid in scrip. By 1933 the auto workers who still had jobs were earning an average of only $20 a week.

As the slow recovery began, so did the intensive organizing efforts of the unions, a chaotic process in which not a few Communist organizers were involved and the leading Detroit industrialists launched a campaign of murder, mayhem, and relentless intimidation of auto workers. Scarcely noticed at the time, but indicative of the hostility of the late 1930s, was a fracas on a Ford assembly line between a young black radical serving as an undercover union recruiter and a white company spy. A racial fight was provoked, and the black man slammed a 36-inch steel bar across the company man's head. Unconscious, the white man was carried out of the plant; the company fired the black man—but Coleman A. Young would return 30 years later as the first black mayor of Detroit.

In 1935 the chaotic plethora of early unions began to solidify in the United Automobile Workers, whose steep climb has been described as the "greatest surge forward of the underpossessed" in the history of industry. The National Labor Relations Act of 1935 required employers to bargain collectively with unions, and after breakthroughs with a number of smaller firms, the UAW in 1937 staged its great sit-down strike against General Motors at Flint and won recognition. Later that year, a similar sit-down strike broke Chrysler's resistance, and by the end of 1937 the UAW had contracts with 400 companies. But old Henry Ford refused to give in; Walter Reuther, for instance, would earn fame in the annals of labor industry as one of the organizers severely beaten by Ford's hired thugs at a confrontation on an entrance overpass at the River Rouge plant in 1937. But in 1941 Ford was finally obliged, following a short strike, to recognize the UAW, and in fact granted it the first union shop and dues checkoff in the industry. After that, the UAW's power grew rapidly and it has since been total master of unionism in the automobile (and now farm implement) field.

Walter Reuther was the central figure of the UAW's history and the most influential single trade unionist of the postwar era in America. Son of an old Socialist German brewery worker, Reuther was an expert tool and die worker at Ford in his early years. Even while he worked a full day at the plant, he worked his way through college. After Ford fired him for union activity in 1933, he took a magnificently educative 33-month trip around the world with his brother Victor, observing trade union activity everywhere. Part of the trip was through the Soviet Union, and Reuther's right-wing enemies would claim for years that the stay there proved his Communist leanings. The fact is that Reuther was always a Socialist, never a Communist, and in fact won the UAW presidency in 1946 after a decisive battle with Communist elements in the union.

Reuther was known as a pugnacious redhead in his younger years and never lost his superb organizing and tactical skills in dealing with the heavies of the auto industry. During his career, the UAW went from zero to 1.6 million members, replaced Henry Ford's prescribed five-dollars-a-day wages with more than five dollars an hour in average wages and benefits, and pioneered such innovations as profit sharing for workers, a cost-of-living escalator in contracts, a guaranteed annual wage for workers (in a formula including unemployment compensation benefits), management-paid pensions, and early retirement plans. There was a time in the 1940s and 1950s when Reuther was the most feared and hated of American labor leaders, called by George Romney "the most dangerous radical in America."

In resistance to Reuther, the big firms also sharpened their negotiating methods and, in fact, since 1958 have worked in perfect tandem in dealing with the UAW. Until Chrysler's 1979 troubles, contract negotiations were almost a matter of routine. After both sides presented and discussed their demands, the Big Three finally presented absolutely identical offers to the union at three locations—Chrysler at its Highland Park headquarters, General Motors at the GM building in Detroit, and Ford at Dearborn. One year the offers were so identical that they contained the same typographical errors. Union officials regret this industry solidarity, because, as one official relates, "in the old days the firms were fiercely independent and that was a great advantage for us because we could play one off against the other." Congress insisted in 1979 that the UAW give Chrysler some breaks, but the union kept the differences among the Big Three to a minimum.

The auto industry is blessed with an absolute minimum of featherbedding and has traditionally registered high levels of productivity. Pay and benefits aside, there is a limit to what the UAW can do to better the everyday working milieu for its membership. The man who spends his life at the monotonous, repetitive job of putting the left front wheel on 60 vehicles an hour can hardly be expected to value his job as a great privilege.*

Both union and company leaders acknowledge that with a work force younger, blacker, and better educated than twenty years ago, worker dissatisfaction with dead-end assembly-line jobs is increasing, as is the turnover on employment rolls. Younger workers think nothing of talking back to foremen, of turning down jobs they think might hurt their health or safety, or of staging wildcat strikes in defiance of their own union leaders. Absenteeism and the use of drugs are on the upswing, and contribute to the soaring recall rate of new vehicles.

Reuther's unusual contribution went beyond solid bargaining-table successes to the unique way he led his massive union. He believed in internal trade-union democracy, and the UAW became the most democratically run major union in America with such devices as an outside grievance procedure to which members can resort when they feel the union is treating them unfairly. Reuther fought hard to get black representation on the UAW board, and later to get a woman on the board as well.

And Reuther's horizons extended beyond traditional union concerns to broad social issues and politics. Following his death in 1970 in an airplane accident, the Washington *Post* editorialized that Reuther "left his imprint upon the social and economic life of the United States more indelibly, perhaps, than any political figure in his time, Franklin Roosevelt excepted. He was part labor leader, part social reformer, part evangelist." During his lifetime Reuther was often faulted for aggressive moralizing, but the fact was that his mind produced an almost endless stream of romantic, imaginative ideas. Some were amazingly farsighted, like his 1945 proposal to convert war plants to mass production of housing and transportation rolling stock (advice the country would have done well to accept). Others were simply a matter of a burning conscience—a dedication to racial equality and nonviolence, to aid for the poor, nuclear disarmament, better medical care and housing, and a cleaner environment. In retrospect, the "radical" tag opponents so often pinned on Reuther simply lacks credibility.

Reuther's leadership skills received national recognition in 1952 when the militant CIO (Congress of Industrial Organizations) chose him as its

---

* Automation, which came some years ago to the stamping and matching plants, reduces some of the most monotonous jobs—though, of course, it threatens jobs, too. GM made a major breakthrough in automating the assembly lines with robot welding machines and other labor-saving devices at its Vega plant in Lordstown, but paid a price. A 22-day strike in 1972 against the monotonous routine spawned widespread concern for boredom on the line, or "blue-collar blues," as it came to be known.

president. Only three years later, however, the CIO merged with the parent AFL (American Federation of Labor), the more conservative and craft-oriented organization from which it had split in the mid-1930s. Reuther became a vice president of the combined AFL-CIO and head of its seven-million-member Industrial Union Department. But he soon began to chafe at what he believed were a lack of devotion to social causes and an absence of the zeal and fervor of the earlier days of trade unionism on the part of the AFL-CIO president George Meany and the governing board of the combined unions. Reuther attacked the AFL-CIO for its unstinting support of the nation's Vietnam policy, for its connections with the Central Intelligence Agency, for alleged failures to organize hard enough in new fields such as technical, professional, and farm workers, for failing to avoid disruptive public-service strikes, and for failing to press hard enough for liberal ideas such as national health insurance.

Much of the fight was one of personalities—Reuther, scrappy and uncompromising, faced by Meany, authoritarian and oriented to past policies as any man in his seventies is likely to be. In 1968 the final break came and the UAW was no longer part of the AFL-CIO.

Within Michigan, the UAW's splitoff splintered the labor movement's once unified political effort. August Scholle, veteran AFL-CIO chief for the state, lost 60 percent of his membership at one fell swoop. ("Gus got sawed off at the knees," one old labor reporter told us.) Of the million-plus union members in Michigan today, the UAW has 500,000, another 270,000 are associated with the regular state AFL-CIO and the remainder are Teamsters * or independent.

Reuther never groomed a single successor during his quarter of a century as UAW president. On his death, the presidency went not to the man some believe he might have preferred—Douglas Fraser, the personable and humane man who headed the union's Chrysler division—but rather to another 35-year veteran of organizational work within the UAW, GM division chief Leonard Woodcock. Some of the "liberals" in UAW leadership circles feared Woodcock might be too centrist for their taste, but Woodcock appeared to surprise them pleasantly, in his first year in office, by showing sensitivity in working with black, Mexican, and student committees, in strong opposition to the Vietnam war. William Serrin, formerly with the Detroit *Free Press* and author of a book on the 1970 auto workers' strike, *The Company And The Union*, reported that "there are those in Detroit labor circles who will say, privately, that [Woodcock} surpasses Reuther in several areas: intellect, ability to analyze problems, and ability to speak quickly and concisely." But clearly, he lacked Reuther's charisma.

As fate would have it, the UAW was headed into contract negotiations at the very moment that Reuther died, and General Motors had already made

* The Teamsters were expelled from the AFL-CIO in 1957 after congressional investigations had disclosed ties with gangsters and misuse of union funds by its officers. It is widely assumed but still unproven that Mafia connections were behind the July 1975 abduction and presumed murder of ex-Teamsters president James Hoffa, last seen leaving a suburban Detroit restaurant.

it clear it would take a stiff stand against runaway labor costs and, if need be, endure a long and costly strike in 1970. As if to prove his manhood and leadership mettle, Woodcock decided to call the first strike against GM since a 119-day strike Reuther had led in 1945. (In the intervening years, Ford and Chrysler had been struck, but never the massive GM complex.) Had Reuther lived, there is no way of telling how the 1970 strike might have turned out. But as the scenario was finally played out in 1970, GM—perhaps anxious not to trigger a rank-and-file revolt in the UAW that might lead to prolonged turmoil in the industry—agreed to a very costly (and potentially inflationary) package including an immediate 51-cents-an-hour raise, improvements in the early retirement plan, and restoration of the landmark cost-of-living plan which had been partially bargained away in 1967. The benefits were more than triple what Reuther had been able to achieve in the historic showdown with GM right after World War II and represented what some called a "fantastic" victory for the union. But the UAW members might well have rejected it if two months of strike had not already drained their union strike fund. (The strike cost the UAW $160 million.)

The 1970 settlement all but guaranteed Woodcock's reelection as UAW president in 1972, and undoubtedly had an impact on the negotiation of 1973. The target in 1973 was Chrysler, and after a 2½-day strike—the shortest on record—the company and the UAW reached an agreement. Three years later, with Woodcock retired and Fraser now the president, it was Ford's turn. That strike lasted almost a month.

In the realm of the bargaining table, the UAW acquitted itself well without Reuther. In other areas, most notably the distance between the traditionally progressive leadership and the newer, younger breed of uncommitted workers, a gulf developed. Reuther had sensed it before his death, had fought its manifestation during the 1968 presidential campaign, in fact. That was the year George Wallace threatened to embarrass the union's long-time ally, Hubert Humphrey, in the presidential campaign. Some local UAW presidents openly supported Wallace, but their effort was offset by a frantic pro-Humphrey drive organized out of Solidarity House. Reuther himself personally got on the telephone to opposition factions around the country to get them to line up for the regular Democratic ticket, a tactic which Wallace campaign managers later recalled with bitterness. When Wallace ran again in 1972, he was making the same inroads, but the UAW had no Reuther to point out the difference between social democracy and populist demagoguery. In the Michigan presidential primary, in the UAW's own back yard, Wallace won a clear majority, with 51 percent, in a campaign heavily tinged with racial appeals associated with the anti-busing fervor gripping urban areas of the state that year. George McGovern picked up only a quarter of the vote, while Humphrey finished with a disappointing 16 percent.

Yet it would be premature to write off the UAW as a potent political force, in Michigan or on the national scene. "The UAW influence is all-pervasive," Detroit *Free Press* political reporter Remer Tyson told us. "It can control the state central committee on a crucial vote and decide who will be party chairman." Take the UAW out of the Michigan Democratic party, and there wouldn't be much party, he was suggesting. While it may be all-pervasive, it is not all-controlling—and that is the crux of its political action efforts in the years to come.

In a sense, the UAW is a victim of its own success. The average assembly line worker can make $18,000 a year with ease, hardly a salary associated with an oppressed proletariat. If he's a craftsman or there's lots of overtime, that figure climbs over $20,000 quickly. Noting their affluence, Tyson compared the UAW assembly line worker to Midwestern Republicans: "They're interested in the same kinds of issues," he noted. It's a cliché by now to point out most UAW workers are property owners, with their own homes in the suburbs, a couple of snowmobiles, and often a piece of vacation land in northern Michigan. Solidarity House has not been immune to the drift toward the middle class, either. On coffee tables in the lobby of the UAW headquarters, brochures advertising UAW vacation tours to Hawaii, the Caribbean, and Europe can be found.

Sam Fishman, head of the UAW's political action activities, vigorously insisted the ideals of Reuther have been carried on by Woodcock and now Fraser. In the same interview, however, he acknowledged the union member of the late 1970s was younger, more educated, and had a different lifestyle ("They smoke pot," he pointed out as an example). "They are a different breed," Fishman noted. "They have a different understanding of the union and a different attitude." None of the younger workers lived through the GM strike at Flint or the Battle of the Overpass at Ford, he noted. Fraser's awareness of this fact was behind his call in 1978 for a "new alliance aimed at transforming the American political system by making it more accountable, responsible, and democratic." It was reminiscent of Woodcock's role in the national Democratic and congressional politics a few years before, as well as a confirmation that the UAW leadership has not forsaken its commitment to social progress.

A glimpse of Fraser's view of the workers was caught by Washington *Post* political columnist David Broder as he explained the message the workers on the line had been sending to Solidarity House. The message when Fraser brought together his political lieutenants earlier to plan for the 1978 campaign was brief and blunt: forget it. "The workers," as Broder went on to explain the prevailing attitude, "have decided that politics is a con game, and they won't be suckered with the same exhortations that have worked in the past. They followed the union's lead and helped elect Jimmy Carter and a heavily Democratic Congress in 1976. But they don't believe their lives are any better—or that they are getting closer to a 'fair share' of the benefits of this society." Broder termed Fraser's call to consciousness a high-risk strategy, because among other things, "It is not certain that the UAW's million-plus members, many of them comfortably middle class, really want a program of militant political action for social change."

Chrysler's 1979 troubles sent some shocks waves through the economically comfortable UAW membership. Fraser used the situation to bring to America one of the most radical ideas out of the European labor movement: in exchange for the union's support of federal aid for Chrysler, he won himself a seat on the Chrysler board of directors. But over the long run, the real dilemma that faces the UAW is: How fast do the members want to move on social change? The racial issue was but one of many confronting the union. The tension of the Wallace appeal, the desertion of Detroit after the riots a decade ago, and the antibusing furor that climaxed in the 1972 campaign all subsided, partly because the massive layoffs of the mid-1970s shifted attention to economic survival. Yet the lack of recent notoriety didn't mean racial harmony reigned in and around the plants, that blacks no longer felt restricted to low-level assembly jobs, or that they now feel they have their fair share of important middle- and high-ranking posts within the UAW. Fishman told us the problem was one of education, but one that has been compounded by the younger workers who have less faith and less allegiance to the union. Fishman recalled that Reuther used to say: "First we organize, and then we have to unionize." For Fraser, and the new generation of leaders succeeding him after his retirement by 1983, that remained the most critical question to the survival of the UAW as a progressive political force: Could middle-class workers be unionized in the social mold of Walter Reuther?

Thrice Transformed Politics—Williams, Romney, and Milliken

Three times since World War II, the politics of Michigan have been transformed, and today they bear little resemblance to the condition that prevailed before 1948. For the better part of a century, the Republican party had ruled with scant opposition from an often scandal-ridden Democratic party that waited to pick up the crumbs of federal patronage. The GOP, dominated by rural conservatives and big manufacturers, had controlled the Michigan governorship for 80 of the previous 94 years and had an iron hold on the legislature and the congressional delegation. As the postwar era dawned, the prospect was for continued conservative Republican domination. In 1947, there were only five Democrats in the 100-member Michigan house and only four Democrats among the 32 senators.

But a series of events in the New Deal '30s and wartime years had created new conditions that would lead to fundamental change. The rise of the UAW, abetted by the Wagner Act, meant that Michigan for the first time in its history had a cohesive, militant trade-union movement with deep interest in politics. And in 1941, the state had passed a strict civil service law that erased the patronage potential which had drawn many old line Democrats as bees to flowers. The state's Democratic party was actually slipping into the control of James Hoffa, then an up-and-coming president of the local Teamsters and a man with little interest in issues or ideology.

In a series of conferences in 1947–48, the decision to bid for control of the Democratic party was made by a coalition of liberal labor leaders and intellectuals. On the labor side, the chief figures were Walter Reuther, his brother Roy, and August Scholle, president of the Michigan CIO. With Reuther's support, Scholle got the state CIO convention to approve labor's becoming an active participant in the Democratic party. But the movement was not labor's alone; also involved were a group of respected and respectable liberals. They included Neil Staebler, a wealthy Ann Arbor oil man and ex-Socialist who would serve as Democratic state chairman for many years,* and G. Mennen Williams, 37-year-old heir to the Mennen soap fortune who had become an ardent New Deal convert in the 1930s.

Williams, an effervescent politician in a perennial polka-dot green bow tie, was chosen as the Democrats' candidate for governor and proceeded to turn in one of the most spectacular performances in modern state politics. Archconservative Republicans helped Williams win his first election in 1948 by failing to support then Republican Gov. Kim Sigler, who had incurred their disfavor; the conservatives apparently figured they could let the boyish soap king be elected and then dispose of him two years later. But the Republicans had underestimated Williams' brains, shrewdness, and ambition and made an egregious tactical error. Reelected by narrow margins in 1950 and 1952, Williams won by landslide proportions in the following three elections and served a record 12 years as governor of the state.

Republicans constantly attacked Williams, either as a "phony" or as a CIO stooge and "a captive of Walter Reuther." But Williams was able to build stature on his own and sometimes made decisions against labor's will. In fact, he may have done as much for labor as labor did for him; John H. Fenton comments in *Midwest Politics,* "Soapy Williams and Neil Staebler proved to rural and small-town Michigan that the Democrat as a labor racketeer or 'drunken Irishman' was merely a stereotype." Power and influence within the Democratic party were truly shared between labor and the business and university liberals; in the early 1960s, when labor made the mistake of ramrodding its own choice for governor (John B. Swainson), the way was cleared for Republican resurgence.

In area after area—civil rights, compulsory health insurance, training programs for the unemployed, public recreation, education—Williams and Reuther sought to make Michigan a laboratory for social democracy. They took advanced stands, ahead of their time, and permanently altered the political complexion of the state.

Business and conservative circles rightly recognized Williams' governorship as the harbinger of vastly increased state taxes and services—of the kind

* Staebler turned out to be one of the most skilled practitioners of citizen politics in the U.S. and later served a term in Congress, only to be beaten by Romney for governor in 1964—the classic case of the political manager who should not have tried to change roles. He is a superb raconteur of politics and likes to recall that when he and his friends set out to revive the Democratic party in Michigan, "there were counties where any known Democrat could be fired from a public or private job —so we used to meet like early Christians in the catacombs." Later Staebler served on the Federal Elections Commission.

which in fact would become commonplace in many states in the 1960s and '70s. In the Republican-controlled legislature, its senate still outrageously malapportioned to the benefit of rural areas, they were able to minimize Williams' achievements. (Williams returned the contempt; as James Reichley wrote in *States in Crisis,* "Williams dealt with the legislature as though setting out to whack the snout of a large and obstreperous hog.") Frustrated in Lansing, Williams often appealed to the people over the legislators' heads and had partial success in such fields as unemployment and workmen's compensation, mental-health reform, and higher teachers' salaries. But his greatest impact was in an area where the legislature could less easily thwart him —appointments to the bench and to regulatory boards and commissions. Here Williams effected a minor revolution by appointments of dedicated liberals, some of whose rulings drove businessmen up the walls.

As Williams' terms went on, the defenders of the status quo became increasingly alarmed about his impact. Opposition was not only rampant in rural areas and among businessmen, but in Detroit, where the mayor criticized Reuther's behind-the-scenes power and the newspapers constantly assailed Williams and his labor allies. "Everybody was trying to hang Soapy by his bow tie and make sure he never became a presidential candidate," one reporter told us years later. The conflict came to a head in 1959 when Williams couldn't get the legislature to approve his then-record budget or to enact the corporate profits tax he demanded to finance it. The corporate tax, with no effect on individuals, was of course a red flag to the Republicans. They took the opposite tack of demanding an increased sales tax instead—anathema to the liberals. Both sides fell back to increasingly intransigent positions, and Williams finally, as a tactic, let state employees go without their paychecks for a couple of paydays.

The tactic backfired. Michigan's government became a national laughing-stock (there was a joke that year about a drink called "Michigan on the rocks"), the state's industrialists compounded the problem by conjecturing on the possible loss of industry to Michigan, and the market fell out of the bottom of bonds with the Michigan name attached. Detroit and out-of-state papers had a heyday at Williams' expense, but the state's national image had suffered greatly. Williams switched to support of a corporate profits and graduated personal income tax, but the legislature bulled through a sales-tax increase instead. Ironically, the Republican businessman George Romney in the governor's chair during the 1960s would enact a flat-rate form of the income tax and boost state taxes to $1.4 billion by 1969—*three times* the magnitude of the 1959 Williams budget that had been labeled so irresponsibly extravagant.

The change in Michigan's Republican party since World War II was slower in coming and less radical, but perhaps of as much significance for Michigan as the Democratic shift. In past years, the Michigan Manufacturers' Association held inordinate power in Republican policymaking through its hold on Republican state legislators. Business tycoons like Arthur Summerfield, the General Motors dealer in Flint who became Eisenhower's Postmaster General, were extremely influential. The policy of the GOP, reflecting its twin pillars of support in big business and the rural hinterland, was in favor of low taxes, minimal government services, and the protection of private property—the diametric opposite of a Democratic party controlled by those who wanted to reallocate the power, goods, and opportunities of the society.

As Williams' years in the governorship wore on, the Michigan GOP became increasingly anemic. By 1957, the Democrats held all the elective state-wide posts in Lansing and the Associated Press was able to report from Washington: "Republican campaign officials said today that for all practical purposes there is no GOP statewide organization in Michigan." The Democrats and labor had, in fact, succeeded in painting the GOP as the kept creature of big business. And the Republicans had succeeded in casting Williams and the Democrats as the handmaidens of big labor. Thus Michigan entered the 1960s with a stalemate in need of a resolution. The man who proved capable of doing that was George Romney, and his contribution looms as large in the Republican history as Williams' does in the Democratic.

Yet it was not originally as a Republican, but as a nonpartisan, civic-minded man above party that Romney first made his mark in politics. He rose to prominence in the 1950s as apostle and chief salesman of the compact Rambler of the American Motors Corporation he headed, arguing that Americans were tired of the "gas-guzzling dinosaurs" then being turned out by the Big Three. The Rambler campaign not only proved Romney's business prowess in one of the most startling corporate success stories of modern times, but it cast him in the role of a sort of David fighting the Goliaths of his industry in behalf of the Little Man. The precedent-shattering profit-sharing plan which Romney negotiated for American Motors with the UAW in 1961 enhanced his independent image. Thus when he finally did enter politics, the UAW and the Democrats had little success in labeling Romney a rubber stamp for big industry—or a typical Republican.

Romney's first major step into the public arena was in 1959 as head of the bipartisan Citizens for Michigan, a reaction to the "cash crisis" stalemate between Williams and the GOP legislature. Other participants in CFM included the League of Women Voters and Robert McNamara, then president of Ford. Romney viewed CFM as a kind of third force to break the impasse, and only in 1961, when he ran for the post of delegate to the constitutional convention which CFM had succeeded in creating, did Romney openly declare himself a Republican. Romney served creditably as an officer of the convention and then in 1962 challenged and beat for the governorship Williams' lackluster successor, John Swainson. The pitch of the Romney campaign was tailor-made to the mood of the times—he attacked the Democrats as dominated by labor, admitted the GOP had been dominated by business, and said that the state needed "a governor who recognizes that the common interests of all the people of Michigan are superior to the special interests of any special group or individual in the entire state." The depth of the Democratic loyalty built up since the war was reflected in Romney's narrow first-time margin: only 80,573 out of 2,764,618 votes cast.

Michigan made a quantum leap forward in the six years that Romney served as governor, a record in no way diminished by the fact that a booming national economy bolstered the auto industry and went a long way toward solving the budget crisis left behind by the Democrats. Romney restored confidence in the Michigan government, won approval of the excellent new constitution, set the state's finances in order through enactment of the first income tax in its history, and finally—despite all his earlier talk of citizen action over party action—revived and reinvigorated the Michigan Republican party and left it an even match for the still powerful Democratic-labor machine.

The new constitution, replacing a 1908 version that had been amended dozens of times, represented a major step forward for the state. State government was reorganized with a reduction of the former unwieldy 120 boards and commissions to 19 umbrella departments. A permanent state civil rights commission was established. The top-heavy ranks of state elected officials were thinned out, a powerful state board of education created, and the judicial system reorganized with a unique authority for the supreme court to control local courts. In what appeared to be a final resolution to the age-old arguments over legislative apportionment, the house was put on a strict population base and the senate on an 80-percent-population, 20-percent-geography basis (a provision later wiped out by Supreme Court reapportionment decrees). Perhaps the most controversial feature prohibited a graduated income tax; this feature particularly aroused the ire of Democrats and organized labor and prompted them to oppose the constitution. But it was approved by the voters, albeit narrowly, during Romney's first year in office.

In 1964, Romney said he would "accept but not endorse" Barry Goldwater as his party's presidential nominee, an apostasy that offended the right wing of his party throughout the country. Finally, in 1966, Romney was ready to abandon his "lonesome George" campaigning style and go to the voters as a full-fledged Republican. The reason, of course, was his desire to win the 1968 Republican presidential nomination as a party man with coattails broad enough to carry in other candidates of the party. After an exceptionally vigorous campaign, Romney won reelection with a 527,047-vote plurality—60.5 percent of the vote, a better showing than even Soapy Williams had been able to achieve in his salad days. And not only did Romney win himself, but he helped interim U.S. Sen. Robert P. Griffin win a six-year term (with a 94,416-vote edge) and guided the Republicans to victory in five marginal congressional districts the Democrats had held. The GOP also regained control of the legislature. Romney's lieutenant governor, William Milliken, would turn out to be the modern-day long-distance runner of the Michigan GOP.

The 1966 Republican sweep was all the more amazing because the man Griffin beat for the Senate was none other than G. Mennen Williams, returned from service as Assistant Secretary of State for African Affairs to reenter the political wars. On the face of it, there should have been no contest: Williams, the proven champion at the polls, favorite of the UAW and liberal wing, almost an institution in himself, opposed by Griffin, a rather modest, quiet veteran of 10 years in the U.S. House described by one writer as a man "with the presence of a certified public accountant."

The Williams-Griffin race suggested that labor and the Democrats would have to move beyond some of the old bromides of labor against capital if they hoped to win in the future in Michigan.

Romney's smashing 1966 victory made him, overnight, the leading contender for the Republican presidential nomination. But the presidency is the Big Time, and George Romney, sincere, moral, the evangelistic Mormon, would prove within a little more than a year that he lacked the depth or staying power required in a campaign for the White House.

Which of the two men—Romney or Williams—left the most lasting mark on Michigan politics? In the wake of Romney's smashing reelection victory in 1966, it looked as if the Republican party were about to compete with the Democratic as a vigorous, issue-oriented, broad-based movement. There were still archconservatives in the Republican party, including even some Birch-oriented district leaders whom Romney tried unsuccessfully to purge. But the rural voice was diminished and the Arthur Summerfield types were gone; business was still a campaign contributor to the GOP but no longer controlled it as it once did. Many middle-management men from the auto industry continued to work in the Republican party, but their politics were not extremist. Without Romney, it is difficult to believe that would have happened. And without the long rule of the liberal-labor wing of the Democratic party, which shifted the center of gravity of Michigan politics so clearly to the left, it is difficult to believe that the old Michigan GOP would ever have accepted George Romney at all. As Neil Staebler told us shortly after Romney left the state, "We made them (the Republicans) become a decent bunch."

Even before Romney's departure for Washington, however, there was evidence that the Republican revival might be paper-thin. In the 1968 elections, the Democrats demonstrated their continued vitality by turning in a 222,417-vote plurality for Humphrey over Nixon—the biggest Democratic presidential margin in any state outside the Northeast. With Milliken installed in the governor's chair, the moderate Republicans lacked their flamboyant leader, and the conservative wing began to reassert itself. In 1970, Milliken beat back his Democratic opponent for governor, but by a slim margin of only 44,111 votes out of 2,656,093 cast.

But William Milliken was to transform Michigan politics for the third time, weaving a pattern of bipartisanship that left some Republicans shaking their heads and many Democrats eager to shake his hand and embrace him.

The folklore around Milliken's home town of Traverse City speaks of his mother raising him from childhood with the idea, not of running the family department store, but of being governor. True or not, Milliken's turn to be chief executive came rather abruptly. Romney called from Washington

Jan. 22, 1969, to say he was resigning to join Nixon's cabinet. The same day, Milliken was sworn into office in a hastily called ceremony by a Supreme Court justice using a borrowed Bible and apologizing for not wearing a formal robe. Milliken's inaugural "address" was only 203 words long. In the minds of many at the time, Milliken would have been a prime candidate as among the men least likely to fill Romney's shoes and to cope with reconstruction of Detroit, the vicissitudes of an economy dominated by the cyclical auto industry, and the political hazards of running a government increasingly populated by Democrats. He did not so much fill Romney's shoes as create a new style of shoes to fit his own political and philosophical predilections.

"You have to look at him as a political craftsman," Detroit *Free Press* political reporter Remer Tyson said nearly a decade after Milliken had been in office. "He's so good, he comes off as a nonpolitician. At first, people thought he was a nice guy but not tough enough. He's kept the soft image, but he acts tough." The hallmarks of his administration have been programs responsive to problems and a successful style finely tuned to the times. Tyson ticked off the key ingredients: an aura of competence and integrity leading to high credibility; a willingness to admit mistakes; the maintenance of an image of a "guy who will try to do the right thing"; a sensitivity to major problems which need attention, and a willingness to try to do something about them. In a state where self-admitted Republicans are a distinct minority (roughly 20 percent is all that identifies with the GOP), Milliken shaped these ingredients to maximize his leadership and maintain control of the governor's office while Democrats were winning almost every other office in sight. In 1978, for instance, he was reelected by a margin of 383,527 votes —a bigger plurality than all but three governors in Michigan history—even while Griffin, though he was Senate Minority Whip, was going down to defeat and Democrats were retaining their control of both houses of the legislature for the third consecutive election and the congressional delegation split 13–6 in favor of the Democrats. Milliken won an extraordinarily high percentage of the black vote for a Republican (about 35 percent) and even carried heavily Democratic Wayne County (which includes Detroit), the first Republican to perform that feat in 32 years.

Government Performance, Milliken, Bipartisanship at Work

It would be a mistake to think that the Williams-UAW years or the Romney regime turned Michigan into an island of far-out socialistic experimentation. Applying the yardsticks of a state's tax effort as a proportion of its personal income, Michigan is significantly ahead of her more "regressive" neighbors, Indiana, Ohio, and Illinois. (Although a spate of legislative indiscretions occurred late in the 1970s, corruption in Michigan government seems to raise its loathsome head less often than in the other large Midwest states, a probable result of the switch from patronage-based politics to issue-based politics.) Reflective of Governor Milliken's policies, Michigan also moved up on the scale of per capita taxing and spending during the 1970s, rivaling on the expenditure side even the high-service state of California although not yet at the level of New York, the other major big-state spender of modern times. With taxes, Michigan's per capita levies put it behind both California and New York, as well as its northern neighbors on the other side of Lake Michigan—Wisconsin and Minnesota.

It is difficult to believe that any of this could have happened, however, had it not been for the Williams years, which gave respectability to socially activist government, pulling Michigan—despite all the screaming and yelling of the oxcart-era legislature—into the 20th century. During the Romney years, the state's administrative and financial house was put in order. And the courts finally forced legislative reapportionment. But what Romney had failed to do was to find any kind of solution for the escalating problems of the cities (especially crisis-plagued Detroit) or to initiate badly needed and fundamental reforms in education and environmental control. Those problems were left for his successors.

From the start, Milliken developed an agenda to deal with the problems of the 1970s, the cities especially, but also the environment, transportation, equitable school financing, and land use. Describing Michigan as "primarily urban," he urged the legislature to make a $5 million bloc grant to Detroit "as evidence of the state's commitment to urban Michigan . . . and a city with unique and awesome problems." An official governor's office was set up in Detroit, and Milliken visited the city frequently. In parceling out benefits of a $100 million bond issue, he fought for and got a substantial share for new recreation facilities in and near cities (battling ruralites and sportsmen who wanted all the money spent for distant parks, fisheries, and wildlife projects).

But that was only starters in Milliken's unflagging commitment to the salvaging of Detroit, an effort which earned him the respect and even tacit political support of Mayor Young (a vice chairman of the Democratic national party). Such an alliance would never have been possible had Milliken not supported his rhetoric with responses that pumped aid into the central city. The rhetoric speaks for itself: "Failure to deal with the cities where the people are now really means we're abandoning the whole country," he told us in a 1977 interview. "When you consider the enormous investment that's already been made in the city with sewage lines, streets that have been laid out, and all the services which are available now, to rehabilitate the cities and revitalize them would cost a fraction of what it would cost to start over anew. . . . The physical facilities to take care of people who come in on a temporary basis are still in the cities. Our investment is there, and I think we have to save our investment."

Programatically, Milliken has concentrated not so much on cure-alls, which raise expectations unrealistically high, but plodding, steady progress. In retrospect, his bipartisan approach may have assured Detroit and the urban areas more state aid than either Williams or Romney could have provided.

The list of creative reponses is impressive. In 1971, Milliken pursued revision of the state's revenue sharing formula with municipalities, replacing the per capita basis for distributing funds (which was crippling Detroit as its outmigration accelerated after the 1967 riot) with a plan based on need and tax effort. By 1979, Detroit's share of the revised pot of state aids came to $105 million, compared to only $30 million had the old program continued. Early in his administration, Milliken had proposed the most radical restructuring of school financing ever officially backed on the U.S. mainland. With local schools largely financed with local property taxes, the inequities of per pupil expenditures were blatant, varying from $1,000 to $3,000, depending on the wealth of the district. Milliken's plan for elimination of local property taxes for school purposes and for state assumption of school costs was undermined, first by the covert opposition of much of the education establishment and ultimately by the voters. In a 1972 statewide referendum on the issue (the same year as the integration and busing issue), Michigan voters resoundingly (1.8 million to 1.3 million) said "no" to state takeover of school costs. But Milliken came back the following session with a package of legislation that ended up providing a $380 million tax cut, increasing school aids 14 percent, and incorporating the "circuit-breaker" concept under which additional state tax credits were given whenever a person's local property taxes exceeded a set percentage of his income.

When Detroit was facing its budget crisis in the mid-1970s and a wave of felonies on the expressways was spreading fear throughout the Motor City, Milliken and Mayor Young worked out a plan to allow state police to patrol the freeways, releasing the undermanned police force to concentrate in other areas. In 1976 Milliken pushed through the legislature a $28 million package earmarking aids for Detroit's transportation system, the library, zoo, health, and other cultural facilities. Other evidences of Milliken's positive role in urban problems—beyond the continued open line of communication between the governor's and mayor's office—were housing and neighborhood improvement grants, job development programs, assistance in the intracacies of municipal financing, and a gubernatorially appointed urban action task force. In interviews, both Young and his chief aides went out of their way to praise Milliken's sensitivity to the city. Indeed, when Young delivered a welcoming address to the National Governors' Conference, meeting in Detroit in 1977, he specifically cited Milliken's support for the city and urged the governors to "take a hard look" at their own cities "and offer the same type of support to your cities that is being offered by the governor of this state. I think it's the key to the future progress of this nation."

Milliken's responsiveness to Detroit's ailments was not without opposition, especially from rural Republicans, some of whom would just as soon see Detroit became a part of Windsor, Canada, across the river. That division was clearly evident in the fight over the $168 million transportation and gasoline tax package that survived in the legislature only through Milliken's active intervention. Republican support for the measure was hard to come by, until Democrats demanded Milliken guarantee GOP votes to make it a true bipartisan bill (and protect Democrats against charges of pouring state tax dollars into the black hole of Detroit). While a sizable part of the new funds would go into Detroit's proposed mass transit system, Milliken's public statements constantly stressed that the new monies also would go into maintenance and improvement of Michigan's 116,000 miles of roads, for bridge repairs, rail preservation, Lake Michigan ferry service, and other transit benefits to the outstate regions. After clearing the house, senate Democrats split, forcing Milliken to convince enough Republicans to get a majority. The final vote in the senate was 19–19, with GOP Lt. Gov. James J. Damman casting the tie-breaking vote. It was another example of Milliken's superb sense of coalition-building.

While one observer noted that Milliken was "in some ways more of a Democrat than some Democrats," he did not ignore the business community nor economic development. His administration saw the elimination of a potpourri of business taxes and the establishment of a single corporate tax. Aware of the trend of companies to locate or expand their operations in the Sun Belt, he also proposed and won passage of Michigan's plant rehabilitation act, designed to grant tax breaks to companies rehabilitating obsolete industrial facilities or building new ones. Chrysler was one of the first firms to take advantage of the program, opting to renovate its antiquated Mack Avenue Stamping Plant in Detroit, saving 5,000 jobs and a substantial tax base for the city. In just two years, the legislation was credited with keeping 32,000 jobs and creating 28,000 new ones in the state of Michigan.* Against Milliken's wishes, however, the legislature broadened it to provide assistance in all parts of the state—rural as well as urban—so that the assistance couldn't be targeted to cities as specifically as Milliken would have liked. There was an additional negative: that Michigan seemed to be getting ever deeper into a tug-of-war with other Midwestern states for industrial locations. The tax write-offs could in the long run prove deleterious to the level of government service to which Michigan had become accustomed.

Milliken's image as a protector of the environment had been formed early in his administration. A new environmental quality commission was set up and, with Milliken's encouragement, Michigan became the first state to ban the sale and use of "hard" pesticides. Environmental proposals contained several measures, including coastal zoning, to protect the Great Lakes. But that image was jeopardized by the furor over the accidental contamination of

---

* The impact of these 60,000 jobs was translated by Fred Osann, Jr., a Chrysler vice president, during a presentation to the National Governor's Conference held in Detroit in 1977. Those jobs provided more than $725 million in personal income each year, enough to support 187,200 people, he said. In addition, it provided mortgage and rent money for 69,600 homes and apartments, taxes to educate 30,600 children, bank deposits totaling $315 million, retail sales adding up to $339 million (supporting 2,400 retail establishments), and support for 45,600 other jobs in non-manufacturing fields. The impact "we especially like," Osman noted, was the fact those 60,000 jobs also provided ownership of 71,400 passenger cars.

livestock feed by a fire retardant called polybrominated biphenyl (PBB), a controversy that lingered throughout the decade. More than 30,000 cattle, 1.5 million chickens, and 7,000 other animals died from the poisoning, causing irate farmers to file $75 million in claims. Complaints of physical maladies and abnormalities in those who had been exposed to the poisoned animals were investigated by medical researchers in the years following the 1973 incident, leading to mixed conclusions. One study said there was a possible link between the PBB and ill health, while another study of children born after the incident could pinpoint no unusual health problems. The contamination and aftermath provided fuel for one of the most sustained attacks on the Milliken Administration, leading to a highly critical television account by the Public Broadcasting System, charges of ignoring the issue, and some controversial accusations as late as the 1978 gubernatorial compaign with the Democratic candidate, State Sen. William Fitzgerald. Michigan did impose standards controlling PBBs even more stringent than the federal limits.*

As Michigan prepared to enter the 1980s, reapportionment again emerged as a major political issue. A decade before, it was thought reapportionment based on one-man, one-vote came too late to help Democrats and the cities. That verdict may have been premature for the Democrats but largely justified for the cities. Originally, suburbs and Republicans were the presumed beneficiaries of the one-man, one-vote reapportionments. But, as it turned out, Democrats were aided more than initially assumed, especially in areas like Macomb County, adjacent to the northeast corner of Detroit. Many of the people moving into Macomb County (population approaching 700,000) were the now middle class, blue-collar auto workers and their families, the symbols of the white-flight syndrome. They accounted for much of the 60,000-plus growth in the county following 1970, making it Democratic country, conservative Democratic full of ethnic enclaves, but Democratic nonetheless. To its west is Oakland County (just shy of one million people), the bastion of the affluent and professionals and long the citadel of Republicanism. The growth there has dwarfed even its neighbor to the east, with more than 76,000 additional residents during the 1970s (including a growing number of middle class black families escaping Detroit—a limited version of black flight from the city). While suburban growth may help Democrats even more in the 1980s, the urban areas of Michigan will not benefit much from greater representation after the 1980 reapportionment. Wayne County lost 252,000 people between 1970 and 1977, equal to 9 percent of its population.** None of the counties with the other leading cities—Grand Rapids, Lansing, Jackson, Muskegon, Kalamazoo, Saginaw, or Bay City—grew more than 4 percent in that period.

* Less than two weeks before Milliken's reelection effort in 1978, a Michigan judge threw out a $250,000 damage suit by one affected farm couple, the first judicial ruling since the 1973 incident. Not only was there not a "shred of credible evidence to support the claims," Judge William Peterson wrote, but he said the disaster had been blown out of proportion, causing needless public fear and livestock slaughter, and the state's (Milliken's) reaction had been reasonable and proper. Given the timing, so soon before the election, the decision raised questions whether it would be accepted as the final word on the issue.
** The other four counties losing population were Branch and Calhoun in the Battle Creek area, Genessee (Flint), and Gogebic, the westernmost county in the Upper Peninsula.

Providing the dramatic growth—with obvious implications when reapportionment maps are redrawn—were the counties in the north central part of the state. Of the 20 counties in Michigan showing population growth of more than 20 percent since 1970, 18 were concentrated in that belt of farms, forests, lakes, and orchards. The growth of the area has been so dynamic that Governor Milliken called a "Northern Michigan Growth Conference" in 1978 to plan for the future, including preservation of the many recreational highlights of the region. "The challenge we face of fostering proper and desired growth," Milliken warned the region's new and old residents, "is no less a problem than the one we faced a few years ago in attempting to escape the distress of unemployment."

Who are the migrants responsible for giving the counties of upper Michigan a population growth rate double the rest of the nation? They are mostly young adults and families, college educated, with white collar skills, fleeing the ravages of urban life, and retirees, drawn to the region's quiet lifestyle and many recreational outlets. They are settling, for the most part, in low density areas, in very small unincorporated towns and villages and in the rural open countryside. While the political complexion of these new growth areas has yet to solidify, the doctrine of one-man, one-vote will at least guarantee that the full weight of their vote is reflected in Lansing and Washington.

Michigan's contribution to the Supreme Court's one-man, one-vote decisions is not generally appreciated but, in fact, was extremely significant. Since the early 1940s, Michigan labor leader Gus Scholle had been fighting for equally populated legislative districts. He filed a landmark court suit for reapportionment in 1959, incurring the opposition even of Democrats who feared offending members of their own party from the Upper Peninsula, which was overrepresented. But Scholle noted the presence of the liberal Warren Court in Washington and felt it was time to press the issue, fearing the opportunity might be lost for decades if the Court later turned conservative. The AFL-CIO counsel, Theodore Sachs of Detroit, did the basic research and then as a countesy passed it on to the plaintiffs in the famed Tennessee suit of *Baker v. Carr*. "Then they beat us into the Supreme Court and got the credit," Scholle lamented.

The net effect of reapportionment in Michigan and other states was not necessarily to make legislatures more "liberal," and in some cases the precise mathematical equality of districts insisted on by the courts has bordered on the preposterous. But as Michigan's experience showed, the reform did clear out the rotten borough deadwood of the largely conservative hinterland and send a younger, more educated, flexible, and modern-thinking generation of men and women to the state capital. In northern states, the reform meant Democrats had at least a chance of winning legislative control—a fact that finally occurred in 1975 in Michigan. And by tightening the partisan balance in the legislature, reapportionment gave blacks a chance to bargain for their interests there. In Michigan, the blacks won a representation consistent with their proportion of the population. The 1969 legislature passed a $100 million bond issue for low-income housing, to be followed by many other urban aid programs during the Milliken years, a clear manifestation of black political power.

A Leader in Public Education

Since 1837—and still today—the Michigan state constitution has declared: "Schools and the means of education shall forever be encouraged!" Michigan had the nation's first state superintendent of public instruction and was the first state to provide free high school education. Despite continuing inequalities between school districts and the problems blacks and other minorities face within them, Michigan's elementary and secondary schools stand slightly above the national average in overall per pupil expenditures and third in the Union in teachers' salaries.

Michigan's system of public higher education, however, is its more distinctive achievement, and many regard her public university complex as second only to California's in quality. The state's huge and virtually autonomous major universities—Michigan State at East Lansing, the University of Michigan at Ann Arbor, and Wayne State University in Detroit—attract enrollments around 118,000. Michigan State and Michigan rank 18th and 19th in the U.S.A. in full-time enrollment, and Wayne State is not far behind. The University of Michigan has long been the intellectual leader of the group with an excellent arts and sciences faculty, as well as internationally known medical and law schools.* It draws a politically activist intelligentsia and the state's natural aristocracy in much the same mode as the University of Wisconsin at Madison. And some of the same problems that Berkeley and Madison face—loss of support among legislators, taxpayers, alumni, and the business community—haunted Ann Arbor in the wake of the student activism days spawned by the Vietnam War and the civil rights movement. In 1970, a Black Action movement and white radicals, partly through physical intimidation, forced president Robben W. Fleming and the regents to agree to increase the black percentage of enrollment from an existing 3 percent to 10 percent of the university's 33,000 students by 1973–74. Since only 6 percent of Michigan high school graduates were blacks at the time, there ensued the spectacle of the university looking all over the U.S. for marginally qualified black applicants and then promising them an average $4,000-a-year support. Not only was the level of assistance discriminatory vis-à-vis qualified but economically deprived white students, but there were early reports of a dilution of the level of classroom teaching, declining faculty morale, and questions

---

* In 1971, the American Council on Education rated Michigan's graduate faculties among the top five in the U.S. in classics, philosophy, anthropology, geography, political science, sociology, botany, population biology, and electrical and mechanical engineering. The university is one of the major social-science research centers of the U. S. It has close tries to the economically independent Survey Research Center, which has pioneered in advanced polling techniques. Its library, with almost 4.8 million volumes, ranks it as the fourth largest university library in the country, behind only Harvard, Yale, and Illinois.

about the university's long-term academic standing. When Fleming announced in 1978 he was leaving to become head of the Public Broadcasting Corporation, some faculty members still resented what they considered a cave-in to pressure. They insisted their predictions of a lower quality student, and implicitly a less prestigious university, had come true. Supporters of Fleming defended the decision, arguing it was an acceptable price to pay to open the doors of higher education to a too long deprived minority.

Michigan State, founded in 1855 and the nation's first land-grant college, was still a sleepy agricultural school when John A. Hannah took over its presidency in 1942. Viewed by friends as a masterful builder of the modern university and by others as a ruthless academic entrepreneur, Hannah stayed in office so long (27 years in all) that some suggested he might be called "the Methuselah of university presidents." But in those years, Hannah transformed Michigan State from a cow college into a major engine of public training—a 5,000-acre "megaversity" with an enrollment of 42,541 and an annual budget of more than $100 million. There was a saying in the legislature: "The concrete never sets on Hannah's Empire." Purists criticized him for making MSU into a big "service station, filling its students with courses like Sewage Treatment or the Dynamics of Packaging." Hannah brushed off the criticism and took it as a compliment: "The object of the land-grant tradition," he said, "was not to de-emphasize scholarship but to emphasize its application." And under his tutelage, MSU also launched an extensive graduate program in virtually all nonprofessional areas. One interesting program was a College of Human Medicine, oriented more to producing general practitioners than specialists. And defying MSU's reputation as a party school, Hannah paid top salary for outstanding faculty.

Not a small part of Hannah's success at MSU was his high-pitch salesmanship in getting money from the legislature; the MSU budget rose at a rate almost twice that of the University of Michigan. Sometimes Hannah's entrepreneurial talents brought embarrassment, as in 1966 when *Ramparts* magazine alleged that an MSU program for training South Vietnam policemen had provided a cover for CIA agents. But Ann Arbor was not free from all criticism either; there, some faculty (especially in scientific fields) made fortunes in spinoff technical companies that sprang up around Ann Arbor.

On the more positive side, it should be reported that University of Michigan students were in the forefront of the national environmental protection movement by the early 1970s, and that an amazing army of 9,500 Michigan State students were giving from three to 10 hours a week without pay to help people in need in ghetto areas, schools, and hospitals. Most MSU students were also pleased in 1969 to learn that their trustees had named a highly competent black man, Dr. Clifton R. Wharton, Jr., as the university's new president. Wharton had once been something of a student activist himself, helping found the National Student Association while a student at Harvard in 1946. Before taking up his duties at MSU, he was vice president of the Agricultural Development Council in New York, a group founded by John D.

Rockefeller III to support teaching and research on economic and human problems of agricultural development. Thus the appointment was in keeping with MSU's land-grant tradition, but also broke new ground because Wharton was the first black to head a major predominantly white American university. Wharton's success in guiding a major campus did not fail to attract the attention of educators elsewhere. In 1977 he was hired away from Michigan State by the State University of New York, where he became chancellor of the country's largest higher education system.

Before he left, however, he made a gigantic imprint on the land-grant concept, reshaping it to the needs of the late 20th century instead of the agrarian philosophy of the mid-19th century. He called it a "modern land-grant philosophy" that provided for expanded concern for adult education, minority enrollments, and urban problems. He told *Saturday Review* magazine in 1972 that a public university would never regain the public support of the 1960s unless it changed "to meet what the public perceives as its real needs." He continued to explain those needs in terms of many educationally neglected groups: "When you talk about people who have been bypassed, you are talking about blacks and other minorities, but not only about minorities. In many instances, you also are talking about rural whites. These unmet needs definitely involve older people—women in their thirties who want something more, highly trained professionals whose skills have become obsolete. Universal access to higher education and lifelong education are going to be realities, whether professors and university presidents like it or not."

More than half of all university students in the United States live at home and commute to college, among them the 34,500 students at Wayne State University in Detroit, the third of Michigan's "big three" universities. Wayne State, which began in the 1890s-vintage Central High School building near center city, is a not untypical example of the potentialities and problems of the commuter college. Already of substantial size at the end of World War II, WSU grew rapidly in the GI Bill era and decided to continue in center city rather than move to the suburbs. And a few years later it was fortunate to have the state of Michigan take over its financial support from the hard-pressed city of Detroit.

Wayne State had 15 percent black enrollment by the start of the 1970s, the highest percentage of any predominantly white university in the U.S. The 1967 Detroit riots swirled through WSU's immediate neighborhood, and since then the institution has striven mightily to relate itself to the Detroit black community through such varied programs as communiy based extension centers, off-hours management and technology training, the Teacher Corps (actually begun at Wayne in 1966), social-work students interning in city agencies, legal-aid assistance, and the clinical staff provided to Detroit General Hospital through the medical school.

A testimony to the efforts and effects of Wayne State's involvement in the needs of Detroit came in 1978, when the Detroit *News* included former WSU President George E. Gullen, Jr., as one of the seven most influential men in the metropolitan area. During his tenure, spanning most of the 1970s, Gullen built alliances with corporate and community leaders to assure the university's quality and to extend its influence into the surrounding neighborhoods, making them both cleaner and safer. He parlayed his experience as a former vice president at American Motors (under Romney) to involve other major corporate executives in his efforts, using his position to deal with pressing education and health issues. Of his role in upgrading education, the *News* said in its copyrighted story, "That makes him a welcome white face among many of Detroit's blacks. Indeed, most blacks new to power in Detroit hold degrees from Wayne State." Even in retirement, Gullen is considered, the *News* said, the "best person in power and academic skill to deal with the most crucial problem in Detroit's future—education."

Americans who have never attended a commuter college have difficulty understanding the obstacles and problems of getting one's education in the hectic on-again, off-again type of schedule of a student who lives at home. Still the model for higher education is the English college system of "houses of scholars" living together in a relaxed, meditative environment designed to develop the "whole man" through concentration and contact with peer and professor. The commuting student's life is precisely the opposite. At Wayne State, more than 75 percent of the students are obliged to hold down full- or part-time outside jobs. Students often arrive exhausted at class from lack of sleep and long commuting trips, and frequently are obliged to skip courses they would like to take because of their complex work schedules or car-pool arrangements. Family pressures on the student living at home are an emotional drain for many. Making friends and social contacts on campus or finding an opportunity to talk informally with faculty is extremely difficult. At Wayne State, study areas and congenial eating places are at a minimum and students are frequently seen studying in their parked cars between classes. The problems for the commuting student will obviously continue to be formidable.

The Statewide Economy, Tourism, the Upper Peninsula

There is an old saw to the effect that "when the U.S. economy catches a cold, Michigan gets pneumonia." Automobiles are one of the most easily postponed consumer purchases, and all the postwar recessions have hit with special vengeance in Michigan. The 1974–75 recession, triggered by the Arab oil embargo, was no exception. While unemployment averaged 8.5 percent for the country as a whole, Michigan's unemployed totaled 12.5 percent of its work force. In Detroit, the figures hovered above 15 percent much of the year, and even more—around 21 percent—for black males. Automobiles are, indeed, the big factor in the Michigan economy. By the same token, when there is an auto strike, all of Michigan suffers; the 1970 walkout at General

Motors, for instance, cost the state government $25 million in lost revenues and added $25 million in welfare costs. To guard against the whiplash effects induced by the auto industry, Michigan approved in 1977 a budget stabilization fund, or a "rainy day fund" as it is called. Its purpose? To set aside revenues during the good times for use during the hard times, be it a strike, recession, or other economic calamity.

But there is a lot of nonautomotive Michigan, too. The state leads in a wide variety of goods ranging from breakfast cereals to steel springs. The 14,500 manufacturers in the state turned out wares that added $32.4 billion in value to the state's economy during 1976. Among the states, Michigan's $64.2 billion in shipments ranked it seventh. A growing diversification of the state's economic base is reflected in employment figures that show that service industries have doubled their payrolls since the mid-1940s while manufacturing jobs slipped from more than half the total in 1947 to about two-fifths today. Few states have such a small percentage of their work force in federal civilian or defense-generated employment.

Mineral production—chiefly of low-grade iron ore on the Upper Peninsula—brings $1.4 billion a year into the Michigan economy. Salt mines (including some under the city of Detroit) are said to have deposits of 71 trillion tons, and the state is one of the nation's foremost salt suppliers, with 10 percent of annual production. Lumbering has passed the exploitive era of the state's early history but forest products still contribute about $255 million to the state's economy each year. A diversified agriculture of dairy products, cattle, wheat, and fruits produces an annual income of about $1.7 billion. The state boasts of being "the bean capital of the world." The Great Lakes—cooling the prevailing winds in summer and warming them in winter—make the lands along their shores ideal for fruit growing; Michigan ranks number one among the states in sweet and tart cherries and she is a leading producer of blueberries, apples, spearmint, peaches, pears, strawberries (a juicy 9.5 million pounds a year), beets, and tomatoes. For those interested in odd facts, it may also be reported that Michigan has no peer in its output of hothouse rhubarb. For many who work the land, farming is a marginal occupation and there are many part-time or "retirement" farmers. On the other hand, large farming operations draw thousands of migrant workers, whose living conditions are a subject of continuing concern.

Woods, lakes and waterways, ski hills, snowmobile trails, and a handful of man-made attractions (like Henry Ford's unique museum and Greenfield Village at Dearborn) make Michigan an important tourist state.

With some concern, one reads in a chamber of commerce report that "an estimated 500,000 outboard motors churn Michigan's waters" and claims that Michigan has more snowmobiles registered than any other state, a development one may see as asset or debit depending on his attitude toward nature. More reassuring is the revival of sport fishing in Lake Michigan. The St. Lawrence Seaway allowed eel-like sea lamprey to infiltrate the lakes; these parasites in turn almost wiped out lake trout before chemicals and electric screens at their spawning grounds stopped the destruction. Then, in 1966, some 800,000 coho salmon from salt waters along the West Coast were planted in streams along the Great Lakes and some had grown up to 22 pounds, providing a bonanza for the sport fishermen. Fear of killing off this new sporting opportunity contributed to Michigan's decision to ban the sale of DDT, traces of which were found in some salmon catches. Yet pollution problems in the lakes continued to threaten fishing; in 1970, for instance, all fishing in Lake St. Clair had to be banned because traces of deadly poisonous mercury, released from chemical plants, were found in lake fish. By the late 1970s, however, pollution controls had curbed much of the wastes that used to flow unchecked into the lake and the Detroit River. Fishermen were beginning to find some game fish in waters where they could not survive just a few years ago.

As if man's contaminants would never cease, a liquid industrial compound called polychlorinated biphenyl (PCB, different from the PBBs that killed livestock) also was detected in Great Lakes water at mid-decade. Early in 1976, the legislature set more stringent levels of PCB content in the electrical equipment, paints, inks, rubber tires, and other manufactured items for which it is used. However, massive infusions of federal EPA dollars ($137.6 million in 1976), coupled with private expenditures, had at least stabilized the level of pollution and sometimes improved the quality of many of Michigan's lakes, streams, and boundary waters.

Michigan's other tourist attractions include the Sleeping Bear Dune between Lake Michigan and Glen Lake and the magnificent old Grand Hotel on Mackinac Island, which claims it has "the longest porch on earth." The Grand Hotel is where Michigan's Republican elite, some thousand strong, gather every other year for what one party leader calls simply "the nicest political event in the country."

Michigan is so far-flung geographically and so cosmopolitan in its ethnic strains that it appears to lack a common personality. Before statehood was achieved in 1837, most of the settlers were from New York and New England. Then came Germans, populating Saginaw, Ann Arbor, and other parts of southern Michigan and continuing their influx well into the 20th century. Starting in 1846, there were substantial numbers of Dutch immigrants; they left their mark in the geography books with western Michigan cities such as Holland and Zeeland. Irish came in substantial numbers; but even more significant were Swedes, Norwegians, Finns, and Italians, many of whom worked in the north Michigan lumber industry that flourished in the past century. From 1910 on, substantial numbers of Poles and other East Europeans arrived, drawn to the factories of the Detroit area. As late as 1970, foreign born and first-generation Americans comprised 19 percent of Michigan's people. Finally, there was the black population influx, starting 70 years ago; the black percentage of Michigan's population was then .6 percent (17,115 out of 2,810,173), today it is 11.2 percent (1,108,560 out of a statewide population of 9,129,000). Michigan still has a high percentage of poor Southern-born whites and their children; the largest club in Pontiac for years was said to be the Arkansas Club, made up of the families of people who came to work in the auto plants.

The Upper Peninsula requires a special word because it is so vast (equal to the combined areas of Connecticut, Delaware, Massachusetts, and Rhode Island), so distant, and so much a stepchild of modern Michigan. First populated by early French explorers, the area was once a great supplier of pelts. In the 1880s, its magnificent pine forests were razed; today some are growing back, but lumbering is not exactly a booming industry. Over the past century, the region yielded nearly 11 billion pounds of copper, but both that industry and iron ore mining are now in decline. Rather intensive explorations of potential copper lodes in recent years have nourished some hopes that not all the metal has been extracted from beneath the barren land. A decade ago, after years of the sons and daughters of the Upper Peninsula leaving for opportunities elsewhere, the region seemed to have little economic future. But the 1970s saw a growth splurge of sorts for the 15 counties in the UP. Only one county experienced a population decline between 1970 and 1977 (Gogebic, the westernmost county on the Peninsula), while the region showed an overall 9 percent surge. The widely scattered, thinly populated towns, the trout-rich streams and woodlands, parks and wastelands, ugly slag heaps left by defunct mines, waterfalls, ski jumps, swamps, and tree stumps all remain, much as when people were leaving. But now, the very quality they all symbolize—the antithesis of urban America—seems to provide the attraction a sizable number of people are seeking. Whether the UP will develop the economic base to sustain its new inhabitants will be an issue the 1980s will have to address.

Detroit: A Born-Again City?

Twentieth-century Detroit has had every reason to be a great, prosperous city. With the fifth largest population among U.S. cities, it has had a convergence of resources—financial, managerial, and in transportation—which should have made it a bulwark of strength for Michigan and the Midwest. Yet repeatedly in the 1960s, in the mid-1970s, and starting again in 1979, the mighty Motor City found itself a metropolis in pain, uncertain about its future and viability.

Yet for a period of time after the mid-1970s recession, and before the oil crisis and start of the collapse of Chrysler in 1979, the city which had nearly been consumed by the riots of 1967, by budget crises of the mid-'70s and other decimating urban ills, seemed to be shaking itself loose from the throes of agony. Many believed it had an excellent chance to rise, phoenix-like, from the ashes.

The pessimism of Detroit at the end of the '60s was vividly captured by Robert Popa in the Detroit *News* on September 21, 1969. Under a page one banner headline, "Is Detroit Dying Because No One Cares?" the article began:

What's wrong with Detroit?
Well, to start with:
Its school system isn't doing the job.
Its downtown heart isn't too strong. Decay has set in.
Its streets aren't very safe or well lighted.
Valuable land sits vacant in the downtown area.
And its civic and industrial leaders haven't been leading.

This searing assessment comes from a most unexpected direction. It was made this week by Dwight Havens, president of the Detroit Chamber of Commerce, an organization usually dedicated to boosterism or apologies rather than to criticism. . . .

Popa's story, appropriately illustrated by a weed-infested empty block in the downtown area, continued with a recitation of building booms sparked by strong civic leadership in Pittsburgh, Dallas, and other great industrial cities —but so obviously missing in Detroit, where everything seemed to be moving to the suburbs or dying. Detroit, Havens pointed out, could boast of being the home of the Big Three auto companies, the Burroughs Corporation, and National Bank of Detroit, one of the nation's largest banks. "Per square foot, we've got more talented leadership in Detroit than any other city of the world," Havens was quoted as saying, "but nobody's doing anything."

As the 1970s matured, the same conclusion could no longer be reached: people cared, people in the bars as well as in the posh executive suites. Max Fisher, the wealthy industrialist and influential figure in Detroit Renaissance, Inc., told the world in 1976 that thousands of Motor City residents were ready to declare, "Detroit ain't down yet!" He went on in a signed column in the New York *Times*:

There is no attempt here to ignore Detroit's problems. We Detroiters are so acutely aware of them that we couldn't ignore them if we tried. But there are many of us who can see both sides of the Detroit balance sheet—the assets as well as the more-publicized liabilities. And with this perspective, we are persevering with the confidence of a tough, resilient city that has tackled and handled monumental jobs in the past.

At about the same time, the New York *Times* interviewed a number of black Detroiters and summed up the predominant feeling with a quote from the owner of a popular black bar: "You can't help but feel this is home now, and it's a good feeling. Blacks are saying now: Detroit's ours now. Let's rebuild it."

Substantiating that wave of optimism was a survey by New Detroit, Inc., a coalition of businessmen and citizens formed after the riots, released in October 1978. It reported a dramatic upswing in confidence about the city's future by residents—black and white—of Wayne, Oakland, and Macomb counties. In 1976, only 47 percent of the residents felt optimistic about the city, the survey found, but the responses two years later soared to 71 percent. On race relations, 51 percent of Detroit's whites saw an improvement since the 1967 riots—compared with 28 percent two years before. Among blacks, 57 percent saw the races progressing together since the riots—compared with 42 percent in 1976.

"The most optimism is among the blacks," said Dr. Barbara Bryant, the survey's research director. "I think that reflects a black power kind of thing, a feeling of being more in control, and that extends beyond Mayor Young. I don't think the suburban optimism about Detroit means a whole lot of suburbanites are going to move back. Their view is that Detroit has 'bottomed out' and can only get better. You have to realize where the attitudes started from."

The new, upbeat feeling about the city probably could not have emerged had control of City Hall remained in the hands of the white power structure. The signal of the shift of the city's population from a white to a black majority came in 1973, when Coleman A. Young was elected mayor, narrowly outpolling former Police Commissioner John Nichols. No one person can claim total credit for the resurgence of hope in Detroit, but Coleman Young must be recognized at least as the right man in the right place at the right time. As the tipping of the racial majority in Detroit approached in the early 1970s, a major uncertainty pervading the city was the type of black leadership which would rise. Although considered radical in his younger days in the auto union, Young has provided a firm, stable influence on this transition, equally sensitive to the fears and needs of his black brethren as well as the remaining whites. To that assessment one must add his astuteness as a politician and a catalyst to downtown development. Some have called him a "black Mayor Daley," but his style and political base are far from Daley's Chicago.

Outside of his own personal gifts of leadership and the barely visible corporate consciousness just emerging from its profit-coated cocoon, Young had little to work with as he became the first black mayor of the city. A magnificent new $100 million Civic Center sat on a handsome 75-acre riverfront site, including Cobo Hall (the largest convention and recreation hall in the world) and Ford Auditorium (home of the Detroit Symphony Orchestra). But with one or two notable exceptions, the new hotel construction needed to permit the city to maximize its convention potential had been stymied and there was a shortage of hundreds of rooms.

Downtown Detroit's skyline was dominated by older, narrow-windowed, high brick office buildings of forbidding 1920s and 1930s architecture. Since World War II, not a single major new building had been constructed in downtown Detroit except for structures that by their nature have no choice other than to be there (banks, public facilities, and the like). Ford and Chrysler headquarters were outside the city borders, and GM's was removed from the downtown. In place of the booming retail center one could expect in center city, Detroit had just one quality department store—Hudson's, a gigantic establishment long considered an institution in U.S. retailing, but fast closing floors on the path toward closure (and replacement by a much smaller Hudson's) in the early 1980s. Downtown and its environs were filled with ugly strip commercial development.

The seminal event in Detroit's physical rebirth occurred in 1977 with the opening of the $337 million Renaissance Center, including a 73-story hotel (the world's tallest) surrounded by four 39-story office towers, touted as the sign of the rebirth of Detroit. Many of Detroit's hopes had been pinned to the success of the riverfront complex ever since Henry Ford II announced six years earlier his company would act as the financial catalyst for the venture involving 51 corporations.

Building revival (of which more later) may eventually prove much easier than transportation reform in the city associated globally with the automobile. Especially at rush hours, downtown Detroit streets (set at disharmonious angles to each other by an ill-conceived or badly executed plan by Pierre L'Enfant), are clogged with cars. Parking remains prohibitively expensive. The Motor City has never had a subway or elevated system—though there's a chance the 1980s might change that. After years of planning and delaying, the city's proposal for an elevated transit loop around downtown (referred to locally as the "People Mover") got a shot in the arm in 1978 when the legislature approved gasoline and license tax increases, part of which would provide state dollars to match federal funds already earmarked for Detroit.

Detroit is blessed with a fine location between Lake St. Clair to the north and Lake Erie to the south; along the busy Detroit River at its very doorstep pass a colorful panoply of great and small ships—grain-, ore-, limestone-, and coal-carrying barges. Set directly in the middle of the river is Belle Isle, a splendid 985-acre park much frequented by the city's people. But the aesthetic and recreational potential of the riverfront is thwarted by scores of obsolete industrial plants. Even now, office, plant, street, and home fill so much of Detroit that relatively little land is left for sports and relaxation; the city's percentage of park and recreation land is much less than New York's, Philadelphia's, Chicago's, or San Francisco's.

Looking west and southwest along the riverfront from center city, the view is of forests of steel and chemical plant smoke stacks. At one time, they could throw a pall across the city and darken the setting sun. Before more stringent pollution control regulations forced industry to clean up their wastes, a climatic inversion would coat Detroit with air pollution once or twice a week, creating a thick haze while the sun was shining just a few miles away.

By the late 1970s, many of Detroit's problems remained: a perilous city budget dependent on heavy federal and state aid, with deficits ever rising despite Milliken's continuing efforts to find new sources of state support; demanding public employee unions; still badly deteriorated schools; scores of unrevived neighborhoods outside of the downtown area; the ever-present unemployment specter. It was clearly too soon to say the city was on a definite, upward path. Many of the newly created downtown jobs, for instance, were going to college-trained whites, leaving most blacks still out in the cold.

Nevertheless, there was a growing cadre of civic-minded people from all walks of life, coupled with public officials, who had replaced the doomsday litany of the naysayers with a hopeful agenda of "can-doism" for the future. To declare Detroit born again might be premature, notwithstanding all the pervasive optimism. Renaissance Center and all the other dynamic developments of the 1970s probably more accurately reflected a conception, not a birth. But a vital change of attitude and expectations had occurred.

Then, starting in 1979, came the renewed crisis of the automobile industry. The Detroit area payrolls of Chrysler, the mainstay of the city's economy, plummeted from 81,700 in 1978 to 47,200 by spring 1980. The city budget was suddenly in as much trouble as it had been a half decade before—a $56.3 million deficit for the fiscal year ending in June 1980 and the prospect of a shortfall of $90 million, or even more, in the fiscal year to follow. Severe layoffs were hitting police, fire, and other vital services, and the total number of city employees was headed for its lowest level since the Great Depression of the 1930s. All of the doubts and fears the city had sought to put behind it in the late 1970s were reemerging. And no one could be sure whether these fresh reversals would be yet another storm to be endured, or whether they represented something far more serious.

Indeed, Mayor Young's 1980–81 budget not only decreed no salary increases for city workers—at a time of double-digit inflation—but an actual overall budget decrease for the first time in 17 years. Deputy Mayor Simmons told us in May 1980 that it might be necessary to actually order salary reductions. There was scarcely any prospect that the city would have fiscal life rings thrown to it by federal and state governments as it had in the mid-1970s. The federal government was paring down, striving for a balanced budget, and there was strong and increasing anti-Detroit sentiment in the state legislature—reinforced by the state's own tight fiscal situation and the gross mismanagement of Wayne County, revealed in 1979, which was unfairly being associated with the city itself. The city's citizens and businesses were already taxed to the hilt, and the reapportionment following the 1980 Census was sure to reduce urban and increase suburban strength in the state legislature even more. City officials frankly despaired in contemplating the fiscal future.

The Hero Mayor and the Great Riot of 1967

For a few Camelotlike years in the 1960s, Detroit seemed to be on its way to salvation under a witty and sophisticated hero-type mayor named Jerome P. Cavanagh. Cavanagh burst onto the political scene in 1961 when the tired old city was laboring under a $34.6 million deficit, auto production was down and unemployment at a high 10 percent, and industry and home-owners were accelerating their flight to the suburbs. Incumbent Mayor Louis Miriani, the builder of Cobo Hall, had the two newspapers and virtually the entire Detroit establishment behind him and was expected to win with ease. A virtually penniless attorney with no elective experience behind him, about all Cavanagh had was youth (he was then 33), a beautiful wife (she was a former campus beauty queen), many children to bolster his Catholic image in a heavily Catholic city, and a keen sense of the deep currents of discontent in the city. He put together what has been described as "a strange alliance of gadflies, young liberals, and crusty old pols" to pull a startling upset victory. A key factor was the black vote, about a third of the total. A few months before, in response to a wave of white murders and muggings, Miriani had ordered a police crackdown which hit the largely innocent black community the hardest. Blacks resented this and provided about 72 percent of Cavanagh's winning vote.

To put the city's financial house in order, he rammed through a 1 percent income tax on city workers (later reduced to .5 percent on nonresidents). For the first time, blacks were given important city posts. The young and vibrant mayor also discovered and perfected what was described as Cavanagh's Law for raiding the federal treasury: think up a program to benefit cities, lobby for its passage by Congress, and then be first in line, palms upward, when the dollar spigot is turned on. Cavanagh became the first man in history to head both the National League of Cities and the U.S. Conference of Mayors simultaneously, and in this halcyon year national news magazines rushed to write laudatory articles on his performance. One of his aides liked to say: "On a clear day, Cavanagh can see the White House."

Then, as Cavanagh headed into his second term in 1966, Camelot vanished. President Johnson began to divert poverty money to Vietnam and it turned out that the city's housing program had succeeded in razing 11,000 slum dwelling units during the Cavanagh regime, but that only a fraction had been replaced—and mostly with middle- and upper-income housing.

Then came Cavanagh's personal problems. His worldly, swinging ways failed to sit well at home where Mary Helen Cavanagh, the typical Irish Catholic girl who wants her husband to stay home, was becoming increasingly estranged. Certainly not all the fault was on Cavanagh's side, but in 1967 she sued him for separate maintenance and messy divorce proceedings followed in which both fought for custody of the eight children.

Five days after Cavanagh's break with his wife became public, the most destructive race riot in the history of the United States broke out in his Detroit. Within a week's time, vast blocks of the city were gutted by flames, 43 persons were killed (33 blacks, 10 whites), 7,200 were arrested, and damage of close to $45 million was inflicted. The death and damage toll would exceed that of Watts or Newark or even of the Detroit race riot of 1943, when 34 died (25 blacks, 9 whites). Yet this new Detroit riot would be of far different complexion from the conflagration of 1943, when gangs of whites and blacks clashed in open street warfare. Summer 1967 was the great season of racial convulsion across the entire U.S.A. One week before, Newark had blown—a spectacle instantly relayed to Detroit and the nation by television. The hallmarks of the 1967 riot were looting and arson, and a chance for hardpressed blacks to pick up a free case of whiskey or television set, and to get revenge on local stores which constantly gave them the short end. No racial gangs clashed; even at the height of the disturbances white reporters were rarely molested in the black areas.

The Detroit riot was all the more tragic because it happened in the city where virtually everyone thought it "couldn't happen," where black-white dialogue was more advanced than in practically any other great American city, where the mayor was intensely sensitive to the black community, where a high proportion of blacks owned their own homes, where the auto industry had helped many earn substantial livelihoods. But as later investigation would show, the chief rioting was not mainly practiced by a "riffraff" of young dropouts, uneducated and jobless. Only 10 percent of those arrested, in fact, were juveniles. A high proportion of the rioters had at least a foothold in middle-class society—of the males, for instance, 83 percent were employed (40 percent by the auto companies), 45 percent were married (and four out of five of them living with their wives), two-thirds had no previous criminal convictions, and the average income, by some estimates, was around $6,000. Why did this group, then, take to the streets? Only tentative answers can be given. One reason may lie in television and increased education: this generation realized what it was missing, was beginning to recognize the white racism built into "the system" for what it was. The repeated incidences of gross police brutality later documented by the Kerner Commission were but a reflection of what the Detroit black had been faced with for years. The white man's promises, the web of false expectations raised by President Johnson and Cavanagh and their poverty program, were recognized as a sham in large part. As Irving J. Rubin wrote for the *Reporter* a few months after the Detroit conflagration: "The riots were an outburst of frustration over unmet demands for dignity and for economic and political power. They were a tragic, violent, but understandable declaration of manhood and an insistence that blacks be able to participate in and to control their own destinies and community affairs."

Cavanagh's own leadership deteriorated rapidly in his last two years in office. The city crime rate continued to soar, race relations polarized more and more as whites reacted in anger or flight from the riots. The financial cushion from the payroll tax disappeared and the city faced a $50 million deficit. (About the only happy development of 1968 was the Detroit Tigers' American League pennant win, its first in 23 years—followed by victory in the World Series. The hysteria and street-corner hugging that followed were utterly color-blind.) Early in 1969, Cavanagh announced his retirement, and by his last months in office he had, in the words of one Detroit newspaper editor, "virtually abdicated."

The Black Transition and Coleman Young

The 1970 Census showed that blacks represented 44 percent of the Detroit city population (up from 29 percent in 1960). At some unchronicled moment in 1972 or 1973, Detroit became a city with a black majority, the largest city in the country with such a distinction. As that point approached, two questions about the political future of the city were frequently raised. One was the economic base that would remain in Detroit—whether it would be dominated by abandoned businesses, the poor and the elderly, or whether the remaining blacks would have a strong enough middle class to be self-supporting instead of a stepchild dependent on county, state, and federal governments. By the late 1970s, the response to those questions remained mixed. On the one hand, some middle class blacks were fleeing to the suburbs too, as quickly as their income would permit it. On the other, some young white couples were returning to the city, lured by the availability of well-constructed old homes which have become the best buys of the metropolitan area (indeed, some phenomenally less expensive than suburban homes of comparable quality).

The second question was the type of black leadership which would control the government and politics. Out of Detroit have come many of the most provocative black-nationalist types of movements—the Black Muslims, the Black Jesus theology, the extremist DRUM movement in the auto plants, and the separatists of the Republic of New Africa. The election of Young in 1973 confirmed the suspicion that those groups commanded no real, broad-based political support among blacks.

That response had seemed likely in 1969 when another black man— Wayne County Auditor Richard Austin—came within 7,000 votes of being elected mayor, receiving a monolithic 94 percent of the black vote and one out of every five white votes. A thoroughly competent contender, he had strong backing from the UAW, Teamsters, and the Detroit *Free Press*, and in 1970 was elected secretary of state.

The man elected mayor in 1969 was Roman S. Gribbs, son of Polish immigrant parents who served previously as county sheriff. Though an overwhelming white vote (about 80 percent) elected him, Gribbs proved to be no racist, starting with appointment of a number of blacks to important city posts. He faced the delicate task of being a transition leader in Detroit's white-to-black development, a painful and difficult process.

Yet four years later, when Coleman Young did actually win election as Detroit's first black mayor, a city judge rated his administration a "dynamic success" even before Young's inaugural address—simply because "the goddamn town didn't blow up" when he was elected. Part of the reason for that was the fact neither Young nor his opponent, former Police Commissioner John Nichols, appealed to racial fears in their campaigns. Still, the racial division of the city was reflected in the results. Young won by about 14,000 votes—231,000 to 217,000. A post-election analysis showed support for each was overwhelmingly split along racial lines: 92 percent of the blacks voted for Young while 91 percent of the whites cast ballots for Nichols.

Intuitively recognizing the black administration of a city split 50–50 racially cannot ignore the new white minority, Young immediately moved to deal with the white power brokers, who still controlled the capital of the city.

Ardent promises of support came from the two symbols of power in the city—Henry Ford II and UAW President Leonard Woodcock. Young was sworn into office by two judges—one white, one black. He refrained from throwing out many of the aides of former Mayor Gribbs, keeping a promise his staff would reflect the racial balance. At the same time, he acted expeditiously to disband an elite police strike force called STRESS (Stop The Robberies, Enjoy Safe Streets), an innovation of Nichols to combat street crimes. STRESS generated hostility in the black community, which felt the unit's white officers were trigger happy and all too willing to crack down on blacks. In their first four months in action, STRESS officers killed eight blacks; in less than two years, one white STRESS officer killed six people. After that, there was no patching up of the antagonism; the unit's abolition was the only answer. Finally, Young showed his determination to be independent and above race. His target was Detroit crime—a source of fear among both the black and white communities.

"I issue a forward warning now to all those pushers, all rip-off artists, to all muggers," Young told a somewhat startled audience in his inaugural speech. "I don't give a damn if they are black or white, or if they wear Superfly suits or blue uniforms with silver badges—hit Eight Mile road." The tone of the Young Administration in Detroit had been set.

For Coleman Young, now approaching the age when most people think of retirement, his election in 1973 and reelection in 1977 would add another stirring chapter in any volume of Horatio Alger rags-to-riches stories. Born in Alabama, he can recall his mother's fear of the "bunch of dudes in white sheets" riding through town. After World War I, his family joined the trek of many other Southerners to Detroit, where he continued to encounter discrimination, molding his liberal line of thinking. (Partly because of his early union organizing activities, he was labeled a radical by some and even a Communist by others, including Walter Reuther in 1946, during Reuther's purge of the UAW, and later by the House Un-American Activities Committee.) Blacklisted by labor and management alike, Young developed a chronic case of what Motor City residents call buzzard's luck—"can't kill nothing, nothing won't die." Politicking was always his first calling, even during his most down-and-out days. Finally, in 1960, he was elected a delegate to the state constitutional convention, built a good reputation, and in 1964 was elected to the Michigan state senate, where he helped write the state's open housing law. Given the chance, he rose rapidly: in 1968, he was elected Michigan's Democratic National Committeeman, the first black in the country to hold that position.

Through it all, Young retained the sense of his roots while taking what he could from the variety of interests which crossed his paths. Essentially, he changed little (except, perhaps, to become even more politically savvy) since Remer Tyson, political writer of the Detroit *Free Press*, described him in *The Nation* shortly after his first election.

A tall, dignified man with a salt-and-pepper mustache, a 55-year-old, happy-go-lucky bachelor, Young mixes the telling idiom of the Old South with back-alley language of big industrial Detroit. The rhetoric reflects the man. On the promise of equal employment during his administration, he says, "that means more at the top for blacks, for there ain't no shortage of blacks out there behind them garbage trucks." On racial separatism: "The last man who tried that was Jeff Davis. He had an army and everything and still didn't win." To whites who have fled to the suburbs: "Like Joe Louis, said, you can run, baby, but you can't hide."

Young's followers swear by him as a one-time poor boy "off the corner," who has shared their struggle. He did come up the hard way, sometimes risking his neck to rebel against racial and economic discrimination. He has stayed in touch and his street people have reason to trust him.

But Young is no longer a poor black man struggling to make ends meet. He wears expensive suits and flashy rings, usually carries a couple of hundred dollars in his wallet. He owns part of a Detroit bar and rib shack, an interest in a Detroit housing complex and part of a Florida land development corporation. Some of his best friends think of him as more a playboy than a politician who pays attention to details. . . . Young is easy to like, delightful to drink and dine with; but it is difficult, if not impossible, to know him down deep.

Detroit, Michigan, and the country have come to know Young by his deeds. Whenever his administration might end, he would leave a lasting legacy to his city—the replacement of hopelessness with hope. Politically, the gains by blacks went beyond City Hall. Ten years after the 1967 riots, Detroit had not only a black mayor but also a black school superintendent, a black police chief, and a black county sheriff. Instead of one black on the nine-member city council, there were four. The school board also had been reorganized, with blacks assuming majority status (seven of 13 members in place of two of seven members on the old board). Young had made the police department, source of so much racial antagonism, one of his first priorities upon taking office. At the time of the riots, 95 out of every 100 police officers were white; crime rates were soaring out of sight when Young took over; murders were climbing before he took office, from 693 in 1972 to 751 in 1973, and continued increasing to 801 in his first year in office. Detroit picked up the unwanted designation as "Murder Capital, U.S.A."

Richard Simmons, Detroit's deputy mayor, told us in an interview that Young realized no one could govern, much less reconstruct a city, in the midst of chaos. Civil order was necessary. "In order for Detroit to become great again," Simmons said, "the mayor first of all had to resolve the very bad feelings toward the protective services, particularly the police." He undertook both structural reorganization and attitudinal reform. Simmons said Young had to make the community know that the "police force, as part of the city government, was under the direction of civilian control. The police . . . as a paramilitary operation sometimes think of themselves as an entity to themselves and I believe that is going too far." According to Louis Martin, editorial director of the black-owned Michigan *Chronicle*, Young had a distinct advantage over his predecessors in dealing with the crime issue.

"Young can lay it on the line to the black community," Martin said, "and he will be listened to, whereas a white man would be met with suspicion right from the start."

Besides the overhaul of the police department (which met with anticipated stiff resistance from many rank-and-file officers), Young initiated an affirmative action effort to hire more black officers. By the end of 1978, 41 percent of the patrolmen on the beats were minorities, 9 of 21 district commanders were black, and a 20-year veteran black officer, William L. Hart, had been chief for more than two years. Young also decentralized the department, creating 46 minipolice stations in the neighborhoods, each with foot patrols, a practice that had disappeared in the 1950s. The crime rate (though crime statistics can prove contradictory conclusions) slowly started declining, while public trust started moving back upward. In 1977, an out-of-town journalist noted that "something very strange happened here this week: the city which is known perhaps as much for its crime as for its cars went six days without a reported homicide." It had been almost a decade since that happened, the account said, a noticeable improvement over 1974 when murders were occurring at a rate of more than two a day.

By no means did every pusher, rip-off artist, mugger, and murderer "hit Eight Mile road," as Young admonished in 1974. Problems continued. In 1976 a wave of youth crime threatened to cut short the economic resurgence of the downtown area. Businessmen with capital needed reassurance that downtown Detroit was worth investing in, especially after a gang of several hundred youthful thugs invaded a rock concert in Cobo Hall. Hundreds of whites and blacks alike were beaten and robbed, and one woman was raped, while Detroit's men in blue, admittedly outnumbered, remained outside the hall and refused to interfere with the pillage. It was the climax to a trail of terror left by the gangs during the summer of 1976, forcing Young to impose a 10 P.M. curfew for everyone under 18, recall 450 policemen laid off as a budget-cutting measure, and fire Police Chief Philip Tannian less than two months after the Cobo Hall incident. The continuing internal dissension within the department, creating low morale among the officers, also was cited by Young for replacing Tannian with Hart. Detroit, by the end of the '70s, had largely erased its notoriety as "Murder Capital," and joggers could be seen out on the streets at six in the morning. Yet from time to time, the specter of past fears continued to crop up.

Young's second major crisis to overcome, if he was to put Detroit back on its feet, was the financial deficits in the city budget. Facing a red-ink figure of $44 million in 1976 and more than twice that in 1977 ($103 million), Young did what few mayors are willing to do—bite the bullet, lay off employees, and cut spending. "It hurt us," the mayor said in his 1976 state of the city message. He detailed the impact of his cutbacks:

Many hundreds of city employees have been laid off permanently. There are more than 4,000 fewer employees on city payrolls today than there were 18 months ago. During this past year we shut recreation centers, museums, and immunization clinics. Both the police and fire departments operated with fewer men and women. Programs had to be delayed.

The coming year will be harder. . . . The first steps we've taken toward a renaissance, toward the building of a better Detroit, will be wiped away if we fail to take hard action now. . . . We can't paper this thing over. We can't play with the books, and juggle the figures. . . . I will do what I have to do.

Compounding his dilemma was the recession from which Detroit and the nation was only emerging in 1976. The year before, with auto production down, the average unemployment in the city was 20 percent, reaching a high of 22.1 percent, according to the Michigan Bureau of Employment Security. That was compared with 14.4 percent for the six-county metropolitan area, 12.5 percent for the state, and 8.5 percent for the country. To the saying that Michigan gets pneumonia when the nation gets a cold, one might add that Detroit gets pneumonia with complications.

After surveying the alternatives (further cutbacks were "irresponsible," he concluded), Young called on outside help—from Lansing and Washington. His conclusions were supported by a Task Force on City Finance, which estimated the city would need to lay off another 4,700 workers to close the projected $103 million budget gap. Lansing and Governor Milliken responded with what Young called a "historic breakthrough" by giving Detroit a $30 million "equity payment" for services, such as cultural facilities, health services, and crime efforts, provided up to then by the city to the state without compensation. The federal government's counter-cyclical aid helped some, as did continued funding of city employees through CETA (Comprehensive Employment and Training Act).

The outside aid also came at the time the economy was taking off again, easing the unemployment rate back to half the level of the recessionary highs. The combination of events allowed Detroit to accumulate a small surplus instead of a $100 million deficit and provided the city with at least a brief respite from the clutches of financial disaster. (As if the "Perils of Pauline" would never end, however, Congress in 1978 put a $7,200 lid on what CETA workers might be paid. At that point, Detroit had 2,400 firemen, policemen, and recreational employees getting all or part of their pay from CETA, and starting policemen, for example, earned $17,500 annually. Congress also abruptly ended the so-called counter-cyclical, or antirecession special aid funds for cities, a program under which Detroit was expecting $17 million for its next year budget. All of this pointed up the dangerous dependence of Detroit and similar cities on federal grants. Indeed, by 1978, for every dollar it raised locally, Detroit was receiving 69.6 cents from Washington.) And there were intimations of even worse financial trouble down the road. Michigan has a law authorizing compulsory arbitration between municipalities and public safety (police and fire) unions, a practice that can lead to devastating consequences for hard-pressed cities. Compulsory arbitration decisions awarded in 1978–79 to Detroit's police and firemen—already the highest paid in the United States—threatened to trigger a $68 million increase in the city's financial obligations, a development almost totally outside the mayor's control. Ironically, Coleman Young as a state senator cosponsored the 1969 legislation. But by the late 1970s he had not only disowned his progeny but was refusing to pay high awards made by outside arbitrators and seeking to have the law overthrown by the courts. "Compulsory arbitration," he said, "destroys collective bargaining and, even more serious for Detroit, compulsory arbitration destroys sensible fiscal management." Arbitrators, he said, are granted "powers so broad that they undermine the democratic process and strip from the people of a community their ability to control their own affairs."

By dealing squarely with the crime and budget issues, Young bought time to nurture his plans for economic revitalization, surely the jewel in his crown of accomplishments. As noted earlier, the gigantic Renaissance Center has been the springboard for other downtown development. Ren Center was called a fortress by some critics—appropriately enough, given the massive blank walls it exhibited at street level, as if it keeps the surly mobs of the city at bay, far from visiting conventioneers in their encapsulated environment. (Someone sarcastically suggested that Detroit was founded as a fort—in 1701 by Antoine de la Mothe Cadillac—and might now die as one.) But the Center did remake the Detroit skyline quite suddenly. The criticism which proved false was that it would create large vacancies in the other, long-struggling downtown office buildings. That did not, in fact, occur. Young could also note that Ford moved 1,800 workers from the Dearborn headquarters complex into one tower, while General Motors moved its entire overseas operation from New York to occupy part of another tower. The argument that Ren Center would be a catalyst was borne out by the renewed interest shown simultaneously in other downtown development. The *Free Press*, Detroit's morning newspaper, constructed a new plant on the river west of Cobo Hall and the Civic Arena, close to the spot where oil millionaire Max Fisher was underwriting the construction of some riverfront apartments. Fisher's apartments, along with others planned on Washington Boulevard and the Lafayette towers and town houses, will be priced for the middle class, both black and white.

In one week in September 1978, Ford announced a joint venture with the Rockefeller family to build two more 21-story office towers east of the present cluster, at a cost of $70 million; General Motors announced the rehabilitation of the New Center neighborhood north of its headquarters, at a cost of $20 million, including $1.3 million from GM; and the Detroit *News* somewhat prematurely announced that Hudson's, the patriarch of downtown department stores, planned to join Sears and Penney's in building a massive shopping center a half-block from its current location and call it Cadillac Center. The local papers fairly gushed about the prospects, with the *Free Press* suggesting the two new office buildings at Ren Center should "silence the doubters once and for all," and the *News* trumpeting, "Money talks. And it made a heartening assertion this week: Detroit is a good investment." Just how good that investment might be remained in substantial doubt in 1980, however, with the department store commitments for Cadillac Square (except for Hudson's) still unconfirmed and even Hudson's trying to pressure the city for more public financial commitment. And a group of historic preservationists remained furious with Hudson's for its insistence that before it built a store in Cadillac Square, it would abandon and demolish the massive downtown building in which it had been doing business since 1928. Architect-planner Victor Gruen told us in 1978, when Hudson's made known its intention to tear down the old 2.8 million square foot store (at 25 stories the world's tallest department store): "This building was a landmark of Detroit in the same way the Eiffel Tower is of Paris. The news that this institution shall close down is an unbelievable horror." And a veteran city journalist told us in 1980: "Hudson's has slowly turned the tourniquet on that downtown store until it's now a pale shadow of its former self—so pale that everyone now agrees it's a reasonable thing for them to prepare to shut it down. You could see it coming five years ago. And Hudson's has continued to build suburban malls all around the city—a dozen in all now."

Even with the laudatory self-congratulations of 1978, the fact that Saks Fifth Avenue New Center store, in the heart of GM's renovation project, announced it was closing after 38 years and moving out to Fairlane Town Center in Dearborn, was all but lost. Fairlane's sponsorship by none other than Henry Ford II has raised some question about Ford's commitment to maintaining the central city. After all, it was the modern shopping center that helped encourage suburban sprawl and the depopulation of the central city in the first place. Other projects, including a $12 million, 380-bed federal detention center in downtown Detroit scheduled for occupancy in 1980, and several other neighborhood proposals, were also used by City Hall to justify their claim of Ren Center as a catalyst. According to Young, $603 million in construction and renovation projects involving 53 downtown buildings could be tied directly to the existence of Ren Center.

"I've never said I expected the Renaissance Center to eliminate crime and deterioration. It's symbolic of a new generation; it's not the final answer," Young replied to criticism of the project. Equally symbolic were the reports of increased shopping and restaurant activity downtown, the completion of the new city-built Joe Louis arena (honoring a native son), success in landing the 1980 Republican National Convention and the 1982 Super Bowl.

One of Detroit's problems in regaining economic self-sufficiency was that its millions of dollars of new construction would not be completely reflected in property tax rolls for years to come. State legislation in the mid-1970s gave a full real estate tax exemption for 12 years to new apartment buildings in the city, delaying the day when their property tax revenues can be counted on. In response to a question whether this loss of revenue worried him, Young told us in an interview: "No, the land was producing no significant tax revenue anyway. We'll pick up much more than the lost tax revenue through sales taxes, general increase in economic activity, and through the thousands of new city residents that will be attracted."

Another worry—population loss, counted at 224,153, or 15 percent of the city's population during the first eight years of the 1970s, was no longer considered as severe a problem (except in the loss of some federal per capita grants) as it once had been. The suburban flight was clearly leveling off by the late 1970s, apparently as all who would leave finally did depart the city. The general expectation was that the population would stabilize—possibly around 1.2 million persons—in the 1980s.

Detroit Schools, Neighborhoods, and Housing

All of Detroit's downtown economic revival and fresh political verve did not, however, obscure some very tough social problems which were still left to be dealt with:

SCHOOLS AND INTEGRATION. In 1972, a racial and a fiscal crisis simultaneously converged on the Detroit school system, prompting a new exodus of those who could afford to flee to head for the suburbs. Early that year, U.S. District Court Judge Stephen J. Roth declared Detroit's schools segregated and later ordered the busing of 150,000 black city children to the suburbs and an equal number of white suburban pupils to the city. The response from the populace was swift and predictably negative.

In addition, the Detroit school system was in one of its perennial fiscal crises. The local voters had already rejected a tax levy increase, and in the fall election the statewide voters would turn down Governor Milliken's proposal for the state to assume school costs. With an average student-teacher ratio of 35–1, the 291,000 pupils then in the Detroit schools—two-thirds of them black—clearly were getting shortchanged on their education. State achievement tests scores confirmed it: they were at the lowest levels. "The conclusion," Judge Roth wrote in his March 1972 decision, "is inescapable that relief of segregation in the public schools of the city of Detroit cannot be accomplished within the corporate geographical limits of the city."

In an election year, the volatility of the busing issue spilled over into the campaigns, especially through George Wallace's primary race, exacerbating the problem and feeding the emotions. Eventually the U.S. Supreme Court agreed with Judge Roth's segregation conclusion but rejected the cross-district busing remedy. When busing finally began, it was almost academic: some 21,200 children out of an already-shrunken enrollment of 247,500 as more and more parents had moved, with their children, to the suburbs. Young told a national television audience in 1975 that "busing within the city of Detroit alone, where already over 70 percent of the pupils are black, can solve no problem. The basic problem with the city of Detroit, and its educational system, is a lack of quality, a lack of money."

Whatever the reasons, the school situation remained an emergency one at the start of the 1980s. Detroit schoolchildren were still scoring persistently below state and national levels in standard tests. Only 28 percent of the 10th and 11th graders passed all three parts of a competency test of grade-level reading, writing, and arithmetic.

NEIGHBORHOOD REVITALIZATION. In his 1977 reelection campaign, Young found himself under attack for concentrating on the Renaissance Center and other downtown development at the expense of Detroit's neighborhoods. The argument apparently had little impact on the voters, as Young defeated Ernest C. Browne, a city councilman, by an overwhelming 218,826–150,404 vote. Yet there was evidence to support Browne's contention.

The visitor could see it when traveling out Woodward Avenue, which extends straight from downtown through Highland to Oakland County and at the Eight Mile Road divides the city in two. It is not the worst part of Detroit, for sure. But the signs of decay are there: the boarded-up, empty buildings, the broken sidewalks with weeds growing through the cracks, the debris-strewn vacant lots, and the inevitable sleazy shops selling X-rated material. One block south of the Detroit Medical School complex, hailed as an urban renewal success, runs Eliot Street. In a block of Eliot, just a couple of blocks east of Woodward, stands Alpha House, a historic old brick house of World War I vintage like many others that once stood in the neighborhood. In the same block, however, six of the other houses stand only as boarded-up sentinels of a bygone era of grandeur. Another remains partly razed, while the rest of the block is empty lots or large former homes sliced up into multiple apartments. Detroit still has thousands of such blocks, its flashy downtown revival notwithstanding.

It took Detroit 10 years to start rebuilding the heart of the 1967 riot area along what was then 12th Street but has been renamed Rosa Parks Boulevard. For part of that decade, the ruins of the fires and looting were left as a reminder of the scourge. Then the area was cleared, still a barren reminder of the community of people who once lived and worked there. Finally, in 1977, ground was broken for a $3 million shopping center with 13 stores on Rosa Parks Boulevard. The stirrings of new life were also apparent in construction of a 100-unit apartment house and 86 new townhouses nearby.

The mayor and his aides responded to criticism by saying neighborhood streets might not be totally safe but were becoming safer, that housing might not be uniformly of the best quality but was improving. And, Deputy Mayor Simmons told us, of every four dollars spent by Detroit's government, three are spent in the neighborhoods. "This is an extremely large city," he said. "It's hard to see other projects that aren't concentrated as those in the central business district."

Where are the other projects? These are most frequently cited:

- The Detroit Medical Center, a 240-acre complex involving six hospitals in the Wayne State University area, site of the city's worst slum during the 1950's. Hailed by the Detroit *News* as a "mammoth symbol of urban renewal success," the project has created one of the largest and most modern medical facilities in the country, employing more than 10,000 people full-time, and its

$500 million price tag is even more costly than the riverfront showplace, Renaissance Center. Even though some question its impact on the community around the Medical Center, others point to new business developments springing up to support the complex.

▪ General Motors New Center rehabilitation, small in scale but potentially significant in its impact, city hall claimed. "It involves a process that might be marketable for renovating housing in other neighborhoods," said Young's press secretary James Graham. GM and other businesses were to put up about $2.6 million (half from GM) to buy and rehabilitate 125 single-family homes and 175 apartment units in the neighborhood adjacent to its corporate headquarters three miles north of downtown. After renovation, they would be resold for about $40,000, a price that will make them one of the housing bargains of the metropolitan area.

▪ Elmwood III, in the heart of the old Black Bottom ghetto, the neighborhood northeast of downtown where Mayor Young grew up. Part of an urban renewal project, on 500 acres bulldozed down 25 years ago, Elmwood III calls for a cluster concept of middle- and upper-income town houses and single-family homes. When they first went on the market, their cost was $45,000; with the high demand for the units, costs have shot upward to $65,000–$70,000. Elmwood area apartment units were down to 55 percent occupancy before the area's revival in recent years. Since then, rents have been raised three times and occupancy stood around 95 percent in 1978.

▪ Harmony Village, in the Livernois section on the northwest side of town, scene in 1975 of a small scale disturbance touched off by the shooting of a black man by a white bar owner. There the city, the state housing authority, and the federal Housing and Urban Development (HUD) Department then collaborated on a project that would eventually provide for 2,000 moderately priced (about $28,000) homes.

▪ Indian Village, an historic district between downtown and the Grosse Pointes. Though a few hundred homes are involved, its attraction is the well built but rundown houses that once were the homes of the giants of Detroit industry. Largely without governmental aid, a person could buy one of the homes a few years ago for $35,000–$40,000. Now they have been snatched up, and a sense of community has developed. When one does go on the market, it will command $100,000 in many cases, one resident said.

▪ Malls, fascades, commercial strip developments. Scattered throughout the city, the malls (smaller models of the one on Woodward Avenue near downtown) attempt to provide a convenient, attractive place for city residents to shop. According to Simmons, the city has spent or set aside about $60 million for these neighborhood developments, mostly from the city public works program and federal community action bloc grants.

For many city residents, a certain quality of life still is missing in the Motor City. William Serrin, former *Free Press* reporter turned urbanscape critic, lives in the Indian Village neighborhood. He talked about the little things that make the difference between the good, comfortable life and life in Detroit. Things like the elm tree stump in front of his house, killed by dutch elm disease: despite repeated calls to the city over a period of a couple of years, it still sits there, with no indication the city intends to remove it. In the winter, snow simply doesn't get removed from many streets, a distinct problem for a snow-belt city. As far as parks go, they are few and poorly maintained. The deterioration in the quality of life "weighs you down, and finally it makes you leave town," said Serrin.

HOUSING. At one time, the U.S. Housing and Urban Development (HUD) Department was the largest homeowner in Detroit, a testimony to the utter failure of its housing policies of the 1950s and '60s. First, bulldozers came in and laid waste to hundreds of acres of homes and stores, with a promise of something better to come. But it never came. The public housing, when built, crammed hundreds of people into socially explosive high-rises. Often, the housing was demolished, never to be replaced. Then came the Housing Act of 1968, with new promises for helping low-income people buy their own homes. An immense scandal, worse in Detroit than any other city, grew out of the speculators and bribers involved in that program. A congressional committee reported in 1972 that HUD had been forced to acquire 8,000 homes in Detroit, and estimated up to another 20,000 properties were in default. The federal government stood to lose $200 million in the program in Detroit alone. Ultimately, about 150 persons were convicted of charges stemming from the wheeling-and-dealing that accompanied the program. "HUD . . . with its arrogant attitude had gutted this city," said Deputy Mayor Simmons.

A major part of Young's second four-year term was dedicated to converting the repossessed, publicly owned HUD housing into rehabilitated homes owned by private taxpayers. In restrospect, Young viewed the HUD blunders as a "disaster which for us becomes a blessing," a reserve stock of unoccupied homes, structurally sound, "that the city can use for its poorer people." By the mid-1970s, as the suburban housing market became both saturated and overpriced, Detroit's cheaper, rehabilitated homes were also becoming magnets for some white middle class couples looking for a housing bargain—and willing to face the vicissitudes of Detroit housing. On new construction, there was nowhere to go but up. In 1979, the town that once called itself "the city of homes" issued fewer than 10 single-family house building permits.

Power in Motor City

As Detroit began its second 10 years after the devastating 1967 riots, it had two things going for it visibly lacking a decade earlier—strong leadership, personified by Young, and concerned civic support from a wide variety of private and quasi-public organizations. When one asks who has real power in Detroit now, no longer is the answer as it was a decade ago: "Nobody." Indeed, the Detroit *News*, in an exhaustive 1978 study of power in the city, concluded: "A personal, reasoned commitment to Detroit by a large majority of power-holders now exists and seems to guarantee not only survival of the city but its continued revitalization."

There were other fascinating conclusions in that *News* survey by Andrew McGill and Barbara Young—too long to relate in detail here. The authors did find that power was more institutionalized, less personal than it had been in the Detroit of earlier years, that the auto industry was no longer "the be-all and end-all of power in and stemming from Detroit," that no "small, elite power structure dominated by white businessmen" controlled the city, that there was evidence of concern about the city on the part of white business leaders and other suburbanites, that organized labor's power may be more circumscribed than most would think, and that blacks—most notably Coleman Young, but not Young alone—had risen to positions of substantial power in Detroit.

The central core of Detroit's establishment, the *News* found, actually consisted of two distinct but linked groups: on one side the rich, socially elite and commercially important people of Detroit, including auto magnates, former board chairmen, bank presidents, top retail merchants, and the like, and on the other side people from working class backgrounds, including politicians, labor leaders, lawyers, ministers, and other professionals. The first circle, it was noted, "comes from upper class kinship lines," the second "is more than half black and includes a number of labor union leaders with a consistent background of militant, left-of-center unionism." Young, out of the latter group, remarked about his close ties with many in the first: "You ain't gotta love 'em to use 'em."

Seven men, the *News* decided, were individually and particularly collectively, when working together, the most powerful in Detroit in the late '70's: Henry Ford II; UAW president Douglas Fraser; Coleman Young ("the personification of government power in this region"); recently retired Wayne State University president George Gullen; lawyer-civic leader Alan E. Schwartz; Peter Stroh, president of the Stroh Brewing Company (an old Detroit firm); and Joseph Hudson, Jr., chairman of the J.L. Hudson Co.

"Each person has power in his own right," the *News* said in a copyrighted series. "But what distinguishes these men is that each, independently, has influence well beyond his own power sphere. Possessing great power, they are usually slow to use it. They are more methodical than dynamic. Yet when they unite—and call on their friends—they control the lion's share of Detroit power today. They can cut across cultural, class, wealth and occupational barriers to bring together diverse people of power. In short, these seven men control the critical power links to make big things happen—or not happen."

Hudson, then in his late 30s, learned in 1968 how dangerous it could be (in the temper of those times) to take a forceful and exposed civic role. He helped to form and became first chairman of New Detroit, an organization to bridge racial lines that became, in fact, the first urban coalition in the country. But within days of that announcement, Hudson found irate customers accusing him of being a do-gooder and "bleeding heart" and returning their Hudson's charge cards by the dozens.

A sign of change in the times was that just a decade later, Hudson could appear at the White House Conference on Balanced National Growth and Economic Development and hold up his own city as an example of productive public-private partnerships:

■   New Detroit, after a rocky start during which the white and black members had some confrontations and misunderstandings, learned to work together, drawing in the top executives of the auto industry, the Burroughs Corporation, major banks, and other business leaders, as well as leaders from neighborhoods and other citizens. New Detroit provided staffing for some community projects as well as seed money for others, its activities spanning such areas as minority jobs, health, drugs, youth and neighborhood stabilization. As one former federal official involved in the early days of New Detroit said, "These people have accomplished something because they forgot the quick fix, combined insight and clout, and learned a whole lot about each other and their town."

■   Detroit Renaissance, composed mostly of the chief executive officers of the 30 largest professional and industrial firms in the area. It was set up by Henry Ford II in 1971 primarily to help underwrite the construction of Renaissance Center. Since then it has moved on to other development projects, including new downtown housing, a jobs development study, and planning for a new downtown shopping center. (Generally unreported in the local press, however, there have been ongoing, sub-rosa antagonisms between the business planners and some of the aggressive blacks working for Coleman Young—thwarting, in fact, some development that might otherwise have moved forward.)

■   The Detroit Economic Growth Council, composed of senior business executives, labor leaders, and public officials. One recent year, its cochairmen were retired GM Chairman James Roche and retired Chrysler Chairman Lynn Townsend. Its major areas of concern are revenue growth for city government, to retain existing businesses and help them expand, and efficiency and management of city government.

Essential to much of that cooperation that began to mark Detroit in the '70s was the close set of ties developing, especially between Young and Ford. To support Young's reelection effort, for instance, Ford sponsored a $1,000 a ticket fund-raiser at that most elite of the establishment retreats, the Detroit Club, where until a very few years ago the only black person to cross the threshold was a servant. "Coleman Young is my favorite mayor," the automaker king said. "And Hank the Deuce is my favorite industrialist," the grinning, erstwhile radical mayor replied. (In addition to making the right friends, Young operated under an informal set of rules divined by William Greider of the Washington *Post*: First, take care of your people—i.e., the black folk who gave you your chief electoral support. Second, choose your enemies wisely, and if you must have enemies choose them for maximum political value—for example, the white-dominated police force. Third, do not speak ill of other politicians you need—e.g., Republican Gov. William Milliken. And fourth, talk in a language that will reassure your people, even if it provokes your opposition—such as advocating busing to achieve quality education.)

A final source of power in Detroit are the two major dailies, the *Free Press* (morning) and *News* (evening).

Of the two, the *News* is the more conservative, had in 1979 a slightly larger circulation (632,000 daily), and profits from its ownership of WDVM-TV in Washington, D.C. It came to own that station in December 1978, when the fear that the Federal Communications Commission would outlaw ownership of a television station and a newspaper in the same city caused the *News* to swap its longtime outlet, WWJ-TV in Detroit, for WDVM (then WTOP-TV), owned by the Washington *Post*. The *Free Press*, somewhat more liberal, breezier in its writing style, has been gaining ground on the *News* in the 1970s. Its 1979 circulation was about 15,000 less (down from 100,000 less in 1970) and its benefits greatly from its ownership by the vigorous Knight-Ridder Newspaper chain. Detroit has been the most strike-prone newspaper town in the U.S.A. since World War II, suffering a 134-day long strike in 1964 and another 267 days in 1968–69—a record length in U.S. history.

The *News* has traditionally been a city-based paper, heavily emphasizing local news, while the *Free Press* has had greater outstate circulation. In 1980, however, there were signs that the *News* was moving aggressively to expand its circulation area. Throughout the Young administration, both papers have been strong boosters of his downtown revitalization efforts.

A fresh and independent journalistic voice in the city, launched in the 1970s, was *Monthly Detroit*, which in 1980 took on as its editor Robert Pisor, a respected ex-*News* reporter and onetime press secretary to Coleman Young.

Suburbia and Detroit Metro

Detroit's geography, from center city to suburb, runs roughly this way: first comes the slowly changing downtown center with its Renaissance Center and Cobo Hall, of which we have spoken; forming a choke collar around this business district is the U-shaped black ghetto, closed off by the river; beyond the ghetto are industrialized and largely white-working-class areas, most of which experienced constant black population pressure into the 1970s.

Two independent towns are actually encircled by Detroit—Hamtramck (population 22,873), a citadel of poor Polish and Ukrainian whites, however one quarter black; and Highland Park (29,173), home of huge Chrysler and Ford plants and a one-time ethnic bastion, now becoming black faster than Hamtramck. Highland Park, in fact, in 1968 elected the only full-time black Republican mayor in the U.S.A., Robert P. Blackwell, an articulate ex-UAW official. No sooner had Blackwell's fellow Republican, President Nixon, taken office in Washington than Highland Park began to receive an amazing flow of federal money, more in a few months than it had received in the previous half a century of its existence. Despite his success in bringing in about $1,000 federal aid for each city resident, Blackwell was voted out of office in 1975 by Jesse P. Miller, a black city councilman and union pension fund employee who sought to make his mark crusading against pornography, massage parlors, topless-bottomless go-go bars, and other dens of iniquity.

By the end of the decade, modest efforts to revitalize Highland Park were underway, sporadically interrupted by Detroit's economic swings. The majority black community initiated in the summer of 1978 an effort to boost citizen pride and participation through a series of community meetings on "Highland Park roots." These featured lectures on the city's rich history (it was the site of the first mass-produced auto and once had parents from around America sending their children to its superior school system), profiles of the accomplishments of current and past residents, and discussions of modern urban problems.

Hamtramck (pronounced Ham-tram-ack) has some interesting claims to fame: it is the headquarters of the Olsonite Company, the world's largest manufacturer of toilet seats; and it appeared at one time to be the most impoverished city in America. The state finally declared the city bankrupt and put it in a receivership in 1971, but only after it had incurred debts of $32 million ($1,000 for every man, woman, and child in the city) with annual revenues of only $4.7 million. "City Hall has been run like a bad Polish joke," said the local weekly newspaper editor. "Everybody had two or three relatives on the payroll. . . . Over the years, when somebody wanted a hundred bucks from the city treasury, he simply took it and tossed an IOU into the box." On top of its financial woes, a federal judge ruled in 1971 that the city had been guilty of using urban renewal projects to oust blacks from the community, a judgment the U.S. Supreme Court upheld in 1974.

A colorful variety of suburbs surround Detroit. Ranging southward along the Detroit River and a few miles inland are a group of factory-dominated, lower-middle-class white cities like Ecorse, Southgate, Wyandotte, and Dearborn. These are some of the areas that most needed the environmental reforms of recent years; Robert Pisor, then of the Detroit *News*, conjectured a few years ago that these cities probably constituted "the most polluted congressional district in the nation: the air stinks, the waters are technicolor, and sky filled with smoke and debris."

Dearborn was long known for the extraordinary longevity of its mayor, Orville Hubbard, a staunch fiscal conservative and rigid segregationist who left office in January 1978 after 37 colorful years—longer than any U.S. mayor save Albany, N.Y.'s Erastus Corning II, who was sworn in five days earlier than Hubbard in 1941 and still going strong at the start of the '80s. Dearborn (population 104,199) is a tight white island of Poles, Syrians, and Italians, proud homeowners who can be seen of a summer evening watering their lawns, standing side by side in their undershirts. The 1970 Census found 13 blacks in Dearborn, but their location is a well-kept secret. Tax money from the huge Ford River Rouge complex pays 57 percent of Dearborn's taxes. The grandiose Fairlane shopping center, another brainchild of Henry Ford II, may help attract more people to Dearborn, and possibly ease the population loss that has plagued the city since 1960 when it had more than 112,000 people.

Just north of the Detroit line are a number of middle class working suburbs like Warren, Royal Oak, and Oak Park in Oakland and Macomb counties. One of these, Warren, gained a measure of fame in 1970 when it became the fulcrum of an effort by the national Housing and Urban Development Department, headed by George Romney, to achieve some measure of racial integration in the white suburban noose around Detroit. Warren is entirely a creation of the postwar population movement of people bent on escaping the grime and crime—and some say, the blacks—of the inner city. In 1950, 727 people lived in Warren, in 1975, 172,755.

A substantial percent of the workers in Warren's auto plants are blacks, but the community has been so hostile to blacks moving in—in 1967, for instance, a mob attacked a house bought by a mixed couple—that Warren had only 28 black families in residence. This stark case of housing discrimination, necessitating a massive "reverse commute" for blacks working in Warren but forced to live in Detroit, led HUD officials to believe they could use Warren as a test case to force suburban integration in return for $3 million in urban-renewal funds the city needed badly for neighborhood development. But angry residents got up a referendum to repeal the city's entire urban renewal program and passed it in November 1970, thus cutting off millions in federal aid—and choking off any chance of integration.

After the close-in middle class suburbs typified by Warren, the northern Detroit suburbs shift to wealthier enclaves like Troy (home of the S.S. Kresge Co.), Bloomfield Hills, Birmingham, West Bloomfield, and Farmington. This is favorite territory of the new generation of young auto and advertising executives and many of metropolitan Detroit's up-and-coming civic leaders.

Further to the north lies the troubled city of Pontiac (76,027 people), one of GM's principal outposts (home of the Pontiac division), a grimy city with a combustible mixture of Southern whites, blacks, and Mexican-Americans. In 1971 a controversial school busing plan was imposed on Pontiac, accompanied by violent demonstrations and the dynamiting of 10 empty buses—a crime the government blamed on six members of the Ku Klux Klan, including the former grand dragon of the state KKK. School enrollments declined 11 percent in the next year, as many parents moved their children into Catholic, Protestant, and other private schools, much to the chagrin of some clergy who saw the inconsistency of the motives with their preachings. Within two years, school officials and some parents were reporting improved racial tolerance among the children. Difficulties remained, but as one mother said, "Many positive things have happened here." Seeking to recoup a more positive image, Pontiac sought recognition in 1974 as an All-American City, partly on the strength of its successful community effort to woo William Clay Ford and his Detroit Lions to the new 80,000-seat Silverdome stadium it built for $50 million.

The specter of school busing between Detroit and the suburbs, raised in Judge Roth's later overturned 1971 decision, prompted a political uproar of immense proportions in the suburban towns. Bitterly opposed grassroots groups, many with determined women at the fore, sprang into being. Many normally liberal politicians scurried for the cover of newly formed antibusing positions. The fears of suburban parents were partly on racial grounds—the fear of violence in the schools, or intermarriage; another concern was subjecting their children to the inferior quality of underfinanced Detroit schools. With the Supreme Court decision in 1974, passions were calmed. But suburbanites might yet have to face the reality of integration. Several knowledgeable observers, not the least of which is Mayor Young, noted the black populations creeping upward in some suburban communities in the '70s. As the trend continued, they prophesied, suburban residents would have to deal with integrated schools or run farther away once again.

One of the great breakthroughs in American mercantile history was made in the early 1950s just north of the Detroit line in Southfield Township, where Hudson's bought a huge tract of land and constructed the spectacular Northland shopping center. "One of the few uniquely American building types," architectural critic Wolf Von Eckardt wrote in those years, is "the new trading post in the exurban wilderness—the regional shopping center." Northland was not only a pioneer of the new breed of marketplaces, but one of the best. Designer-planner Victor Gruen not only consigned the omnipresent autos to the outer periphery but endowed the central shopping areas with trees, flowers, fountains, and quiet protected pedestrian areas.

Despite its architectural success, Gruen didn't believe he accomplished completely in Northland what he set out to do. In a 1978 interview in his native Vienna, Austria, where he retired after 30 years in America, the man credited with inventing the modern shopping mall told us that his concept of a unified, multifunctional center had not come to pass. Surrounding the merchandising areas he had planned apartments, hotels, laboratories, government service centers, medical and amusement facilities, merged together to form one multipurpose center, much like the organically grown European city of Gruen's boyhood. What resulted at Northland, he said, was a series of one-dimensional centers, serving a variety of functions, each surrounded by its own parking area and roads, with no way for pedestrians to travel easily from one center to the next. Northland, however, Gruen said, is far better than most. The typical suburban shopping mall, which he first sketched out in 1943, has been so perverted by "fast buck promoters and speculators" that he is no longer willing to acknowledge "fatherhood," Gruen told us. Most are built in outlying locations that cause long, energy wasting automobile trips, lack identification with existing communities, and have no purpose save merchandising. "I refuse to pay alimony for those bastard developments," Gruen said. (By letter, telephone, and assorted broadsides, Gruen continued from his Vienna apartment to fight sterile and dehumanizing shopping malls, to urge more and more multi-purpose developments in urban settings, and to champion a new and fervent cause of his later years—opposition to nuclear power—until his death in 1980).

Northland's success was so great that it became in many ways the focal point of the entire Detroit area (though, significantly, it is not on the Detroit tax rolls). It threw the city center off base and drained downtown of its life blood. Even the city's blacks often stream out to Northland on weekend shopping expeditions, rather than face the parking problems and other inconveniences downtown.

Curving along the shore of Lake St. Clair just east of the city in a closed-in, compact strip of privilege and cool green shade are Grosse Pointes, dwelling places for *la crème de la crème* of Detroit's nuts-and-bolts society. The auto aristocracy, the top executives of Chrysler, Ford, and General Motors—all make their home in the Grosse Pointes. But inroads also are being made into this enclave of exclusivity. Where once only the barons of industry owned homes here, they have been succeeded first by the corporate upper-middle class. A third wave of people began buying into the Grosse Pointes in the 1970s: younger, well educated, professional, comfortably well off, but not rich, and, yes, even a handful of black families.

A continuing problem of deep concern is the disparity in income and housing quality between Detroit and its suburbs. In the mid-1960s it was found that in some areas of the city, median family income was as low as $3,900 a year; in wealthier suburbs (such as the Grosse Pointes and spots like Bloomfield Hills) it exceeded $20,000 a year. The overall median income in Oakland County was 50 percent again as great as that in the city of Detroit. And while income levels generally leaped forward in the 1970s, the basic disparities seemed to remain. Bloomfield Hills, for instance, had an astounding per capita income in 1976 of $29,849 (multiply that by four to get your average family income), about 6.4 times the per capita income of $4,625 in the city of Detroit. That was essentially the same margin as in the riot-torn late '60s. The disparity between other suburban communities and the city was less startling but substantial still. Poverty statistics pinpoint the disproportionate income distribution in equally revealing terms. In Michigan central cities in 1976, 15.3 percent of the people were below the poverty level, compared with 5.6 percent in the metropolitan areas outside central cities (i.e. in the suburbs), and 9.1 percent in the state as a whole. The poverty among blacks (23 percent) was three times as among whites (7.2 percent).

If there was any optimistic sign among all this, it might be the fact that the median family income in Detroit was higher than in the country as a whole, and considerably higher for black families in Michigan ($11,876) than in the entire country ($9,045), stark testimony that blacks are sharing the economic gains won by the UAW.

By the late 1960s and early 1970s, at least some elements of the Detroit community began to recognize the futility and danger in regarding Detroit and its suburbs as two separate entities. The first initiatives for metropolitan-wide cooperation, significantly, came not from the government but from the private sector—namely, Detroit's Metropolitan Fund, one of a broadening group of areawide nonprofit corporations operating in the U.S. to pull together a broad power structure (business, labor, intellectual, philanthropic) in a concerted effort to approach problems that spill out over several cities and towns.

When we first spoke with Metropolitan Fund director Kent Mathewson and his associate Don Shelton about Detroit regionalism in 1971, they could talk only wistfully about the hope of generating some kind of regional identification in the years ahead. By 1978, they were heartened by the city's apparent comeback, the state equity payment to Detroit (addressing specifically the special services Detroit had historically provided for the suburbs and state as a whole, in every area from prisons to recreation, without compensation), and the "very interesting coalition between the black Democratic mayor from Detroit and the white, out-state Republican governor." Suburbanites who for years had avoided the city were at least now driving in to visit Renaissance Center and show it to out-of-town visitors, they noted. And while Detroit was still at a distinct disadvantage in the legislature, with rural and especially suburban interests so often lining up against it, they noted that Governor Milliken had become the *de facto* "metropolitan mayor," the lead figure in mediating the interregional disputes. (One could only wish more American governors would heed that model.)

Yet in matter of hard fact, deep-seated antagonisms remained between Detroit and its surburbs. Part of this could be attributed to suburban smugness and prejudice, but part too to the implied racism of pronouncements by Coleman Young and his colleagues—perhaps a political necessity, as they saw it, but still a divisive factor in attempting to achieve intraregional cooperation. The city had been far too slow, in the view of some friendly observers, in forming political coalition with its poor, close-in, sometimes black suburbs—not to mention the outstate cities, predominantly white, which were beginning to suffer many Detroit-style problems, from population flight and housing deterioration to poor schools and retail decline.

Michigan's Other Cityscape

There is another industrial Michigan outside of Detroit and its immediate suburbs, consisting of 11 Lower Peninsula cities with populations ranging roughly between 50,000 and 200,000 (in the aggregate, about two thirds of the Detroit total). A startling number of these medium-ranked cities turn out to harbor microcosms of Detroit's black-white dilemma, even maintaining well defined ghettos in which improverished and middle-class blacks alike are confined. The consequences likewise are reflected in a slow growth, or even a negative growth, in most of the cities since the 1970 Census.

At the center of the "outstate" complex is Lansing (population 126,805, down from 131,546), the state capital wth a dependable government payroll. Lansing's first love and big dollar, however, comes from the auto industry; both the Oldsmobile division of GM and Fisher Body are on location. The city has a large contingent of motorcycle-type Southern whites, often in confrontation with blacks who are largely confined to the city's southwest side. Providing additional economic stability to the community is its smaller twin city, East Lansing, home of Michigan State University.

An hour's drive northwest of Lansing and just a county short of the Lake Michigan shore is Grand Rapids (population 187,946), once a placid city of white, blond-haired, Republican conservatives who all seemed to have some sort of Van in front of their surnames. But the high cost of skilled labor drove most of the once prospering furniture business to the South, and the population changed with an influx of Poles and blacks imported to man varied new industries. After a period when the new racial and ethnic mix learned to live with each other, during which some major downtown stores closed and moved to suburban shopping centers, Grand Rapids has been trying to revive itself. Sadly, the change has take a toll, including the demolition of the intriguing old city hall, which was replaced with a multilevel parking lot. But there have been a new main street mall, an expanded convention center, and a new 2,500-seat music hall. By the mid-'70s, older city neighborhoods such as Heritage Hill also were attracting middle class people back into town, and apartment building was being stimulated after an extended dormant period.

Before Gerald R. Ford, Jr., gave up a secure House seat to become Vice President and then President of the United States, Arthur Vandenberg was doubtless the most illustrious man ever to emerge from Grand Rapids (his birthplace in 1884). Americans remember Vandenberg as the isolationist-turned-internationalist who helped write the United Nations charter at San Francisco in 1945 and chaired the Senate Foreign Relations Committee when many of the pioneer postwar international programs were being molded. Ford moved to Grand Rapids at the age of one and was a Vandenberg protégé when he first won election to the House in 1948. But more on Ford later.

Lying south of Lansing and Grand Rapids, pointed in an almost straight line from Detroit to Chicago, are four cities of somewhat lesser magnitude: Ann Arbor (population 103,512), Jackson (43,338), Battle Creek (43,338), and Kalamazoo (79,542). Ann Arbor is the most atypical of the lot; it manufactures some automobile parts and other industrial goods but is chiefly the campus town of the University of Michigan and the research-oriented firms the university has generated. The intellectual community competes for power with a wealthy old conservative Republican faction and the blacks and blue collars.

Battle Creek, the breakfast cereal capital with both Kellogg and General

Foods located there, has initiated a rather unique approach to its growth challenges. It acquired Fort Custer military base, abandoned since World War II, and turned it into an industrial park. City officials also have been active in recruiting foreign investment to the area—especially from Germany and Japan.

Northward, in the vicinity of Saginaw Bay, are two run-of-the-mill GM cities, Saginaw (population 86,202) and Bay City (47,215), the former with so many blacks and Mexican-Americans that a black was actually chosen mayor in the 1960s. Saginaw started early to halt the out-flow of downtown business, but met with only limited success. It updated its plans for stabilizing the central business district in 1976, and enticed significant parts of the private sector off the sidelines to join with public-sponsored improvement efforts, offering greater promise for the future. Nearby Midland (37,434) is the home of Dow Chemical Company, 25th largest industrial corporation in the country. Environmental controversies have frequently swirled around Midland, stemming from both the Dow plant and a nuclear power plant, proposed to be built in the late 1960s but delayed by objections through most of the 1970s.

Finally we come to Flint (population 174,218, down from 193,317 in 1970), the epitome of the blue-collar lunch-bucket city and General Motors town *par excellence*. Sixty percent of the men and women in Flint work at the Chevrolet, Buick, and Fisher Body plants, a total GM payroll exceeding 60,000. No city in the U.S.A. has a higher average workingman's wage. Likewise, no city produced more trucks (434,948) than Flint did in 1977, and only two cities (Detroit and St. Louis) turned out more cars than the 456,459 that rolled off Flint's assembly lines. The city's problem, of course, is the lack of economic diversification; this fact hit home hard in the 1974 recession when 10,000 GM employees were laid off from its plants. GM dominates so totally that the second largest employer in town is the Hamady Brothers Supermarket chain.

Flint has an ample supply of Southern rednecks and blacks and a strangely contradictory race history. In October 1967, the Ku Klux Klan, headed by a pipefitter leading more than 100 Klansmen from "eight Flint units," boldly staged a march down the main street of town, complete with satin robes, hoods, sashes, and insignia. That same year, there were disturbances in the black community and Mayor Floyd McCree walked the streets to calm tensions. Amazingly, McCree was a black man—the first black mayor in the city's history, a salaried foreman for Buick with 23 years seniority and an extraordinarily able political figure. With its huge UAW membership, Flint should be a stronghold of issue-oriented strong Democratic leadership. But instead, most of the Democratic leadership—especially on the white side—is patronage and job oriented.

Lackluster Democratic leadership and organization led in 1966 to a major Republican coup in Flint: ouster of the run-of-the-mill, patronage oriented Democratic Congressman by a dynamic and attractive liberal Republican, 28-year-old Donald W. Riegle, Jr. Michigan would hear more of Donald Riegle.

Flint does have one priceless and unique asset: the Mott Foundation, creation of Charles Stewart Mott, the grand old patriarch of Flint and one of the richest men in America before he died in 1973 at the age of 97. Persuaded by General Motors pioneer W.C. Durant to bring his axle-producing plant from Utica, N.Y., in 1906, Mott became and remained Flint's leading industrialist. He had been a member of the General Motors Board of directors since 1913 and had long been the largest single GM stockholder. Mott served as mayor of Flint in his younger years and in 1920 even ran (though unsuccessfully) for governor. Then, in the mid-1920s, he established the Charles Stewart Mott Foundation, now one of the nation's 10 largest with some $462 million in General Motors stock and other assets. (Stewart Mott, C.S.'s son born when the old man was in his fifties, manages his own inheritance and dispenses hundreds of thousands of dollars in philanthropic and political contributions for liberal causes. He once estimated that the family fortune, including the assets of the foundation, added up to $800 million.)

Interviewing Mott in Flint in 1969, we discovered a still alert and compassionate old gentleman of 94 years who still evidenced a boyish enthusiasm for his town and for the work of his foundation. "Instead of scattering our shots," Mott said, "we have concentrated the foundation's efforts in Flint and tried to make the city a laboratory and proving ground of what can be done to improve education and recreation opportunities." The undertaking of which Mott seemed the proudest—and which others in Flint consider the foundation's most vital contribution—was the program to open the schools after hours for adult education and community programs. If any 10 people in Flint want an adult education course, the foundation will finance it for them. The open schools program (recognized as early as the 1930s by Eleanor Roosevelt as a pioneer in its field) has increased the number of hours that all Flint schools are open each year from 1,400 to 3,800 hours. The theory is that the buildings belong to the taxpayers and they have a right to use them. "What a whale of an increase in the use of property, with adult education classes in these schools," Mott said. In the last decade, the foundation has begun to branch outside its own city, including support for housing in black neighborhoods of Chicago and St. Louis, a group in Washington, D.C. ($1 million) that helps improve the economic health of disadvantaged communities and enterprises, and other self-help efforts, especially those involving enhancement of neighborhoods.

Although C. S. Mott's wealth and resources would have permitted him to rule Flint with an iron hand from behind the scenes, he never chose to do so. He used his power very sparingly, was not a major campaign contributor, and kept his foundation scrupulously clear of politics. Nonetheless, his death left a very real leadership vacuum in the city, according to one former city official. "The gray eagles have left the scene and there is no one to pick up the reins of power that they dropped," he said.

The foundation continues to be a force in Flint's renewal efforts of the 1970s. It contributed $1.1 million toward the Flint Riverbank Park, a flood control, riverbank beautification program, and "community gathering place" on the Flint River. Near the park, a 565-unit housing project (including town-houses and apartments) for the elderly also was built, using $1.5 million from the Mott Foundation. To diversify the economy and create about 2,000 new jobs, the city spent $20 million in community development block grants plus $1.6 million from the foundation to develop a 274-acre industrial park.

Flint received a shot-in-the-arm from other sources too. The University of Michigan relocated its Flint campus to a 40-acre downtown site and expanded enrollments from 3,000 to 10,000 by 1980. The former Sears department store was renovated as part of the downtown campus of Mott Community College (formerly Genessee Community College) which was expected to have an expanded student body of 20,000 by 1980. In a reversal from most municipalities, Flint became only the second major city in 25 years (Albuquerque was the other) to abandon the council-manager form of government in favor of a strong, full-time mayor system.

When one surveys the scene at Flint, about the best judgment one can make is that every city could use a C.S. Mott and his works.

Michigan's People in Washington

Before leaving Michigan, we must note the unique, albeit accidental, contribution the state made to that most wrenching of national traumas, the aftermath of Watergate and the resignation of Richard Nixon as President of the United States. Gerald Ford, the House minority leader after 25 years of representing Grand Rapids, had aspired to be Speaker of the House but became President, the first man to gain that high office without the benefit of a popular mandate. Much has been said about the events leading to Ford's swearing in on Aug. 9, 1974 as our 38th President, and need not be repeated here. Ford, an unspectacular but upright and honest leader, did reestablish in the presidency and federal government a sense of integrity, so sorely needed in the post-Nixon days. His niche in history—as a transitional figure from the "national nightmare," the end of which he spoke of on taking office—is assured.

Yet on other issues, Ford's record as President was distinctly lackluster. The caution, the comfortableness with the status quo, the tendency to be a nonstop partisan acquired over years campaigning for fellow Republican House candidates around the country—these habits proved too deeply in-grained for Ford to break. He could have, for instance, on taking office ap-pointed some Democrats to high positions and proclaimed a "government of national unity" in the wake of the Watergate scandal. Instead, he soon pardoned Nixon for all and any crimes committed in office and was off on the hustings trying to help Republican congressional candidates in that fall's (1974) elections (with predictable lack of success). The fact that Ford barely lost election to the presidency in his own right in 1976 (winning Michigan, incidentally, by a very respectable 53–47 percent margin) was actually an achievement, given Jimmy Carter's heavy early lead in the polls. Ford's final acts in office were to arrange for a smooth transition; then he and his wife were off to retirement in Palm Springs, California—not Grand Rapids.

A special word also must be said about the late Philip A. Hart, the gentle Democratic Senator from Michigan who died of cancer only a few days before his planned retirement in 1976. Some called him the "conscience of the Senate," and his colleagues named a new Senate Office Building after him. From opposite sides of the political spectrum, Hart and Republican Senator Griffin played a national role of greater significance than any Michigan representatives since the days of Arthur Vandenberg.

Hart, a product of the Williams era of Michigan politics, was a soft-spoken man who developed quietly in the 1960s into a highly effective spokesman for liberal Democratic Senators on civil rights and consumer issues. He became the acknowledged leader of the Democratic civil rights bloc, carrying the floor fight for the landmark Voting Rights Act of 1965 and the 1968 open-housing civil rights bill. And the Senate Judiciary Antitrust Subcommittee, the chairmanship of which Hart inherited from the late Estes Kefauver of Tennessee, tackled controversial consumer-oriented issues such as auto repairs and insurance, drug prices, and oil import quotas. Hart was also a leading sponsor of truth-in-lending and truth-in-packaging legislation and an articulate opponent of the antiballistic missile system. In an episode Hart would as soon have forgotten, he carried the unsuccessful floor fight to nominate Abe Fortas as Chief Justice; after President Johnson was obliged to withdraw the nomination, he offered Hart a place on the Court. But the idea came to naught because it was to late in the 1968 session to hope for confirmation.

Hart's great influence as leader of the Democratic liberal bloc was attributed to hard work, good staff, steadily reliable judgment, and as Spencer Rich of the Washington *Post* pointed out, "considerable behind-the-scenes influence and capacity to get things done in the everyday committee work and floor action of the Senate." In this respect, Hart differed markedly from liberal spokesmen of earlier years like Illinois' Paul Douglas and Pennsylvania's Joseph Clark, men often so blunt in debate and intolerant of their opposition that their effectiveness was seriously undermined. Though he was a favorite of the UAW and the liberal wing of the Michigan Democratic party, Hart's genteel manner somehow even gave Republicans in his state the feeling he was one of them; somehow they couldn't believe that a man with a home on Mackinac Island could be such a dangerous liberal.

Robert Griffin, the bespectacled giant killer from Traverse City who brought Soapy Williams to his knees in the 1966 Senate race, seemed—until his 1978 defeat—to be an expert in seizing on seemingly impossible causes and turning them into victories. In 1959, as a House Member, he coauthored the Landrum-Griffin Labor Reform Law which was then passed by a House packed with union-backed Congressmen elected in the 1958 Democratic sweep. Six years later, Griffin was a key strategist in dumping Indiana's Charles Halleck as Republican House Leader, replacing him with fellow Michigander Gerald Ford. In 1968, only two years after entering the Senate, he started out with scarcely an ally to block President Johnson's appointment of Abe Fortas as Chief Justice, and eventually thwarted the nomination.

Again in 1969, Griffin's decision to oppose President Nixon's nomination of Clement Haynsworth to the Supreme Court was a key turning point in the South Carolinian's eventual defeat. And though he was a virtual greenhorn by Senate "club" standards, with only three years service behind him, Griffin in 1969 won election as Assistant Republican Leader (or Whip) of the Senate. Griffin's days, William Serrin reported for the Detroit *Free Press*, "run to 12 hours, his tastes to white shirts and dark blue suits, and his mind to tactics rather than theory. The tactics and the 12-hour work days paid off."

Had Ford won in 1976, Griffin might well have ended up on the U.S. Supreme Court. He tried, following the Ford defeat, to win election as Senate Minority Leader, losing to a more personable and photogenic Howard Baker of Tennessee. In 1978 Griffin first announced his retirement, then was persuaded by the Republican hierarchy to run again so the Democrats wouldn't gain the seat, and ended up losing anyway to Democrat Carl H. Levin. A liberal, Levin served eight years on Detroit's city council (and before that as attorney to the state civil rights commission) and campaigned as "an urban ombudsman," promising to help cut through federal red tape in urban programs.

Hart's successor in the Senate, Donald Riegle, is a man who has made more of a name than a record for himself. Hart was forever associated with his liberal causes; Riegle has been considered a precursor of a political style. Given the erratic path Riegle folowed in becoming a Democratic Senator, beginning as a Republican, it becomes difficult to argue with his success. From the start, when he upset the Democratic incumbent Congressman in Flint in 1966, Riegle has made a splash. In that race, Riegle contracted with the California professional campaign firm of Spencer-Roberts to launch a sophisticated computer and poll-backed onslaught on the sleepy Democrats. Physically attractive, extremely hard-working, possessed of one of the best staffs on Capitol Hill, Riegle did little to hide his presidential ambitions, a fact that aroused no little enmity among state Republican leaders and fellow House members. The fact he became a vocal opponent of the Vietnam War and in 1970 ran with UAW support hardly endeared him to the GOP hierarchy. It shouldn't have been a shock, under the circumstances, when he cut his ties to the Republicans in 1973 and joined the Democratic Party.

Three years later, much to the consternation of many of his new Democratic colleagues, he entered the Democratic primary to succeed Hart. Two other highly respected Democrats were in that race—Richard Austin, the black secretary of state since 1970, and Rep. James G. O'Hara, the thoughtful and astute leader of the liberal House Democratic Study Group. Applying the polling and media concepts he had developed in his congressional races, coupled with the personality so well adapted to his style, Riegle compiled almost half of the primary vote while Austin and O'Hara were splitting a quarter apiece. In the general election, he defeated a former Republican House colleague, Marvin Esch, but much of the latter stages of Riegle's campaign was directed against the Detroit *News*. The *News* revealed in an article that Riegle had had sexual relations with a woman staff member, and the encounters had been taped. Not content with the initial story, the *News* printed transcripts of the tapes. If the paper had been intent on ruining Riegle's career, as he claimed, the tactic backfired. Many people were more repulsed by the *News'* decision to print the intimate transcript than by Riegle's indiscretion in the first place. Shortly after the election, however, the new Senator and his wife announced their plans for a divorce.

Detroit's Rep. John Conyers, Jr., first elected in 1964, took a lead in building a black caucus in Congress and has demonstrated unusual skill and will in rising to the top of black leadership ranks. By the late 1970s, Conyers was beginning to assume leadership in the House by virtue of his seniority. He had, for instance, become chairman of the Judiciary Subcommittee on Crime, an area of key concern to blacks—and his district. He was variously described as "the Julian Bond of Congress," "a New Left Democrat who still thinks the system can be made to work," "a good bellwether on what blacks will do or not do," "a master of organization," "an extreme opportunist," and "grandstander." Anyone who evokes such reactions is sure to be heard from often in the future.

Another black member of the House, Rep. Charles Diggs, Jr., chairman of the District of Columbia Committee, earned a different kind of notoriety. In 1978 he was convicted on 29 charges of arranging kickbacks from his staff members, among other things. Even with the conviction hanging over him (he appealed, lost, and pursued yet another appeal as 1980 began), Diggs ran for his 13th term and won with ease. His House colleagues were not quite so lenient. In July 1979, the House voted 414–0 to publicly censure Diggs for his misuse of office salaries after he admitted to diverting $40,031.66 for his personal use. It marked the first time since 1921 that the House had censured one of their own. Diggs finally retired from Congress, voluntarily, in 1980.

John D. Dingell, whose district covers the southwestern part of Detroit and a number of adjacent suburbs, became a leading conservationist and environmentalist in Congress long before those issues gained the national popularity they have today. It is somewhat ironic that a man with such a fervent environmental interest represents one of the most polluted and industrial districts in the country. As chairman of the Commerce Subcommittee on Energy and Power, he gained a position to be listened to—and heard—in congressional circles.

Among other Michigan House members of note in the '70s was Guy Vander Jagt, Republican Congressional Campaign Committee chairman, member of the Ways and Means Committee, and his party's ranking man on the Government Operations Conservation and Natural Resources Subcommittee—a post which helped him win approval of the Sleeping Bear Dunes Natonal Lakeshore in his western Michigan district. Democrat Lucien Nedzi of Detroit won note as the highest ranking Vietnam "dove" on the House Armed Services Committee but saw his reputation tarnished some when, after appointment as chairman of a special Armed Services Subcommittee on Intelligence, it was revealed he had been aware of the CIA's illegal domestic activities and involvement in assassination plots but never blew the whistle on those operations. James Blanchard, a liberal Democrat first elected in 1974, became the House's chief advocate of sunset legislation to force review and possible termination of government programs.

It would not seem quite proper to close without mentioning a member of Congress who retired in 1974. Former Rep. Martha Griffiths of Detroit won a measure of national fame as the mastermind behind the 1974 passage of the Equal Rights Amendment for women. She was also the first woman to sit on the House Ways and Means Committee. Her retirement after 20 years in the House did not signal withdrawal from political life: in 1976, she was chairman of the Rules Committee of the Democratic National Convention.

A Michigan Postscript

When all is said and done with Michigan, the whole may be something less than the sum of the parts. The auto industry, with its wealth and manpower resources, could and should have been a pacesetter for American business and life, brave enough to take the early plunges—into safer and less polluting cars, into mass transit and city planning, into advanced opportunities for blacks. Instead it waited for Ralph Nader and the Detroit riots, and later for OPEC and the mounting international energy crises dictating smaller automobiles, to spur it to action. Even in 1980, sensitive observers detected a pervasive mediocrity among those in the industry who should have been thinking the most inventively and courageously about the perplexing future of the 1980s. The UAW has, indeed, been an innovative force in American life, but inflationary wage increases over the years suggests the union may not have counted the costs for the U.S.A. as a whole, just as the auto companies failed to count the deleterious national effects of the cars they built. The UAW leadership, though socially progressive, has failed to convince its members of the justice of their policies, raising profound questions about the union's direction once the current leaders retire in the early 1980s.

With its wealth and opportunities, Michigan should never have let Detroit "happen," or for that matter let Lansing or Flint happen quite the way they did. In race, housing, regional government, Michigan is a disappointment. For too long, men of much wealth but little breeding or culture held the ultimate power in Michigan, and even today one sees a growing number of strong individuals but senses a lack of strong forces challenging the power system. Its "renaissance" notwithstanding, can Detroit be brought back into the mainstream of economic life and opportunity in Michigan and the nation —especially since it may be, because of its immense dependence on the auto industry, the one American city that will suffer the most from the nation's hard energy futures? What will happen as the automobile's once dominant role in the U.S. economy continues to shrink? If the state couldn't deal effectively with its racial antagonisms in good times, how will it face them in hard times? Why aren't Michiganders fighting and dreaming and thinking more about their future? They are certainly more awake than they were twenty years ago—events have seen to that. But are they awake enough? And finally comes the most disturbing thought of all: are the financial power and influence of yesteryear so eroded that it is already too late to prepare for anything more than a generation of painful adjustment?

INDIANA

THE POLITICIANS' STATE

IN THE LAST SPRING OF HIS LIFE, as he criss-crossed Indiana in search of votes in the 1968 presidential primary, Robert F. Kennedy could not withstand the temptation to charter a campaign train that would retrace the route of the fabled Wabash Cannonball. And in a way, the very name of Indiana, a place where people called "Hoosiers" live, raises an image of settled Midwestern typicality, of vast cornfields, small villages, and closely held factory cities, of value placed on things familiar and known.

In fact, Indiana is in many ways a microcosm of what America was half a generation ago. Here one does find a people clannish, protective of property, suspicious of government, patriotic. Hoosiers have always taken a perverse pride in letting someone else be first, in clinging to their independence as steadfastly as any rural New Englander. They have viewed with skepticism those outsiders with newfangled ideas infiltrating their borders in the heart of the Heartland.

Still, as we shall see, Indiana is now shedding the political, social, cultural ideals that served it so long. That and not the past will be largely the story of this chapter.

Something of the simplistic and idealized notion Hoosiers had of themselves at one time was captured by William Herschell in his poem engraved
on a plaque hanging in the Statehouse in Indianapolis:

> Ain't God good to Indiana?
> Folks, a feller never knows
> Just how close he is to Eden
> Till sometimes he up and goes
> Seeking fairer, greener pastures
> Than he has right here at *home.*
> Where there's sunshine in th' clover,
> An' there's honey in the comb;
> Where the ripples on th' river
> Kind of chuckle as they flow . . .
> Ain't God good to Indiana?
> Ain't he, fellers? Ain't he, though?

Less pastoral in its imagery, but hardly less inflated was the description
Theodore Dreiser, one of Indiana's truly great gifts to literature, wrote of
his home state: "There is about it a charm I shall not be able to express. . . .
This is a region not unlike those which produce gold or fleet horses or oranges
or adventures." John Gunther, in his *Inside U.S.A.*, detected even at mid-
century a diversity among the Hoosiers often overlooked. Indiana, he recounted, "has a powerful substratum of Germans. . . . These can have lived
in a community for a hundred years, but they will not be Hoosier." Nevertheless, he found widespread evidence of certain traits attributed to the
Hoosiers—shrewd and independent first of all, but conservative, God-fearing,
and unostentatious as well.

Less evident than the Hoosier characteristics is the genesis of the term
itself. One story simply credits it to the Indian word "hoosa," meaning corn.
Another claims it's a vernacular contraction for "who is yer," a common
pioneer greeting. A historian suggested English immigrants brought the word
"hoozer" with them from the Cumberland Mountains to southern Indiana.
Given the greatest credibility, however, is the account of William E. Wilson,
who suggested in his book, *Indiana, a History,* that the word originated with
the men working for Ohio Canal builder Samuel Hoosier. In the 1820s, these
men—with reputations as the hardest working and most reliable laborers—
simply became known as Hoosiers. As the term spread, it took on the conno-
tation of any person with great virtue and virility; often today, to those outside Indiana, the label conjures up the image of a plain country bumpkin
as well.

Hoosier Incongruities

In reality, Indiana is a place of incongruous contrasts. As the state moves
into the final decades of the 20th century, and as the pressures and pace of
the world beyond its borders persistently nudge it to change its ways, the

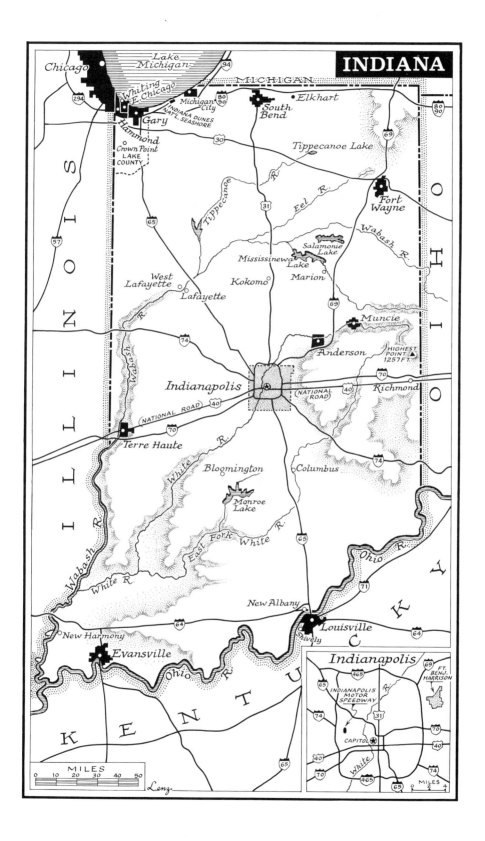

disparities between what was and what is became more vivid. No state had more venal patronage politics, but court decisions and legislation have shriveled the spoils system, all but eliminating even the infamous 2 percent club which guaranteed all appointees would contribute 2 percent off the top of their public paychecks to party coffers. Few legislatures have resisted reforms and full-time status as stringently as the lawmakers in Indianapolis; yet in 1969 they took a step no other northern legislature—not even in the supposedly progressive coastal states—had been willing to take to resolve urban problems: they created a county-wide, consolidated metropolitan government for the state's major city, Indianapolis. Yet even as Indiana entered the 1980s, a fierce debate continued over the need to have a full-time legislature instead of the traditional part-time body it had always been.

Indiana, in the first half of this century, had a history of bigotry unequaled North of the Mason-Dixon line. Indeed, the Ku Klux Klan, hawking its familiar anti-Semitic, anti-Catholic, anti-black propaganda, openly flourished and actually laid legitimate claims to controlling the governor, legislature, and many courts and local governments. Yet Indianapolis was the only Northern city of its size to escape major racial disturbances in the late 1960s and remained calm even though embroiled in the trauma of a major school busing court case during the 1970s. Until only three decades ago, Indiana state laws deliberately subverted the intent of the Constitution's 14th Amendment and subordinated blacks. Anti-Catholicism also was a potent force, thanks in large part to the Klan, and contributed to John F. Kennedy's overwhelming defeat in Indiana as late as 1960. Still, a disparaging word about Notre Dame, America's premier Catholic university, at South Bend, can elicit the ire of more than just the Irish in Indiana.

Indiana too has been the home of the American Legion (its headquarters still are in Indianapolis) and the once ultra-intolerant, ultra-conservative Indianapolis *News* and *Star* (some moderation is detectable in recent years, especially in racial relations), as well as the birthplace of the truculent John Birch Society. As conservative as it has been, Indiana ended the 1970s with two anomalies for U.S. Senators—Birch Bayh, a rural Vigo County (Terre Haute) country-boy Democrat with one of the most consistently liberal voting records in Congress, and Richard Lugar, the Oxford University-educated Republican who was the most visible figure in formation of Indianapolis' metropolitan government.

Shortly after World War II, Indiana's legislators cast a suspicious eye toward offers of federal dollars, passing a vehement resolution declaring all such aid tainted: "We propose henceforward to tax ourselves and take care of ourselves." By the mid-1970s, however, federal aid to Indiana totaled more than $6 billion, 18th among the 50 states, and was a large factor in the 1,134 miles of interstate highways criss-crossing Indiana's fields and cities, more than in any other state of its size. While the highway and certain other aids have become acceptable, those for welfare mothers and cities are suspect. For many, the old attitudes maintain a tenacious hold. "We're less beholden to government and less dependent on it," John Barnett, past president of the State Chamber of Commerce, told us. "When New York City had difficulties, a lot of people said, 'To hell with them; we take care of our problems—let them.' " Stan Evans, former editorial chief of the conservative and influential Indianapolis *News*, explained the attitude this way: "The people of Indiana are self-conscious of themselves, as Hoosiers, as Midwesterners," he said. "A certain hostility toward the East may be assumed. . . . Indiana has in some ways become symbolic to people in the East of something they don't like, and vice versa, and there's a natural antagonism." That attitude is translated into votes, too. In 1968, Indiana gave Richard Nixon his largest margin of victory in any state, and in the 1976 GOP presidential primary, it carried Ronald Reagan to a win over fellow Midwesterner Gerald Ford. "When Nixon speaks here," Evans once said before the former President's downfall, "generally he speaks in generalizations, you know, like 'get out and do good for America,' and something like that, and it carries the state."

A strain of insecurity also seems woven into the Hoosier life-style. Eugene McCarthy picked up the sentiment during his treks through Indiana during his 1968 quest for the Democratic presidential nomination. "There seemed to be a rather generalized defensiveness in Indiana against outsiders," McCarthy wrote later in his book *The Year of the People*. "In northern Indiana, especially Gary, people seemed worried about the prospects of being taken over by Chicago. In the south, they were threatened by Kentucky, in the west by Illinois, and in the east, by Ohio. It was as though in Indiana they have to think Indiana for fear that if they do not, it will be absorbed by the outside world," McCarthy theorized.

No single personality, no single issue, no single city can capture the totality of the metamorphosis underway in Indiana. But a glimpse at the people of Muncie (pop. 83,000) in east central Indiana shows Indiana is no longer in its cocoon. Muncie became famous in the 1920s for its ordinariness, when it was the subject of the classic sociological study by Robert S. and Helen Merrell Lynd. Middletown, the Lynds called Muncie, because it represented the typical America city.* After studying Muncie, the Lynds concluded the city simultaneously grasped the values of the 19th century and struggled to confront the demands of 20th century industrialization and modernization. "A citizen has one foot on the relatively solid ground of established institutional habits," they wrote, "and the other foot fast to an escalator erratically moving in several directions at a bewildering variety of speeds." In the late 1970s, a new research team moved into Muncie and repeated the questions the Lynds had asked half a century earlier. In their study, *Middletown III*, they found the same dichotomy was present: half said the Bible was a "sufficient guide to all problems of modern life"; three-

---

* It was not the first nor last time Indianans were so characterized. In 1900, Mark Sullivan in his *History of Our Times* called Indiana's people "the most typically American" of any in the nation. In World War II, the Office of War Information selected Madison, Indiana, as the typical American town, and during the formative years of political polling, Indiana provided the bulk of the middle America sample.

quarters had unquestioned faith in the U.S.A. as the "best country in the world"; and 47 percent—the same percentage the Lynds found—agreed it was "entirely the fault of a man himself if he does not succeed." While the researchers in the 1970s found no trace of a distintegration of familiar Indiana social values, they nonetheless found some deviating behaviors within the old value framework. The students interviewed enjoyed both bubblegum and pot, churchgoing and pornography. As one 16-year-old interviewed was quoted as saying: "Yeah, we smoke dope all over, in our cars, walking around before class, any time, but that doesn't mean we don't believe in God or that we'll let anybody put God down. That can get you in a fight." (Such logic makes it easier to understand how a plant manager in southern Indiana could in one breath lash out against liberal Democrats and labor for ruining the economy and in the next assert that Birch Bayh "isn't one of them.")

Muncie reflects another changing fact of economic life in Indiana: more and more, its home-grown industry is falling under the ownership of out-of-state and sometimes even out-of-country corporations. Like so many other Hoosier cities, Muncie existed for decades under the patriarchal leadership of the Ball brothers, who came to the city in 1886 with the promise of free natural gas and free land to manufacture their fruit jars. Their legacy is far more apparent than the company that bears their name—so do the university, the hospital, and other buildings, to say nothing of the churches and other civic projects endowed by the philanthropic foundation the brothers set up in 1926. The Ball Corporation, though, is now a diversified, multinational concern, its major operations moved elsewhere, the Ball family is dispersed across the country, its influence in Muncie a shadow of years past. That story—even more familiarly with a direct sale of a local corporation to a national or multinational firm, leaving only branch managers to participate in local civic affairs—is repeated in countless cities up and down Indiana.

What chains of events fostered the narrow provincialism of Indiana? Perhaps it was the state's unfortunate location in the path of America's westward expansion, first just beyond the frontier, then part of the frontier, finally only a gateway for pioneers passing through on the way to the "Wild West." Indiana calls itself today the "crossroads of America," a motto justly deserved, although with ironic overtones. The state has access to both the major waterway systems of the Midwest—on the north, to the Great Lakes through Burns Harbor on Lake Michigan, and to the south, to the Mississippi River through its newer, 1,100-acre Southwind Maritime Centre 10 miles downstream from Evansville on the Ohio River. Even with the growing threat of railway abandonments, Indiana's more than 6,000 miles of track dwarfs the interstate highway total of 1,134 it boasts so much about. But while access to Indiana is easy, so is access through and out of it: many of its sons and daughters left the state to find their fortunes elewhere, leaving behind an increasingly inbred, unwavering white, Anglo Saxon Protestant culture with little imagination and equal innovation. This steadfast devotion to time-proven traditions can be seen today in Indiana's aversion toward public indebtedness. Ever since the state almost fell into virtual bankruptcy in 1840 after it unsuccessfully tried to underwrite large-scale construction of a canal system, the constitution has prohibited debt and promoted the "pay-as-you-go" dictum that prevails still. Indianans are proud that today the state, compared to others in the industrial Northeast and Midwest, ranks absolutely last in indebtedness.

The Civil War doubtless also played a major role in the provincialism. A potent Copperhead movement sympathetic to the slave-owning South flourished in Indiana, especially in the counties near the Ohio River (an area still more Southern than Midwestern). At the same time, a radical Republican governor sent almost 200,000 Indiana men into battle, 25,000 of them never to return home alive. The wartime rivalries lingered for generations, with veteran, son, and grandchild reliving the bitterness and voting by rote either Union (Republican) or Copperhead (Democrat). Such unthinking, fixed attitudes only reinforced the innate suspicions and fierce individualism that already existed.

Indiana's first white inhabitants were the French, who came to trade with the Indians and established in 1732 a fort on the Wabash River that was the forerunner of Vincennes. When the area became part of the old Northwest Territory in 1787, Indiana was planned as a northern free state. But its first significant number of settlers arrived not from the North but the South, a fact which contributed as much as the Civil War to the isolationism that became a Hoosier way of life. From Virginia, the Carolinas, through the Cumberland Gap, and from Kentucky, down and across the Ohio River they came, bringing with them all their cultural, political, religious, and social heritage. To this day, no Northern state has such a large share of Southern white stock as does Indiana. Not the least of this heritage were their slaves, despite the prohibition against slavery included in the Northwest Ordinance of 1787. Far into the 20th century, Indiana carried laws on its books barring interracial marriages. These Southerners also brought with them the Jacksonian brand of democracy, embedding the spoils system as a cornerstone of Indiana politics. To this day, Indiana's highly personal brand of local politics and, only slightly less so, the state politics, comes down to dividing the spoils. Who gets the jobs means far more than good government—a tradition that effectively stifled change and innovation in vast portions of the Hoosier state and encouraged the Progressive and muckraking eras to bypass Indiana.

For years, Indiana had its own Mason-Dixon line, dividing the state roughly along the course of the old National Road, now U.S. Highway 40, the line reaching from Richmond on the East through the Capital City and southwestward to Terre Haute on the banks of the lazy Wabash River. Together, Indiana's two halves span but 236 miles north and south; with its modest 140-mile width, the state totals 36,291 square miles, or 38th in size in the country. Still, it is the smallest state west of the Allegheny Mountains.

The Southerners who came to settle the portion of Indiana below the illusory line failed to pick a very promising area. Southern Indiana is a territory of low-lying hills and barren, clay soil, which allowed only a skimpy sustenance to farmers. Coal mining later flourished in southwestern counties for a few decades, and is still mined there today—with the ready cash benefits for a few and general depression for the many that extractive industries so often bring in their wake.

The immigrants who settled Indiana north of the line came from a different direction—from New England, New York, Pennsylvania, and beyond, across the ocean from Germany and Poland and other countries torn by the Revolution of 1848. The legacy of foreign immigration was still apparent in the 1970 Census, when 6.8 percent of the state's population was still foreign born or first generation Americans, with Germans and Poles ranking first and second. The immigrants to northern Indiana settled first on the flat, black, nutrient-rich soil covering the state between Indianapolis and the Great Lakes. Later, they endured the heat and grime to run the mills and machinery in the Gary-Hammond-East Chicago industrial complex. Many of these industrial workers gave their votes to Alabama's George Wallace during his presidential forays into Indiana in 1964, 1968, and 1972, a delayed reaction to the influx of Southern blacks after World War II. Still, by the 1970s, blacks numbered only 388,600 in Indiana, just 7 percent of the total state population.

Forces of Change

If this neat political and geographic dichotomy were ever true—and there were always scores of exceptions to the pattern—it certainly is outmoded today. Most of the traditional values endure; even brief discussions with locals produce evidence that personal property, patriotism, churchgoing, and conservatism are far from dead. The old values may have been skewed a bit, as Muncie showed, but they still are realities not to be ignored. Geographically, the state seems unchanged. The north is largely unforested, fertile, and flat; the south is hillier, less prosperous, but far more pleasing to the eye. Almost imperceptibly, the land is changing. The unique prairie vegetation and outdoor splendor of the Indiana Dunes, a 2,182-acre park along Lake Michigan, have been encroached upon by industrial expansion and developments, threatening one of the few unique topographical wonders in Indiana. Environmentalists raised their voices in protest, but like most progressive crusaders before them in Indiana, they find only isolated groundswells of support. Suburban communities throughout the state continue to edge outward, replacing some croplands with ranch-style houses on barren lots. Former metropolitan manufacturers, seeking lower taxes, dependable workers, and a better business climate, are finding all three in the small cities of Indiana, and again the new plants are altering the landscape of the countryside.

The forces of change blurring the old North-South division are most starkly illustrated in the political and economic realms. Politically, the loyalties of Hoosiers are mixed, with partisanship and corruption weakened but hardly obliterated (especially at the local level). As in other states, the politics of personality are on the ascendancy, and the nemesis of all professional politicians—the ticket-splitting independent voter—stalks Indiana as determinedly as in any other Northern state. Economically, the exodus from farm to factory has made countless ripples, both for the rural and urban areas.

Indiana now has two great industrial centers. The larger revolves around Indianapolis and its ring of prosperous satellite cities (Richmond, Anderson, and Muncie to the east; Kokomo and Marion to the north; Lafayette and Terre Haute to the west, and Columbus to the south). Within these cities and their environs, 40 percent of Indiana's 5,330,000 people live, producing everything from cars to telephones, furniture to fruit jars. Unlike most other northern states, Republicans thrive in most of these cities, providing genuine competition and in some instances maintaining control of their communities. With seven interstates converging on Indianapolis and with more than 100 truck lines operating out of it, the capital city also is the hub of the motor transport industry, much as Chicago for years was the railhead to the nation.

To the north, congregated in Lake County where Illinois, Indiana, and Lake Michigan meet, is the second great industrial center. Its major cities, Gary, East Chicago, Hammond, and Whiting, are industrial and political cesspools compared to Indiapanolis and the smaller cities. Rough and raw, Gary and environs are more akin to Chicago than to the rest of the Hoosier state. The European ethnics have retreated in the face of the influx of Southern blacks, leaving Gary with a black majority in control of City Hall. In this tiny corner of Indiana, the acrid pollution is not quite as bad as a decade ago, but it still can turn day into dusk. Racial discord only compounded the political corruption epitomized in Gary, although ethnics and blacks avoided confrontations in other parts of Lake County. In good times, when the steel mills are running day and night, wages are plentiful and unemployment is slight. The exception is among the blacks, whose unemployment in the best of times is high and during economic slowdowns reaches frightful proportions. Organized labor is strong in the Gary orbit and noticeably less conservative than its counterpart elsewhere in Indiana. To prove the point, Edward Sadlowski, a reform-minded third generation steel worker, challenged the hierarchy of the United Steelworkers Union in 1974 and won election as director of the Chicago-Gary district, with 140,000 members, the largest in the union.

Geographically separate but still vital in industry, as we will note later, are South Bend and Fort Wayne in the north and Evansville in the south.

The exodus from the farm has contributed to the changing complexion of the industrial centers as well as rural areas. In 1960, Indiana's urban population was 62 percent; by 1977, it was nearly 68 percent. Only half as many people, about 3 percent, were working the land in the mid-1970s, compared with 6.9 percent two decades before. In 1976 there were about 20,000 fewer farms in Indiana than a decade earlier. Even so, the drop-off was significantly smaller than the 40,000 decrease in the 10 years before 1964. The size of farms rose as their numbers decreased, as modern technology, new and expensive equipment, and corporate management converted the family-run farms into big business, often worth upwards of half a million dollars. Many small farmers found costs so high they were forced to take second jobs in nearby industrial plants just to make ends meet. By no means, however, does all this mean Indiana's agriculture is near a state of collapse. Indiana still is a leading farm state. Its cash receipts from farm marketings consistently are in the top 10, totaling more than $3 billion in the 1970s. Nearly three-fifths of that came from crops, chiefly corn, sorghum, oats, wheat, rye, soybeans, and hay, not to mention the popcorn harvest which will rank Indiana either second or third in the country, depending on the year. The exodus from the farm land was hastened by the modernization of Indiana society. The burgeoning new suburbs, the extensive interstate network, and the economic boomlet generated by new plants contributed mightily to the 7.4 percent drop in acreage under the plow during the 1960s and 1970s. All told, Indiana by the late '70s had 1.3 million fewer acres cultivated than it did in 1964.

All of this brought political repercussions. There was a time when the Farm Bureau spoke with a resounding voice in Indiana, but its power in legislative and political circles diminished in proportion to its constituency. Reapportionment of legislative districts on a strict one-man, one-vote basis, reflecting the population shift to the urban areas, further relegated the farm lobby to a secondary stature in the statehouse in Indianapolis.

Reapportionment also debilitated the once entrenched partisanship that so long dominated Indiana. Ed Ziegner, political editor of the Indianapolis *News*, told us seats were not gerrymandered "in the sense they used to be," and added: "The effect is to allow a legislator, whether Republican or Democrat, to be more independent. If he really knows how to get out and work his district and campaigns on a personal basis, while the seat may have been set up as a birthright Republican or birthright Democrat, that doesn't mean that's what it has to remain." As the lawmakers became more independent, they break away from the traditional, rural-oriented values of the Hoosier state, gradually taking on the notions associated with an urban, industrialized society.

As agrarian Indiana declined, industrial Indiana expanded. The first entrepreneurial enterprises in pioneer times were the sawmills and gristmills, established to meet the basic needs of settlers within a day's wagon ride. Now about 10 percent of Indiana's nearly 8,000 manufacturers have foreign markets, much of the goods shipped through Burns Harbor, the Great Lakes, and the St. Lawrence Seaway. By the mid-1970s, Indiana's export trade amounted to $4 billion a year. So diversified had the state's manufacturing base grown that it had 299 of Fortune's 500 top corporations operating either a plant or a subsidiary in the state. The state's industry runs the gamut from mobile homes, raw steel, and electrical machinery to pharmaceuticals, plastic products, and transportation equipment. Truck assembly plants in Fort Wayne, Indianapolis, and South Bend produced 95,375 trucks in 1977. Altogether, employment in motor vehicle and related industries accounted for 29 percent (nearly 500,000 persons in the mid-1970s) of Indiana's workforce. Not surprisingly, the United Auto Workers were the largest independent union in the state. The diversification of Indiana's industry helped it weather the economic downturns during the 1970s better than many industrial states.

No force of change in Indiana has been as pervasive as the federal dollar. Despite the 1947 resolution by the legislature declaring Indiana independent of federal aid, Hoosiers have come to view Washington as less of an alien force and more of a partner—albeit not a completely trusted one. From the late New Deal days up until 1960, Indiana Republicans found a sure-fire election day success formula by opposing the growth of the federal government, opposing acceptance of (most) federal aid, and persistently exhorting less government spending. To this day, many county boards and city councils retain their phobia about federal aid, preferring self-sufficiency even at the price of doing without.

The beginning of the end for obdurate Indiana resistance to all forms of federal aid probably occurred when President Eisenhower inaugurated the interstate highway system, requiring states to put up only $1 for every $9 the federal government held out. Highway aids are not to be put in the same class as welfare aids or dollars for the cities, and Indiana was not about to reject such a deal. As one observer put it, "Hoosiers may be stubborn, but they're not stupid." By the mid-1970s, Indiana was receiving more than $1 billion a year in federal assistance, although the $205 per capita it received in all forms of federal spending in 1976 was the lowest of all 50 states and only two-thirds of the national average. The Tax Foundation Inc. reported in 1978 that Indiana paid $1.43 in federal taxes for every $1 it got back in federal aids, the highest amount (and worst bargain) among all the 50 states. (Among the other Great Lakes States, Ohio and Illinois did not fare much better, paying $1.31 and $1.26 respectively for each $1 of federal aid received. Michigan almost broke even, at $1.01, while Wisconsin had the only bonus, paying only $.88 to get $1 back from Washington.)

"The leaders have been the feds" when it comes to changes in mental health, health and welfare in Indiana, we were told by Ed Thuma, former Legislative Council director and budget chief under Gov. Otis Bowen. In addition, grants by such agencies as the Environmental Protection Agency for sewage treatment facilities have altered the jobs of many town and village clerks, forcing them to choose between wrestling with federal regulations amidst their bookkeeping chores or seeking full-time assistants. For those believing that part-time public officials are preferred over full-time professionals (and there are many in Indiana), the addition of new staff to cope with federal requirements was traumatic. Urban assistance grants were sought with reluctance for years (excepting in Gary under the administration of Mayor Richard Hatcher and in a few other cities), but Indiana's mayors "bleated like lost lambs," as one observer told us, when President Carter trimmed urban aids to balance his budget early in 1980. Dollars flowing from the military contracts and military personnel were always welcome, though. Such contracts themselves totaled $834.8 million in 1976, a certain part of which can be attributed to the location of Fort Benjamin Harrison in Indianapolis, home of the U.S. Finance Center, which issues all checks for the Army.

Leaders overtly advocating change are still relatively rare in Indiana, and with good reason: they can't get elected, or stay elected if they move too far in front of their constituents. But the incessant pressures from outside, forcing change, are having their effect. One politico in Indianapolis confided to us, "It's not a Hoosier state in the old sense. And by Hoosier, I mean, hardworking, friendly, somewhat conservative, commonsense, sort of a pragmatist, little bit suspicious of government, 'I'll do it my own way.' . . . ." There was more than a trace of lamentation in his voice.

Panorama of Politics Past

Traditionally, Indiana spawned a special breed of politician. Those elected seemed to include an inordinate proportion of those who would be either despots or just crackpots waving the American flag, fanning jingoistic fervor, or railing against the nefarious giants on the Eastern seaboard. Albert Jeremiah Beveridge's maiden speech in the U.S. Senate shortly after the turn of the century set a tone for inflammatory rhetoric. Let his words speak for themselves: "God has not been preparing the English-speaking and Teutonic peoples for a thousand years for nothing but a vain and idle self-contemplation and self-admiration. No! He has made us the master organizers of the world to establish a system where chaos reigns. . . . Pray God the time may never come when Mammon and the love of ease shall so debase our blood that we shall fear to shed it for the flag and our imperial destiny."

Those following Beveridge inclined toward protecting Hoosiers from the outside world. Sen. James E. Watson, a staunch defender of high tariffs, isolationism, and business supremacy, was elected to the House of Representatives six times and the Senate three times. A member of the inner circle of Republicans at the national level, he was a communicant in the smoke-filled room in 1920 that finally agreed on nominating Warren Harding for President; Watson was also an ally of Henry Cabot Lodge in rejecting President Wilson's League of Nations. H. L. Mencken, the political critic, derided him as a "mountebank so puerile and preposterous" he made others of his ilk seem dignified. Yet, Mencken accorded Watson recognition as a politician, calling him an "adept professional." Watson lost none of his vituperation as he aged. Eight years after his defeat for reelection in 1932, he was at the Republican National Convention, strenuously, some said viciously, opposing Wendell Willkie's nomination. To Willkie's face, Watson said he had nothing against whores in church; he just didn't go along with them leading the choir on first Sundays.

Another master of invective was William Jenner, the fire-eating right-wing U.S. Senator of Indiana during the 1950s. Nationally, Jenner is remembered as the man who called General George C. Marshall a "living lie" and a "front man for traitors." In Indiana he is recalled as the dominant figure in Hoosier Republicanism for 15 years. Irving Leibowitz in his delightful book, *My Indiana*, picked Jenner as the "perfect symbol" of what Indiana was before the forces of change became widespread in the state:

And what a symbol. He pounds the desk. He cusses. He dramatizes. He shouts. He whispers. He can be warm and gregarious. He can be ice cold. He can turn his emotions on and off.

Jenner has been described variously as a Southern Indiana hillbilly, a demagogue, a wild and woolly vigilante, a witch-hunter, a grant inquisitor and a fascist firebrand.

His political associates picture him as one of the last great patriots, a courageous and militant battler for American sovereignty, the preservation of the U.S. Constitution and the uprooting of the Soviet fifth column.

After two impassioned terms in the Senate, Jenner quit in 1958. He wanted to raise his son Billy in the purer atmosphere of southern Indiana, his friends insisted; his enemies contended Jenner thought he might not be re-elected. Retirement did not mean withdrawal from political circles, however. That autumn, when the Republican campaign faltered in the cities, Jenner caustically advised a closed GOP planning session: "Draw a circle around every single one and don't set foot in them. Forget 'em. Concentrate on the farms and the towns. If we can't win in Indiana, we can't win anywhere. We've got the most conservative press and the most conservative people in America, from Lake Michigan to the Ohio River. Pour it on."

Late in the 1970s, Jenner's health was not what it used to be, but like Watson he had lost little of his virulent impetuosity. In 1978 he spoke at a Republican oldtimers' dinner. One of our political friends in Indiana told us that "Jenner uses some of the rawest language of any politician I've ever known. At this dinner, with a lot of women present, he described (President) Carter as a pimple on the prick of progress. No reporter there could use that, but that's Bill Jenner."

Paul McNutt was another classic character in the annals of Indiana politics, the perfect product of the Hoosier system as it was for most of the 20th century. McNutt, Indiana's Democratic governor during the New Deal Days, was a former state and national commander of the American Legion, a sure-fire ticket to electoral success at the time. (Tarnishing the stereotype, though, was his Harvard Law School degree, a biographical note often lost in his associations with the Legion.) McNutt instituted major economic reforms in the state during his Depression-years administration, but he probably is better remembered as the perfecter of the infamous "2 percent club," the public employee kickback system that filled party coffers for four decades afterwards. He nurtured aspirations for national office, hoping, as one observer put it, to "march into the White House behind a Legion drum and bugle corps." First, he sought a place on Roosevelt's ticket in 1936, then assumed FDR would step aside after eight years, only to be surprised by the President's announcement of a third term. Roosevelt disappointed McNutt for a third time when he bypassed the Indiana governor for the vice presidential place again in 1940, picking Henry Wallace instead. Clearly, McNutt was the favorite of the delegates for the second position on the 1940 ticket. When he strode to the platform in Chicago to announce his support of Wallace, the galleries and the delegates roared their opposition to what they knew he was about to do. "I want . . ." he started. "No!" they screamed back. Seven times he began, only to be choked off by the thundering outcries. Finally, McNutt, always the loyal soldier, got it out: "He is my commander-in-chief," he said of Roosevelt. "I follow his wishes, and I am here to support his choice for Vice President of the United States." Roosevelt did have a consolation prize for McNutt: U.S. Ambassador to the Philippines.*

The Grand Exceptionary Indiana Republican was Wendell Willkie. A small-town boy from Elwood, about 30 miles north of Indianapolis, Willkie made good, not in Indiana, but in New York City as the $75,000-a-year president of the big electrical utility, Commonwealth and Southern. At the time of Willkie's nomination as the 1940 Republican presidential candidate, and to this day, Old Guard Republicans in Indiana swear he was not one of them, but rather an apostate who had rejected his roots. The archconservative, isolationist-minded Hoosier Republican later came to detest Willkie's doctrine of "One World" or his reformation of the party's image from isolationist to internationalist. The New York *Times*, upon Willkie's death in 1944, said he was "as American as the countryside of his native Indiana." But so strong was the distaste for Willkie in his home state that even his son, Phillip Willkie, was quickly crushed when he sought his first statewide office, superintendent of public instruction, in Indiana years later.

Strangely enough, Indiana was also the home state of the famed Socialist, Eugene Debs. Debs came out of the Brotherhood of Locomotive Firemen in Terre Haute, where by the age of 20 he was secretary of his lodge. In 1893 he founded the American Railway Union—historic because it was open to all railway employees. But the union was crushed, and Debs jailed for his role, in the violent Pullman strike of 1894. A year later Debs became a Socialist; in 1900, he received the first of four straight Socialist nominations for President. His followers were legion: in 1912 he received over a million votes. But heavy winds of controversy swirled around Debs because of his bitter oppo-

---

* Indianans had been popular ticket balancers in the past, with four Hoosiers serving as Vice President. Schuyler Colfax was the first, serving under President Grant 1869–73, followed by former Gov. Thomas Hendricks under Grover Cleveland in 1885 (Hendricks died in office), former U.S. Senator Charles Fairbanks under Theodore Roosevelt 1905–09, and Thomas Marshall under Woodrow Wilson during both terms. That made Marshall the first Vice President since John C. Calhoun to succeed himself as Vice President. Marshall made the best of his apparently limited national role with his sense of humor. "The cave of the winds" was his irreverent reference to the U.S. Senate.

sition to U.S. involvement in World War I. He ran once more for President, in 1920, from his cell in Atlanta, Ga., where he had been sentenced to 10 years during the war for violating the Espionage Act. President Harding later commuted the sentence and Debs came back to Terre Haute, sick, tired, old, but heartened by the band that greeted him. Until contemporary times, he was a rarity in Indiana politics—a champion of change.

The last of the Old Guard Republicans to hold major office in Indiana were Homer Capehart and Charlie Halleck. Capehart was a down-home industrialist (his electronics firm made Capehart and Zenith radios) who once sponsored a "cornfield conference" on his farm. He served in the U.S. Senate from 1944 until Birch Bayh unseated him 18 years later. While a contemporary of Jenner in the Senate, Capehart was not of the same mold. While Jenner could never accept Dwight Eisenhower, Capehart made the adjustment. "If you're handed a bunch of lemons, you'd better make lemonade," he liked to remind colleagues. According to one political reporter, "Homer had the skill to accommodate himself to a changing situation. Homer had friends on both sides of the aisle, while I don't think Bill Jenner ever really had any Democratic friends." In the late 1970s, Capehart still ran some of the family businesses, but devoted much of his time as a "kind of patriarch of his family," as one Democrat put it, especially since his son and daughter-in-law were killed in a plane crash, leaving him to make sure their chldren were cared for. Capehart died in 1979.

No Hoosier of recent years moved in such lofty Republican circles as Charles Abraham Halleck, who rose to be regarded as the quintessential Midwestern Republican during his 34 years in the U.S. House. He gained something of a national celebrity status during the 1960s as half of the "Ev and Charlie Show," the loyal opposition's televised critique of the Kennedy and Johnson Administrations which Halleck shared with the indubitably entertaining Sen. Everett Dirksen of Illinois. It was as leader of the House minority Republicans that Halleck earned his accolades as a gutsy and wily practitioner of congressional infighting. William S. White described Halleck as "one of the ablest, toughest party floor leaders of modern times." Of Halleck, Eisenhower said: "You are a political genius."

Halleck's conservatism was tinged by pragmatism, a sense of where the power was and how to achieve it, even when in the minority. Despite his conservative voting record, he never won the full trust of his state's right-wing Republicans. His apostasy was infrequent, but his fellow Hoosier Republicans' memories were long. In 1940 Halleck nominated Willkie for the presidency, garnering plaudits throughout the nation but scowls at home. In 1948 he swung Indiana's delegation to New York's Thomas E. Dewey on a promise of becoming Dewey's running mate. Dewey's doublecross, in selecting Earl Warren instead, left a bitter taste in Halleck's mouth. Four years later, frozen out of the Indiana Republican convention delegation, Halleck went to Chicago and worked assiduously for Eisenhower while Indiana's official contingent was supporting Ohio's Robert A. Taft almost 100 percent. Rising in stature in the House during the 1950s as a chief Eisenhower lieutenant, Halleck arrived in 1959 when he staged a coup d'état and deposed the aging Joseph W. Martin, Jr., of Massachusetts as House GOP Leader. Later he teamed with Southern Democrats to kill or bottle up many Kennedy bills. As time wore on, he encountered image problems and in 1965 found himself on the receiving end of another House rebellion, this one led by Michigan's Gerald Ford: Halleck was given the same unceremonious dumping he had delivered to Joe Martin six years earlier, setting the stage for Ford to become part of a unique chapter in U.S. history. Three years later, Halleck retired.

A footnote to Halleck's retirement: Succeeding the crusty conservative was Earl Landgrebe, winner of the 1968 GOP primary in the Second District with but a paltry 22 percent of the vote. Landgrebe earned a sort of immortality shortly before his own defeat in 1974 by declaring unshakable fidelity to Richard Nixon. The day before Nixon's resignation, Landgrebe uttered his most unforgettable quote: "Don't confuse me with the facts," he blurted out to reporters quizzing him about the possible impeachment of Nixon for Watergate misdeeds. "I've got a closed mind. I will not vote for impeachment. I'm going to stick with my President even if he and I have to be taken out of this building and shot." Back home in Indiana, only 39 percent of the Second District voted for Landgrebe that November, sealing his political coffin with ballots instead of bullets. Just six years after Halleck left a secure conservative Republican seat, the Second District voters had sent a Democrat to Washington to represent them, a harbinger of things political to come.

Partisanship and Politics: The Passing of Venality

Partisan politics, once a deadly serious business in Indiana, with jobs and financial gain at stake, remains a serious game. "We still maintain strong party orientations, but it's weakening every year," one Democratic partisan of long standing conceded to us. Democrats and Republicans alike are philosophically conservative, at least at election time, but politically, Indiana no longer is a Republican state. "The last several governors have not been strongly partisan," a Republican official observed. "Still, compared to other states, Indiana would seem partisan." There has been good reason for that national image of partisanship, frequently spilling over the bounds of respectability into the realm of corruption. Both Republican and Democratic parties once controlled the paths to power (and still do in some county courthouses). Those party organizations were machines in the classic sense of the word, fed by patronage and held in check by old-fashioned bosses tightly controlling nominating conventions, jobs, and contract dispersement. People operating in the system had debts to pay, and Indiana had a finely tuned patronage machine designed to make collections.* The 1970s saw a deterioration of those

* John Fenton, writing in 1966 in his book *Midwest Politics*, conceded that the existence of widespread corruption in Indiana, with an active two-party system, was puzzling to him. "One theoreti-

machines, dismantled largely by forces beyond their control. But the populist from Wisconsin or Minnesota would still be taken aback by the partisanship.

The "2 percent club," the license plate franchises, the solicitation of state contractors, the distribution of insurance premiums—all institutionalized forms of Indiana's "honest graft" for decades continue to exist, but on a greatly diminished scale. The backbone of the Indiana patronage was Governor Paul McNutt's "2 percent club." So successful was the requirement that all state government patronage employees contribute 2 percent of their pay to the party that Republicans adopted the concept after McNutt left and local party organizations applied the technique in the courthouses and city halls. At its zenith, the 2 percent kickback was worth between $500,000 and $700,000 a year to the party in power at the state level alone, although an exact accounting never was made. The system was enforced from time of entry to point of departure. One of the questions on the state job form application read: "Would you be willing to contribute regularly to the Indiana _____ State Central Committee?" Once on the job, refusal to pay the 2 percent was tantamount to asking for a termination notice. Objections to the practice were occasionally voiced over the years by those with a purer ethical code, but it was not until legislation, court decisions, and a change of heart by the enforcers during the 1970s that the club became debilitated.

In the mid-1970s, Indiana's Democratic Rep. J. Edward Roush secured passage of a bill that in essence outlawed partisan considerations in the hiring and firing of public employees. Then, starting with a landmark case which originated in Chicago, the U.S. Supreme Court virtually eviscerated all patronage systems in the country. Gov. Bowen made employees' contributions more voluntary. Employees were still encouraged to contribute 1 percent of their wages in the late '70s, but if they didn't nobody did anything about it. "Time was when they would have been canned," noted Ed Ziegner of the *News*. "But that isn't going to happen anymore and they know it isn't going to happen." The result by the end of the '70s was that the "2 percent club" could count on perhaps $200,000 a year, according to one estimate, and that was shrinking annually, abetted by the smaller proportion of patronage workers, numbering only 7,000 to 8,000 of the 28,000 state employees.

Ironically, advocates of the "2 percent club" over the years defended the practice on the grounds that it was "clean money," without strings attached. It allowed party leaders to operate without becoming indebted to a few large contributors who equated their money with political muscle. With the present-day emphasis on fund-raising dinners and individual contributions, the "fat cats" have a greater opportunity to wield influence, they argue.*

---

cal function of two-party competition is to keep a check upon just such malpractices," he wrote. "A partial explanation for the corrupt flavor of Indiana politics was the dominance in both parties of job-oriented professional politicians to whom issues were unimportant save as they served as a means by which to secure jobs."

* Indiana officials are notoriously slow to comply with financial disclosure laws. After the federal campaign contributions disclosure law went into effect in 1972, Common Cause filed complaints that 91 candidates for nomination to the U.S. House of Representatives failed to submit reports as required. Of those 91, 22 were from Indiana.

Solicitations of contributions from companies doing business with the state, another lucrative source of partisan income in the past, also has become less institutionalized. There was a time when state-run computers tracked every company, the kind and amount of its business with the state, and the amount of its contributions. Few firms hopeful of future business with the state ever declined. New restrictions in the 1970s on corporate campaign contributions curtailed the practice. Only $3,000 could be given by corporations for a state office, and up to $1,000 for lesser offices. Pressure also grew for competitive bidding system for certain contracts. The effect of the political forces of change was not to eliminate the solicitation practices of the past, but merely make them more sophisticated. In 1978, Gordon St. Angelo of the Lilly Endowment, the former State Democratic Party chairman, told us that he suspected "most everybody that does business with the state of Indiana does expect to make a contribution somewhere along the line." He explained the rationale behind the expectation: "It's kind of like your commitment to your religious beliefs in dollars and cents. You make a pledge. But they're not going to take you to court or kick you out of church if you don't make the pledge. But you know when you join the church, you've got some financial obligations."

The increasing sophistication of Indiana's political payoff system was noted by a veteran of many legislative battles, who said that "other forms of patronage" now are vastly more significant. Making policy decisions that affect the business community, contractors, the speed of work, the direction of work, the erection of public buildings and reservoirs were among the examples he cited. "I don't know how many jillions of contracts we process through government," he said. "But I think they are significantly more important than the 2 percent money. . . . It's subtle, but it's there. It's not corrupt, particularly, but it's there." In at least one area, businesses in Indiana have revolted. At one time, more than $100,000 a year in commissions on state insurance policies ended up in the hands of the party in power or its minions. The practice worked this way: the governor appointed one or several of his political favorites to write the policies, for which they were paid several thousand dollars. The actual commissions went to licensed insurance agents designated by the controlling party committees; as a practical matter, the agents were expected to endorse their checks over to the local party organizations. By the late '70s, however, the political affiliation of the insurance agent was less important and some insurance companies simply refused to handle the policies if they are required to kickback to the ruling party.

The patronage gleaned from the sale of license plates continued, however, a glaring reminder that partisanship still lived in Indiana. For every license plate, for every driver's license, for every vehicle title transfer, there continued to be a 50 cents service charge that went directly into the hands of the county chairman of the party in power. (Part of the 50 cents ended up in the state party coffers.) The license branch operations, first initiated back in 1932, were part of the fiefdoms of each ruling party county chairman, who could operate the franchise himself or delegate it to an appointee, usually with the understanding the chairman receive a certain percentage for his own use. Again, the exact amount of booty this generated for the majority party could only be estimated. In 1977, Indiana had 3,585,961 registered cars, trucks, and buses, and about an equal number of registered drivers. One estimate placed the return to a large county like Marion (Indianapolis) at $100,000 annually, while the sum for a small rural county could be better than $15,000 a year. The extent of the institutionalization of this system was seen in the revenue allocation from the personalized license plates Indiana authorized in 1978. Of the $40 cost of the special plate, $15 went to the Republican Party, $15 to the Democratic Party, $3 to the license branch (local party), and $7 to the state public treasury. The equal distribution between Republican and Democratic parties was no gesture of generosity: the legislature was politically divided at the time, and Democrats told the Republicans who proposed the political skim-off that they would go along only if they got part of the action.

Notwithstanding the passing of venality and the lessening of partisanship in Indiana, there is engraved still in the minds of many Hoosiers a cultural addiction to the Jacksonian concept of political employment (to the victor belong the spoils). An aide to Governor Bowen reflected on the depth of this attitude when he discussed patronage in Indiana:

"One of the problems that you get with regard to patronage is a kind of kneejerk reaction to the whole system, the theory that anyone should pay any tribute to anybody for getting a job. I'm concerned still about questions of accountability. If you move everybody outside of the political system, you're going to get a bureaucracy that's bloated and unaccountable, as you seem to have in the federal bureaucracy. You lose accountability, because you can't change any of the actors."

Given the ossified nature of many civil service systems, it was hard to say that he didn't have a point. Easy for outsiders to belittle, the patronage system may not have been as debilitating—or indeed corrupting—as one might think. As former Governor Matthew Welsh, certainly an honest chief executive himself, told us, such practices as license plate sales by county chairmen "warrant only passing criticism by the political purist."

When it comes to government scandals on a widespread scale, Indiana doesn't seem much worse off than other states. The administration of George N. Craig, in the early 1950s, was the last tainted by scandal. (Some Craig associates were brought to the bar of justice for highway scandals, but the governor himself was not implicated.) Indiana municipalities have a far less savory record. Gary and Lake County (of which we will report more later) have been havens for corrupt officials for many decades. While Terre Haute's reputation improved in recent years, corruption there too was once a way of life. As recently as the 1960s, during the generation of antiwar demonstrations and the offbeat hippie culture, people were reminded that Terre Haute was known as a sin city. When Indiana State University's President Alan C. Rankin proposed the closing of the brownstone brothels only a few strides from the college dorms, the mayor, Leland Larrison, blustered: "If the college will get rid of the beatniks, kooks, and hippies there, I'll shut down the houses." Indianapolis too was shaken during the mid-1970s by scandals in its police department, unearthed in a Pulitzer prize-winning series by the Indianapolis *Star*. But similar scandals erupt from time to time in many places across the country.

Not only have changes in the patronage system altered the power of Indiana's partisan machines, but externally a host of statutory and legal changes have begun to reshape the parties, the kinds of candidates coming into politics, and the vise-like hold the bosses used to have. These changes began in the early 1960s and have left untouched few things political in Indiana. In 1976 the candidates for governor were picked by a direct primary for the first time, ending decades of party convention—and party boss-control —over the nominees for chief executive. The direct primary for other major offices was instituted only a few years earlier—though the conventions continued to pick their candidates for secretary of state, treasurer, auditor, attorney general, reporter, and clerk for the supreme court. County chairmen vigorously opposed the direct primary. "It was that old convention system that was a big piece of the glue that held the party system together, and it's broken now," one observer of the political system told us. "The convention was quite a piece of politicking. There were great rewards that went out to the system later on."

The bosses, especially in the more urban counties, also fought to the last elimination of the multimember state legislative districts. With the creation of the single-member districts, would-be lawmakers no longer had to rely on the machine's slating process to assure them of election. "The slating process was almost unbeatable with the multimember districts," a former legislative staff person said. "Now with the single-member districts, legislators have more freedom and can vote their constituents' interests." In the 1960s, reapportionment led to less gerrymandering, to the advantage of metropolitan areas. Then, annual legislative sessions were endorsed, attracting a different kind of politician, more independent, less beholden to the political powers-that-be. Similar reforms in the executive and judiciary branches were shifting power away from the political professionals. The constitutional constraint against more than one term for governor was amended in 1972, and four years later Governor Bowen became the first governor in modern times to win a second consecutive term, greatly enhancing the authority of the chief executive both over lawmakers and party power brokers.

Many judges too were removed one step from the political sphere. While their initial appointments may still have exhibited some partisan colorations, their election was not only nonpartisan but also without opposition. Voters are simply asked the question whether the judge should be retained in office.

If the voters say yes, the judge gets a 10-year term; if they say no, the governor could appoint another. Many court decisions used to be rooted more in political considerations than precedents in the law. In the opinion of many, Indiana judges began to improve in the '60s and '70s: the pay improved, educational training was better, the quality of judicial decisions became less dependent on the political parties involved, and generally, judges were more willing to reflect their new-found independence.

Gordon St. Angelo, with a little tinge of remorse, traced the virtual political revolution in Indiana to the 1968 McCarthy movement and McGovern Commission reforms. "In the opinion of an adherent of a strong party-oriented system like myself," St. Angelo said, this was "the beginning of the end of a strong two-party system in the country." The advent of issue-oriented groups, like Ralph Nader crusades, the women's movement, ecologists, and tax reformers followed soon afterwards, eroding centralized partisanship still further. But even today, single-issue groups find far less sympathy for their activities in Indiana than their counterparts can generate in most other states.

Environmentalists finally translated their rhetoric into governmental action in 1979, when their complaints about the safety of the Marble Hill nuclear power plant under construction on the Ohio River brought the project to a halt. That, up to then, was the exception, but led some to wonder if the antinuclear power lobby was making inroads in Indiana.

Finally, the impact of television and radio removed the insularity of Hoosiers from the rest of the world, a trait the county bosses preferred to continue. Former Secretary of State Larry Conrad said that Indianans were "very much taken by the personalities of politics. . . . They are very conscious of the individual." Ed Thuma, former Legislative Council director, underscored the contribution of the media to the changing Hoosier voter:

"It's all tied together with the weakening of the parties, the strengthening of the media, and the disaffiliation of the voter from either party. . . . Before media developed, the mix of appeals was different. There were more county organizations and door knocking; less literature and less TV spots, fewer billboards, less direct dough pouring into the media. It's true not just here but all over the country. I don't think the average voter scrutinizes the candidate's voting record, unless he does something terrible."

Contemporary Politics: Democrats, Primaries, and the Residue of Conservatism

Neither political party enjoyed dominance in Indiana as the state entered the 1980s. Certainly, the partisanship had subsided, although no one assumed that politics was any less serious for those who remain as professionals. Equally certain, the ticket-splitting voter held the balance of power in any statewide election. Although less conservative, Indiana could hardly be called a liberal state. In every one of the presidential elections between 1948 and 1976, it voted more Republican than the nation as a whole—by an average of 4.8 percent in the eight elections. Only four Democratic presidential nominees have won a majority in Indiana since 1900. In 1968 the conservative streak was manifested in the 261,226-vote margin for Richard Nixon—his largest plurality in any of the 50 states.

It has been in state and local elections that the modern day Hoosier's political schizophrenia has shown up. In any given election, as many as 300,-000 Indiana voters split their tickets, leaving the party professionals to shiver at the thought of what happens in the balloting booth. Presidential primaries offered an early signal that the preferences of party leaders would be ignored when emotionally powerful alternatives were available. The first came in 1964 when Alabama's fiery Governor George C. Wallace made his first foray onto the national scene, picking Indiana (along with Wisconsin and Maryland) as states where he would seek support for the Democratic presidential nomination. The task of slowing the Wallace phenomenon fell to Indiana's governor of the moment, Matthew E. Welsh, a dignified and quiet but brilliant small town lawyer from Vincennes who had created an active civil rights commission which managed to keep Indiana from the racial flash point. Wallace's campaign against civil rights laws and federal intrusions struck home in many parts of Indiana. Race-conscious Lake County, for instance, gave him a majority of its vote. But Welsh, running as a stand-in for a then very popular President Johnson, crushed his protagonist statewide by a vote of 376,023 to 172,646. Wallace received 29.8 percent of the vote.

In 1968, with Wallace heading the American Independent Party in the general election, he received only 12 percent of Indiana's vote, and four years later he lost of Hubert Humphrey in the Democratic primary. "Wallace never carried Indiana," one observer noted in an effort to offset the notion of extensive Wallace appeal in the state. "Many people got the idea Wallace got 90 percent of the vote in Indiana, but he never did. The best he did was 41 percent in 1972 (against Humphrey)," he said. "I'm not saying that's bad, but my point is that people have a general impression that he swept Indiana like Sherman went to the sea in 1864. That's not true." There was, however, also a widespread assumption that Wallace's appeal among Hoosiers was his racial politics. And there was good reason to assume that in Indiana. In the 1970s the state still had the reputation as the strongest Ku Klux Klan state in the North. It was not many years ago that numerous small Indiana towns prominently displayed signs reading: "Nigger, don't let the sun set on you here." A similar sign on the boundary separating Lafayette from West Lafayette was not destroyed until a few days after the assassination of Martin Luther King. Irving Leibowitz recalled the ugliness of Klan activity at its height:

Nearly 500,000 Hoosiers, in white robes and hoods, burned their fiery crosses almost nightly to strike fear in the hearts of their neighbors. Masked Klansmen by the thouands paraded through downtown city streets like an avalanche of snow descending. The Klan preached white supremacy, terrorized Negroes, persecuted Jews, discriminated against Catholics and with a pathological ferocity took unto itself the duties of vice crusading and punishing of immorality.

Such tactics were familiar in Indiana long before the Klan set foot there. After the Civil War, vigilante groups called "regulators" broke up gangs of robbers and counterfeiters. From 1873 to 1893, hooded "Whitecaps" flourished in eight rural southern counties, concerning themselves with eradicating cruelty to children, wife-beating, drunkenness, infidelity, even laziness. Ironically, the beginning of the end of the Indiana KKK came in 1925 when its grand dragon, D.C. Stephenson, was convicted of the murder of a young Indianapolis girl who died after his sexual assault upon her. Institutionalized bigotry died more slowly, however: it was 1949 before legalized school segregation was repealed and not until 1964 that a law forbidding whites and blacks from marrying was taken off the books.

As deep as the racism runs in Indiana, the appeal by Wallace touched far more than that. It struck too the antiwelfare and antibureaucratic sentiments shared by so many. Ironically, Wallace and Robert Kennedy—even though poles apart philosophically—seemed to attract many of the same kind of followers in Indiana, especially among blue-collar laborers. Former Democratic State Chairman Gordon St. Angelo told us he had conducted some tentative voter analysis of the two candidacies and that there was a "surprisingly close" correlation between the tallies for Kennedy and Wallace in counties both men carried heavily. "A fine line separated them," St. Angelo said. "It's only speculation, but I have a tendency to believe they did draw on the same strains."

In Welsh, the Democrats had perhaps their best governor of postwar years to run in the 1964 primary. Among other things, Welsh had won legislative approval of a revolutionary tax reform package which included an income tax and a sales tax, both firsts in Hoosier history. Four years later, the presidential primary was immersed in the national Democratic factional battle stirred by the Vietnam War. The governor in office at the time was a Democrat of a different stripe: Roger D. Branigin, a silver-haired attorney with a crackerbarrel personality, 62 years of age when he left Lafayette to become governor. A conservative Indiana Democrat of the old school, Branigin was determined not to rock the boat. But fate was to put his name in the headlines and on the airwaves of the nation for a few brief weeks in 1968 when he became a stand-in for President Johnson, opposing Senators Robert Kennedy and Eugene McCarthy. When the 1968 votes were counted, Branigin's 30.7 percent placed him second, behind Kennedy's 42.3 percent and slightly ahead of McCarthy's 27 percent. Branigin's defeat was not only a personal one, quickly extinguishing his fanciful ideas about a possible national role, but also a serious setback for both the Democratic party and organized labor, which had gone all out for his candidacy. The notion of a national role was breathed into the campaign when the Indianapolis newspapers owned by Eugene C. Pulliam (a close friend of the governor's) printed reports that Branigin was one of three or four Democrats under serious consideration for the vice presidential nomination. With Branigin unable to enhance a national ticket in any way, it was painfully obvious the stories had been concocted or deliberately inspired by the followers of Hubert Humphrey, who had become the frontrunner when Johnson withdrew from the race.

A brief digression about the Pulliam papers of Indianapolis, the *News* and the *Star*. Eugene C. Pulliam, a right-wing evangelist and hater of things international and Eastern, controlled both papers for a quarter century. A plaque in the lobby of the *Star-News* building quotes Pulliam as saying: "If you forget everything else I've said, remember this: America is great only because America is free." Despite a staff including some distinguished reporters, the papers occasionally would editorialize grossly in news coverage, run front page cartoons, and carry unlabeled editorials for pet candidates. On the day before the 1968 primary, the *Star* saturated its front page with pro-Branigin stories and ran what amounted to an unmarked ad across the bottom of page one: "Vote for Indiana—Vote for Branigin." Pulliam thought John F. Kennedy was unduly influenced by left-wing pressure groups and warned against "buying the White House." In 1968, when Robert Kennedy's campaign staff complained about the "outrageous and callous disregard for fairness" in the primary coverage, Pulliam issued a statement insisting "Kennedy and his entourage received more space in [the two papers] than any other candidate." Later, Reporter Jules Witcover did a painstaking review of the primary season papers for *The Columbia Journalism Review*. Witcover's findings conclusively proved Pulliam's assertions to be fallacious. During the campaign, Branigin got 45 percent more coverage in the *Star*, and 52 percent more in the *News*, to say nothing of the fact that stories about Kennedy often were highly critical while those about Branigin were permeated with adulation.

Pulliam died in 1975, at 86, leaving the papers to his son, Eugene S. The younger man impressed all almost immediately as a more professional newsman and a publisher with greater concern for fairness than his father. A former reporter on the *News* remarked that he could never tell for sure if the papers were following the people of Indiana or the people were following the conservative stance of the papers. The Pulliams have three other papers in Indiana, two in Muncie and another in Vincennes. A former Muncie editor concluded that the Pulliams no longer control the outcome of elections, but they can influence them, even if it's "not as much as before." As another politico observed of the Pulliam papers: "Anybody that buys ink by the barrel has some clout."

By general consensus, Indiana no longer is a solid Republican state. But neither is it solid Democratic. St. Angelo and Conrad both described to us what might be called a "fluke theory" of electoral success for Hoosierland Democrats. According to them, Democrats win statewide office in Indiana only when a fluke occurs. The most telltale signs of an approaching "fluke," or Democratic victory, they said, are a split among Republicans, a public trend toward a new face or a new style of politics, or a strong (for Indiana) presidential candidate at the top of the ticket. Democrat Vance Hartke's 1958 win for the U.S. Senate over Governor Harold Handley, for instance, came in a year when the GOP was divided. Birch Bayh's victory in 1962 exemplified the potency of a bright, fresh, new face appearing on the scene and overpowering the staid and predictable Homer Capehart.

Thus, to equate the willingness of Indiana voters to occasionally veer to the left with the conversion to mainstream national politics would be misleading. A Charles Percy of Illinois or a Jacob Javits of New York would probably find little support from either the courthouse cliques or the rank and file Republican in Indiana. And the only reason Birch Bayh could espouse his liberal convictions and survive was his concurrent attention to such constituents as the farmers and labor union members while maintaining a canny sense of what to publicize back home and what to downplay. The change in Indiana's political direction, then, was not a 180-degree turn, but only a shift of 90 degrees, or perhaps even less. Among the leading Indiana politicians of the 1970s—Bayh, Lugar, Bowen, Hartke, and Hatcher—only the Gary mayor dared to present himself to the voters as something other than a moderate, middle-of-the-road candidate. But Hatcher's constituency and Gary's problems were not typically those of Indiana; they more resembled those of a Newark or Detroit than a Fort Wayne, Evansville, or Indianapolis.

The electoral track record of Birch Bayh helped answer how a senator with a 94 percent favorable rating from both the Americans for Democratic Action (ADA) and labor's Committee on Political Education (COPE) and a zero score from both the National Association of National Businessmen and the Americans for Constitutional Action could win so consistently. For one thing, while Bayh kept on winning, it wasn't by much. Against Lugar in 1974 and another articulate Republican, William Ruckelshaus, in 1968, he received only 52 percent. That opposing 48 percent was a constant reminder to tend to political fence-mending back home often and well. Bayh had also served an excellent apprenticeship—he had grown up in Indiana, gone to college there, and served eight years in the Indiana House (including four years as Speaker). With his soft drawl, even after nearly 18 years in Washington, he still came across in his many back-home visits as one of the boys stopping in for a little talk over the cracker barrel.

In fact, there seemed almost a nonrecognition among Indiana Democrats and independents of Bayh's national reputation as a liberal. In running for the presidency twice, Bayh was considered a potential liberal alternative. In spearheading opposition to Nixon's Supreme Court nominees, he was taking on the man who had convincingly carried Indiana over Hubert Humphrey by 11 percentage points. But his wife's breast surgery cut short his 1971 foray into presidential politics, after he had assembled a savvy and energetic staff and a considerable bankroll. In 1976 he started a step behind the early announced candidates and never caught up: after a bleak 5 percent of the Massachusetts primary vote, good only for seventh place, he decided to concentrate again on his Senate job and his home state.

In the Senate, Bayh produced remarkable mileage from an ordinarily obscure and mundane committee assignment—the Constitutional Amendments Committee. Three of the proposed amendments authored by Bayh cleared Congress during his tenure; before this spurt of constitutional revisions, only one amendment had been approved in 30 years. The 25th Amendment provided for a new line of vice presidential succession, allowing for the selection of Gerald Ford as Vice President when Spiro Agnew resigned and contributing to Ford's elevation to the White House instead of House Speaker Carl Albert. The 26th Amendment established the 18-year-old vote for all elections. Bayh's third successful effort to push a constitutional amendment through Congress, like many of his liberal stances, met with greater favor outside his own state than inside it. The Equal Rights Amendment (ERA), guaranteeing women equal treatment under the law, passed Congress in 1972. When it came before the Indiana legislature in 1975, the house approved it but the senate killed it. Two years later, however, it cleared both houses in Indiana. In 1979 Bayh lost when he sought Senate approval of another constitutional amendment he had backed for a full decade—direct election of the President, replacing the electoral college.

The saga of Vance Hartke provides testimony of the perilous course for liberals in Indiana. From the time of his first election to the Senate in 1958 (he'd previously been mayor of Evansville), Hartke leaned consistently to the left. He was for liberal social programs, against new arms systems, for civil rights acts, against the oil depletion allowance. He became one of the earliest senators to oppose U.S. involvement in the Vietnam war.

A more moderate opponent than archconservative Richard Roudebush might have defeated him in 1970, but Hartke squeaked through by 4,283 votes out of 1,737,697 in a much disputed and recounted election. By 1976 Hartke was clearly ripe for an upset, which Richard Lugar administered. Beyond ideology, Lugar was able to exploit the issue of Hartke's questionable connections with monied interests—most of them outside Indiana. For years, there had been rumors that Hartke was taking better care of special interests in Washington than the public interest. Many of the charges were dredged up from years past, but cynics suggested Indiana had two senators—Bayh and Bought. Hoosiers can tolerate a liberal who pays attention to the needs of the home-folk. They don't tolerate a liberal whose integrity had been successfully challenged—at least in the minds of those who decide elections. Hartke got only 2,500 votes fewer than six years before, but the bright and personable Lugar garnered 400,000 more than Roudebush in 1970. By any standard, the 59 percent majority Lugar piled up—90,000 more than even Gerald Ford—was an avalanche.

Lugar, Unigov, and Congressional Miscellanea

Richard Lugar, a moderate by national standards, is doubtless seen as a suspiciously liberal figure by many Indiana Republicans. Born and reared in Indianapolis, he went away to college, first to Denison University in Ohio, then to Oxford University in England on a Rhodes Scholarship. During these formative years, Lugar acquired an intellectual frame of mind—plus a sophisticated vocabulary and manner of expression rare among politicians anywhere —which he would later carry into public life. Following his education, he returned to Indianapolis to run the family business for 17 years. He became a member of the city school board and was involved in a civic leaders' club called the Greater Indianapolis Progress Committee. On that committee, Lugar began floating plans for metropolitan government reorganization, only to be rebuffed at each turn.

Prior to the 1967 mayoralty election, Lugar's path crossed that of L. Keith Bulen, former state representative and new Marion County Republican chairman. Bulen differed from his doctrinaire, postwar GOP compatriots: he'd rather win elections than philosophical debates. And he sensed Republicans weren't going to do it with the candidates and platforms they were customarily running on. For Bulen, philosophy could be sacrificed on the alter of pragmatism. He saw in Richard Lugar the kind of candidate with the kind of ideas that fitted into his formula for electoral success. Together, they captured control of city hall in 1967, a feat Republicans had accomplished only twice in four decades. Lugar and Bulen were on the way up. Without either of them, their most outstanding monument to the new Republicanism and better government in Indianapolis probably never would have reached fruition. Unigov was the result—the reorganization of government in Marion County, fusing substantial functions of Indianapolis with those of the county. While the ultimate reorganization adopted was the work of many, Lugar remained the brains and Bulen the master political tactician.

The prominence of partisan politics in the creation of Unigov is an instructive case of the way things get done in Indiana. "We used strong political muscle to do this job," Lugar later wrote. "To be effective, a county had best have political muscle in the state Legislature, [and] with the governor. . . ." The first step was the 1968 Republican State Convention, where Secretary of State Edgar Whitcomb, Speaker of the House Otis Bowen, and a Purdue University dean by the name of Earl Butz were vying for the party's nomination for governor. Bulen backed Whitcomb, delivering 294 of Marion County's 346 delegates. (Bowen's chance would come four years later; Butz's call would come from Richard Nixon, to be Secretary of Agriculture.) After Whitcomb won the nomination, Bulen was elected Indiana Republican National Committeeman. The second step in creating a political base to combine the city and county government was masterfully executed in the fall elections: Whitcomb became goverper, Republicans gained 73 of 100 seats in the House and 35 of 50 in the Senate. Not a single Democrat was among the Marion County legislative delegation of eight senators and 15 representatives. With any consolidation plan needing legislative action and gubernatorial signature, the political advance work was critical, especially in Indiana, where partisanship is lived and breathed.

Simultaneously, Lugar, County Council President Beurt R. SerVaas and City Council President Thomas Hasbrook—also Republicans—were testing their ideas out on each other and a small but growing coterie of city and civic leaders, technicians, planners, and lawyers. Even before the fall election, Lugar had formed two task forces to deal with reorganization and develop a plan that would win legislative support. By December, the task force announced its final recommendations in time for introduction in the January session of the legislature.

Nor had Lugar forgotten that the legislature is composed of more than just Marion County. "Throughout 1968, much of the strategy involved my campaigning throughout Indiana in behalf of not only the state candidates, but more particularly of state senators," Lugar later explained. So, when the bill was introduced in the senate early in the session, there were political chits to be called. And every Marion County delegate in both houses had assigned lobbying tasks.

Local popular support was important too. Politically volatile proposals were omitted from the plan during drafting; as a result, Unigov made no suggestions of merging school districts, which might have meant busing of blacks from the central city to suburban schools, or vice versa. But Lugar also took his campaign to the community, speaking wherever there were listeners, sometimes in three places in an evening. Numerous amendments were written as the momentum was carefully built.

When a public hearing was held early in February 1969, the parade of hostile witnesses was long, with a string of arguments equally extensive. But the opposition was fragmented, disorganized, with no common thread woven through their complaints. The vote was 28–16 in favor. In the house, then-Speaker Bowen nearly squelched the bill by delaying its scheduling for final passage. For a week, the country doctor pondered the bill; * then, on March 5 the last day on which the rules allowed legislation to be passed, Dr. Bowen rose above his personal reservations and gave his blessing. When the roll was called, the count was 66 in favor, 29 opposed.

Although the voting was over, the debate was just beginning as to what was accomplished by the consolidation. "Many who oppose this proposition possess a fear of change . . . a fear of representative government," said E. Henry Lamkin, Marion County leader of the house forces during final debate on the measure. "It's the kind of fear that spreads through a city. Indianapolis is a great city. This [bill] will keep it from becoming like so many other

* One reason for the delay was Lugar's precipitous act of handing out Bowen's unlisted telephone number. It was not until after Lugar delivered an abject, handwritten apology that Bowen released the bill.

cities: a doughnut—a suburban circle surrounding a hollow core."

Overnight, Indianapolis jumped from the nation's 26th largest city to the 11th. Its boundaries were pushed outward to the Marion County lines, although certain municipalities with clout—Beech Grove, Lawrence, and Speedway—were allowed to keep their identities. The taxing authority was untouched, too. The county commissioners were abolished, replaced with a new 29-member Common Council with 25 single-member districts and four others elected at-large. Some special district authorities also were left autonomous, but county agencies were reduced from 26 to 6.

What did Lugar and Bulen really accomplish? Some said Unigov was more pomp than substance, that it really changed little in the way of governmental administration. That point has been the subject of many debates, and certainly cannot be resolved here. Blacks also felt cheated after the passage of Unigov, when it became apparent to them they might not be as likely to control or influence the newly created countywide government as they might have the old city government without the annexation of the overwhelmingly white areas. The blacks' expectations, however, may have been realistically beyond hope of attainment, even within the old city boundaries. While their ballots obviously were diluted, demographic projections have indicated blacks were overly optimistic in their anticipation of gaining power; with or without Unigov, the hoped-for black majority in the old borders of Indianapolis wasn't likely to materialize until some time after the year 2000.

What Democrats feared at the time, and experience has borne out, is that Unigov was a political boon to Republicans. Without doubt, GOP control of the metropolitan-wide government—with the addition of many suburban Republicans—has been perpetuated and even strengthened. "My greatest coup," Bulen was to exude later. Bearing this out were the margins of Lugar's mayoral victories, burgeoning from 8,994 in 1967 to 53,697 in 1971. The passage of Unigov made Lugar an overnight star in municipal governmental circles. Many had tried reforming and consolidating municipal governments; Lugar's success ranked him among an elite few. He won acclaim in Republican circles, too, soon becoming known as "Nixon's favorite mayor," and with good reason. Lugar was frequently called to the White House to offer counsel on urban problems and received many appointments to advisory groups. In 1970 Nixon picked Indianapolis as the site of his first out-of-Washington Domestic Affairs Council meeting. While there, he invited Lugar to attend a NATO conference in Brussels to speak on the dilemmas of cities. Unigov became an urban laboratory to test the Nixon Administration's theories about cities, including consolidation of federal grants to reduce red tape.

Such a laying on of the presidential hands made it all the more embarrassing in 1974 when Lugar felt compelled to backtrack on his Nixon connections. In a South Bend speech, Lugar said the Watergate tapes "revealed a moral and spiritual tragedy." Nixon's editing of those tapes exhibited "sorry conduct" which he found "deeply disappointing." True to form, the outraged right wing of the Indiana GOP immediately rushed to field an opposing candidate at the state nomination convention, seeking to punish Lugar for daring to do anything less than stand shoulder-to-shoulder with the disgraced President.

Ironically, while Lugar's stature grew nationally, his mentor, Keith Bulen, was eclipsed for a while on the political scene. A superb political organizer and tactician, Bulen ran afoul of charges of questionable distribution of some liquor licenses. But little proof and no indictments resulted; he kept busy for a while as an attorney and in the harness horse world, and reemerged in 1980 as a deputy director of Ronald Reagan's presidential campaign.

A rundown of other Indiana political luminaries cannot omit the dean of the congressional delegation, South Bend's Rep. John Brademas. First elected in 1958, Brademas by the late 1970s was Majority Whip for House Democrats (third ranking position in the leadership ranks), and fourth ranking Democrat on the influential Education and Labor Committee. He was chairman of the Select Subcommittee on Education, and served as well on the subcommittees on Labor-Management Relations and on Post-Secondary Education. Brademas became Congress' leading expert on the financing of higher education and possibly the most prominent example of the Congressman so devoted to and proficient in specific causes (vocational rehabilitation, for instance) that client groups counted him their chief Capitol Hill ally, the man who could guide and control the elements of the federal bureaucracy responsible for their programs. State government leaders, by contrast, criticized Brademas as Congress' most intransigent categoricalist, unwilling to allow state or local governments any significant discretion in how they administered federally funded programs. In a sense, Brademas symbolized a high degree of responsiveness to social needs, using federal programs and funds to meet them, coupled with arrogant opposition to efforts, in either the federal executive branch or state capitals, to diminish the direct power of his subcommittee or rearrange priorities in the interests of greater efficiencies and economy.

Brademas was both a personal and political anomaly in Indiana: a man of Greek extraction in a district where Germans and Poles are the largest ethnic groups, a Methodist in the district which harbors Notre Dame, a Rhodes Scholar in a state not known for intellectual sophistication. Assiduous fence-mending helped him survive in a district lost by Democratic presidential nominees in several recent elections.

Brademas became the dean of the delegation in 1976, the year Gary's Rep. Roy Madden lost his bid for an 18th term in Congress. The 84-year-old Madden was losing his grip on the district for years, but he was in a position of helping labor and had high seniority, ascending to the House Rules Committee chairmanship in 1972. But Madden's reign over the once powerful Rules Committee degenerated into a farce. Journalists used to attend Rules Committee meetings in 1973 just to get comic relief from the developing Watergate crisis.

The man administering electoral euthanasia to the aging Madden was Adam Benjamin, Jr., a West Pointer, former Gary city official, and a 10-year veteran of the state legislature. In the 1976 primary, Benjamin compiled 56 percent of the vote, against 34 percent for Madden. The general election was anticlimactic for that heavily Democratic district: almost three out of four voters cast their ballots for Benjamin. In the House, he coupled good fortune with hard work to accomplish what some members wait years to do: he became chairman of his own subcommittee in his second term. Former Rep. George Shipley, an Illinois Democrat, surprised many by not seeking reelection in 1978, which left a vacancy on the Legislative Appropriations Subcommittee. Since all the other more senior subcommittee members already were chairmen of their committees, Benjamin ascended to the head of the prestigious committee at the start of his third year in the House, a first for Congress. His diligence and homework suggested he might turn the often obscured subcommittee assignment into a political stepping-stone, much as Senator Bayh took advantage of his role on the Constitutional Amendments Subcommittee.

Governors, Legislators, and Lobbies

As Indiana politics rolled into the 1980s it was clear that it would take an exceptional candidate of either party to equal the spell cast by Governor Bowen—"Doc Bowen," as most people called him—over the previous eight years. Without any of the slickness frequently associated with media-conscious candidates, Bowen cultivated a personality image all his own. "He's such a skillful politician," remarked one political reporter. "He's a country doctor from a little town called Bremen, up near South Bend, and he comes across as a country doctor who still makes house calls for $7." From one of Bowen's staff aides came this assessment: "He has the image of a counselor. If you had to get advice from somebody, and you looked around at everybody that was available, you'd go to Doc, because you figured he'd give you good advice." And from a Democrat of long standing in Indiana: "Everybody hates the AMA. Doctors in general are disliked, but don't say anything about my doctor. And Doc comes off as that old-style doctor, who if you need him at 12:30 at night, he'll come. He probably hasn't made a house call in 80 years, but nevertheless that's the way he comes off."

That image was translated into a popularity without rival in recent times in Indiana. First elected in 1972 with 57 percent of the vote, Bowen won four years later by 309,000 votes, more than any other governor in Indiana history. Throughout his two terms, he maintained a job approval rating—according to both Republican and Democrat-sponsored polls—hovering at the mid-70 percent level, the envy of any chief executive. Even Democrats and segments of organized labor agree publicly it was difficult to find fault with Bowen as chief executive, much less with him personally.

With the exception of his property tax relief program in his first year in office, Bowen's administration had more of a quality of stability than innovation. In his last of seven terms in the house (the final five years as speaker), Bowen energetically supported a property tax relief bill that was killed in the senate due to a veto threat by then Republican Governor Whitcomb. How-ever, Bowen had his issue for the 1972 campaign—property tax relief. Further enhancing his image as the trusted family physician, Doc Bowen delivered on his promise in 1973. Admirers of Bowen like to point out the tax freeze Bowen put into effect in Indiana came five years before Howard Jarvis' Proposition 13 gained credibility in California. Bowen's program reduced the local prop-erty taxes about 20 percent and froze them at that level. Simultaneously, he raised the sales tax from 2 percent to 4 percent, increased the corporate in-come tax, and set aside the additional revenue as local property tax relief and school aids. In 1977 the freeze on the local property rates was eased, allowing a 5 percent increase in 1978, an 8 percent increase in 1979, and nothing (through the insistence of legislative Democrats) in 1980, an election year. School tax levies were held even from 1973–79, when a 1 percent raise was permitted.

No one disputes the political appeal of the program: it became the hall-mark of the Bowen administrations. Before his time, to raise taxes and sur-vive was unheard of in Indiana. Again, the image was critical to the survival. "When he says he's going to tax you, it's like he's holding your wrist and telling you he has to charge $10 for the house call, but you're going to live," a Democrat almost lamented to us. Some municipal officials complained about the tax freeze, arguing it pinched local governments, forced some per-sonnel layoffs, and generally was rigid and inflexible. Indeed, in 1978, a rash of local public employee strikes spread through about two dozen cities, the first time Indiana had experienced such widespread job actions (all public employee strikes are illegal in Hoosierland, but the workers won amnesty pro-visions). The tax freeze, according to local officials, held down what cities could spend and caused the unrest. Bowen could easily argue the positive side of the program, though, and did. He pointed out that the actual statewide property tax rate in 1978 was $7.45 per $1,000; without the freeze and added state relief, it would have been $11.31 per $1,000. As late as 1978, Indiana's property taxes collected were actually less than six years earlier—a situation few if any other states could emulate.

Bowen's budgetary politics reflected another side of him. A moderate and undoubtedly less conservative than many who voted for him, Bowen never-theless has pursued a socially active role for state government long dormant in Hoosierland. "Indiana is very much more socially conscious than we were even a decade ago," said Bowen aide Ed Thuma. "The stereotype of con-servatism isn't completely without foundation in this state, but I think if you look at the record, in the area of human services, we've moved at the same pace as the nation." The problem was, Thuma added, Indiana started out so much further behind most other states. Bowen, with little fanfare, shepherded through the legislature budgets that saw spending for mental health grow from $175 million to $335 million, for health from $67 million to $327 million, and for welfare (that great contributor to sloth and moral perversion, in the minds of many Indianans) from $378 million to nearly $1.1 billion. Reflecting the tax freeze and higher school aids, spending for education nearly tripled from $682 million to more than $1.9 billion. Bowen and his associates more often emphasized the efforts to rebuild the state's prisons (where periodic rebellions occurred during the 1970s) and upgrading the state's parks and natural resources. "We changed philosophy really," Thuma said about state park funding. "We decided we ought to turn them into areas of recreation, and not just scenic beauty, where people could start to have fun in a variety of ways." As a result, many of Indiana's state-owned campgrounds, lodges, swimming pools, and other facilities, largely in a state of neglect a few years ago, were developed and their use promoted.

It is a tribute to Bowen's skill as a politician that he accomplished so much while partisan control of the legislature was so frequently divided. Bowen had a Republican legislature to work with his first two years in office, while pushing through his tax relief package. But after that Democrats captured at least one house until the GOP regained control in 1979. His overwhelming popularity certainly would give Democratic lawmakers pause before taking the governor on in major battle. But beyond that, Bowen, pragmatist that he was and a product of the legislature itself, fully understood the need to work together and compromise as a last resort. "I think that probably Bowen is a very astute reader of the public, and he has been pretty responsive to what he sees their priorities as being," a former legislative staffer said. "I don't think those priorities were there 15 years ago, but they are very much there in the executive and the legislative branch now."

In the Indiana legislature, an intense struggle developed in the 1970s between advocates of the traditional, part-time "citizen legislator" and the new breed of full-time, professional lawmakers. Until then, Indiana unswervingly supported a weak legislative body, its sessions constrained by the constitution to 61 days every other year. While annual sessions were instituted in 1971, the deliberations during even-numbered years still were limited to 30 days. Howard Peckham, in his bicentennial history, "Indiana," reflected the sentiments of many when he wrote of the limited legislative sessions: "By and large, that limitation has been prudent. . . . the state has enjoyed 22 out of 24 months free from legislative meddling; and the consensus has been verified that representatives and senators can make up their minds in two months as well as they can in six or eight or more." Indeed, Indianans are imbued with the notion of the "citizen legislature," the idea that lawmaking ought to be only a part-time vocation. Ivan Brinegar, former executive director of the Indiana Association of Cities and Towns, who left to head the Academy in the Public Service, stated forcefully the basis for the "citizen legislature": "I don't know that we need all the government we seem to have. I don't think we need professionals," he told us. "I think we need people who work in factories, in a law office, or an insurance company, or a schoolteacher, people who have been ordinary tax-paying citizens. Then I think they're obligated to spend part of their time in a regular job. You don't need people who are going to spend full time [in the legislature]. You won't get the kind of competent people we have had. We've had good government, and will continue to be all right as long as we maintain the citizen politician." Besides the abbreviated session lengths, part-time lawmaking was encouraged by the salaries: Indiana legislators in the late 1970s received only $6,000 a year for their services.

Traditional sentiments notwithstanding, Indiana entered the 1980s with adherents of full-time professionals and part-time citizens in the legislature choosing sides. The nature of governing had shifted, demanding more time and technical knowledge than have been previously necessary. During the 1979 legislative session, the citizen legislature advocates sought to reimpose the constitutional limit on session lengths. Even though armed with a statewide poll showing a majority of Hoosiers supporting the part-time legislature, the proponents could not win approval.

The legislature in the 1970s mirrored the political transition underway in Hoosierland. Though it had traditionally been under Republican control, Democrats won control of both houses during President Johnson's landslide election in 1964. The following session found the house Republican and the senate still under the Democrats. From 1969 to 1975, Republicans dominated both houses; split majorities by relative narrow margins, however, prevailed in 1975 and 1977 sessions. The fluctuating majorities changed the complexion of the legislature in more ways than one. Turnover was high, with more than half of the lawmakers late in the 1970s having served only three or fewer sessions. It was not unsual for a second-year, and sometimes even a freshman senator to be a committee chairman. Lacking experience that was a hallmark of their predecessors, Indiana legislators more and more were turning to increased staff to help them grapple with the steadily more technical and complex issues of state government. The trend augmented the pressure for full-time legislators, as well as changed them from an acquiescent body rubber-stamping the wishes of the governor. "They certainly are a much more viable body than they were before," an assistant to the governor said. "They don't necessarily have to take what the governor says any more. They have their own sources of information."

There was a widespread consensus that the quality of legislators had improved as a new breed independent of the county bosses won elections. "The legislature used to be a dumping ground for political hacks in both parties," one observer told us. "That hasn't been true for a good many years now, and we've got a much higher level of education, much higher quality." Among Republicans and Democrats alike, the new lawmakers were younger, more articulate, and more pragmatic than partisan.

For some uninitiated "citizen legislators," the deliberations in Indianapolis resemble the confusion Alice found in her adventures in wonderland. After one four-year term, Ft. Wayne Sen. Graham Richard stepped down, writing for his local paper that the legislature "can be an extremely frustrating experience" for "people who like to be productive." He added: "It is exasperating to shepherd a bill through many meetings and strenuous senate debates only to have it killed by the will of one legislator in the house. The speaker may never assign the bill to committee or the chairperson may never schedule the bill for a hearing. Worse yet, the committee will pass the bill and the speaker might lock it in his safe or hold it hostage for other votes." While Richard conceded the quality of legislators improved during his term, his description of the process undoubtedly showed that all vestiges of the old guard politics have yet to be erased from state government.

Considerable support also can be found in Indiana for the century-old adage of a New York jurist who once expounded that "no man's life, liberty, or property is safe while the legislature is in session." By that standard, less government is better government. And by that standard, Indiana's 1979 session would be judged successful. As the National Civic Review summarized it: "The 1979 Indiana General Assembly adjourned in April without undertaking any major policy changes." Governor Bowen's property tax relief program was continued, the "citizen legislature" issue was left unresolved, and the score was zero for attempts to place more stringent controls on lobbyists, to pass a collective bargaining bill for police and firemen, to repeal the earlier ratification of the Equal Rights Amendment, and to rescind the direct primary nomination of governor and lieutenant governor. For many Indianans, that record of inaction is more of a blessing than one studded with new programs likely to increase taxes.

Indiana has shown no hurry to adopt 20th-century governmental reforms. Six decades after the U.S. Constitution gave women the right to vote, the Hoosiers' 1850 vintage document still stipulated that reapportionment be based upon "the number of male inhabitants, above 21 years of age." (In practice, of course, the provision was ignored.) For 43 years prior to the Supreme Court's 1964 one-man, one-vote decision, Indiana legislators blithely ignored their own constitution's mandate to reapportion every six years. In fact, they refused to reapportion at all, causing grave urban underrepresentation. Only gradually has the state given in to demands of minorities and others to do away with its multimember legislative districting system (through most of the 1970s there were no more than six blacks in the state's General Assembly). And reapportionment, when it came, improved the urban Democrats' strength only slightly because of the strong Republican foothold in Hoosier cities.

Just as the national distinctions between Republicans and Democrats are blurred by Hoosier's conservative nature, so are the activities of Indiana lobby groups that seek to influence electoral and legislative politics. Organized labor in Indiana and the United States grew side-by-side early in the 20th century. Immediately before and during World War II, Indiana was a center of high-level unionism. Indianapolis could boast the headquarters of no less than 11 major international unions, including the powerful United Mine Workers, the Teamsters, and the Carpenters. John L. Lewis, the guiding genius of the

UMW, and William Green, one-time president of the AFL, both had offices in downtown Indianapolis. By the late 1970s, Indiana's 650,000 unionized nonfarm workers were down slightly from a peak earlier in the decade, but the total still was 6 percent higher than the national average, ranking the state among the most heavily unionized in the country. In addition to about 400,000 AFL-CIO members, the progressive and aggressive United Auto Workers could count 100,000 brothers and sisters in the state, mostly around the major assembly plants in Fort Wayne, Indianapolis, and South Bend. As a percentage of the state's total population, that put Indiana's UAW membership second only to Michigan's. And the headstrong Steelworkers, with about 97,500 dues-paying Hoosiers, had more members in only two other states, Pennsylvania and Ohio. Their concentration in the steel mill citadels in Gary and East Chicago accentuated their potency, especially in Democratic presidential primaries and other statewide primaries.

But somewhere along the way, significant blocs of Indiana's organized labor meandered off on a back road, their ideology more in tune with Hoosierland's conservative culture than the liberal ideology espoused by their national counterparts. It is hardly a new phenomenon. John Gunther, shortly after World War II, noted that Indianapolis was "the home of two of the most trenchantly conservative labor leaders in the United States" (Daniel J. Tobin, general president of the Teamsters International, and "Big Bill" Hutcheson, president of the United Brotherhood of Carpenters and first vice president of the AFL). Even today, Indiana's conservatism still tempers the union mentality, fragmenting labor effectiveness in electoral politics, moderating the zeal of the UAW and Steelworkers and undoubtedly contributing to frequent defeats in the legislature. In the elective arena, one long-time observer told us, "unions can't control elections. In a close race, they can tip it, when it's a legislative candidate. But they can't run a statewide candidate." Solidarity in statewide races is infrequent. In 1972, Sen. George McGovern received the backing of the UAW (or at least its leadership), but the state AFL-CIO "remained silent and gave no endorsement." Republicans Richard Lugar and Otis Bowen also were the beneficiaries of certain overt labor support during the 1970s. In the legislature, the unions were usually strong enough to block legislation repugnant to them but lacked the power to pass laws. The last time labor in Indiana won a major legislative victory was in 1965, when a Democratic-controlled legislature repealed the right-to-work law approved eight years earlier. While unity was maintained for that battle, "once this was attained, there was quite a separation of viewpoints as to what was important," state AFL-CIO Secretary-Treasurer Max Wright told us in an interview. Collective bargaining rights for public employees and their right to strike were major sources of contention throughout the 1970s, and remained as victories to be won in the 1980s. Firefighters and police were willing to accept arbitration, while the Teamsters and other unions spurned the possibility. "In the 20 years I've been in this office," Wright said, "every year we've been unable to get this kind of [bargaining] legislation. The unions meet every time the legislature meets, they all agree they'll go along the road together, but when the time comes, they all split their separate ways and as a result, no legislation. I'm sure if they were to unify all the way, there'd be legislation." The inability to overcome the innate Hoosier conservatism was reflected in the many failures of labor to improve benefits for unemployment compensation and workmen's compensation (although some gains in this area came under Bowen).

No single lobby can be said to dominate the Indiana legislature as it enters the 1980s. Certainly, the gargantuan omnipresence of the American Legion during the 1920s and 1930s has no counterpart today. In those days, any man aspiring to statewide office (and women need not apply!) might as well have forgotten it if he were not a legionnaire. The Farm Bureau influence likewise has waned as the proportions of the farm populace shriveled to about 3 percent. Yet the Bureau continues to have its moments of success, and even such a major lobby as the State Chamber of Commerce has its defeats. There is agreement that the truckers, the five big investor-owned utilities (the IOU's, as they are called locally), the rural electric co-ops, the bankers association, and the teachers association (mentioned more frequently than any of the others) are the lobbies with the greatest and most consistent clout in the legislature.

Single-issue, reform-minded groups also surfaced during the 1970s. With few exceptions, these groups found only sporadic and isolated favor at best. Yet several professional politicians, with no little apprehension, told us these reform-oriented groups were likely to wield more and more influence as the political changes of the 1970s took root in the decades ahead.

Education and the Arts

Education in Indiana always has had to shoulder a double-yoked burden: the native financial conservatism and the entrenched sentiment for a privately operated and privately funded school system. From the first days, there were many promises made for a free and open network of schools from elementary through college. But the promises were followed by decades of delay before the tax dollars were produced, especially in the realm of higher education. It was not until the years following World War II that able leadership lifted Indiana University and Purdue University from the ranks of mediocrity.

Indiana's first constitution mandated that the state "provide by law for a general system of education, ascending in regular gradation, from township schools to a state university, wherein tuition shall be gratis and equally open to all." Unfortunately, that grand assurance was qualified by the phrase, "as soon as circumstances will permit." Throughout the 19th century, courts restricting local schools' authority to levy taxes and the innate reluctance to spend public funds hampered the establishment of free and equal schools. Howard Peckham, former director of the Indiana Historical Bureau and a historian in his own right, minced few words in chastising the state's record in education. "Its provision for public schools was nothing short of disgraceful," he wrote in 1976. "As a result, it suffered immoderate illiteracy, persistence of prejudices, industrial lagging, and political primitivism until recent times." The 1850 constitutional provision for free public education, for instance, was for all except what were then referred to as "people of color." It took until 1949 to erase from the law the provision allowing racial segregation in schools. While recent decades have seen some improvement in state aid to local schools, thanks largely to an extremely effective teachers lobby after World War II, the state's overall performance in education still has its share of critics.

Indiana has not been without its educational experiments. The city of Richmond lays claim to the distinction of starting the first junior high school in the country, in 1896. One of the more progressive experiments arose from the social reform community in New Harmony, in southwestern Indiana, founded in 1825 by the wealthy Welsh textile manufacturer, Robert Owen. With his encouragement, some of the most advanced educators of the day made New Harmony their home and introduced their children to a school system that stressed practical, vocational training. In a day of classical learning, it was a novelty, too novel in fact for Indiana. Within three years, internal dissension beset New Harmony, dooming it to failure and perhaps beclouding the success of its educational techniques. Today, New Harmony is being restored by historical benefactors, including the Lilly Endowment of Indianapolis, reviving for 20th-century tourists Owen's vision of a utopian society.

The first real education system in Indiana was established by religious and other private groups. Some have attributed this inclination for private education to the domination of early Indiana by Southern whites, who brought with them their educational traditions tied to the plantations and the churches. In the 19th century, higher education especially was the domain primarily of religious-affiliated institutions. Fifteen church-related colleges founded before the Civil War still flourish in Indiana today. Notre Dame, founded in 1842, is the most widely known, even if for its athletic and not its academic exploits. Both Butler University in Indianapolis (established 1855) and Wabash College in Crawfordsville (1832) are privately endowed with strong traditions of their own. DePauw University in Greencastle (founded by United Methodists in 1837), Earlham College in Richmond (founded by Quakers in 1847), Franklin College in Franklin (established by Baptists in 1834) and Hanover College in Hanover (founded by Presbyterians in 1827) demonstrate the diversity among the small but respectable church-affiliated colleges that have given private education a good name in Indiana.* As racial animosity and fear grew in Indiana during the 1970s, there was a noticeable upswing in

---

* The religious fervor of fundamental Protestantism runs deep throughout Indiana. Max Wright, secretary-treasurer of the state AFL-CIO, told us he was convinced one of the best attractions for any political candidate in Hoosierland would be to campaign with gospel quartet singers. While Wright acknowledged he had been unsuccessful in convincing politicians to put a gospel quartet on stage before the political stumping starts, he was positive it was a sure-fire ticket to election in Indiana. Gospel folksinging concerts regularly drew full houses in Indianapolis, Fort Wayne, Muncie, and Evansville, to name but a few of the larger communities, he said.

some communities in the establishment of new private and parochial schools, further evidence that public schools are not always seen as a universal institution.

The distinction of the oldest institution of higher education in Indiana goes, however, to Vincennes University, the state's only public-supported junior college. When Vincennes was established in 1801, the local gentry held great expectations for its future. Their hopes sank after Indiana became a state in 1816, the legislature seized the 23,400 acres it had received in its federal grant, sold the land, and used the proceeds to support Indiana Seminary, later to be known as Indiana University at Bloomington. But it took 30 years and a U.S. Supreme Court decision to finally settle the argument over the validity of the action. Aside from that initial grant, Indiana University and its sister institution, Purdue University at West Lafayette (founded in 1869), struggled with meager public support until around World War II. Just before the war, Herman B Wells became president of IU; just afterwards, Frederick L. Hovde was chosen to head Purdue. Each was the right man at the right place at the right time, and each is credited with transforming his university from a mediocre, isolated school into an academic institution with growing national prestige. Although Wells retired as IU president in 1962, he remained as a good-will ambassador, fund-raiser, and adviser for many more years.* According to a former president of the IU Alumni Association, Wells and Hovde changed the "whole philosophy" of the two universities, expanding them considerably to reflect the changing society that was creeping into Indiana. In a rare meeting of minds of competing public universities, IU and Purdue consolidated their two campuses at Indianapolis in 1969, and pooled their resources. By the late 1970s, more than 20,000 full-time students, plus 14,000 more in continuing education programs, attended classes at the combined universities' campus just west of downtown Indianapolis. The medical school there is the nation's largest. Altogether, IU enrolls about 80,000 students, while Purdue (which has a stronger emphasis in engineering and agriculture) has about 42,000. Symptomatic of Indiana's slowly developing educational system, the state did not establish a two-year vocational-technical system until 1963. But in typical overpromise fashion, the legislature mandated 13 regional campuses within the Vocational Technical College system but budgeted only $50,000 for the first year. As one board member said, "The lawmakers just gave $50,000, a scrap of paper, and said, 'Start a college.'" In time, however, things picked up and the vocational colleges became ultra-lively with thousands of students and a multi-million-dollar annual budget.

For a state with a reputation of insularity, Indiana nonetheless has produced more than its share of authors, poets, and artists. For half a century before 1921, Indiana writers were in the forefront of America's popular litera-

---

* Some doubted Wells' dedication to academic freedom, but he proved his mettle by sticking up for the most famous member of his faculty, Dr. Alfred C. Kinsey, whose *Sexual Behavior in the Human Male* and *Sexual Behavior in the Human Female* sparked a predictable storm of protest among square Hoosiers in the late '40s and early '50s.

ture. Lew Wallace of Crawfordsville published the best-seller, *Ben Hur*, in 1880. Later came Terre Haute's Theodore Dreiser, one of the early realistic novelists with his *Sister Carrie* and *An American Tragedy*, and the dean of Indiana letters, Booth Tarkington of Indianapolis. Tarkington, winner of Pulitzer prizes in 1919 and 1922, authored *Penrod*, *Seventeen*, the *Magnificent Ambersons*, and *Alice Adams*. (Former U.S. Sen. Albert Beveridge joined the list of Hoosiers winning Pulitzers when his *Life of John Marshall* won the prize for history in 1920.) Probably the favorite of Hoosier writers, though, was the poet James Whitcomb Riley, whose homespun verses captured the speech, mannerisms, and culture of the Indiana of his time. Riley is most often remembered as the author of "When the Frost Is on the Punkin'," "Little Orphan Annie," "The Old Swimmin' Hole," and "The Raggedy Man." Among the more noteworthy of the other Indiana artists are Hoagy Carmichael of Bloomington, composer of "Stardust" and "Georgia on My Mind," and the immortal Cole Porter, who wrote such timeless songs as "Begin the Beguine" as well as the Broadway musicals "Kiss Me Kate" and "Silk Stockings." Quite aptly, that period has been called Indiana's golden age of literature.

In more recent years, the arts in Indiana have benefited substantially from several philanthropists, most notably in Indianapolis. The family of Josiah Lilly, Jr. (of pharmaceutical fame) gave its 45-acre estate overlooking the White River in the capital city to the Art Association of Indianapolis. In addition to the Lilly Pavilion of the Decorative Arts, the Krannert Pavilion, housing pictures transferred from the smaller Herron Art Museum, and the Clowes Pavilion with its Medieval and Renaissance art were built in the 1970s, giving Indianans an opportunity for a taste of culture of considerable quality.

Urban Exceptions to the Indiana Rule: Indianapolis . . .

Indianapolis tempers Indiana's dominant conservatism with economic pragmatism, and Gary flouts it with doctrinaire liberalism and classic corruption. It is symbolic that Indianapolis, Indiana's biggest and the nation's 11th largest city, sits so precisely in the middle of the state, while Gary languishes on the outer fringes of its northern and western boundaries, a province unclaimed except by its own. Even with its economic variety, its tension between political conservatism and contemporary revisions, its urban congestion and pastoral solemnity, Indiana has an overriding homogeneity, a sense of the expected, a quality of middleness interrupted only sporadically by deviations that accentuate the rule. Among the cities, Indianapolis epitomizes the rule and Gary is the exception to prove it.

Indianapolis goes back almost to the inception of statehood, to 1824 when the capital was shifted from Corydon, just west of Louisville near the Ohio River, to a settlement along Fall Creek that then consisted of a few cabins in the woods and 600 hardy pioneering inhabitants. It took two more decades, past the arrival of the National Road in 1830 and the first railway in 1847, before Indianapolis could realistically hope for a prosperous future. Gary, on the other hand, was a creation of the 20th century, founded in 1906. The founder was U.S. Steel, which was seeking a centralized location with transportation outlets for its finished product and an ideal dumping ground for the inevitable waste products that would spew forth from its giant mills. Early Indianapolis was settled by the Southern immigrants, although a handful of New Englanders and Easterners brought with them refinement and integrity that enabled them to have influence beyond their numbers. Gary, from the start, was peopled by foreign stock and later by Southern blacks— all imported expressly to man the mills. Poles, Lithuanians, Serbians, Italians, and Croatians prevail, although a total of 57 ethnic strains were once counted. After 1919, U.S. Steel began importing blacks to break a prodigious strike, and now whites are in the minority of the deteriorated industrial glut that is Gary.

Economically, Indianapolis can boast a diversity in its industry and manufacturing that protects it from the ravages of the recessionary cycles that periodically send Gary's unemployment rate to 15 percent or more. Indianapolis has General Motors Detroit Diesel Allison Division (with 13,500 employees), other multi-thousand-worker plants of Western Electric, Eli Lilly, RCA, Chrysler, Ford, and Chevrolet divisions, the Kroger, National Tea Company, and A & P food chains, plus significant state, federal, and local government employment, and healthy service and financial industry. Gary has primarily basic, heavy industry, with U.S. Steel's 50,000 workers (in the best of times) heading the list. Indianapolis has been under the pall of an air pollution clean-up order from the Environmental Protection Agency (EPA), but its environment is pristine in comparison with Gary's contaminated atmosphere, even in the wake of the recalcitrant steps of U.S. Steel and other industry during the 1970s to curb their outpouring of wastes. And in terms of cultural, recreational, and entertainment activities, there is no comparison at all.

Indianapolis was described to us as an "overgrown small city." It is an apt characterization. One always visits Indianapolis wondering whether its reputation for reactionary, right-wing politics is still justified. A first question is likely to be, "Is the American Legion still here—and as influential as it was?" The answer is yes—and no. The city remains the official home of the Legion (although key parts of it have moved to Washington), thanks to $7.5 million in tax dollars provided by compliant politicians to build the original headquarters in the War Memorial Plaza, plus another $2.5 million set aside by the legislature in 1945 when the Legion threatened to move out of the city. But key parts of the Legion hierarchy have moved to Washington, and the general influence is clearly diminished. It was late in 1958 when Robert Welch and 11 of his right-wing friends sat in the living room of Mrs. Marguerite Dice and formed the John Birch Society. With visions of a million-member organization, Welch, Mrs. Dice, and their cohorts set out to save the world from the great communist menace, taking up where the late Sen.

Joseph McCarthy had left off. Ten years later, assembling in Indianapolis for an anniversary dinner, Welch could claim only 60,000 to 100,000 followers. But George Wallace's presidential bids and American Party movement drained off much of what was left of Birch Society sentiment in Indiana. As late as the mid-1960s, Irving Leibowitz could write that Indianapolis "continues to attract every last-ditch reactionary and screwball in the country." A decade later, that was no longer true. A major catalyst of change was Richard Lugar, who set in motion a revival that had rippling political and economic impacts in the capital city, even if the broadest dimensions of their social implications had yet to be fulfilled by the late '70s. Indianapolis moved decisively away from the right-wing image of the past and proffered a pattern of change tinged with economic pragmatism.

Why the change? The impact of mass communications, perhaps, or the fact of Richard Lugar, Unigov, et al. Or simply a dose of old garden variety civic boosterism. "Many people come to Indianapolis expecting to find a stodgy conservative community which has no color," said Carl Dortch, then head of the city's chamber of commerce. What they find, he insisted, is a community that has "come alive in recent years and has much to offer for a whole spectrum of life styles." To this, the visitor might raise an eyebrow— the idea of Indianapolis becoming a sparkling Atlanta in the Ohio River Valley is a bit much. And there was, indeed, tangible "progress." Since Lugar became mayor, the city constructed a sports arena for the Indianapolis Pacers basketball team, enticed the Hilton and Hyatt Regency chains to build fancy downtown hotels, renovated the nostalgic century-old City Market area, and successfully beautified Monument Circle, which once housed the governor's mansion but has long since been replaced by the Soldiers and Sailors Monument. (Some have wondered whether the grotesquely militaristic monument adds to or detracts from a revitalized downtown Indianapolis.) "We have a desire to move ahead—but not too fast," Mayor William H. Hudnut III observed as the end of the 1970s approached. "We're still a conservative city, but we've become more progressive the past 10 years. People here are home, school, and church-oriented. You don't have a downtown bursting at the seams with entertainment places." (To which one could only say "Amen." Most evenings, for instance, there are so few people in downtown Indianapolis that one could imagine a curfew had been imposed. Except for the Pacers basketball games, entertainment is practically nonexistent. Private parking garages close around 7 P.M. and are often closed on weekends and holidays. Walking the streets of the inner city at night is a bit like strolling through a high-walled catacomb.)

Even Texas cities might envy the intimate business-city hall ties of Indianapolis. Dortch cited an example. "We literally passed the hat," he said, to get private donations to help build the $2 million convention center next to the Hyatt Regency complex. Such private-public sector ties are not new. There is a story told, in fact, that Frank McKinney, a former Democratic National Committeeman, used to run the city from his offices of the American Fletcher National Bank, one of the two banks in the city with more than $1 billion in deposits (Indiana National being the other). The focal point of the business-government alliance is the Greater Indianapolis Progress Committee (GIPC), initiated in the mid-1960s by Lugar's predecessor, Democratic Mayor John J. Barton. Barton, seeking to cultivate support from civic and business leaders, created the GIPC to provide them with a "sense of participation" in his administration. Among his appointees was Lugar, who used the platform as a springboard into the mayor's office itself. As only the third Republican mayor of Indianapolis since before the Great Depression, Lugar immediately dissolved the distrust that had grown between his Democratic predecessors and the business community. Barton used the GIPC as a well-intentioned civic group which could "advise and direct" the mayor, Dortch said. Lugar transformed it into an instrument of political change through which he could guide and direct the business community, a strategy that Hudnut has preserved. Today, the GIPC has a full-time staff and is located in the City-County Building, just a floor below the 25th-story office of the mayor. Membership on the committee generally includes the city's money men and its economic and political movers and shakers, many of whom have a financial stake in the revitalization of Downtown and the overall growth of the community at large. Through it, fund-raising efforts are coordinated, legal impediments to development projects overcome, public opinion molded, and pressure applied where necessary.

Hugh Rutledge, veteran city hall reporter for the Indianapolis *News*, recounted for us the way the city fathers can coalesce in the face of an emergency. For several years, Indianapolis was the home of the U.S. Open Clay Court tennis tournament, but in 1978 the tourney sponsors decided to move the event because the local racquet club facilities were too small. Such a move would be a blow to the carefully protected image of Indianapolis as a growing regional commercial and financial center that had left behind its days as a bush-league city. The public-private alliance swung immediately into action. In short order, the city approved a $4 million bond issue, the Indiana University-Purdue University Indianapolis campus provided the land, the Lilly Endowment added another $2.5 million, and the U.S. Open Clay Court tournament had the promise of a brand new enlarged facility. The sponsors changed their mind, signed a 10-year contract with the city, and the public had a facility it could use the other 51 weeks of the year for tennis and hockey activities as well as concerts. One year later, in 1979, the tournament was played in the already completed facility.

The Lilly Endowment saw its assets dwindle sharply during the 1970s but remained one of the 10 largest philanthropic foundations in the country and almost a second treasury the city can draw on. In 1974, Lilly Endowment had assets of $227 million and stock in the Lilly corporation of more than $900 million. A ruling by the Internal Revenue Service forced it to give grants at a faster rate after that, and by the end of the decade its assets were cut in half. The Endowment was established in 1937 by the heirs of the giant phar-

maceutical firm based in Indianapolis to support primarily religious, educational, and other charitable causes. Eli Lilly, the patriarch of the company
and the guiding spirit of the Endowment, died in 1977 at the age of 91. His
death ended an 81-year association with Eli Lilly and Company that began
when he earned 10 cents an hour grinding green pokeroot herb. It was five
years after the elder Eli became president of the firm in 1932 that the Endowment was formed. The closer a project is to Indianapolis, the better has been
the chance for it to be funded by the Endowment; though grants have extended throughout Indiana and the world, few social or political risks are
taken. The Endowment correctly noted in its 1977 annual report that "in
recent years, a principal emphasis has been the development of the central
city." Among those projects, besides the tennis court mentioned above, Lilly
has been a significant contributor to the Market Square complex (which includes an office building, parking ramp, and sports arena as well as the renovation of the 1886 marketplace) and the Near East Side Community
Organization, whose activities will be discussed later. A local official once
remarked that the Lilly Endowment, from a capital standpoint, has "done
more for the city than the city itself." In some years, he added, Lilly gives
more money to city projects than the $12 million to $14 million received in
federal revenue sharing. The Endowment's proximity to Indiana public life
was illustrated by some of the high-ranking Endowment staff hired during
the 1970s, including James Morris (a former aide to Lugar), Richard Ristine
(a Republican who lost the governor's race to Branigin in 1964), and Gordon
St. Angelo (the former state Democratic party chairman). The parent corporation, Lilly, remained one of the two major home-based companies
(Stokely-Van Camp is the other) in a city now overwhelmingly a branch-
office town.

Richard Lugar's two administrations provided the catalyst for the regeneration—and the "re-Republicanization"—of Indianapolis. Unigov not
only expanded the city's effective boundaries but contributed the political
base that would keep Republicans in City Hall and their economic development ideas entrenched in public policy. As Gordon St. Angelo said, Unigov
"turned out to be one of the bigger political annexations in the history of
this state." Lugar's 1971 reelection by 44,703 more votes than his initial win
verified St. Angelo's assertion. Republican William Hudnut did not fare
nearly as well in his 1975 election, although his job approval rating soared
to above 80 percent through much of his first term. No political "fix" is
permanent, of course. As the 1970s drew to an end, Republicans and Democrats both eyed the erosion of GOP strength and predicted there would be
a "son of Unigov in the legislature one of these days," as one local official
put it. Without it, Indianapolis will slip back into the hands of Democrats
sometime during the 1980s, by the estimate of partisans of both parties.

Hudnut was the hand-picked heir of Lugar and another protégé of Keith
Bulen before the latter fell from grace and power. A strapping six-foot, four-
incher, Hudnut was a third generation Presbyterian minister who arrived in

the mayor's office via Washington. In 1972 he ran for Congress and defeated four-term Congressman Andrew Jacbos in Indiana's 11th District. The local wisdom had it that Hudnut grasped Nixon's coattails in that (pre-Watergate) election in 1972, and "clung on and prayed." It worked only once: in 1974, in a rematch, Hudnut was returned to private life by Jacobs, who has continued to win reelection ever since. (Jacobs, incidentally, for a time had only one of the two congressional votes in his family. He married Congresswoman Martha Keys of Kansas in 1975, and both decided they wanted to keep their seats. Jacobs flew to Indianapolis to campaign on weekends, while Keys continued on to Kansas City and Topeka until her defeat in 1978.)

In office, Hudnut suffered through the inevitable comparisons with Lugar. Both offered impeccable academic credentials, Lugar as a Rhodes scholar, Hudnut as a Phi Beta Kappa at Princeton and summa cum laude from Union Theological Seminary. Unigov, though, had established Lugar as such a successful innovator that Hudnut or anyone else would pale by comparison. But Hudnut maintained the close business-City Hall alliance, exhibited a deft political touch, and was considered a likely future statewide candidate. Only a city like Indianapolis, it appears, offers its mayors that prospect, a commentary on how very different this city's politics are.

In the late 1970s Indianapolis witnessed a miniaturized reversal of the population flow to the suburbs as young working singles and some couples moved back to the neighborhoods ringing downtown, buying up dilapidated properties and rehabilitating them. The restoration of historic landmark areas served as an additional magnet to the neighborhood revitalization. Included in the renaissance is Lockerbie Square, just a few blocks east of Monument Circle, the site of James Whitcomb Riley's restored home, considered by some period experts as one of the United States' most perfect examples of Victorian architecture and furnishings. The areas around President Benjamin Harrison's home and the Morris-Butler Museum and Home, both Victorian landmarks a dozen blocks north of the Circle, likewise have served as focal points for revitalization of those neighborhoods. The reverse migration created a new dilemma for Indianapolis' poor, mostly blacks living in the disintegrating housing surrounding downtown. As the more affluent young working men and women moved into the neighborhoods, buying property and upgrading it, the area suddenly became more desirable places to live, sending property prices and rents beyond the reach of its poor. Only a few years before, the interstate highways and other public construction projects such as the Indiana University-Purdue University campus development saw block after block of housing leveled, displacing many poor and blacks. Regardless of the causes, it seems that the victims of "progress" are always the same.

Lugar sought to build some bridges between the Republican Mayor's office and the blacks and poor in Indianapolis. There was further progress under Hudnut. The embryonic neighborhood associations found ready access to his office. In a first for Indianapolis, he granted the neighborhood groups significant roles in decisions involving their interests, especially the $10.5

million in federal Community Development Block Grants that the city pursued to underwrite the association's wide-ranging activities. But when the federal government asked Indianapolis to build, under the program, units of public housing in middle-class and upper-class white enclaves Unigov had drawn into the city, the city council refused.

Indianapolis today is at least two cities. There is the publicly displayed city, with the downtown its key, the city which the mayor's office, the Chamber of Commerce, and the Greater Indianapolis Progress Committee promote. The city's arena, the 26-story City-County Building, the City Market, the new hotels, the repavement of the Circle, all the new developments are signs of success. But there's another city, too. This is the city the neighborhood associations are struggling to improve, the city that fought for more than a decade the inevitability of racial integration in its schools, the city that resists federal mandates whenever they conflict with the traditional or the economically efficient methods that have always prevailed. This "second" city is reflected in the issues the neighborhood associations staked out as their purview. These associations, nearly a dozen in all, ring the downtown showcase area, and represent the poor or near-poor—the have-nots—of Indianapolis. The Near East Side Community, an umbrella-type group encompassing several activities, is one of the more active associations. It has its own community development corporation, a health center, block clubs, and several satellite organizations involving youth, senior citizens, and businesses. The Old Northside Neighborhood Association and the Herron-Morton Place Association, both on the near north side in the "gold coast" neighborhoods of years past, concentrate on housing renovation, salvaging the stately old homes that often have been carved up into apartments. (Two historic sites, President Benjamin Harrison's home and the Morris-Butler Mansion, have been restored and opened to the public in this area.) One of the most deteriorated sections of the city, the community represented by the Citizens Neighborhood Coalition, is primarily black and poor, abutting the Old Northside community. It is here that the economic displacement issue has been the touchiest, with considerable resentment developing as the whites have restored Old Northside Neighborhood homes and moved into the fringes of the black community, driving up prices and driving out some of the very same poor who were still smarting from their relocation by the interstate highways and from having the misfortune of living in the midst of the old Model City target area for Indianapolis. Not all the black community groups are atop racial tinderboxes. The United Northwest Area represents a more stable neighborhood with significant black single family home ownership.

Racial relations remain an omnipresent but not an overriding problem in Indianapolis. By some quirk of circumstance, race never afflicted Indianapolis with the insidious divisions faced by many other Northern cities. There were none of the racial conflagrations that singed so many other Northern cities during the 1960s, for instance. One factor is that the percentage of blacks (18 percent in the 1970 Census) is not particularly high. But black leaders asserted a continuing pattern of racism in such arenas as the city council, clear through the 1970s. In the wake of the creation of Unigov, blacks had complained that the consolidation deprived them of the likelihood they would have soon gained majority status in the city if the old boundaries had remained in effect. But William M. Schreiber, in a study, "Indianapolis-Marion County Consolidation: How did it all happen?", dismissed the contention that a black majority was imminent in the city. His projections placed that eventuality sometime around the year 2000. Schreiber did concede that blacks were on the threshold of controlling the Democratic party primary vote in the city. "To the extent that Unigov limits black impact in a Democratic primary election, black fears of voting power dilution are justified," he concluded.

Employment for blacks in Indianapolis has never been a problem as in other cities like Gary, Chicago, or Detroit, thanks in part to the diversified manufacturing base and the location of more than 25,000 auto industry-related jobs in the city. Still, segregation in Indianapolis was for many years an accepted and institutionalized practice. In 1927 the Ku Klux Klan-controlled school board built two new high schools—Shortridge, designated for white students, and Crispus Attucks for blacks. This rigid, dual system of education remained in effect until the 1949 state law banned it. But by then the neighborhood school concept in vogue left the effect the same. As a result of a 1968 suit challenging the school's racial policies (filed partly at the urging of the U.S. Justice Department) Federal Judge Hugh Dillin found *de jure* segregation and ordered metropolitan-wide busing to achieve equality. The busing order, the first in the nation (even before similar plans for Detroit and Richmond), originally called for busing even beyond Marion County. Initially overturned in the appeals process, Dillin's decision, after years of prolonged litigation, was finally sustained by decision of the Seventh Circuit Court of Appeals in Chicago. In 1971 faculties were integrated and the start of desegregated high school was agreed to by the school board, but it continued to resist the busing decree. Even after a more compliant school board favoring busing was voted into office in 1975, the legal imbroglio persisted. The impact on the city and the school system was all too plain. David Rohm, the Indianapolis *News* reporter who covered the case from the start, told us school enrollment plummeted by nearly one-third between 1968 and 1979, to only about 80,000. While the black percentage of the city's population was less than 25 percent, the black school enrollments were more than 40 percent and growing by 1.5 percent each year, he said, adding: "A lot of people are voting with their feet."

Late in 1978, community leaders, including Hudnut, began to wonder if continued resistance was worth it. An out-of-court settlement was encouraged, not because of any widespread conversion to the ideals of social justice, however. According to Rohm, the attitude was "if the county is to grow and develop, we can't have this thing hanging over our heads."

No discussion of Indianapolis would be complete without the "Indy 500," that richest of all automobile races that annually attracts 300,000 or more persons to the city. Each Memorial Day weekend, the city all but closes down—except for the bars, restaurants, and motels catering to the racing enthusiasts. Half of them are home-state Hoosiers, but the others come in jets and campers from across the nation to watch the great endurance test of machine and man (and now woman, since Janet Guthrie qualified in the mid-1970s as the first female driver in the 500's history). Auto racing provides a curious attraction: for some it is the speed and the flash of machine encircling the 2½-mile track; for others, it is more morbid, the possibility of a flaming crash and the spectacle of death and injuries, although no racing supporter admits of this inducement. For the drivers, despite the chance of carnage (the worst were in 1965 and 1967), there is both the prestige of the race, the World Series and Super Bowl of auto racing rolled into one, and of course the prize money (above $1 million a year of late).

The Speedway's then-owner, Captain Eddie Rickenbacker, had actually contemplated dividing up the land for real estate development in 1945. But Anton (Tony) Hulman, a Terre Haute entrepreneur, was prevailed upon to buy the track for $700,000 and turned it into the familiar spectacular success of the postwar years. He died in 1976 but his family carried on control.

A final high(er) cultural note about Indianapolis: there are philharmonic and civic orchestras, as well as drama and theater, including the Booth Tarkington Civic Theater, the oldest continuously active civic theater with 60 seasons of entertainment to its credit.

. . . and the Strange World of Gary and Lake County

Gary, so starkly the antithesis of Indianapolis, shares one similarity with the capital city: it survived the permutations of the 1960s and 1970s, and with greater anticipation for the future than before. Its population peaked in 1970 when it hit 188,398; with the flight from the inner city, Gary slipped at least 25,000 in the 1970s, below what it had been in 1960. Somewhere around 1970, the shift of population left the blacks with an absolute majority in Gary; by the end of that decade estimates of the proportion of blacks in the city ranged up to 60 percent.

The transition from a white majority to a black majority, of course, was the most traumatic of all the changes undergone by Gary, a transition dominated by Richard Hatcher, the black mayor first elected in 1967 (the same year as Lugar). As Gary entered the 1980s, it had stabilized considerably; Hatcher was entrenched as an institution and not just an aberration, the exodus of whites and businesses had all but ceased (all who could leave had done so) and a miniscule reversal of the flow was detected. The infusion of federal dollars was beginning to show results; the remaining whites had discovered they could live peacefully in a city with a black majority. Furthermore, a black-run City Hall certainly was no more corrupt than its predecessors and unquestionably far more sensitive to its soul brothers and sisters than any white administration ever had been. Racism still reared its loathsome head, occasionally sparked by suggestions emanating from the mayor's office itself that sounded like the rhetoric of black separatism. The primary difference in the corruption was that blacks probably get a larger share of the rake-offs than they did before Hatcher moved into City Hall (although no major scandal has soiled the mayor himself).

Unfortunately, Gary's economic revitalization barely extended beyond Broadway, the main downtown business strip. Much of the $500 million in federal grants that Hatcher attracted to rebuild the city was channeled into downtown showplace edifices; one had only to walk three blocks off Broadway to find the gutted buildings and vacant lots proving that Gary still had a long way to go before earning the accolade "thriving." While the city had its comfortable neighborhoods—black and white—there remained many grimy ones too, where a house or building vacated could easily become an overnight target for looters and arsonists. Slight increases in construction of new single family homes were detected late in the 1970s, holding out hope for a housing rebound in the 1980s.

The racial and political transition from the hands of the white-ethnic-dominated Democratic party and City Hall was not accomplished without considerable resistance. To be elected Gary's first black mayor, Hatcher had to fight the entrenched regular Democratic machine, led at the time by county clerk and County Democratic chairman John G. Krupa. A fiercely patriotic second-generation Polish-American, Krupa was convinced Hatcher was but the front man for a subversive nationwide conspiracy. During the first election in 1967, Krupa demanded Hatcher repudiate black militants H. Rap Brown and Stokely Carmichael as the price of his and the organization's support. When Hatcher spurned the demand, Krupa fought him tooth and nail, going so far as to attempt tampering with voter registration lists to strike off the names of blacks and add often-fictitious names that would be voted for the machine. The underhanded tactic was thwarted, however, when one of the machine's workers blew the whistle and federal agents came in to protect the integrity of the voting lists. In succeeding elections, the actors changed but the level of controversy surrounding Gary, Hatcher, and his political antagonists did not. His adversaries became black power brokers, like Dozier Allen, the head of the dissident Democratic faction, operating from a political base as commissioner of Calumet Township (which holds considerable political muscle through its distribution of general welfare). Allen ran unsuccessfullly against Hatcher in 1975 and was the power behind another adversary—also unsuccessful—in 1979.

Hatcher's 1967 election catapulted him into national prominence, a man to watch. His repeated capability to survive reelection challenges, stabilize racial tensions, and reestablish some hope where only despair existed earned him a national reputation as a respected black leader. An early supporter of President Carter, he was enticed in 1978 by an offer to join the senior White

House staff as a liaison with cities and the black community, only to turn it down. Locally, Hatcher did not enjoy the same universal adulation. "In Gary's black community, he is not God," one local observer put it. Crime, gambling, and prostitution—after a flurry of clean-up activity in the first years of his administration—reestablished their tenacious grip on the city. There were arguments about the extent of gambling and prostitution compared to pre-Hatcher Gary—but no argument that it still flourished. The corner of Sixth and Adams near downtown remained notorious as a pick-up spot for prostitutes, "in broad daylight and sometimes even in the mornings," we were advised. Hatcher's first police chief, James Hilton, won a reputation as a crime-buster, cracking down on the gambling and other corruption, causing considerable loss to the Mafia and its agents in Gary who had so much invested in long-term payoffs. The syndicate and corruption never were eradicated from Gary, but some thought a new millennium of decency had arrived. It didn't last long. Late in the 1970s, the police department itself was immersed in the cauldron of corruption. Police Chief Charles Boone was twice tried in connection with allegations about misuse of a department drug fund. Although he was never convicted, the ensuing revelations convinced many city residents things had returned to their pre-Hatcher state of venality. Another Hatcher associate, the director of the streets department, was convicted and jailed in 1979 for misuse of federal CETA funds. Ever loyal to his supporters, Hatcher never did repudiate that associate, even after the conviction.

As a champion of Gary and a procurer of federal funds, few could fault Hatcher. Early on, he channeled some of the federal aid into building 3,000 low- and middle-income housing units—the city's first in a decade. Ultimately, $20 million went into building 13,000 units. As the 1970s ended, he had engineered federal guarantees for rehabilitating the stately old Gary Hotel at Sixth and Broadway in downtown Gary for 140 housing units for the elderly. He developed job training programs and job placement programs, moving 6,000 persons onto payrolls in his first term. In the mid-1970s, when the auto plants writhed in the agony of the slump in car purchases and the steel mills banked their furnaces in response, Gary's unemployment shot up to 15 percent. By the end of the 1970s, stability had returned and Gary's unemployed hovered at or under the 6 percent average for the state as a whole. Streets were paved, the police force opened to blacks and Latinos, and garbage collections placed on more or less regular schedules.

Hatcher never shied from confrontations. Whether the target was the local political machine or U.S. Steel, he seemed to revel in the challenge. Asked in 1975 about his attempts to rule by confrontation or by promoting racial divisions, he asserted the problem was his "temerity to be the first black elected and to be independent on top of it and not play the game with the machine." According to him, "I'm always in fights because I don't go along with the machine and others, including businessmen, who want to return to the good old days." At best, Hatcher and U.S. Steel eventually treated each other respectively, after a few fencing matches. With more than $1 billion in capital plant, U.S. Steel was a natural target as Hatcher sought an infusion of money when he first entered City Hall; even a miniscule property tax reassessment would funnel additional millions into the city treasury, a move arduously opposed by the mill. The political, economic, and environmental presence of the mills in Gary cannot be ignored; U.S. Steel rises like a hulk just a few blocks north of City Hall. Besides being the largest employer and taxpayer in town, it's also the largest polluter. Only when unemployment rises (and production tapers off) does the pollution slacken noticeably. When a south wind blows off Lake Michigan, which averages at least once a week, the acrid fumes from the mills leave pedestrians choking for breath. U.S. Steel cannot claim to be the steadfast, good corporate citizen; not infrequently, the interests of stockholders are placed above those of the local citizenry. In 1974 the corporation faced a $2,300-a-day fine for continuing to operate open furnaces which spewed heavy dosages of orange-colored oxides into the air. When a federal court ordered it to pay the fine or close the furnaces, U.S. Steel closed the furnaces, laying off 2,500 workers at a time when unemployment in the city already was nudging the 15 percent level. The court order came after the company had eight years to correct the deficiencies, without the trauma of mass layoffs. U.S. Steel stalled to the last. It finally did install some pollution control equipment, but only after the courts and the Environmental Protection Agency (EPA) had all but keelhauled it to force compliance.

Hatcher discovered in office that old-fashioned exhortation had a place in urban Gary too. When people think of ghettos and Gary, many of them assume the city resembles the aftermath of a total blitzkrieg. One Gary defender reminded us that such an image ignores the many well-kept neighborhoods and stigmatizes the entire community. Gary has a majority of blacks, he remonstrated, but too many people forget blacks are families too. They have concern for their children, they want a good education for them, they don't want to get beat up, they're seeking good jobs, and—far more than many outsiders assume—own and maintain their own homes with all the pride of the Polish ethnics in south Milwaukee or Irish in Chicago's Bridgeport. Much of this evolved after Hatcher took office, forcing the opening of greater opportunity. In 1976 Hatcher himself noted the problems of black people had changed. "We won the battle to get down the formal barriers to black people," he said. "If we are to exploit the opportunity of the open door as well as whites, we must recognize our responsibilities to ourselves." His prescription sounded like a page from the book of adages of a typical small Hoosierland town: self-help, mow your grass, pick up your garbage, paint your house, and then capital will start flowing in to rejuvenate the dilapidated inner city.

Appropriately, Gary's new civic center—built with $12.7-million in federal aid and scheduled to open in 1980—was named Genesis Center. The complex, located at the north end of downtown, just a block from City Hall, was ultimately to include a civil rights hall of fame, bringing its total price tag to nearly $23 million. All of that money came from the federal government—a fact that tells much about the evolution of local-state-federal relations in Gary. The city couldn't afford to pay anything, and the state will not be found among the contributors. Hatcher in recent years has become increasingly critical of the refusal of Indianapolis and the legislature to acknowledge Gary and its problems, much less help it. As far as the state is concerned, Gary is a leper colony and is shunned whenever possible. When Gary needed legislative changes to arrange for federal financing of Genesis Center, it took the lawmakers three years to act, even though they weren't being asked for a nickel. Gary officials know it is futile to approach Indianapolis for any assistance.

The attitude of the state government only mirrors that of the white residents and businesses that fled downtown and the city in the 1960s and 1970s. Planned or not, it is symbolic that the interstate system knifes through the heart of Gary, but the only exits are near the east and west city boundaries, making it simpler to reach the suburbs than downtown. Sears and J.C. Penney were among the first major businesses to abandon downtown, and their vacant buildings stand like cavernous outposts of a former civilization, mute testimonials to the politics of fear and hatred. Progress was hard to achieve —and hold. A new downtown Holiday Inn in Gary early in the 1970s was to herald the dawning of the new age. But it folded at mid-decade, adding to the morbid desolation growing in downtown. But with a $1 million federal grant, the city bought the property and convinced the Sheraton hotel chain that with the new civic center and other developments, downtown Gary had a future worth investing in. In 1979 the Sheraton opened its doors within sight of Genesis Center.

Gary's newspaper, the *Post-Tribune*, deserves a special mention. From the start, it opposed Hatcher and his administration, willing to support any candidate with a shred of respectability (even if machine-backed) against him. Its reporters also constantly nipped Hatcher's heels, probing allegations of misdeeds and occasionally turning up abuses that warranted serious investigations. Unfortunately, there were instances when the paper's zeal exceeded its facts, in the opinion of some, giving Hatcher cause to question the paper. It appeared the antagonism by the *Post-Tribune*, returned in kind occasionally by the mayor, bordered on a vendetta. At one point in the 1979 campaign, Hatcher referred to the paper as "racist," a charge that infuriated its black city editor. Yet, as 1980 neared, the *Post-Tribune* faced a decision about its aging plant, whether to renovate facilities downtown or follow those who had fled. Leaving downtown would be the quintessential rebuke to the mayor, but the paper seemed ready to place civic responsibility above political antagonism and to stay downtown.

The corruption we have noted in Gary is nothing unusual for Lake County; the problem appears endemic and continuous. The populace simply expects one set of rascals to replace another. Take, for instance, the case of George Chacharis, the people's choice for mayor of Gary more than two decades ago. George (or "Cha Cha" as his friends were wont to call him) understood the rules of the game in Lake County all too well: a public trust was a way to build a private fortune, and in politics-à-la-Indiana, to the victor goes all the spoils. The problem Chacharis had was not that he took the usual rake-off on business done with the city, but his timing. In 1959, Arkansas' Sen. John McClellan headed a Senate investigation into crime and corruption in Lake County and concluded: "The illicit operations which appear to have flourished in Lake County since 1950 would have been impossible without the knowledge, acquiescence, and cooperation of some public officials." At the behest of a group of steel and oil executives and some university professors, the Northwest Indiana Crime Commission was funded, a former FBI agent hired, and then-Attorney General Robert F. Kennedy was prevailed upon to appoint a special assistant to the U.S. Attorney for the area. Some months later, Mayor Chacharis was indicted by a federal grand jury for overlooking payment of income taxes on $226,696 obligingly provided by compliant local construction companies. (It was only the pending grand jury indictment that saved President Kennedy from the embarrassment of naming Chacharis to an ambassadorship, a plum he had coming for his faithful delivery of the Democratic vote in 1960.) Even after Cha Cha emerged from jail, he remained popular enough for some to predict he could run for reelection and win again, record or no. Cha Cha had merely maintained the local tradition.

One seasoned observer of the Indiana scene suggested to us there was only one place on the globe comparable to Lake County—Hong Kong. "The two places suffer jointly," he said, "from 'I don't-care-itis,' a disease for which no serum has been found. Whether it's vice, prostitution, politics, or crime, everybody in Lake County has a stake in the action or he's a victim of the same." As if to confirm that observation, Thomas R. Fadell—the successor to Chacharis as crown prince of Lake County's corruption—was convicted in 1979 for masterminding an office payroll swindle. Fadell built his power base as the assessor of Calumet Township. So potent did he become before his downfall that he once retorted to a businessman threatening to appeal his assessment: "I am the law." The conviction on four counts of misappropriation of public funds plus a count each of conspiracy to commit perjury and theft came two years after a U.S. District Court found him guilty of two counts of perjury and five counts of obstructing justice in the same payroll fraud. According to the indictments, Fadell used employees in his assessor's office to work for his private sand mining, land development, mobile home park, and trucking companies—all the time while on assessor's office time and paid with public funds. Lake County Prosecutor Jack Crawford said the guilty verdict marked a "new day in the history of Lake County," noting that people were "fed up with ghost payrolling, misappropriation of public money, and arrogant public officials who feel they are above the law." His words undoubtedly were more for public consumption than public conversion to acceptance of a higher set of morals.

Physically, Lake County is dominated by the image of a steel jungle. Its atmosphere, in spite of all the orders of the EPA and the courts, remains contaminated by the fumes of steelmaking. Its industrial corridor hugging the lake is congested with coal piles, power lines, freight cars, oil tanks, and all the dreary physical facilities indigenous to basic manufacturing. What doesn't befoul the air is poured into the lake or its tributaries, seemingly private reservoirs for the oil refineries, utilities, and steelmakers. While Gary and East Chicago (population 42,979) in fact fit the stereotype well, both have commercial strips fighting to stay alive and residential neighborhoods both well kept and eyesores. Little Whiting (population 7,133) is so filled with oil refining equipment and monstrous tanks that there is precious little space left for people. This same area also embraces Hammond (population 103,229), heavily residential and industrial at once, though its industry is cleaner.

The Lake County pattern is for blacks and other minorities to live closer to the lake and their jobs in the mills, while the whites congregate in such southern suburbs as Merrillville (where a giant shopping mall snatched so much of the commercial enterprises of Gary), Crown Point (the county seat), and a countryside that suddenly engulfs the traveler less than 20 miles south of the lake. A place of cattle and corn and serenity, southern Lake County saw scattered homes transform even that pastoral scene during the 1970s.

Crown Point, near the center of Lake County, lost some of its image as a sleepy little town during the 1970s, aided by several annexations and considerable housing development. By the end of the decade it had grown more than 22 percent to 14,753. Neither the sleepy town nor the burgeoning development is enough to obscure the fact that Crown Point traditionally ruled over probably the most corrupt urban county among the 50 states. (For beginners, it should be reported that not many years ago, the standard kickback on any Lake County contract was 15 percent. Significantly, no one in county government has been caught with his hand in the till in recent years, but it's easy to start an argument over whether this phenomenon should be attributed to cleaner government, more lackadaisical enforcement, or officials' greater sophistication in covering their tracks.)

Part of nostalgic Crown Point was saved from the wrecker's ball during the 1970s. The county courthouse, abandoned in 1974 when a new government and jail complex was built in the north part of the town, was converted to a shopping and entertainment mall. The Lake Courthouse Foundation stopped the destruction, arguing the building was one of the finest 19th century, Victorian-style courthouses in the Midwest and was steeped in history. Among other things, William Jennings Bryan delivered a presidential campaign speech there, and the infamous John Dillinger would have been tried for murder there—if he hadn't escaped from the county jail!

For years, Gary and East Chicago have vied with each other for the distinction of producing the most steel and harboring the most corruption. East Chicago's biggest payrolls are paid out by Inland Steel (with 22,500 workers) and J & L Steel (formerly Youngstown Steel and Tubing). Within its 11 square miles, the city has about as many workers (nearly 50,000) as inhabitants, but the numbers of both have shrunk since 1960, when employment levels hit a high of 70,000 and the population almost 58,000. The city is ugly and dismal, about equally divided between low- and middle-income and between blacks, Latinos, and whites (mostly Poles, Slovaks, Croatians, and Serbians). Simultaneously, East Chicago may be one of the most integrated cities in the country. Races mix block-by-block and even within blocks in some areas. The racial tensions that used to afflict Gary found no fertile ground in East Chicago. It is no city of brotherly love, however; it has been characterized as a city where everyone either is on the take or just wants to be left alone. Perhaps significantly, the successor to Krupa as Democratic County chairman was East Chicago's Mayor, Robert A. Pastrick. East Chicago offers working men its illegal liquor, illegal gambling, and the pleasures of prostitutes who openly work out of the bars and hotels (and sometimes an American Legion post!). Such flagrant defiance of the law occurred with the acquiescence of local officials. When asked why nothing was done to halt the obvious violations, one city official told us: "If you stop gambling and crack down on it, what diversion is there for the guys who work in the mills—especially the single ones? It just can't be stopped. Now what we would like to cut out are the after-hours places, with fighting and prostitutes." In East Chicago, the payoff—at all levels—is the rule, hardly an exception. The city is quintessential Lake County.

The Hoosiers' Lesser Cityscape

To round out our Indiana story, we turn now to the lesser cities of Hoosierland. Fort Wayne, today the state's second largest city, was one of the first white settlements in Indiana. That was even before General "Mad" Anthony Wayne, sent by President George Washington to establish a trading post, had outwitted the Indians at the battle of Fallen Timbers in 1794. Then, where St. Mary's River joins the St. Joseph River to form the Maumee, General Wayne built the outpost which the President designated as Fort Wayne.

Fort Wayne is a comfortable community, blending a mix of generally clean industry and the fruits of the rich farmland around it to produce a community with a minimum of petty squabbling over civic affairs. Magnavox and Central Soya make their home offices here, while General Electric and International Harvester are the biggest employers. About 85 percent of the world's diamond wire dies are made by several local manufacturers. Lincoln National Life insurance also contributes much to the community—both in terms of jobs and with civic leadership.

The city fathers, sensing they were losing industry in the 1950s, undertook a major face-lifting that brought Fort Wayne back from the edge of economic stagnation. By the 1970s, with 185,000-plus people, a per capita income ranking second only to Indianapolis, and its long-time German Lutheran wealth, Fort Wayne appeared vibrant again. It boasted a healthy civic spirit, some good restaurants including an award-winning French cafe, a philharmonic orchestra, a fine arts and performing center, plus two quite vigorous newspapers—the free-swinging liberal Democratic *Journal-Gazette*, the morning paper, and the staunchly conservative and quite Republican *News-Sentinel*, its afternoon counterpart, which was sold to Knight-Ridder in 1980.

And for those always searching for a tidbit of trivia, here are two: Fort Wayne fielded a baseball team of students on the night of June 2, 1883, against a group of Illinois professionals, down in the old League Park at the foot of Calhoun Street, under an arc-lighting system installed by the Fort Wayne Jenney Electric Company (the forerunner of General Electric). That memorable event was the birth of night baseball, or so say the natives of Fort Wayne.

And finally, there's the legendary Johnny Appleseed, named for his proclivity for planting the luscious apple seeds all over the Midwest. On a trip through Fort Wayne in 1845, Johnny contracted pneumonia and died. His grave is in Johnny Appleseed Park, just south of the Coliseum.

To the northwest is South Bend, a Democratic enclave in the heart of the Republican agricultural-industrial belt that starts just east of Gary and runs to the Ohio border. South Bend consistently provided the Democratic votes needed to keep Rep. John Brademas in Congress for 20 years. In the late 1970s, it had Democratic mayors, first Peter Nemeth and then Roger Parent, and usually sent Democrats to the General Assembly in Indianapolis. It's a pleasant and neat community, with few serious crimes and even less slumlike housing.

South Bend used to be thought of as the home of the conservative and staid Catholic university, Notre Dame, and a football team perennially ranked among the nation's best. The Fighting Irish still fill the stadium every weekend they are home, but now they must share the accolades earned with an academic institution. Since Father Theodore Hesburgh became president more than a quarter century ago, South Bend has become the home of the avant-garde Notre Dame, an advocate of change (women were admitted in 1972 for the first time), of increasing academic excellence (the American Council of Education has ranked it among the top 30 private schools in the country), and of openness to ideas not exclusively Catholic (a birth control conference was held on campus). Hesburgh's administration has been marked by an increased social consciousness as well as greater academic freedom. But his changes hardly won unanimous approval. Many alumni, espousing more traditional Catholic views, questioned the openness to change and ideas. "I don't want this place to be a ghetto, or a backwash," Hesburgh responded. "We should discuss all issues. This doesn't mean we agree with them, but we can't hide."

For a school whose disciplinary code and monastic rules earned it a reputation as the West Point of the Midwest, with compulsory Mass every day and prayers before every date, the changes were tantamount to a minor revolution. Hesburgh, called by some the "most influential cleric" in the nation, also carried his theology beyond the campus. For 15 years he was a member and chairman of the U.S. Civil Rights Commission—before President Nixon dumped him after the 1972 elections because of Hesburgh's increasingly caustic comments opposing the Administration's antibusing and Southeast Asian policies. Hesburgh created a civil rights center on the Notre Dame campus, housing one of the nation's most extensive civil rights libraries. He is no stranger to the corporate world, having held at various times directorships on several boards, including the Chase Manhattan Bank.

Some long-time residents of South Bend chafe a bit when people suggest their city is only Notre Dame. There is more to their city of 117,000, they say, which goes back to even before the university was founded in 1842. For one thing, they note, it is a strong industrial community, a fact which helped attract so many Eastern European immigrants as it grew in the 19th century. Bendix, the appliance maker, and Oliver, the farm manufacturer, are but two of the corporations with long traditions in South Bend. The saga of the Studebaker Brothers has been retold endlessly, but they carved a unique niche in Indiana automobile history: they lasted longer than any other car firm started in Indiana.

The number varies, but up to 375 makes of cars have been manufactured in the Hoosier state. Elwood Haynes of Kokomo made one of the first successful horseless carriage runs in Indiana, when he puttered down the Pumpkinville Pike on July 4, 1894. Exactly who made the first successful automobile in Indiana still is hotly contested. Only 16 of the 375 makes survived the competitive automobile industry for more than 15 years, and the Studebaker boys lasted the longest. If you count the years they made their horse-drawn wagons, from 1852 to the turn of the century, they existed in South Bend for 111 years. Once, in 1956, the union at Studebaker voted itself a pay cut, hoping to forestall the inevitable. The move helped only briefly, because in 1963 Studebaker joined the makers of the Dusenberg, the Maxwell, and the Stutz and shut down its assembly lines, leaving the car field in Indiana to the branch plants of General Motors, Ford, and Chrysler.

Part of the reason South Bend holds such a high reputation must be attributed to the city's only newspaper, the *Tribune*. Generally Republican, the *Tribune* has maintained an unshakable independence throughout its existence. Frederick A. Miller was president and editor for many years before he died, and he made sure fairness was pursued diligently and corruption with any political label was a prime target in the paper's news and editorial columns. A fearless opponent of injustice in any form, Miller's *Tribune* was one of the lonely few which dared to speak out against the Ku Klux Klan even at the height of its political power during the 1920s. The paper remains a voice of independence and moderation today.

When it came to vice and gambling, Lake County had a small-town rival in Terre Haute. Its houses of prostitution operated openly for years, but the local sons and daughters rose up in indignation after Mayor Leland Larrison refused to shut them down and seemed even to condone them. "There were only three houses left," Larrison later explained. "And they were such nice houses—as nice as an illegal operation can be. I just didn't want to get involved in shutting them down." It gave William Brighton the issue he needed. *Time* magazine and journalists from as far away as Australia had traipsed into Terre Haute to write about this "sin city." Brighton delivered on his campaign promise and shut down the houses. "We're not sin city any more. We're pride city, the queen city of the Wabash." At least Larrison was consistent: even in defeat, he refused to renounce the error of his thinking. "Instead we've got some very high class massage parlors," he argued. "Now they're in the motels. It's a rich man's game now. It costs you $50 to $75. . . . Ten bucks was the going price when I was in there. The average salesman, he can't sneak $50 onto the expense account."

Terre Haute has had more than its share of economic ups and downs. Early in the century, it was prospering. It had coal, industry, breweries, and distilleries, and was destined to become the "Pittsburgh of the West," local promoters were saying. By 1920, while the rest of the nation was entering an era of unprecedented prosperity, Terre Haute stopped growing. Crippling strikes in the coal mines, prohibition closing the breweries and the distilleries, not infrequent flooding of the Wabash, and a decided void where civic leadership should have been all contributed to the reversal of fortune. Periodic renewal efforts have been made, but Terre Haute and Vigo County haven't put it together.

Terre Haute has given the nation some favorite sons. Eugene Debs preached a message of economic brotherhood. Theodore Dreiser's immortal novel, *An American Tragedy*, struck many sensitive spots in the local gentry, and the book never gained the esteem in his home town that it did nationally. Dreiser's song-writing brother, Paul Dresser, was received more kindly. Dresser's "On the Banks of the Wabash" is the official state song. Sculptor Janet Scudder also came from Terre Haute, as does the senior Senator, Birch Bayh. Besides the better part of the locally owned commerce and industry owned by the Hulman interests, Terre Haute has facilities operated by Anaconda Aluminum, J. I. Case, Pillsbury, Columbia Records, Eli Lilly, and more than 130 other industries.

Evansville did what Terre Haute failed to do: stop the outward flow of industry and rebuild the city. Evansville, located on a bend in the Ohio River, in southwestern Indiana, found itself with unemployment running into the thousands when its major industries—Servel, International Harvester, and Chrysler among them—decided in the 1950s to find new homes. Fear began to spread that the city's disjointed businessmen and politicians would be paralyzed in the face of the threat and let the city float down the river. One factory location survey firm tagged Evansville as a city with a huge "inferiority complex." Suddenly Evansville's businessmen and politicians coalesced and formed a group "Evansville's Future, Inc." The dingy old waterfront was cleaned up, new construction begun, and substantial new industries enticed to the city. Transportation was upgraded. Old industries expanded, including Mead Johnson and Company, makers of Metrecal, the dinner for dieters. Part of the credit went to Vance Hartke, who stepped into his Senate seat after three years as mayor. His leadership reins were ably assumed by Frank McDonald, another Democrat who put harmony above partisanship, and then an equally competent Republican, Russell G. Lloyd (who had the qualities to place him on some future statewide GOP ticket, but was murdered by a woman who burst into his home after he had left office).

Politics in Evansville are of the rough-and-tumble variety, reminiscent of the riverboat days. This was Copperhead Country in the Civil War and for a long time afterwards. D. C. Stephenson parlayed this bigotry into his statewide KKK movement, starting out from headquarters in the Vendome Hotel.

Most travelers would drive through Columbus only on their way to another town—if it weren't for one man. J. Irwin Miller is to Columbus as Cosimo de Medici was to Florence, Italy. Nominally, as he won wide renown, Miller was chairman of the board of Cummins Engine Company, the world's largest manufacturer of diesel engines. Cummins dominates the town economically. But Miller chose to be a patriarch, a patron, and a social conscience. The reason travelers will stop in this community of 28,000, about 43 miles south of Indianapolis, is its architectural splendor. In 1942 the renowned architect Eliel Saarinen designed the First Christian Church of Columbus. But it wasn't until more than a decade later that Miller created the Cummins Engine Foundation that eventually pledged to pay all architectural fees for new and innovative buildings in the city. That has resulted in more than 40 public and private buildings designed by a list of architects which reads like a "Who's Who in Architecture." Probably the most famous of all is the North Christian Church, designed in 1964 by Eero Saarinen, son of Eliel. A 192-foot spire, topped with a gold leaf cross, rises up from the low-lying hexagonal building, a stunning sight in a community surrounded by cornfields and inhabited by people who would be the first to admit they are not cultural cosmopolites. The North Christian Church was the last building created by Saarinen (the younger). "This little church" was among his best, he wrote shortly before he died, "because it has in it a real spirit that speaks forth to all Christians as a witness to their faith."

Miller has not limited his efforts to encouraging fine architecture. Through his leadership, Cummins has sought out and attracted a number of top-level black executives and management trainees for the firm, literally importing them and forcing the community to live and work with and for blacks. Cummins and Miller could run the town if they chose. But Miller has said he prefers to stay in the background, leading more by example than by directive. "We try to play a catalytic role rather than a determining role," Miller said once. "We've always thought people were reasonably innovative here, so whatever we might do hopefully would have some impact."

Without a doubt, Miller has made an impact on practically all that he has touched. In 1968, *Saturday Review* named him businessman of the year. A year before, *Esquire* in a cover story on this Indiana industrialist suggested he possessed better qualifications than any other living American to be elected President. But of course Miller was no politician, and Indiana is the politician's state. Only one Wendell Willkie a century, please.

OHIO

THE MIDDLE-CLASS SOCIETY

OHIO, MOTHER OF SECOND-RATE PRESIDENTS, hung up about its own identity (East to Westerners, West to Easterners), the personification of the middle class society, is the least distinctive of the great industrial states of the U.S.A. New York has its stimulating world city, Pennsylvania its Quaker and "Keystone" traditions, Illinois has brawny Chicago and colorful "clout" politics, Michigan the auto empires and advanced unionism, Texas is its own unique world, California a nation in itself.

But Ohio? What is a "Buckeye"? It's a tree, of course, but historian Walter Havighurst relates that when the authors of the *Ohio Guide* of the Federal Writers' Project in 1940 tried to decide on a cover design, the buckeye was discarded because few Ohioans would recognize the tree. The final design, neatly symbolizing a split character, half industrial, half rural, was a sheaf of wheat over a tire.

If you view the Buckeye as a man rather than a tree, you could say, as one writer has, that he embodies "dedication to the homely virtues of honesty, thrift, steadiness, caution, and a distrust of government." Perhaps the homely virtues could bear reassertion in a modern world all too rife with materialism and a flashy culture. Our editor for this book, Evan Thomas, recalls that his father, the illustrious Norman Thomas (often Socialist candidate for the presidency) told many "tales of the essential decency of his childhood neighbors" in Ohio. "They were hipped on the fundamentalist religions, but they were thoroughly human. In fact, it was mainly because Dad had spent his childhood in Marion that he went through Princeton a Republican, of all things."

But the "wonderful world of Ohio," as the hucksterish governor of the 1960s and 1970s, James Rhodes, called his state, has in recent times cared less for the homely virtues. (In Ohio, Rhodes said again and again and again, "profit is not a dirty word.") By dollar measures of what a state does for its people—in education, health, welfare, mental care, environmental control—Ohio remained near the bottom of the 50-state rankings and in the absolute cellar among the great industrial states (Texas excepted) throughout the 1970s. And there was little color, verve, or great culture to relieve the monotony. Ohio just plowed through history, turning out immense amounts of manufactured goods, shortchanging many of its own people, practicing a politics of indifference. In 1970, Ohio was the scene of the killing by the National Guard of four Kent State students—the first such casualties of the modern student revolution. The following autumn, after a great scandal that wracked the ruling Republicans, Ohio elected John J. Gilligan, a vigorous young Irishman and liberal-intellectual Democrat from Cincinnati, as governor. But Gilligan could last only four years until Rhodes returned to power.

All along, of course, Ohio has had its redeeming graces, its imaginative and dedicated men and women, some innovative institutions. Doughty Cincinnati, decades past her prime, still has a certain old world charm and is in the midst of a graceful renewal; Dayton is one of the cleaner and more progressive of Midwestern cities; there are numerous small colleges of exemplary quality (Antioch, Oberlin, Kenyon, Ohio Wesleyan, and the like).

As John Gunther correctly recorded, "basically, Ohio is nothing more or less than a giant carpet of agriculture studded by great cities." Ohio in 1970 had no fewer than eight cities with more than 100,000 people, 16 metropolitan areas which house 78 percent of the state's 10,652,017 people, and 153 cities with 10,000 or more inhabitants.* One can't be on a highway headed in any direction in Ohio for an hour and not hit a medium-sized city—a Steubenville, a Warren, Niles, Sandusky or Fremont; "our state is really microscopic," one Ohioan told me. Of the major cities, ranging from Cleveland (population 876,000) to Springfield (85,907), we will have more to report later; suffice it here to note that none has the weight of a Chicago in Illinois, a Detroit in Michigan or a New York City in New York; which has not a little to say about the fragmented nature of urban politics in a basically metropolitan state.

Most of Ohio's borders are wet—Lake Erie (color it dirty) to the north and the Ohio River stretching 436 miles along the east and south; there are,

* Between 1946 and 1970, the total population rose 3.1 million, or 48 percent. By 1977–78, it had increased a small additional 44,000 and ranked 6th.

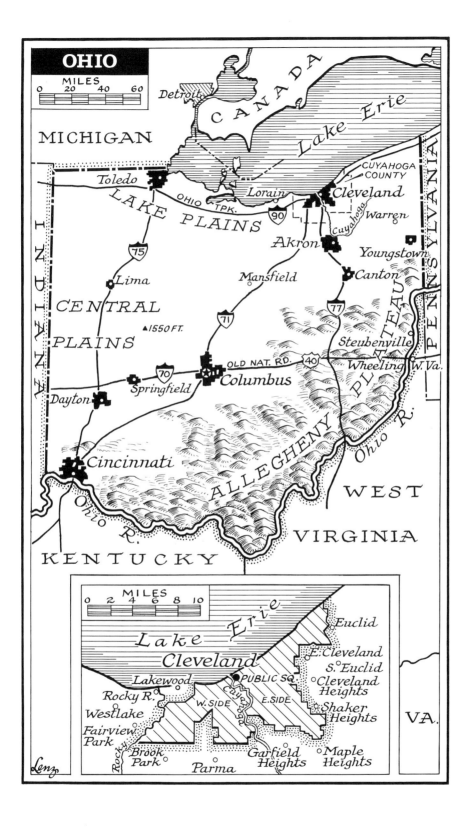

OHIO

MILES
0   20   40   60

Detroit

CANADA

Lake Erie

MICHIGAN

Toledo

LAKE PLAINS

OHIO TPK.

Lorain

90

CUYAHOGA COUNTY

Cleveland

Cuyahoga

Warren

Youngstown

Akron

75

Lima

Mansfield

Canton

CENTRAL

▲1550 FT.

71

77

Steubenville

PLAINS

70

Old Nat. Rd.

40

Wheeling W.Va.

Springfield

Columbus

Dayton

ALLEGHENY PLATEAU

Ohio R.

Cincinnati

WEST

Ohio R.

VIRGINIA

KENTUCKY

INDIANA

PENNSYLVANIA

MILES
0   2   4   6   8   10

Lake Erie

Euclid

Cleveland

E. Cleveland

S. Euclid

Lakewood

PUBLIC SQ.

Cleveland Heights

Rocky R.

W. SIDE

Cuyahoga

E. SIDE

Westlake

Shaker Heights

VA.

Fairview Park

Rocky R.

Brook Park

Garfield Heights

Maple Heights

Parma

Lenz

however, some arbitrary cartographer's lines along the Pennsylvania, Michigan, and Indiana borders, so that the overall impression is more or less square.

The geographers say there are three regions of Ohio. About a quarter of the land area, mainly in the southeast quadrant, is the Appalachian Allegheny Plateau, remnants of the Allegheny Mountains spilling over from Pennsylvania and West Virginia, becoming more gentle as they move westward. Along the shores of Lake Erie from Cleveland to the northwest corner of Ohio is a strip known as the Lake Plains, or the onetime Black Swamp that thwarted early settlers until they found a way to drain it. All the rest of Ohio—the great land bulk, moving out to the Indiana border—is a Central Plains area, gently rolling land similar to the plains of the more westerly states except that the first settlers found practically the entire region covered by forest, not grass.

The rugged, hilly country of the southeastern Allegheny Plateau, a mixture of sylvan wood and land ravaged by strip coal mining, harbors few cities of any note and much rural poverty; along the Ohio River are some heavy industries including steel companies run out of Wheeling and Pittsburgh. Many of these counties are poor in the extreme, with subquality schools and poor public facilities. The original settlers were mostly Virginia and Kentucky woodsmen. On the political scale, this region votes predominantly Republican but is likely to switch to the Democrats in hard times.

Northeastern Ohio is highly industrialized and heavily populated, a smokestack-studded industrial complex of befouled air and great productivity including the cities of Youngstown, Warren, Canton, Akron, Cleveland, and, somewhat farther west, Toledo. These cities are actually part of an identifiable megalopolis called Chi-Pitts, anchored by Pittsburgh on the east, Chicago (or possibly Milwaukee) on the west. John Steinbeck in *Travels With Charley* wrote of passing through these "great hives of production" and "my eyes and mind were battered by the fantastic hugeness and energy of production, a complication that resembles chaos and cannot be." And then Steinbeck added: "What was wonderful was that I could come again to a quiet country road, tree-bordered, with fenced fields and cows, could pull up . . . beside a lake of clear, clean water and see high overhead the arrows of southing ducks and geese." How long those countryside charms can remain, as suburbia gobbles up the farms and industrial pollution exacts its toll, is open to question. Once a haven of New England settlers, this region is now heavily peopled by the children and grandchildren of European workers—Italians, Slovenians, Hungarians, Poles—who were imported to man the heavy steel and rubber industries earlier in this century. Following them came hundreds of thousands of blacks from the American Southland. The political coloration (except for some farm counties and suburbia) is overwhelmingly Democratic.

Finally, occupying roughly half the land and representing half of the state's population, is central and western Ohio, the easterly terminus of the great Midwestern farm belt but also strong manufacturing territory and site of cities great and small, among them Columbus at center state, Dayton and

Cincinnati at the southwesterly corner. Here are the descendants of the Scots, Irish, Pennsylvania German, and assorted Civil War veterans. The German flavor is especially strong in southern Ohio and equals conservatism. Many of the overwhelmingly Republican counties of the U.S.A. are in these central and western regions, but interestingly there are still a handful of counties that have been voting Democratic ever since the Civil War. (The political scientist John Fenton has shown an amazing correspondence between the counties that voted for the Copperhead Democrat Clement L. Vallandigham in 1863 and were still voting Democratic in recent years.) But these old Democratic counties are but a small fraction of the population, and the salient political factors are generally rural and especially small city Republicanism, and the fact that metropolises like Columbus and Cincinnati—despite great industries, labor unions, and black population—have been so dominated by the thought patterns of their conservative establishments that they have registered Republican majorities in most elections.

An Economy of Heavy Industry

Heavy manufacturing dominates the Ohio economy, the natural result of her strategic location between the iron ore deposits of Minnesota and the coal mines of Appalachia, between the St. Lawrence Seaway to the north and the Ohio River to the south, and within 500 miles of two-thirds of the nation's population and three-quarters of its wealth. Her manufacturing output of more than $37 billion a year ranks third among the states; her coke ovens, blast furnaces, and finishing mills place her second among the 50 in primary and fabricated metals production. Ohio is first in the U.S.A. in rubber as a result of the output of Akron's factories, and also ranks high in machinery, automobile assembly, and automobile parts manufacture. But the product lines are a picture of diversity; Ohio is first, according to the promotional literature that pours out of Columbus, in products ranging from business machines to coffins, buckets and pails to Chinese food and Liederkranz cheese, roadbuilding and earthmoving equipment to playing cards and Bibles. Other major factors are coal, lime, and some oil and gas mining, the growing service industries, plus trucking and lumbering. Ohio has a healthy and diversified agriculture (chiefly dairy products, cattle, corn, and hogs) with a total farm income of $2.8 billion a year—11th among the states. Hardly a tourist mecca, Ohio nonetheless picks up several billion dollars a year from travelers passing through.

In a real sense, however, Ohio is musclebound by the dominance of heavy industry, a portion of the economy most susceptible to automation. Announcing proudly that jobs are the answer to every social ill, Governor Rhodes set out in the 1960s to draw thousands of new industries to Ohio. Rhodes' industrial "Raiders" undertook scores of industry-hunting tours around the U.S.A. and several foreign trade missions. A national advertising campaign stressed the already-cited theme, "Profit is not a dirty word in Ohio," as well as the pitch, "In Ohio, government is run as a business." Prospective advertisers were reminded that Ohio had the lowest state and local tax rates in the country and also the lowest proportion of government employees.

The heavy promotional campaign did attract several thousand new industrial jobs, both during the '6os and when Rhodes returned to the governorship in the '7os. But with automation making its impact ever more obvious and the aging facilities in such heavy industries as steel, actual manufacturing jobs in Ohio registered only modest gains in the '6os and declined in the 1970s. Of the actual new factory jobs attracted to Ohio, most were concentrated in heavy manufacturing such as rolling mills, assembly plants, and rubber factories and relatively few in the more exotic, electronic age industries which pay comparatively higher wages. Ohio was adding significant numbers of new positions, but the lion's share of them came in "service" jobs— nonmanufacturing jobs such as mining, transportation, utilities, wholesale and retail trade, food stores, department stores, banking, insurance, and government service. Little of this stemmed from the state's job promotion efforts, which were concentrated heavily on industry.

To attract new firms or expansions, Ohio in the '7os went heavily into the tax abatement game, allowing businesses to avoid up to 100 percent of their property taxes for up to 20 years. First authorized for economically lagging cities in 1973, the tax exemption was widened to virtually all areas of the state—urban, suburban, or small town—in 1977. Economic development officials in the state government and several localities claimed that the exemptions were proving highly successful in luring new firms to the state, and they could point to some big firms that took advantage of the abatements. But there was solid evidence, developed by the Ohio Public Interest Campaign and others, that many of the firms would have selected Ohio locations in any event. Moreover, each tax abatement reduced local property tax yields essential for funding the schools and other public services, thus reducing the state's general attractiveness as a place to live. As officials of the Ohio Public Interest Campaign told us, "Industries that might look to Ohio, including those involved in higher technology requiring a more skilled work force, have to look to the fact that Ohio's per capita level of funding of public education is 49th in the country. That's much more significant in the locational decision than any tax abatement." The state's economic development agency, they claimed, was "acting as an agent for developers and industries in bargaining for public subsidies and has no other reason for being."

There was some local grumbling about Rhodes's give-away programs, especially to foreign-owned companies. One of Rhodes's greatest coups was attracting the first U.S. assembly plant of Honda, the Japanese automaker, to the town of Marysville northwest of Columbus. Near a town of one movie house, four Lutheran churches and no motel, Honda promised to build an assembly plant in a cornfield and hire 2,000 workers. But the state of Ohio planned to spend millions to improve roads, sewers and rail facilities in the area. Union County, whose voters had not passed a school levy increase for at least five years despite critical shortages, agreed to give up Honda's taxes for 15 years. Said Donald Nolan, a local truck driver: "Sure, the guys with money are going to make a lot on that plant, but I'm not. I've been paying taxes since I was 16, I'm a Vietnam vet, I got shot twice and broke my back under an armored personnel carrier and spent 17 months in the hospital, and nobody told me to forget about paying taxes for a couple years."

Reports from various cities also indicated the state economic development officials were peculiarly inept in assisting small entrepreneurs getting new businesses off the ground, or in aiding Ohio businesses in trouble, or when they actually closed their doors, in helping workers or new owners take over those businesses and maintain them as job-providing enterprises. A sure sign of trouble was the low level of new business incorporations, the breeding ground of new job opportunities. In 1977, for instance, Ohio ranked only 46th among the states in fresh business incorporations related to the overall population. The rate was 13.1 per 10,000 residents, compared to 87.0 in Nevada, 26.4 in New Jersey, and 20.0 in the country at large.

Chief responsibility for this generally dismal record could be laid at Rhodes's door. At no point did he show a particular concern for the quality (as opposed to the quantity) of jobs in the state. The tax structure was not adjusted to encourage "think tanks" or advanced industries. The hallmarks of the Rhodes approach were to keep taxes low, to move ahead of all other states in completion of interstate roads, to push tax abatements, to get state financing for industrial bonds to save businesses first investment costs, and to promote the Ohio State Fair until it became the nation's most successful. Rhodes was fond of passing out homilies such as this one (referring to tomato juice production, in which Ohio leads the U.S.): "If every Ohioan drank one quart of tomato juice a year, it would mean 5,000 more jobs in Ohio." Left to future years were the problems of modifying the structure of an old-line economy, heavy industry state so that the people could share more fully in the benefits of the electronic and service-oriented age.

Neglectful State Government: From Lausche to Rhodes

When Frank J. Lausche was first elected governor of Ohio in 1944, he bore all the marks of a true American folk hero: son of a Slovenian-born steelworker, self-made lawyer and outstanding city judge, respected mayor of his home city of Cleveland, disdainer of old-line machine politics, a Democratic candidate who could appeal across all party lines. Gunther devoted the first six pages of his Ohio chapter to an enthusiastic review of the Lausche personality and record, calling him a man of "charm, vitality," of absolute honesty and "sympathy for the underdog" whose only major defects stemmed from "a lack of an academic education and a disinclination to think abstractly." An honored slot in history seemed to be in store for Lausche when he finally left the governorship in 1956.

But in Ohio today, it is hard to find a knowledgeable observer with a kind word for Frank Lausche. For this frugal and conservative Slovenian imposed such a parsimonious, strict pay-as-you-go philosophy in Ohio, akin to the low-spending Byrd regime in Virginia, that the state has yet to regain the position among the states in services to people—in education, welfare, criminology—or mental care—which it held before he took office. Benefiting first from a wartime-generated surplus in the state treasury, and later refusing adamantly to increase taxes, Lausche failed to inaugurate needed capital investments or adequately finance basic state services except in one area—highway construction. Highways of course provided a major political payoff in jobs, campaign money from contractors, and visible achievement. All the time, the children of Ohio were being deprived of educational investment equal to the other states of the Union, especially the large and wealthy states comparable to Ohio. As John H. Fenton points out in *Midwest Politics,*

> In 1956, at the close of Lausche's period in office, some 1,000 boys were in residence at the Boys' Industrial School, which admitted to a rated capacity of about 600. In the sleeping quarters of the school there were as many as 70 beds jammed one against the other so that the only access to beds beyond the outer row was to step from bed to bed. According to Lausche's critics, the reason for spending so little on children's services was that they did not vote.

As for the electoral base that made all this possible, Fenton observed that Lausche was able to attract votes from conservative Republicans. "These votes, when superimposed on the Democratic votes cast by ill-informed low-income voters in the cities, provided him with comfortable majorities in the general elections." Lausche's electoral downfall in fact came not in a general election but in a Democratic primary. He served two terms in the U. S. Senate after leaving Columbus but was finally turned out in 1968 when the liberal leadership of the state Democratic party decided it had had enough of a Senator who usually voted with the Republicans, and it backed John J. Gilligan of Cincinnati in a successful primary race against Lausche.

The first postwar Ohio Governor to make a serious effort to make Ohio government responsive to growing education, mental health, and welfare needs was Michael V. DiSalle, the genial, roly-poly former mayor of Toledo and wartime chief of the Office of Price Administration elected in the 1958 Democratic sweep. But to achieve just a few modest reforms and meet rising state costs, DiSalle had to raise taxes—for the first time in 20 years. (State government had limped along through the Lausche years with status-quo taxes and a couple of bond issues, passed by the legislature over Lausche's opposition.) DiSalle lacked political finesse, the taxes backfired against him seriously, and in 1962 he was defeated by Republican James A. Rhodes, who rode into office on a promise of "no new taxes."

Rhodes shares with Lausche the distinction of having been one of the two most influential men in postwar Ohio history; he was governor from 1963 to 1971 and again from 1975 into the 1980s. His mark will be felt on the state for years to come. A sturdily built man whose personal manner ranges from hearty back-slapping to cold discourtesy, Rhodes was born into rather poor circumstances, his father a coal miner. As governor, he avoided press conferences and confrontations with opponents and delegated the details of administration to a generally competent but nonintellectual staff. In more than three decades of office-holding, Rhodes revealed himself as a robust type, a man's man, fond of golf and poker, given to ribald jokes,* and for the most part, a superbly successful politician. His plurality in winning a second gover- norship term in 1964 was 703,233 votes—an all-time Ohio high.

What the public wanted, Rhodes decided, was no new taxes, and he promised, "There'll be no new or additional taxes as long as I'm governor of Ohio." In his second term, Rhodes finally was obliged to force some tax and fee adjustments through the state legislature. But overall, Ohio had to limp through the 1960s on a regressive sales tax base for state government and ever increasing local property taxes, much to the distress of hard-pressed home- owners and marginal businesses.

The net impact of the Rhodes regimes, in fact, was to continue the Lauschian politics of fiscal status quo in the very years when most American state governments were taking long forward steps. Ohio's tax effort (as a per- cent of personal income) ranked 41st in the nation in 1950, 42nd when Lausche left office, but only 47th by the end of Rhodes' second term in 1973. Even with an income tax added, it had sunk to 50th in the nation by the lat- ter part of the '70s. Whether compared to other Great Lakes states, or the five poorest states of the Union, or the overall national average, Ohio was slipping farther and farther behind. But for the industrial promoters in Co- lumbus, this was a plus, not a minus. They took out full page ads in the *Wall Street Journal* to proclaim: "OHIO'S STATE AND LOCAL TAXES ARE THE LOWEST IN THE NATION! . . . Ohio makes dollars go farther without loss in essential services. . . . Profit is *not* a dirty word in Ohio."

But in the words of David Hess, a reporter for the Akron *Beacon-Journal*, "While the administration fiddles a happy tune, Ohio's education, mental health, welfare and corrections programs sink steadily into indifference and neglect."

Perhaps the most telling indicator of Ohio's neglect of its fundamental public responsibilities has been the treatment of its public schools. From the late '60s through the '70s, Ohio had the dubious distinction of leading the nation in school closings. Local schools are far more dependent than in most states on local property taxes, and there is a statutory requirement that any increase in local school tax levies be approved by a vote of the people. The system in an archaic one, crippling for public education. In autumn 1969, for

---

* At one governors' conference, while Michigan's George Romney was rambling at the speaker's stand, Rhodes slipped a note to fellow Governor Roger Branigin of Indiana. It read: "This guy couldn't sell pussy on a troopship."

instance, more than 19,000 children in 40 Ohio schools were locked out of their classrooms for days or weeks when their school districts were forced to close down for want of operating funds. Between 1970 and 1977, voters in Cincinnati, Dayton, Toledo, Columbus, and Canton rejected a total of 22 proposed tax increases to operate the schools; fearing defeat, school officials in Cleveland, Akron, and Youngstown didn't even submit levies in that seven year period, despite strong inflationary pressures. By the late '70s the situation was even more acute as schools became a whipping child not just of recalcitrant taxpayers but also of opponents of court-ordered busing to achieve desegregation in several of the state's largest cities, including Cleveland, Columbus, and Dayton.

The eventual remedy for the school finance dilemma would have to be either a hefty boost in the state income tax or the less desirable alternative of boosts in already regressive local property taxes, combined with abolition or modification of the local school levy vote requirement. But it was an issue on which Rhodes consistently refused to exert effective leadership, despite the grave dangers to Ohio's public schools and the quality of education afforded the state's young people. The legislature also seemed frozen in inaction, despite an unambiguous requirement in the Ohio Constitution that "the General Assembly shall make such provisions, by taxation or otherwise, as . . . will secure a thorough and efficient system of common schools throughout the state."

Nor could Ohio citizens themselves be absolved of blame for the continuing public education crisis in their state. It was they who were voting "no" on local school levies. And it was they who were electing malfeasant state legislators and governors of the quality represented by James Rhodes.

Where Rhodes made his strongest mark on Ohio—and differentiated himself clearly from the old Lausche approach—was in selling the people, during his first two terms as governor, massive bond issues (totaling some $2 billion in all) for highways, higher education facilities, and other physical improvements. For years under Rhodes, the bonds in effect substituted for new taxes. Half of them went for highways. "We get the most political credit for another mile of superhighway. And don't worry—maintenance won't be a problem; our voters will vote anything for highways," Rhodes's finance director, Howard L. Collier, told us in 1969. The statistics showed that Ohio under Rhodes was spending more on highways than on any other state service.

But Rhodes's breakthrough in facilities for higher education was not to be gainsaid. During the 1960s, a total of $665 million in bond money was provided for bricks and mortar to expand the Ohio educational system from five universities and a college to 12 state universities, a new medical school, and dozens of permanent branch facilities (including the equivalents of junior colleges).* The bulk of these facilities were not completed until he left office in 1971, leaving to his successor the task of raising millions of new money to

---

* In the entire 160-year period preceding Rhodes's terms, only $200 million had been spent by Ohio for higher education facilities.

staff and operate the new educational facilities.

During his third term as governor (1975–78), Rhodes tried to repeat the formula which had served him so well in the '60s: hold down taxes, do nothing in regulatory or tax policy to offend business, and reap the publicity windfall for capital construction for which future generations would have to pay. But this time he was thwarted in a central element of his program. He proposed a huge "Blueprint for Ohio" bonding package in the 1975 elections. The total cost, $4.5 billion, would have been the largest bonding obligation ever proposed in a single year anywhere. Rhodes claimed the program would make Ohio "depression-proof" by financing a massive public works employment program, financing capital improvements in dozens of communities throughout the state, and improving mass transportation. The proposals were embodied in constitutional amendments that would have also created major new tax breaks for industry. But the voters turned down the amendments by overwhelming percentages ranging from 68 to 84.

An extremely harsh but not wholly inaccurate summation of the dynamics of Ohio's special interests-first politics was provided by David Hess in a 1970 article for *The Nation*:

> For the past 75 years, starting with the long reign of kingmaker Mark Hanna, the state's politics have reeked of intrigue and manipulation. Voters have come to expect a certain dissembling, sometimes even mild corruption, from their political leaders. Candor and intellectual integrity are seldom rewarded; more often than not, they are greeted with suspicion and hostility.
>
> The state's most successful politicians—men like Hanna, John Bricker, Frank Lausche, James Rhodes—are those able to move most skillfully among the state's power blocks, wheeling and dealing for favors and concessions while deftly creating a public image of rectitude and incorruptibility. Such men are pragmatic, alert to opportunity, and only superficially committed to any ideology or grand design of government. (The late Sen. Robert A. Taft may have been an exception to the rule.) Such men accommodate themselves to the interests of big business, since great power resides in the directorates of Ohio's giant mills, banks and insurance companies.
>
> They also know that the conservative tone of the urban establishment is endorsed in rural Ohio by the stolid and prosperous farmers. . . .
>
> All of this, along with the rising conservatism of Ohio's trade and industrial unionists, produces a milieu in which human progressivism can hardly flourish. Materialism, social indifference, racial intolerance and economic discrimination are traits shared by both the working and the managerial classes.

Reporter Hess went on to charge that Ohio's major newspapers reinforce the beliefs and myths of the reigning establishment. "In Columbus and Cincinnati, the major papers have for years operated largely as extensions of the banking-industrial elite," Hess wrote, and he went on to characterize Cleveland newspaper management as "uncertain and effete" and to criticize even the generally respected newspapers of Toledo, Dayton, and Akron for hesitating to define social goals, even if they do engage in sporadic criticism of state policy. "There is a tradition, too, of chummy relationships between politicians and newspaper executives," Hess wrote, confirming a judgment we heard from many others in Ohio. Even critics of the establishment acknowledge, however, that in the past two decades the Ohio press has begun to report more fully and accurately on events and issues in the state's public life. The problem is that the speed of change is slow, and it may be years before a truly crusading and consistently independent press emerges in the state. In 1978 *Ohio Magazine* ran an article alleging "The Watchdog Is Dead." The evidence was rather compelling. Of the 98 newspapers printed in the state, 70 were found to be owned by newspaper chains, "many of which are absentee barons controlling their holdings from Illinois, New York, or any one of a raft of other states." In 31 counties, it was reported, chain-owned dailies were the only paper in the county, and in 47 cities they operated without competition. The chain ownership could be expected to sever some ties between local editors and the business establishment, but it was not likely to spur investigative reporting.

From time to time, the Ohio press questioned James Rhodes's personal integrity and indeed showed that he had used at least $54,000 of campaign funds for personal contributions. But the most probing questions about Rhodes came from outside the state. In 1969 *Life* magazine alleged that Rhodes had not only diverted campaign money to personal use but had run afoul of the Internal Revenue Service and acted questionably in commuting the life sentence of Mafia leader Thomas Licavoli when money was reportedly available to buy that convict's way out of prison. No illegal conduct on Rhodes's part was ever proven, but the faint aroma of suspected corruption was probably the decisive factor in his very narrow loss to Robert Taft, Jr., in the 1970 Republican primary for the U.S. Senate.

An unrelated statehouse loan scandal then paved the way for the election as governor of John J. Gilligan, a 49-year-old graduate of Notre Dame and one time teacher of literature at Xavier University in Cincinnati, a man about as unlike Rhodes as one could imagine. In his campaign, Gilligan not only refused to dodge the tax issue but actually insisted on repeating again and again that Ohio would need new taxes to solve its fiscal crunch and provide adequate services in the 1970s.

So it was that in March 1971, Gilligan recommended a $9.1 billion biennial budget for 1971–73, about 50 percent more than Rhodes's last $6.2 billion budget for 1969–71. (Eventually the legislature approved a 43 percent increase.) To finance the increase, largely aimed at bolstering state support of local schools, Gilligan proposed crossing the financial Rubicon: enactment of the first income tax in Ohio's history, applicable to both corporations and individuals. The rate would be steeply graduated and tied to property tax relief. Rounding up support for such a daring program was difficult in a legislature still under solid Republican control (54–45 in the house, 20–13 in the senate). But ironically, it was opposition from organized labor, dead set on tax reform that would put practically all the additional burden on businesses, that blocked a majority for the Gilligan tax package through most of 1971.

Finally, labor relaxed its opposition, and with some Republican help, the income tax passed. It was not a high tax: the maximum rate was 3.5 percent of income. Even with it, Ohio remained near or at the bottom of all states in its relative tax effort. But support for the local schools did rise 70 percent, to about 40 percent of school costs (compared to 28 percent at the end of Rhodes's second term). And there was some money for a "humanization" effort in the state's mental institutions, which had been among the most dismal in the nation.

In 1972 opponents placed a referendum question on the ballot to repeal the new income tax. But the voters, apparently aware of how important the new money was for local schools, defeated the repeal by a margin of better than 2–1. The tax was sustained, in fact, by a majority vote in every county in Ohio. The next year, Ohio voters by a 2–1 margin approved institution of a state lottery, with proceeds to go into the general fund. The lottery, like its counterparts in other states, did begin to produce revenue ($183 million between 1974 and 1978), but as elsewhere, that didn't mean a great deal in the larger state revenue picture since it accounted for only a half of one percent of total state and local revenues. In addition, a whole series of contract scandals arose in connection with the lottery—the kind of influence-buying almost inevitable, at some point, when states descend into the gambling business.

In substantive terms, the Gilligan record in four years as governor was exemplary. In addition to sharply increased appropriations for schools and human services, he created a state Environmental Protection Department, fought for and won a tough strip mine reclamation law, and instituted a consumer protection program. He weakened the hold of middle-aged white males on state boards and commissions by setting out consciously to include more representatives of organized labor, blacks, and women. He set a high moral tone by revealing his own personal finances and income tax returns and insisting that high-ranking associates do the same. Though his proposals were seriously weakened during legislative debate, he did try to get strong ethics and campaign spending laws enacted. (Ohio's ethics record is not very strong; for half a century, a law regulating lobbyists has been on the books, but in all that time only two persons have been convicted of violations.)

Where Gilligan failed—in a way that truncated his political career in 1974—was as a personal leader. A blunt Irishman and liberal-intellectual, often charming and personally generous, he also illustrated at times a brashness and low "boiling point" that got him into political hot water. He made a generous number of failures in staff selection. And when he ran for reelection in 1974 he found himself outmaneuvered and outfoxed by none other than James Rhodes, returning to the political wars in a bid for a third term. Rhodes had far more effective television commercials; his backslapping, garrulous manner contrasted with Gilligan's sometimes cold and aloof manner; he scored political points by attacking the "Gilligan gougers" for taxing "everything in Ohio that walks, crawls, or flies," without mentioning how low Ohio's tax effort still was compared to other states. Rhodes promised more roads, more bridges, a $1,000-a-year raise for all teachers—and no new taxes. Crippled by a low election day turnout in the normally heavily Democratic Cleveland area, Gilligan lost by a margin of only 11,488 votes out of 3,072,010 cast.

After his defeat, Gilligan interpreted the loss as "a personal repudiation of me," noting that the people seemed to have approved of his programs by electing strong Democratic majorities in both houses of the legislature. Gilligan later suggested that his mistake in the campaign had not been to be too candid and outspoken, as many critics said, but rather in not being candid enough. All his campaign advisers, he said, had told him "the one thing you couldn't talk about was the possibility of new taxes." But when he "trimmed" on that issue, Gilligan said, "everybody knew we weren't telling the whole truth. When people pressed me I became defensive, querulous, furious. I wanted so badly to win I fell into the oldest of the classic traps: 'We'll say enough and no more just to get elected, and then we'll be able to do all sorts of good things with a Democratic legislature.' And that was my own fault. In the end, there's nothing worse than a Democratic liberal who loses his belief that his vision of the world can move the electorate."

Whether Gilligan's analysis was correct or not, many intelligent Ohioans deeply regretted the election outcome. As editor Jim Fain wrote in the Dayton *Daily News*, "The defeat of Gov. John Gilligan was a sorry day for Ohio. No chief executive in a half century has done so much for this state. None ever accomplished so much in the face of such difficult odds. . . . In case you're wondering who was the real loser, let me remind you of Pogo's classic line: 'We have met the enemy, and he is us.' "

Four years later, in 1978, Ohioans had another opportunity to vote for a liberal Democrat in place of James Rhodes, and again they chose Rhodes. The Democrats' nominee was a formidable candidate: Richard Celeste, 40, the state's lieutenant governor (he had won by 217,000 votes while his running mate Gilligan lost to Rhodes four years before). Celeste had Cleveland-area ethnic roots, a record as a Yale honor graduate, Rhodes Scholar, and Peace Corps veteran. Celeste laid his campaign plans with ultimate care, assembled a dedicated, young staff, and avoided a primary with a relatively united Democratic party behind him. All that, however, was not enough to undo James Rhodes. The old master (he would be 73 by the end of the term he won) suggested Celeste would somehow double the state income tax, wrapped himself in the American flag in a well done final television commercial blitz, got crucial help from the Ohio Right to Life Committee—and offered Ohio voters the same old familiar platform and name. They bought again, by a margin of 47,536 votes. A crucial reason for Celeste's defeat, it turned out, was a heavy dropoff in the regular Democratic vote in such cities as Cleveland, Akron, Toledo, and Youngstown. Rhodes actually got 93,000 votes less than he had against Gilligan, but the general disaffection in Democratic ranks— probably more a revolt against the Carter administration, and general malaise, than active dislike of Celeste—hurt the Democrats even more.

Issueless Politics: the Bliss Phenomenon

Packed with cities, heavily industrialized and unionized, harboring large populations of East and South Europeans and blacks, Ohio has every reason to be a liberal Democratic state. Polls of basic party preference almost invariably show more Ohioans identifying with the Democrats than with the Republicans. Yet a Republican aristocracy of industrialists and small-city conservatives has dominated Ohio through most of the past century. Democratic presidential victories (as in three of FDR's four elections, or 1948, 1964, and 1976) were exceptions to the rule; with rare exceptions (such as 1958 and 1970), Republicans won the governorship unless the Democratic candidate was equally conservative. Between 1941 and the early 1970s, the legislature was under Republican control three times as often as it was controlled by the Democrats.

In the 1970s there were signs that the Republican-conservative domination was starting to disintegrate. Democrats won control of the house in 1972 and of the senate in 1974; by the 1976 election they had supposedly (but not actual) "veto-proof" majorities of 62–37 in the house and 21–12 in the senate. And in 1976, for the first time since the Civil War, they won control of the Ohio Supreme Court. We will examine the reasons for this Democratic surge, but it first seems necessary to ask what were the reasons for the long-standing dichotomy between the Democratic demography and Republican electoral performance of the state.

Geography was perhaps the most important. Ohio has no single dominating city akin to Detroit in Michigan, Chicago in Illinois, or New York City in New York. Cleveland, Ohio's largest city, casts only 7 percent of the statewide vote. Split asunder into many camps, the normally Democratic groups —labor unions, ethnic coalitions, blacks, intellectuals—lack a single population center in which they can coalesce and begin a bid for statewide dominance. Of the large cities, only Cleveland is dependably Democratic; the Republican business-elite, at least until the 1970s, monopolized the press and public forums of second- and third-ranking Columbus and Cincinnati. All but a handful of the smaller cities were Republican bastions under similar conservative domination and formed the backbone of GOP voting strength in Ohio. Generalizing about the smaller population centers, John Fenton observed:

> The small towns tended to be rather monolithic, with the business community holding sway. The Chamber of Commerce, Rotary Club and other business organizations were virtually the only groups that met and discussed issues. . . . The vice president of the bank was not a faceless, bloated plutocrat to workers in the small corn belt town that he was in the big city. On the contrary, he drank his morning cup of coffee in the same restaurant and often at the same table as the shoe clerk and the mechanic. In these face-to-face situations he presented the

business point of view concerning issues, and his word was accepted by the listeners as akin to law. After all, he was informed and articulate and a "good guy."

History was a second factor. The Republican party emerged from the Civil War years as the party of patriotism and the establishment; virtually the only Democratic counties for many decades were those that had voted for the Copperhead Democrat, Clement Vallandigham, in 1863. The people of these counties often found themselves labeled as "promoters of sedition" and "traitors," but they did hold together a semblance of a statewide party in years when the Democratic party almost disappeared as a functioning unit in states like Michigan, Minnesota and Wisconsin. Thus when the liberal-labor coalition of the New Deal and post-New Deal days appeared on the scene, the Democratic party was not an empty shell that it could seize with ease. Under the manner of a candidate like FDR, the disinherited of two generations—the descendants of Vallandigham's supporters and the foreign born, Catholic, and black population that suffered so much in the Depression—could be drawn together in effective majority coalition. But thereafter their ideological differences surfaced and division ensued; when the statewide Democratic party in 1968 finally summoned up its courage to back liberal John Gilligan against Frank Lausche in the party's Senate primary, the move was more resented by conservative rural Democrats than by ethnic party leaders of Lausche's own heritage.

Another factor in Democratic weakness over many years was the balkanization of the party leadership into separate urban enclaves across the state. Entrenched urban county organizations, especially the one headed for many years by Ray Miller in Cleveland, went their own way with little regard for the perennially anemic statewide Democratic organization; Miller in fact explicitly maintained that his organization had neither legal nor moral ties to a state Democratic party.

For decades, the fragmented condition of organized labor also led to Democratic weakness. Unlike Michigan's UAW, Ohio has no single dominant union; there are scores of unions across the state whose leaders have often preferred to make their own arrangements with political candidates, rather than working in concert. Nor have Ohio's labor leaders been "issue oriented" like those in Michigan; they were often described as a "bread-and-butter" lot for whom politics were a secondary consideration. Only when the interests of all of organized labor seemed in peril—as in 1958, when "right to work" was on the ballot, or in the Goldwater race of 1964—did all elements of organized labor pull together in a concerted campaign. (They won on both occasions.)

Starting in the late 1960s, however, the state AFL-CIO began to take on more of the coloration of its counterparts in other heavily industrialized states. Under leader Warren Smith, the AFL-CIO began to learn the effectiveness of money and computers and showed an organizational talent extending down to the precinct level. To crystallize issues, the state AFL-CIO began publication of a carefully researched, well designed monthly issues and politics pamphlet for all AFL-CIO members in the state; it was the best of its kind we have seen anywhere in the country and contributed significantly to labor unity and effectiveness in the political arena.

Ohio's most powerful unions include the Teamsters, Machinists, and Communications Workers (all spread out across the state); the Ohio Education Association (its 80,000 teacher members are considered by many Ohio's most politically powerful single union); the American Federation of State, County and Municipal Employees (which organized, among others, the bulk of state employees); the United Auto Workers (most numerous in Toledo, Cleveland, Cincinnati and Columbus); the Steelworkers (in Youngstown, Canton, Cleveland, Lorain and other towns), and the Rubber Workers (almighty in Akron).

If the Ohio Democrats have traditionally been a faulty alliance of the have-nots in society, exactly the opposite can be said of the Republicans. John Fenton has shown that a substantial number of the people voting Republican in Ohio today are the descendants of the first settlers of the ancient and all-but-forgotten boundaries of the Virginia Military District and Western Reserve areas, settled early in the past century by Whigs ·vho became Republicans and never thereafter altered their partisan preference. When modern industry came to northeast Ohio in the late 19th century—especially steel and oil refining, the latter in Cleveland under John D. Rockefeller's Standard Oil Company—it was Republicans who owned and managed the new enterprises. That colorful era was well depicted in *The Ohio Guide* prepared by the WPA Writers' Program:

> With industrialism, there arose a new type of politician, whose dealings gave rise to abuse, scandal and corruption. In the 1880s "boss government" flourished, and for a quarter of a century two men, Mark Hanna of Cleveland and George B. Cox of Cincinnati, each boss of his own city, despotically controlled the government of the state. Hanna was an ironmaster who went into politics to protect his business interests, and then made it his life work. Cox was a saloonkeeper. Both were millionaires. At first they quarreled, but later compromised, Hanna taking over the northern part of the state as his domain, and Cox the southern. They named Ohio's national representatives and officials.
>
> Their day was one of almost unchecked abuse, not only in politics but also in all fields of business. Exploitation was ruthless. . . . Hanna's spectacular career reached a climax in 1896 when his protege, William McKinley of Canton, was elected President of the United States. . . . At that time Hanna approached more closely than any other man in history to being "boss" of the United States.*

It is true that there were reform elements in Ohio. Democratic Senator George H. Pendleton, an associate of the prewar reformers of Cincinnati, wrote the Civil Service Act in 1882, and Republican Senator John Sherman, brother of the Civil War general, fathered the Sherman Antitrust Act in 1890. In the early 1900s a group of great reformers took control of Cleveland, Cincinnati, and Toledo from the corrupt bosses. The state government in the

---

* John Gunther's wonderfully quotable remark about Hanna: he "wore a President like McKinley practically as a watchfob."

1910–15 era enacted a number of significant reforms. Yet throughout, it was the Republicans who represented Ohio's privileged—and in 1920 nominated and elected one of their own, Warren G. Harding, as President.

The Republicans of the post-World War II era—businessmen small and large, suburbanites, small townsmen, well-to-do corn belt farmers, members of old families, and relative newcomers—shared one thing in common between themselves and their historic predecessors: they were "on top" and wanted to remain there. Since they were a numerical minority, they recognized the need to coalesce and indeed formed a superb statewide organization. At least until recently, there was a single county—Hamilton (Cincinnati) —which had the wealth and votes to control most Republican primaries, thus giving a focal point of political control and leadership. And finally, the Republicans succeeded because of the handsome bankrolling arranged for them by the Ohio business community.

The chief architect of postwar Republican organizational strength in Ohio was Ray C. Bliss, a man whose modest demeanor (that of a small-town banker, or the Akron insurance broker which he was) belied unusual intensity when it came to matters political. Bliss was called on to head the state GOP after a surprise Democratic sweep in 1948, coming into office as the party's first fulltime and salaried chairman. He had one condition for taking the job—that all fund raising be conducted by the party's independent finance committee, which operates like a political community chest. On only two occasions while Bliss was chairman did the big contributors interfere with party policy—in 1958, when they insisted (over what Bliss later claimed were his vehement opposition and warnings of defeat) on putting a "right-to-work" proposition on the Ohio ballot, and in 1964, when many of them supported the right-wing crusade to nominate Barry Goldwater for the Presidency. (Bliss feared an election day disaster if Goldwater were the nominee and was furious with Governor Rhodes for throwing the delegation to the Arizonan before the convention opened.) Both 1958 and 1964 brought sweeping Republican defeats in Ohio.

As state chairman, Bliss built the prototype of the successful modern state party organization (a model since copied in many states). A permanent full-time staff of about 16 people (and more at election times) was hired. Field representatives worked to foster party organizations in counties throughout the state. A well-oiled public relations department turned out releases favorable to Republicans and negative on Democrats and published the weekly *Ohio Republican News* to warm up the party faithful and propagandize others. Professional polls were ordered to gauge public opinion on issues and candidates. Widespread voter registration drives were undertaken. A speakers' bureau arranged for big-name GOP speakers at party affairs. Special attention was given to state legislative and congressional races, with major emphasis on candidate recruitment and behind-the-scenes work to avoid bloodletting primaries. A full research division kept newspaper morgue-type files. Other divisions took care of Young Republican, women's, and veterans' affairs. Bliss himself worked closely with Republican members of the legislature to develop party positions (especially when there was a Democratic governor.)

The one thing Bliss never, never did as a party chairman was to talk in public about issues. He was essentially a technician, to whom issues were a propaganda tool, not an end. His ideological neutrality assured him longevity on the job in Columbus and made him the natural choice (especially with behind-the-scenes backing from former President Eisenhower and former Treasury Secretary George Humphrey) to be chosen Republican National Chairman after the Goldwater debacle of 1964. Bliss performed fairly creditably in Washington, pouring oil on the troubled Republican waters, running a tight ship at GOP headquarters, but failing—perhaps because national issues were beyond his ken, perhaps because of the independent nature of the state party organs under him—to register the same measure of increased Republican vote he had been able to accomplish in the smaller world of Ohio. President Nixon ungratefully fired him shortly after the 1968 election.

Bliss was the man who engineered Senator Robert Taft's triumphant reelection victory in 1950, when organized labor was determined to defeat the "Mr. Republican" of the U.S. Senate. He was also given credit for the surprise victory of Richard Nixon in Ohio in the 1960 presidential race. But as Fenton pointed out, "Bliss was an effect of a well-knit party rather than a cause."

The Democrats' rise in the 1970s had its roots in the late 1960s, especially a hard-won victory by Gilligan over Lausche in the 1968 Democratic Senate primary. That vote seemed to signal an historic repudiation of the conservative rural bloc in the Democratic party. Gilligan was to lose the general election for the Senate that year to a very popular Republican, William Saxbe. But he used his primary victory, building toward his eventually successful gubernatorial bid in 1970, to take control of the state party apparatus and turn it into a far more aggressive, youth-oriented, socially conscious organ. By capturing many state offices in 1970, the Democrats took control of the Apportionment Board, which set the new district lines for state legislators to the Democrats' advantage. Then, with a well staffed operation utilizing the latest in computers and political analysis, the Democrats started their successful campaign to take control of the Ohio legislature. The previously debt-ridden state Democratic organization began to garner campaign contributions in significant quantities and to coax organized labor into fuller and fuller election time cooperation. All of this remained—despite Gilligan's 1974 defeat—a key factor, for instance, in Jimmy Carter's narrow victory over Gerald Ford in Ohio in the 1976 presidential race. (Carter won the state by a slim margin of 11,116 votes, just a tenth of a percentage point ahead of Ford.)

Ironically, the remnant of what some called a "very strong, street-corner Protestant vote" in many of Ohio's smaller cities and its rural hinterland, especially in the southern part of the state, helped the Democrats with several of their victories of the '70s. It helped former astronaut John Glenn win all 88 Ohio counties in a successful race for the U.S. Senate in 1974; it was a major ingredient in Carter's 1976 presidential primary victory in Ohio over Arizona's Rep. Morris Udall; it helped Carter defeat Ford that autumn.

The Democratic resurgence was eased by fierce internecine conflict in the vaunted Republican state organization, first as a result of the bitter Taft-Rhodes Senate primary fight, and even more particularly the reeking scandal that erupted in May 1970. It was revealed that several leading Republicans —including Rhodes himself, Auditor Roger Cloud, State Treasurer John D. Herbert, and state Sen. Robin Turner—had received thousands of dollars in campaign contributions from Crofters, Inc., a year-old Columbus firm that arranged for private companies to receive hundreds of thousands of dollars in loans from the state treasury. Crofters was headed by former state tax commissioner Gerald A. Donahue, a prominent Republican operative and confidant of Rhodes. The loans, which included $4 million to the Four Seasons Nursing Home Centers of Oklahoma City and $8 million to Denver's King Enterprises (a firm which was seeking to shore up Bernard Cornfeld's International Mutual Fund empire), were determined by a subsequent state investigation to have been illegal because they exceeded the state's statutory limit for commercial investments and did not satisfy state risk requirements.

In the imbroglio which ensued, the Republican State Committee publicly repudiated Herbert's 1970 candidacy for attorney general and Turner's candidacy for state treasurer. Both men, however, refused to withdraw from the already nominated state ticket. The state committee gave a vote of confidence to Cloud, the party's nominee for governor, who claimed his contribution from Crofters had been given to an aide and returned when he learned of it. The scandal, however, was too much for the GOP to overcome, contributing to the Gilligan election for governor that year. (Commenting on the feuds within the state GOP, Gilligan's campaign manager, Mark Shields, could gleefully joke about "civil war in the leper colony.") In time, of course, the Republicans recovered from the jolt; their efficient organization continued; they won a reasonable share of elections. But the image of the statewide Republican organization both managerially adept and totally honest had been irreparably shattered.

Profile of a Legislature

An inveterate reader of state newspapers is struck again and again by the superficial and uninformative nature of reporting on the state legislatures which make so many vital decisions about the rules of American society, the services people will receive, the taxes they will pay. In many states one discovers that the local press had never stepped back to review the major power bases in the state legislature, the changing nature of membership, the real impact of the reapportionments. An exception was a fine series of articles on "How the Ohio Legislature Really Works," written in 1969 by Richard Zimmerman and Robert Burdock of the Cleveland *Plain Dealer*, from which some key paragraphs are quoted:

The General Assembly is made up of four houses—the Senate, House, the lobbyists and the press corps.

The most important work of the General Assembly is done in the Top of the Center restaurant, behind the closed doors of the Neil House, in the bar of the Columbus Sheraton, in closed meetings of the majority party leadership, in the governor's office—and only sometimes in the open committee rooms.

In fairness, it would be said that the Ohio General Assembly is probably one of the better state legislatures. The leaders of both parties are, within a framework that existed long before they came to Columbus, responsible and honorable men. The members, for the most part, believe themselves to be serving the public good, insofar as practical politics permit.

Gone are the days when lobbyists openly paid off legislators in cash in the halls of the Statehouse after they had cast a "right" vote. Gone are the days when "Boss" Hanna arrogantly sat in his Neil House suite and pulled the strings of power, perverting the legislative process as drunken legislators reeled among brass spittoons.

But not gone is the tremendous power of the special interest lobbyists who lurk in the legislative halls. Not gone are the log-rolling and the pork-barreling which waste millions of dollars of tax money in the home districts of particularly powerful committee chairmen. Not gone is a governor who will buy votes with promises of public works projects.

Many if not most of the more complex omnibus bills come directly from Columbus-based lobbyists representing trade, business and professional associations. The insurance industry, for example, practically dictates the laws that are supposed to control that industry. The same can be said of the banking industry, the utilities, savings and loan organizations.

The 33 members of the Senate include 13 lawyers, four educators, two insurance agents, two union representatives, a couple of "public relations" men on payrolls of companies with vested interests in legislative action, a strip mine operator, plus a variety of assorted businessmen. Most legislators have other sources of income which at one time or another will put them in a conflict of interest with their elected positions. . . .

There are only 1,500 to 2,000 corporate members of the Ohio Manufacturers Association, but its influence is tremendous. It represents both big and small firms which make up the huge industrial complex of Ohio. The Ohio Trucking Association has only 800 company members, but it represents a billion-dollar industry with significant local influence, both political and economic. The Ohio Education Association, on the other hand, has 85,000 dues-paying members and maintains a large and efficient staff in its own building in Columbus.

When Democrats are at the helm, labor sups well at the captain's table. (But) as a constantly potent force in Ohio politics, organized labor is only a myth.

The coalition of Republican legislators and business-oriented trade associations is a formidable power structure. As a result, social reforms and needed tax revisions in Ohio are not forthcoming.

The writers then went on to review some lobbyists' tactics, including getting undesirable bills introduced so that they can later get credit with the employers for killing the legislation, or on the other side, "fetcher bills" introduced by unscrupulous legislators to force lobbies to entertain them—or sometimes as out-and-out money shakedowns.

A decade later coauthor Zimmerman had gone to Washington to represent the *Plain Dealer*, but Burdock was still in Columbus—now as publisher of a new, monthly glossy—*Ohio Magazine*. Still keeping a careful eye on the legislature, Burdock told us that the evaluation of 1969 was still substantially correct. The Ohio Manufacturers Association, he said, continued to be the best financed lobby in Columbus, with the largest staff; the Retail Merchants Council was proving very effective, as was the Ohio Bankers Association; through its friends on key committees, the insurance industry was still writing the laws under which it operates in the state. The public utilities, Burdock said, "own the place—they can assemble more money, more influence and votes than anyone—even the teachers." But organized labor, Burdock noted, was showing more political savvy and legislative strength than it had previously.

Even with a Democratic-controlled legislature, Columbus watchers report, the power of business remains formidable. And labor has suffered some significant defeats through inability to enact into law a collective bargaining bill for public employees and the Republicans' successful effort, in a 1977 referendum, to repeal a law which would have allowed election day registration of voters.

There are a number of public interest groups active on the state level—Common Cause, the League of Women Voters, the Ohio Public Interest Campaign, and the Citizens League of Greater Cleveland. Occasionally such groups score successes in lobbying the legislature. But when they come up against major business or labor interests, their scorecard has not been impressive. In 1979–80, the Ohio Public Interest Campaign drew up and gathered 97,000 signatures for an "Ohio Fair Tax Initiative" to deprive corporations of their "direct use" sales tax exemptions, forbid tax abatements, and provide "circuit breaker" tax relief for homeowners, renters, and family farmers. It was claimed the initiative would add $1.3 billion to the 1980–81 budget for schools and public services. Predictably, the Ohio Manufacturers Association tried to prevent the measure even getting to the ballot, mounting some 14 lawsuits against it. All lost in the courts, however, and the measure appeared headed for the ballot.

According to Blair Kost, director of the Cleveland Citizens League, the reapportionment of the legislature effected in the 1960s did tend to produce younger, more intelligent, and more ambitious legislators, and especially increased suburban representation. "The suburbs are now the most powerful bloc, dealing with either the center cities or the cornstalk brigade from the rural areas to form a majority on specific issues," Kost said. While rural and conservative voices are still strong, moderation is more the order of the day.

The reapportioned legislature, Kost said, hired more staff, set up additional work space for legislators and secretaries, voted annual sessions, and instituted centralized bill drafting and a regular research position for each standing committee—all steps recommended by the League.

The Congressional Contingent

No Ohioan of modern times has enjoyed national prominence akin to that of Senator Robert A. Taft; but for the sudden emergence of Dwight D. Eisenhower on the political scene in the early 1950s, Taft would most probably have won the Republican presidential nomination in 1952 and possibly the presidency. Taft would have been the eighth Ohio President, following in the footsteps of Grant, Harrison, Hayes, Garfield, McKinley, his own father William Howard Taft, and Warren G. Harding. Despite his general conservatism, Taft had a progressive record on such issues as aid to education and housing, and no one ever doubted the honesty and integrity of this scion of the aristocratic Cincinnati family. Few legislators of our time have had a more supreme grasp of American law and done their legislative homework more thoroughly. Taft's most brilliant legislative contribution was doubtless the Taft-Hartley Labor Management Relations Act of 1947, the basic labor law of the postwar years. (In retrospect, it is amusing to recall the fury with which the unions fought Taft-Hartley, calling it the "slave labor act" and every other evil name. In reality, American labor has done quite well under the legislation.)

Taft's judgment in other fields, however, is dimmed by the perspective of history. He was fiercely isolationist before World War II, voting against the draft and lend-lease; he was also a bitter enemy of public power development. After the war, he voted against the Marshall Plan and favored a "Fortress America" in the early 1950s. Taft's sobriquet of "Mr. Republican" is really a reference to the pre-New Deal and pre-Wendell Willkie Republicanism that lingered on in the Midwest after the rest of America had accepted its passing. Perhaps the official demise came with Taft's own death in 1953.

Snowy-haired Senator (and onetime Governor) John Bricker of Ohio was once considered a major national figure and actually was selected by Thomas E. Dewey as his vice presidential running mate in 1944. But compared to Taft, Bricker was the shallowest of politicians. He left no legacy on the national scene other than the now all-but-forgotten Bricker Amendment to restrict the President's treaty-making powers. (Interestingly, some suggest that if the Bricker Amendment had passed, the President would have lacked authority to negotiate the SEATO treaty and the Vietnam war might well have been averted.)

Bricker was beaten in 1958 by the irascible, unpredictable Stephen Young, an aging Populist-style Democrat who won some renown during his two Senate terms by refusing to endure abusive letters from constituents, firing back salvos in kind.* In 1959 Young became the first member of Congress publicly to reveal his outside income and securities. He retired from the Senate in 1971.

William Saxbe, the Republican who succeeded to Lausche's Senate seat in 1969, was an even more startling switch from the old industry-satrap style of Ohio Senator. A shrewd country "squire" from a one-stoplight country crossroad called Mechanicsburg, Saxbe had a rustic air about him—chewing tobacco from a red-and-white striped package of Union Workman and spicing his conversation with barnyard expletives and down-home metaphors. In Washington, Saxbe made peace issues his overriding concern, taking a leading role in the fight against the Nixon Administration's antiballistic missile program. He called Vice President Agnew a "witch hunter" and fought President Nixon's nomination of Clement Haynsworth to the Supreme Court. He once described AFL-CIO President George Meany as "a crotchety and rude old man" and called Nixon aides "Bob" Haldeman and John Ehrlichman "Nazis." Of Nixon's protestations of innocence in Watergate, Saxbe said: "He reminds me of the fellow who played the piano in a brothel for 20 years and insisted he didn't know what was going on upstairs." Not long after, a desperate Richard Nixon, in the wake of the "Saturday night massacre" and Elliot Richardson's resignation, turned to Saxbe to be Attorney General. When impeachment proceedings began and Nixon asked the Justice Department to handle his defense, Saxbe flatly refused. Under Gerald Ford, he served as U.S. Ambassador to India. And then he returned to his law practice and farm in Ohio and refused to run for public office again—to the disappointment of a public which had come to treasure his salty independence and public irreverence.

Ohio's Senators in the late '70s were two old rivals in Democratic primary battles—John Glenn, the Marine who was the first American to orbit the earth, on February 20, 1962, and wealthy Cleveland businessman Howard Metzenbaum. Metzenbaum had been the surprise winner over Glenn in the 1970 Democratic Senate primary, only to lose to Robert Taft, Jr., that fall. Gilligan appointed Metzenbaum to the Senate to succeed Saxbe in 1974, but Glenn, a much savvier politician than he'd been in 1970, won the nomination and that Senate seat. Metzenbaum, undaunted, ran again in 1976 and defeated Taft, a thoughtful and pleasant man never able to match the brilliance or political stature of his late father. In the Senate, Metzenbaum lines up predictably with labor and the liberal Democratic wing; Glenn votes a more middle-of-the-road line and has proven a quietly competent Senator. In 1976 he was one of the men Jimmy Carter considered tapping as his running mate.

Through wily redistricting and able candidate recruitment, Ohio Republicans maintained overwhelming control—usually by a 3-1 margin—of Ohio's

---

* To a Cleveland resident who wrote that he looked in the obituary page every day hoping to find the Senator's name, Young, then in his late seventies, wrote: "I am feeling better than you would look if you were to take me on."

23 or 24 U.S. House seats for a quarter century after World War II. By the 1978 elections, however, the Democrats had righted the balance to significant degree: the Republicans still led, but by a more modest margin of 13 seats to the Democrats' 10. The Ohio delegation has harbored its share of mediocrities, but several from each party have risen above the mass. Some have been skilled power brokers, like conservative Clarence J. Brown of rural west central Ohio, who led Republicans on the House Rules Committee, or Michael J. Kirwan, the blunt old Irishman from Youngstown who parlayed his two positions—as chairman of the House Appropriations Subcommittee on Public Works, which dispenses rivers, harbors, and other public works projects for virtually every district of the country, and the Democratic Congressional Campaign Committee, which apportions election funds for Democratic Congressmen—into a position of influence almost unparalleled on Capitol Hill up to his death in 1970. "Kirwan is almost a dictator when it comes to dispensing favors and funds for Congressmen's pet projects," the Cleveland *Plain-Dealer* once commented; others in the press nicknamed him the "Prince of Pork."

But of all the power brokers (and abusers), few if any rivaled Wayne Hays, the man who represented a poor southwestern Ohio district for close to 30 years and rose to the twin pinnacles of power—chairman of the House Administration Committee and of the House Democratic Campaign Committee. Hays wheeled, dealed, placed other Congressmen in his political debt, bullied opponents, fought election law reform, and as the Washington *Post* finally revealed in 1976, placed a mistress (Elizabeth Ray) on his committee payroll. The scandal forced Hays to resign from Congress, a ruined man— though, to general amazement, he was back in the political wars two years later, winning election to the Ohio house.

Other Ohio Congressmen of note include two Cleveland Democrats— Charles A. Vanik, member of the powerful Ways and Means Committee and a leading fighter for antipollution programs to save Lake Erie, and Louis Stokes, brother of former Mayor Carl Stokes, first black member of the Appropriations Committee and chairman of the special House committee investigating the assassinations of Martin Luther King, Jr., and Robert F. Kennedy. Democrat Thomas L. Ashley of Toledo became one of the House's leading experts on housing and national growth policy. Akron's John F. Seiberling voted for Richard Nixon's impeachment on the Judiciary Committee; he is also an Interior Committee member and respected environmentalist. Republican Charles W. Whalen of Dayton, a former economics professor, became an antimilitary maverick and opponent of the Vietnam war and was known for an exceptionally liberal record for a member of his party. He retired from Congress in 1978. On the far right side of Ohio's House delegation, John M. Ashbrook became so upset with President Nixon's overtures to Communist China and embracing of wage and price controls that he mounted a little-noted campaign against Nixon for the 1972 presidential nomination.

Of all the men Ohio has sent to Congress in recent times, none exercised such vital leadership as soft-spoken, diminutive William M. McCulloch, ranking Republican on the House Judiciary Committee. McCulloch was a product of the flat, rich farmlands of western Ohio, some of the most conservative territory in the U.S.A., and for most of his career (1947–73) he was an obscure Congressman whose voting record reflected the cautious conservatism of his constituents. But in the 1960s, McCulloch became an articulate and obstinate fighter to win for American blacks the basic rights he saw as theirs under the Constitution. McCulloch's role in conciliating various proposals for reform, in drafting and then winning the essential Republican support for the civil rights acts of 1964, 1965, and 1968, was essential to their passage. Fighting for extension of the 1965 voting rights act over opposition of his own party's administration in 1969, McCulloch said that the legislation provided "for the thrust of black power in the best tradition of America—at the polling place." Ironically, few of the millions of American blacks to benefit from the legislation McCulloch made possible will have ever heard of the unassuming figure from the Ohio farmlands for whom constitutional and human rights were more important than normal political advantage. Because of ill health, McCulloch retired from Congress in 1973.

Cleveland, Now

> *Cleveland has about as much charm as an automobile cemetery or the inside of a dynamo.*
>
> —*John Gunther*, Inside U.S.A. (1947)

> *Cleveland . . . is the ethnic family trapped in a flat and going to the dogs. . . . It is neighborhood after neighborhood after neighborhood. It is more suburbia than a bulldozer could love. Cleveland is industry: huge complexes that create steel and a Central Avenue that shouts. Cleveland is young, old, middle-aged, and everything else. Cleveland is Lake Erie and those who, from one year to the next, never see the lake at all. Cleveland is the Catholic nun, the train station bum, a thousand housewives, and on that corner the man dressed as a woman. Cleveland is Euclid Avenue, a neighbor named Krtchmareck. Cleveland is expressways and narrow alleys. . . .*
>
> *Yet somewhere in this—between the Cleveland Tower and the melancholy neighborhoods and the pleasing suburbs decked out in early American Formica and the factories and all the people these items feast upon—exists the dream, the beauty, and the anger that is Cleveland. Because Cleveland is much more than an empty terminal lobby, where on days the wind blows cold, old men assemble, waiting to die. Cleveland is not waiting to die.*
>
> —*Dick Perry*, Ohio: A Personal Portrait of the 17th State (1969)

"What is the difference between Cleveland and the Titanic?"
"I give up."
"Cleveland has a better orchestra."
                                                    —*Popular joke* (1978)

"Cleveland has the problems of an old industrial city. It also has the most acrimonious government in Christendom."
                                                    —*Columnist George Will* (1978)

Two million Americans—one out of every 100 residents of the nation —live today in what is called the Cleveland metropolitan area,* a megalopolitan mix of factories, warehouses, docks, high rises, freeways, tenements, bungalows, ramblers, shopping centers, schools and universities, churches, parks, and turgid rivers that stretch some 45 miles along the shores of Lake Erie and for an average of 10 miles inland. Cleveland's first reason for being was as a modest port city, spurred to growth from 1832 onward when it began to receive goods shipped on the Erie Canal, that great man-made transportation invention of the 19th century. Then, after the Civil War, big industry came: steelmaking after the first iron ore shipment arrived from the Lake Superior region in 1852, oil refining dating from 1862 when John D. Rockefeller began the operations that would lead to that monopoly to end all monopolies, the Standard Oil Company.

For as long as any person now living can recall, Cleveland has been a brawny producer, handler, and shipper of industrial commodities. From its factories pour immense quantities of iron and steel, machine tools, industrial equipment, and motor vehicles. Cleveland still refines vast quantities of oil and is deep into petrochemicals; it is a global leader in iron ore management and supply; the printing and publishing industries furnish income, and it is even alleged that the area leads the world in hothouse tomatoes. But the city's manufacturing employment, which hit a peak in 1969, began to decline precipitously in the 1970s; by 1978, 65,000 blue collar production jobs or 20 percent, had faded away. Some analysts viewed the blue collar job loss as part of an irreversible American trend away from industrial production, and the Greater Cleveland Growth Association even launched a major campaign emphasizing the white-collar side of the city. Critics asked, however, whether Cleveland's business leaders had any concern for the "losers" in this economic evolution.

But the industrial loss was only part of a picture of intense malaise that Cleveland presented to the world by the late 1970s. Assessed real estate values were declining even during a period of national inflation of land values. The confrontation between ethnic whites and the ever growing black population seemed almost as intense as it had been in the riot-torn '60s. About a fifth

---

* Cuyahoga County (population 1,559,471), containing Cleveland itself, represents the lion's share of the metropolitan area population, but sometime in the 1950s suburban Cuyahoga surged ahead of the city proper in population, a trend not likely to be reversed in the lifespan of anyone today.

of all families were receiving some income under the AFDC welfare program. Per capita income was well below the state and national average. Retailing was oozing out to the suburbs and suburban-center city income differentials were increasing. Finally, a decade of fiscal sleight-of-hand topped by a roaring political dispute between the power establishment and a pugnacious young mayor out of the ethnic wards made Cleveland the first major city to default on its fiscal obligations since the Great Depression.

Yet as real as all those problems were (and we shall return more fully to the political wars later on), the crises that made Cleveland a national laughingstock masked a picture of economic strength and significant urban revival. Cuyahoga County and regional authorities, far more stable politically than the city, had taken over a broad range of services once under the city's purview, ranging from the zoo, sewer, and transit systems to hospitals, stadium, and major parks. Trying to make the best out of the obvious transition away from manufacturing, the city's promoters were beginning to talk much more aggressively about Cleveland's status—and future potential—as a corporate headquarters city and potential as "an international center of advanced services" for its corporate giants. By stretching to include the big rubber companies in Akron, 35 miles away, the city can claim to be home of 39 of the top 1,000 U.S. corporations, including such heavies as TRW, Republic Steel, Standard Oil (Ohio), White Consolidated Industries, Eaton, and Hanna Mining. Only New York and Chicago have more corporate headquarters. There were some corporate desertions in the '70s—Addressograph-Multigraph and the Harris Corp., for instance, announced plans to shift their headquarters to Sunbelt states—but in general the corporate base was holding firm. Downtown Cleveland, in fact, had a bigger work force than at any time in its history because of the corporate offices and the ancillary services they demanded, ranging from law, accounting, engineering, and finance to research and computer centers.

While the very thought of Cleveland conjures up for many vistas of dingy mills and smokestacks, the city does offer other amenities: an "emerald necklace" of fine parks which ring the city's periphery (though in contrast to those county-run parks, many of the city's own are in a sad state of disrepair); a beautiful, prestigious, and richly endowed art museum, considered one of the nation's finest; the world-famous Cleveland Orchestra, directed until his death in 1970 by George Szell, in more recent years by Lorin Maazel; a public library system, blessed with its own special taxing district, more heavily used than almost any other in America; professional opera and ballet companies; a renewed and thriving theater district around Playhouse Square; and top professional sports teams—the Indians (American League baseball), the Browns (National League football) and the Cavaliers (National Basketball Association). And the city has a prestige university, Case Western Reserve, which resulted from the merger of Case (known for its scientific disciplines) and Western Reserve (liberal arts, medicine, engineering, and law).

First to settle the city were New Englanders, then Irish to dig the canal and build the railroads, then more Easterners, and from the 1870s onward, a flood of Germans, Irish, Welsh, French, Scots, Bohemians, Jews, Poles, Slovenes, Lithuanians, Hungarians, Rumanians, Italians, Czechs, and Russians to man the hearths, refine the oil, and build, build, build the city. At one time three-quarters of Cleveland's people were foreign born; the descendants of these people, called the "cosmos," still fill almost every block of Cleveland's West Side with well-defined little ghettos, each preserving its own customs, languages, religions, foods, and costumes. Cleveland offers, for instance, the only Rumanian folk art museum this side of Rumania; the ethnic festival days are too numerous to count. No less than 63 separate ethnic groups have been identified on the West Side; often their children move out to Parma or other working class suburbs while the old folks stay on in the city to protect their hard-earned homes and vote against new taxes. Except for a couple of black enclaves of many decades' standing, the West Side is all white (and determined to stay that way); block after block of the old wood frame houses and narrow yards march on in what seems to an outsider dreary procession, the residential monotony relieved only by corner stores and markets, churches of a hundred faiths, and a few dismal old fortesslike structures called schools. There is intense local pride in many of these communities, however. And the West Side also harbors Ohio City, in recent years the scene of substantial resurgence by young families (many of them professionals) buying late 19th-century Victorian, Colonial, and Greek revival homes. Ohio City has a large and illustrious farmers' market, a Neighborhood Housing Service performing small wonders in helping low-income people renovate their homes with low-interest loans, and Cleveland's best parochial high school (St. Ignatius). Cleveland has not had the amount of neighborhood revival noted in many East Coast cities, but Ohio City is a symbol of the potential for the future.

The great preponderance of residential neighborhoods on Cleveland's East Side are as black as those on the West Side are white. Between the two there is the natural barrier of the Cuyahoga River, twisting filthily through center city and lined by warehouses, terminals, and railroad tracks. Blacks have lived in Cleveland since early in the 19th century, but the great black influx began with World War I and continued until the late 1960s. Gradually the blacks forced the cosmos out of old neighborhoods like Hough (scene of a cataclysmic riot in 1966) and Glenville (where black militants and police staged a celebrated shoot-out in 1968). The visitor to Hough today sees hundreds of deserted buildings, refuse-strewn lawns, streetfront churches, metal grills on store windows, and evidence of the revival in the wake of the 1966 upheaval: community development centers, health and day-care centers, and one of the Great Society's revival efforts—the $3.4 million Martin Luther King Plaza, with stores (some boarded up) and apartments atop them.

There are few pockets of true racial integration among Cleveland's neighborhoods. One of the exceptions, however, is on the East Side: the community of Buckeye, once known as the largest Hungarian settlement outside of Budapest. Heavy black incursions led to ugly confrontations in the late '60s: blacks abducted and raped a white woman, for instance, and whites shot up and bombed the homes and businesses of black newcomers. But in

1970 the Buckeye Area Development Corporation emerged out of the old Hungarian Tradesmen's Club, persuaded the police to establish an outreach center which nipped vigilantes, created a skills center for the unemployed, and was cited as a major reason for selection of Buckeye for the house-to-house rehabilitation program of the Neighborhood Housing Service. Merchants along Buckeye Road, long famed for its Hungarian meat markets, pastry shops, and restaurants, began to restore their dilapidated red brick buildings, many with architecturally interesting turrets and balconies, to their former old world village charm. The political ferment for constructive change was kept alive by an integrated, militant organization, the Buckeye-Woodland Community Congress.

Massive population shifts in the postwar era set the stage for Cleveland's racial outbreaks of the '60s, busing tensions in the '70s, and efforts to create a more satisfactory modus vivendi between the two races. Between 1950 and 1970, the population of Cleveland proper declined from 914,808 to 750,903, a loss of more than 150,000. But what is most fascinating about the net loss of population is that more than 300,000 whites fled the city during the 20-year period, while at the same time the black population rose about 100 percent (to 287,841). In 1970 the city was 39 percent black, by 1976 42 percent; no one could say for sure whether the black share of Cleveland's population would continue to rise or level off because of possible white middle-to-upper-income return to the city, eventual stabilization of the cosmo neighborhoods, or the flow of black people to suburban towns (East Cleveland, directly abutting Glenville, in particular). A key but not often articulated problem for Cleveland's blacks was the fact that they were losing a substantial number of their leaders to the suburbs.

The overwhelming population fact of the '70s was the rapid overall population decline of the city. By 1978 the population was estimated to have dropped to 600,000. That meant that since 1970, a fifth of the city's entire population had left—almost as severe a population loss as Cleveland suffered in the entire previous 20-year period.

A chief irony of Cleveland geography is that the swank suburbs lie to the east of the city; the well-to-do white commuters to center Cleveland must pass through the black population belt on their way to downtown and back home each day. Shaker Heights remains the most famous of Cleveland's upper crust suburbs, though in fact it has accepted, with remarkable success, a significant minority of Jews and blacks in recent years. The most exclusive, posh suburbs now lie further east of the city: Pepper Pike, Hunting Valley, Gates Mills, and others.

Cleveland's center remains its Public Square, dominated by the grim old 52-story Terminal Tower. The square harbors a ghastly war memorial and is the hub from which the great avenues—Euclid, Superior, and Ontario—spoke out to all directions save north, a course which would soon land one in Lake Erie. For more than a generation, center city atrophied; then in the 1960s came the $250 million Erieview urban renewal project between the

Public Square and the lake. In 1973 Ada Louise Huxtable of the New York *Times* visited Cleveland and took dead aim at the 163-acre Erieview project. It "stands as a kind of monument to everything that was wrong with urban renewal thinking in America in the 1960s," she wrote. "There is a large, abortive plan by the architect I.M. Pei, long on desolate, overscaled spaces, destructive of cohesive urbanism, and defiantly antihuman." Huxtable described "bland new buildings stamped out of a common commercial mold," surrounding "a huge, bleak, near-empty plaza with a complete set of nonworking fountains and drained pools." Erieview symbolized the problem of modern downtown Cleveland: a relatively busy world of office workers during the daytime; a rapid exodus around 5 P.M.; a virtual ghostland at nighttime.

Around 1970, however, a construction boom began along Superior Avenue and other sites in the city's core, including banks and corporate headquarters buildings, luxury apartment buildings, government buildings, and the like. A kind of Bohemia—renovated lofts and warehouses, antique and ethnic arts and crafts shops, waterfront restaurants and taverns—sprang up in the Flats, an old industrial district beside the river. A multimillion-dollar revitalization of Public Square began with a symbolic tree planting in 1977. Euclid Avenue, the city's premier shopping and business district, was the subject of an imaginative proposed plan by a New York-based nonprofit group, Project for Public Spaces, to broaden the sidewalks dramatically, ban parking altogether and private autos most hours of the day, and create a limited transit mall more hospitable to pedestrians. (In addition to top department stores, Euclid Avenue is home of a multi-storied Arcade built in the 1890s, a charming precursor of the less charming luxury retail malls of more recent times.)

Finally, the prospect of reborn Cleveland nightlife emerged in Playhouse Square, several blocks down Euclid Avenue from Public Square. Earlier in the 20th century, Marcus Loew, Edward Albee, and other entertainment kings had constructed a group of splendid art deco theaters there, offering such stars as Houdini, Lynn Fontanne, and Judy Garland. But the area declined precipitously until only one of the theaters was still in use; two of them almost succumbed to the wrecker's ball (to be replaced by a parking lot) in 1972. But a dedicated group of citizens worked to save the area; "big name" entertainers were brought in at cut rates; two shows ("The All Night Strut" and "City Lights") were offered absolutely free. Clevelanders from all walks of life began to flock to the area, drawing nearly 500,000 patrons during 1977. The Cuyahoga County government stepped in to purchase the Loew's building, housing the Ohio and State Theatres, leasing the theaters back to the nonprofit Playhouse Square Foundation. Formerly dormant cafes and restaurants began to prosper; plans were begun for full-scale retail and hotel redevelopment at Playhouse Square to complement the arts renaissance.

Several blocks beyond Playhouse Square is the campus of the new Cleveland State University, which brought Cleveland its first public higher education in the '60s and had 40,000 students by the mid-'70s. The other area of principal growth was University Circle, home of the art and natural history museums, Severance Hall (where the Cleveland Orchestra plays), parks and gardens, and Case Western Reserve, a commuter school which went through hard financial times in the '70s as it struggled to become a university of national stature.

Few world cities ever so despoiled their natural environment, or moved so close to choking on their own pollutants, as Cleveland. The symbol of this was the slimy, chocolate-brown Cuyahoga River, bubbling with subsurface gases, filled with phenols, oils, and acids from the steel mills and refineries along its banks. (Among the denizens of the Cuyahoga's downtown "flats" area are Republic Steel, U. S. Steel, Sherwin-Williams Paint, Standard Oil, and National Sugar Refining.) The Cuyahoga, indeed, was the only river of the U.S.A. to be officially declared a fire hazard; one June day of 1969, its oil-slicked waters burst into flames and burned with such intensity that two railroad bridges that span it were nearly destroyed. The Federal Water Pollution Control Administration declared that "the lower Cuyahoga has no visible life, not even low forms such as leeches and sludge worms that usually thrive on wastes."

By the late 1970s, however, the Cuyahoga River seemed to have gained something of a new lease on life. Under the gun of federal and local anti-pollution rules, the steel firms and other industries had installed relatively effective water treatment plants; the oil slicks had disappeared and some species of fish were even returning. Federally funded sewage treatment facilities helped as well; by 1983, some $430 million worth of improvements to three treatment plants were scheduled for completion, and a $100 million large interceptor sewer was to be finished by 1980. Over many years, the city's archaic sanitary storm sewer system had overflowed into sewer mains in heavy rains, discharging untreated household wastes into the much afflicted Cuyahoga. There were also reports of notable improvement in Cleveland's air quality, fifth worst in the U.S. in the late '60s as a result of the cumulative assault of steel mills, power plants, building furnaces, and automobiles. Particulates in the air decreased about 50 percent in 10 years, largely as a result of $600 million worth of air pollution equipment installed by industries in the eight-county region surrounding the city.

There was even hope that Cleveland might reverse, at least in part, the egregious planning errors which have so sadly separated it from the view of the lake which first gave it birth. In sharp contrast to Chicago, which preserved inviolate the view to Lake Michigan across open parkland, Cleveland allowed its access to Lake Erie to be cluttered by the nation's first lakeside expressway and by a wide swatch of industrial no man's land dotted with power plants and junk-strewn empty lots. Few American cities have shown such a callous disregard for their greatest natural asset. But in 1977 the city finally reached agreement with the state of Ohio to transfer ownership of the lakefront parks, yacht clubs, and marinas to the state government, which was preparing to spend millions on improvements. An official of the Cleveland Foundation predicted that the park redevelopment would stimulate development of adjoining private property; "in 25 years Cleveland will look like Chicago on its lakefront."

A brief word on rapid transit, perhaps the only area in which Cleveland of late can be said to have made more progress than its sister cities. Cleveland introduced the country's first new postwar rapid transit service in 1955, part of a line that has stretched to 19 miles—an S-shaped route that runs from East Cleveland, through downtown, and out to the Hopkins International Airport. The airport extension, completed in 1968, made Cleveland the first U.S. city to provide a direct rapid transit line for its airport travelers. The right-of-way, however, was one of the ugliest known to man: it became a "castaway alley" of garbage, tires, unkempt backyards, and industrial no-man's land. In 1976, however, a citizens' clean-up campaign, "Rapid Recovery," was formed to survey the entire right-of-way, engage the aid of artists and landscape architects for beautification projects, paint gigantic wall murals, and get homeowners and businesses to clean up their backyards and in some instances landscape the sections of their property visible to transit riders. The project promised to be a national model of transit right-of-way beautification and citizen cooperation.

Power in Cleveland

Over Cleveland's history, corrupt political machines and waves of reform have come one after the other. The major political parties have switched places in ascendancy. Mayors and city governments have come and gone. But one thing has remained constant for a century: the steady hand of self-interested control by the powerful moneyed and industrial forces. Under Mark Hanna's rapacious regime, the control was blatant and direct. But business control remained firm behind the scenes during the reform movement that gave Cleveland one of America's most progressive governments early in the century; neither did it abate during the period of undisputed cosmo control from the early 1930s to the 1960s, or when blacks eventually began to demand and get major offices. In 1967, in fact, it was the decision of the business elite that made the black man Carl Stokes mayor of Cleveland, a decision which cynics said was based less on a belief in equal rights than a desire to buy peace and protect Cleveland against racial riot and the destruction of property.

Indeed, like so many other currents in Cleveland life, the role of the power elite is best explained in ethnic terms. Cleveland urbanologist Thomas E. Bier has done just that by showing that the most powerful—and enduring—ethnic group in the city has been and is British. The root goes back to Connecticut, at the time of the 1790s settlements of the "Western Reserve," and from there to England, Scotland, and Wales. As industrialization took hold in the 19th century, Cleveland's British lost their superiority of numbers—but they controlled, some becoming extraordinarily wealthy, the rapidly expanding new economic enterprises. Many of the most powerful, Bier notes, lived on or near the famous millionaires' row of Euclid Avenue; the economically weak—Hungarians, Italians, Lithuanians, Poles, and others —were left the least desirable land along, above, and downwind of the industrialized Cuyahoga River. Starting in the 1870s, the "plague of commercialism" began to eat up Euclid Avenue. The British ruling class, riding newly invented electric rail transit, moved to Shaker Heights, Cleveland Heights, and other suburban refuges. Yet, Bier notes:

As the British moved to the suburbs and beyond, they left behind their direct political power in the city but not their economic power. They continued to occupy the seats of power as did their fathers, grandfathers and great-grandfathers.

Today, as a hundred years ago, the British dominate the boards of Cleveland companies and corporations, banks, universities, hospitals, and philanthropic, charitable, cultural and service organizations. They dominate the ranks of top executives in industrial corporations and law partnerships.

Bier speculates that as lower-income folk—white and black—continue their migration away from center city, many to the suburbs, and as middle class people pave the way in places like Ohio City, the stage may be set for many of the British elite to one day return to the center city they deserted so long ago. In any event, he notes, they still control, through their economic power, the downtown area, and through their philanthropic activities, University Circle. One can imagine, says Bier, "the two islands expanding over several decades or more with facilities for the economically stronger and eventually linking to form a corridor of essentially 'new city' between University Circle and downtown."

All that, however, was still speculation in the 1960s and 1970s as Cleveland remained locked in a bitter struggle between black, cosmo, and the nonresident but still powerful ruling elite. We do well to pick up the story in 1967 when Cleveland chose Carl Stokes as the first black mayor of a major city in American history.

Why did a city still 63 percent white elect a black mayor? One reason was clear enough: Carl Stokes, risen from the East Side streets and poolrooms to wartime service, college, law school and the state legislature, was an articulate man of immense personal charm who could deal on equal terms with the people of both the ghetto and the business-political elite. Stokes won his two terms (the second in 1969) by narrow margins; the fact he won at all was a reflection of the growing desperateness of many Cleveland leaders. As the Cleveland *Press* wrote, by the mid-'60s Cleveland was "a city on dead center— shut off from federal funds, slum-ridden, air and water polluted, streets grimy and unsafe, crime rising, funds short, taxes high, schools inadequate, racially tense, saddled with a costly yet inadequate public transportation system." For a quarter century, the town had been afflicted with a series of caretaker mayors, the last of them, Ralph Locher, so incompetent that the Federal Department of Housing and Urban Development felt obliged early in 1967 to cut off several millions of dollars for already-approved urban renewal projects.

Race relations had been deteriorating steadily since 1964 when a young white minister threw himself before a bulldozer at a protest at a school site and was crushed to death. Hough had erupted in the summer of 1966 in a five-day battle of firearms and firebombs, followed by more violence in April 1967. Locher's police chief was photographed in Hough during the riots wearing sports slacks, carrying a hunting rifle, and promising to get him one. Thus the blacks were totally unified, the business establishment appalled about what might happen next, and there was the candidate—Carl Stokes—a black man everyone found hard to dislike, his candidacy made respectable by the *Plain Dealer* endorsement. To pick up the white support he needed, Stokes crossed over to the West Side and radiated the image of the sincere young man, fair-minded on race and aware of issues, at countless small gatherings. A Ford Foundation grant to the Cleveland chapter of CORE helped get blacks registered. On primary day, Stokes picked up better than 95 percent of the black vote and 15 percent of the white vote. Because blacks voted in far greater numbers, he won. In the general election, essentially the same pattern was repeated to give Stokes his victory over his moderate Republican opponent, Seth Taft, nephew of the late Senator; in 1969 the pattern worked again to win Stokes reelection, this time over a "cosmo" type opponent.

Stokes's candidacy had a cathartic effect on the black people of Cleveland; their attitude after the Stokes election was exultant and possessive: "He's *our* mayor," or as one of Stokes's campaign workers put it, "Where there was no hope at all for black people, now they got hope."

The primary effect of Stokes's first years was psychological, reversing the pessimism and despair prevalent during the Locher years. The federal spigot for every type of aid was turned on again, the city's credit rating was restored, a port authority necessary for future economic growth was voted, as was the $100 million sewage bond issue. Within two years, 5,000 units of low-cost housing were going up—more than in the entire previous two decades. In the wake of Martin Luther King's assassination, Stokes walked the ghetto streets for five days urging the black community to stay cool, and it did. A multimillion-dollar program called "Cleveland: Now!" was announced, encompassing every possible federal aid for the city along with renewal aids by the business community; the program was mostly a public relations gimmick, but it had its intended psychological lift for the city.

But like every "hero mayor," Stokes began to encounter problems. Some he inherited—including a blatantly racist police force hostile to the idea of a black mayor. But many problems stemmed from Stokes' unwillingness to deal with members of the powerful city council—an unwieldy 33-man body that reflects Cleveland's multiple ethnic nuances—or with others on a basis of mutual respect. Stokes' major legislative proposals were presented on a take-it-or-leave-it basis as emergency legislation, offending natural allies. Even black councilmen were treated in a cavalier fashion.

For a long time the newspapers and establishment forces in the city remained friendly to Stokes, seeing him as the one man who could keep peace in the city. But eventually they became disillusioned with the lack of concrete performance and the mayor's abrasive ways. In 1971 Stokes decided to retire (later to become a television newsman in New York City). He egregiously mishandled the political maneuvering leading to election of his successor—so egregiously, in fact, that in the general election with a white Democrat, a black Democrat, and a Republican all running, the Republican won.

Ralph Perk, Cleveland's new leader in 1971, was The Ethnic Mayor, a scrappy favorite of the cosmo communities. (As one correspondent reported, "Perk can speak Czech, dance Slovak, sing Polish and pray Bohemian—not to mention that he married an Italian girl.") Perk had promised in his campaign to "unshackle" the police department and restore fiscal integrity to City Hall. Neither promise was very well fulfilled. The police, by the end of his tenure in 1977, were thoroughly demoralized. And stuck with a no-new-taxes promise, Perk and his financial advisers made ends meet in the city budget simply by issuing bonds, allegedly for capital outlays, and expending the proceeds for operating expenses. Immediate cash was also garnered by relinquishing city control of the sewer and transit systems to regional authorities. Cleveland was one of the, if not *the* lowest taxed city, on a per capita basis, in the country. But three times during the early '70s the voters turned down increased taxes, sowing the seeds of the fiscal disaster which would await Perk's successor in 1978.

Enter now Dennis J. Kucinich, only 31 years of age (yet already a veteran of 10 years as a Cleveland officeholder, first as councilman, then as clerk of courts) when he defeated Perk and a fellow Democrat to win the mayoralty in 1977. Born just after World War II to a Croatian-American truck driver father and Irish-American mother, Kucinich was the oldest of seven children, leaving home at 17 to escape an unstable family life. Like Perk, Kucinich had firm roots on the ethnic West Side. Physically, he was an unimposing candidate: barely five feet, seven inches tall, he bore a striking resemblance to *Mad Magazine* cover boy Alfred E. Newman. He was also a young man of supreme self-confidence, determination, and visceral pugnaciousness. Every public issue was subjected to hysterical treatment in which Kucinich employed the most pejorative words he could about opponents. Within a few months of taking office, for instance, he had called members of the still-balkanized Cleveland City Council everything from "buffoons" to "lunatics," "the most reactionary group of fakers ever to hold office." Equally unpleasant words were found to describe the business leaders of Cleveland. Kucinich found it so necessary to make them whipping boys at every turn that he missed a chance to leverage any business commitments for rebuilding of the city.

Kucinich's verbal venom and transparent paranoia should not, however, divert one from his perception of the "new urban populism" which he saw himself as representing. In an October 1978 speech to the National Press Club in Washington, Kucinich defined his position quite clearly. Some excerpts:

The November 1977 Cleveland mayoral election brought about a shift in the center of power, from the major corporate interests, the banks, the utilities, the real estate trusts, to the poor and working Clevelanders. . . . Big Business found that no longer did City Hall rubber stamp the demands of those who were economically powerful. A people-oriented city government which places human values over corporate or corrupt financial gain represented a dramatic turn in Cleveland and presaged confrontation.

We have required big business to pay a fair share of the property taxes in Cleveland. We have stood up to the corporate extortionists who threaten to pull up stakes unless the city capitulates to millions of dollars of property tax abatements. By refusing tax concessions to commercial developers we stopped the shift of taxation from those who are best able to pay onto those home owners for whom property tax rates are becoming confiscatory. . . .

We're enforcing air and water pollution laws, a policy which puts us in conflict with the wealthiest industries in the community. . . . We're resisting the gimmick of county-wide government which reduces the influence of city residents in determining their city's destiny.

All too often people in a major city are deprived of a close relationship to their city government. But I begin the first hour of every day taking phone calls from the general public. . . .

The Kucinich speech also proposed controlling inflation through excess profits taxes on corporations, a stop to migration of industries to the Sunbelt by requiring that companies announce plant relocations years ahead of time, and "constructive utilization" of government pension funds for urban economic redevelopment rather than investment in corporations.

The hostile reaction of Cleveland business circles to such oratory and policy thrusts was quite predictable; it was equally clear why some of the long put-upon blue-collar folk of the West Side may have thought they finally had a spokesman, someone to articulate their frustrations and name the knaves responsible for their problems. That would have left Kucinich in a strong political position—the business elite largely resided out of town, while the West Side voters would remain on his side. But a series of foolish actions began to undercut Kucinich's position almost from the day he took office, suggesting that the young man whose master's thesis was a study of confrontation politics may have been far more adept at theory and rhetoric than the hard business of governing.

He selected a 25-year-old financial director with almost zero financial experience, a 24-year-old community development director, a 26-year-old light commissioner, a 21-year-old woman as assistant public safety director. It was not just the youth, but the personal qualities of most of these appointees—abrasive, arrogant, vindictive—that caused the most problems. The most feared member of Kucinich's team was 48 years old, Sherwood Weissman, a former peace activist and United Auto Workers official who took glee in firing recalcitrant city officials and was depicted as a kind of backroom Rasputin of the administration.

Kucinich's most outstanding appointee was Richard Hongisto, former reform sheriff of San Francisco, to be police chief. An innovative and unconventional law enforcement official who worked seeming miracles in reforming the San Francisco jails, Hongisto began to provide the Cleveland police with their first firm and capable leadership in years. (There had, in fact, been eight police chiefs in nine years.) Preferring roaming the streets to hours behind his desk, Hongisto stopped to visit precinct houses, personally collared burglars, helped stranded motorists during snowstorms. He became quite popular, in both white and black neighborhoods and within police ranks. But the new chief's favorable publicity irked Kucinich; tension mounted between the two; Hongisto complained publicly of "unethical things" the Kucinich inner circle was trying to get him to do; in a bizarre scene on television, Kucinich publicly fired Hongisto. It was a nearly fatal move for the young mayor. Citizens were angered; Kucinich appeared a petulant and vindictive person. Within days, a strong recall movement was underway. Some 39,500 Clevelanders signed recall petitions; the city's two daily newspapers, the black press, the AFL-CIO, the local Democratic party, and the black political faction led by City Council President George Forbes all lined up against the mayor, attacking the entire tone and thrust of his administration. But his real enemies, Kucinich claimed, were those big business interests he had been fighting all along. With heavy West Side support he survived the recall vote by a paper-thin margin of 236 votes.

Just a few months past that confrontation, Cleveland plunged into its fiscal crisis of 1978 that eventually resulted in Kucinich's defeat. For the city's general financial plight, Kucinich could not be held responsible. When he took office the city's bookkeeping was in such tangled shape that outside examiners had declared the books virtually inauditable. The accountants declared, however, that more than $40 million was missing from the city's bond fund, having been used to cover operating expenses during the Perk years. The continued refusal of Clevelanders to raise their taxes simply compounded the situation, so that on the fateful day (December 15, 1978) there was simply no more money left to pay $15.5 million in notes owed to six Cleveland banks.

The temptation to compare Cleveland's plight with New York's was strong—but perhaps misleading. First, the order of magnitude of problem was entirely different: Cleveland's immediate problem was in the millions, New York's in the billions. As the New York *Times* noted in an editorial: "Cleveland tried to ease personal hardship by keeping taxes low. New York tried to make up for private job losses through public employment. New York far outspent its revenues. Cleveland failed to impose enough taxes to cover its basic costs." But there was a common factor: "Both cities borrowed for capital investments and used the money for operating expenses."

The Cleveland default was not, of course, a necessity. The banks might have "rolled over" (i.e., renewed) their loans to the city; immediate tax boosts might have been ordered; the city might have sold off some property. But there were practical and political reasons that all these things did not happen —evidence that the confrontation Kucinich had sought had led to total stalemate. Indeed, it was worse than stalemate; the negotiations among the mayor, council, business community, and the state on how to solve the problem dissolved into the same orgy of personal abuse which had characterized Cleveland ever since Kucinich took office.

The most severe disagreement centered on the insistence of business and many councilmen, but the fervent opposition of Kucinich, to the idea of selling off the city's publicly owned utility, Muny (Municipal Electric Light and Power System), to the area's big private utility, the Cleveland Electric Illuminating Company (CEI). Muny had been founded early in the century by Cleveland Mayor Tom Johnson, a giant of the Progressive movement and a hero figure to Kucinich. Profitable during most of its existence, it held down power rates for its 45,000 consumers. But in the 1960s Muny fell victim to sloppy management and political payroll padding. By the late '70s its own power plants were in disuse and it was deeply in debt to CEI, from which it was obliged to buy power. Muny supporters alleged that CEI was in fact trying to kill off Muny to gain a total local monopoly. By 1978 CEI was moving to seize hundreds of pieces of Muny equipment in payment of the debts, but the city had lodged a $325 million antitrust suit against CEI. (A federal investigation had indeed found that CEI had engaged in a series of anticompetitive acts designed to enable the utility to take over Muny.) Kucinich's camp argued that if Muny were sold off to CEI, the antitrust suit would become moot, together wth the potential $325 million payment; the business camp insisted there was no other choice than to sell Muny for the proffered $158 million price to end the city's fiscal impasse. Kucinich argued for keeping Muny as a cornerstone of his platform of "urban populism" and "power to the people"; the city's banks made the sale of Muny the decisive factor in whether they would renew their loans to the city. And chief among the banks insisting on that condition was the Cleveland Trust Company, Ohio's largest bank with some $4.5 billion in assets. Two of Cleveland Trust's directors were also directors of CEI, and the bank was one of CEI's largest stockholders—a situation prompting Kucinich to charge that "Cleveland Trust and CEI have surfaced as a hydra-headed economic Loch Ness monster ready to destroy anyone in its path." Kucinich even got consumer advocate Ralph Nader to come to his defense: "Kucinich has refused to give in," Nader said. "He is bringing to the public's attention one of the more important issues of our time: who runs our cities? Is it the political government duly elected by the people, or the unduly elected corporate government?"

Kucinich charged that Cleveland Trust had made sale of Muny a direct condition of renewing its loan to the city; board chairman Brock Weir denied that, saying his only concern was a workable financial plan to cover Cleveland's debts. But he told reporters: "We had been kicked in the teeth for six months. On December 15 we decided to kick back." (In his own way, Kucinich kicked back too. He invited reporters to watch as he withdrew $9,197 of his personal funds from Cleveland Trust, which he charged with "trying to destroy a city government through blackmail and intimidation. I am going to take my clean money out of this dirty bank." The publicity effect was dampened, however, by the same-day arrest of the mayor's younger brother

Perry on a charge of robbing another Cleveland bank of $1,396.)

Through all the negotiations, Kucinich and the city council remained in bitter, personal dispute. Only after default was agreement finally reached to place two measures on the city ballot in February 1979: sale of Muny, and raising the city income tax from 1.0 to 1.5 percent. The vote resulted in 2–1 voter approval of the tax hike (most of which would be paid by commuting suburbanites). But a similarly overwhelming margin was registered *against* selling Muny Light, a significant victory for Kucinich and defeat of the business establishment, the Cleveland newspapers, Citizens League, and opponents on the city council.

Kucinich's paranoid behavior increased, his political base declined, and on November 6, 1979 the grand experiment in urban populism went down to defeat. The new mayor, George V. Voinovich, epitomized all that Kucinich hated: he was James Rhodes's lieutenant governor and had close ties with the business community. Voinovich campaigned on a pledge not to sell Muny Light, however. The new administration started off by asking for volunteer financial and management support from the business community to cope with the city's financial problems—and got an overwhelmingly positive response, with several months of help from 80 major executives. (The business establishment seemed so relieved to have Kucinich gone that it would react positively to almost any reasonable request from Voinovich. But one could argue that without the Kucinich nightmare, such capitalist interest in the city would never have been forthcoming.)

Cleveland's problems seemed so overwhelming, however, that when Voinovich—a quietly effective behind-the-scenes operator—took office he could say he felt as if he were going off to war. The news from the accountants he hired to figure out where the city stood fiscally supported such feelings: Cleveland's deficit was $111 million. The requirements for clearing away the debt: borrowing $50 million under a new state law designed to clean up Cleveland's finances (normal borrowing sources were closed off after the default), raising taxes and city fees and cutting back services through personnel layoffs.

Remarkably enough, one department head in Cleveland's city government, first appointed by Carl Stokes, survived through the Perk administration and was retained under Kucinich. He was Norman Krumholz, a refreshingly different city planner who was espousing—in a quieter way, with more substance—urban populism years before Kucinich. Krumholz rejected the idea that planners could afford, in a city with Cleveland-scale problems, to rely on abstract models of some "best future" for "the city beautiful." Rather, he said, they should plunge into the battle as advocates of the poor and near-poor people who make up the vast bulk of the city's population. Massive urban freeways and big downtown complexes, he suggested, might line the pockets of developers and construction unions, but what is their effect on poor people and city neighborhoods? Thus when new highways, office projects, rapid transit plans, or sales of city properties were proposed, Krumholz systematically raised such basic questions as: Will the project provide more jobs at livable wages for Cleveland residents? Will it stem the tide of neighborhood deterioration? Will it return more, rather than less, tax money to the city so that public services can be maintained and expanded? Such intervention blocked a new West Side highway, forced council debate on city payment of $15 million in bridge and road improvements for a proposed "Tower City" of downtown office buildings and apartments, and forced a much better deal for transit dependent Clevelanders (a third of the city's families own no car) in negotiations to transfer the ailing Cleveland Transit System to a regional authority. In the transit negotiations, Krumholz and his planning staff demanded—and got—reduced fares, expanded bus service, and agreement to spend about $1 million a year for a "dial-a-ride" prenotification pick-up and delivery service for elderly and infirm transit-dependent passengers.

Krumholz was a pioneer, Columbia University's Herbert Gans suggested, in "cutback planning"—charting for an era of population and economic decline in aging cities like Cleveland. He was also one of the country's first planners to insist that the residue of poor left in center cities not be forced to pay inordinate costs in the era of decline, especially if proposed city policies would provide much greater benefits for large businesses and suburban commuters. But at each step Krumholz provided careful research and was willing to negotiate calmly with the business powers and others whose interests might be thwarted. Had Dennis Kucinich demonstrated the same qualities he might have been more effective and made his points without sowing the seeds of such bitter discord.

In addition to the banks, which gained unusual visibility in their showdown with Kucinich, the Cleveland power establishment includes all the public utilities (not just CEI), as well as the city's great industrial firms and most of its huge legal establishment (some 5,000 lawyers). But the power of the establishment is less than it was in decades past—not only because of the resistance of a Kucinich or Krumholz, but also because of assertive black power and a general spreading of spheres of effective power. No longer can a committee of the elite meet at the Union Club and make decisions to which the rest of the city will necessarily adhere. Special spheres of power also belong to the board of education, private welfare organizations, and especially the Cleveland *Plain Dealer.* Quiescent in earlier years, the *P-D* was sold to the Newhouse chain in the 1960s but nevertheless moved to more vigorous leadership under editor Thomas Vail. *P-D* news coverage often was first rate, though in the 1970s there was an increase of complaints by reporters that stories in controversial areas were quashed. The *Plain Dealer* received especially heavy criticism for its handling of Kucinich, his recall, and the stakes in the fiscal crisis—even though the paper, ironically, had supported Kucinich in his 1977 race for mayor. Vail has personally impressed us as a highly committed civil leader.

Concurrently, the Cleveland *Press* has become more timid in its news coverage and editorial stands, perhaps as a result of the retirement in the mid-1960s of veteran editor Louis Seltzer, a strong-willed little bantam rooster of a man who delighted in playing the role of kingmaker in Cleveland and statewide politics. Every Cleveland mayor from Frank Lausche to Ralph Locher (Stokes' predecessor) was picked by Seltzer, and the Seltzer blessing had not a little to do with Rhodes' rise to power. The *Press*, a Scripps-Howard paper, circulates most widely among Cleveland's sturdy working classes, while the *P-D* is read more by the intelligentsia and throughout much of northern Ohio.

The word may never have seeped through to the man in the street, but Cleveland in the '60s and '70s developed an irrepressible gadfly pamphleteer in the Tom Paine tradition, a man whose editorial barbs (despite critics' allegations of inaccuracies) often caused intense discomfort among the city's top leaders. He was Roldo Bartimole, a former *Plain Dealer* and *Wall Street Journal* reporter who said Cleveland was "a city incestuous in its civic and business interlockings." Bartimole repeatedly alleged that "the same people who run the corporations control the civic, cultural and political life of the community," resulting in "inbred chauvinism." The *Plain Dealer* and publisher Vail were frequent targets. Though Bartimole's *Point of View* newsletter had a tiny circulation, its barbs were often long remembered. An example: while Cleveland leaders were boasting the city led the nation in per capita annual United Way giving, Bartimole discovered that many corporate moguls were squeezing "fair shares" from their workers while personally contributing little or nothing.

No review of the Cleveland scene should omit the powerful, progressive leader of its philanthropic world, the Cleveland Foundation, the country's oldest (founding was in 1914) and largest community foundation (assets of well over $200 million). The foundation contributes over $10 million annually to a wide variety of programs in such fields as health, family planning, care of children and the aged, scholarships, university development, and culture. Its hand is found in practically every innovative and forward-looking activity in the community, from neighborhood group revitalization projects to downtown planning and a project such as Playhouse Square. Close to 2,000 Clevelanders have made gifts or left bequests to the foundation since its founding, most with no instructions save an admonition to use the funds for the Cleveland community. Thanks to outstanding leaders—James A. Norton in the '60s, Homer C. Wadsworth, former head of a similar foundation in Kansas City, in the '70s—the Cleveland Foundation has rarely backed away from controversial issues. Predictably, its 11-member board has often been regarded as the soul of the Cleveland establishment; by the late '70s, however, it included two blacks and two women.

Columbus: Complacent and Prospering

Well-scrubbed, provincial, and complacent, Columbus is a spacious plains city whose spirit is entirely Midwestern and logical: set almost dead center in Ohio because it is the state capital, laid out on an orderly grid system, with the inevitable central square at its very center, and in the middle of that square, the State House. About the only unpredictable thing about Columbus is the State House itself, an example of pure Doric architecture with thick limestone walls and a funny sawed-off cupola absolutely atypical of American state capitols. Columbus, said the city's mayor of the 1970s, Tom Moody, is quite content to be characterized as the "largest small town in America."

It is hard to believe that Columbus now has more than half a million people (an estimated 533,000 in a metropolitan area of 1.1 million); somehow the old rural flavor lingers on and on, even if (as the Cleveland *Plain Dealer*'s Richard Zimmerman once suggested) the image is now more of a farmer's market grown fat and sleek. There is also ample *lebensraum* (shared, significantly, with another Midwest city doing quite well, Indianapolis). The Columbus land area was vastly expanded—from 40 square miles in 1950 to 175 in 1978—to make it Ohio's biggest city geographically and in fact one of the largest in the U.S. This expansion, complete with inner belt, outer belt, split-level suburbs, and industrial parks, was in stark contrast to Cleveland, which remained hemmed in by strong suburban neighbors. Today there are fewer than 30 cities in Franklin County, in which Columbus is located, but more than 100 in Cuyahoga.

Columbus' character was shaped decisively by its proximity to southern Ohio and that area's early settlement by nonslaveowning yeoman farmers from Virginia and Kentucky, folk naturally self-reliant and suspicious of government. Except for an influx of Germans in the 1840s, Columbus never received a significant European ethnic injection.* The black percentage—only 18.5 by 1970—was well below that of Cleveland and other Northern cities; significantly the city suffered only minor racial disturbances during the tumultuous 1960s. Fresh migration, even to this day, tends to be heavily Appalachian; indeed it is jokingly said that the mountain people are products of "the three R's"—reading, 'riting and Route 23, the main highway link to Columbus from West Virginia. No major city of Columbus' size seems so homogeneous and middle class in every way.

Columbus failed to share in the explosive manufacturing growth and large tides of European immigrants in the late 19th and early 20th centuries. The result, as Wilford L'Esperance noted in a 1970s report for the Mayor's Economic Development Council, was that Columbus experienced a growth "parochial, locally-oriented and orchestrated by a power structure with a

* The most lasting physical legacy of that German immigration is German Village, a half-square-mile area just south of center city built with many red brick cottages reflecting Old World rather than American architectural styles. Once a flourishing ethnic neighborhood with its own community centers, churches, restaurants, and foreign language newspapers, German Village declined so far in the post-1920 era that by the 1950s the city had actually designated it as an area for urban renewal clearance. But the Frank Fetch family, longtime residents, started a preservation movement; by the early 1960s the city took cognizance and rezoned the entire area from commercial to residential, with required "certificates of appropriateness" in style for building permits. The net result: a neighborhood with human scale, identity, pleasing ambiance. But in recent years the prices of restored houses have been $100,000 or more, suggesting the need to spread preservation activities to other neighborhoods. Just that was happening in another older area, Victorian Village on the near north side, by the late 1970s.

southern small-town perspective consisting of bankers and merchants." The extremes of poverty and wealth noted in many of the industrial cities also failed to appear in Columbus; the results can be seen today in fewer slums and less deprivation, a weaker labor movement, and little of the spillover of inherited wealth that created distinguished cultural institutions in such cities as Toledo, Cincinnati, and Cleveland. (When Samuel Hanna died in the 1950s, L'Esperance observed, he bequeathed a sum of $30 to $40 million to the Cleveland Art Museum, helping it become one of the world's renowned centers of art. "Personal wealth of this kind and size was not created in Columbus," L'Esperance noted.)

Maynard E. Sensenbrenner, Columbus mayor during the '50s and '60s, was a Democrat, a conservative, and a deep believer in brotherhood. In 1965 he received the Fiorello LaGuardia Award for being the best mayor in the nation; the record, in fact, shows he inaugurated the aggressive annexation drive from which the city still benefits so strongly. Sensenbrenner's style was another matter; an aggressive patriot, he wore an inch-square rhinestone-encrusted American flag in his lapel and was fond of telling visitors that the key to the success of his All-American city was not just "planning and doing and letting everybody have his say. No siree," Sensenbrenner insisted, "you need a lot more than that—a dynamic faith in God and a dynamic faith in the United States and a dynamic faith that you can be anything that you want to be. And that old spizzerinktum. Now that's 1000 percent better than enthusiasm. If you've got it, you've got everything." (In 1969, however, Columbus' carefully nurtured image as a "clean city" was tarnished a bit when Justice Department officials charged that "almost every member of the vice squad" had been paid off by gamblers and that the Columbus police had obstructed efforts at a federal crackdown.)

Tom Moody, the Republican who defeated Sensenbrenner in 1971 and then remained mayor during the 1970s, was a perhaps duller—but much more impressive—man. A thoughtful student of cities and their problems, he led in urban conservation work for the National League of Cities and became that organization's national president. Less recognized locally for his skills, he was a bit of a prophet without honor in his own land. But he ran a highly efficient city government, with excellent local services on Ohio's lowest local tax rate. (Relatively docile local government unions plus a lack of high social service demands by the Appalachian poor helped make that job easier.) Late in the '70s, Moody took a key role in peaceful implementation of a federal desegregation order involving busing.

Columbus' industrial development has been on a strong upswing ever since 1940, when the federal government erected a large aircraft plant later taken over by private interests. Initially low wages, especially compared to northern Ohio, attracted many industrial plants, which could draw on an ample labor supply in neighboring rural Ohio and the Appalachian belt; eventually many highly trained technical and professional personnel were hired as well. Today, Columbus' largest industrial payrolls are those of firms like Western Electric, Westinghouse, General Electric, North American Rockwell, and GM-Fisher Body. Fortuitously located at the intersection of two interstates, Columbus has attracted major distribution centers for J.C. Penney, Sears Roebuck, and more than 70 industrial office and research parks in the city and its surrounding outerbelt. The area's labor market has been Ohio's fastest growing since 1966; even in recessions, unemployment has averaged 20 to 25 percent below the national average. Some of the resiliency is, of course, due to such "recession proof" industries as the state government and Ohio State University (enrollment 51,000, largest of any single university campus in the nation). Financial institutions (bank holding companies, insurance firms, three banks which rank among the country's top 200) have grown in recent years. National Insurance, expanding strongly in the 1970s, built a new headquarters building in downtown Columbus, the tallest structure in the city's history. Borden moved from New York all its middle and top level managers, leaving only formal corporate headquarters behind. Fast food franchise headquarters flourished in the city. The Battelle Memorial Institute, advertised as the world's largest independent nonprofit research organization, continued its global research activities, primarily in scientific and engineering fields. But it also branched more into social/behavioral sciences. A court suit and settlement with the Internal Revenue Service forced Battelle to distribute $80 million from the will of its founder; Columbus share in the benefits. Thirty-six million dollars, for instance, were contributed to a new downtown convention center. Battelle also provided the major funding for the Academy for Contemporary Problems, a major research resource of the national public interest groups, such as the National League of Cities and National Governors Association. Some of the Academy's best studies were on the modern-day economic problems of the Midwest.

The downtown physical evidence of all the new Columbus activity was apparent to any visitor. Between 1960 and 1970, $145 million was invested in center city projects; in the 1971–78 period alone, $585 million in development occurred, including buildings by Borden, Nationwide, and Motorists Mutual, a 41-story State Office Tower, a new Federal Office Building, Banc Ohio Plaza and Galleria complex, and others. With scores of new shops, luxury hotels, and the like, there was a grave danger that Columbus' old small-town, rural atmosphere might someday drift away entirely.

For a touch of traditional Columbus, however, one had only to walk into the building of the Columbus *Dispatch*, which faces the central square a few yards from the State House and is topped with a great red neon sign proclaiming the *Dispatch* "Ohio's Greatest Home Newspaper." Inside the foyer, one discovers two of the grimmest portraits of *homo sapiens* we have ever seen: the cold, arrogant, calculating faces of Robert Frederick Wolfe and Harry Preston Wolfe, founders of what grew to be the most powerful and ruthless single-city-based communications and economic establishment of the United States. Though laughed and sneered at (usually in private), the Wolfe empire enjoyed an iron grip on Columbus for decades after the founders had gone onto their reward. Not until the 1970s—due to change within the family, as well as the diversification of Columbus' economy—was the grip finally relaxed.

The Wolfe brothers made their first fortune by founding the Wolfe Wear-U-Well Shoe Corporation, which turned out to be a fabulously successful manufacturing and retail operation. Then, early in this century, they got control of the *Dispatch*. Next came bank acquisitions leading to formation of Banc-Ohio, a far-flung holding firm which by the 1960s controlled 22 central Ohio banks, including the largest in Columbus, with deposits of some $700 million. Other Wolfe-controlled enterprises included the Ohio Company, a large underwriting firm in municipal bonds, ownership of thousands of acres of choice Ohio farmland, and the Columbus radio and television stations WBNS. (The call letters stand for Wolfe Banks Newspapers & Shoes.) The Wolfes also owned the Neil House, for decades the city's leading hotel, plus extensive other downtown real estate.

For many years the only significant counterforce to the Wolfe group in Columbus was the prestigious Lazarus family, owner of Columbus' leading department store (and the Federated Department Stores chain). The Lazarus family showed little taste for an open power struggle with the Wolfes. But in 1969 we interviewed Trent Sickles, then an elderly gentleman associated with the Lazarus management, who offered his startling private views of the Wolfes as "a clan arrogant with power and money . . . a fantastic octopus, with tentacles everywhere." Another Columbus businessman, less extreme in his view than the now-deceased Sickles, said: "The Wolfe clan is involved in all that transpires. You bank with them, you may rent from them, you hire your employees through their newspapers, you advertise your goods in their papers, you get your view of the world from the news they carry in their papers and on their television stations." For decades, the Wolfes have had close connections to politicians, especially Republicans; at their summer place, called the Wigwam, they have been entertaining GOP bigwigs ever since the days of Hoover and Landon. John Gunther reported that at the Wigwam the Wolfes kept pet wolves.

By the end of the 1970s the Wolfes remained the most important economic entity in Columbus by virtue of the immense amount of economic activity they still controlled. During the decade they had prospered; we heard one estimate of their wealth at a minimum of $100 million, probably several times that. But the sheer fact of the economic diversification of Columbus during the decade made the Wolfes less all-decisive in the city's affairs. Also, the family experienced a number of deaths and retirements that had the net effect of reducing direct family influence over civic affairs. Preston Wolfe, a small man with a cold stare (at least for outsiders) who was the real ruler of the clan for decades, retired as publisher of the *Dispatch*, turning the reins over to his nephew, Edgar Wolfe. But Edgar died in 1975 when the Wolfes' private plane crashed into a radio tower in Washington, D.C. In his early thirties, Preston's own son, John Frederick Wolfe, then became the *Dispatch*'s publisher; a man trained in business rather than newspapering, he moved slowly and cautiously in his leadership position, though some observers believed that a slow but significant improvement in the *Dispatch*, long considered a pedestrian paper, resulted from his influence. (Day-to-day decisions at the *Dispatch* were made by executive editor Carl DeBloom, an honest veteran newsman, loyal to the Wolfes but interested in producing a good paper. The *Dispatch*'s editorial policy remained strictly Republican-conservative, but some columnists of other persuasions began to appear. Improvement was also noted at the Scripps-Howard-owned morning *Citizen Journal*, under a new editor, Richard Campbell. The *C-J*, however, depends on the *Dispatch* for advertising selling and printing, an arrangement which hampers heady independence.)

An important sign of opening up of Columbus journalism occurred in the '70s with appearance of the *Columbus Monthly*, a sprightly glossy magazine not unwilling to report openly (as no one dared before) on power arrangements within the city. In the late '70s it reported that John Walton Wolfe, chairman of the Ohio Company—"like other leaders of the Wolfe family before him, a complex and enigmatic man"—was the single most powerful person in Columbus. The report said John Walton Wolfe had strong influence with Governor Rhodes and the Franklin County political establishment, acted decisively and well in money matters, and tended to get involved only in civic projects where he could maintain control.

Second on the *Monthly*'s power list was Charles Y. Lazarus of the department store company and vice president of Federated Department Stores. Third was John W. Galbreath, owner of his own company and chairman of the Pittsburgh Pirates, the man whose money and influence made John Bricker, a builder and sportsman with activities and projects around the world. Far-away interests often kept Galbreath out of the mainstream of Columbus activity, though (even in his eighties) he remained a major player in most downtown developments. (In a 1977 speech to the Columbus Chamber of Commerce, Galbreath praised the city for its reliability, for "not being out to prove anything" in the style of a New York or Los Angeles, and because "we just know in our hearts that Columbus—politically, socially, economically —isn't going to be caught up in excesses of any sort.")

To the world, Ohio State University is known far more for football than its academic achievements (though it does have a few outstanding departments, in such fields as optometry, pharmacy, and education). The Woody Hayes era came to an abrupt halt in early 1979 with the firing of that veteran coach (who finally let his emotions get away from him and took a swing at an opposing team's ballplayer). Whether OSU will soon shed its football mania is another question. A young man preparing a doctoral dissertation at OSU in the early '70s found that of a scientific cross-section of 2,000 Columbus citizens, an amazing 85 percent had attended at least one OSU game and that football interest in the city was so extensive and deeply ingrained that people were "not free" to say if they were indifferent to the OSU team. "If a person expresses no interest, he is going against huge normative social pressures," said researcher Albert Schwartz. "He is in the category of a freak."

OSU was believed to have one of the more docile American student bodies until 1970, when the campus erupted in a series of demonstrations in which 26 persons were wounded by shotgun blasts and scores were injured, and Governor Rhodes ordered 1,200 National Guardsmen onto the campus. The OSU disturbances rivaled—except for the casualties—those at Kent State, 120 miles to the northeast of Columbus.

But it was the Kent State incident—with demonstrators' vandalizing of downtown stores, the burning of an ROTC building, and then the National Guard killings of the four students—which aroused the entire nation. The President's Commission on Campus Disorders later reported that the deaths were "unnecessary, unwarranted, and inexcusable." The resultant trials and suits accomplished little in pinpointing culpability and left troublesomely unanswered the questions of how such a terrifying chasm in attitudes and standards could have opened between the staid burghers of the middle-class society and their children on the campuses. For all of the excesses which may have been traceable to some students, it remains difficult to forget James Rhodes' words at a spring 1970 news conference. The demonstrators, he said, were "the worst type of people we harbor in America," "worse than brown shirts and the Communist element." Two days later came the fatal National Guard shootings at Kent State.

The autumn after Ohio State and Kent State erupted, there was another great mob scene in Columbus as thousands of students surged along High Street, lighting bonfires, drinking, and smashing bottles. But now the police were all smiles, for the occasion was a different one: celebrating Ohio State's defeat of its undefeated archrival, Michigan, thus assuring the home team a berth in the Rose Bowl. "The [police] condone football because this is how things were 30 years ago," a coed senior from Toledo told a reporter. "But if we demonstrated against the war or on local issues, they'd come down hard on us."

Cincinnati: Soft Charm in a Heartland City

> And this song of the Vine,
> This greeting of mine,
> The Winds and the birds shall deliver
> to the Queen of the West
> In her garlands dressed
> By the banks of the Beautiful River.
> —Henry Wadsworth Longfellow

Before Chicago was, and while Cleveland struggled to be more than a village, Cincinnati was one of America's great cities. Set fortuitously on America's early mainline to the West, the Ohio River, Cincinnati prospered as a port city, an early industrial center, a place of culture in the early 19th century, winning the sobriquet of Queen City from Longfellow and others before him. Her list of illustrious past residents includes John James Audubon, the artist-naturalist; Stephen Foster, the great songwriter; and William Homes McGuffey, author of the first children's readers. Harriet Beecher Stowe lived here and gathered material for *Uncle Tom's Cabin* when Cincinnati was a key station on the Underground Railway. In 1843, Charles Dickens passed through and described Cincinnati as "a beautiful city, cheerful, thriving, animated." For decades, she was the largest American city west of the Alleghenies and north of New Orleans; in 1860, she was one of three American cities with a population of more than 100,000 people.

After the Civil War, the Ohio River was eclipsed as a main route to the West and Cincinnati began a long decline in relative population and importance; today her population (410,441 in 1976) places her 30th among American cities. But her charm and grace, what Gunther called "a certain stately and also sleepy quality, a flavor of detachment, soundness," lingers on in this most untypical of all heartland cities.

Geography and ethnic strains combine to give Cincinnati its unique flavor. The setting is not unlike a giant amphitheatre, with the legendary seven hills surrounding a lower central Basin along the grand curving sweep of the Ohio River. Some of the hills are steep in the extreme; many were vineyards in earlier times. Heights and water combine to give drama and excitement to the scene; one of the grandest urban vistas we have seen in America was from the blufftop home of Governor Gilligan just east of the city, seeing the twisting golden cord of the river in the late afternoon sun, the constant commerce of boat and barge along the great waterway, the riverside city, enveloped in the haze of a dying day.

The first Cincinnatians were Virginians, Welsh Quakers from Pennsylvania, and New Englanders. Then, from the 1850s onward, came a great rush of Germans, a liberty-loving and cultured lot but examples of a lower-middle-class conservatism still typified in scores of Cincinnati savings and loan associations and resistance to all rapid change. At one time, the Germans were concentrated in an area north of Mill Creek known as Over-the-Rhine; urban renewal of the '50s and '60s blew out the core part of the West Side so that more outlying West Side neighborhoods such as Westwood, Cheviot, Mt. Airy, and College Hill are the great Geman strongholds. Up to World War I, German as well as English was taught in the public schools. Summertime German festivals are a way of life to this day, with quantities of beer, bratwurst, and Limburger cheese. And the city still has some fine old German restaurants. (In fact, it has the only group of really excellent restaurants in all of Ohio.) The second immigration wave was Irish, as conservative as the German and now scattered through many parts of the city (including Mt. Adams, Hyde Park, and Mt. Lookout) and, in ever increasing measure, intermarried with the Teutonic stock. For decades Cincinnati has had a small but influential Jewish community.

While middle and upper class people pushed first out to the hilltops, and then into outlying suburbia, the Basin has been the receptacle for the city's poor: blacks over many decades (now 135,000 strong) and, especially in recent years, poor Southern Baptist white folks from Appalachia.* On the eastern outskirts are the wealthiest suburbs, places like Hyde Park and Indian Hill, home of the aristocratic Tafts (who have been in Cincinnati since 1839) and other families of privilege like the Gambles, Guyers, Pogues, or Lazarus clan. These families have traditionally formed a rigid caste system and their clubs have had restrictive racial and religious membership policies. But great wealth is no longer a Protestant monopoly; increasingly Catholics share it as well.

Cincinnati has long been said to have the most honest and efficient government of any large American city, and it is one of the largest with a city manager. It was not always so. From the 1880s until 1925, the city was in the grasp of a corrupt, conscienceless Republican machine. The leader for almost 30 years was a former saloonkeeper named George B. Cox, who became a bank president and millionaire but never lost his touch for predatory politics, keeping a card file on the personal lives and arrests of citizens, dispensing city jobs to ward heelers and many incompetents (including some illiterates). Occasional reformers tried to clean out the Augean stables of city government, but lacked staying power; permanent change did not come until the 1920s when influential and dedicated rebels, mainly Republicans, persuaded the long-abused citizens of the city to approve a new home-rule charter including introduction of the city manager form of government. To keep the city government honest and efficient, the city manager for many years was paid one of the highest public salaries in the United States.

The Charter party early made the basic decision to continue as a party on its own, competing with the Democrats and the conventional Hamilton County Republicans. For years the Charterites were either a majority of the city council or—because of the unique system of proportional representation which Cincinnati kept for many decades—a potent and influential minority. The early Charter base was primarily in the silk-stocking hilltop areas, but during the New Deal the blacks and other underprivileged of the Basin joined as well. Trouble began to appear in the postwar era when increased city reliance on federal aid led Republican and Democratic Charterites to split more and more frequently. In the '60s the Republicans took total control of the council; between 1968 and 1972 there was a Republican-Charter alliance again; following that a Democratic-Charter alliance took control. The ethical standards of city government are still of the highest; since this was the first Charter goal, one must conclude that the movement was one of the most successful citizen reform efforts of modern urban history.

A Charterite from the start and doubtless the most distinguished Cincinnati citizen of the past half century has been Charles P. Taft, a warm-hearted

* The Appalachian whites, Gilligan pointed out to us, were brought into Cincinnati to man the factories when manpower was scarce and then regurgitated in periods of labor surplus, much like California and Texas' use of Mexican wetbacks.

and public-spirited man with enduring interest in liberal Republicanism, phi-lanthropies, and national church work. "Charles Taft's loyalty and enthusiasm for bipartisan innovation," political scientist William H. Hessler wrote a few years ago, "have never wavered, despite the fact that his defiance of the regular Republican organization at the local level has surely cost him a dis-tinguished career in national politics." Taft was elected a Charter council member in election after election, until he finally stepped down in the late 1970s at the age of 80 following 31 years in the office. His long continuity made it possible for Cincinnati to institutionalize its reform. When we last interviewed Taft in 1976, he said he was still enjoying his job despite two metal hips and two bad knees. "I'm not up to Clemenceau yet," he quipped, then drove off in an old car with a 12-foot gold canoe with a Charlie Taft for City Council bumper strip on it. A bitter footnote about the Tafts: Charles' brother Robert stuck with the regular Republican organization for life and never lost a chance to disparage or oppose the reform program in his home town.

Cincinnati has remained fortunate in the quality of its city managers in recent years—E. Robert Turner, an influential man with the power structure, leader in downtown development, and a past president of the International City Management Association, who served up to 1975, and William V. Donaldson from then to 1979. Donaldson brought a touch of humor and unconventionality—along with a penchant for management innovation—into staid Cincinnati. (His early career had included stints as a theological stu-dent in Toronto, a night embalming clerk and waterworks employee in Den-ver before serving as city manager in Scottsdale, Ariz., and Tacoma, Wash.) Faced by a yawning deficit and taxpayer refusal to increase the city's payroll tax ("our Proposition 13," Donaldson told us), he decided it was time for the city to start some major contractions. Almost 100,000 people had left in 20 years and 3,500 manufacturing jobs had disappeared and there was no rea-son to believe some magic relief would appear "to lay on the gold and get us out of our long-term fix," he noted. Donaldson reduced the permanent work force from 9,200 to 7,200 in three years and looked around for longer-term solutions.

One idea was to enlist citizen aid; as he saw it, citizen participation too often boils down to people "yelling" at government to provide new services or pick up the garbage more often. His alternative: to say to citizens, "What are the things, with minimal city assistance, that you can do for yourselves?" As an example, when neighborhoods complained about unclean streets, the citizens were told that if they really wanted clean-ups, the city would provide public service workers as "whitewings"—the people who push buckets along with brooms—provided the neighborhoods would finance their uniforms and agree to keep track of their time. And to the displeasure of many city pro-fessional workers, Donaldson encouraged citizen volunteers on many projects. "We seem to have convinced people they can't do things for themselves," he noted. "We've lost the idea of being self-reliant. But there are a lot of things government does that people could and would do for themselves." For example, with the recreation budget shrunken, citizen volunteers began to take on major responsibility for junior league baseball and other sporting events.

Donaldson also instituted a number of ingenious productivity programs into city government, developed a "team" approach to tackle tough development issues (and walk around the lethargic civil service), and evangelized for catching up with the city's $200 million backlog of deferred maintenance in roads, sewers, and other public facilities instead of investing heavily in new capital projects. Finally, Donaldson pushed the city government deep into economic development, including technical information to businesses to prevent their flight, new service jobs for blue collar workers, new downtown housing (to give that area a pool of around-the-clock residents, thus reducing crime and the deserted-after-5 P.M. effect), and aggressive efforts to hold the city's existing downtown retailing and prevent major new stores from going to the suburbs instead. Donaldson told us he made no apologies for having the city act as an entrepreneur. Cities, he observed, started out as entrepreneurial enterprises, exploiting rivers, highways, or railroads. "But somehow we changed into being Giant Janitors," he said. "We picked up the trash, locked up the bad guys, and put out fires. If cities are going to come back, they've got to become entrepreneurial again."

A few months later, feeling he had dealt with enough problems of the Cincinnati political menagerie, Donaldson moved on to make a profession of a lifetime interest by becoming president of the Philadelphia Zoo. He had found, Donaldson said, that "the zoo can make a real contribution to the improvement of the quality of life for people who live in cities, to open a window to the wild for people in central cities whose other total contact with nature seems to be pigeons, rats, and cockroaches."

Cincinnati has long had strong neighborhood identity, a natural social outgrowth of the sharp line of demarcation provided by a setting of deep ravines between plateaus. And since the early 1960s the city has also developed one of the country's superior models of relating to neighborhoods. Not that the idea originally came from City Hall: a series of crises in such areas as zoning, freeways, schools, and recreation motivated new community councils to organize and older civic organizations to renew themselves. The city government was originally stung by the new combative spirit but soon began to help neighborhoods draw up community plans and to welcome suggestions of what each neighborhood would like to see included for itself in the upcoming year's city budget. In 1978 the National Municipal League, after a study of Cincinnati's 47 community councils, concluded that despite some shortcomings—uneven participation and effectiveness of the councils, plus questions of their official status—Cincinnati still deserved "its reputation as a leader in the neighborhood movement."

Of Cincinnati's neighborhoods, the one that has undergone the most illustrious rebirth of recent years is Mt. Adams, on one of the fabled seven hills. Mt. Adams has a rich history. Nicholas Longworth bought it up in

1830 and turned it into a vineyard where he developed the great Catawba grape; a few years later he donated four acres for an observatory which was built by public subscriptions in a burst of civic enthusiasm for scholarly pursuit. Former President John Quincy Adams came to dedicate the observatory in 1834, and the hill was promptly named for him. When a destructive blight struck the vineyard (which had been immortalized in Longfellow's poem), Longworth's son Nicholas donated the land for what is now 184-acre Eden Park, which in turn became the site for the Cincinnati Art Museum, a conservatory and natural history museum, and most recently the illustrious new Playhouse-in-the-Park. From Eden Park and most sections of the hill one has an expansive view of downtown Cincinnati, the river, and the Kentucky hillsides and flats with the dormitory communities of Newport, Covington, and Dayton on the other shore. More than a century ago, most of Mt. Adams (excepting the parkland) was laid out in small building lots— typically 25 feet wide, 100 feet deep—which attracted the striving German and Irish immigrants to build their shoulder-to-shoulder homes. Mt. Adams became a strong Roman Catholic community, dominated by the spires of the German and Irish churches. To one of these, the Church of the Immaculate Conception, thousands have made the long climb from Columbia Avenue every Good Friday for more than a century now, praying step by step.

As the suburban rush of the 1940s and 1950s gathered steam, Mt. Adams found itself increasingly a backwater. Many of the old homes—an architectural salad of Federal, Victorian, and nondescript structures—were literally falling apart, some turned into $30-a-month cold-water flats. A couple of old Cincinnati families had bought and restored homes with especially magnificent views, but the general future seemed bleak. Then, in 1959, a young man named Neil K. Bortz, just out of Harvard Business School and a former student of writer-urban critic Lewis Mumford, bought his first old house on Mt. Adams—starting, through his own enthusiasm and skill, one of America's most vigorous and colorful private renewal efforts. With two partners, Bortz founded Towne Properties, Inc., a firm which bought and restored scores of properties on Mt. Adams and by the late 1960s was doing more than a million dollars a year in construction and renovation on the hill. In partnership with Indiana industrialist J. Irwin Miller, Bortz also developed strikingly modern new town houses, thrust out from Mt. Adams on pilings driven into bedrock, each with a spectacular view of river, city, and hills. Countless others were inspired to undertake renewal on their own, in modern and traditional style, the exteriors of the refurbished homes proclaiming their freshness in every shade of the rainbow. And in their wake, vigorous small businesses— quaint saloons and restaurants, shops and art galleries—were attracted as well. Young professionals, the remnant Irish and German population, artists, hippies, and college students all mingled along Mt. Adams' steep and narrow streets in an urban scene of special vitality.

A neighborhood which has gained new life against even more difficult odds is Mt. Auburn, set atop another one of the seven hills with breathtaking views of the river and city flats below. In the 19th and early 20th centuries there was no "finer" or more socially prestigious Cincinnati address. Great mansions of Italian Villa, Second Empire, or Greek Revival style lined Auburn Avenue, known as Cincinnati's Fifth Avenue. In one of those homes William Howard Taft, the future President, was born in 1857; in another, the grandmother of one of this book's co-authors in the 1860s.

By contrast, one's best guide to Mt. Auburn in the 1970s was a black, bearded master of street language and historic preservation—Carl Westmoreland. But in his determination to make Mt. Auburn a proud community to live in, it would probably be safe to say Westmoreland matched any of the elite of yesteryear.

Soon after World War II, serious blight was visited on Mt. Auburn. Highway construction uprooted longtime residents and led to blight and general disinvestment. Some of the fine old homes (not yet preserved as a national historic district) were chopped up into professional buildings or demolished for parking lots. Blacks displaced by West End urban renewal began to flood the area. By 1970 Mt. Auburn was three-quarters black; vacancies and abandonments were high; there were many drug pushers, pimps, and petty thieves. From the late 1960s onwards, however, a community council and Good Housing Corporation (headed by Westmoreland) began to provide a model case of self-generated neighborhood improvement. With remarkable nerve and persistence, Westmoreland importuned city officials and business leaders for assistance—and began to get it. The housing foundation started with a $7,000 gift from a corporate executive in 1967; by the late 1970s it had rehabilitated or built hundreds of housing units and several office and commercial buildings with a total value of well over $9 million. Routinely, the foundation bought up buildings that were the scene of one type of illicit activity or another and turned them into community assets. An example was Auburn House, an historic structure built by the man who owned Cincinnati's first streetcar line. Over the years it had declined into a house of prostitution, but the police turned a deaf ear to community demands to close it down. "So we raised $186,000 cash and bought it," Westmoreland noted. "We restored it pretty much to its original condition. Now it's our health center and our central offices. What was a 27-room brothel is now a 27-room office building."

That type of self-sufficiency was the key to Mt. Auburn's revival. "It's our neighborhood," Westmoreland said, "and we decided that if we're going to live here, then we're going to own it. We've done that, and it's given us more political clout, more impact with the police, with everybody. When we go to City Hall to talk about public improvements, we're not going now like beggars. We're going as people who've done something in our own community, and deserve some consideration that goes beyond charity."

Mt. Auburn's worst slum was "The Hole"—a series of tall old tenement buildings on Glencoe Place where stabbings, drug traffic, and other crimes had terrorized inhabitants. "We couldn't deal with the slumlords, so we bought them out," Westmoreland noted. "We felt we had to redo the entire environment, so we reduced the density from 500 to 99 units, tearing down several buildings for mini-parks, for parking, to let sunlight in. You can't put but so many people in this gully. Black ain't but so beautiful." The restored buildings, with their high ceilings and distinctive exterior brickwork, were most attractive. But the new tenants found Westmoreland's approach had a steely toughness. No one could occupy one of the foundation's housing projects without a credit and police check and an interview by a screening committee of residents. Tenants failing to pay rent or engaging in vandalism were quickly evicted. "We've got to be tough," Westmoreland insisted, "because come the first of the month the bank doesn't care if we're nonprofit or black. It wants its money. This isn't a social experiment. We live here. The value of my house, or the quality of the school where my kid goes, is affected by what happens in this building."

The new spirit of confidence proved contagious in Mt. Auburn. In the Prospect Hill section, for instance, under-30 designers, office managers, and teachers were snapping up condemned properties—many picked over by vandals—and restoring them at a rapid clip by the mid-1970s. Westmoreland was even beginning to complain that middle class "speculators" were beginning to buy up the neighborhood and displace poor black folk.

The process of revival was yet more difficult in a third historic Cincinnati neighborhood—Over-the-Rhine, a once cohesive German working class area close to the central business district. As Phyllis Myers and Gordon Binder of the Conservation Foundation noted in a 1977 report:

> Over-the-Rhine has been torn apart socially and physically in recent decades by many forces. After achieving a degree of affluence, the Germans and newer Italian residents left for the suburbs. Into the housing came thousands of unskilled Appalachian whites, seeking jobs in the city. Displaced blacks from other neighborhoods were relocated here. The Findlay Market [Cincinnati's sole remaining open air market, with a distinctive peak-roofed building of 1902 vintage] deteriorated. Stores became vacant. In place of its former ethnic homogeneity, Over-the-Rhine became a series of fragmented sub-neighborhoods: business people who lived elsewhere, social service personnel, clergy, blacks, poor whites, elderly Germans. The indices of social malaise—crime, welfare, transiency, and vacancy —soared.

It was a story echoed in virtually all older American cities, though with a somewhat "happier" ending. Some 600 houses and 3,000 units were renovated under federal housing programs; that failed on its own to reverse the physical deterioration of many blocks of houses and stores, still evident in the mid-1970s. But the Findlay Market was refurbished and by the end of the decade it seemed likely that the pressures for inner-city recycling and revival, apparent in so many cities, would sustain the effort to give Over-the-Rhine a new lease on life.

When Gunther visited Cincinnati at the end of World War II, he found the slums in the Basin "among the most insufferable in the nation." A businessmen's group formed in the late '40s spearheaded the first step of renewal, clearing a monotonous square mile of grimy slums in the West End for a modern industrial-commercial complex with ready access to rail sidings and loading docks. In 1962, again at the businessmen's urging, Cincinnati voted $150 million toward partial or complete demolition and replacement of eight major downtown blocks. A $10 million convention exhibition hall rose, along with new high-rise office buildings, overhead pedestrian walkways, an underground garage beneath Fountain Square, a new Contemporary Arts Center, and a $40 million sports stadium for the Cincinnati Reds baseball team and a National League football team. Downtown emerged elegantly refurbished, a place of shape and character. In fact, even in the late 1970s Cincinnati, in its typical careful and conservative way, was still implementing a plan developed in the 1940s which consciously shrank the size of downtown to maintain its relative compactness (15 square blocks) and character. All development, as envisioned 30 years before, still fell away from Fountain Square, the highest point (and a particularly charming one with its ornamental bronze-and-porphyry monument brought from Munich in 1871). Only one new building was of clearly substandard design (the Kroger Building, described to us by one local leader as "a triumph of the public works school of architecture"). A downtown covered skywalk passed *through* the Convention Center, banks, restaurants and department stores. In 1977 the city decreed that no one could tear down a center city building for a parking lot: "We want to keep the buildings and keep downtown walkable," City Manager Donaldson said.

Power in Cincinnati was traditionally held by an overwhelmingly Republican business-industrial elite, some of whom were Social Register types, some self-made men. Unlike Columbus, no single family ever dominated—Cincinnati had too many powerful home-owned industries for that. Members of the elite were found on the interlocking boards of the great corporations, as chief supporters of the United Appeal campaigns, as powerful fund-raisers on their own, and as the finance and organizational backbone of the Hamilton County Republican organization. Gradually the old order has lost its absolute grip. In 1969 the Cincinnati *Enquirer* quoted a successful local businessman saying: "Forty years ago you could have said the city was run from the Queen City Club. Then a Geier or a Kroger could do as he damn well pleased. But those days are gone." A decade later we were counseled to include in our list of power points, with which the business elite must deal, the neighborhoods (given their increased organizational and political clout), the black community (black Charterite Theodore Barry was mayor, for instance, for three years in the '70s), and the Roman Catholic Church. "It's necessary to get the blessing of the Archbishop for any major moves," one city official said.

Cincinnati has never aspired to be a city of heavy industry like Akron or Cleveland, but she is no slouch in producing goods for a nation. Procter and

Gamble, which started in 1837 with two brothers making and peddling tallow candles, lard oil, and German soap, is now the 20th largest industrial corporation of the U.S.A. (annual sales $7.3 billion).* The city has many medium-sized specialized industries that employ skilled workmen; many of these firms turn out machine tools; indeed Cincinnati bills herself as the machine tool capital of the world. She also produces the most playing cards of any city, and is big in everything from tin cans, chemicals, mattresses, and shoes to anchovy pizzas, jet engines, and pianos. Cincinnati's economy today is so diversified that she seems almost depression-proof; the city is one of the last to feel a slump in the economy. In addition to P & G, her largest employers include Cincinnati Milacron, General Electric, and Monsanto. The city is also a banking and financial center and headquarters town of the Lazarus-owned Federated Department Stores and the Kroger Company. Federated had grown to a position of enviable power in U.S. retailing by the end of the 1970s; among its divisions were such famous stores as Filene's (Boston), Abraham & Straus and Bloomingdale's (New York), I. Magnin (San Francisco) and Rich's (Atlanta). Sales by 1979 were close to $6 billion annually. To its credit, the firm refused to close downtown stores in the flight to the suburbs and was making large downtown investments in Brooklyn, Boston, Columbus, and Oakland.

And still there is the river, the lusty, busy Ohio coursing 981 miles from Pittsburgh (where the Allegheny and Monongahela Rivers meet) to Cairo, Illinois (where the mighty Mississippi awaits). The river made Cincinnati, and she is still its chief port city, even as the day of the side-wheelers and stern-wheelers recedes further into history. Today the Ohio carries twice the freight tonnage of the Panama Canal and three times the design capacity of the St. Lawrence Seaway, and it is practically all great bulk stuff in huge tows of as many as 20 steel barges loaded with 20,000 pounds each—coal, iron ore, oil, chemicals, metals, salt, sand, gravel. The Ohio River Valley has been called the Ruhr of America, but it is a classic case of the son outgrowing the father: since World War II, there has been the development of four Ruhr Valleys in the stretch from Pittsburgh to Cairo. Coal is the greatest freight item, much of it from West Virginia and Indiana fields destined for huge steam generating plants along the river which furnish the needs of industries (especially aluminum) with great electricity demands. Other coal barges will be destined for Ohio towns like Steubenville, a place that breathes smoke and fire and exhales great slabs of hot searing steel for the industrial machine of the heartland.** Cincinnati watches the industrial flotilla pass her doorstep but prefers for herself, if you please, a less gross way to make money.

---

* P & G could be a driving civic force but is so slow and cautious, both in business and public affairs, that its bright young men tend to leave.

** Steubenville, having topped the listing in some national studies of particulate emissions such as dirt, smoke and soot, may be the dirtiest city in America. A few years ago enterprising reporters found the air so dirty that the grass turned blue, houses turned black overnight, and cows' teeth fell out.

Down the Population Ladder: Toledo—Akron—
Dayton—Youngstown—Canton—Springfield

Brawny, thriving industry . . . downtown decay and the glimpse of renewal . . . ring on ring of suburbia . . . shopping centers with their parking
lots eating up the green earth . . . the world of the interstate road . . . and
somehow, an incessant insularity, even in the age of instant communications
—these are the hallmarks of Ohio's middle-ranked cities, down the population ladder from Toledo (358,677) to Springfield (74,018). Here is a quick
tour:

Set at the westernmost point of Lake Erie, not far from Detroit, Toledo
is a port of no mean proportions that receives thousands of ships each year,
many from distant points of the globe—but the city has about as much international flavor as Omaha or Kansas City. As writer Dick Perry points out,
"Few youngsters running away to sea head to Toledo."

A multiplicity of ethnic groups make their home in Toledo, and the city
comes complete with a substantial black segment. The Democratic party has
been traditionally all-powerful and traditionally liberal in its outlook. Downtown Toledo is in transformation from down-at-the-heels to modern steel-and-
glass renewal, the east side of town is well described as grimy and melancholy,
close-in old neighborhoods harbor thousands of the lower middle class, and
the forever growing suburbs show a newer if dull face. Recent years have
witnessed a wave of new corporate investments, including a promised $100
million world headquarters for Owens Illinois and highly controversial (and
expensive) state office building. Yet despite all the emphasis on commerce
(Toledo is one of the world's largest soft coal shipping ports, a great handler
of grain, big in oil refining, a leader in glass production) there is also culture:
the art museum and zoo claim to be in the top dozen or so in the United
States.

For long decades the rubber center of the universe, Akron (pop. 244,265)
was made by, sustained by, totally dominated by the single product. This was
the home of four of the five great rubber makers, all in the $1 billion a year
and up category—Firestone, Goodyear, General Tire, and Goodrich. The
great rubber names were everywhere—on schools, banks, country clubs, and
residential sections. When the winds were unfavorable, the piercing smell of
concentrated rubber chemicals pervaded the town. But they were a sweet smell
for Akron businessmen, because rubber meant money.

But in the 1970s the rubber giants began to fulfill an Akron nightmare.
One by one, they closed their aging plants in the city, moving the jobs off to
the Sunbelt and other spots far afield. In 1978 alone the city lost some 3,000
factory jobs, adding to the 25,000 that had deserted the city since 1950. Goodyear announced it would invest $75 million in an Akron research and develop-
ment center. But Firestone—incorporated in Akron in 1910—announced it

was merging with Borg-Warner Corporation of Chicago, casting doubts on how long the firm would have significant operations in the city. Picking up much of the slack of industrial closings was a strong growth in the white collar service industry area, however.

Power in Akron has long gravitated toward the rubber executives (frequently meeting at the Portage Club to exchange trade gossip), the now declining United Rubber Workers union, a strong local Democratic party, and the Akron *Beacon-Journal*, a paper of moderate-to-liberal persuasion regarded by many as the best in Ohio. (The *Journal* was the original paper in the Knight chain, which grew to include the prosperous Miami *Herald*, Detroit *Free Press*, Charlotte *Observer*, and Philadelphia *Inquirer*, all papers of some distinction.)

For decades, Akron suffered from decay in its rundown business core, with more and more vacant buildings as the suburban shopping centers sprouted and prospered. The city's solution was to rip out almost its entire downtown in one of the biggest urban renewal binges in America. During the 1970s there was, however, substantial downtown building and up rose such structures as Cascade Plaza, a formidable office-hotel complex, and a restored Quaker Oats Company mill converted to house small restaurants and shops. But in late 1978 Polsky's, a 98-year-old department store second largest in the town, closed its doors forever. Natives still talked of their downtown, particularly at night, as a "dead" place. Perhaps this is due to the population mix, which includes thousands of country folks from southeast Ohio, Kentucky, West Virginia, and Tennessee—plus a substantial black ghetto. Akron has a symphony orchestra, but its real interests have always run more to hometown events like the national Soap Box Derby (born in Akron), the American Golf Classic, and the World Series of Golf.

Set in a rich agricultural valley of southwestern Ohio, Dayton (pop. 197,744) is a clean, well-governed town with a great deal of civic pride—the counterpart of other successful Midwestern cities in its population range, such as Fort Wayne in Indiana, Grand Rapids in Michigan, and Rockford in Illinois. The good government tradition goes back to 1913, when Dayton became the first major American city to adopt the commissioner-manager form of government—an indication of the early hope of reformers to "remove politics from government." In the early '70s Dayton leaped ahead of practically all other U.S. cities when the city manager inaugurated a plan of task forces of department heads and principal subordinates to transcend the narrow specializations inherent in functional city departments. The department executives were evaluated as much by their task force operations as by their direction of their own departments—a sharp break with the normal hierarchical (and increasingly rigid and bureaucratized) structures of most city governments. Dayton's good government habit has spread to the Miami Valley Regional Planning Commission, which has taken a positive interest in maintaining a viable city even as the rest of the county has grown. Among other things, the commission conceived and inaugurated a rather effective "fair share" housing plan to introduce reasonable percentages of black and other low-income hous-ing units into the suburbs.

Dayton used to be a safe Democratic area and was the home city of Governor James M. Cox, the 1920 Democratic presidential nominee. But with the suburbs, conservatism has grown, and the overall area is now mar-ginal politically. Cox's old paper, the Dayton *Daily News,* has had the repu-tation of being Ohio's most liberal daily, counterbalanced in its home town by the moderately conservative Republican *Journal-Herald.* The Dayton area was the homeplace Richard Scammon and Ben Wattenberg chose for their typical American voter, a housewife whose husband works in a factory and whose brother-in-law is a policeman, in the book *The Real Majority.*

The 1960s and '70s saw Dayton beset by a move of businesses and resi-dents to the suburbs or further afield. The black share of the population rose to a third, and a huge suburban shopping center, Dayton Mall, imperiled the downtown shopping area. With mixed success, the city has battled to mini-mize its problems. There has been intensive urban renewal and downtown rebuilding, including one large office building-department store project, Court-house Square, into which the city sank substantial sums of money and to which it offered substantial tax abatements. The payoff for city coffers would have to wait for years, but the project did help to spur new, adjoining de-velopment. The city had one of the country's best model cities programs in the '60s, worked hard to improve law enforcement through community co-operation with police, and could be credited with successful efforts to keep the peace with the exception of a major racial disturbance in the summer of 1966. Racial problems were formidable because, in addition to its blacks, the city has a large population of not-always-docile Kentucky and West Virginia mountain folk on its East Side. Yet in 1970, a black man became mayor. Later in the decade, several of the city's deteriorated neighborhoods, aided by city "leveraging" of funds to attract investment, were clearly on the rebound.

The industrial "greats" of Dayton have traditionally been National Cash Register (it was here that James Ritty's "mechanical drawer" began the cash register industry) and General Motors' Frigidaire Division. But National Cash Register went to automated equipment in the '70s, reducing employment drastically, and GM later sold the Frigidaire Division to White Consolidated Industries, which proceeded to close the plant and throw thousands out of work. Between 1969 and 1979 some 30,000 industrial jobs were lost in the city; whether the hemorrhaging could be averted before an irreversible down-ward spiral occurred remained an open question at the end of the '70s.

Youngstown (pop. 129,875) and Canton (pop. 98,044) form with Akron a smoky, clanging triangle of heavy-industry towns southeast of Cleveland. Steel and gangsters are the two commodities for which Youngstown was most famous over the years—until, in 1977, with the precipitous closing of Youngs-town Sheet & Tube's Campbell Works by the company's conglomerate-owner, the Lykes Corporation, 4,650 workers suddenly lost their jobs and Youngstown became the symbol of the older city suddenly thrown onto the economic ropes by the obsolescence of the industrial plant that once made it prosper. In the case of the Youngstown Sheet & Tube closing, it was not only obsolescence of equipment and the lack of water transportation for raw materials but also the fact that the New Orleans-based Lykes Corporation, after acquiring the plant in 1969 from local owners, did virtually nothing to make the facility viable through modern furnaces, pollution control equipment, and the like.

The Youngstown shutdown apparently qualified as the biggest nondefense industrial layoff in U.S. history. Many workers had never known any adult occupation save steelmaking. The Mahoning Valley had seen its first blast furnace in 1803, so that heavy metal manufacturing was woven into the very character of the area: a culture of massive steel mills flanked by churches, union halls, bars, and workers' homes. In immense numbers they had come to man the steel mills, passing the work down through generations—Germans, Poles, Slovakians, Hungarians, Italians. Yet overnight, with the Youngstown Sheet & Tube closing and others threatened, the entire local culture and sustenance seemed in danger of crumbling.

Led by a Roman Catholic and an Episcopal bishop, a coalition of 186 Ohio religious leaders was rapidly formed under the name of the Ecumenical Coalition for the Mahoning Valley. The coalition mounted a "Save Our Valley" campaign with the intent of attempting what seemed the most promising course: reopening the steel mill as a largely worker-owned enterprise. Within a few months over $4 million had been raised in Save Our Valley savings accounts by churches, unions, business people, and local citizens. The federal Department of Housing and Urban Development commissioned the National Center for Economic Alternatives, led by independent-minded economist Gar Alperovitz, a man long fascinated by the possibilities of worker ownership of major enterprises, to draw up a feasibility study. Predictably, Alperovitz found the plant could be reopened and made profitable—but at a cost exceeding half a billion dollars, including a federal loan guarantee of well over $200 million. After much hemming and hawing, the Carter administration decided that was too much of a risk for the federal government to undertake for a single facility. And despite the attractive idea of worker ownership and the potentials for productivity and community cooperation it might bring, the fact was that very high federal guarantees were being asked for a facility that would recreate only some 1,500 of the jobs lost when the Campbell Works closed down. A far better-balanced, reliable way for the area to recuperate lay in government investment of rather moderate sums in semiprivate corporations to provide venture capital and technical assistance in large numbers of independent small new businesses in the area. (That idea, advanced by an economist, Michael Kieschnick, was circulated to Washington departments involved with economic development but was originally ignored by all. Politics, presumably, requires either a publicized "big fix" or inaction; less flashy but practical strategies have great difficulty being "sold," even to community groups, such as the Ecumenical Coalition, which should see their value.) By the end of the decade, unemployment rates were down in Youngstown, but surveys indicated many steelworkers had moved away or taken lower paying jobs.

Labor strife, including killings, plus all sorts of vice and crooked dealings in city government, were the order of the day in Youngstown for decades. The city is a strong contender for the title of ugliest in the U.S.A. Labor dominates Democratic politics and in turn is dominated by the Steelworkers Union and the United Auto Workers, though Republicans sometimes stage breakthroughs (including the mayoralty). Youngstown is one of those places where voters delight in turning down school tax increases and where unions are strong (and strike prone) even in government. In early 1980 when Mayor George Vukovich refused to negotiate for a police and firefighters' wage increase the city would not be able to pay for, the public workers struck for six days. Vukovich sadly told the Boston *Globe*, "There is no solution for Youngstown. I shouldn't be saying this. I love this place, but if I were looking for a future I wouldn't look for it here."

Canton is a workingman's town one would expect to vote solidly Democratic on the basis of its strong unions, heavy Catholic element (Polish, Rumanian, Italian, Hispanic), plus a formidable bloc of black voters. But it is actually a swing area, has had a Republican mayor—Stanley A. Cmich—for close to two decades, and has been known for sending ultraconservative Republicans to the state legislature. The town was once vice-ridden, with widespread gambling and prostitution, but cleaned itself up some years ago. A physical clean-up has also hit center city, with distinctive urban renewal projects. The biggest employers are Republic Steel and Timken Roller Bearings. (The latter corporation, paternalistic and violently antiunion, distinguished itself by sponsoring the right-thinking news programs of Fulton Lewis, Jr., and his son. But it could also take credit for support of an advanced vocational high school, the Timken Mercy Hospital, a cultural center, and one of the finest county historical societies in the U.S.) The city newspaper, the Canton *Repository*, has traditionally stood somewhere to the right of Canton's most illustrious past citizen, President William McKinley, whose remains are forever encased in a Canton mausoleum almost 100 feet tall. Another architectural monstrosity in Canton is the 1963-vintage National Football Hall of Fame, which is topped by a 52-foot dome shaped like a football. The city has been nuts about football since the days of the early professional Canton Bulldogs, practitioners of a nose-bashing brand of ball; today more than 25,000 fans will turn out for a local high school game, and Ohio State University is the only Ohio school which draws more football fans than McKinley High School each season.

Finally, there is Springfield (pop. 78,018), a town in sad eclipse. Located some 43 miles west of Columbus on old National Road (now U. S. 40) that first opened up the heartland to surface travel, Springfield has a rich cultural history—home of Wittenberg University (founded in 1845), the place where hybrid corn began, birthplace of the 4-H Clubs, and a literary-publishing center through the Crowell-Collier Publishing Company (founded in the 1880s).

But today, Springfield is an aging town of old frame houses and dingy brick buildings at its core. Many of the old family-owned businesses hold on, and the city still has its distinctively German-Lutheran-conservative flavor. But Crowell-Collier folded in the 1950s, the tax structure is deteriorating, public transportation is sick, and the population has declined sharply in recent years. The only noticeably positive report from Springfield in the '70s was that it had begun to pioneer in joint labor-management committees to smooth out operations of its city government.

Mansfield, Ohio

The heart of Ohio, and its typicality, may well lie not in the great cities which we have, perforce, been discussing, but in the vast numbers of smaller cities that account for so much of its population and so much of its conservatism—places like Lima, Middletown, Marion, Zanesville, Lancaster, Portsmouth, Kent, Athens, Alliance, Chillicothe, Ashtabula. Occasionally one will pop up in the news for some civic breakthrough: Middletown (population 50,000), for instance, was declared a 1978 winner of the "downtown development awards competition" of the New York-based Downtown Research and Development Center. The city had revitalized a 300-acre downtown with a $45 million mall, City Centre Plaza, that enclosed in a fully weather controlled space two former business streets in the town center, together with a new arts center, city building, senior citizens' apartment complex, and the like.

Before we depart the Buckeye State, let us pause a little longer in one of these "middling" cities—Mansfield, a manufacturing and supply center halfway between Columbus and Cleveland. In many ways, Mansfield is indeed a microcosm of small-city Ohio and the American Midwest. Power shifted early in the century from the farmers to the industrialists, who remained unchallenged until the 1970s, when new voices arose—and industry began to flee. Visiting Mansfield in 1969, we found a rather complacent, prosperous city where no one was too anxious to rock the boat. "Mansfield wants to conserve and protect what it has," D. K. Woodman, the local newspaper editor then, commented. But a decade later, the complacency had fled. "There's a new sense of need for some change," said the new editor of the Mansfield *News-Journal*, Robert May. "We need to be more imaginative and bold or the community will be in a real crisis."

Mansfield's fears lay in a slow crumbling of the industrial base on which it had so long depended. Industry had arrived in the late 19th century with such firms as Ohio Brass and Tappan Stove, followed later by a Westinghouse plant, a rubber factory and steel mill, and Fisher Body in the 1950s. For years this diversity seemed to protect Mansfield—from the worst effects of the Great Depression, then from the early postwar recessions. By the late 1970s, however, the rubber firm—Mansfield Tire Company—had closed its Mansfield plant, opened a new plant in Tupelo, Miss., and was thinking of moving its corporate headquarters away. The Westinghouse plant had become part of White Consolidated Industries and harsh labor-management difficulties were developing. Overall unemployment was mounting, while the population (which had risen from 37,154 in 1940 to 55,047 in 1970) was starting to decline.

To cure its industrial job loss problems, Mansfield was no longer looking for big industries to come to town: it knew that was unlikely to happen in any event. Instead, the search was for high-technology, light industry—a search likely to prove frustrating, of course, because thousands of American communities were competing for the same handful of new light industry plant locations at the same time. There were some hopeful indications: a Project Care had been formed, for instance, to counsel workers who lost their jobs on how they might find new opportunities through retraining. Mansfield had yet to grasp, however, the immense opportunities for generating indigenous small industries, the types of firms shown by economists to be the best providers of new jobs in the American economy.

In 1969 the old industrialist power structure, making the essential decisions for Mansfield at places like its exclusive Fifty-One Club in an old downtown building, still held the town in its cautious, conservative grasp. But a decade later, editor May said, "The biggest problem of this town is that it has no leadership any more—no group to galvanize plans. There is less thought about the community in general." One reason, he suggested: that so many home-grown industries had become parts of national corporations. Hired managers, with scant loyalty to or interest in Mansfield, were sent to run those plants for a few years, then withdrew. If there was to be a new power structure, May suggested, it might lie in academicians, lawyers, and other professionals. One major source of activity was the Mansfield campus of Ohio State University, which not only offered a full college program but also harbored the North Central Technical College, offering various types of technical-vocational training.

Where the old establishment and whatever powers succeeded it were still failing was in saving the downtown area, a dreary mixture of old brick buildings and some old Victorian wooden homes. The downtown began to decline in the 1960s, and before long all but one of the major stores had fled. Year after year, Mansfield talked about urban renewal and did nothing about it. The number of abandoned and empty stores continued to mount. In 1979 came a demoralizing blow—the decision of the biggest local bank to expand with computer operations in a suburb rather than downtown. Plans were afoot for streetscaping with new trees and sidewalks as a first step toward redevelopment. Outside consultants were telling Mansfield to make itself into a center of specialized stores and urban ambiance—but there was no guarantee that would come to be, especially if the chronic bickering between merchants and the city government continued as it had for so many years.

Typically, suburban shopping centers—in particular one large mall, located in the adjoining town of Ontario and drawing customers from a six-county area—proved to be the undoing of downtown Mansfield. Built on vacant land, soon surrounded by chain fast-food stores and other satellite establishments, the mall (built in 1969) was where the action—and the fresh investment—could be found. Like so many cities, downtown Mansfield had failed to see the dangers, failed to remain competitive or remake its own image and facilities at the right time. It would be paying the price, in abandonment and a reduced tax base, for decades to come.

All its problems notwithstanding, Mansfield had some things going for it as it approached the 1980s. Black-white relations, always relatively good, remained that way, with a minimum of fuss over school integration. (The black standard of living was low but superior, ironically, to that of the Appalachian hillfolk from Tennessee and Kentucky who settled in Mansfield to work in the plants and continued to reject all offers of help.) In past years Mansfield had suffered under severe air pollution problems, with a huge yellow cloud over the Empire Steel plant, airborne particles from the brass company, and soot from the tire firm. Government regulations (and some closings) had effectively cleaned up the air by 1980. The Mansfield *News-Journal*, part of a chain owned by Harry Horvitz, a man who made his home in Shaker Heights near Cleveland, had undergone a couple of management upheavals; it remained moderately conservative but far more open to change (and encouraging new departures) than in times past. In addition to its university campus, Mansfield had a fairly new arts center, a symphony orchestra of some quality, and handsome horticultural gardens widely renowned for their annual tulip displays. The surrounding area was quite a recreation center, with two ski runs and lodges and three man-made lakes (great canoeing meccas).

A touch of glamor has long applied to Mansfield, perhaps separating it from many other smaller Ohio cities. More than a century ago, railroad financiers used to meet in Mansfield, and Abraham Lincoln's name was first mentioned in regard to the presidency at such a Mansfield gathering. Senator John Sherman of Antitrust Act fame was from Mansfield, and it was the birthplace of the late Pulitzer-prize winning author Louis Bromfield, who turned his famed Malabar Farm outside the city into a conservation showcase and gathering place for writers and entertainers. Kay Francis, movie star of the '30s, used to come and dance with her shoes off; another visitor was John Gunther, traveling the country to write *Inside U.S.A.* But nothing more famous ever happened at Malabar than the 1945 marriage of Humphrey Bogart and Lauren Bacall; as if nothing were holy, their nuptial bed can still be viewed on daily tours of the home.

By 1980, however, it was a long time since Bogart and Bacall bedded down at Malabar and one could well ask: Was Mansfield's sun—and those of Ohio's other towns and cities—on an irrevocable downward course? Could the middle class society in the state of heavy industry look forward to a rewarding tomorrow? When one considered just Ohio's inbred complacency, its continued paralysis of government, its inadequate schools and indifferent public administration, the answer had to be negative. But there were those few fresh signs of movement, of reassessment, of fresh powers rising and new challenges fermenting. Enough, in any event, to offer a small glimmer of hope.

PERSONS INTERVIEWED

THE FOLLOWING PERSONS kindly agreed to interviews in the preparation of this book. Affiliations shown are as of the time of the interview.

ADAMANY, David, Secretary of Revenue, State of Wisconsin, Madison, Wis.

ALLEN, Janenne, Administrative Assistant to Lt. Gov. Richard Celeste, Columbus, Ohio

ANDERSON, Gerald, Urban Redevelopment Consultant and Member, Cleveland Transit System Board, Cleveland, Ohio

ANDREWS, John S., Chairman, Republican State Committee, Columbus, Ohio

ARLOOK, Ira, Executive Director, Ohio Public Interest Campaign, Columbus, Ohio

ARONOFF, Stanley J., State Senator, Cincinnati, Ohio

BACHELDER, Glen, Politics & Program Division, Executive Office of the Governor, Lansing, Mich.

BAIRD, William, Correspondent, Lansing *State Journal,* Lansing, Mich.

BARNARD, William C., Chief Editorial Writer, Cleveland *Plain Dealer,* Cleveland, Ohio

BARNES, Linda, Director, Office of Intergovernmental Relations, State of Michigan, Lansing, Mich.

BASS, Andrew, Director, Bureau of the Budget, Cleveland City Council, Cleveland, Ohio

BECHTEL, William, Federal Co-chairman, Upper Great Lakes Regional Commission, Washington, D.C.

BERNDT, Ray, Regional Director, United Auto Workers, Indianapolis, Ind.

BIRGE, Evie, WFBM-TV, Indianapolis, Ind.

BLISS, George W., Director of Investigations, Better Government Association, Chicago, Ill. (deceased)

BLISS, Ray C., Former Chairman, Republican Ohio State & National Committees, Akron, Ohio

BOWES, David, Editorial Page Editor, Cincinnati *Post,* Cincinnati, Ohio

BRENNINGER, Ivan, Executive Director, Academy in the Public Service, Indianapolis, Ind.

BREUSCHER, Harvey, Director of Statewide Communications, University of Wisconsin, Madison, Wis.

BRUNNER, J. Terrence, Executive Director, Better Government Association, Chicago, Ill.

BULEN, L. Keith, Republican National Committeeman, Indianapolis, Ind.

BURDOCK, Robert, Publisher, *Ohio Magazine,* Columbus, Ohio

BUSH, James A., Coalition Against Redlining, Detroit, Mich.

CALLAHAN, Gene, Administrative Assistant to Secretary of State Alan Dixon, Springfield, Ill.

CARLEY, David, President, Carley Capital Group, Madison, Wis.

CATTANACH, Dale, Director, Wisconsin Legislative Audit Bureau, Madison, Wis.

COLLIER, Howard L., Director of Finance, State of Ohio, Columbus, Ohio

CONRAD, Larry, Secretary of State, Indianapolis, Ind.

COOK, Herb Jr., Associate Publisher, Columbus *Monthly,* Columbus, Ohio

COUSINEAU, Stanley, Rouge Plant, Ford Motor Co., Dearborn, Mich.

COUTURIER, Jean J., Graduate School of Management, Northwestern University, Chicago. Ill.

CRELLIN, Jack, Labor Reporter, Detroit *News,* Detroit, Mich.

DALY, Robert, Appointments Secretary, Office of Gov. John Gilligan (Ohio)

DAY, William, Retired Executive Director, Illinois Legislative Council, Springfield, Ill.

DEDMON, Emmett, Vice President & Editorial Director, Chicago *Sun Times & Daily News,* Chicago, Ill.

DE GRANDIS, Paul, Deputy Director, Cleveland Board of Elections, Cleveland, Ohio

deGRAZIA, Victor, Director, The Kate Maremount Foundation, Chicago, Ill.

DE VISE, Pierre, Professor of Urban Sciences, University of Illinois at Chicago Circle, Chicago, Ill.

deZUTTER, Henry, Education Writer, Chicago *Daily News,* Chicago, Ill.

DONALDSON, William V., City Manager, Cincinnati, Ohio

DORTCH, Carl, President, Indianapolis Chamber of Commerce, Indianapolis, Ind.

DOYLE, James E., Federal Judge, U.S. District Court, Western District of Wisconsin, Madison, Wis.

DREISKE, John, Political Editor, Chicago *Sun-Times,* Chicago, Ill.

DREW, William, Commissioner, Department of City Development, City of Milwaukee, Wis.

DUBOIS, William, Executive Assistant to Governor Otis Bowen, Muncie, Ind.

EGAN, Very Rev. Msgr. John, Presentation Church, Chicago, Ill.

ENGLE, Glenn, Bureau Chief, Detroit *News,* Lansing, Mich.

ENGLEHART, Gordon, Indiana Correspondent, Louisville *Courier Journal,* Indianapolis, Ind.

FARRELL, Joseph A., Administrative Assistant to Sen. Charles Percy, Chicago, Ill.

FERMI, Mrs. Laura, Author and Civic Leader, Chicago, Ill.

FINNEY, Leon, Director, The Woodlawn Organization, Chicago, Ill.

FISHMAN, Sam, Director, Community Action Program, United Auto Workers, Detroit, Mich.

FISHER, Francis B., Regional Administrator, Department of Housing & Urban Development, Chicago, Ill.

FLANIGAN, Jack, Republican State Committee, Columbus, Ohio

FRASER, Douglas, President, United Auto Workers, Detroit, Mich.

FRY, Rev. John, First Presbyterian Church, Chicago, Ill.

FUERST, J. S., Professor of Political Science, Loyola University, Chicago, Ill.

GILLIGAN, John J., Governor of Ohio

GOLDBERG, Bertrand, Architect, Chicago, Ill.

GORDON, Robert, Director, Indiana Regional Office, Anti-Defamation League of B'nai B'rith, Indianapolis, Ind.

GOVE, Sam, Director, Institute of Government and Public Affairs, University of Illinois, Urbana, Ill.

GRAHAM, James, Press Secretary to Mayor Coleman Young, Detroit, Mich.

GREENLEAF, Charles, Politics & Program Division, Executive Office of the Governor, Lansing, Mich.

GRUEN, Victor, Architect and Urban Planner, Vienna, Austria (since deceased)

HAGA, Thomas H., Chairman, Genesee County Planning Commission, Flint, Mich.

HALL, John H., Assistant Executive Secretary— Governmental Services, Ohio Education Association, Columbus, Ohio

HANDLEY, Harold W., Former Governor of Indiana

HARRINGTON, Fred Harvey, President, University of Wisconsin, Madison, Wis.

HASSETT, Paul, President, Wisconsin Association of Commerce and Manufacturers, Madison, Wis.

HAWK, David, City Hall Reporter, Gary *Post-Tribune,* Gary, Ind.

HAYDEN, Martin, Editor, Detroit *News,* Detroit, Mich.

HERNANDEZ, Ernest, Reporter, Gary *Post-Tribune,* Gary, Ind.

HOGE, James F. Jr., Editor, Chicago *Sun-Times,* Chicago, Ill.

IRWIN, William P., Professor, Department of Political Science, Case Western Reserve University, Cleveland, Ohio

IVORY, Marcellius, Director, Region IA, United Auto Workers, Detroit, Mich.

JACKSON, The Rev. Jesse, Director, Operation PUSH, Chicago, Ill.

JAFFY, Stewart R., Attorney, Columbus, Ohio

JANOWITZ, Morris, Professor, Department of Sociology, University of Chicago, Chicago, Ill.

JOHNSON, Roland H., Staff Associate, The Cleveland Foundation, Cleveland, Ohio

JONES, Sam, Director, Urban League of Indianapolis, Indianapolis, Ind.

JORDAHL, Harold C. Jr., Chairman, Community and Natural Resource Development Programs, University Extension, University of Wisconsin, Madison, Wis.

KAY, Norton, Press Secretary to Gov. Daniel Walker, Springfield, Ill.

KEAST, William R., President, Wayne State University, Detroit, Mich.

KELLEY, Clifford, Alderman, City of Chicago, (Chairman of Black Aldermanic Caucus), Chicago, Ill.

KELLOGG, James, Director, Politics & Program Division, Executive Office of the Governor, Lansing, Mich.

KELLY, Edward, Research Director, Ohio Public Interest Campaign, Columbus, Ohio

KENNEDY, Robert E., Associate Editor, Chicago *Sun-Times,* Chicago, Ill.

KLEIN, Bernie, Controller, City of Detroit, Detroit, Mich.

KLEIN, Howard B., Chairman, Cleveland Planning Commission and President, Burrows Booksellers, Cleveland, Ohio

KLESSIG, Ed, Farmer, Cleveland, Wis.

KNOWLES, Robert P., President of the Wisconsin State Senate, Madison, Wis.

KOST, Blair, Director, Citizens League of Ohio, Cleveland, Ohio

KOTZBAUER, Robert, Editorial Writer, Akron *Beacon-Journal,* Akron, Ohio

KRAUS, William, Aide for Communications to Gov. Lee S. Dreyfus, Madison, Wis.

KROMHOLZ, Norman, Planning Director, Cleveland, Ohio

KULSEA, William, Correspondent, Booth Newspapers, Lansing, Mich.

LaFOLLETTE, Gerry, Correspondent, Indianapolis *News,* Indianapolis, Ind.

LAVIN, Allen S., Attorney for The Metropolitan Sanitary District of Greater Chicago, Ill.

LAWTON, John A., Attorney-at-Law, Lawton & Cates, and Member, State Natural Resources Board, Madison, Wis.

LEONARD, Richard H., Editor, Milwaukee *Journal,* Milwaukee, Wis.

LEVIN, Sander M., State Senator, Berkley, Mich.

LEWIS, David L., Professor, Graduate School of Business, University of Michigan, Ann Arbor, Mich.

LITTLEWOOD, Tom, College of Journalism and Communications, University of Illinois, Urbana, Ill.

LONGSTAFF, Robert, Lansing Bureau Chief, Booth Newspapers, Lansing, Mich.

LUCEY, Patrick J., Governor of Wisconsin

LUGAR, Richard G., Mayor of Indianapolis, Ind.

MAIER, Henry W., Mayor of Milwaukee, Wis.

MAIER, Irwin, Publisher, Milwaukee *Journal,* Milwaukee, Wis.

MARTIN, Louis, *The Defender,* Chicago, Ill.

MATHEWSON, Kent, President, The Metropolitan Fund, Inc., Detroit, Mich.

MAY, Robert, Editor, Mansfield *News-Journal,* Mansfield, Ohio

McALLISTER, Robert L., Director, Realtors' Ohio Committee, Columbus, Ohio

McCLORY, Robert, Free Lance Writer, Chicago, Ill.

McCREE, Floyd, Former Mayor of Flint, Mich.

McELROY, John M., Assistant to Governor James Rhodes (Ohio)

McNALLY, Joel, Reporter, The Milwaukee *Journal,* Milwaukee, Wis.

MEEGAN, Joseph B., Executive Secretary, Back of the Yards Neighborhood Council, Chicago, Ill.

MIKVA, Abner, U.S. Representative from Illinois

MILLIGAN, Thomas S., Indiana Republican State Chairman, Indianapolis, Ind.

MILLIKEN, William, Governor of Michigan

MINOW, Newton, Attorney, Former Chairman, Federal Communications Commission, Chicago, Ill.

MOODY, Tom, Mayor of Columbus, Ohio

MORGAN, James R., President, Wisconsin Taxpayers Alliance, Madison, Wis.

MOTT, Charles Stewart, Mott Foundation, Flint, Mich. (deceased)

MOTT, Harding, Mott Foundation, Flint, Mich.

MUHAMMED, Imam Wallace Deen, President, Black Muslim Church, Chicago, Ill.

MULLER, Will, Columnist, Detroit *News*, Detroit, Mich.

NELSON, Bryce, Correspondent, Los Angeles *Times*, Chicago, Ill.

NEWMAN, William, Architecture Writer, Chicago *Daily News*, Chicago, Ill.

NORTON, James A., President & Director, The Cleveland Foundation, Cleveland, Ohio

OGLIVIE, Richard B., Governor of Illinois

O'GRADY, Eugene P., Chairman, Democratic State Committee, Columbus, Ohio

O'HARA, Richard, Correspondent, Dayton *Daily News*, Dayton, Ohio

OLIVER, Jack L., Chief, Bureau of Information, Cleveland City Council, Cleveland, Ohio

PASTRICK, Robert, Controller, City of East Chicago, Ill.

PATRIARCHE, John, Executive Director, Michigan Municipal League, Ann Arbor, Mich.

PETRIE, Thomas, State Senator, Green Bay, Wis.

PICKUP, Robert, Executive Director, Citizens Research Council of Michigan, Detroit, Mich.

PISOR, Robert, Editor, *Monthly Detroit,* and former Press Secretary to Mayor Coleman Young, Detroit, Mich.

POPA, Robert, Correspondent, Detroit *News,* Detroit, Mich.

PROTESS, David, Better Government Association, Chicago, Ill.

PULLIAM, Eugene S., Publisher, Indianapolis *News* and *Star,* Indianapolis, Ind.

QUELLER, Robert, Citizens Research Council of Michigan, Detroit, Mich.

QUINN, Michael, Executive Director, Indiana Association of Cities and Towns, Indianapolis, Ind.

RAWSON, Mrs. Barbara, Assistant Director, The Cleveland Foundation, Cleveland, Ohio

RAYNER, A. A. Sammy, Alderman, 6th Ward, Chicago, Ill.

RECKTENWALD, William A., Investigator, Better Government Association, Chicago, Ill.

REDDIN, John, Editorial Page Editor, Milwaukee *Journal*, Milwaukee, Wis.

REDMOND, Mary, Head Librarian, Illinois State Library, Springfield, Ill.

RESTLE, Roland, Investigator, Better Government Association, Chicago, Ill.

ROBERTS, Edwin Jr., Editorial Page Editor, Detroit *News*, Detroit, Mich.

ROHN, David, Education Reporter, Indianapolis *News*, Indianapolis, Ind.

RUBIN, Irving J., Director, Detroit Regional Transportation & Land Use Study, Detroit, Mich.

RUTLEDGE, Hugh, City Government Reporter, Indianapolis *News,* Indianapolis, Ind.

SALAS, Jesus, Program Coordinator, United Migrant Opportunities Services, Inc., Milwaukee, Wis.

SALZARULO, Frank, Farm Editor, Indianapolis *News,* Indianapolis, Ind.

SARGENT, Steven, Executive Director, Illinois Municipal League, Springfield, Ill.

SCAMMON, Richard M., Director, Elections Research Center, and former Director of the Census, Washington, D.C.

SCARIANO, Anthony, State Representative, Park Forest, Ill.

SCHILDHOUSE, Burt, Public Relations, Columbus, Ohio

SCHMITT, John E., President, Wisconsin State AFL-CIO, Milwaukee, Wis.

SCHOLLE, August, President, Michigan State AFL-CIO, Lansing, Mich.

SCRIVEN, D. E., Ford Motor Company, Dearborn, Mich.

SERRIN, William, Author of *The Company and the Union,* Former Reporter, Detroit, Mich.

SHELTON, Donn, The Metropolitan Fund, Inc., Detroit, Mich.

SICKLES, Trent, Assistant to Management, Lazarus Department Store, Columbus, Ohio (deceased)

SIMMONS, Richard, Deputy Mayor, Detroit, Mich.

SIMON, Paul, Lieutenant Governor of Illinois

SIMPSON, Dick, Alderman, City of Chicago, Ill.

SLAUGHTER, Guy, Correspondent, Gary *Post-Tribune,* Gary, Ind.

SMITH, Henry, Director, Public Information Office, Bureau of the Census, Washington, D.C.

SMOLLER, W. Jeffrey, Director of Information, State Department of Natural Resources, Madison, Wis.

SOGLIN, Paul, Mayor of Madison, Wis.

STAFF, Charles, Drama and Music Critic, Indianapolis *News,* Indianapolis, Ind.

ST. ANGELO, Gordon, Program Officer, Lilly Endowment, Inc., and Former State Democratic Chairman, Indianapolis, Ind.

STANTON, James V., President, Cleveland City Council, Cleveland, Ohio

STEVENSON, Adlai, III, State Treasurer of Illinois (subsequently U.S. Senator from Illinois)

STEWART, R. Jaffy, Attorney, Columbus, Ohio

SWAN, James D., State Senator, Elkhorn, Wis.

SYKES, Donald, Executive Director, Community Relations-Social Development Commission, Milwaukee, Wis.

TAFT, Charles P., City Councilman, Cincinnati, Ohio

TAGGE, George, Correspondent, Chicago *Tribune,* Springfield, Ill.

TALBOTT, Basil Jr., Political Editor, Chicago *Sun-Times,* Chicago, Ill.

TEER, Fred L., Director, Model Cities Agency, East St. Louis, Ill.

TEETER, Robert M., Market Opinion Research, Detroit, Mich.

TENEBAUM, Robert, Associate Editor, Columbus *Monthly,* Columbus, Ohio

TER HORST, Jerry, Washington Correspondent, Detroit *News,* Detroit, Mich.

THOMPSON, James, Governor of Illinois

THUMA, Ed, Budget Director, State Board of Health, Indianapolis, Ind.

TOWNSEND, Leonard, Attorney-at-Law, Detroit, Mich.

TYSON, Remer, Political Reporter, Detroit *Free Press,* Detroit, Mich.

USHER, Brian, Capitol Correspondent, Akron *Beacon-Journal,* Columbus, Ohio

VISSER, Paul, Administrative Assistant to Rep. Donald Riegle, Flint, Mich.

WADSWORTH, Homer, President, The Cleveland Foundation, Cleveland, Ohio

WAGNER, Thomas J., Administrative Assistant to Sen. Adlai Stevenson (Ill.)

WAHNER, James, Assistant Majority Leader, Wisconsin Assembly, Madison, Wis.

WALKER, Dan, Governor of Illinois

WASHINGTON, Lawrence, Ford Motor Company, Dearborn, Mich.

WASHNIS, George, Administrative Assistant to the Mayor, East St. Louis, Ill.

WEEKS, George, Administrative Assistant to Governor William Milliken, Lansing, Mich.

WEISMAN, Joel, Journalist, Chicago, Ill.

WEENING, Richard, President, Rainbow Publications, Milwaukee, Wis.

WELLS, Herman B., Former President and Chancellor, Indiana University, Bloomington, Ind.

WELSH, Matthew E., Former Governor of Indiana.

WESTMORELAND, Carl, President, Mt. Auburn Housing Foundation, Cincinnati, Ohio

WIDNER, Ralph, President, Academy for Contemporary Problems, Columbus, Ohio

WILHELM, Al, Flint *Journal,* Flint, Mich.

WINDHAM, J. C., President, Pabst Brewing Company, Milwaukee, Wis.

WLODARCZYK, Rita, State Coordinator, Wisconsin Women's Political Caucus, Monona, Wis.

WOOD, James, President, Wisconsin Center for Public Policy, Madison, Wis.

WOODMAN, D. K., Editor, Mansfield *News-Journal,* Mansfield, Ohio

WRIGHT, Max, Secretary-Treasurer, Indiana State AFL-CIO, Greenwood, Ind.

WYATT, Robert H., Executive Secretary, Indiana State Teachers Association, Indianapolis, Ind.

WYNGAARD, John, Green Bay *Press-Gazette* and Appleton *Post-Crescent,* Madison, Wis.

YOUNG, Coleman, Mayor of Detroit, Mich.

ZEIDLER, Frank, Former Mayor of Milwaukee, Wis.

ZIEGNER, Edward, Political Editor, Indianapolis *News,* Indianapolis, Ind.

ZIMMERMAN, Richard, Columbus Bureau Chief, Cleveland *Plain-Dealer,* Columbus, Ohio

BIBLIOGRAPHY

In ADDITION TO THE EXTENSIVE INTERVIEWS for these books, reference was made to books and articles on the individual states and cities, their history and present-day condition. To the authors whose works we have drawn upon, our sincerest thanks.

NATIONAL BOOKS

Barone, Michael, Ujifusa, Grant, and Matthews, Douglas, *The Almanac of American Politics— 1972, 1974, 1976, 1978 and 1980.* Boston: Gambit Publishing Co., published biennially.

Birmingham, Stephen, *The Right People—A Portrait of the American Social Establishment.* Boston: Little, Brown, 1968.

Book of the States. The Council of State Governments. Published biennially, Lexington, Ky.

Brownson, Charles B., *Congressional Staff Directory.* Published annually, Washington, D.C.

1970 Census of Population and Subsequent Population Estimates, Bureau of the Census, Washington, D.C.

Churches and Church Membership in the United States—An Enumeration by Region, State and County, by Douglas W. Johnson, Paul R. Picard, and Bernard Quinn. Washington, D.C.: Glenmary Research Center, 1974.

Citizens Conference on State Legislatures. Various studies including *The Sometime Governments: A Critical Study of the 50 American Legislatures,* by John Burns. New York: Bantam Books, 1971.

David, Paul T., *Party Strength in the United States, 1872–1970.* Charlottesville: University Press of Virginia, 1972.

Editor and Publisher International Year Book. New York: Editor and Publisher. Published annually.

Encyclopedia Americana. Annual editions. New York: Americana Corporation. (Includes excellent state and city review articles.)

Facts and Figures on Government Finance. Published annually by the Tax Foundation, Inc., Washington, D.C.

Farb, Peter, *Face of North America—The Natural History of a Continent.* New York: Harper & Row, 1963.

Federal-State-Local Finances—Significant Features of Fiscal Federalism. Published periodically by the Advisory Commission on Intergovernmental Relations, Washington, D.C.

Guide to U.S. Elections (Washington: Congressional Quarterly, 1975).

Gunther, John, *Inside U.S.A.* New York: Harper & Row, 1947 and 1951.

Jacob, Herbert, and Vines, Kenneth N., *Politics in the American States: A Comparative Analysis.* Boston: Little, Brown, 1971.

Life Pictorial Atlas of the World. Editors of *Life* and Rand McNally. New York: Time, Inc., 1961.

The National Atlas of the United States of America. Geological Survey, U.S. Department of the Interior, Washington, D.C. 1970.

Ranking the Top Colleges, Chronicle of Higher Education, 1979.

Rankings of the States. Prepared annually by the Research Division, National Education Assn., Washington, D.C.

Regional Economic Trends, prepared by Bureau of Economic Analysis, U.S. Department of Commerce, for the White House Conference on Balanced National Growth and Economic Development, 1978.

Saloma, John S. III, and Sontag, Frederick H., *Parties: The Real Opportunity for Effective Citizen Politics.* New York: Knopf, 1972.

Sanford, Terry, *Storm Over the States.* New York: McGraw Hill. 1967.

Scammon, Richard M., ed. *America Votes—A Handbook of Contemporary American Election Statistics.* Published biennially by the Government Affairs Institute, through Congressional Quarterly, Washington, D.C.

Sharkansky, Ira, *The Maligned States: Policy Accomplishments, Problems, and Opportunities.* New York: McGraw Hill, 1972.

State Government Finances. Published annually by The U.S. Department of Commerce, Bureau of the Census, Washington, D.C.

Statistical Abstract of the United States. Published annually by the U.S. Department of Commerce, Bureau of the Census, Washington, D.C.

Survey of Current Business. U.S. Department of Commerce, Bureau of Economic Analysis, Washington, D.C., monthly. April and August editions contain full reports on geographic trends in personal income and per capita income.

These United States—Our Nation's Geography, History and People. Reader's Digest Assn., Pleasantville, N.Y., 1968.

Uniform Crime Reports for the United States. Published annually by the U.S. Department of Justice, Federal Bureau of Investigation, Washington, D.C.

Who's Who in American Politics. (New York: R. R. Bowker Co., published biennially).

The World Almanac and Book of Facts. Published annually by Newspaper Enterprise Assn., Inc., New York.

REGIONAL BOOKS AND SOURCES

Midwest Politics by John H. Fenton (New York: Holt, Rinehart & Winston, 1966) remains the best analytic book on the region's varying state political cultures, and their contrasts, to appear in recent times. Insights into many aspects of the region's life appear in *The Heartland,* by Robert McLaughlin (New York: Time-Life Library of America, 1967).

Among the more helpful reports on the region have been *The State of the Region: Economic Trends of the 1970s in the Northeast and Midwest,* prepared by the Northeast-Midwest. Congressional Coalition, the Northeast-Midwest Senate Coalition, and the Northeast-Midwest Institute, Washington, D.C., 1979; *Projections of Population and Employment for the Upper Great Lakes States, 1970–2000,* by the Population Studies Center of the University of Michigan, prepared for the Upper Great Lakes Regional Commission, 1979; *Upper Great Lakes Regional Atlas: Economic, Social, Environmental Indicators,* Upper Great Lakes Regional Commission, Washington, D.C., 1979; *Stimulating the Economy of the Great Lakes States,* survey for the Committee for Great Lakes Action, prepared by the Academy for Contemporary Problems, Columbus, Ohio, 1977; *Milwaukee and the Economic Future of Mid-America,* a position paper by Milwaukee Mayor Henry Maier, May 25, 1978; *A Statement by the Committee for Great Lakes Economic Action on Regional Growth and Development* Issues, prepared for the White House Conference on Balanced National Growth and Economic Development by the Academy for Contemporary Problems, Columbus, Ohio, 1978; and *Midwest State Profiles,* by the Northeast-Midwest Congressional Coalition and Northeast-Midwest Institute, Washington, D.C. September 1978.

Regular analyses of regional issues appear in *The Northern Perspective,* syndicated weekly newspaper column by Michael J. McManus appearing in many Midwestern and Northeastern newspapers.

Helpful individual newspaper and magazine articles on the region include: "Special Report: Government and the Auto," *National Journal,* Jan. 3, 1976; "Federal Jobs 'Flee' Cities, Panel Says; Chicago Loses 5,497 in 10 Years," by Ed McManus, Chicago *Tribune,* March 11, 1979; "Decrease in Farm Population Accelerates; Figures Show a 14% Decline from 1970–75," by Robert Reinhold, The New York *Times,* April 15, 1977; "Exporting Jobs," by Bill Curry, Washington *Post,* Oct. 10, 1977; "Zenith Losses Force Shift Overseas," by Jerry Knight, Washington *Post,* Sept. 29, 1977; "Years of Choking Paper Mill Wastes," by Casey Bukro, Chicago *Tribune* Press Service, Oct. 18, 1975; "'Heartland' Cities Rebound," by Richard J. Cattani, *The Christian Science Monitor* Aug. 25, 1978.

On environmental issues: "Life on a Dying Lake," by Peter Schrag, *Saturday Review,* Sept. 20, 1969; *Lake Erie Report,* from the Federal Water Pollution Control Administration, Department of the Interior, Washington, August 1968; "Great Lakes Pollution Poses Two Problems," by Seth S. King, New York *Times,* Feb. 6, 1970; "Indiana Harbor Winning in its Long Battle with Pollution," by Casey Bukro, Chicago *Tribune* Press Service, Oct. 25, 1970; "Great Lakes Pollution Fight Is Gaining," by William K. Stevens, New York *Times,* May 23, 1974; "Indiana Harbor Canal Cleaner, But Still Polluted," by Casey Bukro, Chicago *Tribune* Press Service, Oct. 3, 1975; "Cleanest Lake Threatens Life," by Casey Bukro, Chicago *Tribune* Press Service, Oct. 13, 1975; "Ailing Great Lakes Slowly Recovering," by Margot Hornblower, Washington *Post,* July 25, 1976; "Price of Pollution: the Fight to Clean Up Lake Erie is Proving to be Long and Costly," by Craig R. Charney, *The Wall Street Journal,* Aug. 31, 1976; "The Lagging Cleanup of Great Lakes Pollution," *Business Week,* May 29, 1978; "Comeback for the Great Lakes," *Time,* Dec. 3, 1979.

ILLINOIS

Excellent though slightly dated accounts of the Illinois political scene appear in the Illinois chapter of John H. Fenton's *Midwest Politics* (New York: Holt, Rinehart & Winston, 1966) and Austin Ranney's *Illinois Politics* (New York: New York University Press, 1960). A more recent general review of the state's background appears in *Illinois: A History,* by Richard J. Jensen (New York: W.W. Norton & Co., 1978). A number of excellent essays on Illinois' past and present appear in *Prairie State,* Paul M. Angle, ed., University of Chicago Press, 1968. Ovid Demaris' *Captive City* (New York: Lyle Stuart, 1969) is a frightening

but well documented account of organized crime and corrupt politics in Chicago. Other books used as background for this chapter, or quoted in the text, include: Arthur M. Brazier, *Black Determination: Story of the Woodlawn Organization* (Grand Rapids, Mich.: William B. Eerdmans Publishing Co., 1969); Baker Brownell, *The Other Illinois* (New York: Duell, Sloan & Pearce, 1958); *Boss: Richard J. Daley of Chicago,* by Mike Royko (New York: E. P. Dutton, 1971); *Clout: Mayor Daley and His City,* by Len O'Connor (New York: Avon Books, 1975); and *Don't Make No Waves ... Don't Back No Losers,* by

Milton Rakove (Bloomington, Ind.: Indiana University Press, 1975).

Other sources—Regular coverage of the Chicago *Tribune*, Chicago *Sun-Times*, and *Illinois Issues*, the serious monthly magazine on Illinois government and politics published by Sangamon State University, Springfield.

CHICAGO "Portrait of a Lusty City," by Russell Owen, New York *Times Magazine*, April 6, 1947; "The Cities of America: Chicago," by George Sessions Perry, *Saturday Evening Post*, Nov. 3, 1945; "The Chicago the Delegates Won't See," by Leon M. Depres, *The Progressive*, August 1968; "Chicago Stretching Its Seams," by Donald Janson, New York *Times*, Jan. 6, 1969; "Chicago!", by Harvey Arden, *National Geographic*, April 1978; "Chicago a Heavy Loser in Pentagon Tax Budgeting," by Bruce Ingersoll, Chicago *Sun Times*, March 13, 1979; "How Chicago Keeps Downtown Attractive," by Nancy Iran Phillips, *Christian Science Monitor*, May 24, 1974; "Chicago Thoroughfare Emerges as a Mecca for Wealthy Shoppers," by Frederick C. Klein, *Wall Street Journal*, March 3, 1976; "State Street Mall: Chicago's Retail Hope," by William Robbins, New York *Times*, June 20, 1978; "Chicago, Ill.: Scene of Cooptation," chapter in *The City Poor of the 1960s*, by Milton Viorst, The Kettering Foundation, 1977; "Chicago's Reaction to 'Aces,' " by Robert McClory, *Illinois Issues*, September 1978; "The Local Effort Led the Way," by Rochelle Stanfield, *National Journal*, June 3, 1978.

POLITICS *The Chicago Politics Papers*, a series sponsored by the Center for Urban Affairs, Northwestern University, and the Institute of Government and Public Affairs, University of Illinois (1979): "The Last of the Great Urban Machines and the Last of the Great Urban Mayors, Chicago Politics 1955–1977," by Kathleen A. Kemp and Robert L. Lineberry; "The Political Machine, the Urban Bureaucracy, and the Distribution of Public Services," by Kennety R. Mladenka; "Black Machine Politics in the Post-Daley Era," by Michael B. Preston; "Latinos and Chicago Politics," by Joanne M. Belenchia; and "Mayoral Voting in Chicago: the Daley-Bilandic Era," by Joseph Zikmund II.

"Daley of Chicago," by David Halberstam, *Harper's Magazine*, August 1968; "New Life in Old Politics," by R. W. Apple Jr., New York *Times*, March 19, 1970; "Voting in Chicago West Side Ghetto Is Mockery of Democratic Process," by Rowland Evans and Robert Novak, Washington *Post*, Nov. 11, 1968; "The Chicago Coalition Is Still Holding Together," by Dick Griffin, *Fortune*, Sept. 11, 1978; "Chicago Without Daley—New Cards in the Old Game," by Paul Delaney, *The Nation*, May 28, 1977; " 'Calamity Jane': A Civic Drama Plays Windy City," by Kathy Sawyer, Washington *Post*, Feb. 12, 1980; " 'Calamity Jane? Quarrelsome Style of Chicago's Mayor Stirs Political Heat," by Frederick C. Klein, *Wall Street Journal*, Jan. 30, 1980.

HOUSING, TRANSPORTATION AND EDUCATION "U.S.-Baekel Chicago Test Offers Suburban Life to Ghetto Blacks," by Robert Reinhold, New York *Times*, May 22, 1978; "Charge Suburb Housing Rules Bar Low-Income Families," by Don DeVeit, Chicago *Sun-Times*, Jan. 26, 1979; "Chicago Loses $20 Million in Aid in Housing Dispute," by Joel Weisman, Washington *Post*, Jan. 15, 1972; "Chicago's Loop: Metamorphosis," by Seth King, New York *Times*, Sept. 23, 1973; "Transit Body Set for Chicago Area," by Seth S. King, New York *Times*, Dec. 2, 1973; "Chi-

cago School Desegregation: Will Access Work?", by Vicki Gerson, *Illinois Issues*, September 1978; "City Schools Face Funding Cutoff," by Linda Wertsch, Chicago *Sun-Times*, May 12, 1978; "School Integration in Chicago," by Paul Delaney, New York *Times*, May 16, 1977; "Schools Get 3 Months to Fix Hannon Plan," by John McCarrol and Meg O'Connor, Chicago *Tribune*, Dec 17, 1978; "White School Enrollment Dips to 21.5%," by John McCarron, Chicago *Tribune*, Dec. 14, 1978; "Joseph Hannon Digs in His Heels," by Vernon Jarrett, Chicago *Tribune*, Dec. 17, 1978.

BLACKS "Black Powerlessness in Chicago," by Harold M. Baron, *Trans-Action*, November 1968; "Jesse Jackson: Heir to Dr. King?", by Richard Levine, *Harper's Magazine*, March 1969; "Black Hope-White Hope," by John Pekkanen, *Life*, Nov. 21, 1969; "Chicago's Operation Breadbasket is Seeking Racial Solutions in Economic Problems," by John Herbers, New York *Times*, June 2, 1969; "Interview: Jesse Jackson," *Playboy*, November 1969; "Black Panther Killings Leave Chicago a City on Edge," by Edward Shanahan, Detroit *Free Press*, Dec. 21, 1969; "Jesse Jackson Organizing Push to Aid Poor in Urban Areas," by William Greider, Washington *Post*, Jan. 2, 1972; "A Mix of Black Pride v. Showmanship," by Joel Dreyfus, Washington *Post*, Sept. 20, 1973; "Black Protest: Room For All?", by Ellis Case, Chicago *Sun-Times*, Sept. 24, 1972; "Jackson Curbed on Registration," by Seth King, New York *Times*, Sept. 17, 1972; "Rights Groups' Hopes for '75," by Paul Delaney, New York *Times*, Jan. 5, 1975; "Give the People a Vision," by Jesse Jackson, New York *Times Magazine*, April 18, 1976; "Country Preacher Jesse Jackson Launches New Black Liberation Effort: People United to Save Humanity," by Charles Sanders, *Ebony*, March 1972; "Rave Reviews Fade for Jackson," by Robert McClory, *Race Relations Reporter*, March 1971; "What Makes Jesse Jackson Run," by Dorothy Gilliam, Washington *Post*, Jan. 15, 1975.

STATEWIDE ILLINOIS "The City and the Plain," by Robert Paul Jordan, *National Geographic*, June 1967; "Illinois—Mid-American Empire," *Fortune*, January 1968; "The Prairie State—Illinois," New York *Times*, Oct. 2, 1956.

POLITICS "That Other Illinois Primary," by Albert R. Hunt, *Wall Street Journal*, March 11, 1976; "How Illinois Stacks up Against the Other States," by Neal R. Peirce and Jerry Hagstrom, *Chicago*, November 1977; "Vote Power: Suburbs Up, Cities Down," by Peter W. Colby and Paul Michael Green, *Illinois Issues*, November 1978; "Downstate Holds the Key to Victory," by Peter W. Colby and Paul Michael Green, *Illinois Issues*, February 1978; "Voting Patterns in the 96 Downstate Counties," by Peter W. Colby and Paul Michael Green, *Illinois Issues*, August 1978.

"Illinois Politics Feeling Effects of Gov. Walker," by Francis Ward, Los Angeles *Times*, Nov. 14, 1973; "Illinois 'Maverick' Governor Shuns 'Politics as Usual' Path," by Godfrey Sperling Jr., *Christian Science Monitor*, March 10, 1978; "Gov. Walker of Illinois, Who Walked to a Win, Runs into Problems," by Frederick Klein and Jonathan Laing, *Wall Street Journal*, Dec. 27, 1974; "Illinois Walker: A Dark Horse in Populist Silos," by Joel Weisman, Washington *Post*, Jan. 5, 1975; "Illinois Governor Looks to 1976 Bid," by Seth S. King, New York *Times*, July 21, 1974.

"GOP'S Big Jim 'Cases' the White House," by Louise Sweeney, *Christian Science Monitor*, April 20, 1977; "A Candidate with White House Potential," by David S. Broder, Washington *Post*,

Oct. 17, 1976; "Jim Thompson Acting Like Candidate Carter," by Jack Germond and Jules Witcover, Washington *Star*, May 4, 1977; "Thompson Adopts Politics of Personality, Modest Expectations," by Bud Farrar, Decatur *Herald and Review*, May 29, 1977; "GOP Governor has National Ambitions," by Lou Cannon, Washington *Post*, June 6, 1977; "Secret Bilandic-Thompson Deal Disclosed," by Larry Green, Chicago *Daily News*, June 17, 1977; "Big Jim," by Gary Delsohm, *Illinois Issues*, September 1977; Big Jim Thompson for President?", by Michael Kilian, *Inquiry*, May 15, 1978; "Gov. Thompson: What Kind of Politician is He?", by Milton Rakove, *Illinois Issues*, October 1977; "State of the State Message," by Gov. James Thompson, March 2, 1977; "Big Jim Thompson—Moving the Landslide Slowly," by Neal R. Peirce, *National Journal*, July 16, 1977.

CONGRESSIONAL DELEGATION "The Other Ev Dirksen," by Charles Roberts, *Newsweek*, June 16, 1969; "Everett McKinley Dirksen," *Congressional Quarterly*, July 26, 1968, p. 1904; *Dirksen: Portrait of a Public Man*, by Neil MacNeil (New York: World Publishing Co., 1970); "Ev Dirksen: The Complete Senator," by Robert Novak, *Book Week*, Nov. 22, 1970; "The Adlai III Brand of Politics," by William Barry Furling, New York *Times Magazine*, Feb. 22, 1970; "Adlai Hits 'Feudal' Party," by John Dreiske, Chicago *Sun-Times*, Sept. 18, 1968;

"Illinois' Adlai Stevenson," *Time*, Nov. 16, 1970; "Charles H. Percy: The Middle Man," a chapter of *The Republican Establishment*," by Stephen Hess and David S. Broder (New York: Harper & Row, 1967); "Sen. Stevenson's Uncertain Search," by F. Richard Ciccone, Chicago *Tribune*, Feb. 9, 1979; "A Frustrated Adlai Irked with Carter," by Aldo Beckman, Chicago *Tribune*, Feb. 3, 1979.

OTHER "Illinois' Shrinking Farmlands," by James Krohe Jr., *Illinois Issues*, December 1978; "Managing Community Change," by Cecilia McCartney Hoffmann and Michael D. Rancey, Municipal Management Innovation Series No. 28, International City Management Association, Winter 1978–79; "Cement Bribery Trial," by Mike Lawrence, *Illinois Issues*, December 1976; "Fable for our Times," *Forbes* Magazine, March 1, 1973; "East St. Louis Faces Removal of Officials in Fund Inquiry," by Nathaniel Sheppard Jr., New York *Times*, March 25, 1975; "East St. Louis: Indicted," *Time*, Nov. 18, 1974; "Politics in Peoria County," by Carolyn Botarsky, *Illinois Issues*, August 1976; "Peoria," by David R. Pichaske, *Atlantic*, November 1974; "U.S. Rights Report Cites Racial Bias in Cairo, Ill.," by Peter Reich, Washington *Post*, Feb. 7, 1973; "Some Integrated Towns Draw Fire for Efforts to Keep Racial Balance," by Frederick C. Klein, *Wall Street Journal*, Jan. 8, 1979.

WISCONSIN

Being the progressive and forward-looking state it is, Wisconsin also seems to have a larger share of literature devoted to it than most other Midwestern states. Among the most valuable sources in preparing the chapter were *Wisconsin: A Story of Progress*, by William F. Ranney (Appleton, Wis.: Perin Press, 1963); "Programmatic Politics in Wisconsin," a chapter in John H. Fenton's *Midwest Politics* (New York: Holt, Rinehart and Winston, 1966); *Politics in Wisconsin*, by Leon D. Epstein (Madison: University of Wisconsin Press, 1958); *Wisconsin: A History*, by Robert C. Nesbit (Madison: University of Wisconsin Press, 1973); *Political Reform in Wisconsin*, by Emanuel L. Philipp (Madison: State Historical Society of Wisconsin, 1973); the excellent historical section of *Wisconsin*, by the Wisconsin Writers' Project (New York: Duell, Sloan & Peace, 1941); *A Personal Narrative of Political Experiences*, by Robert W. LaFollette (Madison: Robert M. LaFollette Co., 1911); *Joe Must Go*, by Leroy Gore (New York: Julian Messner, Inc., 1954); *The New Citizenship*, by David P. Thelen (Columbia, Mo.: University of Missouri Press, 1972); *Wisconsin: A History*, by Richard Nelson Current (New York: W.W. Norton & Co., 1976); and *The People of Wisconsin*, a public opinion poll published and copyrighted by the Wisconsin Center for Public Policy, 1605 Monroe St., Madison, Wis. 53711, 1978.

The chapter was enriched by regular political-governmental coverage of the Milwaukee *Journal* and Milwaukee *Sentinel*, Madison *Capital Times*, Wisconsin *State Journal* and Green Bay *Press Gazette* (home paper of John Wyngaard's valuable column on state affairs).

GENERAL AND POLITICS "Wisconsin: State of Insurgents," by William Barry Furlong,

New York *Times Magazine*, April 3, 1960; "Wisconsin Survey Leads to Master Plan for Urban Growth," by George H. Favre, *Christian Science Monitor*, Nov. 26, 1968; "Wisconsin Groups Map Resurgence of Democrats in 1970," by Tim Wyngaard, Washington *Post*, Sept. 4, 1969; "Wisconsin Crossovers Worrying Democrats," by David S. Broder, Washington *Post*, April 11, 1972; "Top Wisconsin Vote-Getter Not Assured of Most Delegates," by David S. Broder, Washington *Post*, April 2, 1972; "Three April Primaries Appear Pivotal to Convention Vote," by R. W. Apple Jr., New York *Times*, April 4, 1976; "In Wisconsin, Despite Ads, Udall Isn't Familiar Name," by Joseph Lelyveld, New York *Times*, April 4, 1976; "Close Udall-Carter Battle Shaping Up in Wisconsin," by Seth S. King, New York *Times*, April 4, 1976; "Lucey of Wisconsin: How One Governor Does His Job," by Eugene C. Harrington, Milwaukee *Journal*, (Reprinted from The *Nation*), June 19, 1976; "Lucey Brought Change By . . . ," by Eugene C. Harrington, Milwaukee *Journal*, Oct. 17, 1974; "Lucey: Resolute Reformer," by Eugene C. Harrington, Milwaukee *Journal*, Feb. 29, 1976; "Maverick in Wisconsin," by David S. Broder, Washington *Post*, Oct. 17, 1978; "No Anti-Tax Fever in State, Study Says," by K. S. Kinney, Milwaukee *Journal*, Nov. 19, 1978.

"Gaylord Nelson and the Myth of the White Knight," by Walter Shapiro, *Washington Monthly*, July-August 1975; "The Perplexing Mr. Proxmire," by Martin Tolchin, New York *Times Magazine*, May 28, 1978; "Report From Washington," by Martin Nolan, *Atlantic*, December 1970; "Reuss (D-Wisconsin), A Demanding Man," by Frank Aukofer, New York *Times*, March 2, 1975; "Laird's Years: The Big Price for Keeping the Brass Off His Back," by Michael Gerler, Washington *Post*, Jan. 2, 1973.

"University of Wisconsin is Facing Grim Struggle for Survival," by Eric Wentworth, Washington *Post*, Sept. 13, 1970; "Compulsory Education: The Plain People Resist," by Stephen Arons, *Saturday Review*, Jan. 15, 1972: "25 Years of Desegregation: A 'New Mythology' is Undermining the 'Moral Imperative' That Got School Integration Started," by David I. Bednarek, Milwaukee *Journal*, March 18, 1979.

BUSINESS AND ENVIRONMENT "Despite Cold Weather, High Taxes, Wisconsin Keeps Luring People," by Paul Ingrassia, *Wall Street Journal*, Sept. 16, 1977; "State's Big Business: Who's Who: Here's Roadmap to Location, Size and Profitability of Wisconsin's Major Corporations," by David L. Beal, Milwaukee *Journal*, Sept. 17, 1978; "Farm Economy Not so Healthy for Beginners," Wisconsin *State Journal*, Jan. 21, 1979; "Who Rules the Foam?" *Forbes*, Dec. 15, 1972; "Schlitz and Pabst: Giants Fighting Back," by Stephen R. Byers, Milwaukee *Journal*, May 21, 1978; "The Spirit of Wisconsin" (advertisement), *Forbes*, April 17, 1968.

Series on lake cleanup by Quincy Dadisman in Milwaukee *Sentinel*, October 1978; "The Laws of the White Man Have Hurt the Menominee," by William E. Farrell, New York *Times*, Jan. 10, 1975; "OK $501 Million Plan for Sewer Separation," by Ron Marose, Milwaukee *Sentinel*, May 25, 1979; "Lampreys in Fox River May

Ruin Success Story," by Thomas J. Hagerty, The Milwaukee *Journal*, April 22, 1979; "Peninsula Offers Lure from a Frantic Pace," by Dan Chabot, Milwaukee *Journal*, May 28, 1978.

MILWAUKEE Wells, Robert W., *This is Milwaukee*, Garden City, N.Y.: Doubleday and Company, Inc., 1970; "Racial Issues Dominate in Milwaukee's Politics," by D.J.R. Bruckner, Los Angeles *Times*, March 10, 1968; "Maier's Head Respected In, Outside City of Suds," by William C. Barnard, Cleveland *Plain Dealer*, Feb. 12, 1969; "Milwaukee Mayor Fights Joint News Ownership," by Donald Janson, New York *Times*, May 4, 1969; "Milwaukee's Mercurial Henry Maier," by Ralph Whitehead Jr., *City*, March-April, 1972; "Aldermen Grumble at Bit at Minor Roles," by Michael Bauman, Milwaukee *Journal*, April 19, 1979; "Boston to Milwaukee: Here's Looking at You," by Nathan Cobb, Milwaukee *Journal*, Dec. 10, 1978; "Milwaukee: Livable but Not Problem Free," by William E. Farrell, New York *Times*, Sept. 29, 1975;

"Milwaukee's Melting Pot Fails," by John Keefe and Patricia Simms, Wisconsin *State Journal*, Feb. 29, 1976, and following articles in series: "This Town Was Built Segregated," Feb. 29, 1976; "School Fears Fester in Milwaukee," March 1, 1976; "Milwaukee Marks Time on Issue of Busing," March 2, 1976; "Education Quality Big Milwaukee Problem," March 4, 1976; and "Milwaukee's Time, Options Limited," March 5, 1976.

MICHIGAN

An excellent review of the state's political trends appears in the Michigan chapter of John H. Fenton's *Midwest Politics* (New York: Holt, Rinehart & Winston, 1966); valuable background material may also be found in *Political Party Patterns in Michigan*, by Stephen B. and Vera H. Sarasohn (Detroit: Wayne State University Press, 1957); in *Michigan: A History*, by Bruce Catton (New York: W.W. Norton & Co., 1976); and *PBB: An American Tragedy*, by Edwin Chen (Englewood Cliffs: Prentice-Hall, 1979). Also of use were several publications of the Citizens Research Council of Michigan (a non-profit group, supported by state businesses, that furnishes excellent research material on the state's tax structure), as well as material from the state chamber of commerce. Reference was made to several reports of the Detroit Regional Transportation and Land Use Study, to population projections by the Southeast Michigan Council of Governments, and to such government documents as *Cities in Transition* (report of the Michigan state government Urban Group to Gov. William Milliken, December 1977), and annual reports of state agencies and gubernatorial addresses.

The chapter draws on ongoing coverage of several Michigan newspapers, especially the Detroit *News* and *Free Press*, as well as the following articles in particular.

POLITICS "Soapy, the Boy Wonder," by Beverly Smith, Jr., *Saturday Evening Post*, Nov. 9, 1957; "Romney: A Tough Act to Follow," by Glenn Engle, Detroit *News*, Jan 19, 1969; "Bill Milliken May Look like a Boy, but He's a Man," by Will Muller, Detroit *News Magazine*, Jan. 5, 1969; "A New Governor Finds Civility Pays," by Anthony Ripley, New York *Times*, Feb. 2, 1969;

"Happy Campaigner Milliken," by Robert L. Pisor, Detroit Sunday *News*, Sept. 29, 1974; "'72 Primaries: Michigan an Orphan," by David S. Broder, Washington *Post*, May 11, 1972; "Parties Feel Tensions in County Battleground," Washington *Post*, Dec. 12, 1971; "A Close Call for Carter; Black Vote Gave Him Narrow Edge over Udall," by Jules Witcover and Joel D. Weisman, Washington *Post*, May 20, 1976; "Factory Workers Turning to Nixon," by Duncan Spencer, Washington *Evening Star* and *Daily News*, Sept. 14, 1972; "A New Democratic Coalition," by David S. Broder, Washington *Post*, Oct. 18, 1978; "Tax Panel Studies State School Financing," by Angelo Baglivo, Newark *Sunday News*, May 9, 1971; "Michigan Tries School Aid Reform," by Allen Phillips, *The Christian Science Monitor*, Sept. 7, 1973.

CONGRESSIONAL DELEGATION "Michigan's Hart Emerges as Ball-Carrier for Liberals," by Spencer Rich, Washington *Post*, Feb. 15, 1970; "Establishment Rebel: Michigan's Senator Philip Hart," by Saul Friedman, Detroit *Free Press*, March 1969; "'Mother of the Era': Ex-Rep Griffiths Is No Radical Crusader, Though," by Mary Russell, Washington *Post*, July 13, 1976; "What Grand Rapids Did for Jerry Ford—and Vice Versa," by Robert Sherrill, New York *Times Magazine*, Oct. 20, 1974; "Gerald Ford a Congressman in the White House," by Lou Cannon, Washington *Post*, Oct. 24, 1976.

AUTOS "Henry Ford, Superstar," by Dan Cordtz, *Fortune*, May 1973; "The Small Car Blues at General Motors," *Business Week*, March 16, 1974; "The Energy Trauma at General Motors," by Marylin Bender, New York *Times*, March 24, 1974; "Detroit Turns Against the Gas Guzzlers," by Charles G. Burck, *Fortune*, January 1974;

"Detroit Thinks Small," *Newsweek,* April 1, 1974; "Automotive Recalls: The Plague of the '70s," by Douglas D. Armstrong, The Milwaukee *Journal,* Oct. 1, 1978; "How G.M. Turned Itself Around," by Charles G. Burck, *Fortune,* Jan. 16, 1978; "Crisis At Chrysler," by Guy Darst, Milwaukee *Journal,* Aug. 5, 1979; "Can Iacocca Save Chrysler?" by Jerry C. Davis, Chicago *Sun-Times,* March 21, 1979; "Lateness Is Iacocca's Big Worry at Chrysler," by Tom Kleene and Gregory Skwira, Chicago *Tribune,* March 4, 1979; "Desperate Chrysler Was Its Own Enemy," by William J. Eaton, Madison *Capital Times,* Aug. 10, 1979; "Can Ford Put It Back Together?" by Kirk Cheyfitz, *Monthly Detroit,* April 1980; "Annals of Industry: The Downsizing Decision," by Joseph Kraft, *New Yorker,* May 5, 1980.

LABOR "Workers Increasingly Rebel Against Boredom on Assembly Line," by Agis Salpukas, New York *Times,* April 2, 1972; "Factory Boredom: How Vital an Issue?", by Walter Mossberg, Wisconsin *Star-Journal,* March 23, 1973; "Blue Collar Blues Hit Auto Plants," by Edward S. Lechtzin, Atlanta *Journal and Constitution,* July 8, 1973; "Beyond Boredom—A Look at What's New on the Assembly Line," by Daniel Zwerdling, *Washington Monthly,* July/August 1973; "Compulsory Overtime Plagues Auto Workers," by Peter Milius, Washington *Post,* Aug. 5, 1973; "Auto Industry Facing Lasting Changes," by Agis Salpukas, New York *Times,* Dec. 14, 1973.

DETROIT "The Cities of America—Detroit," by George Sessions Perry, *Saturday Evening Post,* June 22, 1946; "Detroit: A City in Pain," by Jerry M. Flint, New York *Times,* May 1, 1969; "The Changes the City Has Felt, the Problems That Change Has Brought," Detroit *Free Press,* March 9, 1969; "Is Detroit Dying Because No One Cares?" by Robert A. Popa, Detroit *News,* Sept. 21, 1969; "God Help Our City," by William Serrin, *Atlantic Monthly,* March 1969; "Detroit Club's Members Help Change the World but Keep the Club Unchanged," New York *Times,* Oct. 12, 1969; "How One Big City Defeated Its Mayor," by William Serrin, New York *Times Magazine,* Oct. 27, 1968.

"Coleman A. Young: Street Wise and Canny," by Remer Tyson, *The Nation,* Dec. 24, 1973; "Detroit Hangs in There: Mayor Young a Year Later," by Remer Tyson, *The Nation,* March 1, 1975; "Three Mayors Speak of Their Cities," *Ebony,* February 1974; "Detroit Struggles to Save Itself," by Susanna McBee, Washington *Post,* Feb. 20, 1973; "In Detroit, Auto Slump No Longer Means Hard Times," by William K. Stevens, New York *Times,* April 3, 1974; "Impact is Wide When Detroit Goes Flat," by Leonard Silk, New York *Times,* Dec. 8, 1974; "The Top

47 Who Make It Happen," by Andrew R. McGill and Barbara Young, Detroit *News,* Sept. 17, 1978, and the following seven in the series: "Portraits of Power: Seven at the Center," Sept. 20, 1978; "They Made It in their Ways," Sept. 24, 1978; "Who Really Runs the Show," Sept. 27, 1978; "Business Power Gets Around," Oct. 1, 1978; "Getting It Done, Together," Oct. 4, 1978; "One Man Shakes A City," Oct. 8, 1978; "The Powerful Share a Look at the Future," Oct. 14, 1978.

"Detroit's Woes as Bad as New York's But Different," by Francis Ward, Los Angeles *Times,* March 28, 1976; "A Long Hot Summer for Detroit," *Time,* Sept. 6, 1976; "Blacks See Detroit as Their Own, and Hope to Rebuild," by William K. Stevens, New York *Times,* July 26, 1976; "Detroit's Downtown Gets a Tonic," *Business Week,* Aug. 9, 1976; "Damon Keith: Judge on the Firing Line," by William Grant, *The Nation,* Dec. 24, 1973; "Detroit U.S. District Court Judge Damon J. Keith Uses Law Creatively to Right Social Wrongs," by Alex Poinsett, *Ebony,* March 1974; "Detroit Chief: Cities' Future Vital to All: Question and Answer," by Judy Flander and Coleman Young, Washington *Star,* Feb. 6, 1976; "Coleman Young Has His City Rolling in the Right Direction," by William Greider, Milwaukee *Journal,* July 30, 1978; "Survey Finds New Optimism in Detroit," by Stephen Cain, Detroit *News,* Oct. 15, 1978.

"New Optimism Builds in Detroit 10 Years After Devastating Riots," by Reginald Stuart, New York *Times,* July 24, 1977; "Developers Call Detroit Complex the Renaissance, but There is Skepticism That it Signals a Rebirth," by William M. Bulkeley, *Wall Street Journal,* April 15, 1977; "Downtown Detroit Gambles on 'Ren Cen' for Rejuvenation," by William H. Jones, Washington *Post,* Aug. 21, 1976; "New Homes in New Center," by Louis M. Heldman, Detroit *Free Press,* Sept. 19, 1978; "GM Spearheads Renewal of Detroit Neighborhood," by Douglas Williams, Washington *Post,* Sept. 30, 1978.

"Detroit Suburb That Recalled its Mayor Voting Today on Recall of His Successor," by William K. Stevens, New York *Times,* Feb. 19, 1977; "Newcomers Alter Face of Exclusive Grosse Pointe," by William K. Stevens, New York *Times,* Nov. 5, 1974; "Hamtramck Strives to Retain its Polish Character," by William K. Stevens, New York *Times,* Oct. 6, 1974; "Clean Water Hopes Sink in Polluted Saginaw Bay," by Casey Bukro, Chicago *Tribune Press Service,* Oct. 8, 1975; "Tough Old Detroit Is Running Scared," by Carey English, Detroit *Free Press,* May 12, 1980; "When Chrysler Hurts, Detroit Hurts," by Donald Woutat, Detroit *Free Press,* May 13, 1980; "Detroit Vision: Renaissance Built on Eroding Present," by Iver Peterson, New York *Times,* April 28, 1980.

INDIANA

One of the most entertaining and insightful books on any American state is *My Indiana* (Englewood Cliffs, N.J.: Prentice-Hall, 1964), by Irving Leibowitz. Leibowitz was managing editor of the now defunct Indianapolis *Times.* An excellent short review of Indiana's politics appears in a chapter by Edward Ziegner, political editor of the *Indianapolis News,* in *Indiana: A Self-Appraisal,* Donald F. Carmony, editor (Bloomington: Indiana University Press, 1966).

Other useful general source books on the

state include *Indiana: A History,* by Howard H. Peckham (New York: W.W. Norton & Co., 1978); *Indiana: A Guide to the Hoosier State,* compiled by the WPA Writers' Program (New York: Oxford University Press, 1941, republished 1973); *Indiana Fact Book,* published by State Planning Services Agency, Indianapolis, 1976; *Here Is Your Indiana Government,* Indiana State Chamber of Commerce, Indianapolis, 1977; *Indiana Almanac and Fact Book,* published annually by the Sycamore Press, Indianapolis, Ind.; McDowell,

James L. and Perry, Robert T., *Indiana State Government,* Washington, D.C. and Indianapolis, Georgetown University Graduate School and the Academy in the Public Service, 1977.

Ongoing coverage of Indiana as a background for this chapter was culled from the Indianapolis *Star* and *News* and Louisville *Courier-Journal.*

POLITICS AND GOVERNMENT "Kicking Back Pay Is Way of Life in Indiana for Employees of State," by Jonathan R. Laing, *Wall Street Journal,* April 8, 1971; "Kickbacks Still Thrive in Indiana," by John Kifner, New York *Times,* July 11, 1971; "Interim Report on Lugar, Bayh," by Edward Ziegner, Indianapolis *News,* Sept. 21, 1974; "Patronage Rules in Indiana County," by David S. Broder, Washington *Post,* June 15, 1975; "An Indiana Tossup: HHH or Wallace?", by George Lardner Jr., Washington *Post,* April 30, 1972; "Sen. Bayh: The Hoosier at Home," by Rowland Evans and Robert Novak, Washington *Post,* Sept. 21, 1974; "Country Ham and Hard Ball," *Time,* Nov. 3, 1975; " 'Nixon's Favorite Mayor' Seeks New Tag," by R. W. Apple, Jr., New York *Times,* June 13, 1974; "Richard G. Lugar: 'Time to Trust Democracy'," *National Journal,* Dec. 16, 1972; "The Indiana Primary and the Indianapolis Newspapers," by Jules Witcover, *Columbia Journalism Review,* Summer, 1968; "Hesburgh of Notre Dame," by Thomas J. Fleming, New York *Times Magazine,* May 11, 1969.

INDIANAPOLIS "Indianapolis - Marion County Consolidation: How Did it All Happen?", unpublished study by William Matthew Schreiber, 1972; "Unigov: Local Government Reorganization in Indianapolis," by York Wilbern, in Advisory

Commission on Intergovernmental Relations publication, *Regional Governance: Promise and Performance,* Vol. II Case Studies, May 1973; "Getting Back on the Move," *Nation's Business,* November 1976; "Indianapolis: 'Some 5,000 Negro Households . . . Want, Can Afford, But Cannot Get Higher Quality or Better Located Housing'," by Gordon Englehart, *City,* January-February 1971; "It's the Richest Race, But Glory Means More in the Indianapolis 500," by N. R. Kleinfield, *Wall Street Journal,* May 23, 1974; "The Indianapolis Formula for Racial Peace," by Arthur Whitman, Indianapolis *Star,* Dec. 8, 1968.

GARY "A Tax Assessor Has Many Friends," *Harper's* Magazine, November 1972; "Hatcher's Landslide," *Newsweek,* May 17, 1971; "Black Mayor Urges New Approach," by Morris S. Thompson, *Wall Street Journal,* Nov. 8, 1976; "Gary's Decline an Issue in Mayoralty Race," by T. R. Reid, Washington *Post,* May 7, 1979; "Closing of Last Steel Furnaces Alarms Gary, Ind.," by William E. Farrell, New York *Times,* Jan. 5, 1975; "Indiana Assessor Gets 3 Years' Fine in Perjury Case," Chicago *Sun-Times,* Feb. 4, 1978; "New Mayor Finds Gary a Handful," by Bernard D. Nossiter, Washington *Post,* March 9, 1969.

OTHER CITIES "Architecture a Part of Life in Small City," by Bryce Nelson, Los Angeles *Times,* Nov. 7, 1976; "Middletown Revisited: Muncie Adjusts to Change," *Time,* Oct. 16, 1978; " 'They Didn't Realize Who They Were Jazzing With'," by John H. White, Washington *Post,* March 23, 1975; "Open House in Terre Haute," *Time,* Feb. 21, 1969; "Versatile Indiana Industrialist," by George J. Barmann, Cleveland *Plain Dealer,* April 21, 1969.

OHIO

In addition to personal interviews and observations, major reliance was placed on the outstanding analysis of the state's politics in the Ohio chapter of John H. Fenton's *Midwest Politics* (New York: Holt, Rinehart & Winston, 1966). For local color, we turned to *Ohio—A Personal Portrait of the 17th State,* by Dick Perry (Garden City, N.Y.: Doubleday, 1969). Interesting background appears in *The Heartland,* by Robert McLaughlin (New York: Time-Life Library of America, 1967); and *Ohio: A Bicentennial History,* by Walter Havighurst (New York: W.W. Norton & Co., 1976). Among the sources used for miscellaneous facts and figures were the *Ohio Almanac,* published by the Lorain *Journal,* as well as various publications of the Ohio state government.

Reference was made to ongoing news coverage of the Cleveland *Plain-Dealer,* Cleveland *Press,* Cincinnati *Post,* Columbus *Dispatch,* Akron *Beacon-Journal,* and other newspapers and magazines, including the *Ohio Republican News* and *AFL-CIO Focus.* Articles of special use included:

STATE POLITICS AND GOVERNMENT "The Decline of Ohio," by David Hess, *The Nation,* April 13, 1970; "How the Ohio Legislature Really Works," by Richard Zimmerman and Robert Burdock, a series in the Cleveland *Plain-Dealer* between Dec. 29, 1968, and Jan. 3, 1969; *Expenditures and Revenues of the State of Ohio 1950–1967, A Comparative Analysis,* by

John F. Burke, Jr., and Edric A. Weid, Jr. (Institute of Urban Studies, Cleveland State University, 1969); "Ohio: Law and Order Vies with Scandal," *Ripon Forum,* November 1970; "Scandalous Doings Rock Ohio Politics, but Who Can Profit," by Mark R. Arnold, *National Observer,* Sept. 14, 1970; "The Lottery is a Loser," Cincinnati *Post,* Nov. 15, 1978; "Contract Scandal Slows Ohio Lottery," New York *Times,* Dec. 10, 1978; "Ohio Gov. Rhodes: Coming up Roses, Despite Everything," by David Broder, Washington *Post,* June 4, 1978; "In the Knack of Time," by Abe Aaidan, *Ohio Magazine,* January 1979; "Explaining the Ohio Fair Tax Initiative," by Paul Ryder, Cleveland *Plain-Dealer,* May 10, 1980.

CLEVELAND "Why Cleveland is Different," New York *Times,* Dec. 19, 1978; "Letter from Cleveland: Battling to Keep its Headquarter Status," *Business Week,* Feb. 13, 1978; "Cleveland is a New Britain," by Thomas E. Bier, Cleveland *Plain Dealer,* Oct. 11, 1977; "Outmigration Bucks History," by Thomas E. Bier, Cleveland *Plain Dealer,* April 13, 1977; "Homes for Hough," by Wolf Von Eckardt, Washington *Post,* Nov. 25, 1978; "Cleveland: City Where Politics Has Failed," by Bill Peterson, Washington *Post,* Dec. 28, 1978; "Cleveland's 'New Generation' Mayor," by James Ring Adams, *Wall Street Journal,* June 9, 1978; "Cleveland Mayor Faces Recall Vote," by Roldo Bartimole, *In These Times,* July 5, 1978; "Kucinich Defines 'Urban Populism'," by Dennis J. Kucinich, Cleveland *Press,* Oct. 3, 1978; "Dennis Kucinich: The Punking of Cleveland," by Edward P. Whelan, *Esquire,* Dec. 5, 1978; "Dennis," by Abe Zaidan, *Ohio Magazine,* July 1978; "Cleveland: A Mayor, A City on the Brink," by Susanna McBee, Washington *Post* Aug. 12, 1978; "Cleveland on the Brink," by Thomas J. Brazaitis and George P. Rasanen, Cleveland *Plain Dealer,* Aug. 3, 1978; "Boosterism in Cleveland," by Terrence Sheridan, *More,* August 1973; "The 10 Worst," *More,* May 1974; "Invaluable Pain in the Neck," by Dave Rothman, *The Nation,* Oct. 29, 1973; "Tom Vail and His Magic Pencil," by Terrence Sheridan, *More,* November 1973; "Cleveland's Press Gadfly," by John Arnold, *Progressive,* June 1974; "Despite Debts, a Change Has Come Over Cleveland," by Iver Peterson, New York *Times,* May 9, 1980.

COLUMBUS "The Economic Ethos of Columbus, Ohio," by Wilford L. L'Esperance, *Bulletin of Business Research,* October 1976; "Columbus Enjoying a Quiet Prosperity," by Reginald Stuart, New York *Times,* Nov. 20, 1978; "Power in Columbus," by Max Brown, *Columbus Monthly,* March 1976; "Neighbors View German Village," by Larry Ford and Richard Fusch, *Historic Preservation,* July - September 1978; "Cleveland vs. Columbus: A Tale of Two Cities,"

by Abe Zaidan and Brian Usher, *Ohio Magazine,* May 1979; "Columbus's Inferiority Complex," *Columbus Monthly,* March 1978; "The Kids," by Julia Osborne, *Columbus Monthly,* February 1977; "Footballtown, U.S.A.," by Robert Vare, *New Times,* Sept. 20, 1974.

OTHER CITIES "A Revitalized Cincinnati Blends Old and New Spirit," by George Vecsey, New York *Times,* Sept. 8, 1972; "Cincinnati," by William Marlin, *Saturday Review,* Aug. 21, 1976; "Neighborhood Conservation—Lessons From Three Cities (Cincinnati)," by Phyllis Myers and Gordon Binder, Conservation Foundation, 1977; "Campbell Works Plan is Unveiled," by T. V. Petzinger Jr., Youngstown *Vindicator,* Dec. 12, 1977; "The World Blow," Youngstown *Vindicator,* Sept. 20, 1977; "Ohio City Will Try to Run Steel Mill," by Peter Behr, Baltimore *Sun,* Dec. 16, 1977; "Ohio's Other Cities: A Rather Mixed Bag," by Iver Peterson, New York *Times,* Feb. 25, 1979; *Middletown,* by Robert S. Lynd and Helen Merrell (New York: Harcourt, Brace and World, 1929); "'Small Town U.S.A.' Prepares for Impact of Cornfield Converted into Honda Plant," by Iver Peterson, New York *Times,* Feb. 11, 1980; "Mayor: This City Is Dying," by Robert Levey, Boston *Globe,* May 19, 1980.

INDEX